◄O►◄O►◄O►◄O►◄O► MEXICANOS

MEXICANOS

A HISTORY OF MEXICANS IN THE UNITED STATES

Second Edition

MANUEL G. GONZALES

INDIANA UNIVERSITY PRESS · Bloomington and Indianapolis

This book is a publication of

Indiana University Press
Office of Scholarly Publishing
Herman B Wells Library 350
1320 East 10th Street
Bloomington, IN 47405 USA

www.iupress.indiana.edu

The paper used in this publication meets the minimum
requirements of American National Standard for
Information Sciences—Permanence of Paper for Printed
Library Materials, ANSI Z39.48-1984.

Manufactured in the United States of America

Library of Congress Cataloging-in-Publication Data

Gonzales, Manuel G.
  Mexicanos : a history of Mexicans in the United States /
Manuel G. Gonzales. — 2nd ed.
      p. cm.
  Includes bibliographical references and index.
  ISBN 978-0-253-35368-9 (cloth : alk. paper) — ISBN
978-0-253-22125-4 (pbk. : alk. paper) 1. Mexican Ameri-
cans—History. I. Title.
  E184.M5G638 2009
  973'.046872—dc22
                                    2009021537

6 7 8 9 10   21 20 19 18 17 16

For
CINDY

and our daughters,
VANNA AND AMALIA

CONTENTS

ACKNOWLEDGMENTS

◄O►◄O►◄O►

I continue to be in the debt of all those friends and colleagues who contributed their time and effort to the first edition of Mexicanos. In addition, I wish to thank the many individuals—some of them repeat offenders—who aided me in updating this new edition. These include professors Elizabeth Coonrod Martínez, California State University, Sonoma; Juan Mora-Torres, DePaul University; Armando Alonzo, Texas A&M University; Arnoldo De León, San Angelo State University; Lorena Oropeza, University of California, Davis; Lisa Jarvinen, LaSalle University; and Vanna Gonzales, Arizona State University.

As always, archivists Christine Marín, Arizona State University, and Lillian Castillo-Speed, University of California, Berkeley—both consummate professionals—provided valuable counsel; as did National Association for Chicana and Chicano Studies stalwarts Kathryn Blackmer-Reyes and Julia Curry Rodríguez. I am also indebted to my old college friend Walter Brem, formerly with the Bancroft Library at the University of California, Berkeley, who continues to share his bibliographical expertise.

I want to express my gratitude to Rogelio Agrasánchez Jr. for his generosity in providing materials from his incomparable Mexican film archives, but even more for his unfailing moral support throughout the past three years. It would be hard to meet a nicer person. Carlos Larralde continues to be a loyal collaborator. My good friends Richard Delgado and Jean Stefancic have also been very supportive. David Weber, as always, remains a model and an inspiration.

The staff at Indiana University Press has been wonderful. I feel honored to have worked, once again, with Robert Sloan, certainly one of the best editors in the business. Mr. Sloan, his assistant, Anne Clemmer, and their colleagues at IUP have been unfailingly kind and helpful, and working with them has been a sincere pleasure. My copy editor, Carol Kennedy, did an outstanding job.

Finally, I wish to thank my wife, Cindy, for reading and correcting this manuscript, as well as all the others. Her unwavering support, through thick and thin, has meant more to me than words can express.

MEXICANOS

INTRODUCTION

Today the systematic study of Mexicanos in the United States is known as Chicana/o studies.[1] Its genesis is to be found in the turbulent decade spanning the late 1960s and early 1970s, when Mexican American students at California and Texas colleges and universities, inspired by the tenets of Chicanismo, hence calling themselves *Chicanos,* initiated a search for the historical roots of the *movimiento* (movement). From its inception, this discipline, like ethnic studies generally, met with considerable skepticism and resistance in established academic departments across the country. Traditionalists were disdainful of the first works in the fledgling field. Among the most vocal of these critics were the historians Arthur Schlesinger Jr., Jacques Barzun, and Diane Ravitch. And, truth be told, these early efforts in the new ethnic scholarship suffered from a number of academic deficiencies.

Many pioneering works in Chicano studies lacked a strong theoretical framework. Other early attempts by Chicanos to record the story of their people for the first time were unabashedly celebratory, calling into question their intellectual objectivity. Yet, the mainstream criticisms of these young iconoclastic scholars were often exaggerated, and in many cases completely misguided. It should be noted, too, that the foundational literature of any new discipline is bound to lack the intellectual rigor others might desire. This was as true of the emerging social sciences in the late nineteenth century as it has been for the plethora of other new disciplines spawned in the 1960s and 1970s. Nevertheless, fair or not, the integrity of the entire discipline was called into question, which represented a challenge that needed to be addressed sooner or later.

I am reminded here that the icy reception accorded Chicana/o scholarship was not unlike that encountered by another group of would-be revolutionaries who were also on the cutting edge of their field—the French Impressionists of the late nineteenth century. The establishment scoffed at the paintings of these young

Parisians; they seemed amateurish and lacked substance. Distressed by this wide-spread criticism, and yearning for some degree of respectability in the art world, Paul Cézanne famously charted a new path. Breaking with Impressionist colleagues, Cézanne, an outsider from the provinces, resolved to move in a new direction, what art historians would later label "Post-Impressionism." He yearned, as he put it, to create works as "solid and lasting" as those hanging in museums.

Ten years ago, in this same spirit, I felt that it was imperative to embark on a fresh path in tracing the history of Mexican-origin communities in the United States, to initiate a new, or at least a different, kind of ethnic history than what was being attempted by Chicano scholars, one that would win the respect of the gatekeepers of academe. Trained in European history, I did not fully identify with the emerging Chicano perspective. As with the example of Cézanne, this outsider status allowed me to question some of the assumptions of the new wave. However, like him, I had no desire to repudiate the efforts of maligned colleagues but to build on them. What was needed in these studies was a greater degree of objectivity.

Ultimately, I wanted to construct a realistic portrait of Mexicans in this country, warts and all. In an effort to win wider credibility for the emerging field of Chicana/o studies, I wished to examine Mexicanos in the same way as other U.S. immigrant communities had been scrutinized by respected scholars in the past, for example, the Jews by Nathan Glazer or the Irish by Kerby Miller. Judging by the number of times *Mexicanos* has been cited in the bibliographies of mainstream U.S. history textbooks in recent years, it seems reasonable to conclude that these efforts have not been in vain. And, of course, the book's modest success largely reflects continuing demographic trends, notably the massive immigration from Mexico and other Latin American countries—allowing Latinos to overtake blacks as the country's leading ethnic group—and the transformation of Mexican Americans from a regional into a national minority.

Unlike many other minorities in the United States—blacks and Native Americans, for example—the history of Mexicanos has largely been written by insiders, members of the ethnic community.[2] However, this is not completely true. Indeed, the first serious attempt to uncover their history was made by the eminent journalist and civil rights activist Carey McWilliams (1905–1980), whose enormous impact has been so widely recognized by Chicanos themselves that he was selected the initial Scholar of the Year—an honor he shared with the renowned folklorist Américo Paredes—by the multidisciplinary National Association for Chicana and Chicano Studies (NACCS) in 1981.[3] Many other non-Latinos have made important contributions to the field of Chicana/o studies. Among historians these include such stalwarts as Leonard Pitt, Matt S. Meier, Sarah Deutsch, James A. Sandos, and David J. Weber, the latter contributing not only as an indefatigable researcher but also as a leading mentor to aspiring minority scholars. Moreover, with only a few notable exceptions, the early history of Hispanic peoples in North America, the Spanish phase, continues to be the exclusive preserve of non-Latinos.[4]

Nevertheless, since the advent of ethnic studies in the 1960s, it is Mexican-origin and other Latino scholars who have dominated the study of Mexicans in the United States. A product of the Chicano Movement, these youths prided themselves on community involvement; Chicanos saw themselves as scholar-activists. It should be made clear at the outset that most Mexican Americans who currently teach or research Mexican American history do not belong to NACCS.[5] In fact, only a small number of them are members of Chicana/o studies departments or centers. In other words, the militant perspective characteristic of these programs is a distinct minority viewpoint among historians who specialize in the study of the Mexican American past.

However, it has been these movement scholars who initiated the new academic interest in Mexicanos. Moreover, most of the cutting-edge work in the emerging field of study has emanated from these same scholar-activists. The reason is simple: committed to a multidisciplinary approach, these movement scholars experience and are more open to fresh perspectives, not only within their own umbrella discipline (Chicana/o studies), but also from allied and related fields that challenge "the master narrative," such as queer studies and women's studies, as well as programs that focus on other ethnic minorities.

The most noteworthy of these pioneering scholars has undoubtedly been Rodolfo (Rudy) Acuña, the quintessential scholar-activist. By 1968, when he earned his Ph.D. in Latin American history, Acuña was heavily involved in the Chicano Movement in southern California,[6] and almost immediately became its leading intellectual. Unfortunately, his campus and community activism have often obscured his academic production and impact. Practically single-handedly, Acuña established the main lines of Chicano historical inquiry. His textbook *Occupied America,* which has gone through five revisions, each of them almost completely rewritten, remains "the Bible of Chicano Studies." His emphasis on victimization and resistance dominated early Chicano historiography and still continues to resonate with many scholars.[7]

Professor Acuña and his generation created a firm foundation for the study of Chicano history. Influenced by studies in a variety of disciplines, however, the field has become ever more sophisticated. The initial focus on brown working-class Catholic men living in the Southwest has expanded tremendously. By the 1980s, the study of *mujeres* (women) was well under way, a trend initiated and still dominated by Chicanas themselves. The geographical dimensions were then broadened, first into the Midwest, where a Latino presence was long-standing, as Mexican immigrant communities sprang up across the country. Chicano social mobility has sparked an interest in exploring class as a subject of historical investigation. More recently studies have been initiated into the rise of Protestantism in Latino communities. The study of sexuality seems to be the last frontier; but, mirroring vast social changes, there is evidence that at long last traditional resistance to research in this controversial sub-area is being surmounted in the discipline.

As the historian Antonio Ríos-Bustamante chronicled in a comprehensive survey of Chicana/o historiography in 2000, movement colleagues, experimenting with a wide variety of methodologies and interpretive models, had already produced an impressive body of solid scholarship.[8] Since his sanguine assessment of their output a decade ago, Chicano academics have only redoubled their efforts, in the process opening up many more areas of investigation, such as Hispanic participation in sports and the military.

As a result, many Chicano scholars have now won wide and well-deserved recognition beyond Chicana/o studies. Richard Griswold del Castillo, Arnoldo De León, Juan Gómez-Quiñones, Mario T. García, Ignacio García, Gilbert González, and Dennis Nodín Valdés are among the most renowned of the marquee names who have won the respect of their colleagues in the historical profession. Several of them, including Albert Camarillo, Félix D. Almaráz Jr., and Vicki Ruiz, have been elected to head prestigious historical associations. Aside from Professor Ruiz, prominent Chicanas in the field include Deena González, María Montoya, and Antonia Castañeda.

A cadre of young scholars is currently revitalizing the field. Several established scholars have taken on the important work of cultivating the youth. Perhaps the most dedicated of these senior mentors have been Camarillo, at Stanford University; and, once again, the hardworking Ruiz, at the numerous institutions where she has taught. Talented newcomers include Lorena Oropeza, Andrés Reséndez, Miroslava Chávez-García, Stephen Pitti, and a host of others. This influx of youth guarantees that Chicano history will continue to be what it has always been: an innovative field characterized by new interpretive frameworks and groundbreaking discoveries. Given the extensive and innovative achievements in the study of Chicano history made by this vibrant academic community in recent years, this edition of *Mexicanos,* even more than the first, is a synthesis, and to a large extent, a celebration of the great strides made by Chicano scholarship in history and virtually every other academic discipline.

Although I have never been an activist and by temperament am inclined to avoid affiliation with any group, I consider myself a Chicano historian; that is, I experienced the movimiento, and it affected me in a positive way. While I sometimes take Chicano colleagues to task, my criticisms have more to do with differences of interpretation than with fundamental principles. I should also make it clear at the outset that my academic training in the history of Western civilization has made me more sensitive to class than to race. As a college student at the University of California at Santa Barbara, I was strongly impacted by Marxism, like many other Chicano scholars who received their education in the 1960s and 1970s. Although I still accept Marxism as my main theoretical model—that people are moved primarily by self-interest is undeniable, in my view—this perspective is a secondary rather than a primary theme in my work.[9]

What I hope to accomplish is a concise and balanced account of the history of Mexicans in the United States, including background information beginning in the sixteenth century. I propose to incorporate the latest findings on the subject, paying particular attention to the work found in professional journals of history and related disciplines. In keeping with the most recent trends in the discipline, this second edition of *Mexicanos* tries to be inclusive; as I noted in my first introduction, even *vendidos* ("sell-outs") have a history.

As with all scholars, my work is informed by my view of my particular discipline. Not all Chicano historians agree on the nature of history and historical study. Committed to a multidisciplinary approach from its very beginnings in the sixties, Chicana/o history has been receptive to many innovative approaches both from within and from outside the broader field of Chicana/o studies. External influences come from many academic areas, including but not limited to literary studies, women's studies, cultural studies, queer studies, and other ethnic studies. As a consequence, Chicano historians have employed a wide variety of theoretical models. The most popular of these have been internal colonialism, world systems analysis, generational approaches, and historical materialism (the model I personally find most useful). A score of others, some of them quite exotic, have appealed to my colleagues in the field from time to time. No one model has been universally acclaimed.[10] Theories, of course, are useful because they permit students of the human condition to look at things in new ways.

However, it is important to maintain perspective. The study of history, in my view, boils down to asking three essential questions: What happened? Why did it happen? What difference did it make? For students of history, models are simply tools to provide answers to these basic questions; they are means to an end, not an end in themselves. In some of the other social sciences, theoretical models have taken on a life of their own. One result is that for laypersons some of these monographs are virtually unreadable. History, though, is not generally a discipline that emphasizes theory, and my work is no exception to the rule. Unencumbered by excessive theoretical baggage, I hope I have related the stories of Mexicanos clearly and concisely.

Since I am sometimes critical of what have become mainstream interpretations in Chicana/o studies departments during the past forty years, many of my Chicano colleagues will continue to find my work generally conservative. This perception may have something to do not only with the generation gap but also with the fact that my academic training in modern European and Latin American history has encouraged me to look at Chicano history with a certain sense of detachment. However, as I mentioned, being an outsider has its advantages. Moreover, I believe that there is room in the field for moderate as well as radical interpretations. In fact, there is a good deal of diversity among Chicano historians, a trend that will become more rather than less pronounced as time goes on.

As is true of most thoughtful scholars during the last ten years, some of my views have evolved. One change, in particular, is relevant here: my perception of what constitutes objectivity. When I began my synthesis of Mexican American history, reacting to a major deficiency in Chicano historiography, I promised an "objective" study. The reaction was delayed but inevitable. Soon after publication I was taken to task by a few Chicano scholars, who assured me that this goal— noble, at least in the abstract—was impossible.[11] While not entirely convinced by their arguments, in retrospect, I must agree that their criticisms were basically sound. Postmodernism has little to offer historians. However, it *does* provide one very important insight: truth is in the eye of the beholder. As a Marxist, I appreciate this criticism. Marx, after all, had cautioned that ideas were the products of a changing material environment. This healthy skepticism of what constitutes truth is shared by all the major thinkers who have taken a Marxian perspective, from Charles Beard through E. H. Carr to Michael Parenti, my most recent intellectual mentor. Among Chicanos, the Marxian view is best expressed by Professor Acuña, who writes, "Truth is socially constructed, not discovered. Strip away the political and cultural coverings that pass as 'truth' in each society and the power of hegemonic interests [is] exposed."[12]

My own recent appreciation of this important insight, however, has less to do with intellectual currents than with personal experience. Like most Americans, I was strongly impacted by the events of 11 September 2001 and their consequences. Forced to get involved politically—I have been a staunch supporter of the anti-war movement—it was not long before I came to realize that many of my friends and colleagues, most of them very intelligent people, disagreed with me on my assessment of the war and the Bush administration. Only then did I come to truly appreciate the subjective nature of historical inquiry. My views of people who disagree with me are less judgmental than before.

It follows, then, that in this second edition I am more understanding of divergent viewpoints expressed by my colleagues in Chicana/o studies. My expectations of their scholarship are more realistic. This change, too, stems from a better understanding of their work. Moreover, as indicated above, the field itself has evolved, and I propose for the better. There is a much greater degree of professionalism in the discipline, in part a result of better-trained young scholars entering the field.

Possibly the single most momentous change during the past decade has been the growing presence of Chicanas in the discipline. When *Mexicanos* was first published, I noted the dearth of female scholars in the field, which went a long way in explaining the scant coverage of *mujeres* in the historical literature. Happily, this deficiency is being addressed. Thus, women loom much larger in historical narratives today. Moreover, this growing literature, while mainly a product of female scholars, has also reflected a growing interest by their male colleagues. Following this trend, this edition of *Mexicanos* will be able to expand its coverage of *mujeres* significantly.

Finally, a word on terminology is in order. Based on interviews conducted in 1989–1990, the Latino National Political Survey (LNPS), the first nationally representative sample to provide solid empirical evidence about how Latinos see themselves, concluded that the most popular self-referent among people of Mexican background in the United States was *Mexican* (*Mexicano* in Spanish). According to Rodolfo O. de la Garza, a respected political scientist at the University of Texas and one of the authors of the study, 62 percent of people of Mexican heritage born in this country preferred this term, as did 86 percent of the immigrant population.[13] In light of these surprising findings, many Chicano scholars have abandoned the term *Chicano* for the term *Mexicano* in their writings, a practice that I too will employ, especially since I plan to investigate newcomers as well as the native-born. When there is a need to distinguish between native-born and immigrants, I will use *Mexican Americans* for the former and *Mexicans* for the latter. To avoid confusion, the term *Chicanos* (and/or *Chicanas*) will be employed to specify members of the ethnic community who, during the 1960s and subsequently, endorsed the major tenets of Chicanismo; that is, Mexican Americans who, as the journalist Rubén Salazar defined them, came to embrace a non-Anglo image of themselves. Although Chicano historians generally dislike the term *Hispanics,* mainly because they feel that it stresses the European legacy to the complete exclusion of indigenous roots, I will use the term, which is commonly used by others, interchangeably with the preferred *Latinos* (and/or *Latinas*) when referring to Americans of Latin American descent; that is, all Spanish-speaking people in the United States, exclusive of Spaniards and their descendants. *Tejanos, Californios,* and *Hispanos* (and/or their feminine forms) will designate native-born Spanish-speaking inhabitants of Texas, California, and New Mexico, respectively.

SPANIARDS AND NATIVE AMERICANS

PREHISTORY–1521

1

Mexican American is a term devoid of meaning before 1848. The number of Mexicans residing in the United States before the Mexican Cession was negligible. Yet it would be a mistake to begin this history with the Treaty of Guadalupe Hidalgo, for the roots of Mexican American history are buried in the distant past. In order to understand the people and their culture it is necessary to go back at least to the sixteenth century. Like most other Latin Americans, Mexicans are predominantly *mestizos;* that is, they are products of race mixture. When Spaniards invaded the New World in the 1500s and initiated contact with Amerindians in Mexico, the genesis of the Mexican community in the United States began.

After a period of political and economic stagnation in the fourteenth century, the Renaissance, centered primarily in Italy, witnessed not only a momentous expansion of Europe's intellectual and artistic horizons but also an enormous widening of its geographical limits. The Age of Exploration represents the first major expansion of the Europeans, who subsequently came to dominate much of the globe, thanks primarily to their superior technological development. Inspired by God, Gold, and Glory, Europeans pushed their frontiers in all directions, with their most meaningful acquisition being the New World. America was named after an Italian explorer, Amerigo Vespucci, but in the forefront of the process of discovery and conquest were the Spaniards, the chief beneficiaries of this initial wave of Western imperialistic activity.

THE SPANIARDS

Who were the Spaniards and why were they so successful? Building on the solid foundation laid by such notable twentieth-century giants as Américo Castro, Salvador de Madariaga, and Ramón Menéndez Pidal, modern-day Spanish scholars have found answers to these crucial questions in their country's vibrant past. They have discovered that like other Europeans, Spaniards are a product of a multiplicity of cultures. Spanish history can be traced back to the Upper Paleolithic period (35,000 BCE–10,000 BCE), when primitive people dwelling in the Iberian Peninsula began to leave evidence of an emerging culture. Cave paintings, like those discovered in the 1890s in Altamira, near the northern port of Santander, illustrate the amazing creativity of these early inhabitants. These ancient pictures, mostly abstract depictions of animal life, have led modern scholars to designate the Upper Paleolithic the Cradle of Art.

The following millennia are shrouded in mystery, but the Iberian Peninsula, a natural bridge between two continents, must have attracted a variety of people. Among them were Iberians, "dwellers along the Ebro River," as they came to be called by the Greeks; Basques, whose origins are still much debated; Celts, who dominated the region in the period 900 BCE–650 BCE; Phoenicians, contemporaries of the Celts, who established colonies from their base in the eastern Mediterranean; and Greeks, who came at around 600 BCE to settle the coastal areas.

Undoubtedly, however, the most influential of the ancient peoples to arrive were the Romans.[1] Victors against Carthage, a Phoenician colony in modern-day Tunis, Roman legions acquired Hispania, their name for Spain, as a prize in 202 BCE, at the end of the Second Punic War. The Celt-Iberians put up a mighty resistance, but in the end Rome's famed legions prevailed. Though exploited as colonials, the natives received valuable concessions from the Romans. Some of them went on to win fame and fortune within the Empire. Seneca, the brilliant Stoic philosopher, and Hadrian, one of Rome's most powerful Caesars, were from Hispania. The cultural contributions Rome bestowed far outweighed the material riches it extorted from its conquered subjects. Rome imposed its laws, one of its finest achievements. It contributed Latin, which eventually gave rise to Castilian Spanish, a language so beautiful that reading it is still an emotional experience, as well as Catalán and Gallego. Rome also brought a belief system, Christianity, which was made the official religion of the Empire in the fourth century and became a force second to none in shaping the emerging national character of the people.

Increasingly beset by political and economic problems, the Roman Empire weakened after the third century of the Christian era; and, overrun by Germanic tribes who administered the coup de grâce, the western half collapsed by the fifth century. Vandals now controlled North Africa, Franks reigned supreme in France, and even Italy found itself occupied, first by Ostrogoths, later by Lombards. The Visigoths, following other northern tribes, settled in Spain, establishing their capital in Toledo. However, Germanic ascendancy proved to be short-lived.

"Africa," Spain's detractors are fond of saying, echoing a statement originally attributed to Alexandre Dumas, "begins at the Pyrenees." In fact, the impact of African culture has been profound on the Spanish psyche, something Spaniards were unwilling to concede until recently. Taking their cue from the eminent philosopher Miguel de Unamuno, Spanish intellectuals in the early part of the twentieth century began to reassess the role of the Moors in their history. Now most Spaniards find the Moorish legacy a source of considerable pride. The distinguished historian Américo Castro felt that Spanish history began with the arrival of the Moors in 711, when Tarik ibn Zizad led seven thousand Berber troops, recent converts to Islam, on a religious crusade across the Strait of Gibraltar. The campaign was a huge success; the peninsula was overrun at breakneck speed. The Moors (Berber and Arab Moslems) penetrated into western Europe as far north as modern-day Poitiers or Tours—scholars differ on the precise location—where, with their religious zeal waning and their lines of communication overextended, they were finally stopped by Germanic Franks under Charles Martel. Retreating across the Pyrenees, Moslems began to consolidate their conquest of the Iberian Peninsula, the western frontier of a vast empire. Islamic Spain came to be known as al-Andalus.

As Europe declined during its Middle Ages, the mantle of civilization shifted to the East—to Constantinople, the center of the Byzantine Empire, and to the Islamic world beyond. Moslem strength reached its zenith in the eighth century, when Islamic ships gained control of the Mediterranean, putting the Byzantines on the defensive. The caliphate was transferred from Damascus to Baghdad, in modern Iraq, in 750; and during the next few decades wealth from throughout the far-flung realm poured into that magnificent city, fueling an enormous upsurge of intellectual activity. Thereafter, the Islamic world itself began to weaken, mainly because of internal problems. In the year 1000 there were three caliphates instead of one, as Baghdad was now rivaled by Cairo in north Africa and Córdoba on the Iberian Peninsula. By this time, Moorish Spain, completely independent of Baghdad, had created a brilliant culture.

Moors occupied the Iberian Peninsula for over 750 years. During this period their influence came to permeate every aspect of life, especially in the south, in today's Andalucía, where they established their major cities, including Sevilla, Córdoba, and Granada. During their heyday in the tenth, eleventh, and twelfth centuries, they developed a civilization that was the envy of their northern neighbors. Moorish scholars not only helped to preserve the classical heritage of the West, but also made significant contributions of their own, notably in the arts, literature, mathematics, and philosophy. The most original Moorish man of letters was Ibn Rushd, known to the West as Averroës (1126–1198), an authority on Aristotle and a powerful influence on Christian thinkers during the late Middle Ages.

The culture of al-Andalus was also enhanced by Jewish scholars. The diaspora into Iberia, which began as early as the second century CE, had produced a flourishing Jewish community in Moorish Spain, which, though open to exotic elements, largely maintained its own traditions, a freedom conceded by Tarik and his successors. The Jews of *Sepharad* (the Hebrew word for Iberia) prospered. "Andalusia," the historian Howard M. Sachar observed, "offered Jews an arena for commerce unparalleled since the glory days of Rome."[2] They established academies in Barcelona, Córdoba, Granada, and Toledo. They translated the Talmud into Arabic. Their men of letters were renowned throughout the realm. Undoubtedly the most celebrated of these Sephardic thinkers, possibly the greatest philosopher Spain has ever produced, was Moses ben Maimon, or Maimonides (1135–1204), who lived in Córdoba, like his contemporary, Averroës.

While the Moors enjoyed a happy coexistence with the Jews—at least until 1146, when a fanatical Islamic sect from Morocco, the Almohades, introduced religious intolerance—their relationship with the rest of the conquered population was far more complicated. From time to time the two peoples, colonizers and colonized, got along reasonably well; trade took place and intermarriage occurred. Some Christians, called *mozárabes,* assimilated Moslem culture. These amiable relations, however, were the exception rather than the rule. For the most part, there was animosity on both sides. From the very beginning of Moslem colonization, a small enclave of resistance emerged in Asturias, in the mountainous northwestern part of the peninsula. Under the leadership of the legendary Pelayo, this liberation movement, called the *Reconquista* (Reconquest) by Spanish historians, was modest at first. But by the thirteenth century, when Christian successes, notably the famous victory by King Alfonso VIII of Castilla at Las Navas de Tolosa in 1212, forced the Moors to take refuge in Granada and its surrounding area, it had become a mass movement.

By now religion had come to play a vital role in Spanish life. Every campaign against the Moors was a holy crusade. Although the Age of the Christian Crusades is generally assumed to have begun in 1095, when Pope Urban II launched the first crusade against the Saracens in an effort to regain the holy city of Jerusalem, Spanish knights by this time had a long tradition of warring against their Islamic adversaries under the banner of Santiago (Saint James), their patron saint. As in Ireland after the Protestant Reformation, religion in Spain came to be wedded to nationalism. The result was a very militant form of Catholicism. The Spaniards' fanatical devotion to their faith, reflected later in the Holy Office of the Inquisition (1479–1812) and in the zeal with which they proselytized Amerindians, is rooted in these early military campaigns.

The Moors had a far-reaching impact on Iberian culture, on agriculture, music, and language; but none was more momentous than the profound religiosity that they wove into the fabric of life of the Spanish people. Thus, it is generally agreed,

"Spain is perhaps the most avidly Roman Catholic country in Europe, both in the sense of its official affiliation with the church in Rome and to the degree that the culture is permeated and uniquely colored by it."[3]

The marriage of Prince Ferdinand of Aragón and Princess Isabella of Castilla in 1469 paved the way for the final stage of the Reconquest. *Los Reyes Católicos* (the Catholic Kings), as they styled themselves, were deeply religious. However, both monarchs were equally absorbed with achieving political ends, especially Ferdinand, who was later used as a model by Machiavelli. In early January 1492, the mountainous kingdom of Granada, the last Islamic stronghold, was taken through force of arms, and the Moors were expelled from the country. Jewish expulsion followed two months later. The unification of Spain was now complete.

Both ethnic minorities, it should be added, could avoid expulsion by converting to Catholicism. Both Moorish and Jewish *conversos* (converts), however, were now subject to the Inquisition, which reached the height of its power under the infamous Tomás de Torquemada, who served as inquisitor general from 1483 to 1498.

The religious zeal that had resulted in the campaigns against *judíos* (Jews) and *moros* (Moors) was soon transferred overseas. In 1492 a New World was discovered with millions of potential converts, and Spain was anxious to propagate the faith. The Spaniards were ideally situated to play this pioneering role not only because of their early creation of a unified national dynastic state but also because of their geographical position. Jutting out into the Atlantic, the Iberian Peninsula would be the launching pad for the early voyages of exploration.

It was the Portuguese, Spain's Iberian neighbors, who got off the mark first. Up to the twelfth century, Portugal was part of León, one of several provinces which emerged from the lands reclaimed from the Moors. During these years there developed a distinct Portuguese sense of nationalism as well as a separate language. By the end of the twelfth century, a robust dynastic state was competing with those in other parts of the peninsula. The most famous of the Avis, the ruling family that rose to power in the fourteenth century, was the son of King Joao I, Henrique, better known as Prince Henry the Navigator (1394–1460), who is credited with initiating Portugal's interest in overseas exploration and settlement. This fascination was primarily economic in nature. At first, the Portuguese sought to monopolize trade with West Africa, which was rich in gold reserves. Eventually, as is well known, they became obsessed with the quest for an all-water route to *Las Indias* (the Indies), a vague geographical area that consisted of Southeast Asia and its offshore islands, the source of the coveted spices which had enriched Indian, Arab, and especially Italian middlemen. The fantastic profits made by the *veneziani* (Venetians) and *genovesi* (Genoans) go a long way in explaining the Italian Renaissance. By the mid-fifteenth century, Portuguese mariners trained at Sagres, a maritime academy established by Prince Henry on Portugal's southernmost cape, were venturing out into the Atlantic. Having some knowledge of Africa's contours, apparently based on Phoenician sources, the Portuguese felt that by sailing south they could get around the continent, thus arriving on the Indian Ocean, the gateway to the vast riches of the Orient.

During the course of these epic fifteenth-century voyages, the Portuguese discovered and laid claim to several valuable islands, the Azores and the Madeiras being the most attractive to mainland entrepreneurs. They also initiated the slave trade in West Africa, the pernicious traffic in human beings which yielded fantastic financial profits to Europeans until its demise in the nineteenth century. A long series of arduous expeditions culminated in 1488 when Bartholomeu Dias rounded the Cape of Good Hope. Ten years later, in what is arguably the greatest maritime voyage of the Age of Exploration, according to the Spanish historian Felipe Fernández-Armesto, Vasco da Gama reached Calicut in India, thus inaugurating Portugal's short-lived golden age. In fact, this voyage brought about a momentous transformation in the balance of power. In the aftermath of da Gama's successful mission, the world's major theater of commercial activity was rapidly transferred from the Mediterranean Sea to the Atlantic Ocean, a shift signaling the economic decline of Italy, and ultimately of its cultural hegemony, and the rise of Western Europe. The primary beneficiary of this imperious change, however, was not Portugal, which declined so rapidly during the course of the sixteenth century that it was taken over by the Spanish Hapsburgs for sixty years beginning in 1580, but rather its larger and more powerful neighbor, Spain.

One of the supreme ironies in history is that the most famous figure in Spanish history, Christopher Columbus (1451–1506), should be an Italian. The Genovese Cristoforo Colombo was a native of a peninsula with a proud and glorious past but one rapidly eclipsed during his lifetime by his adopted homeland. Though ironic, Columbus's role is not surprising. The Renaissance was a cosmopolitan period when nationalism was only just emerging—in many parts of Europe, regional allegiances continue to predominate over national sentiments to this day—and movement between emerging nations, while limited by technological and financial impediments, was relatively easy. At a time when maritime skills were highly valued, Italian mariners, the best in Europe at the time, found their services much in demand, and they displayed little temerity in hiring out to foreign employers. Giovanni Caboto, who sailed for the English under the name John Cabot, and Giovanni da Verrazano, a contemporary and one of France's leading explorers, are good examples. Columbus himself seemed to have few qualms about living in Spain and serving its rulers.

The details of Columbus's life are vague, but its general outlines are clear enough. The son of a wool weaver, Cristoforo spent his youth learning the skills of seamanship, and by his early twenties he was already making regular trips throughout the Mediterranean aboard Italian vessels. Eventually, in 1479, he wound up in Lisbon, where he married Felipa Perestrello e Moniz, daughter of an Italian mariner and a member of one of Portugal's oldest families. They settled down in Porto Santo, a small island, part of the Madeira Archipelago, where Columbus went into the chart business.

This livelihood was but a means to an end; Columbus dreamed of tapping the enormous wealth of the Spice Islands, known as the Moluccas to the Portuguese. He was aware of Portuguese expeditions moving south along the African coast, but he came to believe that the fabled lands, rich in silks, spices, and gems, could best be reached sailing westward. He initiated a series of petitions in an effort to win financial backing to prove his theories. Upon the death of his wife in 1485, he left for Spain. After an initial rebuke, followed by many trials and tribulations, he convinced Queen Isabella, apparently won over by his charm and bulldog determination, to back the risky enterprise.

The *Niña,* the *Pinta,* and the *Santa María* left the port of Palos de la Frontera on 3 August 1492. Taking on supplies at the Canary Islands, the tiny ships then struggled across the Atlantic. Having miscalculated drastically, the admiral was forced to alter his ship log to bolster the flagging morale of his men. On 12 October, his crew on the verge of mutiny, Columbus sighted land. He had arrived somewhere in the Bahamas. Sailing southwestward, the expedition came upon Cuba and Española, islands which would later be used as a springboard for exploration in every direction. Columbus returned to Spain with a small number of natives and just enough gold to convince his patrons of his success; and incidentally, as Alistair Cooke aptly notes, to initiate "the longest, most determined, and most brutal gold rush in history."[4]

The Admiral of the Ocean Sea made three subsequent voyages to the New World. Although these expeditions were largely disappointing, since they earned him little fame or fortune, Columbus believed he had reached Asia, a misconception he apparently maintained to his death on 20 May 1506.

It is not easy to assess Columbus's role in history. In the past, most historians have agreed with the eminent biographer Samuel Eliot Morison, who saw in Columbus not only a great mariner but also the most remarkable figure of his age. Today, however, the Italian explorer is perceived less favorably.[5] Given the current loss of faith in Carlyle's Great Man Theory of History, scholars are less impressed by elites than they used to be. More importantly, however, Columbus is currently associated with European imperialism, a discredited and much-maligned phenomenon of the postcolonial world. Critics, especially in societies where multiculturalism has become increasingly popular, charge that Columbus saw Indians as inferior and treated them accordingly. His legacy was not confined to the exploitation of peoples; he is also vilified for initiating the European assault on the virgin environment. Kirkpatrick Sale in his popular 1990 work *The Conquest of Paradise: Christopher Columbus and the Columbian Legacy* argues trenchantly for this revisionist interpretation.

While Columbus was guilty of ethnocentrism and exploitation of peoples and resources, he was typical of his age. Although the period of the Renaissance and Reformation was an epoch of almost unprecedented artistic and intellectual achievement, it was also an age of barbarism and intolerance. "It was . . . a time much given to terror, war, pestilence, famine, slavery and religious persecution, most emphatically not one to encourage gentleness or ecological concern."[6] While Europeans took advantage of native Americans, it is also true that they victimized each other. Nor were the native peoples morally superior. "The innocence of the indigenous Americans," John Noble Wilford reminds us, "was more imagined than real. To one degree or another, they knew warfare, brutality, slavery, human sacrifice, and cannibalism."[7] Certainly, there was nothing peculiarly European about exploitation; the Age of Columbus would not be the first time that the strong would take advantage of the weak, nor would it be the last. Finally, it can be argued, if Columbus was no better than his contemporaries, he was certainly no worse. While this era is sometimes called the Age of Titans, few of these so-called titans were noted for their saintly qualities—certainly not Machiavelli, nor even Luther. These individuals suffice to remind us that greatness is not defined by moral character but by influence. Perhaps the best assessment of the much-maligned explorer is given by Felipe Fernández-Armesto: "The real Columbus was a mixture of virtues and vices like the rest of us, not conspicuously good or just, but generally well-intentioned, who grappled creditably with intractable problems."[8]

THE AMERINDIANS

"Wherever I go, and people ask where I am from, I tell them I am Purepecha and I have a language and culture and a history."[9] This terse, but eloquent, declaration of identity, expressed by a proud immigrant from Michoacán about to be evicted from his ramshackle trailer park in the southern California desert, reminds us that the indigenous people of Mexico have a long and glorious past; one, moreover, that continues to define Mexicans and Mexican Americans.

Although Europeans often saw the Americas as "virgin" territory, at the time of contact, according to current estimates, the two continents were occupied by almost one hundred million inhabitants. Under the mistaken assumption that he had reached Las Indias, Columbus referred to the people as *Indios,* and the term *Indians* came to be applied to them. Today, however, many tribal Americans prefer the term *Native Americans* (*Indian* and *Native American* will be used interchangeably in this work). From the very beginning, there was enormous heterogeneity among the native peoples of the Americas; indeed, as the historian Wilcomb E. Washburn has pointed out, there was probably more diversity among Native Americans than there was among the various European ethnic groups who came to colonize the area.[10] This diversity belies a common origin.

The question of Indian origins is still the leading question of New World archaeology. While it can be stated categorically that Native Americans did not evolve from lower forms of animal life independently in the New World—the genesis of human beings apparently occurred in east central Africa some three to five million years ago—there is much speculation as to their migration. One famous theory, endorsed by the Church of Jesus Christ of Latter-day Saints as well as a few non-Mormon scholars, is that all or most Indians are descended from people who migrated from the eastern Mediterranean basin. The most prominent hypothesis, however, has its origins in 1589 when a Spanish Jesuit, José de Acosta (c. 1539–1600), guessed that Native Americans were descended from Asian peoples, a notion based on physical characteristics.[11]

The rise of modern science has tended to substantiate this latter theory, now called the Bering Strait Hypothesis, though in a much more sophisticated form. According to this view, the first nomads entered the Americas via an ice or land bridge connecting modern-day Siberia and Alaska sometime between 50,000 BCE and 10,000 BCE, the end of the last Ice Age. Today this body of water is the Bering Strait, hence the designation of the theory, named after Vitus Bering (1680–1741), a Danish navigator who sailed through the passage during the eighteenth century. The consensus of informed opinion is that the first immigrants were a small band of hunters and gatherers who came in search of large game animals in about 30,000 BCE. They were probably *Homo sapiens sapiens;* that is, anatomically they were identical to humans living today, though scholars are not in agreement here. It appears there were several incoming waves of nomadic hunters, with the Eskimos representing the last large-scale migration, sometime shortly before the time of Jesus Christ. Penetrating south along the slopes of the Rockies, these nomads eventually diffused in all directions over the course of several millennia, finally arriving at the southern tip of the Americas sometime around 8,000 BCE. This theory of Mongolian origin and north-to-south migration is supported by the artifact record, as well as specialized studies of blood types, dental records, and linguistic analysis.

When Europeans first encountered them, Native Americans were found everywhere in the Western Hemisphere. However, they were not living uniformly throughout the two continents. Clearly, there was a tendency by these early immigrants to avoid less attractive areas, tropical rain forests and deserts, and to seek healthier environments, preferably in moderate zones, or, when forced into the tropics, in highland areas. When Europeans arrived in the Americas, there were two large centers of population concentration: the Andean altiplano and Mesoamerica.

While the tribal peoples of South America are fascinating, they are not essential in explaining the roots of the people of Mexico and their communities in the United States. It is the tribes of Mesoamerica that provide the key to an understanding of the Mexicans' Indian legacy.[12] The heavy population density of Mesoamerica reflected the advent of agriculture. The transition from a nomadic to a sedentary society seems to have occurred first in the highlands of south central Mexico. Certainly it was there, according to studies made by the Canadian anthropologist Richard S. MacNeish in the Tehuacán Valley in the state of Puebla, that corn, or maize, the basis of all Mesoamerican civilizations, was initially cultivated around 5,000 BCE. From this source, the cultivation of maize spread both north and south. By the time Europeans arrived in the Americas, corn had been introduced into the Southwest and throughout the eastern part of North America via the Mississippi Valley. Amerindians cultivated a variety of crops, including beans, squash, tomatoes, avocados, potatoes, and pumpkins; but it was corn that made possible the rise of cities, the urban revolution which inaugurates the rise of civilization.

The first of the pre-Columbian civilizations of the Americas developed in the lowlands of southern Vera Cruz and Tabasco, near the shores of the Caribbean Sea, not far from the cradle of agriculture on the central plateau. Discovered in the late 1930s by the American archaeologist Matthew W. Stirling, the ruins of these first cities, San Lorenzo and La Venta being the most impressive, have been dated as early as 1,200 BCE. Built by a people who came to be called the Olmecs, after a later tribe of the same name, these initial urban clusters were actually ceremonial centers rather than full-fledged cities.

The artifact record permits scholars to reconstruct a general outline of Olmec life. The economic mainstay of this advanced society, of all pre-Columbian civilizations, was agriculture. In addition to corn, farmers cultivated squashes, peppers, and tomatoes. However, there was also some manufacturing and considerable commerce. Having abandoned a nomadic lifestyle, the Olmecs, like other peoples in similar circumstances, began to develop a stratified society. At the top were priests, who exerted political power, which they shared with the nobility. Since warfare was common—the rise of civilization increases the amount of strife in society wherever it occurs—the nobles were a warrior aristocracy. Merchants and artisans constituted a small percentage of the population, but they had an impact far greater than their modest numbers might indicate, as there is evidence of an extensive trading network. The majority of the people, the commoners, were peasants. They lived on the outskirts of the ceremonial centers and in the surrounding countryside. At the bottom of the social pecking order were undoubtedly slaves, probably war captives from other tribes and Olmec citizens who forfeited their freedom because of mounting debts.

The relative affluence of Olmec society permitted the rise of a complex and advanced culture. A rudimentary hieroglyphic writing system (not yet deciphered) evolved, perhaps, as in Mesopotamia and other early civilizations, an innovation introduced by merchants to facilitate financial transactions. A calendar permitted farmers to keep track of time. Another remarkable element of Olmec culture was art. Some experts have argued that the Olmecs superseded all pre-Columbian peoples in this regard. Their most prominent artistic creations were massive monolithic stone heads. Made of basalt, most stand about eight feet high. Evidence of a high degree of specialization, these beautiful colossal heads may reflect an African influence. Undoubtedly, as New World archaeology progresses, scholars will discover that there were many transoceanic contacts between the Americas and other continents, including Africa, only fifteen hundred miles from the Brazilian coast.

The most vital aspect of Olmec culture was religion, which impacted every aspect of life. The Olmecs believed in a variety of deities (polytheism). These gods were highly revered; and there is good reason to believe that they exacted, through their priests, continual sacrifices, including human offerings, one of the outstanding characteristics of virtually all Mesoamerican civilizations. In general, these civilizations displayed amazing similarities, especially, as the Mexican scholar Enrique Florescano has demonstrated, in their religious beliefs, which suggests that they had a common heritage, probably the Olmecs.

In the epoch between 300 CE and 900 CE, the classical period of New World civilization, there was an extraordinary flowering of culture in Mexico. During this golden age, a number of remarkable civilizations rose to prominence. One centered on Monte Albán, an elaborate ceremonial citadel discovered in the 1930s in the southern Mexican state of Oaxaca. Built by the Zapotecs, the city, high atop an artificially flattened hill, was the focal point of an extensive empire impacted by both Olmecs and Mayas. Dominated by a powerful priesthood, Monte Albán flourished until the ninth century. Occupied thereafter by Mixtecs, a neighboring tribe to the west, the city was eventually abandoned; and, overgrown with jungle, it soon sank into oblivion.

In the Valley of Mexico, site of present-day Mexico City, the classical period witnessed the rise and fall of another mighty urban society, Teotihuacán, "the place of the gods," as the Aztecs later called it, though contemporaries knew it by the name Tollan. With a population which may have reached two hundred thousand at its zenith in 600 CE, it represents the largest metropolis in Mesoamerica up to that time. Its hub was the ceremonial center dominated by two gigantic monuments, the Pyramid of the Sun—its base larger than that of the Pyramid of Cheops in Egypt's Giza Valley—and the smaller Pyramid of the Moon. Dedicated to commerce, Teotihuacanos—it is not known what they called themselves—extended their economic sway over most of southern Mexico before their sudden and mysterious destruction around 750 CE.

The preeminent civilization of the classical period, indeed the most advanced of all New World societies, was the Mayan. Beginning at about 300 CE, a major cultural awakening took place in the inhospitable rainforests of Belize, Honduras, El Salvador, Guatemala, and neighboring parts of Mexico, where the Mayas established their initial city-states. Tikal, located in the Petén district of Guatemala, was the largest of these. Thought at first to be ceremonial centers like those of the Olmecs, with the population always dispersed in the surrounding area, it now appears that some Mayan sites were true cities. Cultural heirs of the Olmecs, the enterprising Mayas carried their inheritance far beyond their predecessors. Given their primitive technology, the advances made in the intellectual realm were astonishing. At their height in the eighth century, the Mayas tracked stars, developed the concept of the zero, and had the ability to perform simple brain operations. Their astronomers traced the path of Venus with an error of only fourteen seconds a year. They created the only true writing system in the Americas—their hieroglyphics have recently been deciphered—and an elaborate calendar which was more accurate than that used in Europe before the Gregorian calendar of the late sixteenth century. In addition, Mayan art and architecture, well represented in Mexico City's renowned National Museum of Anthropology, are extraordinary accomplishments.

While they excelled in arts and sciences, the ancient Mayas, like the Greeks in the Old World, were unable to overcome their political differences. Divided into city-states controlled by warrior-kings, among the most celebrated being Pacal of Palenque, Shield Jaguar of Yaxchilan, and Yax-Pac of Copán, they proved incapable of creating a true empire. Warfare was endemic among them. Scholars since the 1960s have discovered that human sacrifice was at least as characteristic of their society as it was of the Aztecs. Wars may also account for the decline of urban life at about 900, when the Mayas mysteriously abandoned their cities in the southern highlands and migrated to the Yucatán Peninsula, which had been a peripheral area before. While the archaeologist Sir Eric Thompson attributed the exodus to peasant uprisings, most scholars today emphasize ecological problems, most notably soil exhaustion.

Yucatán witnessed the rise of new centers, including Chichén Itzá, Uxmal, and Mayapán. The northern migration revitalized their culture during the next few centuries, but the Mayans never regained their former eminence. The final decline began after the mid-thirteenth century. When the Spanish encountered the Mayas in the sixteenth century, they were a mere shadow of their old selves, their days of glory practically forgotten. During the postclassic period, from 900 to the Spanish Conquest, there were few intellectual and scientific advances.

Physical evidence discovered at cities in Yucatán, especially Chichén Itzá, indicates that during this postclassic era the Mayas were impacted profoundly by some alien culture, possibly that of the Toltecs. Scholars know that this warlike tribe entered central Mexico from the northern arid steppes sometime around the tenth century. Establishing their capital at Tula, north of Teotihuacán, an abandoned city by that time,[13] in the modern state of Hidalgo, the Toltecs assimilated the superior culture of the tribes of the Valley of Mexico, whom they came to dominate as they adopted an aggressive expansionist policy. Perhaps it was the opposition by these tribes which eventually forced the Toltecs to forsake Tula in the twelfth century and descend from the highlands to the shores of the Caribbean. They bequeathed a number of impressive aspects of their culture to the people they subjugated, among them their chief deity, the benign Quetzalcóatl. Often depicted as a plumed serpent, this god was incorporated into the religious beliefs of both Mayas and Aztecs.

Like the Toltecs, the Aztecs trace their origins to the northern deserts of Mexico, a term derived from *México,* which is what they called themselves, though the site of their mythical homeland, Aztlán, continues to be the object of intense speculation. Náhuatl speakers, both tribes emerged from the Chichimecs ("the dog people"), a generic name for the wild tribes of the North. The Aztecs appeared in the Valley of Mexico, which they called Anáhuac, sometime in the early thirteenth century. Despised by stronger and more advanced tribes, they were forced to continue a nomadic existence in search of a homeland for many years. According to ancient prophecies, the sight of an eagle perched on a cactus plant with a serpent in its mouth would signal the spot where they were to stop, build a capital, and inaugurate their quest for hegemony. Apparently this event came to pass in 1325—scholars are able to decipher their calendar, which differs significantly from that of the Mayas—for in that year they began to build Tenochtitlán, present Mexico City, in the midst of Lake Texcoco. By the time of the Spanish conquest, according to the Mexican anthropologist Miguel León-Portilla, the city's population "must have amounted at least to a quarter of a million."[14]

Having constructed their capital, the intrepid Aztecs embarked on a series of military campaigns which resulted in the creation of a vast empire at a phenomenal speed. By the end of the fifteenth century, a Triple Alliance, consisting of Tlacopan, Texcoco, and Tenochtitlán, had been forged, but the Aztecs were first among equals. When the Spaniards entered their expanding domain in 1519, they encountered a militaristic and theocratic kingdom of more than six million inhabitants stretching throughout southern Mexico. The quest for material wealth and a desire for war captives, dictated by a mystical religion which demanded continuous human sacrifice, seemed to motivate Aztec conquests. The most bloodthirsty of their deities was Huitzilopochtli, their war god. Not all sacrificial casualties were war captives; occasionally, their own citizens were offered up to the gods. "There is no indication of voluntarism among victims," Inga Clendinnen notes, "although some appear to have acquiesced in their fate."[15] Like the Romans, whom they resemble in many ways, Aztecs were master builders as well as valiant warriors. An extensive system of highways helped consolidate their power. Trade became as pivotal as warfare in spreading Aztec culture. What they contributed to their vassals was not insignificant.

Given the massive destruction wrought by the conquest, there are few surviving Aztec relics, but the written records of the *conquistadores* indicate awesome achievements. Tenochtitlán itself, the greatest of New World cities, with a population that was rapidly expanding by 1519, is testimony to their genius. According to its conquerors, it resembled Venice, a city acknowledged by these veterans of military campaigns throughout the Mediterranean world and beyond as the most beautiful in Europe. Only Naples and Constantinople could rival Tenochtitlán in grandeur. Rising magically from the depths of a blue lake, its center traversed by canals and crowned by brightly colored temple-pyramids, the city must have seemed a veritable heaven on earth to its conquerors. While powerfully affected by the Mayas, via Teotihuacanos and Toltecs, Aztec culture never quite achieved the lofty heights of the older civilization. But it should be pointed out that this culture, centered on the Valley of Mexico, was still in the process of developing when the Spaniards arrived. How far the Méxicas could have advanced had their society not been suddenly and completely demolished by external forces is a question that is as intriguing as it is futile.

THE CONQUEST OF MEXICO

The conqueror of the Aztecs was Hernán Cortés (1485–1547), the archetypal conquistador. Cortés was born to a relatively well-to-do family of minor nobility in Medellín, in the western Spanish province of Extremadura. At the age of thirteen, he was sent off to the University of Salamanca, established in 1243, then the most prestigious university on the peninsula, but he found academic life less than inspiring. Abandoning his studies, Cortés soon determined that his future lay overseas. His career was not unique; like young sons of England's noble families of a later date, many ambitious members of the Spanish aristocracy sought fame and fortune in the expanding empire. The young Spaniard arrived in Española in 1504 at the age of nineteen. He took up farming until 1511, when he distinguished himself in the conquest of Cuba, where he had a series of adventures before settling down in Santiago, the island capital. An able administrator, he became a man of some political prominence, even serving as mayor.

Meanwhile, rumors began to circulate of a vast inland empire on the mainland where natives were surrounded by incredible riches. When Diego Velásquez, governor of the island, decided to send an expedition to investigate, Cortés, with his immense energy and charisma, became the logical choice of a leader. The small fleet, consisting of eleven ships and about six hundred men, sailed for Yucatán on 18 February 1519. Following the coast northward, the ships landed several days later at a site Cortés christened La Villa Rica de la Vera Cruz, near present-day Vera Cruz. By now Cortés and Velásquez had had a falling out, and the crew was divided in its allegiance. Such personal animosities and intrigues would be characteristic of Spain's emissaries to the New World throughout this early period. Legend has it that the enterprising Cortés exposed his enemies by scuttling all but two ships, much to everyone's dismay, then promised that those who chose to do so might return to Cuba aboard one of the surviving vessels. However, upon taking the vote, the wily captain destroyed the promised craft, leaving no avenue of escape. The story may be apocryphal, but the fact remains that though he was roundly criticized then and later, Cortés was not only calculating, he was also fearless and single-minded in pursuit of his objectives. After this episode, there would be no turning back. Leaving some of their comrades to defend their beachhead, 450 men marched off to meet their fate.

Good fortune smiled on the expedition from the very beginning. An Indian slave girl, Malintzin Tenepal (1502?–1527?), whom the Spanish named Doña Marina, later called La Malinche, was a peace offering given to them by a tribe of Tabascans.[16] A speaker of Náhuatl, Doña Marina would serve as their faithful guide on the arduous journey. She proved to be invaluable; it was mainly because of her help that the Spaniards were able to survive a series of pitched battles against tribes friendly and unfriendly with the Méxicas. Almost three months after they started, the soldiers of fortune arrived at the Valley of Anáhuac, situated atop Mexico's central plateau, some seven thousand feet above sea level.

Moctezuma II Xocoyotzin had been emperor of the Aztec nation since 1502. Like Cortés, he would be a main player in the drama that would unfold in the next few months—surely one of the most incredible adventures in the annals of human history. Unlike the Spanish captain, he would prove unequal to the task. Mexican nationalists have not been kind to Moctezuma, who proved weak and vacillating under pressure; and yet, in retrospect, it is hard not to feel a certain empathy for the vanquished leader. His priests had prophesied that one day the god Quetzalcóatl, bearded and light-skinned, would return from the East, where he had disappeared in exile sometime in the dim past, a legend inherited from the

Toltecs. It is one of the remarkable coincidences in history that Cortés and his army appeared precisely at the time Quetzalcóatl was supposed to return. Impressed by their timely appearance, Moctezuma came to believe that the strangers might be gods, a suspicion fortified by the Spaniards' apparent invincibility.

Adopting an excessively cautious stance, the curious priest-king permitted the Spaniards, less than four hundred in number, to march into Tenochtitlán on 8 November 1519. With only token resistance, Moctezuma wasted one of his most precious advantages, the city's magnificent strategic position in the middle of Lake Texcoco. Once inside the city, Cortés played his cards flawlessly, first gaining Moctezuma's trust and then gradually turning the gullible emperor into a prisoner in his own palace. Using him as a hostage, the Spaniards, whose numbers fluctuated in the next few months as they reestablished contact with Cuba, extorted from the native peoples vast amounts of gold and silver, treasures brought in from all corners of the empire.

Eventually, the Méxicas rebelled. Disillusioned with their impotent and re-signed leader, an obvious pawn in the hands of their enemies, they staged an angry demonstration in which Moctezuma was fatally injured, leaving Cortés and his men to face the prospect of imminent destruction. In dire straits, they took a desperate gamble: under cover of darkness in the early hours of 1 July 1520, *la noche triste* (the sad night), they attempted to sneak out of the city, their horses' hooves muffled, and their pockets stuffed with loot. A fierce battle ensued. Fighting in total darkness and badly outnumbered, the Spanish faced formidable odds. Many of them, some 450 troops, perished in the bloody battle. Cortés himself barely avoided capture. At daybreak, the survivors, weak from exhaustion, gathered themselves on the mountains high above the Aztec capital, where, according to legend, their commander, discouraged and mourning the losses suffered, wept under an ahuehuete tree. Bernal Díaz del Castillo, one of the survivors and the leading chronicler of the epic undertaking, reports that the Spaniards, their numbers reduced to about four hundred men, staggered back to Tlaxcala, whose inhabitants proved to be faithful allies in this hour of extreme need.

Several months later, fortified by Tlaxcalans and other friendly natives, the irrepressible captain returned to gain his revenge. His objective was Tenochtitlán itself. Using Indian labor, the Spaniards constructed thirteen ships to be used in an amphibious attack on the Aztec stronghold. Weakened by disease and hunger, after a three-month siege, its inhabitants braced for the last assault. Mexican resistance was tenacious, but in the end, supported by native auxiliaries, the undaunted Spaniards prevailed. The fateful day was 13 August 1521. Surrounded by their enemies, the end in sight, many warriors preferred suicide to ignoble defeat, as they hurled themselves from atop the pyramids. Twenty thousand defenders died in the decisive campaign. Those who survived, including their heroic leader

Cuauhtémoc, had nowhere to go, for during the last assault their homes had been systematically leveled and their temples dismantled stone by stone. Mopping-up operations would take many years, the southern jungles providing the most resistance. Still, given the vertical nature of the empire, where all authority—in theory, at least—emanated from the center, the conquest was virtually achieved with the destruction of the Aztec capital.

The victory, given the disparity in numbers between Europeans and Amerindians, especially in view of how quickly it was accomplished, seems improbable. Less than one thousand Spaniards made the final assault on Tenochtitlán. They faced an empire reputedly numbering in the millions. Nor should it be forgotten that the Aztecs were the finest and most successful warriors ever known in the Americas. However, European advantages were numerous. Horses were among the most telling of these. Though the horse had originated in the Americas, it had been extinct for thousands of years. Aztecs were much in awe of these spirited animals. Cortés, appreciating the possibilities, was quick to take advantage, sending in his cavalry to wreak havoc among his opponents at every opportunity. And the Spanish were marvelous riders; they were so adapt at horsemanship that the Méxicas, according to their own accounts, initially thought that horse and rider were one single animal. Mastiffs, too, were effective weapons, given that their victims had no experience with large and ferocious dogs.

Indian allies, some two hundred thousand of them, were also valuable. William Hickling Prescott, whose nineteenth-century account of the Mexican Conquest is a literary masterpiece, was exaggerating only slightly when he concluded that the conquest was essentially an Indian victory.[17] At first, the Spaniards probably saw the empire as a monolithic whole. Almost immediately, however, it became clear that there were deep-seated divisions among their adversaries. In fact, most tribes had been subjugated by force and were ruled through terror. Particularly repugnant to the vassal states was the demand for human tribute, slaves to be sacrificed to the gods. An intense hatred of the Aztec ensured that many tribes, notably the Tlaxcalans, who had maintained their independence under the most trying circumstances, would conclude that the Spaniards were the lesser of evils; hence, the disparity between the two armies was less one-sided than one would expect.

Disease was another key factor that favored the Spaniards. In 1520 an epidemic raged throughout the empire, killing tens of thousands of inhabitants; a demographic revolution had been initiated, one that would ultimately reduce the Indian population by 90 percent. "Clearly," the University of Chicago historian William H. McNeill reasons, "if smallpox had not come when it did, the Spanish victory could not have been achieved in Mexico."[18] Native Americans had virtually no immunity to European diseases, which indicates that though there may well have been numerous transoceanic contacts with other parts of the world prior to the appearance of the conquistadores, these contacts involved only modest transfers of population. It seems clear that even before the battles began, morale was flagging among the Méxicas, a marked contrast to the robust energy and confidence displayed by their adversaries.

Finally, the difference in technology, in the opinion of the British historian Hugh Thomas, was perhaps the paramount factor in explaining the Spanish triumph.[19] In possession of cannon, crossbows, harquebuses, and steel armor, the Spaniards were more than a match for native troops using primitive weapons. During the next four centuries, Europeans would be helped immeasurably by their superior technology. Only when this material advantage was lost did European hegemony in the world erode.

The physical destruction of Tenochtitlán was decided by the conquistadores but mostly carried out by their native allies, who hardly needed encouragement. The vehemence that other Indians displayed in seeking revenge serves to remind us that the Aztecs were widely despised by their neighbors. Méxica priests and warriors, after all, had committed terrible atrocities. Their contemporaries clearly feared them more than they respected them.

As mentioned previously, pre-Columbian America was hardly the paradise some romantics have imagined. On the contrary, for most indigenous people at the time life was probably "solitary, poor, nasty, brutish, and short," to borrow the words of Thomas Hobbes. Still, something very valuable was lost with the destruction of this traditional society and its forcible incorporation into a strange and alien culture increasingly characterized by spiritual poverty. Even the most zealous advocate of Western supremacy would find it difficult to remain unmoved by the pathos expressed in an elegy written by a post-Conquest Aztec poet:

> We wander here and there
> In our desolate poverty.
> We are mortal men.
> We have seen bloodshed and pain
> Where once we saw beauty and valor.
>
> We are crushed to the ground;
> We lie in ruins.
> There is nothing but grief and suffering
> In Mexico and Tlatelolco,
> Where once we saw beauty and valor.[20]

The Aztecs' cultural accomplishments were extraordinary, and many aspects of their lives were admirable and worthy of emulation. Most importantly, the Aztecs and the other indigenous people of Mexico, civilized or not, have left an imposing legacy to the emerging nation. Octavio Paz (1914–1998), arguably the best interpreter of the Mexican national character, puts it best: "Not only the popular religion of Mexico but the Mexicans' entire life is steeped in Indian culture—the family, love, friendship, attitudes toward one's father and mother, popular legends, the forms of civility and life in common, the vision of death and sex, work and festivity."[21] Because the Indian legacy was especially strong among the lower classes, who represent the overwhelming majority of Mexican immigrants into the United States, it is hard to disagree with the renowned Native American scholar Jack D. Forbes, who claims that Mexican Americans are the largest Indian tribe in this country.[22]

Today, almost five hundred years after the Conquest, both Mexicans and Mexican Americans continue to exalt their Indian roots (*indigenismo*) while denying or condemning their Spanish past. This is a vast change in perspective from the early twentieth century, when the exact opposite was the case. It is currently in vogue to condemn the Spaniards for their past transgressions, especially their ill-treatment of Amerindians, whether it was Columbus in the Caribbean, Cortés in Mexico, or Junípero Serra in California.

Of course, this was the central argument employed by its enemies in the past—when France, England, and the Netherlands attempted to discredit Spain by charging that its people were uniquely cruel and avaricious, what Spanish historians call *la leyenda negra* (the Black Legend). Historically, however, Spain's first and most damaging critic was a Spaniard himself, the sixteenth-century Dominican Bartolomé de Las Casas (1474–1566), so perhaps it should not be surprising that at present Spain's most animated critics come from within the Hispanic community.[23] That the Spanish were religious fanatics, given the zeal engendered by centuries of crusades against the Moors, is undeniable. On the other hand, in its attitude toward Native Americans, as well as Africans, and, more importantly, its treatment of them, Spain rates as more humane than most of its detractors, as Mexican writer Carlos Fuentes has pointed out.[24]

Like Las Casas, many segments of Spanish society, notably the monarchy and the clergy, saw Indians as *hijos de Dios* (sons of God); and although the treatment of native peoples was characterized by extreme exploitation, it is also true that genocide was rarely practiced. Indeed, marriage between Indians and whites was sanctioned and even encouraged. Cortés himself—who is buried in Mexico, according to the terms of his will—set the precedent when he took La Malinche as his mistress. The mestizaje that came to characterize society in New Spain, including its northern frontier, has no meaningful parallel in the United States before the twentieth century, for economic as well as religious and historical reasons.

Moreover, whether its sins were great or small, undeniably Spain left a profound and lasting imprint on the peoples of the Americas, not just in the matter of race but in every aspect of their life. This is certainly the case with religion and language, the most basic elements of a people's culture. The fact remains that although Protestantism has made major inroads in recent years, Latin America, with its enormous population, is the leading Catholic region on the globe. Then, there is the language. The Chilean poet Pablo Neruda once exclaimed: "What a great language I have, it's a fine language we inherited from the fierce Conquistadors. . . . Wherever they went, they razed the land. . . . But words fell like pebbles out of the boots of the barbarians, out of their beards, their helmets, their horseshoes, luminous words that were left glittering here . . . our language. They carried off the gold and left us the gold. . . . They carried everything off and left us everything. . . . They left us the words."[25] Mexico today has the largest Catholic as well as the largest Spanish-speaking population in the world; in significant ways it has become more Spanish than Spain itself.

Mexicanos in the United States have a rich heritage. Their culture is the product of a wide variety of influences. The most recent of these is that of the dominant Anglo society: albeit slower than with most immigrant groups, assimilation inevitably, though often reluctantly, is taking place. A community of humble means, Mexicanos also have much in common with other people who occupy the lowest socioeconomic levels, what the anthropologist Oscar Lewis termed the "culture of poverty." Catholicism continues to be another key factor shaping Mexican American life. Indeed, according to the scholar Roberto R. Bacalski-Martínez, "Traditionally, the greatest single cultural force in Mexican American society has been the Roman Catholic Church."[26] However, the Spanish and Indian elements which fused after the collapse of Tenochtitlán in 1521 are what give the culture its distinguishing characteristics. It was at this crucial juncture that the foundation was laid for the emergence of a unique people whose fascinating history is only now coming to light. Perhaps this is what Richard Rodríguez, the celebrated though controversial Mexican American writer, has in mind when he concludes: "My life began, it did not end, in the sixteenth century."[27]

THE SPANISH
FRONTIER
1521–1821

On 12 July 1893, Frederick Jackson Turner (1861–1932), a young professor from Wisconsin, gave a scholarly presentation entitled "The Significance of the Frontier in American History" at the annual convention of the American Historical Association in Chicago. The most influential work ever written by a U.S. historian, this seminal essay proposed that the key to understanding the American people was to be found in their frontier experience, or, as he put it, "the existence of an area of free land, its continuous recession, and the advance of American settlement westward, explain American development."[1] A product of three hundred years of westward movement into an environment with immense resources but few people, exactly the opposite of Europe, the national character came to be characterized by a strong work ethic, rugged individualism, and an unflagging optimism. Yet the most profound legacy of this adventure into the wilderness was democracy. While he discovered many other character traits, not all of them flattering, it was Turner's description of Americans as paladins of democracy that left a lasting impression; by the time of his death in 1932, the idea that "democracy was born on the frontier" had been elevated to an article of faith among his countrymen. A brilliant analysis of the American past, the Turner thesis soon became the dominant interpretation of the United States and what the nation stood for.

Today Turner's views remain popular, and rightfully so, but they are no longer universally endorsed. Among the most severe critics of the Frontier thesis in recent years have been Chicana/o historians, who tend to emphasize the racism and oppression that accompanied the westward movement. These scholars also question, as others have done in the past, the notion that the American national character can be explained exclusively by the westward movement of English-speaking people. They point out that the Spanish also left a meaningful legacy in the United States. This contribution, mostly found in the Southwest, has generally been neglected by textbooks on American history. Moreover, as the Jesuit historian John Francis

Bannon, one of the few scholars dedicated to studying the Spanish Borderlands, has justly observed, "A study of the Spanish frontier, the Borderlands, will show that the Anglo-American experience, magnificent and thrilling though it was, actually was not quite as unique as it is sometimes pictured and chauvinistically thought to be. The Anglo-American frontier can be better understood and more properly evaluated by process of comparison."[2]

SPANISH EXPLORATION OF THE FAR NORTH

After the conquest of the Aztecs and the destruction of their capital, the Spaniards fanned out in all directions in search of God, Gold, and Glory, the same quest which had brought them to the New World in the first place. In the forefront of this march was Hernán Cortés himself, who led an expedition westward to the sea that bears his name. Although the land of the Chichimecas to the north was at first neglected, before too long, conquistadores began to venture into that mysterious region as well, the northern frontier of the Viceroyalty of New Spain (Nueva España), the name Spaniards christened present-day Mexico.[3]

The first Europeans in the Far North, however, were not motivated by God, Gold, or Glory; Álvar Núñez Cabeza de Vaca (1490?–1557?) and his men arrived purely by chance. While sailing to New Spain from Florida, which had first been explored by Juan Ponce de León in 1513, a Spanish expedition consisting of several rafts was caught in a tropical storm in 1528, and most of the men perished. Some crew members managed to reach the shores of Texas (named after a local Caddo Indian tribe). Before too long, only four men were left: Cabeza de Vaca, a native of Andalucía; two other Spaniards, Andrés Dorantes and Alonso del Castillo; and Estevánico, a Moor. These strangers, the first whites and the first black to enter what is now the American Southwest, were objects of curiosity and awe. Their survival among the various tribes they encountered must be accredited to the extraordinary ability of their self-appointed leader, Cabeza de Vaca. Possessing a rudimentary knowledge of herbs, the resourceful Spaniard was able to pass himself off as a medicine man. Thanks to his creative ability, the small party survived, sometimes as slaves, sometimes as free men, meandering throughout the Far North for several years, hoping to find their way back to the cities of central Mexico. Finally, in 1536, the motley group, more Indian than white in appearance by now, was rescued by a Spanish expedition in the wilderness northwest of Mexico City, the viceregal capital.

The men had had incredible adventures, as Cabeza de Vaca's memoirs graphically illustrate.[4] They told tales of exotic peoples and strange flora and fauna. As often happens in similar circumstances, the stories were embellished as they circulated among listeners eager to validate their own aspirations. In time, rumors had it that Cabeza de Vaca had actually sighted the famed Seven Cities of Antilia, later called the Seven Cities of Cíbola, legendary towns adorned with gold. The rumors stimulated a fascination with the lands beyond the northern frontier, and in 1539, Fray Marcos de Niza, a Franciscan, was sent north to investigate. His reports were encouraging. In fact, the friar reported seeing the fabulous cities. Soon three major expeditions were underway in an effort to find the coveted wealth.

In retrospect, it seems odd that the conquistadores, cold and calculating in many respects, could be so gullible during the Age of Exploration. On the flimsiest of evidence they were ready to risk life and limb in a quixotic quest for beautiful women, unimaginable wealth, and even eternal life. Of course, they failed to find the Amazonian beauties of the fictitious island of California; the gold-laden lake where El Dorado, the Indian chief who was covered in gold from head to toe, took his annual bath; and the fabled Fountain of Youth, not to mention a multitude of other mirages. But it should be remembered that the medieval mindset, with its preoccupation with the magical and the supernatural, characterized Western society during the Renaissance and persisted well past the Scientific Revolution in many corners of Europe. And Europeans *had* made one amazing discovery after another since the time of Marco Polo. "Moreover," the historian David J. Weber adds, "Hernán Cortés and Francisco Pizarro had proved the existence of great kingdoms and extraordinary wealth."[5]

The first Spanish thrust into the north took place along the Caribbean shores of North America. In May 1539, the governor of Cuba, Hernando Méndez de Soto y Gutiérrez Cardeñosa, set out to explore Florida with about six hundred colonists. Venturing far and wide, the expedition eventually came upon the Mississippi River—possibly the first white men to cast their eyes upon this wonder—before reaching present-day Arkansas. In search of wealth, Soto lost his life in a futile effort to find it. He died of a fever on 21 May 1542. The survivors of the ill-fated expedition eventually made their way back to New Spain late in the following year.

As the Spanish explored the American Southeast, they also stretched across the continent to the American Southwest.[6] The second attempt to uncover the alleged riches of the North was led by Francisco Vásquez de Coronado (1510–1554), the most famous of the early Spanish explorers of North America.[7] The scion of a wealthy and respected family from Salamanca, Vásquez de Coronado arrived in the New World as a young man of twenty-five. He quickly established himself as the leading political presence on the northern frontier after his appointment in 1538 to the governorship of Nueva Galicia, the coastal province lying northwest of Mexico City. Shortly thereafter he was selected by Viceroy Antonio de Mendoza to head an expedition which would resume the search for the Seven Cities where Fray Marcos de Niza had left off.

In February 1540, Vásquez de Coronado set out from Compostela, in Nueva Galicia, leading an expedition that numbered about eleven hundred men, women, and children, including some seven hundred Indians. The route he selected was similar to that taken by the friar, north along the western coast of the mainland, through the Sonoran desert, and into the area now known as Arizona. The expedition gradually made its way into present-day New Mexico, where the explorers encountered the Zuñi. Farther east, they came across other Pueblo tribes along the Rio Grande, or the Río Bravo del Norte, as it would come to be known. At this time, there were roughly forty thousand Pueblo Indians living in some ninety towns. Failing to find the Golden Cities—Cíbola turned out to be the villages of the Zuñi—but convinced by natives that farther to the north there existed an equally wealthy kingdom, the Gran Quivira, the conquistadores pushed on. Crossing what is today the Texas Panhandle, Vásquez de Coronado went as far as modern-day Kansas, where he arrived in early 1542. At this point, Vásquez de Coronado realized he had been misled by his Indian guide, who was promptly tortured and executed. Abandoning the venture, the disillusioned explorer returned in disgrace to Nueva Galicia in the early summer, having squandered a fortune.

The return of Vásquez de Coronado coincided with the beginning of the third major attempt to expand New Spain's northern borders, this time along the Pacific Coast. The protagonist of this ill-fated effort was Juan Rodríguez Cabrillo, a native of Andalucía, not a Portuguese, as is often claimed. He was the first white man credited with seeing the present-day state of California, designated Alta California at that time to distinguish it from the land to the south, Baja California. Cabrillo sailed from the port of Navidad up the west coast of New Spain in the summer of 1542. After exploring San Diego Bay, sighted on 28 September, the expedition proceeded north along the coast as far as the islands off the Santa Barbara coast. There, Cabrillo suffered a leg injury, which proved fatal. He died on 3 January 1543 and was buried in an unmarked grave, probably on one of the channel islands. Undaunted, the expedition continued up the coast as far as present-day southern Oregon, before returning to Navidad. Survivors reported that the lands they had visited were heavily populated and had a multitude of natural resources, not the least of which was the balmy Mediterranean climate so reminiscent of Spain itself. But there was no gold. Moreover, the voyage north against the strong Japanese current made travel to Alta California exceedingly difficult. Consequently, it would be another sixty years before the Spaniards attempted another foray into the seductive coastal lands beyond Baja California.

The failure of the conquistadores to find the Golden Cities discouraged further efforts to explore the Far North for almost a half century. In addition, there were many obstacles to expansion in that direction, among them arid terrain, vast distances, and the increasing hostility displayed by native inhabitants. The gravest impediment, however, was the apparent absence of precious minerals. Moreover, in the mid-1540s, rich silver lodes were found immediately northwest of Mexico

City, in Zacatecas, and soon after in nearby San Luis Potosí and Durango. Prospectors now poured into this desolate region, most of which became the province of Nueva Vizcaya in the 1560s. The line of settlement remained nearly static until the early 1580s, when two expeditions ventured into New Mexico: the first led by the Franciscan Agustín Rodríguez and the soldier Francisco Chamuscada, and the second by a wealthy entrepreneur, Antonio de Espejo. Neither party encountered much success and colonization of the area was delayed for another decade.

SETTLEMENT OF NEW MEXICO

The *entrada* (incursion) that led to permanent settlement of New Mexico occurred in the 1590s, not because the mines of the interior were exhausted, nor because of the declining Indian labor force given the catastrophic impact of European diseases, but rather because of the threats, real and imagined, posed by European interlopers in the northern region. Having been explored previously, only now were the lands slated to become the American Southwest in the distant future occupied by Spanish *pobladores* (settlers).

The most immediate challenge seemed to come from the English. While England had been quick to capitalize on the discovery of the New World, efforts to follow up on these early voyages of exploration had been put on hold by the religious and political problems associated with the Reformation. As the Elizabethan Compromise gradually took shape, English ships were encouraged to venture far and wide in an effort to expand the Crown's sphere of influence. The most successful of Queen Elizabeth's sea captains was Francis Drake, who circumnavigated the globe in 1577–1580. During the course of this risky adventure, the bold Englishman initiated a series of raids on Spanish ships and even had the audacity to attack the leading city in South America, Lima. The Spanish feared Drake because of the menace he posed to their shipping, but there were larger issues as well. They suspected that Drake's visit to California in the summer of 1579 would pave the way for further explorations along the Pacific Coast and perhaps to the discovery of the fabled Strait of Anián, the Northwest Passage, a waterway connecting the Atlantic and Pacific oceans which European explorers continued to seek for the next two centuries. At any rate, a British presence in the north would jeopardize Spanish expansion there, and possibly even New Spain itself, with its lucrative mining interests.

The formidable task of establishing the northern colonies, a thousand miles beyond the established frontier, fell on the shoulders of Juan de Oñate y Salazar (1549?–1628?), a truly outstanding frontiersman in Mexican history.[8] Oñate grew up in Zacatecas, where his Basque father made a fortune in mining and became one of the most prominent silver barons in the province of Nueva Galicia, the vast

administrative region centering on his native city. Following in his father's footsteps, Juan de Oñate devoted many years to public service on the frontier, earning
a reputation for valor in fighting Chichimeca tribes. Rich and daring, he seemed
the logical choice to initiate Spanish settlement of the Far North. The expedition,
recruited over a period of several years and numbering about 130 soldiers, some
accompanied by wives and children, finally commenced on 26 January 1598.
Oñate entered New Mexico in early May and a few weeks later founded San Juan
de los Caballeros on the upper Rio Grande as his headquarters. During the course
of this momentous journey Don Juan and his party had blazed what would become
one of the most significant overland routes on the North American continent, the
eighteen-hundred-mile road from Mexico City to Santa Fe which the Spanish called
the Camino Real de Tierra Adentro (the Royal Road of the Interior), popularly
known as the Chihuahua Trail.

A string of small settlements, usually adjacent to Indian pueblos along the
river, soon appeared. Among them was San Gabriel del Yunque, which became
the provincial capital for a short time, and is now an archaeological ruin. Oñate's
men were assigned *encomiendas* on the surrounding area; that is, they were given
the right to exploit the labor of the native inhabitants of the land in return for
protecting and civilizing them. Appointed governor of the territory, Oñate served
until 1607, when he resigned and left for Mexico City to face charges of mismanagement. He never returned to New Mexico, but the Spanish consolidated their
hold by increasing the number of settlements along the river. The most important
of these towns would be the Villa Real de Santa Fe, founded by Pedro de Peralta,
Oñate's successor, in 1609 or 1610—the records are unclear—the oldest state
capital in the United States. The pattern of settlement, like many developments in
the Spanish frontier, would be dictated by the native American population. The
colonists settled among the Pueblos because the indigenous people represented
potential Christian converts and a much-needed labor force.

When the Spanish entered New Mexico at the end of the sixteenth century,
there were two competing lifestyles among the Indian tribes, sedentary and nomadic.[9] The former were represented by agriculturalists who resided in *pueblos*
(towns). Apparently descendants of the Anasazi—or "the ancient ones," whose
advanced culture centered on the Four Corners region, where modern-day Utah,
Colorado, New Mexico, and Arizona come together—these tribes had immigrated
south sometime after 1000 CE. Some settled in the desert, among them the Hopi,
the Zuñi, and the Ácoma, tribes known as the Western Pueblos; the majority, the
Eastern Pueblos, resided in a series of towns along the Rio Grande, where irrigation
was much easier. In either case, their lifestyle was dependent on the production of
corn, which had been cultivated locally since about 1000 BCE, when it had been
introduced from central Mexico.

Nomadic tribes were recent arrivals into the region. They had preceded the Spanish by only a few centuries, perhaps even a few decades. Enemies of the sedentary tribes, these wanderers made their living by preying on their relatively affluent neighbors, as well as hunting and gathering. Arriving via the Great Plains, the nomadic tribes maintained some traditions associated with native peoples of that cultural province. Like the Pueblos, the nomads were divided into a number of distinct tribes. Among the most powerful were the Apache, the Navajo, and, somewhat later, the Comanche. During most of the year, the sparse resources of an arid environment necessitated the division of these nomadic tribes into smaller bands. The Jicarilla, the Mescalero, and the Chiricahua, for instance, were all bands of the Apache that would later inspire terror among the pobladores. Small in numbers, the roving tribes were more of a nuisance than a bona fide threat to both Pueblos and Spaniards until the introduction of the horse, which dramatically changed Indian life. Especially after the beginning of the eighteenth century, the nomads, and in particular the Apache, came to dictate the way of life that grew to be characteristic of the present states of northern Mexico from Tamaulipas to Sonora and the American Southwest.

In recent years, much has been written about the treatment of the Native American by the Spanish, but the subject remains controversial. Practically the only point on which there is general consensus is that it is difficult to generalize about the relationship between the two peoples on the northern frontier. There was a sizable discrepancy between attitudes and treatment, particularly on the part of the Spanish. Moreover, neither group was homogenous. There were vast differences among both settlers and tribal peoples. For their part, the sedentary tribes differed markedly from the nomads, and in turn there were crucial distinctions among the agriculturalists themselves. The Zuñi, the Hopi, and the Pueblos of the Rio Grande Valley were separated by language, customs, and traditions. Every tribe took for granted its superiority over its neighbor. Thus, generalizations about Indians, even when limited to the heart of the Southwest, are difficult at best. The same is true for the Spanish intruders. Colonists, missionaries, and soldiers were rarely in agreement on matters pertaining to native communities. Attitudes and behavior also changed from time to time, depending on many factors—political, social, and economic. Consequently, although it is desirable to trace general patterns of behavior, it is also necessary to understand that there were always substantial crosscurrents.

The Spaniards' attitude toward Indians of the Far North, regardless of their cultural level, was similar to their view of the natives of the interior of New Spain: they saw them as inferior beings. In this respect, Spaniards were hardly unique. Like other Europeans, they were guilty of ethnocentrism. Ignorance breeds contempt, and the Spanish saw many things they did not understand. Being tolerant is a relatively modern ideal; few Europeans saw toleration as a virtue until the Age of the Enlightenment.

Yet among the European nations expanding their frontiers, the Spanish position is a subtle variation on the general theme. These differences are explained by a unique historical experience, notably Spain's long contact with the Moors. Inspired by centuries of crusading zeal, as we have observed, the Spanish people of the sixteenth century had developed a religious faith bordering on fanaticism. During the course of the 1500s, this fervor was fanned by the wars of the Reformation. Under the great Hapsburg ruler of the Holy Roman Empire, Emperor Charles V, recognized as King Carlos I in Spain, the Spanish prided themselves on being the paladins of Catholicism. This missionary mindset, this blinding zeal, created a rationale for the many atrocities Indians suffered throughout Spain's American possessions.

A prime example is Ácoma. The famous Sky City in western New Mexico had been initially sighted by Vásquez de Coronado's men. More than fifty years later, the Spaniards returned to the area and attempted to establish contact with the mesa dwellers; but in 1598, a party sent out by Oñate was ambushed by the inhabitants of the pueblo, and as a result the irate governor chose to make an example of the recalcitrant natives. Ácoma was conquered after a brief but violent siege, and revenge was swift. Five hundred men and three hundred women and children were massacred in cold blood; some five hundred women and children and eighty men were taken alive, tried, and found guilty of treachery. All those over the age of twelve were condemned to twenty years of slavery; the men over twenty-one had one foot cut off as an additional penalty; and the children were distributed among the priests and soldiers to be used as slave labor.

On the other hand, the influence of the Moorish crusades also had a positive impact on race relations in the Americas. Given the lofty achievements of their civilization, Moors could hardly be seen as racially inferior. Unlike many other Europeans, then, the Spanish did not automatically equate dark skin with innate inferiority. While many Europeans, especially the English, came to regard Indians as "savages," practically indistinguishable from wild animals, among the Spanish the notion developed that Indians were hijos de Dios; which is to say, though they were ignorant, like children they were still human beings with souls and intelligence, hence potentially equal to Spaniards. This concession allowed the massive mestizaje which came to characterize Hispanic America—a phenomenon not found on the English frontier to any appreciable extent, Pocahontas notwithstanding. Yet, as the historian Antonia Castañeda reminds us, the absence of Spanish women and the propensity of conquerors to ravage native women should not be minimized as other crucial factors resulting in a merging of the two peoples.

Spain's critics, both now and in the past, have been unwilling or unable to appreciate the complexity of Spanish Indian policy. In fact, the Spanish attitude toward the Indian was highly ambivalent. Consequently, there were broad inconsistencies in the management of Native Americans. Spain treated Indians both better and worse than did other imperial powers of the Age of Expansion. Indeed, given human nature, what is remarkable is not so much that the Spanish mistreated the Indians but that a key element within Hispanic society was willing to ameliorate their plight.

All segments of Spanish colonial society exploited the Indians, but the Church tried to also give them something in return: civilization—which to most clergymen meant Catholicism, first and foremost, and then Spanish, "the language of God." So convinced were the missionaries of the righteousness of their cause that many were willing to risk martyrdom to spread the holy faith. Fray Agustín Rodríguez and two Franciscan colleagues lost their lives in 1581–1582 at the hands of the Pueblos. More fortunate was Fray Juan Ramírez, still another Franciscan, who arrived in Ácoma some thirty years after it had been crushed by Oñate's men, and converted its entire population with nothing more than a crucifix. From a historical perspective, the power of religious faith, especially during the Age of the Reformation, should not be underestimated.

Wherever the Spanish went, they set up missions, perhaps the most characteristic of their institutions on the frontier.[10] Missionary work was entrusted to the regular clergy, whose job it was to convert and Hispanicize the neophytes during a lengthy process of instruction. Following conversion, the native peoples would be turned over to the secular, or diocesan, clergy. Needless to say, as in the Old World, competition between regular and secular clergy continued, with the former only grudgingly giving way to the latter.

The two most active monastic orders on the Spanish frontier were the Franciscans and the Jesuits, though other monks, notably the Dominicans, were employed by the Crown from time to time.[11] The first missionaries in New Spain were the Franciscans, the Order of Friars Minor, who quickly came to monopolize religious instruction in major Mexican cities and sought to maintain that hegemony on the northern frontier.

It was the Franciscans who accompanied Juan de Oñate into New Mexico. They were entrusted with the apostolic mission of administering to the spiritual needs of the numerous Pueblo settlements in the region. This province extended along the Rio Grande from El Paso del Norte, present-day Ciudad Juárez, where a mission, Nuestra Señora de Guadalupe de los Mansos del Paso del Norte, was founded on 8 December 1659, to the Upper Rio Grande Valley and as far north as the Spanish could expand their authority.

The *presidio,* or garrison, was the other major institution which appeared on the Spanish frontier. As in other European frontiers, the function of the fort was to provide protection against foreign interlopers and to pacify native populations. Unlike other frontiersmen, soldiers were generally not enthusiastic about immigrating into the inhospitable periphery; they were sent there by the Crown, oftentimes with their families, and were expected to endure long enlistments. Once their tenures of service were up, soldier-settlers were enticed to remain on the frontier by generous land grants supplied by the king or his designees.

Crowded into small settlements and surrounded by a hostile population who saw them as a force of occupation, Spanish citizens, both colonists and soldiers, developed close ties with one another. Indeed *presidiales* (presidial troops), as mentioned earlier, were also settlers. The sense of community was strengthened by the limited availability of marriage partners. Perhaps the most compelling factor in solidifying the community, however, was the common perception of the Indian. Both colonists and soldiers grew to fear and hate the Apache and other warlike tribes. Occasionally, relations improved as trade became mutually profitable or alliances against common enemies made cooperation desirable. Late in the colonial period, for example, a flourishing trade was carried out with the Comanches, who supplied pobladores with Indian slaves. In general, though, conflict characterized the relationship between Spaniards and nomadic tribes.[12]

The Spanish attitude toward the neighboring Pueblo peoples was much different than toward *indios bárbaros,* as the Spaniards referred to unconquered Indians. Converts to Christianity and providers of cheap labor, the Pueblos were naturally seen in a more positive light. Fearful of the Apache and other hostile tribes, the Pueblos, for their part, were often willing to cooperate with whites. Indeed, some interracial marriages occurred, though most were outside the aegis of the Church in this early period.

Nevertheless, the prevailing view of the Pueblos among both soldiers and colonists was that they were inferior peoples, a convenient attitude which justified colonial exploitation. As settlement expanded, a rift developed between the missionaries and the rest of the Spanish community, as happened throughout the empire. The clergy attempted to ameliorate the worst abuses of the native people, while the Spanish citizenry, intent on extracting as much work as possible, called for a laissez-faire policy toward the conquered. Ironically, however, it was the friars themselves who ultimately drove Indians to the breaking point. Although a prolonged drought and increased labor demands by pobladores played a role, it was the missionaries' unrelenting and heavy-handed efforts to undermine traditional religious beliefs which did most to alienate their wards.

The result was the great Pueblo Revolt of 1680.[13] Led by the medicine man Popé, from the town of San Juan, Pueblo villagers along the Upper Rio Grande Valley staged a massive uprising on 10 August of that year. Caught by complete surprise, the colonists, who numbered no more than twenty-eight hundred at that time, were no match for their incensed foes, who received help from some of the nomadic tribes. Almost four hundred settlers were killed, as were most of the thirty-three Franciscans serving the province. Spanish villages of the Upper Rio Grande Valley were quickly abandoned as their panicked inhabitants fled south, to the Franciscan mission at Paso del Norte. For one of the few times in recorded history, a European overseas frontier was actually forced to retreat in the face of popular resistance. It took a decade before the Spaniards were able to gather sufficient reinforcements from central New Spain to reestablish their dominance.

The task of reconquering the lost lands was entrusted to an energetic and capable military commander, Diego de Vargas Zapata y Luján Ponce de León, who was appointed governor of the province of New Mexico in 1688. It took four years before all the preparations were made. Santa Fe was recaptured on 16 September 1692, signaling the beginning of the reconquest. A protracted campaign ensued, during which the governor gained the ascendancy as much by diplomacy as by military prowess. By mid-1694, that victory was assured, though mopping-up operations would drag on for years. Spaniards had now made striking inroads in disrupting the traditional life of the native inhabitants, as reflected in the fact that Pueblo Indian auxiliaries actually played a major role in the campaigns against their brothers.

Resolved not to risk another debacle of the kind suffered in 1680, Spanish administration was tightened. More importantly, reforms, like the abolition of the encomienda, were instituted. The worst abuses were also soon abolished, paving the way for pacification of the area. The missionaries, who gradually lost their influence during the following years, were as conciliatory as was the government. While the exploitation of the natives was not ended altogether—indeed many natives found themselves reduced to peonage—relations between the Spaniards and Pueblos would improve markedly during the eighteenth century.

The Spanish not only rebuilt their old towns, but also began to expand into outlying areas. Among the many new settlements were Santa Cruz de la Cañada, Albuquerque, and Bernalillo, where De Vargas died of a fever in 1704. While it may seem that this expansionist policy was ill-advised given their scant numbers and the strength displayed recently by their native adversaries, a more crucial consideration was weighing on the conquerors, the prospect of foreign invasion. By now, the French appeared to pose a far greater threat to the Spaniards than the English ever had. Colonization of Texas became imperative.

SETTLEMENT OF THE NORTHERN FRONTIER
BEYOND NEW MEXICO

René-Robert Cavelier, sieur de La Salle, made his epic voyage down the Mississippi to the Gulf of Mexico in 1682. He claimed the vast interior of North

America, which he named Louisiana after his monarch, Louis XIV, for the French. His intention was to set up a vast network of trading posts, where valuable furs would be collected from the Indians and taken down the Mississippi to a French city which would be constructed on the delta. La Salle failed to realize this grandiose scheme; he was killed in Texas by mutineers in 1687. But the prospect of a peltry empire centered on the lower Mississippi continued to fascinate his countrymen for many decades to come.

The Spanish, meanwhile, were not oblivious to these heady visions. In fact, they tended to exaggerate the threat posed by the French on their periphery. In the late 1680s, determined to forestall French encroachment there, the Spanish Crown dispatched several expeditions into the eastern part of Texas, which was officially designated a frontier province in 1691. This initial attempt at colonization failed because of serious manpower shortages and Indian resistance.

French persistence, however, forced the Spaniards to refocus their energies on east Texas, and in June 1716, this area was reoccupied by an expedition under the command of Captain Domingo Ramón. A presidio at Los Adaes and several missions were set up on the eastern periphery, but the most pivotal settlements were established at an intermediate location between these isolated communities and the Rio Grande. Here, on the San Antonio River, an expedition led by Martín de Alarcón founded a mission, San Antonio de Valero, and presidio, San Antonio de Béxar, in 1718. Significantly, this very year the French constructed New Orleans, meant to be the great entrepôt La Salle envisioned. On the San Antonio River, a civilian population joined the missionaries and soldier-settlers in 1731, when the town of San Fernando de Béxar was founded by fifty-five immigrant families from the Canary Islands. These white Canary Islanders, the Isleños, were destined to dominate the economic and political life of San Antonio, which became the provincial capital in 1770. However, as the historian Jesús F. de la Teja has shown, the presidiales were numerous and highly regarded enough that the Isleños never established a complete monopoly.[14]

Meanwhile, thwarted by the French, the second attempt to colonize east Texas, the Ramón mission, had had to be abandoned. In the long run, though, this failed 1716 initiative brought some benefits, as the historian Donald E. Chipman makes clear: "The reestablishment of missions and a presidio in East Texas was very important historically, because it gave Spain a valid claim to land north of the Rio Grande, did much to determine that Texas would be Spanish, not French, and helped advance the eventual boundary between Texas and the United States to the Sabine River."[15]

Near San Antonio, a number of smaller outposts were constructed during this period, notably La Bahía, farther down the San Antonio River in 1721. Other small settlements, among them Laredo, were built along the Lower Rio Grande

Valley in the 1740s by pobladores under the command of José de Escandón, governor of the newly established province of Nuevo Santander. Still another wave of immigrants arrived during the economic crisis that gripped the vicekingdom in the mid-1780s.

However, the Texas frontier remained relatively depopulated during the eighteenth century. By 1800, there were only about thirty-five hundred Tejanos in the neglected province. The French threat never really took on the dimensions anticipated, and in 1763, in the aftermath of the Seven Years' War, this preoccupation disappeared altogether with the Spanish acquisition of Louisiana. The lack of sedentary tribes to provide needed labor to the region also proved to be a major obstacle to effective colonization, as did the hostility of the nomadic tribes. It was the Comanche, above all others, who stymied Spanish designs on the northeast frontier. Immigrating into the southern plains from the Rockies in the early 1700s, the Comanche soon displaced the Apache as the Spaniards' chief adversaries on the Texas grasslands. During this period, they were acquiring the horse and mastering its use as a military weapon. Monopolizing this knowledge, they soon dominated neighboring tribes, establishing their reputation in the process as Lords of the Southern Plains. Spanish settlers were nearly as defenseless against the Comanche as other Indians were. Horses gave the tribe a sway disproportionate to its modest numbers. Under these circumstances, it is clear why presidios and missions maintained a precarious existence in Texas throughout the colonial period.

Meanwhile, the northwestern frontier of New Spain was also moving forward, in fits and starts. Like Texas, present-day Arizona witnessed the entry of the Spanish in the late seventeenth century. Compared to the eastern thrust along the Caribbean, movement up the western corridor of mainland Mexico, between the Gulf of California and the Sierra Madre Occidental—and neighboring Baja California—owed more to religious considerations than to imperial concerns.

Migration north along the Sea of Cortés was initiated early. By the mid-1500s, the province of Nueva Galicia, extending beyond Culiacán, founded in 1531, in Sinaloa, was reasonably well established. In the following decades, expansion proceeded slowly. The failure of Vásquez de Coronado to find treasure was a factor. So was the manpower shortage in the Sinaloa region; settlers preferred the mining areas opening up farther inland, in Nueva Vizcaya, now the states of Durango and Chihuahua. The prospects for expansion changed dramatically, however, in 1591, when the Jesuits were given permission to set up missions on the northwestern frontier.

The Black Robes arrived in New Spain in 1572 anxious to do missionary work on the frontier. Since their services were required in the densely populated core area and the Franciscans had established a monopoly on the periphery, they were forced to postpone their plans for a generation. Their chance came once the

Crown, stirred to action by news of Drake's foray into California and the prospect of foreign settlement there, decided that Spanish movement toward the northwest was imperative. Beneficiaries of this imperial concern—Franciscan friars were already overextended—the Jesuits were only too glad to take advantage of the opportunity to pursue their own goals of propagating the true faith. No sooner had they received permission to carry out their new assignment, a product of years of intense lobbying, than they dispatched late in 1591 two missionaries to the Sinaloa frontier, Gonzalo de Tapia and Martín Pérez.

Dedicated and hardworking, Jesuit priests were indomitable in their proselytizing campaign. Their persistence became proverbial, and their efforts were generally crowned with success. During the course of the seventeenth century, they made steady progress moving up the western corridor. Traveling in pairs, they established missions among the Yaquis, the Opatas, and the numerous other tribes of Sinaloa and Sonora. Already by 1620, fifty-five individual missions had been founded.

Although there were many Jesuit fathers who served with distinction, one man stands out among the rest, Eusebio Francisco Kino (1645?–1711), who was among the most remarkable explorers anywhere in the Americas. An Italian by birth, Father Kino was born in the Tyrolese town of Segno. Drawn to the Church at an early age and anxious to escape life in a small provincial hamlet, he opted for the Society of Jesus, the most dynamic order of the day. In Bavaria, he received the best education available and then embarked for the New World.

Kino was one of the first foreigners given permission by the Spanish Crown to enter New Spain. He served briefly in Baja California, where a plan to found missionary centers proved abortive, before arriving in 1687 on the expanding Sonora frontier, where he spent the rest of his life. Practically single-handedly, Kino pushed the mission into the Pimería Alta, today's northern Sonora and southern Arizona. At what was then the northernmost fringe of the province of Sonora, he entered a land inhabited not only by the Pimas but also the Tohono O'odham (or Pápago), the Sobaípuri, and a variety of Yuman peoples. From his headquarters at the mission of Nuestra Señora de los Dolores, in the middle of the Pimería Alta, he disseminated the faith in all directions. During his lifetime Father Kino was responsible for the construction of twenty-four missions from northern Sinaloa to southern Arizona, a truly remarkable record of achievement. If, as one scholar has observed, "Sonora represented one of the most successful mission endeavors of the Jesuit order in the New World, possibly on a par with its organization in Paraguay, established about the same time," much of the credit certainly belongs to the Padre on Horseback.[16] But Father Kino's historical reputation is based only partly on his prodigious proselytizing efforts. He also had a keen interest in science, and he put this fascination to good use conducting experiments in his missions which resulted in improved crops and livestock. His real passion, though, was geography, and his many explorations led to the first accurate maps of the Spanish northwest. Perhaps his most notable accomplishment, in this regard, was his discovery that Baja California was a peninsula rather than an island, a long-held suspicion that he confirmed once and for all, thus rekindling interest in a land route to Alta California.

Eusebio Kino is known as the Father of Arizona. In fact, at least fourteen of his expeditions were made into the area that constitutes the present-day state of Arizona, where on several occasions, he went as far as the Gila River, the northernmost limit of effective Spanish settlement during the colonial period. Eventually, he established three missions there, with the most successful being San Xavier del Bac in 1700. The last years of his life were spent consolidating this northern frontier; and when the Jesuit priest died, he chose to be buried there, at Magdalena, a mission just a few miles south of today's Arizona-Sonora border.

During the twenty years after the death of Father Kino, missionary activity along the Arizona frontier waned, in part because of increased pressure from indios bárbaros, the Apache and the Seri being the most aggressive, and in part because of the lack of sufficient numbers of missionaries available for duty. While the Indian threat did not abate at all, after about 1730 fresh recruits were able to breathe new life into the proselytizing effort. A number of abandoned missions were reactivated, among them Tumacácori and San Xavier del Bac. The efforts of one priest in particular deserve mention, the Bavarian Jacobo Sedelmayr, who carried on the tradition of Father Kino by combining both intense missionary work and geographic exploration. The conversion of the Tohono O'odham during the early eighteenth century is accredited more to him than any other individual. His explorations took him north beyond the Gila River in 1744 and did much to increase Spanish knowledge of the area.

These missionary efforts were only partially successful. The northern frontier erupted again in 1751, when the Pimas, led by Luis Oacpicagigua, rose up in rebellion. Some one hundred frontiersmen, mostly miners and soldiers, lost their lives—apparently, no one bothered to record the number of Indian casualties. It took several months before the revolt was quelled, but the Arizona-Sonora frontier remained unstable throughout the second half of the eighteenth century.

Encouraged by Kino, missionary efforts were initiated in Baja California in 1697 by his friend and colleague, Father Juan María de Salvatierra, another Italian Jesuit.[17] Despite the paucity of its native population and meager natural resources, greatly inferior to those of Sonora, Jesuits were intent on expanding their spiritual realm to the peninsula just as they had previously done eastward, across the Sierra Madre Occidental and on into Chihuahua. The Crown was not adverse to the project. In fact, since its discovery in 1533, Baja California had tempted viceregal authorities; but efforts at colonization, beginning with Cortés in the 1530s and continuing to the time of Kino, had been half-hearted, and hence unsuccessful.

Despite its limited resources, Baja California continued to be enticing. It was the gateway to Alta California, which held immense promise. The Spanish conquest of the Philippines in the 1560s paved the way for a lucrative trade route between the islands and New Spain. Laden with eastern luxury goods, Manila galleons, following the swift Japanese current, made their annual trip along the coast of California to the Mexican port of Acapulco. Vulnerable to pirate raids and in need of supply stations, the Pacific convoys gave California a new significance: a potential base of operations against pirates and better access to supplies.

The search for suitable harbors resulted in two authorized expeditions along the California coast. The first took place in 1595, when Sebastián Rodríguez Cermeño, sailing from the Philippines, led his men down the coast from Cape Mendocino. The second occurred in 1602–1603, when Sebastián Vizcaíno explored the coast north from Mexico and brought back glowing reports of a harbor he named Monterey. Neither expedition, however, found the Bay of San Francisco, and nothing short of this kind of discovery would convince the Spanish Crown to invest its limited resources in the risky venture of settling an area so remote and difficult to access.

From the time of Vizcaíno, the Jesuits clamored for the opportunity to set up missions along the well-populated coast of Alta California. Baja California would be a stepping stone in that direction. So enthused were they about the prospect of a string of missions extending the entire length of the California coast that by the end of the seventeenth century, they were willing to finance the venture themselves, through the Pious Fund of the Californias that they established for this purpose. Spared the cost of the enterprise, with nothing to lose and everything to gain, the Crown could do no less than give its approval.

During the late eighteenth century, the only northern frontier to make significant progress was along the coast of Baja California. In other areas, movement was barely perceptible. In Texas, for example, the removal of the French threat dampened enthusiasm for the continued occupation of that region. Nor did the Spanish acquisition of Louisiana in 1763, following the Seven Years' War, improve the situation. Although the peltry trade should have been a natural magnet, drawing Spanish frontiersmen into the recently acquired area, the vastness of Louisiana and the scarcity of available manpower kept Spain from taking advantage of these new opportunities.

Another obstacle impeding movement into the Far North was again the hostility of the Indians. The 1751 Pima revolt illustrates the tenuous nature of the conversions among neophytes. The most persistent problems, however, came from the nomadic Indians. In the early 1700s, Spanish settlements in the upper Rio

Grande, as well as the neighboring Pueblo villages, began to be assailed by Utes from the northwest and Comanches from the eastern plains. In Texas, the Comanches, moving south, grew so bold that on several occasions, particularly in the 1770s, the province faced the real possibility of extinction. Equally troublesome were the Apaches, who preferred to raid the isolated cattle ranches and mining communities of Chihuahua and Coahuila, but who roamed throughout the northern frontier from Sonora to Texas. Having acquired horses from the Spanish in the 1600s and European weapons from the French, the English, and later the Americans, Apaches were now able to inspire terror far and wide. They were particularly menacing in the Upper Rio Grande Valley. As the historian Marc Simmons has illustrated, during the eighteenth century, despite the ancient Iberian municipal tradition, New Mexican pobladores began to leave the villages to live close to their crops, a pattern of settlement which made them increasingly vulnerable to attack.[18]

The general instability of the frontier encouraged a major administrative reorganization of the northern half of New Spain in the late eighteenth century. The Bourbons, who had succeeded the Hapsburgs to the Spanish throne in 1701, were avid reformers, and they now sought to impose reforms overseas. José de Gálvez (1720–1787), a special agent of the Crown, a *visitador-general* (inspector general), was dispatched from Spain in 1765 to evaluate the situation, develop a plan of action, and carry it out. Practical results were finally achieved in 1776, with the creation of a new administrative structure, the Comandancia General of the Interior Provinces, which united the Californias, Sonora, Sinaloa, Nueva Vizcaya, New Mexico, Coahuila, and Texas. Under a *commandante-general* (inspector in chief), these provinces were expected to perform their administrative functions more efficiently and combat the Indian problem more effectively. Intended primarily to create a more centralized empire, the Bourbon reforms, of which administrative reorganization was only one part, helped to stimulate progressive changes on the frontier after the 1770s. An expansion of the livestock industry, an increase in trade, and a population explosion were among the most wide-ranging consequences. It would seem that despite the prevailing view today, these changes, as the sociologist Thomas D. Hall argues, "collectively lend credence to the claim that the last years of Spanish control of the Southwest were years of prosperity."[19]

At about this time, the decision was made to also colonize Alta California, the brainchild of the visitador himself. The traditional explanation for this expansion is that the Spanish sought to forestall Russian entry into this frontier, and indeed these intruders were one factor taken into consideration, but the decision was made primarily to enhance Gálvez's reputation: by bringing vitality to a moribund frontier, he would ingratiate himself to the Crown and advance his career. The decision was encouraged by the Church, which stood most to gain by the initiative. As it ultimately turned out, and despite Gálvez's intentions, Alta California would become a missionary colony; the soldiers who accompanied the monks would merely serve to ensure their safety.

The entrada into Alta California was carried out by Franciscans, not by their rivals, the Jesuits, who had run afoul of the Crown and had been officially expelled from the Empire by Carlos III in 1767. One of Gálvez's charges, during his lengthy *visita* (1765–1771) in New Spain, was to carry out this edict. The Jesuit missions in the northwest were then entrusted to the mendicant order. The friars in Baja California were designated by Gálvez to make the push north, with the ultimate destination being Monterey, which Vizcaíno had extravagantly praised so many years before. Two men were put in charge of the "Sacred Expedition," as Gálvez called it: Gaspar de Portolá y de Rovira (1718–1786) and Junípero Serra (1713–1784).

Captain Portolá had served many years on the frontier, where he had earned the reputation of a loyal and able servant of the Crown. Governor of Baja California, he was the natural choice to lead the expedition into Alta California. His job was to escort the friars across the wilderness and then return south once the missions were established, leaving his subordinate, Lieutenant Pedro Fages, in charge of presidial troops.

The giant in the enterprise, however, would be Father Serra. Born in Petra, a small village on the island of Majorca, he joined the Franciscans and became a professor of theology at the local university. In his midthirties, he decided to abandon the classroom to pursue a missionary career in New Spain. He served first on the northeastern frontier, in Nuevo Santander. When the Baja California missions were transferred to his order, Father Serra was dispatched to Loreto as father-president, the head of the entire mission system on the peninsula. On the northern trek to Alta California he was accompanied by one of his former students, Fray Juan Crespí, who became his chief aide.

The drive north consisted of two overland parties, assisted by three ships. The first party left Velicatá, Baja California's northernmost mission, on 24 March 1769, and arrived in San Diego on 14 May 1769; and the second party, headed by Serra and Portolá, followed a few weeks later. The difficulties of travel are abundantly illustrated by the mortality rate: most of the three hundred or so men on the expedition died before arriving at their destination.

Undaunted, Serra commenced his work in Alta California with the founding of its first mission, San Diego de Alcalá, on 16 July 1769. Eventually, twenty-one institutions were erected, the first nine by Serra. The last and northernmost mission, Sonoma's San Francisco Solano, was built in 1823, two years after the end of Spanish rule in Mexico.

The mission system came to dominate life in Alta California during the remaining decades of the Spanish era, at a time when it had been eclipsed by the presidio in other stretches of the frontier and had apparently outlived its usefulness, according to many anti-clerical critics. The mission consisted not only of the church buildings themselves but also of thousands of surrounding acres, which were meant to sustain the padres and their Indian wards.

The native peoples, of course, were the raison d'etre of the entire missionary system. Essentially, Alta California was settled because of the enormous numbers of potential converts to be found in the area. According to the foremost authority on the subject, the late Sherburne F. Cook, these numbers exceeded three hundred thousand in 1769, probably the greatest concentration of Native Americans anywhere in North America. Fortunately for the Spanish, most of the Indians lived along the coast, where there were abundant resources for hunting and gathering as well as fishing. The missions established along this narrow strip were easy to link, both via the ocean and overland along the *camino real* (king's highway). While the tribes in the interior, beyond the coastal range, were never brought under effective control, those on the coast, in sharp contrast, were coerced into a life of virtual slavery with surprising ease, even considering the enormous disparity in technology between natives and immigrants.

In the absence of strong resistance, which surfaced only sporadically at the outset, Franciscans were able to produce results that surprised officials in Mexico City. The number of conversions was relatively modest under Serra, but under his successor, Fray Fermín de Lasuén, who served as father-president from 1785 to 1803, the number of converts came to exceed fifty thousand. Neophytes were taught agriculture and stock raising, as well as a variety of crafts. However, the positive achievements of the missions were outweighed by the deadly toll taken by Euroasiatic diseases, as was true throughout the frontier, and perhaps even more severely, as scholars Robert H. Jackson and Edward Castillo argue, by the debilitating effects of slavery.[20] The Indian population along the coast declined from about sixty thousand in 1769 to about thirty-five thousand in 1800.

Alongside the mission, as in other parts of the Far North, was the presidio. The first garrison was erected in San Diego in 1769 by Captain Portolá, who was also responsible for the second presidio, in Monterey in 1770. He returned to Baja California, according to plan, that very year, leaving Lieutenant Fages in charge.

From the very beginning, problems developed between missionaries and military men. Serra and Fages, in particular, did not get along at all. The clash went beyond personalities. The most substantial point of contention had to do with decisions about where and when missions would be built. Serra wanted to extend the mission system with all due haste; Fages disagreed, arguing that his troops had insufficient strength to ensure the safety of isolated missionaries. In addition, it was not clear who had precedence, religious or civilian authorities.

As vexing as the question of authority, supplies and manpower were a concern in the first few years. It was discovered almost immediately that the missions could not be supplied adequately from the south. Not only was Baja California barren, but movement north, by either land or sea, was slow and dangerous. The only alternative was to open a trail between Alta California and the Arizona settlements of northern Sonora. This arduous task was entrusted to one of the most extraordinary and fascinating of Spain's frontiersmen, Juan Bautista de Anza (1735–1788).[21] Captain of the presidio at Tubac—founded in 1753, in the aftermath of the Pima Rebellion—he led a party of some thirty-five men across the Colorado River and over the southern California desert to Mission San Gabriel, where he arrived on 22 March 1774. Anza was accompanied by Fray Francisco Garcés, worthy heir to Kino and Sedelmayr on the Sonora frontier. Anza continued on to Monterey before making his return trip to Tubac. In 1775–1776, he made a second trip to California, this time bringing a company of 240, most of them settlers. Led by Lieutenant José Joaquín Moraga, members of this second Anza expedition were responsible for founding the outpost of San Francisco on 17 September 1776. Anza himself returned to Arizona, the region which continued to supply Alta California during the next few years.

In July 1781, however, this modest but vital commerce ended abruptly. An uprising of Yuma Indians who lived along the trail resulted in the massacre of 104 people, including Father Garcés. This grisly episode discredited the route, and as a result, the Spanish population of Alta California failed to increase to any appreciable extent in the aftermath. In 1800, there were only about twelve hundred non-Indians in the area.

MAJOR TRENDS

The settlement of the coastal region of Alta California at the end of the eighteenth century brought to an end the era of Spanish expansion in the north. During the last half century of the colonial period, exploration continued in many directions, including the Pacific Coast as far as Yakutat Bay, Alaska, but the limit of effective settlement had been established. As one surveys these northern colonies during the last decades of the Spanish frontier, an interesting pattern emerges. Essentially, the Far North consisted of three fingerlike projections extending into North America. On the Pacific Coast were the California missions; two towns of any consequence, San José and Los Angeles; and four presidios, located in San Diego, Santa Barbara, Monterey, and San Francisco. In the center were the New Mexican settlements of the Upper Rio Grande, the most heavily populated area on the frontier, with forty thousand inhabitants in 1821, a quarter of them Pueblo Indians. Santa Fe continued to be the capital and leading city, but nearby Albuquerque, founded in 1706, and Paso del Norte, far to the south, were also key towns along the Chihuahua trail that linked this pivotal province with the Mexican interior. In Texas, the third colonial extension, there were scattered settlements here and there, including some in east Texas, but the only city of any consequence was San Antonio.

Between the fingerlike projections, the frontier was virtually uninhabited by non-Indians, except in northern Sonora, where a garrison was established in Tucson in 1776 and continued a precarious existence on the edge of the Gran Apachería, the land of the Apaches. These areas of settlement were isolated from one another, as well as from northern Mexican towns and the chief population centers on the central plateau. Several attempts were made to link the three sparsely colonized areas but with little success. The abortive 1776 effort by Franciscans Silvestre Vélez de Escalante and Francisco Atanasio Domínguez to establish a trail between New Mexico and California, across present-day Utah, was only the most notable of many such ventures. As a consequence, distinct ways of life developed in the various pockets of settlements on the northern rim of New Spain. And yet, for all their diversity, there were many commonalties among these Hispanic communities.

Frontier society by about 1800 was notably different from that which evolved in the Mexican interior during the course of the eighteenth century. The main difference was that the societies of New Mexico, Texas, Arizona, and California were relatively open compared to the hierarchical structures that had crystallized in the great population centers of New Spain toward the end of the colonial period.

As in other parts of the Hispanic world, in the core area of New Spain the family stood at the center of existence. Family life was remarkably stable throughout the Spanish period, regardless of social class. The Hispanic family generally consisted of a husband, his wife, several children, and assorted relatives. The husband was the patriarch, who, in theory at least, made the most important decisions, a consequence of his status as the breadwinner of the family. His wife controlled the household, raising the children and performing most of the domestic chores. For their part, the children were taught to respect and help their parents. Boys, if they were lucky, received the rudiments of an education; girls were trained in domestic skills. Marriages were often arranged, especially among the most affluent, and occurred at an early age; women tended to marry when they reached the age of puberty.

On the frontier, this pattern generally prevailed as well, but local conditions necessitated substantial modifications. For example, in this peripheral setting, life was much more precarious than in the interior. The historian Alicia Vidaurreta Tjarks, author of several valuable demographic studies on the Far North, is clear on this point: "Life was shorter in the borderlands; permanent warfare against the Indians, the fight for subsistence in a hostile environment, a deficient and limited diet, and, above all, epidemic diseases like smallpox and *matlazahuatl* fever, which specially ravaged Texas (as most of New Spain) during the years 1785–1786, resulted in the loss of many lives, particularly among the infant population."[22]

Frontier life was hard for both men and women, as well as their children. Mothers often died while giving birth. Indian depredations, however, took an even greater toll on their husbands. The number of widows was always high on the frontier. This was true even after the Spanish period. In Abiquiú in 1845, for example, 91 out of a total of 338 households, almost 27 percent, were headed by widows. The average life expectancy, for both men and women, was about forty.

One major difference between established society and frontier society was the relatively greater freedom available to women in the latter. That so many women were widowed was one factor, but the absence of a clear-cut division of labor on the frontier was perhaps more telling. Women often worked outside of the home. *Curanderas* (medicine women) and *parteras* (midwives) were not uncommon. In fact, there were times when women were expected to help men defend the community against Indian raids. The women of New Mexico were especially "liberated," an observation made by many astonished outsiders at the end of the Spanish period and throughout the Mexican period. Unlike their American counterparts, Hispano women were allowed to smoke, drink, and gamble, which often led American observers to conclude that these ladies were lascivious and immoral. In point of fact, these privileges were manifestations of more meaningful freedoms afforded women in Hispanic society. They were at liberty to run businesses, divorce their husbands, own property, and sue in court. These rights were largely theoretical in central New Spain, but they were exercised on a regular basis by the women of colonial New Mexico. The historian Albert Hurtado feels that women in Hispanic California followed a more traditional pattern.[23] It is likely, though, that New Mexico was the rule rather than the exception on the northern frontier.

If gender roles were blurred on the frontier, the same appears to be the case with social classes. Mexican society was highly stratified by the eighteenth century, but society was relatively fluid on the frontier. For one thing, the caste system appears to have totally broken down by 1800. Ethnic boundaries, says the historian Adrian Bustamante, "became blurred, causing the system to become muddled and largely ineffective."[24] No longer was there a tight correlation between color and class, though a preoccupation with racial status continued to be evident in official documents all through the Spanish period. Greater social mobility was also due to the scarcity of labor, which was even more chronic on the periphery than in the heartland. Under such circumstances, the acquisition of land was relatively easy. Regardless of the specific frontier area, most pobladores were landowners.

The trend toward greater democratization increased because the extremes of wealth and poverty found in the established communities of New Spain were largely absent on the frontier. Even though there was a tendency to separate society into those who were better off and those who were not, to label them *ricos* (rich) and *pobres* (poor) respectively, at this point in time, is misleading. The lifestyles of the elite and the rest of the population were similar, if not identical, throughout the northern rim of New Spain; both struggled to make a living in the hard frontier environment. This holds true even in New Mexico, where some scholars see the establishment of an "aristocracy" during the colonial period.[25]

The relatively modest socioeconomic status of the elite is well illustrated by the Chicano historian Antonio José Ríos-Bustamante in a valuable study of Albuquerque based on an analysis of the 1790 census, the most complete census undertaken during the entire Spanish period. In a town population of 1,155, seven individuals listed their occupation as rancher, the most lucrative and prestigious category; and, tellingly, only twelve individuals identified themselves as servants, the lowest occupation on the town's social and economic scale.[26] Even taking into consideration that most servants were children, and thus were missing from the record, it is clear that the elite, itself quite small, was hardly leading a life of leisure. Don Vicente Armijo, for example, one of the seven ranchers—and one of only four men in town to bear the honorary title of "Don"—had four servants, possibly the most of anyone.

Moreover, in New Mexico and throughout the frontier, members of the upper and lower class were often related by marriage and by *compadrazgo* (coparenthood), which ameliorated the relations between the two segments of society. Perhaps most compelling in binding the community, however, was that Hispanic peoples, whether they were white or mixed-bloods, what the Spanish called *castas,* shared a common culture as *gente de razón,* literally "people of reason"; something that was not true of, and distinguished them from, Indians, who were known as *gente sin razón,* "people without reason."

Despite some local differences from place to place, frontier society was similar throughout the Far North. Other commonalties existed as well. In particular, during the closing years of the Spanish period, frontier life was dominated by three key issues: the Indian problem, mestizaje, and American contact.

During the course of the eighteenth century, the Indian threat to frontier settlements escalated precipitously. Frontier communities faced a multitude of problems, but by the 1770s, none more pressing than the Indian Question. The nomadic Indians committed depredations seemingly at will—often provoked by Spanish atrocities, including rapes and kidnappings. The provinces, left to their own meager resources, were unable to curb the violence. Many policies were attempted, ranging from extermination to bribery. But with the absence of an overall plan coordinating local and national efforts, the shortage of men and money, and the ability of the mounted warriors to move from one province to another in no time at all, pobladores were left completely at the mercy of indios bárbaros. Often entire towns were abandoned, putting the frontier economy in disarray. However, by the turn of the century, the situation, if not completely resolved, improved considerably, and relative security was restored.

This amelioration was a result of an Indian policy which had been formulated several years before. In 1777, Teodoro de Croix was made commandante-general of the Internal Provinces. Making alliances with some of the warlike tribes against other indios bárbaros, often hereditary enemies, he experienced modest success in pacifying the frontier. In the early 1780s, however, the viceroy himself, Bernardo de Gálvez, nephew of José de Gálvez, formulated a more effective plan of action. Rather than adopting a purely defensive and reactive policy against Apaches and other indios bárbaros or relying completely on tenuous alliances, he determined to aggressively subjugate them by invading their strongholds. Exterminating recalcitrants in the process, and requiring that the vanquished tribes settle down near presidios, he sought to undermine their traditional lifestyle, hence forcing them to rely on their conquerors for survival. Essentially, their cooperation, in this last phase, would be ensured through bribery. The ambitious plan was put into operation, and it worked remarkably well in pacifying the frontier. Employing both carrot and stick, Bernardo de Gálvez's successors enjoyed considerable success during the next few years. In fact, the Far North was reasonably secure for a lengthy period, which came to an end only in 1810, when the outbreak of the Mexican war for independence necessitated removal of troops from the frontier and encouraged nomadic Indians to again resume hostilities. Yet, in some areas, such as Arizona, the truce held into the 1820s.

A second striking theme during the Spanish period, one that also relates to Indian-settler relations, is race mixture. It is clear that mestizaje was initiated as soon as colonists arrived in the Far North. There is a good deal of disagreement among scholars, however, as to the extent that this process was carried out. Since Indian-Mexican unions could be illicit as well as Church-sanctioned, it is difficult to arrive at a conclusive answer. The written records of the times, of which the most relevant are census and church records, are not much help either. The authorities, both clergymen and servants of the state, were very conscious of race, and in their documents they often alluded to it. However, as many students have pointed out—Manuel Servín, Alicia Vidaurreta Tjarks, Antonio José Ríos-Bustamante, and David Weber, among others—*español,* a term indicating that the person in question was white, the most common designation for the non-Indian population on the frontier, was a highly unreliable measure of race since it was often applied to castas, people of mixed blood. Many pobladores would identify themselves or others as español as long as they weren't obviously Indian or African. While the use of this term reflected the anti-Indian prejudices of Hispanic society, it was also employed to denote that the individual had adopted a European lifestyle; that is, the term was often used as a cultural rather than a racial category. Given the difficulties in studying race mixture, and the lack of research in this area, any conclusions made at present must be tentative at best.

The first settlers to arrive in New Mexico with Juan de Oñate were mostly white. Race mixture in central Mexico, where the pobladores initiated their expedition, was very gradual—as late as the first decades of the nineteenth century, the majority of New Spain's inhabitants were still Indians—and it follows that the same would have been true during the sixteenth century. According to the geographer Richard L. Nostrand, "Of the 210 documented soldier-settlers going to New Mexico in 1598 and 1600, a majority in each year were born in Spain (110), followed by New Spain (55), Portugal and elsewhere (13), and unable to locate (15), or not given (17)."[27] Once in the Upper Rio Grande Valley, pobladores built their settlements away from Pueblo villages, a separation that was encouraged by the Indians themselves as well as the Franciscans, who sought to protect their charges.

But miscegenation began immediately.[28] In New Mexico, and throughout the frontier, especially in the states that constitute northern Mexico today, Spanish frontiersmen were accompanied by substantial numbers of Mexican Indians. Tlascalans (or Tlascaltecos), Tarascans, and Opatas were well represented among these Indian settlers. During the colonial period, these tribes gradually lost their separate identity. Undoubtedly, some of them married Pueblos, but many of them must have married Europeans. Moreover, the settlers occasionally married into local Indian society; Pueblos, after all, were accorded full citizenship rights, including the right to marry into the gente de razón. Missionary efforts to segregate the two communities were not always successful. A 1749 census indicates that 570 Indians resided in Santa Fe and another 200 were to be found in Albuquerque. The opportunity for miscegenation, it seems, was readily available.

Finally, among Hispanic colonists, much of the miscegenation was with genízaros, generally defined as captives and slaves of nomadic tribes who had been ransomed by the Spanish government, though, as Frances León Swadesh, a specialist on the Spanish-Ute frontier, has shown, Pueblo Indians were also represented in this group in striking numbers.[29] Estimates of the genízaro population by 1776 range as high as one-third of the entire population of the province. Some of these detribalized Indians were allowed to go off to the edge of the frontier to build their own settlements, San Tomás de Abiquiú being the best-known example, as buffers against the Plains Indians. The majority became servants in Spanish households, where they gradually blended in with their masters. Mestizaje, then, was the rule rather than the exception. By the end of the eighteenth century, according to a 1776 census of New Mexico, the majority of its inhabitants were designated as mestizos.[30]

Racial blending may have occurred more rapidly in the Texas area, where the non-Indian inhabitants were predominantly of mixed origins by the end of the Spanish period. Race mixture had little to do with the indigenous population in Texas. Most tribes were nomadic and warlike, making marriage with the colonizers unlikely. However, the overwhelming majority of newcomers to Texas during the period before 1821 already consisted of mestizos, mostly from the northern Mexican states of Coahuila, Nuevo León, and Nuevo Santander. As the historian Andrés Tijerina has pointed out, "Most of the Mexican settlers and soldiers who inhabited the communities and presidios of Texas had come from staging areas in northern Mexico where racial mixing had been prevalent."[31] It is important to note that even more than in New Mexico, the genetic pool was impacted by Africans. Blacks and mulattoes were among the immigrants entering Texas from Louisiana to the east, as well as from Nuevo León and Coahuila to the south. The Isleños, who insisted on marrying within their own community, preserved their European bloodlines longer than other Tejanos, but even they had become thoroughly integrated into the emerging melting pot by the end of the Spanish period.

In Sonora, which included Arizona, the situation was similar to Texas in that many of the native tribes were nomads. Where there were sedentary tribes, the Jesuits succeeded in congregating the neophytes into missions. Missionization, of course, did not encourage race mixture. The mission fathers, who were more or less celibate themselves, discouraged Indian contact with whites, who were thought to have a corrupting impact. They also sought to protect their wards from labor exploitation, miners being the chief threats.

Most of the newcomers to the Sonora frontier, be they ranchers, miners, or soldiers, tended to be mestizos. "Practically all those who wish to be considered Spaniards are people of mixed blood," Ignaz Pfefferkorn, a Jesuit priest who served eleven years in Sonora before his expulsion in 1767, later recalled.[32] Nevertheless, in 1821 the one place on the frontier where a large white population remained well-represented was Sonora, where in the late eighteenth century—particularly after 1770, when the Apaches were placated and economic opportunities improved—colonists entered directly from Spain in substantial numbers. Another group, the priests and monks, were white, though it is unlikely that they would have had a meaningful impact on the genetic pool.

Settled in the late eighteenth century, when mestizaje was well-established in central Mexico, particularly among the lower classes, Alta California was colonized by people who were much different racially from those who had accompanied Oñate on his entrada into New Mexico. As Manuel Servín, one of the first Chicano historians to study the Borderlands, points out, the overwhelming majority of men who entered California with Portolá and Serra were either Indians or people of mixed blood; only eight Spaniards spent any time at all in the province.[33] More-over, two-thirds of the men who settled San Francisco and San José in 1776–1778 were Indians or castas. And of the twenty-three colonists, mostly from Sinaloa and Sonora, who founded the town of Los Angeles in 1781, only two were white.[34] The great majority of troops who came into California in the late eighteenth century were of mixed blood, and the same was probably true of enlisted men throughout the frontier.

Though interethnic marriages were allowed and occasionally even encour-aged, for the most part the Franciscans strictly forbade settler-soldiers in California from dealing with neophytes, so interethnic marriages were rare on the northwest-ern frontier. The incidence of rape, as soldiers took advantage of Indian women, may have been relatively common, as the historian Antonia I. Castañeda asserts.[35] However, it must be remembered, children that resulted from these attacks were generally killed by the tribe. The evidence, then, suggests that unlike mestizaje in New Mexico, the mixture of people in Alta California occurred with Indians from the Mexican interior rather than local indigenous populations.

It is safe to conclude that by the end of the Spanish colonial period, substantial racial mixture through a variety of means had occurred on the northern frontier. Certainly, there was more mingling of the races there than in central Mexico, despite the larger pool of native peoples in the south. Undoubtedly, most "Spaniards" on the frontier in 1821 were mestizos rather than white. Many, perhaps most, of the new arrivals were already mestizos. Once they were on the frontier, unions, legal and illicit, between so-called Spaniards and Indians were not uncommon, especially in New Mexico, where colonization had a long history and both soldier-settlers and Pueblo Indians were well-represented numerically.

One ethnic peculiarity of the New Mexican frontier, incidentally, was the ap-parent presence of significant numbers of Jews among the settlers. The expulsion in 1492 had resulted in a number of Jewish conversions to Catholicism in Spain, but many of these conversos continued to practice their ancient faith clandestinely. The New World provided these "crypto-Jews"—known as *marranos* in the Spanish realms—the opportunity to escape the close scrutiny of the Inquisition, an institu-tion that was much weaker overseas—pagans, after all, were not subject to the Holy Office—and some of them migrated to New Spain. The northern frontier was ap-pealing, since there they could best preserve their cultural and religious traditions, though always surreptitiously. Many Mexican Americans today are products of this Sephardic background. According to Frances Hernández, professor of English and comparative languages at the University of Texas at El Paso, there may be some fifteen hundred families in the Southwest who "have retained an unbroken chain of Jewish matrilineal descent."[36]

The third and final theme dominating the last years of the Spanish frontier is the advent of the *norteamericano,* the American. Though Spain's mercantilist philosophy had theoretically precluded the entry of foreigners into its possessions, the system was very loose in reality, and there was never a time when foreigners were completely absent from New Spain. This was even more true of the Far North, which like any frontier environment was hard to regulate. Moreover, unable to satisfy the material needs of its frontiersmen, Spain found that its outposts on the periphery were often anxious to carry on contraband trade with outsiders. Frenchmen, in particular, seem to have penetrated into the northern rim with some regularity in the eighteenth century, even before the incorporation of Louisiana into the Spanish Empire in 1763. In fact, visitors arrived from all over the globe and for many reasons. Americans were the last but, given their imminent hegemony in the area, the most consequential of these interlopers.

By the time of their independence from England, recognized by the Treaty of Paris in 1783, Americans were beginning to develop an interest in expanding their sphere of influence to the Pacific, the gateway to the wealth of the Far East. In the 1790s, Yankee ships began to visit the California coast, where they carried on illicit trade. The first of these ships arrived in 1796. The most famous of the visitors was Captain William Shaler, who saw California in 1803 and published a glowing description of the province two years later. While singing the praises of the land and its resources, he was less complimentary of its Spanish residents, suggesting that their lethargy made progress impossible. Only American energy and diligence, he insinuated, could develop the vast potential of California—one of the first expositions of a sentiment later labeled Manifest Destiny.

Meanwhile, on the Texas borderland, the influx of norteamericanos reached alarming proportions after the Louisiana Purchase of 1803. Already by that date, there were a number of Americans who had settled in Texas legally, many coming in from Louisiana, where the Spanish had actually encouraged Yankee settlement before the territory had been returned to the French in 1800. The cotton gin, invented in 1793, had revitalized the cotton economy in the American South, and new lands were opening up for planters along the Gulf Coast. It was only a matter of time before the United States and Spain would have trouble along their common border, where the new boundary line was in dispute. Problems were precipitated by American citizens, who recognized that the Blackland soils of the eastern parts of Texas, with their many rivers emptying into the Gulf of Mexico, were ideal for both agriculture and ranching. A series of unsuccessful Yankee filibustering expeditions into east Texas, where Spanish control was precarious at best, were staged in the next few years. American land hunger and its own difficulties in enticing settlers into Texas alarmed the Crown. Spanish fears were allayed in 1819, however, when the governments of Spain and the United States agreed on a precise border in the Adams-Onís Treaty.

American contact in New Mexico was less worrisome because the number of Yankee sightings there was so small. The few Americans who straggled into Santa Fe and surrounding villages after 1805 were solitary fur trappers and traders who seemed content to exchange goods. Consequently, Americans met with a mixed reception. Completely dependent on Mexican merchants to the south for their imports, and thus subject to exorbitant prices, New Mexicans sometimes welcomed Yankee mountain men, who sold them pelts at reasonable prices. At other times, outsiders were expelled unceremoniously. One American whose presence was highly unwelcome was Zebulon Montgomery Pike, who, suspiciously, wandered into Santa Fe in early 1807. He pleaded that he had been sent by the American government to find the headwaters of the Arkansas and Red rivers but had lost his way, which may have been the case. It was suspected, though, that he was on a military reconnaissance mission to probe Spanish defenses in preparation for an invasion. Interrogated and sent to Chihuahua City, he and his men were released later that year.

At the time of the Pike episode, Spanish authorities in Mexico City were slowly coming to the realization that the fledgling nation to the northeast posed a legitimate threat to their northern possessions. But when the day came that the confrontation proved inevitable, Spain would be but a memory on the borderlands.

The Spanish and American frontiers share many similarities, but the differences are more meaningful.[37] For one thing, religion had a much greater impact on the northern rim of New Spain. The most characteristic institution on this frontier was the mission, which played a relatively minor role in the westward movement.

The attitude toward the Indian, it follows, was also distinct. Few Anglo-American frontiersmen saw Indians as human beings, a view that was common in the Far North. Whether treatment of the native peoples was more humane is a hotly debated question. The Spanish exploited the Indians heavily, at times instituting slavery. Occasionally, too, they adopted a policy of extermination against the most intractable of the nomadic tribes. On the other hand, miscegenation was widespread, both a cause and a reflection of their more positive attitude toward indigenous peoples. On balance, Indians on the expanding frontier of the United States were probably treated worse than among their counterparts to the south. While genocide may be too strong a term to use here, ultimately, the choice given Native Americans on the Anglo-American frontier was life on a reservation or death.

Finally, while the Spanish frontier was never as authoritarian as imperial theory would suggest and the Anglo-American frontier was never as democratic as Frederick Jackson Turner would have us believe, the fact remains that there was a sizable gap between the mindsets that emerged in the two areas. Individual initiative was more characteristic of the movement west; northern expansion of New Spain was largely a product of government policy, and frontier life was heavily regulated.

In the last analysis, though, it may be unfair to compare Spanish frontiersmen with American frontiersmen; perhaps it would be more profitable to compare life in the Far North with life in the Mexican interior. Only then can we truly appreciate the strengths of the men and women who established a firm foundation for the Indo-Hispanic culture which continues to thrive in the United States.

THE MEXICAN
FAR NORTH

1821–1848

3

The Mexican period of Southwest History was very brief, lasting from 1821, when Mexico achieved its independence from Spain, to 1848, when the fledgling republic lost its northern territories to the United States with the signing of the Treaty of Guadalupe Hidalgo.[1] The most fateful trend in the Far North during this period was the continuing influx, in ever increasing numbers, of norteamericanos. Beset with a multitude of difficulties, which it shared with other emerging Latin American nations after the demise of the Spanish Empire in the New World, Mexico was unable to devote adequate attention to its northern border regions. The chief problem, as it had been for Spain, was the inability to populate an enormous area over which it never established effective control. The advent of the United States, a nation with seemingly unlimited resources and a burgeoning population, a people, moreover, brimming with a confidence that bordered on arrogance, could mean only trouble for their southern neighbors. What Mexico needed desperately in the first decades of its existence as an independent nation was a long period of peace, but it was its misfortune to find itself sharing a common border with the Colossus of the North.

MEXICAN INDEPENDENCE

The collapse of Spain's empire had a host of causes. External factors included the influence of the European Enlightenment, which undermined the old order, as well as the examples of revolution both in North America, where the English colonists proclaimed their independence in 1776, and in France, where a decade of unrest was initiated in 1789. As has justly been observed, the Latin American upheavals that followed were part of an Atlantic phenomenon during a period that the noted American historian Robert R. Palmer has labeled the Age of the Democratic Revolution.[2]

More momentous still were internal considerations in Spanish America itself. While economic and political problems were ubiquitous, as was true in both France and the thirteen colonies, social inequalities seem to have played a larger role than in the other two areas. The Latin American revolutions were instigated by *criollos* (creoles), people of Spanish ancestry born in the Americas. Creole discontent during the colonial era was caused by the virtual monopoly exerted by Spanish-born citizens over the administrative hierarchies of both the colonial Church and State. Called *peninsulares* or *gachupines,* these Europeans dominated economic and political life, effectively shutting out American-born residents from positions of power. By the last decades of the colonial period, resentment against the privileged elite was widespread, but while neither Indians nor mestizos, much less blacks, were in a position to challenge the social order, the creoles came to believe that because of their education and wealth, they were destined to replace their fathers, or at least share the positions atop the socioeconomic pyramid. At the same time, they had no real sympathy with the lower classes, a common American origin notwithstanding, and the last thing they wanted was a race war and the destruction of the social order. While the Latin American revolts may have resulted in enhancing social and political democracy, this ideal was almost completely unanticipated by the emerging creole malcontents.

The occasion for the Latin American revolutions was the conquest of Spain by the French during the Napoleonic wars. When Napoleon invaded Spain in 1808 and replaced King Ferdinand VII with his own brother, Joseph Bonaparte, the people rose up in rebellion. This upsurge of Spanish patriotism proved to be the beginning of the end for Napoleon and his dreams of French hegemony in Europe, but the resulting chaos on the Iberian Peninsula also had dire repercussions for Spain in the New World. By 1825, its American empire would be in complete shambles.

In New Spain, as in other parts of the empire, creoles were in the forefront of the revolutionary surge. Although a member of this class, the hero of Mexican independence was a very unlikely insurrectionary—the Catholic clergyman Miguel Hidalgo y Costilla. Born in Guanajuato and educated in Valladolid—now Morelia, capital of Michoacán—Hidalgo was ordained a priest in 1778. His unorthodox religious beliefs and liberal lifestyle soon got him in trouble with his superiors. In 1803, the fifty-year-old priest was exiled to Dolores, present-day Dolores Hidalgo, a small village near his hometown. By now, he had come to embrace a host of revolutionary doctrines. These included the beliefs in Mexican independence and, even more radical, the equality of all people, including Indians, who constituted more than half of the colony's six million inhabitants. The revolution was launched on 16 September 1810, when the courageous priest delivered his famous "Grito de Dolores" (Cry of Dolores): "Long live our Lady of Guadalupe! Death to bad government! Death to the gachupines!" This historic day, the *Diez y Seis de Septiembre,* is now celebrated as Mexican Independence Day.

Marching on a circuitous route toward Mexico City, the revolutionary army grew enormously, which accounted for its early successes. Unfortunately, indiscriminate looting and killing quickly alienated the propertied classes, and the criollos, the natural leaders of the independence movement in other parts of Latin America, drew back in horror before the daunting prospects of social revolution. Having lost creole support, Father Hidalgo's peasant armies proved no match for well-trained and disciplined Spanish soldiers. The backlash was unusually ferocious. Hidalgo himself suffered a martyr's death in 1811. A fellow priest, José María Morelos y Pavón, a mestizo, tried to keep the revolutionary impetus alive, but his capture and execution in 1815 appeared to be the death knell of the movement.

Events in Spain, however, conspired to keep discontent smoldering in New Spain, ultimately bringing about independence—ironically, under the banner of conservatism. In 1812, with victory against Napoleon's army of occupation in sight, the Cortes, the Spanish legislative assembly, drafted a liberal document establishing a constitutional monarchy. But after his restoration, Ferdinand VII reneged on his promise to abide by its terms; and the Constitution of 1812 was repealed, causing a deep rift between the king and his people. Discontent mounted, especially in the army, where liberal sympathies were particularly strong. Late in 1820, Spanish troops at Cádiz, about to embark for the Americas, where they were needed against rebel armies, revolted against the Bourbon monarchy. Under the leadership of Colonel Rafael Riego, the malcontents demanded the restoration of the 1812 Constitution. Eventually, the Riego uprising would prove abortive, as the major powers, the Concert of Europe, intervened to put an end to this threat to the established order. But in the meanwhile, conservative elements in New Spain, panicked at the prospect of living under an "atheistic" regime, determined to break with the mother country. They found their champion in a creole army officer, Agustín de Iturbide (1783–1824), who declared independence in late 1821 and soon proclaimed himself emperor of the new nation.

Unlike liberation movements in other Latin American colonies, then, national independence in Mexico occurred under the aegis of conservatism rather than liberalism. However, conservative ascendancy was ephemeral. Iturbide's abuse of power served to discredit his political philosophy, as well as the empire; and in February of 1823, he was deposed by his liberal adversaries, who now established a republican form of government patterned on that of the United States. The following decades were to be turbulent ones in Mexican history. It was only with the greatest of difficulties that Mexico would maintain its sovereignty.

In the Far North, the transition from Spanish to Mexican rule occurred with little violence. During the civil war itself, the pobladores of the northern frontier remained largely unconcerned about the issues being contested by royalists and patriots. Only in Texas was there any genuine enthusiasm for independence, as witnessed by popular though abortive revolts led by Juan Bautista de las Casas in early 1811 and Bernardo Gutiérrez de Lara in 1812–1813. But given the modest size of the local populations and the vast distances from the major theaters of action, the impact Texan rebels exerted was negligible. By and large, the residents of the northern rim remained spectators during the tumultuous decade of revolution.

Still, it was not long before the repercussions of the hard-fought struggle were felt by *fronterizos,* Mexican borderlanders. The most momentous consequence in the Far North was the resurgence of the Indian threat. The need to combat the rebels forced the Spanish Crown to transfer many of its presidial troops from peripheral areas to the capital and the surrounding areas, centers of Mexican resistance. The abandonment of its northern garrisons encouraged local tribes, especially the various Apache bands, to resume their raids on the unfortunate pobladores, now left to their own meager resources. The revolutionary wars almost completely ruined the nation's mining industry. Devoid of its major source of revenue, independent Mexico was less able than the Spanish Crown to provide military protection on the frontier. The deterioration of the presidial system, more than any other factor, accounts for the revival of the Indian threat after decades of relative calm. The hard-earned alliances the Spanish government had forged with the Comanche, Ute, Navajo, and Jicarilla Apache crumbled in the 1820s. Still another cause of disruption was the impact of American traders, who provided the natives guns and a market for goods, which encouraged raids on southern settlements. "Few historians," notes a prominent Borderlands scholar, ". . . have understood the extent to which American expansion upset the delicate balance between independent Indian peoples and pobladores in Mexico's Far North, from Texas to California."[3] Indian problems would plague the region throughout the period of Mexican rule.

Another fateful trend during the Mexican period was Anglo immigration. The weakness of the Mexican government, together with the land hunger that characterized America's westward movement, ensured that the steady stream of Yankees during the last years of Spanish colonial rule would only swell after 1821. Ultimately, the norteamericano proved to be a formidable threat even more menacing than the Indian.

The pobladores of northern Mexico faced a set of common problems, but it should not be assumed that life on the frontier was homogeneous. Then, as now, there were meaningful distinctions between the residents of California, New Mexico, Arizona, and Texas, as a quick survey of the political, economic, and social life of these areas will illustrate.

CALIFORNIA

Far removed from the center of political life, California took no direct part whatsoever in the epic events that resulted in Mexican independence. The majority of Californios, some thirty-two hundred people by 1821, had no special feelings about independence one way or the other, and they quickly resigned themselves to the new order. Among the small upper class, however, opinions were sharply divided. News of Mexico's independence was received with genuine satisfaction by some members of the military, among them several young officers representing the region's emerging rancho aristocracy. Disappointed over the lack of support Spain had provided the California provinces, they felt that change could only be for the better. The Franciscans, on the other hand, virtually all of them peninsulares, were hostile to the revolution, especially after the collapse of Iturbide's empire and the apparent triumph of liberalism, a "godless" ideology, with the adoption of the Constitution of 1824. Given the long tradition in Spanish history of a union of throne and altar, the intransigence of the clergy was not unexpected.

The political life of the Mexican Republic during its first decades would be extremely chaotic. Well into the second half of the nineteenth century, a virtual civil war was waged between liberals, who opposed strong central authority and stressed civil liberties, and conservatives, who found an antidote to the country's many ills in a powerful central authority, a solution favored by the authoritarian tradition of the colonial period. Because the advocates of the two philosophical positions were unable to impose their wills on their opponents, a power vacuum was created which paved the way for the rise of the infamous General Antonio López de Santa Anna (1794–1876), an opportunist who came to dominate Mexican politics to midcentury.

Political life in Alta California at this time was also confused. But in the province the struggles had little to do with ideology; virtually all Californios, save the clergy, resented central authority and advocated federalism and liberalism. Ideologically united, the leading families nonetheless engaged in chronic infighting. Insurrections, almost always bloodless, became a regular feature of political life. Californios fought among themselves, as well as against the governors Mexico City would periodically try to impose on them. Usually these factions divided along geographical lines, with the southerners, *abajeños,* opposed to the northerners, *arribeños.* Among the most prominent representatives of the former were José Antonio Carrillo, Pío Pico, and Juan Bandini; of the latter, Juan Bautista Alvarado, Mariano Guadalupe Vallejo, and José Castro. At stake were the governorship and political control of the province.

Beyond their suspicion of Mexico City, particularly after 1834, when the centralists, under Santa Anna, gained control of the national government, the other sentiment that united the liberals of the province was their hostility to the Church. Anti-clericalism was a central tenet of nineteenth-century liberalism.[4] Moreover, the clergy had further alienated liberals, at both the provincial and the national level, by their vociferous and virtually unanimous support of the Crown. The result was the confiscation of ecclesiastical property, the secularization of the California missions, in 1834–1845.

Ideology was stressed at the time by proponents of secularization and was undoubtedly a consideration prompting the legislation. It is likely, however, that economic motives were at least as weighty in explaining the land seizure as were high-minded ideas, as the results of secularization amply demonstrate. Franciscan missions controlled the most valuable land in the province, some fourteen million acres along the fertile and accessible coast from San Diego to Cape Mendocino. Rancheros resented this monopoly—as they had throughout the Far North—although their complaints were generally veiled in protests about the mistreatment of the indigenous mission population.

Secularization, however, did little to alleviate the plight of the "poor" Indian. Under the legislation, half of the mission lands were to go to the neophytes who had previously worked them, and the other half to the government. In fact, virtually all lands fell into the hands of some two hundred families who would subsequently dominate the economic and political life of the province. Through a variety of means, some legal, some illegal, virtually all in violation of the spirit if not the letter of the law, the hapless natives were divested of their inheritance. As for the half that was intended for the public domain, provincial governors soon redistributed these holdings, in the form of generous grants meted out to family, friends, and political allies. During the Mexican period, about five hundred private rancho land grants were made, compared to about twenty during the Spanish period. Secularization of the missions made possible the rise of the rancho aristocracy commonly associated with the halcyon days of Early California.

By the 1840s, with the gradual disappearance of the missions, the California economy came to be dominated by ranches. These large landed estates were virtually self-sufficient. A great assortment of crops were grown, including corn, potatoes, tomatoes, wheat, oranges, lemons, and grapes. More valuable than the agricultural products, though, was livestock. Horses multiplied rapidly; herds were so vast that they were often permitted to run wild without any supervision whatsoever. Cattle were even more plentiful, and more lucrative, for they were the source of hides and of tallow, used for soap and candles. By the 1840s, foreign vessels regularly visited coastal ports to exchange manufactured goods for these commodities. The cattle industry and the commerce it fostered were rapidly transforming life in Alta California on the eve of the Mexican-American War. "In no small way," the political sociologist Tomás Almaguer observes, "the magnitude of the early economic trade carried out between California and New England maritime interests was to help lay the foundation for its later political incorporation into the United States and formal integration as a semiperipheral and then core zone of the capitalist world-economy."[5] While commercial capitalism was in its infancy, signs of affluence, a recent phenomenon, were everywhere.

The chief recipients of this new-found wealth were the rancheros, popularly known today as the "Spanish dons." Whether born in Spain, Mexico, or California, members of this pastoral elite were predominantly white. At the top of provincial society, they and their families constituted less than 10 percent of the colony's population. Many of them ex-soldiers, most were recipients of generous land grants between 1821 and 1848. A few had acquired lands under the Spanish Crown. Their families were usually large, reflecting the relatively healthy and affluent lifestyle that had evolved in the province.[6]

As in other Hispanic societies, the husband and father had an inordinate amount of power. Women, however, maintained a surprisingly lofty position. Not only was the upper-class woman held on a pedestal, but she also wielded real authority. She had legal rights which were withheld from women in the United States at the time. It is telling that practically all Anglo accounts of life in California during this period comment, mostly in a derisive fashion, about this independence. Among privileges accorded women, as the historian Miroslava Chávez-García points out, was the right to own land.[7] Doña Juana Pacheco, for example, widow of Miguel Pacheco and mother of twelve children, received a grant of 17,734 acres in what is now central Contra Costa County in 1834. There were many kinds of grants, and altogether some seven hundred were recorded before the American takeover, of which fifty-five, nearly 13 percent, were awarded to women.

José de la Guerra y Noriega (1779–1858) and Mariano Guadalupe Vallejo (1808–1890) were perhaps the best examples of the rancho oligarchy during this period. Born in the Spanish town of Novales, Captain De la Guerra joined the military in New Spain. Eventually, he was sent to Santa Barbara, where he served from 1815 to 1842 as the fifth commandant of the local presidio and functioned as treasurer for the Franciscan mission system before its demise. At one time, he owned six ranches, totaling over three hundred thousand acres, on which he ran more than fifty thousand head of cattle. He was also the leading merchant in the pueblo.

Vallejo was born in Monterey, where he was educated with Juan Alvarado, a nephew, and José Castro, a cousin.[8] He became a soldier, like his father before him, and was appointed commandant of the San Francisco presidio in 1831. Four years later, Colonel Vallejo was sent into the area north of San Francisco Bay to establish a defensive outpost at Sonoma against the Russians and to pacify the local Indians. Like Captain De la Guerra, he benefited handsomely from the secularization of the mission system; eventually, Vallejo became the largest landholder in the province.

Below the elite and larger in numbers were non-Indians, mainly mestizos, who constituted something of a middle class. Some were soldiers; others were craftsmen. A few even made their living as vaqueros, an occupation highly regarded in this pastoral society. Like the majority of the upper class, these mestizos were illiterate. Disparaged as lazy by Yankee visitors, who were appalled at the number of fiestas in this Catholic society, mestizos worked long hours the rest of the time, especially vaqueros, who performed hard physical labor, often under dangerous circumstances.

Indians remained at the bottom of Californio society. By the 1840s, their rising mortality rate had leveled off, but conditions had not otherwise improved noticeably. In many cases, their situation may have deteriorated, as these native peoples were now at the mercy of ranchers who were intent on extracting as much labor from them as possible. The paternalistic Franciscans, on the other hand, had felt an obligation to provide for their spiritual welfare.[9] The status of native peoples during this period approximated that of serfdom, but the extent of their exploitation is hard to gauge since the descriptions of their plight were generally written by outsiders intent on finding atrocities which would justify foreign intervention. At any rate, the treatment of the neophytes would worsen after the United States' acquisition of the province.[10]

Beyond the coastal range were indios bárbaros. Before secularization, they continually fomented rebellion among the mission Indians and provided a haven for runaways. After secularization, their numbers swelled as many dispossessed neophytes had nowhere else to go but the inner valleys. Throughout the Mexican period, the interior tribes posed a major threat to coastal settlements, to a considerable extent a reaction to Mexican raiding parties. Mistreatment of indigenous people on the northern frontier was worst in California, it has been argued, probably because of the military weakness of its native inhabitants compared to those of other regions.[11]

NEW MEXICO

Like California, New Mexico experienced remarkable changes during the Mexican period. Generally speaking, historians tend to see New Mexicans as very conservative people; and, given their isolation, this description seems quite appropriate. But between 1821 and 1846, life in New Mexico was altered almost as much as in the maritime province.

Politically, however, little changed for New Mexicans immediately after national independence; it was still difficult to maintain contact with Mexico City, sixteen hundred miles away, so the people of the territory continued to go their own way with minimal interference. Under normal circumstances, this neglect might have been acceptable. Unfortunately, the renewed Indian offensive of Apaches and Navajos required increased military aid from Mexico City when none was available. The beleaguered settlers continually petitioned the central government for military reinforcements throughout the 1820s and the early 1830s, but to no avail. New Mexican discontent only worsened after the mid-1830s, with the rise to power of the centralists in Mexico City.

Unable to help New Mexico solve its Indian problems but intent on reining in the independent-minded pobladores of the Upper Rio Grande, the central government imposed an unpopular governor, Albino Pérez, who arrived in Santa Fe in May 1835. Perceived as unsympathetic to local concerns, Governor Pérez soon incurred the wrath of the local citizenry. His attempt to impose Santa Anna's centralist constitution of 1836 proved to be the last straw.

In August 1837, a rebellion broke out among the Pueblos and Hispanic settlers living in the area north of Santa Fe. Led by a genízaro, José Gonzales, the insurrectionists went on a rampage, killing the governor and sixteen other officials. The propertied classes of New Mexico, who had initially sustained the malcontents, turned against them when the violence got out of hand. Their champion was Manuel Armijo (1792–1853), ex-governor of the province. Himself an early partisan of the rebellion, he now became its most implacable foe. Armijo's execution of Gonzales on 27 January 1838 brought the rebellion to an abrupt halt and earned him the gratitude of the region's leading citizens. Subsequently, serving as chief executive on two other occasions, Armijo would come to dominate New Mexican politics during the remainder of the Mexican period.

Given the arid nature of the land, sheep rather than cattle became the mainstay of the New Mexican economy. In climate and terrain, the area resembled the central plateau of Spain, so it was only natural that Spaniards would foster an industry that had been so profitable in the Old Country. The largest sheep ranches were established in the Rio Grande Valley south of Santa Fe, the provincial capital, in the Río Abajo area centered on Albuquerque. The highland areas north of the capital, the Río Arriba, home of two-thirds of the population, could sustain only small holdings. Consequently, families there did not achieve the wealth and prominence of the southerners.

In both regions, settlers tended to reside close to the Rio Grande, which was indispensable for irrigation. Forced to be self-sufficient, rancheros relied heavily on agriculture. Corn, the ancient staple, continued to be popular; but peppers, potatoes, and a variety of European crops were also cultivated.

Manufacturing was negligible. Discouraged by the mercantilist policies of the colonial era, as well as meager local resources, industry was practiced only on a small scale, forcing New Mexicans to depend on the large cities of central Mexico for the great bulk of their necessities other than food. These commodities were transported on mules across the Chihuahua Trail, which emanated from the population centers of the interior and wound its way through a number of northern frontier settlements before entering New Mexico via El Paso del Norte. As the name of the route indicates, the most important of these settlements was Chihuahua, the chief city of the province of Nueva Vizcaya. Chihuahua merchants monopolized the trail trade. While the basis of their wealth was often the rich mines of the surrounding area and the cattle industry it fostered, by the end of the Spanish period, the Chihuahua elite made their largest profits by pursuing mercantile endeavors. In order to purchase manufactured goods, *Hispanos,* Spanish-speaking residents of New Mexico, paid exorbitant prices to southern merchants, which grew to be an acute source of discontent. Yet, as in California, the Mexican period brought dramatic economic changes to New Mexico, and the most portentous of these was in the field of commerce.

The year of Mexican independence, 1821, witnessed the appearance in New Mexico of William Becknell. A trader from Missouri, Becknell hoped to initiate trade with New Spain. Unaware of Mexican independence, the American entrepreneur took a calculated risk that he would receive a warm welcome in Santa Fe. His gamble paid off handsomely. Not only did he blaze the Santa Fe Trail, one of the most famous arteries of transportation and commerce in the annals of the American West, but he also reaped a handsome profit.

In time, trade along the Santa Fe Trail brought huge dividends to norteamericanos who followed Becknell, but it had even greater consequences for the inhabitants of New Mexico. The increase in the volume of trade with the Yankees helped break the Chihuahua monopoly. Hispanos now had access to cheaper and more abundant merchandise, and the Mexican entrepreneurs could not compete. Moreover, Americans were willing to pay top dollar, in the form of manufactured goods, for mules, furs, blankets, and other commodities that nuevomexicanos produced.

Life in New Mexico became more convenient and comfortable. As in California, the chief beneficiaries of this affluence were large landholding families. They were eventually able to accumulate enough capital to enter into mercantile ventures themselves, ultimately competing very successfully against both Yankee and Mexican traders. In fact, as David A. Sandoval has noted, during the next twenty years, New Mexican families such as the Pereas, Chávezes, and Armijos gradually came to dominate trade on both the Santa Fe and the Chihuahua trails, now a single artery linking Mexico and the United States, mainly because of their enviable position as middlemen.[12] Commerce also opened up in other directions. In 1829–1830, Antonio Armijo, apparently a distant relative of Governor Armijo, blazed a trail, via southern Utah, between Abiquiú, New Mexico, and San Bernardino, California. The Old Spanish Trail, as it came to be called, created a vast market for Hispano sheepmen and was well traveled by the time of the Mexican-American War. As on the Pacific Coast, the Mexican period witnessed the advent of an affluent elite, widening the gap between rich and poor.

From 1821 to 1846, New Mexican society was experiencing unusual ferment, compared to the tradition-bound society of colonial days. At the top were the ricos, a small number of families, centered in Albuquerque and the surrounding area, who monopolized the pastoral and mercantile life of the province. Perhaps the most powerful was the Armijo family, whose best-known representative was Manuel Armijo, the dominant political figure of the times.

Governor Armijo, who was as much a businessman as he was a politician, is one of the most colorful and controversial figures in New Mexican history. American traders, who were asked to pay heavy duties for conducting business in the province, painted an unflattering portrait of him as a ruthless tyrant,[13] and his own people saw him as a coward who refused to defend New Mexico against American invaders in 1846. Virtually all contemporaries agreed that he was venal and corrupt. No doubt, Armijo had many personal foibles; but, as Janet Lecompte, a sympathetic biographer, has argued, he was also a hardworking and dedicated public servant who tried to preserve New Mexico's autonomy vis-à-vis both American interests and Mexican central authority.[14]

Beneath the elite were the pobres. Since they resided in the same areas, and in isolation from the rest of Mexican society, they were usually related to the ricos, a situation tending to mute class antagonisms. Like the upper class, pobres were predominantly mestizos. In rural areas, they worked as sheepherders and peasant farmers. In the towns, they performed menial labor, together with genízaros, who occupied a lower social status.

At the bottom of New Mexican society were Pueblos, about nine thousand strong in 1821, exclusive of the Hopi. While some lived among "whites," working as servants or day laborers, sometimes as virtual slaves, most Indians were permitted to reside in their own towns. Among the largest of these villages, about twenty in number, were Taos, San Ildefonso, and Santa Clara. Encouraged to adopt Catholicism, most indigenous people came to practice a syncretic religion heavily influenced by indigenous beliefs. Some Pueblos rejected Christianity altogether.

As in Alta California, and indeed throughout the northern frontier, women continued to be seen and treated as second-class citizens. As was true on the western periphery, here too their condition was mitigated by certain legal protections unavailable to women living in the United States at the same time.[15] Moreover, as the historian Deena J. González has documented, Hispanas discovered a variety of strategies that helped them improve their status.[16] In fact, some of them became quite wealthy. Among the better known success stories were Manuela Baca and María Gertrudes Barceló, known as "La Tules," who made their money in ranching and entrepreneurship, respectively.

ARIZONA

Arizona fared poorly throughout the Mexican period. On the northern rim of Sonora, the pobladores of the Santa Cruz Valley looked to the south—Arizpe, the district capital, in particular—for military and economic support. There were only two settlements of any consequence in the valley, both of them presidios: Tubac, just above today's United States–Mexican border, and Tucson, a few miles farther north. On the edge of the Apachería, both settlements suffered terribly throughout the entire period as Apaches resumed their raids on Sonoran ranches, terrorizing both pobladores and sedentary tribes such as the Pimas and the Tohono O'odham, who relied on the presidios for protection. So intense was the pressure exerted by Apaches that the mission of San Xavier del Bac had to be abandoned temporarily in 1829, and the presidio at Tubac disappeared altogether in 1848. Indeed, throughout the Mexican period, the Santa Cruz Valley, like the rest of Sonora, suffered a steady decline of its fronterizo population.

What little is known about the inhabitants of these northern outposts in this period indicates that they lived in constant fear. Death came not only at the hands of hostile tribes but also as a result of childbirth and disease. The fear of Indians, in particular, made for tightly knit communities. The hardscrabble life left little time for amusement. Religion offered some consolation.

Despite the dangers, however, the pobladores were not totally isolated. As the life of Teodoro Ramírez (1791–1871), Tucson's leading businessman during this period, illustrates, even at the height of the Apache threat, communication with the southern settlements—Altar, Santa Ana, and Santa Cruz, as well as Arizpe—remained constant, though sporadic.[17] The Ramírezes and almost all the families in Tucson and Tubac were closely linked with families in these Sonoran towns through marriage and commercial ties that required continual movement back and forth.

TEXAS

In Texas (after 1824 a part of the State of Coahuila y Tejas), pobladores, though plagued by some of the same thorny problems, were better off than those in northern Sonora. The Spanish-speaking population was confined principally to San Antonio and La Bahía, renamed Goliad in 1829, both along the San Antonio River. But there were two other important clusters of Tejanos. One was in east Texas, centering on Nacogdoches, and the other along the lower Rio Grande—technically part of the State of Tamaulipas, which extended up the Gulf coast as far as the Nueces River—where the leading settlement was Laredo. The number of frontier residents had dropped precipitously at the end of the Spanish period. However, the first years of Mexican independence, coming on the heels of the Adams-Onís Treaty, brought renewed optimism; and, as the historian Andrés Tijerina shows, many pobladores left these presidial towns to establish ranches, particularly along the river valleys.[18] In so doing, however, they exposed themselves to the wrath of the indigenous population. The Indian menace resurfaced immediately, as it did throughout the northern fringe of the new republic. Clearly, the Mexican government was no more able to encourage emigration from the interior nor pacify the Comanches than had been the Spanish Crown before it. Even San Antonio, a town of some fifteen hundred citizens in 1821, was vulnerable to Comanche attack. High expectations quickly gave way to bitter disappointment.

THE CLASH OF CULTURES

The central government was also discredited, in time, by its inadequate response to another pressing problem: the renewed pressure of Anglo immigration in east Texas. American interest in the rich agricultural lands of the Texas plains goes back to the beginning of the nineteenth century, when American filibusters, "the 'illegal aliens' of their day," as Patricia Nelson Limerick calls them, began to make forays into Spanish territory.[19] The Adams-Onís Treaty of 1819 seemed to put an end to this threat, but the independence of Mexico two years later brought renewed interest in Texas by American frontiersmen. As early as 1821, the Iturbide government, having gained a false sense of security as a result of the recently signed treaty, determined that rather than following the traditional policy of impeding foreign immigration, it might be wiser to encourage and regulate the entry of American settlers. Unlike Mexican citizens, after all, Yankees were eager to come into Texas. Government policy, which continued after the fall of Iturbide's empire, was to recruit norteamericanos to enter Texas. By using American agents, called *empresarios*, to entice their co-nationals, Mexican officials hoped to populate the vast expanse of Texas once and for all and transform it into a productive part of the republic.

The most famous agent was Stephen F. Austin (1793–1836). His father, Moses, a Missouri mine operator, had successfully petitioned for an empresario license from Spanish authorities in 1821, shortly before his death. The son inherited the undertaking. After renegotiating with Mexican officials, young Austin was eventually permitted to bring in some three hundred families, who were given approximately five thousand acres apiece along the Brazos River on the condition that they abide by Mexican laws, learn to speak Spanish, and renounce Protestantism in favor of Catholicism. Stephen Austin himself was given a generous grant for his services and the right to collect duties from his recruits. By the mid-1820s, the colony, centered around a town named in his honor, San Felipe de Austin, was thriving. Other Anglo grants were nearly as successful.

As a consequence, thousands of Americans started to enter Texas, many without bothering to obtain Mexican authorization. By 1830, Anglos outnumbered Mexicans twenty-five thousand to four thousand. Tejanos grew alarmed. Not only were they being overwhelmed, but many of the newcomers, it seemed, had no intention of assimilating into Mexican society. A cultural conflict grew increasingly apparent. Anglos and Mexicans were separated by vast linguistic, religious, and political differences. The most crucial element of this cultural gap, however, had to do with race.

Arnoldo De León, the foremost Chicano expert on Texas history, has demonstrated conclusively that the racial animosity of Texans toward Mexicans was well-rooted in the period before 1836.[20] The color issue was predictable since "three-quarters of the Anglos in Texas were southerners who were committed to slavery."[21] The central government in Mexico City was slow to appreciate the magnitude of the problem. However, a series of laws were finally enacted in 1830–1832 to ameliorate the situation. Anglo immigration into Texas was forbidden. At the same time, Mexican families were encouraged to colonize the area. In addition, economic ties between Anglos in Texas and the United States were discouraged through a tough tariff policy. The Mexican response was a case of too little, too late. The laws served only to antagonize Anglo-Texans.

Anglo immigration into Mexico in the 1820s was not confined to Texas; Yankees began to penetrate into the republic all along its northern rim. Everywhere the primary motivation was the prospect of economic gain. The potential wealth of the region was obvious to outsiders well before this period, but it was only with the ouster of the Spaniards and the relaxing of immigration and commercial regulations that Yankees were given an opportunity to enter the territory legally.

Americans arriving in New Mexico during the Mexican period came primarily to trap beaver, to engage in the trail trade, or to do both. By the second decade of the nineteenth century, the fur trade, which had been introduced into North America by the French, was centered on the Rocky Mountains, where American and British mountain men competed to gain economic domination. It was at this time that traders and trappers began to make their appearance in New Mexico. Eventually, some of these mountain men elected to settle in the province and set up mercantile establishments. Taos became their chief center of operations. Among the most successful of the Taos traders were Ewing Young and Kit Carson. Like Carson, who married into the Jaramillo family, most of these foreign-born merchants were reasonably well integrated into Hispano society. According to the historian Rebecca McDowell Craver, fifteen of the twenty-two Americans in Taos in 1841 were married to or lived with Mexican women.[22]

The volume of trade in New Mexico increased dramatically with the opening of the Santa Fe Trail. At first, Missouri merchants were content to conduct their business in New Mexico on a seasonal basis, but before long they saw the opportunity to reap huge profits by setting up permanent mercantile establishments in or near New Mexico. The most celebrated of these early outposts was the "fort" established in 1833 by the Bent brothers, William and Charles, along the Arkansas River.

In California, the appearance of Americans occurred in three waves before the mid-1840s.[23] These have been labeled the maritime interest, the trapping interest, and the pioneering interest. The first of these consisted of Americans and other foreigners who arrived, mostly after 1821, to participate in the hide-and-tallow trade. Yankees were the most active participants in this lucrative enterprise. "It is estimated," according to the historian Bernard L. Fontana, "that Boston traders alone may have carried more than six million hides and seven thousand tons of tallow out of California between 1826 and 1848."[24] After coming around Cape Horn from New England, their clipper ships spent the next few months sailing from one California port to another, exchanging American goods for hides and tallow. They returned home by retracing their initial route. The entire trip lasted two and sometimes three years. The most famous of these voyages was described in 1840 by Richard Henry Dana in *Two Years before the Mast,* an account of his experiences aboard trading vessels along the California coast in 1834 and 1835.

While most seamen only visited the maritime province, a few decided to make their homes there. More typically, though, it was company agents stationed in the port towns of Santa Barbara and Monterey who established residence among the Californios. These individuals married into upper-class society, assimilated the dominant culture, learning Spanish and sometimes practicing Catholicism, and acquired large land grants. The prime example of these outsiders who flourished in California by "going native" was Abel Stearns, who arrived in the province in 1829 and settled down in the Los Angeles area. Stearns married into the family of Juan Bandini, one of the most prominent residents of San Diego, and eventually the likeable and well-connected immigrant became the largest landowner in the southern part of the province.

Stearns's success in the south was mirrored by that of the enigmatic John Sutter (1803–1880), another outsider, in the north. He, too, had been a trader, but his business had been conducted on the Santa Fe Trail. The German-born immigrant arrived in Alta California in 1839. A recipient of a huge land grant in the Sacramento area, Sutter, as his biographer Albert L. Hurtado vividly illustrates, was one of the central players in the momentous events unfolding in the province at midcentury.[25]

After the midtwenties, another wave of foreigners arrived—the fabled mountain men. Mostly Americans, these newcomers came looking for peltry. Unlike the maritime interest, trappers followed overland trails; and once in California, they generally kept to themselves in the interior valleys, thus sustaining little or no contact with the Hispanic population on the coast. The first of the mountain men to reach the province was also the most celebrated, Jedediah Strong Smith (1799?–1831), who entered the Great Central Valley via the Mojave Desert in 1826.[26] Other well-known trappers who visited the province were James Ohio Pattie, Joseph Reddeford Walker, and James Beckwourth.

By the mid-1840s, on the eve of the Mexican-American War, the largest stream of immigrants began to penetrate the area. These were farmers who followed overland trails blazed by the mountain men and who sought fertile land on the coast. Most of the early emigrants succumbed to "Oregon fever" and headed for the Willamette Valley. In 1841, however, the Bidwell-Bartleson train chose to take a southwesterly route from the Snake River, across the Nevada desert, and into California, thus beginning a mass migration of pioneers that would continue throughout the nineteenth century. Most California-bound immigrants were agriculturalists who came from the Midwest with their families looking for land in the Great Valley. Among them was the infamous party led by John and Jacob Donner, which was stranded in the Sierras in the winter of 1846–1847.

THE TEXAS REVOLT

By the early 1830s, given their superior numbers and the increasing antagonism they felt toward both the Mexican government and the Mexican people, Anglo settlers in Texas were rapidly enlisting in the movement favoring independence. All that was needed was a leader and an excuse. The leader appeared in the person of Samuel Houston (1793–1863). So much hagiographic nonsense has been written about Houston by admiring Texas historians that it is almost impossible to separate fact from fiction. Nevertheless, it is clear that he was an extraordinary person with enormous charisma. Born in Virginia of Scots-Irish stock, Houston moved to Tennessee with his family when he was still a boy. Fiercely independent, he ran off into the wilderness while a teenager and lived with the Cherokees, who adopted him into the tribe. He developed an admiration for Native Americans that he would always maintain, a rarity on the frontier. Returning home after an absence of three years, Houston served in the military under Andrew Jackson, won a seat in Congress in 1823 as a delegate from Tennessee, and became governor of the state four years later. After resigning political office in 1829, he first entered Texas in 1832, and he settled there permanently three years later. Although some historians have speculated that he was dispatched to Texas by Jackson, who became president in 1829, to engineer an American takeover,[27] there is no concrete evidence to sustain this interpretation. But the fact remains that from the very beginning, he became the leader of the Texas faction which called for immediate independence from Mexico, in opposition to Austin and his followers, who wanted a more conciliatory policy.

The occasion for independence arose in 1835, a year after the federalist government in Mexico City was defeated by Santa Anna and the centralists. The new government was determined to squash movements for local autonomy throughout the country, now deeply fragmented politically. Their efforts to divest the Texans of recent political gains were so arbitrary that the centralists succeeded in alienating even the Mexican residents of Texas, most of whom would remain neutral in the coming conflict. Austin and Houston now closed ranks. In 1835, the Texans initiated their rebellion against the Mexican government.

The most famous battle of the war occurred on 6 March 1836, when General Santa Anna and his army of some five thousand men attacked the rebel stronghold at the Alamo, an old Franciscan mission in San Antonio, killing 187 defenders.[28] Among the dead were James Bowie, Davy Crockett, and Colonel William B. Travis, the commander of the garrison. While every Texas schoolchild recognizes these names as heroes of Texas independence, few people know that eight martyrs at the Alamo were Mexicans: Juan Abamillo, Juan Antonio Badillo, Carlos Espalier, Gregorio Esparza, Antonio Fuentes, Galba Fuqua, José Toribio Losoya, and Andrés Nava. In fact, many Tejanos actively supported the cause of Texas, some fighting bravely to achieve independence. First and foremost were José Antonio Navarro (1795–1871) and Juan Seguín (1806–1890), members of prominent San Antonio families.[29] Whether these men were heroes or traitors is a question that divides Chicano historians today. What is certain is that anti-Mexican feeling became so vehement during the conflict and its aftermath that the Mexican contribution at the Alamo was virtually annihilated from public memory until recently.[30]

The Mexican victory was short-lived. One month after the Alamo, Santa Anna and his troops were surprised by Houston's army at the Battle of San Jacinto. The Mexicans suffered some six hundred deaths, the rebels lost eight men. The capture of Santa Anna, Mexico's president, virtually ended the conflict. Although the vanquished *caudillo* signed the Treaty of Velasco under duress and the Mexican Senate refused to ratify the pact, the country was in such complete disarray that there was nothing the government could do to repair the damage.[31]

During the next decade, Texas existed as an independent nation. Texans asked for immediate admission into the American republic upon winning their freedom from Mexico, but the petition was denied by Congress. The United States feared alienating its southern neighbor, which threatened to go to war over Texas annexation. However, there was a more sensitive question to consider. A balance of slave and free states had been achieved, and Texas's admission would jeopardize the precarious truce between the two sections of the country. During the next nine years, the Lone Star Republic was beset with a multitude of problems. One of the most pressing was encouraging settlement of the country. Among the agents who were used to recruit American colonists, interestingly, were Henry Castro and Jacob de Córdova, Sephardic Jews who soon became successful real estate moguls. Another major concern of the Republic was mending fences with its neighbor to the south and placating its own Mexican population.

Under the Lone Star Republic, Tejanos found themselves treated as foreigners in their own land, a process well documented by Arnoldo De León. The negative stereotype which had haunted them before—they were said to be lazy and vicious by nature—was reinforced and used as justification for the seizure of their lands. Almost immediately, triumphant Anglos began to portray the Alamo as the site of "the cradle of Texas liberty," a symbol that was "profoundly anti-Mexican."[32] Despised and abused, many Mexicans fled south beyond the Nueces River, now a disputed boundary with Mexico. Some crossed the Rio Grande, where they found greater security. One of these disillusioned exiles was Juan Seguín himself, who discovered that neither his prominence in the community nor his distinguished service to the independence movement had spared him from the hatred and envy of Anglos intent on ridding Texas of all vestiges of Mexican influence. Border raids by disgruntled expatriates and common bandits alike served only to reinforce the Anglo notion that all Mexicans were criminals and must be dealt with accordingly. Tejanos who paid the heaviest price were generally those who refused to leave their homes. Racial violence was widespread during the entire period, but while blacks and Indians suffered horrible abuses, Mexicans endured the worst treatment. Not surprisingly, during the coming Mexican War, "almost no Tejanos" supported the Americans.[33]

The loss of Texas was a bitter pill for the proud Mexicans, and the treatment of Tejanos by the Lone Star Republic only added insult to injury. As for Anglos in Texas, their recent success encouraged expansionist sentiments, which Mexico's obvious weakness did nothing to curb. In 1841, the Texans made an attempt to invade New Mexico. They were repelled by their aroused enemies. Governor Armijo claimed full credit for the victory, but it was the Texans' own incompetence that doomed the enterprise to failure from the very beginning. Tensions increased steadily between the two nations thereafter; it seemed only a matter of time before hostilities would resume.

THE MEXICAN WAR

Expansionist sentiments by the 1840s were hardly limited to Texans. By this time, many Americans, particularly on the western frontier, were intent on territorial gains, by force if necessary. Their immediate objectives were the Oregon territory, soon to be acquired from the British, and Texas, the gateway to California. The strength of these bellicose sentiments can be gauged by the election of James K. Polk to the presidency in 1844. An unabashed advocate of expansion, Polk was swept into office on the promise that he would "reoccupy" Oregon and "reannex" Texas.

The election was interpreted as a mandate. In fact, one of the last acts of the ousted Tyler administration was to annex the Lone Star Republic in early 1845. So powerful was the desire to gain Texas, a prelude to the acquisition of California, that Americans were willing to jeopardize the uneasy truce between North and South over the slavery question. From across the border came a howl of protest. Mexican nationalists had suspected that the United States was behind the Texas revolt, and now these suspicions appeared to be confirmed. Incensed, some of the younger members of the Mexican Congress called for war.

Despite the impassioned reaction, Polk initiated efforts to purchase California from the Mexican government in the autumn of 1845, which speaks volumes for the president's insensitivity. So incredible were these obtuse efforts that one must question whether he was acting in good faith. Naturally, his agent John Slidell was refused an audience in Mexico City. Given the anti-American mood of their people, Mexican diplomats understood that any compromise with the United States at this time was tantamount to political suicide.

It was at this point that Polk determined to use war as an instrument of diplomacy. After all, once the Mexicans had refused to negotiate, there was absolutely no other way to acquire California; the Mexican claim was well established, and the maritime province was adequately populated by Mexican citizens. The American president concluded that the ends justified the means; but, adroit Machiavellian that he was, Polk also realized that he had to appear to be acting in self-defense. Only then would Americans be willing to make the sacrifices that an armed conflict required. Moreover, the country's strong Puritan legacy required a "just" war. How to get the Mexicans to initiate hostilities—this was the practical problem that Polk faced. He found the solution in the boundary dispute that the United States had inherited with the annexation of Texas.[34]

When Texans achieved their independence, they argued that the common border between their territory and Mexico was the Rio Grande. The Mexican government countered by pointing out that the province of Texas had been separated historically from the rest of the country by the Nueces River, 150 miles north of the Rio Grande. What was at stake was not only the entire Lower Rio Grande Valley, but the eastern half of New Mexico as well. When Texas entered the Union, the issue was still pending. The American claim was shaky. The Mexicans were so sure of their position that they were willing to submit the question to international arbitration. The United States had no intention of permitting the British to mediate the dispute.

At this point, Polk decided to take a gamble. In the last days of March 1846, he instructed General Zachary Taylor to occupy the disputed territory. Once fired upon by the Mexicans, Polk could go to the Senate, in good conscience, asking for a declaration of war. Preparing his war message, the president awaited the outcome.

But the Mexicans vacillated, and Polk grew nervous, fearing British intervention in Mexico unless he moved quickly. Finally, on 23 April 1846, the Mexicans declared war on the United States. Polk's ploy had worked, but for the moment he was ignorant of the war declaration. Intent on acquiring California, he convinced himself that the British had the same designs. He felt he needed to act quickly before his imagined adversaries had a chance to react. Early in May, determined that delay would be too risky, he made up his mind to seek a war declaration, with or without Mexican cooperation. Fortunately for him, he now received word that Mexican troops had attacked Taylor on 25 April. On 11 May, President Polk went before the Senate, where he delivered his famous speech declaring that "Mexico has passed the boundary of the United States, has invaded our territory, and shed American blood on American soil." "The message," the historians Michael C. Meyer and William L. Sherman have concluded, "was remarkable for its distortion and provocative to the absurd."[35] Some Americans were skeptical. Young Abe Lincoln, then a member of Congress, had serious reservations about whether the disputed territory was indeed American property. Nonetheless, the U.S. declaration of war was passed overwhelmingly—the House of Representatives voted 174 to 14, and the Senate voted 40 to 2—and so was initiated one of the most popular and successful wars in American history.

The Mexican War, known as the "War of 1847" to Mexicans, basically consisted of three campaigns, all of them American offensives against opponents who were divided and outmanned.[36] The most consequential thrust was initiated by General Taylor, who led his troops into northern Mexico. His objective was Mexico City. His adversaries put up a stubborn resistance—ultimately, the war would claim fifty thousand Mexican lives. Several tough engagements were fought in the north, notably at Monterrey in Nuevo León and Buena Vista in Coahuila, before the path to the capital opened up. The last stage of the victorious campaign was a seaborne invasion of Vera Cruz, led by General Winfield Scott, who then marched on the capital, tracing the route that Cortés had followed centuries before. On 13 September 1847, Scott's marines entered the Halls of Montezuma, and the war was over, for all intents and purposes.

In the meantime, the American Army of the West, under Colonel Stephen Watts Kearny, marched over the Santa Fe Trail and entered the New Mexican capital in August 1846. The initial takeover was relatively uneventful. While many of his advisors were prepared to defend the province, Manuel Armijo, still governor, went through the motions of preparing a defense, before fleeing south into Durango at the last moment. It is rumored that this ignoble retreat was prompted by a bribe provided by James W. Magoffin, an American trader who had been active on the Santa Fe and Chihuahua trails for years. Devoid of leadership, New Mexicans resigned themselves to their fate. In some quarters, notably among Anglo traders, there was even genuine enthusiasm for U.S. occupation.

Kearny did his best to pacify the native population. He then headed for California in late September 1846, leaving a small garrison in Santa Fe. His soldiers' mistreatment of local residents, however, combined with the New Mexicans' hatred of Anglo and Hispano collaborators, resulted in a brief but bloody uprising. Centered on Taos, the revolt erupted in January 1847. Before it was over, insurgents had slaughtered several prominent New Mexicans, including newly appointed governor Charles Bent. As in the 1837 rebellion, though, the rebels, mainly Pueblo Indians, came to be perceived as a threat by the privileged classes, and the uprising was quelled by the local elite. The Taos revolt makes it clear that the notion of a bloodless conquest of New Mexico, perpetrated by a number of U.S. historians, was a complete myth. In fact, nearly three hundred Mexicans and more than thirty Americans were killed before order was restored.

The war in California seems to have broken out independently of events in Texas. Attractive not only because of its splendid resources, particularly its fine harbors, but also because of its value as an entrepôt for the China trade, California represented the primary objective of American foreign policy at midcentury. Stymied in his efforts to purchase the Pacific province, Polk was determined to use the Texas border dispute as an excuse for a war that would win him the coveted prize. However, the wily statesman also concurrently pursued other avenues toward this end. His primary agents in these schemes were Thomas O. Larkin and John C. Frémont.

Larkin, a Massachusetts Yankee who arrived in California in 1832, was one of the most prominent members of the maritime interest. He acquired large properties, but he did not marry into local society. Nor did he assimilate the native lifestyle, though he made friends with many well-to-do Californios. Refusing to burn his bridges behind him, he was a logical choice to be American consul in the province, an appointment he won in 1844. A firm advocate of U.S. expansion, Larkin yearned for the day when California would enter the American sphere of influence. On 17 October 1845, he was given the opportunity to further American designs when the U.S. government sent a secret dispatch appointing him "confidential agent in California." James Buchanan, Polk's secretary of state, instructed him to convince prominent Californios, his friends and colleagues, that it would be in their best interests if the province were to secede from the Mexican union. They were not informed, however, of the next step after secession—absorption into the United States. Larkin's efforts were fruitless. While Californio oligarchs did meet in Santa Barbara on 15 June 1846 to debate the issue of secession, the contentious delegates were unable to come to any agreement. Many of them reaffirmed their allegiance to the Mexican nation. In fact, the historian Michael J. González maintains that the love of the homeland was pervasive, at least in the Los Angeles area,[37] a claim that gains some credence thanks to the stiff military resistance the Americans would soon encounter.

Captain John C. Frémont, the self-styled "Pathfinder of the West," was a member of the American military and a man of enormous ambition. He, too, became an agent for Polk, who felt that the officer might achieve through force what the consul hoped to accomplish through persuasion. Toward this end, Frémont and a party of sixty-two armed men appeared in California in December 1845, ostensibly on a "scientific" expedition. A few weeks later, the party advanced into the Salinas Valley, practically on the doorstep of Monterey, the provincial capital. Confronted by José Castro, the military commandant of the area, who no doubt was perplexed by the Americans' interest in the province's flora and fauna, they were asked to leave the territory. Offended by the commandant's brusque manner, Frémont threatened violence—apparently it did not occur to him that he was in a foreign country—before grudgingly agreeing to leave California for the Oregon territory. Frémont and his men then headed north, where they met with American mountain men. The result of this parley was the Bear Flag Revolt. The insurrection broke out on 10 June 1846, and culminated four days later, when William B. Ide and his men arrested Mariano Vallejo in Sonoma. Frémont, who had been riding toward the Oregon border when he heard the news, quickly returned to Sonoma to assume command of the small army of irregulars. The Americans advanced south along the coast, eventually entering Monterey, which had been taken in the first days of July by marines belonging to Commodore John D. Sloat's Pacific squadron. During the following weeks, the combined American forces captured the Mexican coastal settlements; with the occupation of Los Angeles in mid-August, the conquest appeared to be complete.

Disgruntled Californios, led by Captain José María Flores, made one last desperate effort to reverse the momentum. On 6 December, at the Battle of San Pascual, an Indian village near San Diego, Mexican lancers under Andrés Pico inflicted a surprising defeat on Kearny's troops, recently arrived from New Mexico. But victory was ephemeral; within a matter of weeks, resistance was broken, and the insurgents were forced to recognize the loss of California in the Treaty of Cahuenga, signed on 13 January 1847.

Even before American troops had marched into Mexico City, President Polk dispatched Nicolas P. Trist to the Mexican capital to negotiate the peace treaty. While negotiations were being conducted, American war aims suddenly escalated. Mexico lay prostrate. Many senators now wondered why the entire country might not be annexed. Some suggested that all of Central America was ripe for the taking. There were even those who advocated U.S. hegemony all the way to the tip of South America. Oblivious to these arguments, Trist negotiated a pact, signed on 2 February 1848, which most of his countrymen found excessively lenient. Polk himself was outraged at Trist's failure to respond to the new situation. But, in the end, unwilling to prolong acrimonious debates, the president accepted the Treaty of Guadalupe Hidalgo, named after the Mexico City suburb where it was negotiated. The agreement was ratified by the U.S. Senate on 10 March 1848.[38]

The territorial settlement imposed by the treaty shocked and incensed the defeated people. Many Mexicans, among them Benito Juárez, soon to become the republic's greatest president, preferred to go on fighting rather than accept the dictated peace. Mexico not only had to surrender the vast lands of California and New Mexico, but it was forced to recognize the humiliating loss of Texas. Altogether, the defeated republic lost 947,570 square miles of land, almost half of its national territory, though less than 1 percent of its population. "The Treaty of Guadalupe Hidalgo," Juan Gómez-Quiñones, speaking for virtually all Chicano scholars, opines, "is one of the harshest treaties between countries of the last two centuries with regard to territorial acquisition."[39] Mexicans in the conquered territory were given the alternative of packing up and moving south into Mexican territory—an onerous option that only about two thousand of the one hundred thousand eligible candidates chose—or remaining in what had become the American Southwest. Mexican residents in the conquered territory were guaranteed "all the rights of citizens of the United States" including "free enjoyment of their liberty and property," according to Article IX. Irate nationalists were hardly placated by a payment of $15 million to the vanquished nation by the American government, which also agreed to assume Mexican debts to U.S. citizens to the tune of some $3 million—compensation for territorial losses, which the proud Mexicans saw as blood money.

The Mexican Republic paid a heavy price for its setbacks at midcentury. "The loss of Texas and the war with the United States," scholars have concluded, "contributed more to Mexico's impoverishment, its apparent sterility, its xenophobia, its lack of self-esteem, and its general demoralization than any other event of the nineteenth century."[40] This troublesome legacy still plagues Mexicans, on both sides of the border.

And so ended one of the sorriest chapters of the American epic. Until very recently, in the aftermath of the Vietnam debacle, U.S. historians have been reticent to deal with this embarrassing episode. When the 1846 war was mentioned at all, it was the Mexicans who were saddled with the responsibility.[41] Such, for example, is the interpretation offered by the most celebrated American study of the inglorious conflict, Justin H. Smith's *The War with Mexico* (1919), a two-volume work which offers this odd conclusion in explaining the role of the Mexican Republic:

> Her treatment of Texans and Americans violated the laws of justice and humanity, and—since there was no tribunal to punish her—laid upon the United States, both as its nearest neighbor and as an injured community, the duty of retribution. In almost every way possible, indeed, she forced us to take a stand. She would neither reason nor hearken to reason, would not understand,

would not negotiate. Compensation for the loss of territory, in excess of its value to her, she knew she could have. Peace and harmony with this country she knew might be hers. But prejudice, vanity, passion and wretched politics inclined her toward war; her overrated military advantages, her expectations of European aid, the unpreparedness of the United States, and in particular the supposed inferiority of Taylor and his army encouraged her; and she deliberately launched the attack so long threatened.[42]

Making this judgment seems about as rational as arguing that World War II was a product of Polish aggression against Nazi Germany. While the case for Mexican aggression may not be quite as outrageous, it is clear that Smith's conclusion is baseless. Admittedly, there was a good deal of hawkish posturing in Mexico on the eve of the conflict, but there is no conceivable reason why the Mexicans might want to fight the United States . . . unless they actually strove for dismemberment. Sheep do not normally attack wolves. The gaping discrepancy in casualty figures between the two armies, once the battles began, amply illustrates what both Americans and Mexicans knew before—Mexico was woefully inadequate to the task of competing against the United States, a nation that Alexis de Tocqueville, author of *Democracy in America,* was already touting as a superpower by the 1830s.

The Mexicans may not have wanted war, some scholars might argue, but once American businessmen established themselves on Mexico's Far North, pulling the pobladores into the orbit of the U.S. capitalist system, the die was cast. Even some Mexican historians have bought into this argument. Andrés Reséndez, for example, concludes: "Against the background of a generally stagnant Mexican economy, the Far North inevitably gravitated toward the American economy as frontier residents' livelihoods came to depend on keeping the lines of communication with the United States wide open."[43] This capitalist expansion, "the de facto economic integration of Mexico's Far North into the American economy during the 1820s and 1830s," he suggests, practically ensured U.S. annexation. Certainly, economic integration was a contributing factor, but if commercial links were of paramount importance, all of Mexico would belong to the United States by now. No, clearly human agency had something to do with the way things turned out.

President Polk must shoulder much of the responsibility for the war with Mexico. Admittedly, the smoking gun has never been found, but a survey of the president's actions suggests that his most plausible goal was an armed conflict. What was suspected by many of his contemporaries, who labeled the military engagement "Mr. Polk's War," is often conceded today by students of diplomacy. His political enemies in 1846 accused the commander in chief of being the instrument of a conspiracy of southern slaveholders who sought to extend the Peculiar Institution westward—like fellow Tennesseans Andrew Jackson and Sam Houston, Polk was a slaveholder. While this interpretation may be suspect today, the presumption of the president's bellicose intentions rings true. Not that he ever admitted it. His conduct, he insisted, was motivated by the need to protect American sovereignty, and most U.S. historians have taken him at his word.

Polk's credibility is suspect, to say the least. His duplicity throughout is well documented. His fondness for secret diplomacy went as far as recruiting Santa Anna's help on the eve of the war, when the unprincipled but ambitious caudillo was in Cuban exile. American diplomats have traditionally appealed to high principles . . . and behaved like everyone else. Such was the case with President Polk, who talked of honor and duty, and who declared at the beginning of the war that he was not interested in annexations of territory. What Polk did in 1846, when he instigated a war and blamed the Mexicans, was no different than what Bismarck and Cavour would do in Europe during the next few years or what the United States would do on the Persian Gulf in the early twenty-first century. The American president was a pioneer in the use of *Realpolitik*.

Ultimately, however, James K. Polk was not the determining factor. The clash of arms would have erupted with or without him. In fact, the war very nearly broke out in 1842, before the president began his machinations. In that year, Commodore Thomas ap Catesby Jones, the commander of the American Pacific squadron, heard a rumor that war had been declared. He had nothing specific to go on, but he headed straight for California. He launched an attack on its capital, Monterey, before occupying the port on 20 October—only to discover, much to his embarrassment, that there was no state of war. He had been misinformed. Although his superiors disavowed his actions, Jones escaped with only temporary suspension from naval service. He was not even reprimanded. This pathetic episode illustrates not only the commodore's incredible audacity; more significantly, it indicates that war was in the air, and that practically everyone in the United States knew who the adversary would be and what was at stake. Jones simply jumped the gun.

The Mexican War has been attributed to the American belief in "Manifest Destiny," a term coined by John O'Sullivan, an American journalist, once hostilities had begun, and best defined by Walt Whitman, the Poet of Democracy, as "the great mission of peopling the New World with a noble race."[44] Of course, there was no mission, nor was there even a belief. The lofty concept was a rationalization for baser motives. The armed conflict occurred for many reasons, but mostly because Americans wanted war, or rather what war would provide. The naked truth remains that Mexico had what its northern neighbor craved—land.

THE AMERICAN
SOUTHWEST
1848–1900

Chicano historians have tended to neglect the second half of the nineteenth century. When they began their work in the late 1960s, this period was generally viewed as a hiatus between two much more promising epochs: the age of Mexican sovereignty before and the decades of massive Mexican immigration afterward. It was the latter period, the twentieth century, which tended to dominate historical interest. One reason was that Chicano scholars are generally descended from twentieth-century immigrants and identify very little, if at all, with the so-called Spanish dons. Moreover, many of them pride themselves on being scholar-activists; consequently, they believe that it is imperative not simply to describe what happened in the past, but to change it, an orientation that naturally leads to a preoccupation with more contemporary issues. Still another reason for the neglect of this period was the abject condition of the Mexicano population in the Southwest before 1900. Small and powerless, they were despised and oppressed by mainstream society. It is a sad and depressing story, but one that needs to be told nonetheless. Adversity, after all, left a lasting impression among Mexicanos; many attitudes today are products of the trials and tribulations endured at the time. Happily, Chicano scholars have come to appreciate this perspective, and today it is recognized that the period was a crucible on which the modern Mexican American has been forged.[1]

GRINGOS AND GREASERS

Anti-Mexican attitudes during the second half of the nineteenth century were ubiquitous throughout the Southwest, as many historians have noted. These sentiments arose for a variety of reasons. Perhaps the most obvious was the legacy of bitterness left by the recent war of conquest. While the fighting had not lasted very long, deep animosities created during the conflict persisted on both sides for many years. Subjugated by their enemies, Mexicanos adopted an attitude that is perfectly understandable. The response of the conquerors is more complicated. As in other American wars, enemies were portrayed as evil and unworthy of respect.

This perception of Mexicanos was accentuated in the immediate postwar period by the success of Spanish-speaking immigrants in the gold mines of California. Envious of their good fortune, some Anglo Americans inflamed public opinion against these "greasers" as a means of expelling their competitors from the mother lode country. The conflict over land ownership, which inevitably arose after the military campaigns, would likewise encourage the portrayal of Mexicanos as a foreign and unfriendly element.

Religious prejudice was another source of anti-Mexican feeling. Vehement anti-Catholicism had been characteristic of England since the sixteenth century, a legacy that remained relatively dormant in its American possessions, given the insignificant size of the Catholic population. Nor was there much concern with Catholicism in the new republic during its first decades of existence. The massive influx of Irish Catholics in the mid-nineteenth century, however, rekindled Anglo fears of popery, concerns that were not assuaged in the least when in the midst of the Mexican War several hundred Irish Catholics serving in the American army deserted to the Mexican side. Led by Captain John Riley, the Saint Patrick's Brigade performed valiantly, and today the *San Patricios* are honored as heroes in Mexico. Both Irish and Mexican Catholics came to be seen as lazy, irresponsible, and priest-ridden minorities, largely incapable of assimilation.

Finally, there was the crucial element of race. The folklorist Arthur L. Campa is correct in his assessment when he states: "Cultural, political, and religious differences tended to polarize Mexicans and Anglo Americans, but the most persistent reason for the prejudice felt by Americans was that Mexicans were dark-skinned people. Despite the rhetoric used to rationalize prejudice in the Southwest, the lack of acceptance of darker skins by most Europeans is by and large the most obvious."[2] The second half of the nineteenth century witnessed the rapid growth of racism throughout the Western world, and the United States was no exception. In the American West, where whites encountered people of color in large numbers, racism was widespread among the emigrants. It was primarily racial factors that led to the intense xenophobia experienced by the Chinese in California, prompting the enactment of the 1882 Chinese Exclusion Act, the first instance of an entire ethnic group being barred from entering the country. While racial attitudes toward Mexicanos were never quite as hostile as toward Asians—most Mexicanos, after all, had some trace of European blood—these prejudices were sufficiently powerful to justify their confinement to the most menial positions in the emerging capitalist economy of the Southwest.

The sociologist Tomás Almaguer feels that fellow Chicano scholars have tended to overestimate the amount of racism experienced by their forebears in the nineteenth century, arguing that Mexicanos, in fact, received meaningful legal protection, notably in the Treaty of Guadalupe Hidalgo, not accorded other racial minorities in the West.[3] While Professor Almaguer has correctly pinpointed a deficiency among many colleagues, who tend to stress race to the exclusion of gender and class considerations, he underestimates the amount of racial prejudice encountered by the Spanish-speaking population. Legal protection was often the theory rather than the practice. Ken Gonzales-Day has documented 350 lynchings in the Golden States between 1850 and 1935, and most of the victims were Latinos.[4] Moreover, it is dangerous to generalize based on the experiences of Mexicanos in California, as Almaguer does; if we look at Texas, admittedly the most extreme example, the preeminence of race as the basis for anti-Mexican prejudice and discrimination is perfectly clear.

In fact, relations between Mexicanos and Anglos, the most important theme in Mexican American history during the second half of the nineteenth century, were complex, far more complex than Chicano scholars realized when they began to examine this relationship in the 1970s. Although there was much hostility between the two ethnic groups, this was not uniformly the case. Some Mexicanos, especially among the old elite, adjusted better to the new regime than did others. For their part, some members of the Anglo community rose above the common prejudices of the time. A few—Arnoldo De León refers to them as "our gringo *amigos*"—even formed bonds of friendship with Mexicanos.[5] Interethnic marriages were surprisingly common in some areas. Moreover, the passage of time brought changes in attitudes. Finally, there were substantial differences that manifested themselves geographically. Consequently, the best way of understanding the complexity of Anglo-Mexican relations is by surveying the major areas of Mexicano settlement, one at a time.

CALIFORNIA

The most complete and insightful study of Mexican-Anglo relations in the Golden State during the aftermath of the war of conquest was written in 1966 by the historian Leonard Pitt, who established the main areas of inquiry that Chicano scholars would later pursue. In his *The Decline of the Californios,* the author makes it clear that the status of the Spanish-speaking population in California rapidly deteriorated after the Mexican-American War. While the relations between the two ethnic communities were bound to be troublesome in the aftermath of the war, they were exacerbated immediately by the gold rush.

On 24 January 1848, a little over a week before the Mexicans signed the Treaty of Guadalupe Hidalgo, gold was discovered at Coloma, on the south fork of the American River. The discovery was made by James Wilson Marshall, a Scottish

carpenter employed by John Augustus Sutter, while in the process of constructing a sawmill. The two men attempted to suppress news of the discovery, but it
was not long before it became common knowledge. During the course of 1848
miners began to penetrate the Sierra foothills from far and wide. By the following
year, the trickle became a flood as over one hundred thousand argonauts poured
into the recently acquired territory. Among the most successful of the early miners
were Latin Americans who arrived from the Andean highlands of South America
and the Sonora region of northern Mexico, both areas with rich mining traditions.
Their success, however, was due only in part to their skill; geography dictated that
Hispanic miners would reach the gold fields long before most of their competitors,
including the huge wave of prospectors arriving from the eastern United States.

Envy and racism, as well as the desire to eliminate economic competition,
perhaps the key consideration, soon resulted in the attempt to drive Spanish-
speaking peoples, all of them indiscriminately lumped under the offensive category
of "greasers," from the gold fields. Violence, never far beneath the surface in frontier
society, was soon directed against Mexicans, both native-born and immigrants, as
well as toward other people of color. Though they were not as oppressed as Native Americans, who were subjected to genocide as their lands were invaded, or
Asians, who encountered intense hostility from the time of their initial entry into
the Golden State in 1851, the Mexicano population nevertheless suffered many
indignities.

Their dire situation was made even more precarious thanks to the widespread
use of vigilante law. The rise of vigilantes was predictable, given the lawlessness occasioned by the overwhelming temptations of easy profits, together with the absence
of state police agencies. While few would argue that anarchy was a better alternative,
vigilantism, with all its deficiencies—the burden of proof was on the accused, the
punishment rarely fit the crime, and witnesses were often intimidated—proved to
be a poor substitute for regular law enforcement. Its failure was most evident when
the accused were minorities, given the intensity of racist sentiments at this time.

The outstanding example, one of many, of the oppression of Mexicanos at
the hands of vigilantes was the infamous case of Juanita. In the summer of 1851,
Juanita—her real name was apparently Josefa Segovia—a young Mexicana, killed
an Anglo miner who was attempting to break into her cabin in Downieville, a small
mining town in the mother lode country. She pleaded self-defense; his friends
charged murder. Haled before a makeshift court consisting of the dead man's friends,
Juanita was judged guilty of murder and sentenced to death. She was hanged on
5 July 1851, the first woman lynched in the state of California. Had Juanita been
an Anglo, even if found guilty, she would not have been executed, so exalted was
the status of a white woman in western mining camps. It would be disingenuous to
avoid the conclusion that race was the determining factor: Juanita was a "greaser,"

her unforgivable sin. Such was also the case with Chipita Rodríguez from San Patricio, who was lynched in Texas in 1863, under almost identical circumstances.

The law was used in other ways to the detriment of minorities. Mining codes which excluded Mexicans, as well as the Chinese, from the diggings were enacted in camp after camp. Discrimination was not confined to the local citizenry. In 1850, the California legislature, reflecting the pervasive anti-foreign sentiments of the fledgling state's population, enacted the Foreign Miners' License Tax, requiring that miners who were not U.S. citizens pay a tax of twenty dollars a month for the privilege of mining American gold. The tax was not levied on Europeans; only Hispanics and Asians were required to pay. As with the local mining codes, then, it was clear that discrimination had as much to do with race as with eliminating economic competition. The twenty-dollar fee was exorbitant, and the enforcement of the law was subject to much abuse. By the time the act was repealed in 1851, its goal was largely accomplished: over two-thirds of the fifteen thousand Mexicano miners in Calaveras, Tuolumne, and Mariposa counties, the "southern mines," which they had dominated, were driven away, most returning to their homes south of the border. Among the victims were many Californios, whose rights were denied in violation of the Treaty of Guadalupe Hidalgo.

The failure of the pact to protect the state's Mexicano population was even more egregious in regard to the question of land ownership. The land question was precipitated by discouraged miners who began to occupy Spanish and Mexican land grants in the Great Central Valley by 1850. Discovering vast tracts of fertile land, apparently unoccupied, squatters did not hesitate to avail themselves of the opportunity to become property owners. The grantees, including a number of prominent Anglos such as Sutter and Frémont, as well as the Mexicano majority, resisted encroachment. Faced with superior numbers, however, they were soon overwhelmed. Both sides, ranchers and squatters, appealed to the federal government to validate their claims. After a series of investigations, the federal Congress responded with the Land Act of 1851, which provided that individuals granted land in California by the Spanish and Mexican governments must produce documents to that effect. A board of three commissioners, sitting mostly in San Francisco, would make the final decision, subject to appeal in the court system. Essentially, this piece of legislation placed the burden of proof on the grantee, not the government. In the case of Mexicano claimants, it was also a clear violation of both the spirit and the letter of the Treaty of Guadalupe Hidalgo.

Rancheros faced many difficulties in proving ownership. Deeds were required to be extremely specific in terms of boundary lines, but given the vast tracts of land and the relatively small numbers of gente de razón in the province before 1848, as well as the cost involved, neither Spanish nor Mexican authorities had found it necessary to be very precise. Moreover, the overwhelming numbers of Spanish-speaking grantees knew no English and were largely ignorant of Anglo American legal principles, both serious drawbacks in presenting their case to the American board. Invariably, Mexicano landholders were forced to rely on Anglo lawyers, with predictable results.

On paper, it does not seem that the rancheros fared too badly. Three-quarters of the claims submitted to the land commission, which heard cases from 1852 to 1856, were confirmed, some nine million acres of prime land, most of it along the coast. However, these statistics tell only part of the story. Litigation was long and costly, especially when an appeal was involved—the average time of appeal was seventeen years. Consequently, the rancheros, who were land rich but money poor, wound up surrendering large portions of their domain in attorneys' fees. Furthermore, Mexicano claimants, most of them unable to monitor their English-speaking lawyers very effectively, were bound to be less successful than Anglo colleagues in retaining their holdings. Eventually, after the validation of titles, immense amounts of land were lost through outright fraud.

In the northern part of the state, which was steadily overrun by Anglo newcomers even before the completion of the transcontinental railroad in 1869, the loss of land by Mexicanos was unusually rapid. While there were exceptions— Mariano Vallejo managed to preserve extensive holdings around Sonoma despite the loss of most of his property—Californios in the north retained little economic power by the late 1850s. In the south, the land base was preserved a little longer in the absence of massive Anglo immigration. Indeed, the expanding mining frontier stimulated demand for beef and resulted in high meat prices, which enabled southern rancheros to pay their debts and protect their holdings.

The halcyon days of Old California, however, were numbered. The droughts of 1862–1864 were the beginning of the end for southern rancheros. A depression ensued, which was only made worse during the nationwide panic of 1873. The cattle industry never fully recovered from this setback. Heavily in debt, landholders had a hard time fending off creditors. The crowning blow came in the 1880s, when a massive land boom promoted by the railroads brought thousands of newcomers from the East. Mexicanos were reduced to a tiny minority. Most ended up performing menial labor, notably in construction and the nascent citrus industry. "Contrary to past misconceptions," Antonio Ríos-Bustamante notes, "these economic conditions applied to most of the native-born Californios, as well as to more recent immigrants. . . . With few exceptions, the native-born and more recent immigrants merged into a common community."[6]

The process was not uniform throughout the southland, as the historian Albert Camarillo has well illustrated.[7] The displacement of the Hispanic population occurred most readily in the Los Angeles basin, where the town of Los Angeles was transformed almost overnight. During the 1860s, Anglos came to outnumber

Mexicanos; and by 1880, only about one-fifth of a town population of more than eleven thousand was Hispanic. In Santa Barbara, on the other hand, Mexicanos maintained their numerical majority until the last decades of the century, a state of affairs which permitted the local Hispanic elite, which looked to the de la Guerra family, to preserve political power far longer than was the case elsewhere. By the turn of the century, the town had witnessed dramatic changes, though it never totally lost its Hispanic flavor.

The quarter century following the Mexican-American War and the gold rush witnessed the nadir of Mexicano-Anglo relations in California. The ill-treatment of their people has been documented thoroughly by Chicano historians. Many injustices were inflicted on the Hispanic population, of which the loss of land was only the most spectacular example. The attitude of the dominant society toward the dispossessed added insult to injury. Not all Anglos entering the state despised Mexicanos as an inferior race, but genuine compassion and respect were rarely extended to the defeated people.

Naturally, the vast majority of Mexicanos came to resent the arrogance they encountered. One consequence was the rise of lawlessness, which often took the form of banditry. Lawlessness was not uniquely characteristic of the oppressed Mexicano population; it was rampant on the frontier, especially during this period. Indeed, some historians have seen a lack of respect for the law as an American tradition. Still, the fact remains that there were many more Mexicano bandits in the 1850s and 1860s than their relatively small numbers would warrant. Some came from the ranks of prominent families, including the Castros, Sepúlvedas, and Vallejos. During the decade preceding the U.S. Civil War, roughly 20 percent of San Quentin's inmate population was Spanish-speaking. This phenomenon has prompted most Chicano scholars to conclude that "social banditry," a concept made popular by the British historian Eric Hobsbawm, is perfectly applicable to what was occurring in California, and throughout the Southwest, during these troubled times.

Briefly, this theoretical model suggests that brigands, individuals or groups, are frequently members of conquered minorities who have been victimized by exploitation, often accompanied by racism, and that their oppressed status is the source of their criminality. This model has its limitations when applied to nineteenth-century Mexicanos in the United States. After all, there were many Anglo bandits in the American West at this time. Moreover, banditry was also popular in Mexico, even before the European intervention of the 1860s. Still, social banditry remains the best way of explaining the spontaneous and widespread incidence of lawlessness in the beleaguered community.

The first, and most storied, of the Mexicano bandits was the legendary Joaquín Murietta, who apparently initiated his criminal career after Anglo miners invaded his mining claim in the Sierras, raped his wife, Rosita, killed his brother, and left Joaquín himself for dead. Bent on revenge, the enraged youth began a series of depredations which took him all over the state. In the process, he terrorized Anglos and was given shelter by the Mexicano community, who protected him as one of their own. Joaquín and his lieutenant, Three-Fingered Jack, the story goes, were finally killed in 1853 by a posse led by Captain Harry Love, who collected a handsome reward from the California state legislature.

Now firmly a part of California folklore, Murietta has been accepted as a historical figure by a number of scholars, including the historian Manuel Rojas.[8] It is likely, however, as Leonard Pitt has ably demonstrated, that the tale is more myth than reality. Harry Love was real enough, and so was the reward, but there was no Robin Hood of the El Dorado. After extensive research, Pitt found that there were several Mexicano banditti operating in California in the early 1850s who happened to have the first name of Joaquín. As criminal activity grew, mass hysteria ensued; soon they merged into one single individual, who eventually was transformed into the romantic hero.

There was no one Joaquín Murietta, but the conditions that fostered the rise of rebels like Murietta were real enough. The very existence of the myth is a testimony to this fact. The legend, which the Mexicano community helped preserve, served a psychic need: it provided the marginalized population with a much-needed symbol of resistance against oppression, a function the myth continues to perform today.

Those in need of real live heroes should not despair, for though Joaquín Murietta may not have actually lived, there were other Mexicano bandits whose lives resembled those of the legendary figure and whose existence is beyond dispute. Tiburcio Vásquez, the last of the famous bandidos in California, is a case in point. Born in Monterey on 11 August 1835, Vásquez was the son of an Indian mother and a Mexican father. In the early 1850s, the youth was wrongly accused of being an accomplice to the murder of an Anglo lawman and forced to flee for his life. In 1857, he was tried for horse stealing and sentenced to San Quentin. Freed, he was back in the state penitentiary a few years later, this time serving a sentence for robbery. Upon his last release from prison, Vásquez organized a gang of outlaws who operated with reckless abandon in central and northern California. Occasionally, they ventured as far as the southern part of the state. It was on one of these forays that the increasingly bold gang leader, now with a generous reward on his head and facing a murder charge, was finally apprehended for the last time, betrayed by one of his confederates. Reportedly, he was visited by thousands of visitors while awaiting trial at the Santa Clara county jail in San José. Most of them, according to newspapers, were women eager to catch a glimpse of the infamous Tiburcio. Charged with a murder committed during an 1873 robbery attempt, Vásquez was found guilty and sentenced to death. He was hanged on 19 March 1875, leaving an ambivalent legacy. While most Anglo contemporaries saw him as a vicious and unrepentant criminal, the Mexicano community identified with and protected Tiburcio Vásquez.

The fascination of Chicano historians with Mexicano bandits has obscured the fact that accommodation by the conquered population was much more common than resistance. Generally speaking, the higher the socioeconomic status, the greater the propensity to accept entry into Anglo society. This tendency was most pronounced among the Hispanic elite, a trend reflected in the rate of marriage between members of their class and Anglos.[9] Mariano Vallejo, for example, had eight children who married Yankees, as did three of his sisters.

Clearly, many of the unions which occurred were intended to strengthen political and economic ties. The marriages of their daughters were usually arranged by the patriarchs of upper-class families. Undoubtedly, too, the desire to "whiten" their line was a consideration among the elite, who attempted to distance themselves from lower-class mestizos. As rancheros lost their privileged status, these interethnic marriages became less common, a clear indication that Anglos were now firmly in control, although the arrival of more desirable Anglo women into the state was another weighty factor.

The degree to which upper-class Mexicanos embraced American institutions and customs varied from family to family. Generalization in this area is almost impossible. Some families, among them those of Santiago Argüello, Juan Bandini, Miguel de Pedrorena, and Antonio M. Pico, were eager to ally themselves with their counterparts in the Anglo community, though none of them were as successful as Vallejo in accomplishing their goal. Most prominent Californios, however, were reluctant to abandon their native traditions altogether, especially those who felt the sting of Anglo injustice. Many were resentful of their more accommodating neighbors. Mariano Vallejo, more than any other individual, was the object of their scorn; "I have seen men of pure blood, famous in provincial history, leave the room at the name of Vallejo," observed the historian Charles Howard Shinn in 1890.[10]

Pablo de la Guerra (1819–1874), on the other hand, was a ranchero who made his peace with Anglos, but on his own terms, a position that won him the admiration and respect not only of the majority of the old elite but of the masses as well. Before the American takeover, Pablo de la Guerra, like his father José, had been a steadfast opponent of Yankee annexation, despite the fact that two of his brothers-in-law were Americans. Indeed, during the U.S. invasion of California in 1846, de la Guerra joined the armed resistance, and consequently spent time in prison. Once the conflict ended, though, Don Pablo realized that the clock could not be turned back. He pragmatically accepted the new order, creating a political machine that controlled Santa Barbara for several decades, thus ensuring that his family patrimony stayed reasonably intact. Like a number of the old elite, he also fought to protect the rights of his people, of all ranks in society.

The contrast between Vallejo and de la Guerra in their response to American-ization serves to remind us that the elite reacted as individuals rather than a cohesive class. To dismiss these men as vendidos, pure and simple, as a number of Chicano historians—Rodolfo Acuña in particular[11]—have done in recent years is certainly to find a pattern where none exists, as well as to fail to appreciate the tough choices embattled rancheros throughout the territory were forced to make.

As for the Mexicano masses, those who had never had a privileged position in Californio society, their reaction to Americanization was also complex. Land-less, most Mexicanos had little to lose in the way of material possessions after the conquest, so there was scant incentive to establish relations with Anglos. In fact, they had few alternatives: despised as racially inferior, they were unable to compete with Anglos on the same level, even had they wanted to. On the other hand, resis-tance was also impractical, given their modest numbers—some fifteen thousand people during most of the late nineteenth century—and the massive migration of Yankees into the state beginning immediately after the conquest. Moreover, while they felt oppression, they had always suffered indignities, the fate of poor people in all societies of privilege. For the most part, the great majority of Mexicans, both native-born and new immigrants, resigned themselves to Yankee domination. They gained a measure of security by forming ethnic enclaves, both in cities (barrios) and in rural areas (colonias), and adapted other strategies for survival that might be available to them. In many cases, especially in rural areas, it is possible that Mexicano families continued to eke out an existence at the turn of the century very much as they had before, barely impacted by Anglo society.

ARIZONA

The signing of the Treaty of Guadalupe Hidalgo in 1848 left the Mexicano population of Arizona, which resided exclusively south of the Gila River, under Mexican sovereignty. Almost immediately, though, there was strong pressure in the United States to extend the international boundary farther south. By now it was evident that a railroad line would be needed to connect Texas with California, and it was determined that the most feasible route would run through the Mesilla Valley and south of the Gila. An agent, James Gadsden, was sent into Mexico to negoti-ate a new boundary in 1853. Badly in need of money, the Mexican government of Santa Anna, now at the end of his long and undistinguished career, agreed to sell the Americans thirty thousand square miles of land for some ten million dollars. On 30 December 1853, Santa Anna signed the Treaty of Mesilla, as the Mexicans called it. Ratified by the U.S. Senate in the spring of 1854, the agreement went into effect immediately.

The Gadsden Purchase created the present-day border between Mexico and Arizona—as well as southern New Mexico—thus incorporating the isolated and impoverished Mexican settlements of Sonora's northern rim into the United States. Administratively, Arizona was made part of the Territory of New Mexico until 1863, when it would be established as an independent territory; but economically and culturally, it maintained close ties to the Mexican communities of Sonora for several decades. Mexicanos in Arizona were largely confined to Tucson, an outpost of some five hundred inhabitants. Most *Tucsonenses* regretted the change of flags, but in some quarters there was genuine enthusiasm for American annexation.

On the periphery of the Mexican nation, the pobladores of Arizona had been chronically neglected by Mexico City, and even the recent conflict against the United States had failed to arouse any real sense of nationalism among the forgotten frontier communities. At midcentury, moreover, the resurgence of the Apache threat, begun during the late 1820s and accelerating during the recent international conflict, was at full force, prompting the settlers of the Santa Cruz Valley to look to the United States and its military might for the protection that Mexico had been unable to provide.

There were few Anglos in southern Arizona at midcentury. A desert area plagued by Indian problems, the region never enticed foreigners during the Mexican period the way other northern frontier provinces had. The first Anglos to enter were mountain men during the Mexican period, followed by a handful of soldiers who occupied Tucson during the war. But by 1854, most Anglos in the area were argonauts on their way to the California mines who chose to settle down locally for a variety of reasons. During the height of the gold rush, Texas cattle had been driven through the territory to California, where the hungry miners were willing to pay top dollar. Some cowboys settled down in Tucson, becoming either merchants or stockmen; but most of the newcomers eked out a living in local silver mines, a hazardous and largely unprofitable enterprise given Apache resurgence.

During the first years under American sovereignty, antagonism between Anglos and Mexicanos was considerable, a residue of the recent clash of arms. Race was also an issue, especially among the Texans. Still, by 1860, when Anglos numbered 168 in a town population of 925, there was ample evidence of bicultural cooperation. Interethnic marriages were both a cause and an effect of this improvement. Among recent arrivals who married Mexicanas were A. P. K. Safford, Sam Hughes, Hiram Stevens, and William S. Oury, all prominent members of Arizona's political and economic elite during the next few years.

Ultimately, the relations grew to be quite close; in fact, nowhere in the Southwest did Anglos and Mexicanos get along as well before 1880 as in southern Arizona, a sanguine legacy still in evidence in the Old Pueblo today. Demographics undoubtedly played a role. The disparity in numbers dictated that Anglos had to accommodate to the dominant Hispanic-Indian culture in order to pursue their livelihood. But perhaps the strongest incentive for interethnic cooperation was the common enemy, the Western Apache. Hatred of indios bárbaros was pervasive. Indeed, even the Tohono O'odham and Pimas, sedentary Indians in the region, were willing to make peace with the townspeople when faced with the prospect of Apache depredations, which intensified after the Civil War. The depth of this animosity was demonstrated most graphically in April 1871, when more than one hundred Aravaipa Apache, practically all of them women and children, were slaughtered in a surprise attack at Camp Grant by a combined force, led by William Oury and Jesús María Elías, of Tucson's Anglo and Mexican citizens and their Tohono O'odham allies.

A small Anglo population also ensured that Mexicanos would continue to play a vital role in the regional economy prior to the arrival of the Southern Pacific Railroad, which reached Tucson on 20 March 1880. During this early period of territorial history, ranching reemerged, and silver mining, centered on the Santa Rita Range to the south, revived; but both enterprises made little progress as long as the Apache were on the warpath. The most lucrative economic endeavor in the 1860s and 1870s was long-distance freighting. The isolated settlements of northern Mexico and the American Southwest were in desperate need of food and other commodities. The expansion of U.S. military posts also favored entrepreneurial activity. Freighters were willing to respond to the demand, given the prospects of immense profits, especially when they set up their own mercantile establishments.

Tucson was ideally situated to service both the pueblos of Sonora—many of them, like Arispe and Alamos—becoming wealthy, thanks to the rich silver mines nearby—and the New Mexican settlements, notably the new town of Mesilla, along the Rio Grande, which had access to Yankee goods from the East. Tucson blossomed during the 1870s. By the end of the decade, its population exceeded eight thousand. At this time, the Old Pueblo was widely acknowledged as the leading commercial entrepôt between El Paso and Los Angeles.

Among the most active of the freighter-merchants were members of the Aguirre family. The patriarch of this remarkable clan was Pedro Aguirre, a Chihuahua rancher and businessman who immigrated to New Mexico in 1852. Four of his sons subsequently became active traders on the Santa Fe–Chihuahua trails. Eventually, after Don Pedro's death, the family transferred its center of operations to Tucson, where they continued to expand their freighting and mercantile activities, while also acquiring vast ranches.

The most respected of the Arizona traders, however, was Estevan Ochoa (1831–1888). Like the Aguirres, he too was a *Chihuahuense* who profited from the Santa Fe–Chihuahua trail trade. At the age of twenty-eight, he established a store at

Mesilla, which he ran in partnership with Pedro Aguirre Jr. In 1859, Ochoa found a new partner in Pinckney Randolph Tully. Tully, Ochoa and Company, headquartered in Tucson, came to be the most successful freighting firm operating in southern Arizona and northern Sonora. Its operations extended as far east as Kansas. Retail stores were established in Tucson and surrounding towns. Mining and sheep raising were other enterprises that contributed to Ochoa's growing fortune.

A major benefactor, Estevan Ochoa encouraged educational and other civic pursuits. He was also active politically. He was elected to the territorial legislature on three occasions as a representative for Tucson, followed by his crowning political achievement, his election as town mayor in 1875; he was the only Hispanic to hold this position during Arizona's territorial period (1863–1912). The arrival of the locomotive brought the collapse of his freighting empire and cost him his hard-earned fortune, but it did not diminish Don Estevan's immense popularity with his fellow citizens, Anglo as well as Mexican.

The advent of the railroad signaled the end of an era in Arizona in many ways. Not only did the railroad reorient the major commercial routes east and west, instead of north and south, thus effectively ending the lucrative freighting connection with Sonora, but it also stimulated the rise of a powerful copper-mining boom in southern Arizona in the 1870s and 1880s, which required enormous amounts of capital. The advent of corporate capitalism spelled disaster for the Mexicano entrepreneurs of Tucson.

As the economic power of the Hispanic elite waned, Anglos realized there was less to gain by cultivating their friendship. The elimination of the Apache threat, which occurred a few short years before Gerónimo's capture in 1886, had the same effect. But the most telling factor in the erosion of interethnic harmony was the huge influx of newcomers from the East made possible by the railroad and attracted by the expanding mining frontier. Despite continuing immigration from Sonora, the Mexicano population of the territory was being overwhelmed by Easterners, who had few ties to the local native population and were less tolerant of cultural diversity than their predecessors had been. As Anglos headed for outlying mining areas, Tucson lost population during the 1880s, the result of an economic stagnation which grew increasingly worse before hitting rock bottom during the nationwide depression of 1893. Economic troubles fanned interethnic strife. The easy relations which had existed in the 1860s and 1870s between the two communities in Tucson waned as they drifted apart.

The deterioration of the relations between Anglos and Mexicanos and the ill-treatment of the latter were observed with mounting apprehension by the Hispanic elite. Among their number were individuals who stepped forward at this crucial juncture to provide much-needed leadership for the beleaguered Mexicano populace. The most active of these community spokesmen were two recent immigrants from Sonora, Mariano G. Samaniego (1844–1907) and Carlos I. Velasco (1837–1914).

Samaniego and his mother, a recent widow, immigrated in the early 1850s from Sonora, then in the midst of escalating turmoil caused by Apache depredations, to Mesilla, on the Chihuahua Trail. The family opened up a mercantile establishment, which apparently prospered, for young Mariano was sent off to study in Missouri, graduating from Saint Louis University in 1862. Upon his return to New Mexico, Samaniego took up long-distance freighting, supplying American army posts along the Mexican border. His marriage into the Aguirre family gained him powerful business allies, and in 1869 he transferred the seat of his freighting operations to Tucson. Though he was forced to abandon freighting with the coming of the railroad in 1880, he successfully made a transition to cattle ranching, mining, and stage coach transport, thus escaping the fate of his friend Estevan Ochoa.

Like Don Estevan, Mariano Samaniego was fascinated by politics, an involvement that began as soon as he arrived in Tucson and lasted for some thirty years, during which time he held a variety of offices in city, county, and territorial government. The civic-minded leader was also a member of the University of Arizona's first board of regents in 1886, president of the Arizona Pioneers' Historical Society on several occasions, and one of the chief supporters of the local Catholic Church.

Throughout his career, Samaniego sought to protect the rights of fellow Mexicanos, a concern that dominated his public career after the 1880s, when the strength of nativist sentiments began to alarm the Mexicano community. He organized the Spanish-speaking masses and encouraged their participation in electoral politics. Waging a tireless campaign to combat negative Mexican stereotypes, he defended the rights of his people to retain their own culture, doing everything possible to promote traditional customs and practices, including Mexican patriotic holidays and fiestas. He also sought to ameliorate the deteriorating economic conditions in the fledgling Mexicano barrios by promoting the organization of mutual-aid associations. By the 1890s, Don Mariano was the acknowledged *patrón* (boss) of Tucson's Mexicano community.

Samaniego's electoral successes were supported by Carlos Velasco, editor of the local Spanish-language newspaper. Like many Sonorans of the time, Velasco had moved north to escape political turmoil at home. Political instability, which had been endemic in Mexico since independence, had worsened after the crushing defeat of 1848. The struggle between liberals and conservatives continued unresolved, adding to the nation's ills. Mexico's weakness again invited intervention. As a consequence, during the American Civil War, Napoleon III, anxious to expand French influence wherever possible, was able to impose a puppet government on the Mexicans in the person of Archduke Maximilian of Austria. The ouster of the French army and the execution of the Austrian emperor by Mexican patriots, led by Benito Juárez, paved the way for a liberal victory in 1867 at the expense of the conservatives, who had collaborated with the Austrian ruler and his French benefactors. But the triumph of liberalism did not come easily. Political problems continued to plague Mexico well into the *Porfiriato,* the era of Porfirio Díaz (1876–1911), who was able to fully impose his authority only by the 1880s.

In Sonora, the triumph of liberalism meant the rise of Ignacio Pesqueira, who prevailed over his political rival Manuel María Gándara during the late 1860s. Immediately thereafter, however, Sonoran liberals began to fight among themselves, as was generally the case throughout the country. It was only when General Díaz consolidated his power at the national level that he was able to put an end to chronic violence on the northwestern frontier.

In the meantime, Arizona became a haven for Sonorans, of all political factions, who found themselves in disfavor at home. Generally, they came seeking temporary asylum, intent on returning to their homeland when the violence abated or when their particular champion gained the upper hand. Consequently, Sonoran immigration into Arizona, which peaked in the 1870s, consisted not only of impoverished masses seeking economic opportunities in the mines, but also of middle-class émigrés such as Velasco.

A member of the Sonoran elite, Carlos Velasco was trained as a lawyer in Hermosillo but soon developed a passion for liberal politics and aligned himself with General Pesqueira. This affiliation gained him a number of key political posts. But in 1865, when the *pesqueiristas* were routed by their opponents, the supporters of Maximilian, Velasco was forced into northern exile, eventually taking up residence in Tucson. Returning to his home in 1870, after Pesqueira reestablished his control in Sonora, Velasco occupied a number of key political offices during the next few years, including state legislator. The Pesqueira dictatorship, however, grew increasingly unpopular, and when the government was overthrown in 1877, the forty-year-old lawyer escaped to Arizona, this time permanently.

Velasco had had some journalistic experience in Sonora, and in the Old Pueblo he quickly perceived the need for a Spanish-language newspaper that would cater to the territory's growing Mexicano population. He initiated publication of *El Fronterizo* in 1878, an enterprise that would continue to 1914, an amazingly long life for a frontier newspaper, especially one written in Spanish. Though he never ran for political office, choosing to retain his Mexican citizenship, Carlos Velasco, like Samaniego, became one of the leading citizens of Tucson. More than his compatriot, who needed Anglo votes, Velasco concentrated his efforts on behalf of Spanish-speaking residents of the city. His major influence was exerted through his newspaper, which he used to educate his audience to the leading Mexican intellectual currents of the time and to promote the culture of the Old Country. Don Carlos was not alone in this endeavor; Spanish-language newspapers in the Southwest were first published in the 1850s, with more than 130 established by the turn of the century. Velasco and other editors, sometimes in spite of themselves, played a pivotal role in promoting a bicultural community, a trend that became more pronounced in the twentieth century.

The need to protect the Mexicano community became crucial in the early 1890s in the face of a growing tide of anti-Mexican sentiment sparked by the economic depression of the times. In 1894, the American Protective Association, the leading nativist organization in the country, made its appearance in Tucson. The Hispanic elite was mobilized into action by Velasco, ably supported by Samaniego. The result was the creation of the Alianza Hispano-Americana, which was founded on 14 January 1894 by some forty distinguished members of the Spanish-speaking community. These included native-born citizens as well as immigrants. A *mutualista* (mutual-aid society), the Alianza was set up primarily to protect the threatened rights of Mexicanos in the Territory of Arizona. A brainchild of the elite, the organization cut across class lines, incorporating workers as well as businessmen. So successful was the association that lodges were soon established in the major population centers of the Territory and beyond. Eventually, it became the first Mexican American association to achieve national prominence. By the late 1930s, the height of its power, the Alianza had over seventeen thousand members in the United States and Mexico.

The Alianza was not the first mutualista formed by Mexicanos; these fraternal associations began to appear in the Southwest in the 1870s. Ultimately, mutual-aid societies were formed wherever Mexicano communities were established, both in and out of the Southwest. Their significance is best expressed by the political scientist Mario Barrera: "It is no exaggeration to say that after the family, the mutualistas were the most important social organization among Chicanos from the late nineteenth century to the 1930s."[12] Typically, they came to be named after distinguished Mexican patriots, such as Benito Juárez or Ignacio Zaragoza, the Texas-born general who defeated the French at Puebla on 5 May 1862—a victory commemorated at annual *Cinco de Mayo* celebrations. The functions of these associations were varied. In the words of a respected Chicano historian:

> Mutual aid societies met the material needs of their members with emergency loans and other forms of financial assistance, job-seeking services, and death and illness insurance. They also offered their members leadership experiences in civic affairs, sponsored other institutions like newspapers and private schools, provided their communities with popular community events for entertainment and socializing, and offered public forums that addressed the important issues of the day. Mutualista organizations thus gave their members and communities a sense of belonging and refuge from an often alien and inhospitable environment. The community, in turn, accorded the members and especially the officers the highly respected status of responsible, civic-minded individuals. A lesser-known characteristic of mutualistas is that they served as a major point of organizational unity that spawned local and regional political struggles.[13]

As Chicano scholars have pointed out, the rise of these mutualistas clearly illustrates that many Mexicanos refused to resign themselves to an animal existence in a hostile environment. Indeed, Spanish-speaking men and women initiated and sustained a variety of associations—mutualistas were among the most effective of them—to better their lives. They were not the docile and apathetic population that many Anglo accounts of the time would have us believe.

NEW MEXICO

In New Mexico, the Hispanic population during the second half of the nineteenth century was better able to preserve its heritage than in other parts of the Southwest. The reasons were largely demographic. The Upper Rio Grande Valley had always been the most densely populated area of the northern Hispanic frontier before 1848—there were some sixty thousand Mexican citizens in New Mexico at the time of American occupation—and the relatively sparse Anglo immigration into the Territory during the next decades, given its geographic isolation, meant that Hispanos would retain their numerical dominance until about the time of World War II.

It is customary to refer to the native Spanish-speaking population of New Mexico by the term *Hispanos* in historical accounts—a practice that will be employed in this narrative—but in the nineteenth century, nuevomexicanos referred to themselves as *Mexicanos*. Despite the indiscriminate use of the term, however, Mexicanos in New Mexico in the late nineteenth century were hardly a homogeneous population. A variety of factors tended to divide them, not the least of which was social standing.

During the Mexican period, as we saw, the growing affluence of the region, due primarily to expanding trade, began to create a substantial gulf between those families who were able to accumulate some wealth and the majority of the community, those who were not. By the time of the American occupation, Hispano society, as the anthropologist Nancie L. González indicates, tended to break down into two fairly rigid classes: ricos and pobres.[14] The rapid expansion of stock raising, both cattle and sheep, after the Civil War, would continue to accentuate the class dichotomy.

Hispanos did not live in total isolation, of course, especially during this period. Both Native Americans and Anglo Americans occupied the Territory and developed a series of complex relationships with the Spanish-speaking communities which have been only partially understood. Both exerted a decided impact on Hispanos that can still be felt today.

When the United States acquired New Mexico, it also gained some forty thousand native Americans. Indian society was no more monolithic than that of their

Hispanic neighbors. As before, the native population of New Mexico was divided between the nomadic plains tribes and the sedentary Pueblos. By the time of the American occupation, Mexicanos had long since established a modus vivendi with the latter. Pueblo land grants were meted out by the Spanish Crown, and during the Mexican period, they continued to be honored. Moreover, Pueblos were accorded full rights of citizenship, something that was not true under American rule. Hispanic paternalistic policies met with moderate success; Spanish and Mexican influences permeated both Eastern and, with the exception of the Zuñi and the Hopi, Western Pueblos. The Pueblos also had an impact, though more subtle, on their conquerors. The two cultures were bridged by natives who abandoned their traditional lifestyle and adopted Hispanic values and customs, as well as by inter-ethnic marriages. Both peoples were united, too, in their opposition to the warlike Plains Indians, their common enemies.

After the occupation, however, the relations between Pueblos and their Hispanic neighbors were often strained, in part because of Mexicano encroachment on tribal lands. Resentment on both sides would persist into the twentieth century.[15] Pueblo hostility was perfectly understandable given the Hispanic invasion of their lands and persistent efforts to erode their traditional culture. On the Mexicano side, there was resentment because Pueblo communities were protected by the federal government after the occupation, at a time when Hispanics were forced to fight a losing battle while trying to preserve their grants. Then, too, there was the hatred of indios bárbaros, which was bound to impact Mexicano attitudes toward all Native Americans.

Hispanos were less ambivalent about their relationship with indios bárbaros. Generally speaking, they were as intent on wiping out the warlike tribes as were their Anglo counterparts.[16] Surrounding the tiny Hispanic settlements of the Upper Rio Grande, these tribes included the Utes and Navajo to the northwest, the Jicarilla Apache to the north, the Comanche to the east, the Mescalero Apache to the south, and the Chiricahua and Western Apache to the southwest. When the Americans acquired New Mexico, its embattled Spanish-speaking inhabitants were in the midst of a fratricidal campaign with most of these tribes.

The Comanche were a notable exception. They continued to honor their truce with nuevomexicanos throughout the nineteenth century, and generally maintained good relations with *Comancheros* (Hispano traders), mostly members of the lower classes, who supplied them with essential goods. The Utes, a major source of Indian slaves, sometimes cooperated, as well.

The renewed aggression of the plains peoples at midcentury was a product of not only the weakness of the Mexican government but also the expansion of the Hispanic population into new areas previously considered Indian country. In the 1820s, the Estancia Valley was settled; in the 1830s, Las Vegas and Mora were occupied; and in the 1840s, the Mesilla Valley, just north of El Paso, witnessed an arrival of large numbers of settlers, mostly Mexican immigrants from the south. Expansion continued after the American occupation, as Hispanos migrated from their ancient strongholds in the Upper Rio Grande Valley, motivated by land hunger and a desire to preserve their traditional lifestyle from encroaching American influences. The main thrust was to the north, via the Chama Valley, into the San Luis Valley of southern Colorado in the 1850s and the San Juan basin in the 1870s. This northward movement is described in lavish detail by Frances León Swadesh, who notes "that the pattern of Hispanic community development in northern New Mexico has been one of multiplying, not enlarging, single units."[17] Concurrently, the rich grasslands of eastern New Mexico were attracting Mexicano sheepmen, who ventured as far as the Oklahoma and Texas panhandles. The most adventuresome of these Hispanos was Casimero Romero, who led his *pastores* (shepherds) into the Canadian River Valley.

Under the terms of the Treaty of Guadalupe Hidalgo, the United States pledged to pacify the Indians in the newly acquired territory, and after some halting steps in this direction in the 1850s, the American cavalry began to effectively subjugate the nomads during the Civil War, when both the Mescaleros and the Navajo were forced to the Bosque Redondo reservation at Fort Sumner in eastern New Mexico. Although local residents were discouraged from participating in these military campaigns, settlers continued to form citizen militias to go against their old nemesis, motivated in part by the desire to acquire Indian slaves.

The most famous Hispano Indian fighter was Manuel Antonio Chaves (1818–1889), a nephew of Manuel Armijo. Chaves hated indios bárbaros with a passion—in his old age, he recalled that he had lost more than two hundred relatives to Indian depredations—and he was not above committing atrocities at their expense.[18] On 22 September 1861, for example, soldiers under his command were instructed to open fire on a group of Navajo during a minor dispute; a dozen women and children were shot down in cold blood.[19] Admittedly, Chaves was an extreme case, but his attitudes toward hostile natives differed only in degree from those of other pobladores. The same sentiments that resulted in the Camp Grant massacre in Arizona were typical of the frontiersmen of the Rio Grande Valley.

Only a few Anglos settled in the Upper Rio Grande Valley immediately after the Mexican-American War. Of those who did, a number married into Hispano families. Cross-cultural marriages muted ethnic hostility. Unlike Arizona during the immediate postwar period, then, there was relatively little strife between the two societies. Interethnic marriages would continue to be popular even after the Civil War. Darlis A. Miller has noted that by 1870, these marriages were very common in the Mesilla Valley: in Las Cruces, 90 percent of married Anglo men were married to Hispanas; in Mesilla, 83 percent; and in Doña Ana, 78 percent.[20]

American sovereignty did expand commercial possibilities in New Mexico, which enticed Anglo entrepreneurs, but these were probably outnumbered by immigrants from Mexico, especially to the Mesilla Valley. The chief beneficiaries of enhanced business opportunities, however, were the local oligarchs. Undoubtedly, many of the ricos had been reluctant to see the change of flags, but fears were quickly allayed as economic opportunities expanded and the Indian menace faded.

Among rico families who prospered from increased commerce were the Chávezes, Armijos, Pereas, and Oteros. Continuing to invest heavily in the trail trade, they were able to establish impressive mercantile establishments up and down the Rio Grande Valley, along the trail linking them to both Missouri and Chihuahua.

The expanding mining frontier and the establishment of military posts in the Southwest accentuated the importance of freighting and merchandising, which favored those families with business experience. Moreover, many of these entrepreneurs, having accumulated sufficient capital, were now able to get involved in land speculation, buying up town lots as well as ranches, large and small. While speculation had always been popular on the Anglo frontier, in the American Southwest it seems to have dated from the Mexican period, when American investors introduced this profitable business. Soon, some Hispanos were competing on an equal footing with the newcomers. Among the most successful of the nuevomexicanos in the field were José Serafín Ramírez and Juan Estevan Pino. More fortunate still was Donaciano Vigil, who made such a fortune on real estate that he abandoned a highly successful political career in the mid-1850s.

Hispanic women played a notable role in the commercial expansion, a contribution which has not been recognized until recently. Perhaps the most famous woman in New Mexico during the nineteenth century was the aforementioned La Tules, who ran a gambling casino in Santa Fe and made a fortune, which she increased by investing in the Missouri trade.[21] By the time of her death in 1853, she was one of the wealthiest citizens of the territorial capital. Female entrepreneurs were active in virtually all trail stops in New Mexico. In Socorro, for example, Frances García was the proprietress of a lumberyard, and Rufina Vigil de Abeyta served as a director of the Socorro County Bank.

Some women who ran businesses were widows, who made up a substantial percentage of the population during the middle third of the century, when Indian warfare took a terrible toll. A good example is Doña María Gregoria Rodela de Amador, who arrived in the Mesilla Valley from El Paso in 1846 with her three children.[22] In the 1850s, she established a mercantile store in Las Cruces that formed the basis for the vast merchandising enterprises of her son, Martín Amador. The Amadors, among the first families of Las Cruces, were linked with many of the most prominent families of northern Mexico, notably the Terrazas-Creel clan of Chihuahua.

As prosperity increased in New Mexico, its inhabitants chafed under the territorial status they had been accorded in 1850. Given their overwhelming numbers and potential political clout, Hispanos were anxious to achieve statehood. Congress, fearful of the dubious allegiance of the conquered population, was reticent to go along. But doubts about New Mexican loyalty to the Union were unfounded, as the Civil War demonstrated.

The outbreak of the war in 1861 found New Mexicans divided. Confederate sentiment was confined mostly to the Mesilla Valley, where many Anglo immigrants were Southerners. Led by Lieutenant Colonel John R. Baylor, a Confederate force invaded the Mesilla Valley in 1861, routing the small Union garrisons in the area and setting up a temporary government in the town of Mesilla. A small Rebel force was sent in 1862 to Tucson, which was occupied briefly. The main thrust, however, was up the Rio Grande Valley. The leader of this expedition, General Henry H. Sibley, was led to believe that the influential rico elite, fearing that the abolition of slavery would imperil the institution of peonage, which had taken root in the large estates in the Albuquerque area, would cast their lot with the Confederacy. Some rico families, including that of Miguel A. Otero, *were* swayed by this argument. However, the majority of Hispanos had no stake in peonage. Moreover, New Mexicans detested Texans, an antipathy that antedated the Texan invasion of 1841, and most of Sibley's troops came from the Lone Star State. Finally, the vast majority of Hispanos believed in the Union. The failure to gauge the strength of this sentiment proved to be the decisive factor in upsetting Sibley's plans.

The campaign began well enough, as the invading force encountered little effective resistance, even in Albuquerque and Santa Fe, which were occupied without too much trouble. Spurred on by these easy victories, the Confederate army marched on Fort Union, not far from Santa Fe. Unfortunately for the Rebels, pro-Union Colorado Volunteers, led by Major John M. Chivington, arrived just in time, and by taking a shortcut through the Sangre de Cristo Range, they were able to surprise their foes at the Battle of Glorieta Pass on 27 and 28 March 1862. This pivotal battle sealed the fate of the Confederacy in New Mexico. The remains of the Rebel army beat a hasty retreat back to Texas.

The hero of Glorieta was Manuel Antonio Chaves, who had led the Coloradans through the Sangre de Cristos. This was his finest hour. Even his dubious record as an Indian fighter has failed to tarnish the reputation of the Little Lion of the Southwest.[23]

The aftermath of the Civil War brought large numbers of Anglos into New Mexico, many of them ex-soldiers. The arrival of the railroad in 1880 increased this migration significantly. Many newcomers headed for the mines on the periphery, but some settled in the heart of what the geographer Richard L. Nostrand calls the "Hispano Homeland."[24] Anglos who entered this area were especially drawn to Albuquerque, at the junction of the Atchison, Topeka, and Santa Fe and the Atlantic and Pacific railroads, which became the Territory's leading industrial center by the turn of the century and its biggest city ten years later. For some Hispanic residents, this development proved to be beneficial; however, for the majority it turned out to be more of a bane than a blessing.

Rico families continued to make huge profits on the trail trade, permitting further expansion of land holdings, particularly in the eastern portion of the Territory. Much of the land was devoted to stock raising, which had become extremely profitable after the American takeover because of the opening up of eastern markets. While cattle raising remained important, it failed to keep pace with sheep raising, which peaked in 1880, when New Mexicans owned four million sheep. Under the *partido* system, which governed the industry, the sheep were divided among small herders, the *partidarios,* who received a share of the yield; but it was the large rancher who reaped the major benefits.

While large landholders prospered, owners of small and medium-sized holdings floundered, a process that had begun even before 1848. Evidence now indicates that even during the Mexican period, overgrazing had created serious problems for ranchers of the Upper Rio Grande Valley. Their troubles were compounded after the American occupation, when "the land grant business became the territory's major industry."[25] Oftentimes, as in California, they were unable to clear land titles. Taxes took their toll. Ignorant of business procedures, some grantees found themselves swindled out of their inheritance, often by their own people. Dispossession occurred much slower than in California but had equally devastating results. Ultimately, more than 80 percent of the grant holders lost their lands.[26]

Legal chicanery was most pronounced after the Civil War, when the Territory came under the political domination of a group of unscrupulous lawyers and businessmen who have been labeled the Santa Fe Ring. Led by Thomas Benton Catron and Stephen B. Elkins, this Republican political machine was able to maintain its power from the end of the Civil War into the 1890s, the most corrupt period in the history of American politics. Based in the territorial capital, the ring was active throughout New Mexico, especially in Taos, Colfax, Lincoln, and Grant Counties. It included upper-class Mexicanos, whose support was solicited vigorously because of the voting strength of the Hispanic community—the territorial legislature was predominantly Hispanic prior to 1886. Although the ring eventually fell apart as it lost its political clout, its members reaped economic benefits galore. Catron, himself a lawyer, amassed two million acres in property and was part owner of four million more. His greatest coup was the acquisition in 1883 of the Tierra Amarilla Grant near the Colorado border, which amounted to nearly six hundred thousand acres. Political rings arose in California, Arizona, and Texas after the Civil War, but none were as successful as the Catron machine.

This postwar period saw the breakdown of law and order throughout the Territory. Violence was most pronounced in the eastern grasslands, where Texas cattlemen began to establish their ascendancy in the 1870s and 1880s. During these decades, they drove Hispanic stockmen from areas settled only a few years before. Often, the violence took the form of range wars between Texas cattlemen and Hispanic sheepmen. Perhaps the best example is to be found in the Lincoln County wars of 1869–1881, in which race was only one aspect of a complex and confusing series of events involving a multitude of issues. San Miguel County and the San Luis Valley were other areas which experienced extraordinary racial violence. At times, the bloodshed was due only in part to ethnic animosities, which appears to be the case in the deaths of two prominent rico political leaders: Francisco Chávez, a Democrat killed in 1892, and Colonel J. Francisco Chaves, a Republican assassinated twelve years later.

As in California, though later than in the Golden State, New Mexico witnessed the rise of Mexicano bandits. Among the most notorious were Mariano Leiba of Bernalillo and Vicente Silva of Las Vegas. Although these bandits might not qualify as defenders of the Mexicano community, there is no question that the *Gorras Blancas* (White Caps) fall into this category. A secret Hispano organization operating in the northeastern section of New Mexico—their stronghold was San Miguel County—in the late 1880s and early 1890s, the Gorras were established to protect Mexicanos from Anglo encroachment of their lands. They engaged in a variety of acts of defiance, including cutting fences and burning buildings. Despite their extreme methods, they were supported by some of the most prominent members of the community, among them the influential editor of *La Voz del Pueblo*, Félix Martínez, a resident of Las Vegas.

Hispanos tried to protect their culture as well as their livelihood, particularly through the agency of the Penitente Brotherhood, which was specifically dedicated to preserving traditional religious practices. The chronic shortage of priests in New Mexico during the Spanish period resulted in the formation of a number of *cofradías* or *confraternidades*, lay brotherhoods, that helped to fill the spiritual vacuum. The most celebrated of these grassroots associations was La Confraternidad de Nuestro Padre Jesús Nazareno (the Confraternity of Our Father, Jesus the Nazarene), usually referred to as the Penitentes.[27] The organization's origins are obscure, some scholars tracing them to sixteenth-century Spain. According to Fray Angélico Chávez, however, the Penitentes arose sometime in the late eighteenth century, introduced from the Mexican interior, and before too long the lay society dominated the villages of northern New Mexico.[28]

In the meantime, the Catholic Church continued to be hampered by the chronic shortage of clergymen. Moreover, the few priests in the Territory set less than a shining example. Concubinage was common among men of the cloth. Even Padre Antonio José Martínez, possibly the leading Hispano intellectual of his age, as well as the most respected cleric among his contemporaries, kept a mistress. After the American occupation, the new Catholic hierarchy determined that a thorough reform was necessary. The attempt to reestablish the Church's authority was initiated in 1853, with the appointment of Jean Lamy as bishop of New Mexico. The austere Frenchman was zealous in his efforts to accomplish his charge, as was his successor, Jean-Baptiste Salpointe, who became bishop in 1885. Both reformers, though united in their disdain of local religious observance and ethnic culture, accomplished a good deal, paramount being the foundation of a solid Catholic educational system in the Territory.

Other reforms met with stiff resistance, most notably the attempt to rein in the Penitentes, who represented a mystical brand of religious zeal which has always threatened the Church as an institution. Its annual practice of corporal penance, however, was the reason the Church gave for its opposition. As the Penitentes were persecuted, they increasingly went underground and succeeded in maintaining the allegiance of the villages of northern New Mexico and southern Colorado well into the twentieth century. Its members looked to the Brotherhood to provide a modicum of economic security as well as to administer to their spiritual needs, undoubtedly one reason why mutualistas were less popular in the northern Hispano villages than they were in other parts of the Southwest. By the late nineteenth century, the Brotherhood, while continuing its religious and social activities, also began to organize politically. In many rural areas it was impossible to win an election without its blessing. Its foray into the political area, more than anything else, illustrates its transformation into a vehicle for the protection of traditional village culture.

Ultimately, the preservation of a land base proved to be impossible, especially after the turn of the century, when much of the land in the territory was taken over by the federal government and transformed into national parks. Hispanos, though, had better success in protecting their traditional way of life. The historian Marc Simmons puts it best: "Gradually, of course, by a process of accretion, American ways made inroads. Yet the framework of Hispanic culture was kept intact and continued to serve as the principal point of reference by which the people viewed their past and measured the future."[29]

TEXAS

Texas was the area where Anglo-Mexican relations were at their worst during the second half of the nineteenth century. Mutual animosity had been evident since at least the time of the Texas Revolt and persisted throughout the era of the Lone Star Republic, but it intensified during the Mexican-American War. Texans made up a good part of the invading American force into Mexico, and when they committed numerous atrocities there, some Tejanos, probably the majority of the eleven thousand residing in the state, found themselves in sympathy with their old homeland, where many of them still maintained family ties. Naturally, the violence before the war continued afterward. The conflict was most pronounced along the Mexican border, where flagrant attacks on the Spanish-speaking community were waged with impunity.

Diversity characterized the Mexicanos in Texas, just as it did in the rest of the Southwest. As Arnoldo De León ably demonstrates in a number of excellent studies, their experiences were markedly different in the three major zones of Tejano occupation: San Antonio and surrounding areas (Central Texas), the Lower Rio Grande Valley (South Texas), and El Paso and neighboring communities (West Texas).[30] These experiences were largely dictated by economic considerations.[31]

In Central Texas, Anglos came to dominate political and economic life immediately after its acquisition in 1836; certainly, this hegemony was established in San Antonio before the Mexican-American War. In the postwar period, when Tejanos lost their numerical edge, the rate of interethnic marriages declined, and the Tejano elite in San Antonio was able to preserve some semblance of power only with the greatest of difficulties. Often, in fact, they were forced to sacrifice the interests of the community in order to maintain their own status. "They comprised probably the most reactionary and sycophantic leadership to be found in the Southwest," according to Juan Gómez-Quiñones.[32]

The erosion of the Tejanos' land base continued after the war, and, as in other parts of the Southwest, it was accomplished in a variety of ways, including litigation, taxes, and outright violence. Moreover, as marginal farmers and ranchers, the bulk of the Tejano population was especially vulnerable to economic downswings, necessitating land sales at below-market prices.

Tejano merchants fared no better. They had a difficult time competing against more aggressive Anglo rivals from the very outset, and their financial plight became precipitous after the so-called Cart War in 1859.[33] Throughout the early nineteenth century, Tejanos had established a thriving overland trade between San Antonio and the Gulf Area, the merchandise transported on carts. This lucrative enterprise continued to be their exclusive preserve even after Texas entered the Union in 1845. In an attempt to break the Tejano monopoly, Anglo competitors initiated a series of physical attacks on the *carreteros* (teamsters) in 1859. By the time this violent campaign of harassment was stopped, many wagon owners had been forced to abandon their livelihood. The subsequent decline of the cart trade was a major catastrophe for San Antonio's Tejano merchants, who had invested heavily in the enterprise.

The Mexicano population of South Texas, the Lower Rio Grande Valley, managed to retain economic and political power much longer than in the Alamo City, mainly because Anglos were slow to enter the region. Still, by the end of the century they too came to be seen as second-class citizens.

The aftermath of the Mexican-American War saw a trickle of Yankee immigrants into the region, most of them ex-servicemen. These newcomers tended to marry into the local elites. Typical was Richard King, who arrived in the 1850s and acquired enormous holdings. A benevolent patrón, King maintained the loyalty of his Tejano ranch hands, the *Kineños,* until his death in 1885. The first significant penetration by Anglos into South Texas, however, came at the time of the American Civil War. Their arrival signaled the beginning of the dispossession of native rancheros. Land was acquired through the usual methods, including marriage with the native elites. By the turn of the century, Anglo dominance in South Texas was not only economic but also political, as the machines that characterized political life along the border were controlled by the newcomers, Jim Wells of Brownsville being only the most successful of a host of ambitious carpetbaggers.

Anglos entering South Texas were attracted primarily by the prospect of acquiring lucrative cattle ranches. The cattle industry in the United States boomed after the Civil War ended. The heyday of the Texas cowboy occurred between 1865 and 1885, when longhorns raised on the southern Texas grasslands were driven to northern railheads. During these two decades, beef prices soared and South Texas ranches prospered. However, the gradual expansion of the railroad network ultimately made the long drive superfluous. The cattle boom was over. Many ranchers went under, with Tejanos, owners of smaller holdings, being especially vulnerable.

The end of these bonanza days was a catastrophe in more ways than one for the Mexican population of the Lower Rio Grande Valley. With ranching no longer profitable, farming slowly emerged as the economic mainstay of the area. By now many technological innovations had been made in agriculture; and in order to compete, the expanding farms needed to modernize. By the late 1880s, commercial farming had made its appearance in some of the southern counties, initiating an economic revolution which would continue to unfold almost to the outbreak of World War II. Tejano ranchers, land rich but money poor, were at a distinct disadvantage during this transitional period. Only a few of them managed to preserve sizable holdings, among them Hipólito García and Dionisio Guerra.

The fate of the rancheros was mirrored by that of their workers. Increasingly Tejano vaqueros, some of whom were ex-landholders already forced to accept a decline in status, were reduced to working as wage laborers on large farms, a process well illustrated by the sociologist David Montejano. By the turn of the century, the proletarianization of the bulk of the Hispanic community, continuously reinforced now by impoverished Mexican immigrants from across the border, was complete.

Racial subjugation in South Texas was accompanied by massive violence. Dispossession of Mexican holdings was often the result of physical attacks on native inhabitants. The Texas Rangers, instead of helping the situation, only made it worse since this constabulary was blatantly anti-Mexican, as the renowned folklorist Américo Paredes, relying on a vivid oral tradition, clearly illustrates; and selective law enforcement succeeded in inflaming passions on both sides of the border.

Some of this endemic border violence took the form of resistance to Anglo domination by Tejanos. The rise of Juan Nepomuceno Cortina (1824–1892), the most celebrated of the Texas bandidos, must be seen in this context.[34] Born in the Mexican state of Tamaulipas, Cortina was a member of a prominent ranching family with holdings on both sides of the border. Already embittered by the theft of local ranches by unscrupulous newcomers, Cortina was in Brownsville on 13 July 1859 when he spotted an Anglo city marshal pistol-whipping a Mexican prisoner. Attempting to protect the hapless victim, Cortina killed the lawman and fled across the border. Enraged by the incident, Anglo citizens of Brownsville initiated a reign of terror against "greasers." Cortina, at the head of a small army, responded with a raid on the city in September, an attack that initiated a long period of virtual warfare between Anglos and Mexicanos. The so-called Cortina War took many lives on both sides of the border; but its chief victims were Tejanos, most of them innocent men, women, and children caught in the crossfire. Border lynchings and other atrocities became commonplace throughout the 1860s.

While much of the fighting by Mexican raiders was mere banditry, motivated primarily by the quest to gain wealth, or occasions for personal vendettas, Cortina himself, as his biographers Carlos Larralde and José Rodolfo Jacobo convincingly argue, had a loftier goal: he believed he was fighting to vindicate the rights of his people. Most Chicano scholars attribute genuine revolutionary potential to Cortina's movement. That the campaign never achieved this potential was due not only to the strength of the opposition—the Rangers were ruthless in their fury—but also to the divisions among the oppressed people, who were separated both by class and, since they lived on both sides of the border, by nationality. His opponents included some of the most powerful Mexicano ranchers in the region, among them the political boss Santos Benavides. Interestingly, too, more than twenty Mexicanos served in the Texas Rangers during its long history. His ultimate failure notwithstanding, Juan Cortina, the Red Robber of the Rio Grande, became a hero among the residents of South Texas during his lifetime. Perceived as a champion against Anglo injustice, he was immortalized in a number of *corridos* (folk ballads), some of them still current today.

Another Tejano of the time who also achieved immense renown, and apparently for the same reasons, was Gregorio Cortez (1875–1916), the subject of some of the most popular corridos along the Texas-Mexican border.[35] Born in Mexico, near Matamoros, Cortez moved with his family to Manor, Texas, in 1887. There, on 12 June 1901, he shot Sheriff Harper Morris dead after the lawman tried to arrest him for a crime he had not committed. Cortez fled, initiating the longest manhunt in Texas history. The fantastic ten-day flight, the subject of intense media coverage, ended when Cortez was tracked down by Texas Rangers. He was brought to trial and sentenced to life imprisonment. After years of fighting the unjust verdict, the proud prisoner, now a celebrity, was pardoned by Governor Oscar B. Colquitt in 1913. The ballads commemorating Gregorio Cortez represent a protest against Anglo injustice on one level, but on another level, they are a tribute to all Mexicanos who had the courage to stand up for their convictions.

Catarino Garza (1859–1902) is a third symbol of resistance from South Texas.[36] Garza was born in Mexico, like Cortina and Cortez, but he was raised in Brownsville, which he considered his home. A journalist, he constantly inveighed against Anglo injustice at home and political tyranny in Mexico, where Porfirio Díaz ruled the country with an iron hand. In 1891, Garza recruited a small army in South Texas and captured the Mexican village of Guerrero, hoping to initiate a popular uprising. The masses failed to respond. Disillusioned, Garza and his men returned to Texas. Harassed by the authorities for the next few years, the hapless crusader eventually fled to Cuba, then to Colombia, where he died.

Anglos did not penetrate into West Texas in massive numbers until the railroad arrived in El Paso in 1881. Nevertheless, even before this date, they exerted a substantial influence on the area's economy. In 1848, the Mexican population of the El Paso Valley was clustered in a series of small settlements along the river, of which El Paso del Norte was the largest. El Paso had had a strategic advantage from the very beginning since it connected the New Mexican towns of the Upper Rio Grande with central Mexico. The opening up of the Santa Fe Trail had increased the volume of goods flowing back and forth along the Chihuahua Trail, augmenting the commercial importance of the city, to the immense satisfaction of its Mexican residents, the *Paseños*. Mexican merchants from the south poured into the valley during the last years of the Mexican period to take advantage of the new business opportunities.

The Treaty of Guadalupe Hidalgo established the Rio Grande as the international border, leaving El Paso del Norte on the Mexican side. Given the huge economic potential of the area, it was not long before five small American settlements were established on the opposite bank, the most substantial of which were Magoffinsville and Franklin. These villages grew slowly during the next few years. When El Paso County was created in 1850, San Elizario, a larger Mexicano town downriver, was made county seat. Franklin became the nucleus of a city soon to be called El Paso, incorporated as such in 1873—creating a problem of identity with its sister city nearby, a confusion cleared up only when the Mexican town adopted the name Ciudad Juárez, in honor of Mexico's most revered president, on 16 September 1888.

After the Mexican-American War, the Chihuahua trade was hurt by Mexican tariffs on American goods. The Apache were also a lingering threat during these years. Under these adverse circumstances, the area attracted only a small number of Anglo entrepreneurs. The arrival of John Butterfield's Overland Mail in 1858, however, revived the sagging economy of the El Paso Valley, encouraging immigration from the east.

W. W. Mills, an early pioneer, recalled years later that relations between Anglos and Tejanos were remarkably cordial in the valley in the period between the Civil War and the arrival of the railroad.[37] In fact, West Texas was spared the racial strife that was endemic in other parts of the state during this era, as Anglos integrated well into local society. Like their predecessors, many Anglo newcomers during the Civil War married into Paseño society, thus creating a bicultural environment, which characterizes the valley to this day. Of course, these contacts were established almost exclusively with the native ranching and mercantile elites.

However, the advent of the railroad would drastically alter the relations between the two ethnic communities in the El Paso Valley. A harbinger of things to come was the Salt War of 1877. The source of this conflict was a recent Anglo monopoly of the Guadalupe lakes east of El Paso, as Franklin was now called, and the salt they produced, a commodity which the local Mexican community had traditionally collected free of charge. When irate residents protested, one of their spokesmen was killed, inciting the marchers to violence. The war took on racial overtones, much to the dismay of El Paso's Anglo population, which constituted only one-tenth of the city's eight hundred residents. After several Anglos were killed, Texas Rangers were called in and promptly took bloody reprisals. For a time, it appeared that Mexico and the United States might go to war over the incident. In the end, Tejanos regained their rights to the salt beds, but the two ethnic communities remained estranged for many years.

The Southern Pacific arrived in El Paso on 19 May 1881, and the new line was soon united with the Texas and Pacific Railroad, which linked the western part of the state to San Antonio. The coming of the railroad was undoubtedly the most momentous event in the history of West Texas. As in other parts of the Southwest, the railroad increased property values and stimulated the local mining interest, which in turn attracted the inevitable parade of Anglo entrepreneurs and speculators. The city's population surged in the next few years. El Paso was transformed into an Anglo town almost overnight. In 1884, the county seat was transferred from Ysleta, a city located in the midst of a string of Mexicano settlements to the south, to the mushrooming railroad center, a change that signified the end of Tejano political power in El Paso County.

Economically, local workers were increasingly proletarianized and their wages depressed by the growing number of impoverished immigrants from Mexico—the arrival of the Mexican Central in 1884, linking the Mexican interior to the El Paso Valley, was perhaps as consequential as that of the Southern Pacific—who were re-cruited to toil both in mines and on railroads. Immigration from the south increased steadily throughout the 1890s, when El Paso became the major American port of entry from Mexico; and by the turn of the century, the city, with a population of almost sixteen thousand, was again predominantly Mexicano.

One of the most valuable contributions made by Carey McWilliams in *North from Mexico* was to explode the myth of what he called the Fantasy Heritage.[38] As pointed out in this pioneering work, during the late nineteenth century, especially in California, there developed the popular romantic notion, promoted for economic as well as sentimental reasons, that before Anglo entry into the Southwest, frontier society basically consisted of two classes: the "Spanish dons," a white ranchero elite, and "Mexican peons," the Indianized masses. Those elements of the culture judged to be positive came to be identified with the former; negative characteristics were seen as typical of the latter. As McWilliams notes, there are many problems with this popular analysis. Historically, he has shown, the Spanish/Mexican dichotomy has been used to justify the selective discrimination of lower-class members of the Spanish-speaking community, while at the same time glorifying the Spanish presence in America. Moreover, the portrayal of the Hispanic elite was highly inaccurate. In point of fact, Indian blood permeated Hispanic society, from top to bottom, though clearly mestizaje was more complete among the lower classes.

Another criticism of the Fantasy Heritage, one which McWilliams does not emphasize enough, is that the class system was much more complex than the popular perception would have us believe. There were pobres and there were ricos, but by the second half of the nineteenth century there was also a substantial middle class throughout the Hispanic Southwest.

Although some of the middle-class elements were native to the area, nota-bly in the Upper Rio Grande Valley, many of them were recent immigrants, lured north by the prospect of wealth and security. Despite the common perception, Mexican immigration into the Southwest was not exclusively a twentieth-century phenomenon; Mexicans entered the United States throughout the second half of the nineteenth century. While most of these immigrants were impoverished, they were accompanied by more fortunate compatriots who had education and entrepreneurial skills, especially from the border states of Chihuahua and Sonora.

THE GREAT MIGRATION

1900–1930

The dominant theme of Mexican American history in the twentieth century was immigration. With the one exception of the 1930s, every decade witnessed a substantial increase in the number of Mexican immigrants entering the United States, and there is little reason to believe that this movement will be stemmed in the near future. The first major push of immigrants occurred during the first three decades of the twentieth century. Although statistics pertaining to immigration from the south are highly unreliable, it appears that over one million Mexicans entered the country at this time, joining the half million already in residence. Most settled down in the Southwest, though Mexican colonies began to appear in other sections of the country as well. Given the magnitude and impact, Chicano historians have labeled this transnational movement "The Great Migration."[1]

MOTIVES FOR MEXICAN IMMIGRATION

It is entirely possible, as some students of American immigration suggest, that more Mexicans have immigrated into the United States than any other single national group, including both Germans and Italians. One observer recently went so far as to conclude that Mexican movement north constitutes "the greatest migration of people in the history of humanity."[2] This statement appears rather grandiose, but Mexicans may indeed rank first among peoples who have made the United States their home. It is a claim, however, which is hard to substantiate, given inadequate statistics relating to the Mexican population. As hard as recordkeeping is today, it was even more difficult prior to 1930.[3] The primary problem, then as now, was the surreptitious nature of much of the exodus. In fact, probably most Mexican immigrants in 1900–1930 entered the United States illegally, or at least through irregular channels.

During and immediately after the First World War, a series of laws were passed, culminating in the Reed-Johnson Immigration Act of 1924, regulating immigration into this country. While this legislation was aimed primarily at stemming the massive wave of southern and eastern Europeans, immigration from the Western Hemisphere was also affected by literacy requirements and entry fees. However, given the labor needs in the country during the economic boom of the war and postwar periods, there was no serious attempt to enforce these laws as they applied to Mexicans, who were only too glad to bypass the bureaucratic red tape. Consequently, many of them entered the country without official authorization, a trend that continues today.

The best way to look at Mexican immigration in 1900–1930 is still, as Carey McWilliams did in his pioneering work on Mexican Americans, as a movement motivated by a push-pull process; that is to say, there were certain factors in Mexico forcing citizens to leave the country, and simultaneously there were other factors in the United States, specifically the Southwest, attracting them.[4]

THE MEXICAN REVOLUTION

Let us look at Mexico first. Recent interpretations of the Mexicano experience in this country have tended to accentuate the problems encountered in American society. There can be no denying that incoming Mexicans have faced severe problems, more than most immigrant groups, including racial prejudice and discrimination. Yet the fact remains that since the turn of the century, Mexicans have willingly entered the United States in huge numbers, as they continue to do even today, when they are under no illusions about what life holds in store as they head north; and many have opted to remain in this alien environment, so far from the psychological security of their native villages and cities. Why have they come? Why do they continue to do so? An impartial observer must recognize, at the very least, that with all the problems they encounter, the United States still offers immigrants significant advantages over the Old Country. It would seem, life in Mexico is even more oppressive than life in the United States.

Certainly, this was the case in the first decades of the twentieth century, a period of Mexican history dominated by the Revolution, a conflict which in itself indicated massive discontent among the populace. In contrast to a purely political uprising, a true revolution impacts every aspect of life—politics, economics, culture, society itself. The upheaval that Mexico experienced in 1910–1920 qualified in every respect; it was one of the few true revolutions of the twentieth century.

Its origins were rather modest. It began as a protest movement initiated by Francisco I. Madero, a bespectacled intellectual and member of the landholding elite from the state of Coahuila, on 20 November 1910, after he lost a fraudulent election for the presidency to the incumbent, Porfirio Díaz (1830–1915). While Madero's motives were almost completely political, the revolt quickly escalated into a full-fledged social revolution, so profound was popular dissatisfaction with the Porfiriato.

The roots of the 1910 cataclysm can be traced far back into Mexican history. Some scholars today find its genesis in the agrarian discontent already in evidence by the late eighteenth century. Popular disaffection increased throughout the following century as the peasant masses were gradually incorporated into world capitalist markets, a trend culminating during the late nineteenth century, a fateful period dominated by General Díaz. A partisan of liberalism and a lieutenant of Benito Juárez, Porfirio Díaz gained immense popularity early in his military career when he helped General Ignacio Zaragoza repel the French invasion at Puebla in 1862. The death ten years later of Juárez, by now a political rival, paved the way for the ascendancy of Díaz, who gained the presidency in 1876. Determined to end the chaos that marked the political life of the struggling republic—the presidency changed hands seventy-five times from 1821 to 1876—Díaz gradually consolidated his position, ultimately establishing a one-man dictatorship, which he maintained until his ouster in 1911.

The Porfiriato had popular support in the beginning. Mexico had paid dearly for the political and economic instability that prevailed after its independence in 1821. The loss of its northern territories to the United States in 1848 was only one, albeit the most catastrophic, of the setbacks encountered by the young nation. Corruption at all levels of government was rampant, years of weak and ineffectual leadership encouraged the breakdown of law and order, the economy was in shambles, and social problems abounded. Díaz was determined to resolve the most pressing of these problems, and Mexicans, tired of years of violence and insecurity, were sympathetic to these efforts. Still, divisions were typical. The Church, in particular, fought frantically to preserve its privileges against the "godless" liberals. Díaz was forced to impose his will over recalcitrants using strong-arm methods. Lacking a democratic tradition, many citizens were convinced that there were no viable alternatives to these measures. Moreover, Díaz's policies appeared to work reasonably well in the beginning.

The top priority of the new administration was to restore the power of the central government at the expense of the state legislatures, something which was accomplished by the 1880s. Díaz then turned to strengthening the economy. Mexico was rich in subsoil resources and cheap labor but lacked technological expertise and capital. Díaz sought to remedy the situation by turning to foreign entrepreneurs, especially British and even American investors, the latter not very popular given the recent war. Foreign capital, enticed by generous grants of land and favorable tax laws, poured into the country; and, as Mexico was inexorably incorporated into the global market under the aegis of capitalism, the economy did improve dramatically. The mining industry was revived, with copper now rivaling silver as the most valuable ore. Oil production began in 1901, and nine years later some thirteen million barrels were produced, mostly for export. A vast network of railroads was constructed linking the most strategic state capitals to one another and to American border towns, notably Laredo—a crucial link to San Antonio— and El Paso. By 1892, Mexico had built 6,876 miles of railway; and by 1910, the figure reached 12,000 miles. After the turn of the century, the government also succeeded in establishing an iron and steel industry centered on the northern city of Monterrey. Díaz had promised order and progress, and even his enemies were forced to concede that he had been able to deliver the goods to a surprising extent by the last years of his presidency.

By this time, however, there were many dissidents who had come to question whether the impressive material gains warranted the immense sacrifices asked of the masses. No doubt Díaz had brought his people more security, but at the expense of liberty. Moreover, while a small but powerful minority in Mexico, the Europeanized upper class, was able to share the material benefits of Díaz's reforms with foreign entrepreneurs, the great majority of the citizenry found that its economic status had hardly improved at all or had even deteriorated, in part because Mexico's population soared during the Porfiriato from 8.7 million to 15 million inhabitants. The railroads themselves, as George J. Sánchez has argued, while helping to integrate formerly isolated villages into the larger community, also disrupted traditional patterns of life, causing deep discontent in peasant society.[5]

The most unfortunate victims of progress were Indians. At the end of the nineteenth century, the indigenous community in Mexico was still enormous; more than a third of its inhabitants were listed as Indians in official records, and some two million of them spoke native dialects exclusively. Díaz, who ironically was part Mixtec himself, was convinced by his advisors, above all his treasury secretary José Ives Limantour, that the native population was hopelessly backward and that their very existence posed a grave obstacle to modernization. *Ejidos,* Indian communal holdings, were rapidly divided under Díaz and the land redistributed, the chief beneficiaries being foreigners and the Mexican upper class, mostly whites. Luis Terrazas of Chihuahua, for instance, amassed lands totaling nearly five million acres by 1910, at a time when only 3 percent of the nation's population owned any land at all. Generally, Indians were reduced to working as peons on large haciendas, where they lived in squalor as virtual slaves, one of the most disruptive effects of the rapid incursions made by capitalism into Mexican agrarian society. Those who refused to cooperate were dealt with in severe fashion. Among the intransigents were Yaquis from Sonora who were shipped off to toil in the henequen haciendas of Yucatán after the turn of the century. Making matters worse, the alienation of ejido lands was accompanied by growing anti-Indian prejudice, the Mexican variation of the racism that increased everywhere in the Western world as the nineteenth century waned.

Ultimately, most scholars feel, the single most substantial cause of the coming upheaval was agrarian discontent. The economic crisis brought on by the widespread loss of land by the peasants was the key factor. Could the Mexican elites have nipped the revolutionary fervor in the bud, asks the historian Michael J. Gonzales, had they closed ranks more effectively against the masses? "Given the breadth and depth of the agrarian crisis," he concludes, "this seems doubtful."[6]

Serious resistance to the regime began to develop after the turn of the century. Anti-Díaz sentiment focused on the border states of the north, which became the seedbeds of rebellion. It was here that Ricardo Flores Magón (1873–1922), the most memorable precursor of the Revolution, got his start, as a cofounder of the Partido Liberal Mexicano (PLM) in 1901. Dedicated to overthrowing the Díaz regime, and ultimately the capitalist system, party leaders, including Ricardo and his brothers, were exiled to Texas within a few years. Headquartered first in Laredo and later in San Antonio, now becoming the center of exile politics, the *magonistas* initiated a series of rebellions in northern Mexico in 1906. Persecuted by the U.S. government for violating neutrality laws, PLM leadership fled first to St. Louis, Missouri, then, in 1910, to Los Angeles. In the meantime, Ricardo Flores Magón had abandoned liberal ideas and had begun to espouse anarchism, a transition that can be traced in *Regeneración,* his influential newspaper founded in 1900. In 1911, magonistas attempted an invasion of Baja California from their base in the north, where Ricardo Flores Magón remained to direct operations. The uprising proved to be abortive, as the insurgents failed to arouse popular support among the masses. Crestfallen, the survivors retreated to the United States, where they suffered ongoing persecution by U.S. authorities. During this period, the uncompromising opposition leader also worked to construct a working-class movement, based on anarchist principles, among the Mexicanos of the Southwest.

In February 1915, an attempt to overthrow U.S. rule and reclaim the Southwest was initiated in southern Texas. The insurrection was announced in the mysterious *Plan de San Diego*—a document apparently drawn up in the Duval County town of San Diego—the origins of which remain obscure.[7] Mexicano insurgents, some from across the border, others U.S.-born, numbered as many as five thousand individuals. Their leaders included Aniceto Pizaña and Luis de la Rosa. The 1915–1917 revolt, however, dissipated in the face of repression in Texas, during which hundreds of Mexicanos were killed, and the disavowal of the irredentist movement by President Venustiano Carranza of Mexico.

While this bizarre episode seemed to be fueled by the loss of lands to aggressive Anglo entrepreneurs, made possible by the recent arrival of the railroad into South Texas, and leadership was provided by local Mexicano elements, the magonistas, despite their denials, were apparently implicated in the plot; the San Diego manifesto was vaguely anarchist in spirit. The U.S. government, determined to eradicate the PLM, stepped up its efforts to prosecute party chiefs; Ricardo Flores Magón spent the last years of his life in a Kansas prison, where he died under suspicious circumstances in 1922. The magonistas failed, mostly for the same reasons that all anarchist-inspired movements have died out—lack of organization and an unrealistic program. Its legacy, however, as recent scholarship has demonstrated, was profound.[8] It was Ricardo Flores Magón who first openly challenged the Díaz regime, exposing its vulnerabilities and laying the foundations for the Great Revolution of 1910.

Francisco Madero, scion of a wealthy hacendado family from Coahuila, was no friend of anarchism, but he was able to tap the discontent that the magonistas had accentuated when he launched the Revolution with his *Plan de San Luis Potosí,* issued in San Antonio in November 1910. The bulk of his support came, however, from the middle class rather than the workers. While the bourgeoisie, which constituted a little less than 10 percent of the population, had fared relatively well under the Porfiriato, a financial debacle in 1907 had abruptly altered their prospects for the future, alienating them from the government. According to the historian Ramón Eduardo Ruiz: "One event, as so often happens, ignited the fuse of rebellion. The financial crisis of 1907, which marked the swan song of prosperity, revealed the flaws in Mexico's economic and social fabric and became the watershed of rebellion. Until the depression paralyzed mining, commerce, and industry, the people paid homage to the Mexican success story; with its onset, even disciples of the Old Regime began to listen to the disciples of change."[9]

The ease of his initial success must have surprised Madero. Taking over power, however, was one thing; consolidating that power was an entirely different matter. Like Father Hidalgo before him, Madero unleashed forces he could not control. After ascending to the presidency on 6 November 1911, he was assassinated by counter-revolutionists three months later, the beginning of a lengthy period of intermittent civil strife, at times bordering on complete chaos. While political principles may have been paramount at the beginning, the rebellion soon deteriorated into a series of power struggles as one caudillo after another attempted to gain control of Mexico City, efforts that often resulted in political assassination. Emiliano Zapata, the most dedicated of the revolutionists, an Indian leader who fought for "land and liberty," was killed in 1919; as were Venustiano Carranza, the Coahuila strongman and architect of the famous 1917 Constitution, in 1920 and Pancho Villa, as much a bandit as he was a revolutionary, three years later. These executions were simply the tip of the iceberg. Between 1.5 and 2 million men, women, and children lost their lives during the Revolution.[10] This cataclysmic figure contradicts the common stereotype in the United States of the "cowardly" Mexican.

Despite the obstacles, many Mexicans were able to flee the country even during the periods of most intense violence. Some eight thousand refugees, for example, crossed the border from Piedras Negras, Coahuila, to Eagle Pass, Texas, in a single day in October 1913; and in one week in June 1916, almost five thousand Mexicans poured into El Paso. The numbers increased dramatically, however, once the violence abated.

The Revolution created as many problems as it solved. Massive destruction, the result of pillage, looting, and burning, was everywhere, especially in the areas west and north of the capital, the Bajío. Mexico City was the objective of the various rebel armies and their leaders, most of whom swept down from the north—Madero and Carranza from Coahuila, Villa from Chihuahua, and Álvaro Obregón from Sonora—and it was in the Bajío that the heaviest fighting took place as government troops, the *federales,* moved north to defend the capital. These strife-torn states, which included Guanajuato, Michoacán, and Jalisco, were also among the most heavily populated in Mexico, and the destruction of their crops left the population on the verge of starvation.

Difficulty in acquiring land in an area where the hacienda system was so firmly entrenched also compounded peasant discontent. The end of the Revolution in 1920, with the triumph of Obregón, alleviated the situation somewhat, but it did not solve the basic problems. Agrarian reform, the most popular demand of the landless peasants, was enacted all too slowly by the triumphant Sonoran faction headed by Obregón and Plutarco Elías Calles. In the end, it was clear, there was not nearly enough arable land to meet the needs of the desperate rural population.[11]

Peasant disillusion with agrarian reform was in part responsible for the Cristero Rebellion which broke out in western Mexico in 1926–1929, but other factors added to the crisis. The most immediate cause of Catholic dissatisfaction was the anti-clerical legislation of the postrevolutionary period. The Catholic Church had made itself unpopular with the revolutionaries by its support of conservative elements during the conflict. A champion of the status quo, the Church found itself extremely vulnerable with the fall of the Porfiriato. President Calles, Obregón's successor, and the most anti-clerical of Mexico's revolutionary presidents, was determined to weaken the institution through a series of tough measures, including the expulsion of foreign clergymen and the closing of parochial schools. The attempt to curtail clerical privileges produced an unanticipated reaction in the countryside. Government leaders had miscalculated the extent to which parish priests had won over the hearts and minds of the peasantry, generally the most conservative element in any society. Devoted to their priests, mestizos and Tarascan Indians (*purépechas*) in Jalisco, Michoacán, and Colima rallied to their defense.

Violence swept through the towns and villages of western Mexico as the government eschewed a policy of reconciliation and insisted on fighting fire with fire. It is estimated that some eighty thousand lives were lost in this holy war. Peasants, many of them innocent bystanders, were driven off their small plots of land, their only means of survival. In Arandas, Jalisco, for example, thirteen hundred inhabitants fled north for fear of reprisals by government troops.

The years immediately after the revolutionary upheaval, the decade of the 1920s, witnessed the largest exodus from Mexico, particularly from the western states of Guanajuato, Jalisco, and Michoacán. Flight was facilitated by the reconstruction of the railroad lines, which had been largely destroyed during the years of heavy fighting. Altogether, during the Revolution and its aftermath, a million people, some of them political exiles representing every class of society, most of them starving peasants, moved north to seek a better life across the border.

In fact, large numbers of Mexicans had been entering the United States even before the Revolution. As Chicano historians have discovered recently, beginning in the 1880s, with the arrival of the railroad in the Southwest, many immigrants, mostly from the northern border states, had moved north from Mexico.[12] These early immigrants, like later arrivals, found economic conditions in the Old Country stultifying. Dissatisfied with the Porfiriato, some political malcontents preferred life abroad. After the turn of the century, the numbers of people moving north increased sharply. The historian Lawrence A. Cardoso believes that as many as half a million Mexicans entered the United States during the first decade of the twentieth century.[13]

While political exiles before the Revolution were almost exclusively liberal in their sentiments, those who came during the upheaval itself—when they made up about 10 percent of the total—and especially in the aftermath, tended to espouse conservative positions. Whatever their politics, however, these émigrés, mostly of urban and professional backgrounds, came to be the backbone of the small middle class that developed in the colonias of the Southwest. Their most popular destination was San Antonio, where they settled in the Mexicano barrio on the West Side. In these ethnic enclaves, as Arnoldo De León persuasively argues, these elites came to play an important role in preserving traditional culture:

> They promoted a Mexican past through the distribution of Mexican books, magazines, musical records, and Spanish-language newspapers from Mexico City. They sponsored speaking engagements and theatrical performances and editorialized or extolled the virtues of *la patria* (Mexico, their native country). Meantime, they formed their own clubs and held exclusive cultural activities. They maintained a commitment to preserving Mexican nationalist sentiments within the community of immigrants.[14]

THE ECONOMIC DEVELOPMENT OF THE SOUTHWEST

The immigrants, whether they came in the 1880s or the 1920s, set their sights on the American Southwest. The most attractive destination was Texas, whose Mexicano population increased from 71,062 in 1900 to 683,681 in 1930, according to official statistics—the actual numbers would have been substantially greater. California, the second leading magnet, had 368,000 Mexicano residents by this time.

A variety of factors drew these immigrants into the Borderlands. For one thing, Mexicano colonies were already established here and there throughout the region. Once a part of Mexico, the Southwest continued to be familiar territory, especially for the residents of the northern Mexican states, where the climate and terrain were virtually identical to those of the arid lands north of the border. In fact, as John R. Chávez argues, Mexicanos saw themselves as indigenous to the region, a perception that made it easier for them to make the move.[15] Distance was another factor. The Southwest was the most accessible part of the United States. Railroad lines linked the teeming population centers of central Mexico to American cities such as El Paso and Laredo, both of them directly to the north, and eventually to Nogales, where a railway line to Guadalajara was completed in 1927. Also, as Chicano scholars have emphasized recently, based on their studies of participant narratives, many immigrants were lured into the area by encouragement and financial aid extended by family members who had previously made the journey; that is, many newcomers were part of a chain migration.[16] Oftentimes, large numbers of people from the same village in Mexico came to live together in the United States.

Still, the most compelling attraction exerted by the Southwest was the abundance of jobs. Mexicans found work as laborers on construction sites, in public works systems, in service and food establishments, in lumbering camps, and on ranches. The overwhelming majority, however, came to work in three main industries: mining, railroad maintenance, and agriculture.

At the turn of the century, the best employment opportunities were to be found in the mines. The pacification of the Apache in the mid-1880s had permitted Americans to enter the heart of the Southwest, the territories of New Mexico and Arizona, where they discovered a superabundance of mineral wealth—coal, silver, and copper. Southern Arizona was particularly rich in precious metals. Acquired as part of the Gadsden Purchase in 1853–1854, the area south of the Gila was thought to be worthless by both governments, except as a corridor through which a railroad connecting Texas and southern California could be built. However, by the mid-1880s, Tombstone, though difficult to reach from other parts of the United States, was the hub of a thriving silver mining industry. A lack of labor was all that prevented the full exploitation of the territory.

Just across the border, in Sonora, was a reservoir of cheap labor with a long tradition of mining going back to 1640. In that state, moreover, a mining resurgence, centered at Cananea after 1899, drew large numbers of workers from the Mexican interior at the end of the Porfiriato. Eventually, these miners became the backbone of the Arizona silver and copper mining industry. "Moving from Mexican to American mines," as Linda Gordon has pointed out, "was easy because Americans owned both."[17] By the mid-1920s, Mexicanos composed 43 percent of the state's copper-mining work force. New Mexico, too, developed a booming mining industry, especially in the southern region. Soon after the turn of the century, nearby El Paso became the site of the largest smelting operation in the world. At this time, too, Mexicanos were active in the coal-mining fields further south along the Rio Grande Valley; by 1910, according to the historian Roberto Calderón, Mexicanos and Tejanos represented 98 percent of all the miners in Maverick and Webb counties.

As they had during the time of the California gold rush, Sonorans came to dominate many mining areas, notably along the border. In contrast to the earlier period, they now worked for large corporations, among them Kennecutt and Phelps Dodge, under a highly regimented system of contract labor. The hazards they faced in the tunnels and pits, as well as the smelters, only begin to describe their plight. Segregated from white miners, who earned more than they did for the same jobs (the infamous dual-wage system), and at the mercy of employers who forced them to live in substandard housing in company towns and pay exorbitant prices at company stores, Mexicano miners endured the worst conditions of any of their countrymen in the United States. And yet, they continued to perform their duties; Carey McWilliams estimated that 60 percent of the mine workers in the Southwest in 1900–1940 were Mexicanos.[18] During these years, they were also well represented in the mining fields of Oklahoma, Colorado, Utah, and Nevada.

By the first decade of the twentieth century, Mexicanos were beginning to compete in another industry which required heavy physical labor—railroad work. The railways of the Southwest, first and foremost the Southern Pacific and the Atchison, Topeka, and Santa Fe, were constructed in the 1870s and 1880s, mostly by recent European immigrants, particularly the Irish, Greeks, and Italians. In an effort to take advantage of generous subsidies, the lines were built hastily and sometimes very carelessly. Maintenance became a pressing problem almost immediately. Finding better job opportunities in other occupations or moving up the railroad career ladder into skilled positions as conductors, engineers, firemen, and machinists, the old immigrants tended to abandon the track crews as soon as they could; and the more recent arrivals from Europe were reticent to make the long trek across the continent, once again opening up opportunities for Mexicano workers. Since repairing railroad lines did not require special skills, there were no serious impediments to employing the predominantly inexperienced laborers, who were needed to unload rails, lay switches and ties, and level roads. From 1900 to 1940, 60 to 90 percent of the section and extra gangs employed on eighteen western railroads were of Mexican origin. This dominance was most pronounced in the Southwest, where, according to a 1922 survey, they composed some 85 percent of the track workers.

While most of these laborers remained close to the Mexican border, residing either in boxcars or in labor camps situated at regular intervals along the railroad lines, some were transferred to other sections of the country by railroad companies in dire need of a cheap and pliable labor force. They ended up in major rail terminals such as Omaha and the twin cities of Kansas City, Kansas, and Kansas City, Missouri. Undoubtedly, the most popular destination outside the Southwest was Chicago, where during the late twenties, Mexicanos represented more than 40 percent of the track labor force.

In the early decades of the twentieth century, however, it was the Southwest that attracted the overwhelming bulk of immigrants from the south, for it was at this time that the region experienced an amazing transformation from a pastoral to an agricultural economy, a development that became heavily dependent on cheap Mexicano labor. By the 1920s, when immigration from Mexico assumed flood proportions, neither the mines nor the railroad lines could compete with agriculture in attracting the Mexican immigrant.

While meaningful farming enterprises had appeared before the turn of the century, notably in the cotton fields of Texas, the sugar beet fields of Colorado, and the wheat fields of the Great Valley of California, the true beginning of agricultural development in the Southwest dates from the enactment of the Newlands Reclamation Act of 1902.[19] This path-breaking legislation provided for a series of irrigation projects that were to transform arid lands into rich farming country.

By 1929, the Southwest was producing 40 percent of the total fruit and vegetable output in the United States. The enormous cost of irrigation required massive outlays of capital, which ensured the dominance of large corporate enterprises rather than the small family farms typical of the Midwest. Factory-farms required huge numbers of workers, and by the 1920s, only Mexico was in a position to provide them.

Europeans continued to enter the United States at the turn of the century. Indeed, they came in record numbers. But most of them were not attracted to agriculture; and those who were preferred to settle in the Midwest, where, taking advantage of the 1862 Homestead Act, they were still able to acquire their own farms. During the First World War, European immigration waned; and after the war, the immigration acts of 1921 and 1924, which imposed quotas on Old World migration, effectively stopped the entry of virtually the only Europeans still willing to make the transatlantic journey.

Asians were the other potential source of competition for farm work, but after the turn of the century they slowly disappeared from the fields. The Chinese Exclusion Act had shut off the most substantial source of Asian field labor in California, as well as other Pacific Coast states; and under the terms of the Gentlemen's Agreement, a series of notes in 1907 and 1908 between the United States and Japan, immigration from the latter nation was also curtailed. In the 1910s, laborers were brought in from India, the so-called Hindus, but their numbers were modest, and they displayed the same propensity for climbing the socioeconomic ladder as their predecessors had. As Asians remaining in the United States abandoned the fields, some becoming farm owners, others leaving agriculture altogether, the labor shortage intensified, especially during the Great War, when agricultural production in the West expanded rapidly.

By the 1920s, Mexicanos dominated farm labor in the greater Southwest. Their only competition came from Filipinos, who arrived in California after 1923, but who were at a distinct disadvantage, given the vast distance separating their island homeland from the American mainland. By 1930, they were outnumbered by Mexicanos ten to one in the fields of California.

The expansion of southwestern agriculture produced a wide variety of crops. Well over two hundred products would ultimately be cultivated in California alone. Each crop required an enormous amount of labor. Cotton was the best example. Unlike the harvest of other commodities, such as melons, which required only brute strength and therefore discouraged the use of women and children, cotton picking could be done by the entire family, one reason why more Mexicanos were employed in this crop than any other.

Before the twentieth century, cotton culture was largely confined to the Deep South, where African Americans performed most of the physical labor. During the last twenty years of the nineteenth century, cotton culture spread into Central Texas, where Mexicanos were recruited as sharecroppers. By 1900, however, Texas cotton was being harvested by migratory laborers, most of them Mexicanos who found employment over a seven-month period by making the "big swing" from the southern part of the state into central and northern areas, before returning home via western counties.[20]

The expansion of cotton from Texas into the heart of the Southwest coincided with the period of the Great Migration. By 1910, cotton was being cultivated in both West Texas and the Imperial Valley of southern California. Shortly thereafter, the Mesilla Valley of New Mexico and the Gila River Valley in Arizona began to produce the valuable commodity. After the turn of the century, as Devra Weber documents in her fine study *Dark Sweat, White Gold* (1994), cotton was reintroduced into California's San Joaquin Valley, where the first "Mexican harvest" occurred in 1920. In the six years from 1924 to 1930, from September to February, an average of fifty-eight thousand Mexicanos made the seasonal trek into the Central Valley, where cotton had become the dominant crop, and they constituted more than three-fourths of the total work force. During the twenties, cotton production in the Golden State increased by 400 percent. Until the cotton harvest was mechanized in the 1950s, huge farms employed tens of thousands of *campesinos* (farmworkers), who picked the crop by hand three times seasonally.

The harvest was the most labor-intensive task, but there were many other jobs that had to be performed before the cotton could be picked: once the land was cleared, the cotton had to be planted, thinned and spaced by hoe, weeded, and irrigated. The entire operation up to the ginning process was done by unskilled labor. The same kinds of tasks were required for each and every crop. The amount of work to be performed was staggering. Given the magnitude of the labor problem, then, one can appreciate why Mexicanos were considered indispensable to the economic life of the Southwest by the 1920s.

THE IMMIGRANT

Driven out of Mexico and attracted to the Southwest for political, religious, economic, and a variety of other reasons, thousands of immigrants, most of them destitute peasants, made the hazardous trek north during the halcyon years of the early twentieth century. What was life like for the immigrant during the period of the Great Migration? Each experience was undoubtedly unique, and yet certain thematic motifs emerge over and over again. On the basis of these common threads, it is possible to construct a composite biography of the immigrant during this momentous thirty-year period, and thus understand how this immigrant experience differed so radically from that of other newcomers to America.[21]

José Martínez, our typical modal immigrant, was born at around the turn of the century in a small village in western Mexico, a town like Arandas in Jalisco or La Piedad in Michoacán.[22] He was a mestizo, like the great majority of his friends and neighbors. His schooling was rudimentary; impoverished, the Martínez family saw education as a luxury, and young José was soon pulled out of school to help provide income. Too young to take part in the early stages of the Revolution, José made a living as a *peón* (peasant), much like his father had. Illiterate and unskilled, he faced the prospects of living out the rest of his life toiling on a hacienda. As the military campaigns dragged on, and generals grew desperate for men, he and other youths were recruited as foot soldiers by either the federales or their opponents. Politically apathetic, like most villagers, he was ignorant of the larger issues and preferred to be left alone. Neither a coward nor a hero, José did as he was told.

Fighting alongside his boyhood friends and relatives, he gradually convinced himself of the righteousness of the cause. However, as the conflict deteriorated into a blood bath, and it became impossible to tell friends from foes, his faith began to waver, and eventually survival became his overriding objective. The chaos during the closing stages of the Revolution allowed José to return to his native village, one of the fortunate survivors. He now married his childhood sweetheart, María, and tried to a resume normal life.

But for many people, especially ex–fighting men, a return to the status quo ante bellum proved impossible. On the one hand, some things had changed dramatically. Old rancors from the Revolution now divided communities, and violence, though diminished, continued to permeate society. On the other hand, other things had not changed enough. Poverty was still rampant, and perhaps even worse than before. Massive destruction and a population increase, notwithstanding the high mortality caused by the bloody civil war, put a severe strain on limited resources. The much-anticipated agrarian reform proved a major disappointment. If and when land did become available, the plots were often insufficient in size and of poor quality. The old elites resurfaced, and little changed for the masses.

José, unable to make a good living, but convinced that a better life was possible, one of the most positive legacies of the Revolution, was prepared to try his luck in the United States. Friends and acquaintances, most of whom had never been there themselves, assured him there was plenty of work to be found in *el norte* (the north). In fact, the postwar depression of 1921–1922 was over in the United States, and labor needs were soaring in the Southwest. His wife, who was destined to remain behind, living with her in-laws, was less enthusiastic. Eventually, however, María was won over to the idea. She was reassured that José would return soon, with enough money to acquire a small business, possibly even a ranch. Borrowing money from relatives, he purchased a railroad ticket for about twenty dollars—several months' wages—and headed north with high hopes. The year was 1923.

Several days later, the weary traveler arrived in El Paso and entered the United States without any trouble whatsoever. It was Mexican immigrants like José who would increase the population of this west Texas town, the Queen City of the Southwest, from a little over thirty-nine thousand to about fifty-eight thousand during the decade of the twenties. While he was required to pass a literacy exam and pay a modest head tax of eight dollars, there was minimal effort to enforce these regulations. Even after the establishment of the Border Patrol a year later, it was well understood that cheap labor was essential for the success of large-scale capitalistic enterprises, such as the railroad.

On his way to El Paso, José met and befriended countrymen bound for New Mexico, where, they had heard, they could secure jobs on *el traque,* literally, "the tracks," repairing railroad lines. His new friends invited him along, and soon José found himself working on railroad maintenance crews for "el SP," the Southern

Pacific. Later, he did a variety of other jobs requiring a strong back and few skills. On one occasion, he was recruited to go to southern Colorado, where he worked in the coal mines near Trinidad. There were plenty of jobs available, and he was a good worker. Nevertheless, it took José two years before he could save enough money to send for his wife. By now, he had abandoned his original plan. It had become clear that his family would have to work several years in the United States before they could raise enough money to live comfortably in Mexico.

By the time José met María at the bridge linking El Paso and Ciudad Juárez, he had purchased a secondhand Model T Ford. Rather than return to the backbreaking and hazardous job of repairing railroad tracks, he now chose to live the life of an agricultural worker, an occupation more congenial to his peasant upbringing. For the next few years, José, María, and their children worked as migratory farm laborers, following the crops throughout the Lone Star State. During the periods of seasonal unemployment, they made their home in the predominantly Mexican communities of the Lower Rio Grande Valley, in Mercedes, let us say, where they became part of a growing Mexican subculture.[23] It was in "the Valley," too, that most of their children were born. As the family grew, they came to rely increasingly on the cotton harvest, making the "big swing" that took them through the cotton belt to the northeast. While the wages were meager, given the enormous labor pool consisting of African Americans as well as Mexicans, cotton, grown throughout the state, provided work for the entire family.

After the Depression, as Texas agriculture increasingly mechanized, the Martínez family, having by now abandoned the notion of ever returning to Mexico, would often follow the migratory trails out of state. They ventured throughout the Southwest and even beyond, on occasion. In the spring, they would chop cotton at home. In the summer, they journeyed to California's Central Valley, where there was an abundance of jobs, especially on the Westside, where agricultural empires were being developed by such powerful land barons as Russell Giffen in Mendota (Fresno County) and J. G. Boswell in Corcoran (Kings County).[24] The family might move north in time for the berry harvest in Oregon's Willamette Valley. The beet fields of northern Colorado were another option. Some of their friends preferred midwestern destinations. Yet autumn found the family back home in Texas picking cotton, when other migrants were doing the same in California, or working in the sugar beet harvest in the Great Lakes region or the nearby Red River Valley of Minnesota, or picking potatoes in southern Idaho. Eventually, after World War II, the Martínezes tended to gravitate more toward the Golden State, where wages were significantly higher than in Texas, before finally settling down in one of California's agricultural valleys in the 1950s.

Life for Mexican migratory laborers like José Martínez and his family in the years before the Depression was not easy. What they contributed to the American economy was much more than they received in return. Year in and year out, they toiled in the fields under the most trying of circumstances. They did monotonous stoop labor, often under adverse climatic conditions. Given the seasonal nature of the jobs, they were forced to travel vast distances and to endure frequent periods of unemployment. When they found jobs, hours were long, especially when working with perishable crops, and wages were pitiful, the lowest of any job category in the United States. There was no overtime pay nor health benefits.

The living conditions of migrant workers were equally wretched. They typically lived in isolated labor camps, some of them populated by thousands of temporary residents. In the 1920s, they were generally housed in tents or one-room shacks. Sanitation was usually poor. Living next to the fields where they worked, they endured not only the stench of rotting crops, but also invasions of insects and rodents attracted by the agricultural waste. Disease was rampant, especially tuberculosis, which reached endemic proportions prior to World War II; and health care was sadly deficient. The great influenza epidemic of 1918 took a horrible toll in Mexicano colonias, as did the 1924 outbreak of the plague in Los Angeles. Education for the children was nearly impossible under these woeful conditions, so there was little social mobility from one generation to the next. For decades thousands of migrant laborers toiled in anonymity under conditions that would be difficult for outsiders to imagine. Happily in the last few years a whole series of autobiographies by former campesinos have appeared, giving farmworkers a voice at long last.[25]

There were exceptions to this cycle of poverty. One of them was Anthony Quinn (1915–2001), the eminent actor, who was brought to the United States via El Paso as an infant of four months by his mother on 2 August 1915. Manuela Oaxaca Quinn herself appears to have been an extraordinary person, according to her son's autobiography, *The Original Sin* (1972), a valuable memoir chronicling a vital aspect of the Mexican experience. Born in the state of Chihuahua in dire poverty, Manuela fell in love with a young man from a moderately well-to-do family, Francisco Quinn, son of an Irish immigrant and a Mexican mother. She joined him as a *soldadera* (a woman soldier) when he went off to fight in the Revolution as an officer under Pancho Villa.[26] After Manuela became pregnant by Francisco, he, under pressure from his widowed mother, who looked down on Manuela for her humble Indian origins, refused to see the young woman. Leaving her in the city of Chihuahua, he went off to Texas when the Revolution took a turn for the worse. Confused and left utterly destitute with her infant son, Manuela began her search for the father of her child. After experiencing many hardships, she found him in El Paso. Impressed by her devotion and persistence, Francisco agreed to accept Manuela as his wife; in time, he even grew to love her.

During the next few years, the family of five, which now included Anthony's younger sister as well as his grandmother, traveled throughout the Southwest as

Francisco eked out a living performing a variety of backbreaking jobs. Manuela's life was not much easier than it had been in Chihuahua, but she rarely complained as the family moved from one railroad or mining camp to another. Not only did she perform her duties as wife and mother but, like most lower-class Mexican women in her position, she was forced to work outside of the home to make ends meet. On one occasion, she even toiled alongside her husband repairing railroad tracks in southern California! Anthony Quinn recalls his mother telling him: "I suppose nowadays all this sounds unbelievable. It might even sound strange, a young girl working on the railroad, but we Mexican women were used to it. We fought beside our men and found it only normal to work beside them. I loved working hard beside Francisco. When we came home at night we were both tired and hot. We understood each other's pains. That is almost more important than sharing each other's happiness."[27]

When her husband died at the age of twenty-nine in an accident, Manuela was left in East Los Angeles with two young children and a mother-in-law to support. She made it through this trying period by working the night shift at a Goodyear Rubber plant. In many ways, Manuela cuts a heroic figure, and there can be no doubt, even making allowances for a son's natural partiality, that she was an usually strong individual. But she was hardly unique; during these tumultuous times, thousands and thousands of Mexicanas were forced to make extraordinary and incredible sacrifices.

THE CONTRATISTA

Anti-Mexican sentiment was pronounced wherever Mexicanos went, a bitter legacy from the nineteenth century. The most extreme animosity occurred in Texas, where the memory of the Alamo combined with the exaggerated racial attitudes of Southerners to make life especially difficult for the immigrant. However, living in their own isolated communities and segregated from whites in the work force, most Mexicanos had few contacts with Anglos during the 1920s. In many parts of the Southwest, they remained an "invisible minority" until well after World War II. The discrimination they suffered was inflicted institutionally by large mining, railroad, and agricultural concerns rather than directly by individual citizens. As was true of practically all immigrants, the capitalist economy took advantage of Mexicans, who—despite well-intentioned efforts by Chicano scholars to stress their "agency," their ability to shape their situation—were largely at the mercy of their employers. Despised as Mexicans, the immigrants, as Chicano scholars have shown, increasingly developed a sense of ethnic nationalism; that is, they came to identify with Mexico rather than their native villages.[28]

Not all the injustice came at the hands of the dominant society. Like other newcomers to the United States, Mexicans often discovered that the most shameful exploitation came from within their own ethnic communities. This should not be too surprising since the massive influx of new immigrants predictably created tension with established Mexican American communities. Problems were most severe in New Mexico and southern Colorado, where the native Spanish-speaking population, anxious to be accepted as "Americans" and afraid to be confused with recently arrived *cholos* (lower-class immigrants), came to identify themselves as "Spanish" or "Spanish Americans" in the years preceding the Great War. This defensive mindset, predicated on the false notion that the Indian heritage was negligible in their own development, was pervasive among Hispanos until the 1960s, and continues to have some currency even today. Generally, however, this haughty attitude did not translate into major conflict between old-timers and newcomers given the relative absence of labor-intensive agriculture in New Mexico.

Undoubtedly, the worst abuse from within the ethnic community emanated from *contratistas*. Sometimes immigrants themselves, though more often native-born, these labor contractors served as intermediaries between Mexican laborers and their employers. They were indispensable to the workers since they had access to the one thing the newcomers needed most—jobs.

Some contratistas felt a genuine concern for the welfare of their workers—as was true, too, of some farmers—and it cannot be denied that at times real bonds of affection were forged between the worker and his patrón. But the extreme vulnerability of the immigrants and the considerable power they wielded over the workers invited exploitation, a temptation few contratistas were able to resist. The greatest opportunities for abuse occurred in agriculture, where the transient work force made it especially susceptible to coercion. The contratista, who was generally given a lump sum of money by the grower to have his crop harvested, tried to pay his workers as little as possible to increase his own profits. One way this might be done was by paying workers an hourly wage during the height of a season, when the harvest was plentiful, then switching to piecemeal wages, paid by the unit, when *la pisca* (the picking) thinned out. In this way, the cards were stacked against the unfortunate workers. Yet what was to prevent them from abandoning the fields before the entire crop was in? It was not unusual in this case for the contratista to withhold a percentage of the wage until the last day of the picking season to ensure that harvesters would stay to the end. This money, popularly called *los bonos,* though it was hardly a "bonus" at all, reverted to the contratista if workers failed to meet their obligations, whether it was their fault or not.

There were many other ways of taking advantage of the powerless. For example, a cotton contractor, when weighing a sack of cotton, might claim a weight much lower than that registered on the scale. Since it was considered bad form to check the scale, which always faced the contractor, the hapless workers might not realize that they had been bilked. An incredulous and unusually bold worker who would question the accuracy of the reading would simply be told that, yes, his registered weight had been higher, but a few pounds had been deducted to compensate for cotton that was too wet or a canvas sack that was heavier than it should have been. Protests were futile; the contractor invariably had the final say. Tampering with scales was not uncommon. There were extreme cases, too, when a contratista would simply abscond to Mexico with the entire payroll.

There were more subtle means by which a contratista could turn a nice profit. Most of the workers were *solos,* married men traveling alone, or *solteros,* bachelors, so *borde,* room and board, was often provided. Since the labor contractor had a monopoly on the food concession in the fields, he could charge as much as he pleased, often an exorbitant rate. He might also pay his workers in scrip, which could be redeemed only at *his* store. Many contractors were entrepreneurs who owned businesses, especially *cantinas* (bars). In addition, when the contratista did favors for his workers, altruism was rarely the dominant motive. He would bail a worker out of jail, write a letter for him to his relatives in Mexico, drive him from the labor camp to attend Mass on Sundays—all for a price.

RURAL LIFE

The exploitation Mexican immigrants suffered in industry and agriculture was galling, but the options for these workers were extremely limited. Unable to speak English and ignorant of their legal rights, most were forced to endure indignities in silence. Those who protested found themselves blackballed or, worse still, expelled from the country as illegal aliens, a lesson others took to heart. Moreover, as Mario T. García has pointed out, rather than acknowledging their position at the bottom of the socioeconomic ladder in the Southwest, this first generation of immigrants tended to compare their present status with that which they had occupied in the Old Country, a perspective which softened the sting of injustice. It must be remembered that the overwhelming majority of immigrants came believing that they would soon return to Mexico, with plenty of money, so they felt that the sacrifices they were asked to make would not be more than they could bear. This resignation was most pronounced among laborers in the countryside.

The historian Gilbert G. González has noted that Chicano colleagues in the discipline tend to display an urban bias in their research, often neglecting the rural environment that typified the lives of their forebears.[29] Certainly this is true of studies done on the period of the Great Migration. For example, it is sometimes pointed out that the 1930 census indicated that 50.8 percent of immigrant and native-born Mexicans lived in urban areas. Yet this statistic is extremely misleading. Mexicanos living in the countryside, many of them migratory, were prone to be undercounted. Moreover, there is an enormous difference in the lifestyle of a

Mexicano living in Los Angeles in the 1920s and one living in a small town of three thousand inhabitants in the Lower Rio Grande. But both individuals would be considered urban dwellers by the U.S. Census Bureau in 1930 because both communities had populations exceeding twenty-five hundred.

Unquestionably, most Mexicanos in the United States lived in rural settings as late as the 1920s. To be sure, there were those who resided in true urban communities, places like Albuquerque, El Paso, San Antonio, Los Angeles, and Chicago. But this was not true of miners, railroad workers, or the majority of agricultural workers, especially migratory farm laborers. In fact, some Mexicanos lived in labor camps on a permanent basis. For example, workers in the citrus industry of southern California, as Professor González shows, worked year-round and were expected to maintain permanent residence near the orange and lemon groves. However, not even migrant workers, like José Martínez, could be expected to spend their entire existence living exclusively in labor camps. On the eve of the Depression, the majority of Mexicans resided in small country towns at least part of the year. These rural communities displayed remarkable diversity, depending mainly on the kind of economic function they served, but they could hardly be called "urban."

To achieve an accurate picture of what life was like for Mexicanos between 1900 and 1930, it should be noted that the population was highly transient. Farm and railroad laborers had seasonal jobs, and it was not unusual during this time, a point emphasized by Devra Weber, for a person to work in agriculture, mining, and railroad maintenance, all within a span of a few months, which of course necessitated considerable mobility.[30] Even urban dwellers reflected this impermanence; many workers residing in major urban areas, notably the suburbs of Los Angeles, would follow the crops seasonally.

While most Mexicanos continued to live in rural environments and consequently out of the American mainstream, they were not completely isolated from outside influences. To be sure, they rarely interacted with Anglos. Still, despite segregationist policies, they sometimes worked alongside European immigrants in the mines and railroads in the Southwest; and in Chicago and other cities outside of the Borderlands, in other industries as well. They were familiar with African Americans, not only in the cotton fields of Texas, but also in California, where blacks worked in the Imperial Valley as early as the 1910s. Mexicanos also came into intimate contact with Asians, who worked in the fields as wage earners or small farmers.

A striking example of this intimacy occurred in the Imperial Valley. Immigrants from the Punjab—Hindus, Moslems, and especially Sikhs—arrived on the Pacific Coast shortly before the turn of the century. Some sixty-eight hundred entered the United States between 1899 and 1914. They suffered intense discrimination; conceding that Indian immigrants were Caucasian, the Supreme Court in

1923 nonetheless ruled that they were not white, making them ineligible for U.S. citizenship. Most of them settled in the agricultural valleys of California, where the men—the immigration was almost exclusively male—often married Mexican women. The phenomenon occurred first and remained most pronounced in El Centro and the surrounding area, where 93 percent of "Hindu" marriages before 1949 were with Mexicanas. As Karen Isaksen Leonard has discovered, "Family life and the development of a Punjabi-Mexican community began and flourished best in the Imperial Valley, with settlement in other regions of California and the western states fanning out from there."[31] Interestingly, while children of these mixed marriages were more acutely impacted by their Mexican rather than their Indian heritage, they tended to identify with the latter as they grew older, so entrenched were anti-Mexican feelings in the community at large.

MEXICANOS BEYOND THE SOUTHWEST

Several Chicano scholars, notably Juan R. García, Louise Año Nuevo de Kerr, Zaragoza Vargas, and Dennis (Dionicio) Nodín Valdés, have indicated that even during the period of the Great Migration, a significant percentage of the Mexican population ventured beyond the confines of the old Spanish Borderlands. Their history has recently been incorporated into the larger American mosaic. While some went directly to urban centers, where they worked in industry, most were migratory farm laborers.

The initial movement of Mexican-origin agricultural workers out of the Southwest occurred in the South Platte River Valley at the turn of the century. Stimulated by the 1897 Dingley Tariff, which imposed heavy taxes on imported sugar, the culture of sugar beets spread rapidly throughout the United States at this time, and northeastern Colorado became one of the leading producers. Workers from the south flocked to the newly planted fields. Some of these daring newcomers were Hispanos from New Mexico and the San Luis Valley in southern Colorado; others were Mexican immigrants, many of them arriving from western and southern Texas, which served as vital staging areas for the industry. Entire families were contracted to do the labor-intensive job of harvesting sugar beets by large agribusiness concerns, especially the Great Western Sugar Company.[32] By the 1920s, immigrant and U.S.-born Mexicans had effectively displaced the old workforce, consisting mostly of Belgians, German-Russians, and Japanese.

By this time, too, many *betabeleros* (Mexicano sugar beet workers) had begun to move into other Rocky Mountain states, notably Utah and Idaho, as well as into the North Platte Valley of western Nebraska. Most of these migrants returned to homes in the Southwest seasonally, but eventually some of them settled in the intermontane plateaus, which now became bases for other migratory circuits.

The chief thrust, according to the Chicano historian Erasmo Gamboa, was westward into the Pacific Northwest. In the twenties, the first Mexicano families entered the Yakima Valley of eastern Washington from the mountain states. During the following decade, they were joined by a second wave, workers from South Texas, mainly from the area around Edinburg. By World War II, Mexican rural communities were well established in the Pacific Northwest, notably in the Yakima and Willamette valleys.

Eventually, Mexicanos made their way as far north as Alaska. By the mid-1990s, an estimated twenty thousand Mexicanos would settle in Juneau, Fairbanks, and other mainland cities, working mostly in hotels and restaurants; and a sizable colonia was to be found on Kodiak Island, working in salmon canneries. Unfortunately, this immigration into the Far North has thus far attracted little scholarly interest.

The other major migration northward occurred east of the Rockies, across the Great Plains and into the Great Lakes region.[33] The primary crop attracting Mexicano labor to the Midwest was, once again, sugar beets. Betabeleros first entered the region in meaningful numbers during World War I, lured by higher wages than they could earn in the Borderlands. By 1927, some fifty-eight thousand Mexicanos toiled in the sugar beet farmlands extending from Colorado to Ohio. At this time they represented more than three-quarters of the beet workers in Michigan, Ohio, Indiana, Minnesota, Iowa, and the Dakotas.

The first Mexicano migrants were foreign-born, but by the twenties, they were gradually replaced by the native-born. In either case, they came primarily from Texas, where they were heavily recruited by agents of the sugar industry. The main enlistment center was San Antonio, which had the largest Mexicano population in the country before the mid-1920s. Other major recruitment sites included El Paso, Fort Worth, and even Dallas, which began to see the appearance of barrios as early as the 1870s and 1880s. As in other parts of the country, migrants quickly established networks to help one another. "Mexican migration to the Midwest," according to Zaragoza Vargas, "was not haphazard; each sequence of the journey was well planned by the migrants and involved consultation with family members or friends and especially with those who had already made the extended trip north."[34] During the Depression, Tejano penetration of the northern beet industry would be helped by the formation of an American Federation of Labor–sanctioned agricultural workers' union among European beet workers in the upper Midwest. The union threatened to raise wages, prompting growers to recruit more heavily in the Lone Star State.

By the Depression, many midwestern cities, notably Detroit and Chicago, had witnessed the growth of large Mexicano barrios, as field workers increasingly chose to settle down closer to the farms employing them or abandoned agricultural work altogether. Northern migration was only just beginning. By 1930, the estimated three hundred colonias of the Midwest contained less than 6 percent of the Mexican-origin population in the United States, more than three-quarters of them from Mexico's central plateau. During this early period, according to the historian Juan R. García, in contrast to the Southwest, men vastly outnumbered women in these northern enclaves.[35]

MEXICAN AND EUROPEAN IMMIGRATION: A COMPARISON

The massive influx of Mexicans into the United States which came to an end during the Depression has often been compared to the European immigration which ended abruptly about a decade earlier, when the Golden Door swung shut. In point of fact, the immigrant experience of Mexicans in 1900–1930, especially in the Midwest, was quite similar, in many ways, to that of Europeans entering the country from about the mid-nineteenth century to the First World War, a view best articulated by John Bodnar.[36] The contratista, for example, had his counterpart in the Italian *padrone* and the Irish politician. All were liaisons with the host society. Immigrants, whatever their origin, shared common motives for emigrating, notably the disruption of village economies caused by encroaching capitalism, and difficulties in adjusting to American society. Both relied on the same kinds of institutions as coping mechanisms, such as mutual benefit societies and, above all else, the family. The differences between Mexicans and the various European ethnic groups, however, were more striking and ultimately of greater consequence.

One major difference was the mindset of the two groups. The overwhelming majority of Europeans entering the United States came expecting to become permanent residents or quickly adopted that orientation. Separated by vast distances from their homelands, and a strenuous ocean voyage, they tended to burn their bridges psychologically once they left their native villages. It is true that many newcomers grew disillusioned and ultimately returned to their homelands. According to the immigration scholar Walter Nugent, some 40 percent of Europeans who migrated to Argentina, Brazil, Canada, and the United States in the half-century before World War I eventually repatriated.[37] Still, these "birds of passage" were a distinct minority within every ethnic group; the decided majority chose to make America their home.

In contrast, most Mexicans did not sever their emotional ties with the Old Country. Close family bonds and other sentimental reasons, as well as the ill-treatment many of them experienced in an alien environment, kept the attachment strong. Moreover, the proximity of Mexico made it relatively easy to return home. And because legal restrictions aimed at Mexicans were few in number and badly enforced, a unique pattern of immigration developed, as Emilio Zamora has observed, with Mexicans crossing back and forth between the two countries on a regular basis, sometimes seasonally.[38]

Geography is pivotal as well in another way: it dictated, to a large extent, the kind of jobs immigrants would perform. Europeans landed in the East. Early arrivals, like the Germans, were able to penetrate into the Midwest; but most remained in the mushrooming eastern cities, where they were employed in the rapidly expanding industrial job market. While wages were low and the work monotonous, these "urban villagers" were able to establish roots, mainly in ghettos, permitting their children to gain an education. Conditions would soon improve because the first effective labor unions appeared in industrial centers, especially in the Northeast. On the other hand, Mexicans entering the Southwest found employment opportunities largely restricted to mining, railroad maintenance and repair, and agriculture: occupations that required hard physical labor and oftentimes a migratory existence, which made gaining an education difficult. Working conditions improved very slowly, and social mobility was limited within these established occupational categories.[39] What little progress Mexicanos made was wiped out by the onset of the Great Depression.

While many European peasants managed to purchase land as they entered the American heartland, Mexicans were unable to acquire a land base, a salient characteristic, according to the labor historian Ernesto Galarza:

> As a small farmer, as a husbandman, as a yeoman, the Mexican failed. Even though he was unquestionably a dedicated and industrious worker of the land, he acquired none of it for his own in the United States. And this was not because of a prejudice in American society working notoriously and exclusively against him. It was because even small-family farming—the only kind accessible to the landworking Mexican—was beyond his means, and because family farming was proving no competitor for agribusiness.[40]

The nature of entry into the United States was very different for the two groups. Europeans were overwhelmingly legal immigrants. They arrived at government reception centers—the most famous being Ellis Island in New York Harbor, established in 1892, which saw 12 million immigrants pass through its waiting rooms—and after a lengthy certification process, only those eligible for entry were admitted. Mexican immigration was substantially unregulated. Most immigrants from the south entered the country without their papers. Devra Weber estimates the figure to be as high as 80 percent among migrant workers at this time. This irregular status, except for the 1921–1922 economic slump, was generally not a problem during the 1920s, a decade when severe labor shortages required the importation of cheap Mexican labor. Beginning in 1929, however, when federal legislation made it a felony to enter the United States illegally, their pattern of irregular entry created many difficulties for *indocumentados* (unauthorized immigrants).

Race was an obvious difference: Europeans were white and Mexicans, in general, were not.[11] This is extremely significant. Although most European immigrants after the 1840s suffered intense and widespread discrimination, especially those who represented religious traditions other than the Protestantism of mainstream Anglo society, their skin color was rarely a factor, notwithstanding sporadic attempts made by nativists to label the Irish and Italians *racial* minorities. The same cannot be said of Mexicans. Those who immigrated to the United States were peasants, for the most part, and therefore predominantly mestizo and Indian, a fact that nativist organizations never tired of broadcasting. The nonwhite status of Mexicans would not have been a problem if U.S. society were color blind; but this was, and remains, far from the truth. From the very birth of this nation, beginning with our Founding Fathers, Americans have been absorbed with race, which has always been "at the very center of America's social and political history."[42] In fact, as critics of the dominant Eurocentric perspective argue, out and out racism, rather than simply a disinterested fascination with race, has been characteristic of this history. More pronounced at certain times than at others, it was particularly virulent during the 1920s, when the belief that whites were superior to nonwhites was so pervasive that even some people of color came to accept it. Racism not only provided a justification for the exploitation of Mexicans, and other racial minorities, but also accounted for much of the ill-treatment they received. In this respect, the plight of Mexicans was surely worse than that of their European counterparts.

The strength of anti-Mexican sentiment among Americans had much to do, too, with the unique relationship that had been forged historically between the United States and Mexico. Having enticed Mexico into a major war through a Machiavellian policy and having forcefully divested Mexicans of half their territory, Americans found justification for their aggression by blaming the victims. Moreover, the economic penetration of American capitalism into Mexico during the Porfiriato, based as it was on the exploitation of cheap native labor, fortified the nearly universal belief that Mexicans were meant to be subservient to whites. Unlike their European counterparts, Mexicans entering the United States found themselves marginalized from the very outset.

The many differences between European and Mexican immigration into this country, as well as the fact that the major waves of Europeans came several decades before the Great Migration, help to explain the notable discrepancy between the two groups today in terms of social, economic, and political power. While the Irish, Italians, and Jews have been absorbed into the middle class, Mexicanos, possibly as many as three-quarters of them, continue to be predominantly working-class people.

This apparent lack of socioeconomic progress has been especially frustrating to Chicano intellectuals who predicted some years ago, based on favorable demographic trends, that the 1980s would be the Decade of the Hispanic. This golden age never materialized. The standard explanation given by most Chicano historians for this failure to fulfill their potential is that Anglos have consciously and callously kept Mexicanos in a state of subservience.[43] Although overstated, there is something to be said for this point of view. Certainly, the policies of the Republican administrations of Ronald Reagan and both Bushes go a long way in explaining the depressed status of Mexicanos and other working-class people today. Nor should the needs of corporate capitalism be minimized as factors contributing to racial and other kinds of oppression. But there is a more basic problem, namely, the gigantic influx of Mexican immigrants into the United States at present. As long as this immigration continues on the same massive scale—and given Mexico's burgeoning population and the continuing affluence of the United States, there is every indication it will—the Mexicano community in this country will continue to occupy a position at the lower end of the American socioeconomic spectrum.[44]

Still, as is often the case, there is a silver lining. While most Mexican Americans will make modest gains or no gains at all in the near future, some Mexican immigrants will raise their standard of living substantially, as will some middle-class elements. Moreover, from a broader perspective, America can only benefit from the large numbers of people entering the country. After all, while U.S. citizens may give lip service to the work ethic, it is the immigrants who are prepared to make the sacrifices, a point of view sustained by immigration experts Alejandro Portes and Rubén G. Rumbaut: "Above all, immigrant laborers provide a source of highly motivated, hardworking men and women whose energies expand the human resources of the nation."[45] As was true during the Great Migration, Mexican immigrants will continue to be indispensable in many sectors of the American economy.

THE
DEPRESSION
1930–1940

6

The 1930s was a decade of economic hardship for the United States. All segments of the American population suffered from the shrinking job market. Mexicanos were no exception. Material deprivation was only part of the story. Prior to this decade, anti-Mexican sentiment had been on the rise, but in many parts of the country "the Mexican Problem" was hardly a major issue. With the onset of the Depression, however, Mexicanos became a popular scapegoat. By now many Mexicanos had begun to move into towns and cities; no longer were they an invisible minority. Even their traditional defenders, the large mining, railroad, and agribusiness interests of the Southwest, were reticent to speak out on their behalf. Employers had access to a huge reservoir of cheap domestic labor thanks to the influx of Dust Bowl immigrants; Mexicano workers were now expendable.

By the thirties, though, many Mexicanos were beginning to view "los Yu-naites Estaites," as they called it, as their home. Indeed, many were now citizens by right of birth. Their means of resistance were limited. Not surprisingly, then, many Mexicanos joined the struggling labor movement, now radicalized by the desperate conditions of the working masses. In the end, the unions were forced to their knees by their powerful enemies. For Mexicanos, the defeat was especially vexing. By the mid-1930s, thousands repatriated to Mexico. Some did so voluntarily, others were forced to leave. The legacy of this humiliation is still felt in Mexicano communities to this day.

THE DEPRESSION

The Great Depression is generally dated from the collapse of the New York stock exchange in October 1929; but the roots of the economic slump, the most catastrophic in history, can be traced back to the Great War itself. The global clash had witnessed a vast increase in American economic production, since the United States had to supply its allies, their dwindling resources practically exhausted, as well as meet its own escalating needs. American factories continued to produce at a fantastic rate even after the devastating conflict. However, an agrarian crisis in the twenties severely hampered the buying power of farmers, leading to overproduction. Most Americans hardly realized the difficulties that beset the farming community at the time; they were too busy enjoying life during the Jazz Age.

Unfortunately, much of the affluence which seemed to characterize the period was based on credit, a form of gambling. During the 1920s, Americans discovered the luxury of buying on the time plan, and they took advantage of their opportunities with a vengeance. As businesses began to fold and workers lost their jobs, they were unable to meet their financial obligations. Many debtors lost everything, including their homes. By 1932, the nadir of the slump, about a quarter of the American work force was jobless, and many more were only marginally employed. By this time, world production had been cut in half. Investments in industry practically ceased, falling from ten billion dollars in 1929 to one billion dollars in 1932. The most heavily industrialized countries were the most vulnerable. Germany and the United States were hit the hardest.

Less industrialized than other sections of the United States, the Southwest, where the great majority of Mexicanos resided, appeared better able to weather economic fluctuations. Both mining and railroads, however, were forced to make major cuts, and southwestern farmers, whose operations were already heavily mechanized and who sold their products nationwide, were not much better off.

The collapse of the economy left Mexicanos in the Southwest and other sections of the country in dire straits. Even those retaining jobs found that wages were barely enough to make ends meet. Many Anglo Americans who had previously shunned the strenuous and low-paying jobs Mexicanos were accustomed to now found themselves with no alternatives but to enter these fields. Wages inevitably plummeted as competition for jobs increased.

URBANIZATION

One of the most momentous consequences of economic dislocation for Mexicano *obreros* (workers) was that many were forced from the countryside into the cities. While food was more difficult to access there, urban centers offered compensating advantages. Work remained scarce, but there was a wider array of opportunities, and people could make ends meet by going from one subsistence job to another. The welfare programs that were established as part of President Roosevelt's New Deal were mostly city-based. Of course, large numbers of Mexicanos were ineligible for welfare either because they were indocumentados or because they failed to meet residency requirements; and, in point of fact, the government was not very sympathetic to their plight. Nonetheless, welfare services helped many Mexicano families survive, especially in the winter, when rural jobs tended to vanish.

The Depression was only a catalyst, however; urbanization among Mexicanos antedates the 1930s by many decades. Indeed, some Mexicans were to be found in an urban environment from the time of the Treaty of Guadalupe Hidalgo. Reacting to a popular misconception that Mexicanos became city dwellers only after World War II, Chicano historians such as Richard Griswold del Castillo and Albert Camarillo have pointed out in recent years that the Southwest contained sizable urban populations by 1900. In truth, the number of Mexicanos living in urban barrios was rather modest at that time. However, remarkable demographic changes begin to occur shortly after the turn of the century. The number and size of barrios increased dramatically during World War I, thanks to immigration from Mexico, as well as the influx of rural laborers seeking to improve their lives in the expanding urban-industrial sector occasioned by the war itself. True urbanization among Mexicanos began at this time. During the 1920s, the movement accelerated at a rapid pace, particularly in the Midwest, and continued into the following decade.

Perhaps the Mexicanos most impacted by the Depression were the Hispanos of northern New Mexico and southern Colorado. During the course of the early twentieth century, as their land base contracted, villagers in this impoverished area found themselves fighting to survive. The men were forced to make ends meet by turning to wage labor, which meant seasonal migrations into the sugar beet and mining industries of Colorado. The decline of these enterprises during the Depression, though, cut off these vital sources of revenue, causing a major crisis. Unable to pay taxes and conservation district assessments, some eight thousand Hispanos lost their farms and ranches. The collapse of the regional economy in the early 1930s, well documented by the historian Sarah Deutsch, inevitably forced many families to abandon village life for the cities.[1] In Denver, for example, the Mexicano population tripled during the troubled decade.

While the transformation of traditional Mexican culture was not as dramatic in other parts of the Southwest, urbanization was a region-wide phenomenon. The main destinations of city-bound immigrants continued to be the major barrios created in the previous century. By 1940, the largest of these were found in the West Side of San Antonio, El Paso's Chihuahuita in the southern part of the city, and, most of all, in Los Angeles, particularly east of the downtown area.

The City of Angels illustrates the dynamics of the urbanization experience for Mexicanos better than anywhere else, and today it contains the largest Spanish-speaking population in the United States. Special attention has been given to the evolution of *Angeleños* by many Chicano historians. Founded in 1781, Los Angeles remained a Mexican pueblo until the giant land boom of the 1880s transformed it into a flourishing Anglo metropolis. By the turn of the century, the Mexicano population, a small minority, was mainly confined to the area slightly west of the Los Angeles River, centered on the old plaza. The site of the original pueblo, the plaza was now the city's central business district. After about 1910, "Sonoratown," as it was known to outsiders, was rapidly transformed into a modern commercial center. As real estate prices skyrocketed, Mexicanos fanned out in several directions, aided by the expansion of the interurban railway system, creating a host of new barrios, which grew along with the city; the population of Los Angeles mushroomed from about one hundred thousand in 1900 to over a million in 1930. The main thrust from the city center went east, to and beyond the river. By the outbreak of the war, Mexicanos had entered the Belvedere-Maravilla area; and in the 1920s, they were in the process of penetrating neighboring Boyle Heights, lured by economic opportunities created by the construction of factories nearby. By 1930, more Mexicanos resided in East Los Angeles, the collective name for the eastern barrios, than in the historic central plaza barrio. The population grew not only because of natural increase but also because the barrios there came to serve as a magnet for the migratory farm labor force from throughout southern California. Indeed, Los Angeles itself, as the historian Douglas Monroy reminds us, "continued as an agricultural city at least until World War II, in spite of its rapid urbanization and industrialization."[2] In addition, some residents arrived directly from Mexico, which was also the case in a number of other southwestern cities, notably San Antonio and El Paso, which served as distribution centers for Mexicano labor to the north. By 1930, Los Angeles, with 97,116 Mexicanos living within its city limits, had the second-largest Mexican population in the world, surpassed only by Mexico City itself.

The way of life in the Mexicano barrios of East Los Angeles and other parts of the city in the 1930s was not much different than in other barrios scattered across the Southwest. Life was extremely difficult during the Depression; a sense of stultifying poverty was the first and most vivid impression made on the visitor. In fact, social and economic conditions were wretched even before, as the Mexican Fact-Finding Committee commissioned by Governor C. C. Young, which focused on Los Angeles County, made clear in its oft-quoted 1930 report. The Depression accentuated all the problems. Housing was dilapidated and overcrowded. Few residents owned homes, though Mexicanos in Los Angeles were better off in this regard than in most other places. Sanitation was deficient, not much better than in underdeveloped Mexico itself. Other woes included seasonal employment at low wages and a rudimentary education for the children, usually in segregated schools. The administration of justice left much to be desired. "Throughout the 1930s," notes California state historian Kevin Starr, "the LAPD and the sheriff's deputies made war on young Mexican men in the continuing belief that such young men were by definition criminal in fact and intent. . . . Beatings were frequent, as were frame-ups of Mexican men who talked back or otherwise resisted arrest. A number of young Mexican men were shot dead in the street by trigger-happy officers."[3]

As F. Arturo Rosales has shown, relations between Mexicanos and the police were consistently bad during the interwar period not just in southern California but throughout the country, and they were worst in big cities such as Los Angeles, Phoenix, and Chicago.[4] One of the main reasons mistreatment of people of color was more pronounced in large urban settings was, undoubtedly, because police departments there, especially in the Midwest, tended to be dominated by members of newly arrived European immigrant groups, who not only shared the racial prejudices of mainstream society but were also competing against Mexicanos head to head in the workplace.

Problems abounded in the community, and yet barrio life represented a multitude of positive features, even in the depths of the economic slump, as old-timers looking back on their experiences remembered years later.[5] The barrio offered—and still offers—the kind of security that immigrants and their children could find in no other place. The surroundings were familiar, the reason barrios were often labeled "Little Mexicos" by both friendly and hostile observers. Spanish was the dominant language. It was heard everywhere—at home, in the streets, in businesses, and at church. Much of the social life of the barrio revolved around the Catholic Church, especially for *la gente decente,* the "more respectable elements," though Protestants, including Aimee Semple McPherson, were also beginning to administer to the needs of the community. While women spent a good deal of time in church, men preferred cantinas and pool halls, where drinking and gambling were the most popular pastimes. Cock fights were another masculine passion. Everyone enjoyed fiestas, dances, parades, and picnics in the park.

Movie houses, showing the latest films from Mexico as well as the United States, and touring *carpa* theaters, which also helped to preserve ties with the Old Country, were generally packed.[6] Barrio dwellers were served, too, by Spanish-language radio, which gained a great following. By the early 1930s, folk singer and radio personality Pedro J. González had achieved iconic status among his Mexicano audiences in Los Angeles. Radio programs naturally concentrated on Mexican popular music. The level of popular culture, however, could be surprisingly high, as corridos had to share the air waves with Italian operas, French military marches, and other kinds of classical music, not to mention the poetry of Rubén Darío. Community life was vibrant.

The barrio population was highly transient, even in the more industrialized colonias of the Midwest, as a large number of residents were migratory workers much of the year. This spatial mobility would suggest that the community was certainly not a restrictive environment where inhabitants felt trapped and alienated. Chicano scholars today generally see the barrio in a positive light, challenging the widely held belief that ethnic ghettos are predominantly breeding grounds for crime and poverty. In the words of the Chicano historian Ricardo Romo: "[T]he distorted ghetto image of barrios ignored the fact that the majority of Mexican immigrants, for reasons of language, kinship, and folk customs, chose to live together in barrios. These barrios provided a sense of identity with the homeland and a transition into American society. Thus modern ghettos or barrios are not necessarily homes for losers and sinners."[7]

URBANIZATION IN THE MIDWEST

The most urbanized Mexicano population by the Depression was to be found in the Midwest.[8] It has been suggested that Mexicanos began entering the region almost immediately after 1848.[9] However, given the large number of European immigrants available to meet labor demands there, it is highly unlikely that their numbers were very big. The history of Mexicanos in the Midwest, as previously mentioned, really begins at the turn of the century, when small groups of Mexicano migrants made their appearance in the sugar beet fields which began to proliferate throughout the region. By World War I, Mexicano railroad workers had also arrived in the area following the rails from Texas to Chicago via Dallas, Omaha, and other railroad towns on the plains. The greater metropolitan area of Kansas City, for example, a major railroad center on both sides of the Missouri-Kansas state line, already had a Mexicano population of three thousand by 1914. Since farm labor and railroad work were highly seasonal, both contributed heavily to emerging urbanization.

In the beginning, factory owners found this spontaneous migration satisfactory for their needs. During and immediately after the war, though, labor agents began to actively recruit workers directly from Mexico and Texas and to ship them into the urban industrial centers by rail, so acute was the labor shortage. Not only had wartime industries expanded, but the global conflict and the 1917 Immigration Act had cut off the flow of European immigrants, previously the mainstay of heavy industry in the North. Some Mexicanos were brought in as strikebreakers, most notably during the nationwide steel strike of 1919, which resulted in their recruitment as far east as Bethlehem, Pennsylvania. Mexicanos found employment in the industries with the most urgent need: steel, automobile, cement, and meat-packing plants. Omaha, St. Louis, and Kansas City witnessed the steady growth of colonies during or soon after the war. Such was the case in the industrial cities of the Great Lakes as well. In Detroit, the center of automobile manufacturing, the country's biggest industry, Mexicanos made their appearance in 1918, when the

Ford Motor Company began to recruit them successfully by offering the same wages it paid white workers. Two years later, the Motor City had a Mexicano population of three thousand, with the largest barrio located southwest of the downtown area, close to the factories. In 1923 they built Our Lady of Guadalupe Church, forming the first exclusively Mexicano parish in the Great Lakes region. Other automobile manufacturing centers in Michigan, such as Flint, Pontiac, and Saginaw, also enticed Mexican labor.

The densest concentration occurred, however, in the Chicago metropolitan area, where there were almost thirty thousand Mexicanos, mostly young foreign-born males, on the eve of the Depression. The hub of the nation's railroad network, it was inevitable that the Windy City would attract a significant Spanish-speaking population. Other Mexicanos, however, found work in the packing plants and steel mills of the city and its suburbs. In Chicago proper, already the second largest metropolis in the country, barrios surfaced in three areas. The largest was in the Near West End, near the city center, where Italians were the predominant ethnic group. Among the settlement houses here that catered to Mexicano needs was Jane Addams's Hull House. South Chicago, next to the Indiana border, where Spanish-speaking newcomers lived and worked with Poles, had a smaller though better-integrated Mexicano population. Our Lady of Guadalupe, the city's oldest Spanish-speaking Catholic church, founded in 1928, was located here. The smallest community was in the Packingtown/Back of the Yards district, between the other two colonies, where they got along best with their neighbors, mostly Poles and Irish. Mexicano communities immediately began to expand eastward from the southern part of the city along the southern shores of Lake Michigan (the Calumet) into East Chicago, thirty miles from the Windy City, and nearby Gary, steel centers in northwestern Indiana. By 1930, these two satellite cities and surrounding communities reported the presence of some nine thousand Mexicano residents, with the largest colony located in Gary's southside. Many Mexicanos in the Calumet region worked at the Inland Steel Company in East Chicago's Indiana Harbor, the largest employer of Mexicanos in the Midwest after the Ford Motor Company.

Other Mexicanos lived in medium-sized towns such as Davenport, Iowa; Omaha, Nebraska; Lansing, Michigan; and Toledo, Ohio. By 1930, according to census figures, there were approximately fifty-eight thousand Mexicanos in the Midwest, of which the majority were urban dwellers. Most of the men (53.6 percent) were employed in factories.

Early studies by Chicano scholars such as Valerie Mendoza and Gilbert Cárdenas, following Carey McWilliams, likened the experiences of Mexicanos in the Midwest to those of the European immigrants who had preceded them into the region.[10] Thus, they felt that Mexicanos lived lives there which differed markedly from those of their compatriots living in the border area.

There were, in fact, outstanding differences between the two Mexicano communities. First, midwestern Mexicanos were more heavily urbanized, which means they generally received higher wages and a better education. Second, midwestern Mexicanos, being more urban, were less isolated from outsiders, often living and working with European immigrant populations. Although there was ongoing tension, as both groups competed for the same jobs, even in the worst of times there were some interethnic marriages between Mexicanos and other Catholic populations. Exogamy was certainly more pronounced among midwestern Mexicanos than among their compatriots who settled in other regions. Third, their distance from Mexico made it harder for midwestern Mexicanos to maintain ties with their native roots, which, together with the other differences mentioned, resulted, according to most of the early studies, in a greater degree of assimilation than occurred along the southwestern border region.[11] The use of English, as University of California economist Paul S. Taylor reported in the 1920s, was appreciably higher in the northern cities. Even Dennis Nodín Valdés, the dean of Chicano midwestern historians, has asserted: "Early twentieth-century Chicano/a history in the Midwest has more parallels to European immigration history than in the American Southwest."[12]

More recent studies by Chicano scholars, however, tend to emphasize similarities between the Midwest and the Southwest. While these newer studies recognize the diversity of Mexicano communities in both regions—especially between rural and urban populations—they argue that, generally speaking, the rate of assimilation in both areas was about the same: very modest.

In truth, even contemporary observers noted that the assimilation rate of midwestern Mexicanos lagged behind that of the European immigrants they worked and often lived with. Of course, the bulk of the Europeans preceded the majority of Mexicanos into midwestern cities, but this is only one reason for the disparity. More telling was the level of resistance they faced. Discrimination against Mexicanos ("spicks"), the presence of African Americans notwithstanding, was more intense and widespread than early scholars realized. Other immigrants feared economic competition and felt superior to the dark-skinned newcomers. Moreover, beginning in 1919, as the labor historian Lizabeth Cohen has illustrated in her highly acclaimed study of Chicago workers during the interwar period, factory owners encouraged racial tensions by employing both Mexicanos and African Americans as strikebreakers.[13] The historian Gabriela Arredondo makes a convincing argument that the abuse of Mexicanos was most extreme in the Windy City, and much of it came at the hands of the police department, staffed largely by hostile white immigrants and their children.[14]

Under these extreme conditions, while most Mexicanos were able to acculturate, assimilation proved elusive. In fact, so intense was the hostility that the beleaguered immigrants were forced to withdraw into their ethnic communities, where they made a concerted effort to maintain their cultural traditions, setting up a variety of patriotic, religious, mutualist, and other associations. Of greater consequence, *Mexicanidad* (Mexican nationalism) was embraced and zealously defended in barrios—more so with the immigrants than their children—a mindset that served to further distance them from their neighbors. Ironically, too, this ethnic nationalism came to be more pronounced among these and other Mexicano communities in the United States than it was in Mexico itself—although there, too, especially under President Lázaro Cárdenas (1934–1940), government efforts to instill national pride were beginning to bear fruit.

THE "MEXICAN PROBLEM"

As might be expected, the collapse of the economy in the 1930s exacerbated racial tensions, which augured ill for Mexicanos, both in the Southwest and outside that region. In fact, anti-Mexican sentiments, as the account above indicates, were evident well before the Depression. In the 1920s, during the aftermath of the Great War, nativism was pervasive. Many people felt the need to keep America "pure." The Ku Klux Klan, with a membership of some five million in the mid-1920s, was only the most outspoken of a large assortment of white supremacist organizations, which included the American Legion, the Daughters of the Golden West, and other patriotic groups. Although these animosities mirrored the impoverished conditions among some segments of the American population in the 1920s, nativism may have had more to do with the xenophobia engendered by the war. It was these insecurities which were primarily responsible for the legislation enacted after 1917 restricting European immigration.

Nativist fears fed the growing perception of Mexicanos as a problem in the 1920s, a concern intensified by their appearance in cities. The "Mexican Problem" was a popular topic in the national press throughout the interwar period. Spearheading this anti-immigrant campaign was the widely read *Saturday Evening Post*. Madison Grant was the most strident of the many critics who called for legal restrictions on the "mongrel" Mexicans. Although statistical evidence was rarely presented, the "Mexican element" was accused of increasing community crime rates, lowering educational standards, and creating slums.

These negative perceptions, as Arnoldo De León and many other Chicano scholars have documented, began as soon as Anglo newcomers came into contact with Hispanic residents of North America in the early nineteenth century. Incorporated into the powerful myth of Manifest Destiny, the view that Mexicans were dirty, lazy, and violent gained widespread currency during both the Texas revolt and the Mexican-American War. Yankee success seemed to confirm their worst suspicions of their opponents. The creation of a tourist industry in the Southwest at the turn of the nineteenth century, moreover, encouraged the construction of a fantasy heritage which, as Carey McWilliams argued, elevated the status of the Spanish dons by contrasting them with a lower class of lazy half-breeds, a view of the Mexican masses that became pervasive during the First World War and the years that followed, when destitute Mexican immigrants poured into the country.[15] The rise of truly national media during the Jazz Age ensured that negative stereotypes of the Mexican would gain universal acceptance in mainstream society. Undoubtedly the most powerful media influence was exerted by the fledgling film industry. As Chicano film critics have shown, Hollywood popularized many stereotypes of Mexicans, most of them negative, first and foremost the view of Latinos as "greasers."[16] By the late 1920s, thanks to these stereotypes, Mexicans were widely perceived by nativists as a foreign and unfriendly people who were unassimilable.

There was just enough truth in these nativist arguments to sway public opinion. The naturalization rate of the Mexican, less than 6 percent in 1930, was the lowest of any immigrant group, and problems abounded within the colonias, though detractors rarely mentioned that Mexicanos were more often victims than perpetrators.

Stereotypes of Mexicanos invariably had a racial basis. A classic example is provided by Dr. Roy L. Garis, an economics professor at Vanderbilt University, who saw Mexicanos as "human swine" and described them in this way in 1930:

> Their minds run to nothing higher than animal functions—eat, sleep, and sexual debauchery. In every huddle of Mexican shacks one meets the same idleness, hordes of hungry dogs, and filthy children with faces plastered with flies, disease, lice, human filth, stench, promiscuous fornication, bastardy, lounging, apathetic peons and lazy squaws, beans and dried chili, liquor, general squalor, and envy and hatred of the gringo. These people sleep by day and prowl by night like coyotes, stealing anything they can get their hands on, no matter how useless to them it may be. Nothing left outside is safe unless padlocked or chained down.[17]

The popular aversion to Mexicanos in the racially charged atmosphere of the 1920s was not unique. All ethnic Americans were suspect. The lingering stereotype of the Italian American as a Mafia gangster, for example, has its origin in the interwar period.

The so-called Mexican Problem was both a cause and a consequence of a campaign waged in Washington throughout the 1920s to stem the flow of immigrants from south of the border by the enactment of restrictive legislation. The quota acts of 1921 and 1924 had exempted immigration from the Western Hemisphere, thanks to the efforts of southwestern business interests, who insisted that Mexican labor was vital to their survival. Critics demanded that this exemption be terminated. Nativist groups were the leading supporters of this concerted anti-immigrant campaign, but organized labor was a powerful ally. Though racism played a role, unions generally opposed New World immigration on economic grounds: the new immigrants, it was feared, would depress wages and steal jobs. The leading spokesman for labor in the fight to exclude Mexicans was Samuel Gompers, president until 1924 of the American Federation of Labor.

In Congress, the campaign to restrict Mexican entry was led by Representatives John C. Box (D-Tex.) and Albert Johnson (R-Wash.) and Senator William Harris (D-Ga.), all of whom sponsored bills to curtail immigration during the twenties. Their opponents in Congress agreed that Mexicanos were racially inferior, but they countered with the argument that Mexicano labor was indispensable. In the end, as is usually the case, the economic argument prevailed. However, while the representatives of southwestern corporate interests were ultimately able to defeat the exclusionary bills, popular opinion was so adamant that Congress was forced to pass legislation in 1929 making illegal entry a criminal offense.

REPATRIATION

The restrictionist campaign did not end in the 1920s, but the Depression made additional immigration laws unnecessary: the economic slump choked off immigration from the south. Mexicans, after all, had been attracted to the United States by the prospect of making money, but now jobs were virtually nonexistent. Although it had problems of its own, agrarian Mexico, on the periphery of the world economy, looked far more attractive to its citizens than an industrial United States apparently on the verge of collapse. Moreover, it seemed foolhardy to make the hazardous journey to the north, where anti-Mexican sentiments were pronounced and discrimination was pervasive, when Mexicans could remain in the familiar and secure environment of their native villages, close to friends and relatives. In fact, in the 1930s, many Mexicans living in the United States returned to their homeland.

Altogether, it has been estimated that about one-third of the Mexicano population in the United States left the country during the Depression, though some authorities, according to Lawrence A. Cardoso, believe that the true figure may be closer to half.[18] The most intense period of repatriation occurred in 1929–1935, when, Abraham Hoffman, the leading authority on the subject, estimates, some four hundred thousand Mexicanos were involved.[19] Not all of these repatriations were voluntary. Possibly as many as half of those who left did so against their will. Some of the methods employed to get Mexicans to return home were subtle, some were heavy-handed, and occasionally some were even illegal. County, state, and federal government agencies were all involved. During the course of this hugely popular campaign, civil liberties were violated on a regular basis, as American-born children of immigrants, now U.S. citizens, were often denied the option to stay in the country when their parents were deported. Harassment and discrimination against remaining Mexicanos were also common.[20]

The exodus began in the first months of 1931, when the federal government launched a massive deportation drive centered on southern California. By the end of the year, somewhere between fifty thousand and seventy-five thousand Mexicanos had left the southland for Mexico, most of them intimidated by government scare tactics. During the next few years, Los Angeles would lose roughly one-third of its Mexican-origin residents.

Mexicano communities in the Midwest, however, witnessed the most losses relative to the total population. A 1934 study by Paul S. Taylor found that while only 3.6 percent of Mexican nationals in the United States lived in Indiana, Michigan, and Illinois, this region provided over 10 percent of the *repatriados* (repatriates).[21] By this time, Chicago had lost 30 percent of its Mexicano population, some four thousand people. Detroit was hit as hard, if not harder by the deportations.

The plight of Mexicanos during these tumultuous times was perhaps worst in Texas, where repatriation, heightened racial tensions, and a depressed economy— only intensified by the Agricultural Adjustment Administration policy of eliminating hundreds of thousands of acres from cotton production—forced them out of the state in droves. Although many of the state's Mexicanos, particularly immigrants, headed south of the border, others scattered throughout the United States, a Texan diaspora that paralleled the better-known migration of so-called Okies from the Dust Bowl.

THE DUST BOWL MIGRATION

Between 1929 and 1933, farm income in the United States dropped by two-thirds. Already weakened by the financial reverses of the Depression and threatened by growing mechanization—the tractor, first and foremost—tenant farmers in the lower Great Plains were struck a death blow by Mother Nature in the mid-1930s. Drought conditions, which actually appeared as early as 1931, combined with windstorms, made life in what had once been labeled the Great American Desert precarious at best. A single storm, on 11 May 1934, carried away some three hundred thousand tons of topsoil from the plains states. Thousands of destitute families were forced to abandon their homes, a migration immortalized in the stunning photography of Dorothea Lange, wife of Paul Taylor. Some parts of the Dust Bowl lost up to 40 percent of their population. Eventually, more than a half million people were involved in this exodus. Some moved into the industrial centers of the North, but work was difficult to find there. The number of jobs had shrunk dramatically, perhaps more than in any other part of the country. Moreover, the mass migration of black laborers from the South, initiated during World War I, was well under way, and these northern cities were now witnessing a phenomenal growth of African American communities. Lacking industrial skills, Dust Bowl immigrants were reluctant to compete for jobs in the unfamiliar northern metropolises. The only other alternative was to move west.

Car caravans began in 1935. Entering the Southwest via Texas and New Mexico, some families found jobs and established roots in those states. Others settled down in Arizona. Most, however, perhaps three hundred fifty thousand, continued on to the promised land, California, a trek graphically described by the novelist John Steinbeck and, more recently, the historian James Gregory. A few ventured beyond, into the Pacific Northwest. The agricultural valleys of the Pacific Coast were soon swamped with poor white farmers looking for work. While, as Professor Gregory has shown, almost half of the Okies entering the Golden State settled in Los Angeles or the San Francisco Bay Area, the most popular rural destination proved to be the Great Valley, especially the southern section.[22] Bakersfield and the rest of Kern County grew an astounding 63.6 percent from 1935 to 1940.

The impoverished status of Mexicanos, already extreme, was only worsened by the new arrivals, who often settled down in the very places Spanish-speaking workers had previously dominated—the agricultural valleys. Whereas Anglos had accounted for only 20 percent of the state's migratory labor force in 1929, they represented about 85 percent of the total by 1936. Problems were bound to surface, since, as regional writer Gerald W. Haslem has pointed out, "many Okies were Southerners in their racial attitudes, and some had left their native states rather than do 'nigger work.'"[23] Tensions remained high between the two groups for decades, a situation that was only exacerbated when Okies moved out of the fields to better-paying jobs in packing sheds, canneries, ice plants, and cotton gins, which they then attempted to monopolize, with considerable success.

LABOR STRIFE

The adverse conditions caused by the Depression led to a prolonged period of intense labor unrest in factories and fields throughout the country. "In fact," one astute observer has noted, "for five years, from the middle of 1933 to early 1938, America witnessed a full-scale outbreak of class warfare such as had not been seen for generations."[24] The Southwest was among the bloodiest battlefields. As Emilio Zamora, Rodolfo Acuña, Juan Gómez-Quiñones, and other Chicano labor historians have documented clearly, Mexicanos were active participants in the strikes that characterized the region during this tumultuous period. This activism, though, did not originate during the Depression; as Gómez-Quiñones has shown, obreros had fought to raise wages and improve living conditions from the nineteenth century and even before.[25] The beginning of the twentieth century witnessed accelerated efforts by Mexicanos to improve their economic status. A brief survey of this agitation from 1900 to 1930 will suffice to illustrate an essential Mexicano contribution to American history that continues to be neglected by mainstream historians. Literally hundreds of strikes took place. Only the most well-chronicled episodes will be covered here.

It should be made clear at the outset that Mexicanos have had to struggle to improve their lives without much help from established labor unions. The U.S. labor movement was in its infancy at the turn of the century. Less political and ideological than their European counterparts, the first American unions concentrated on organizing skilled workers. Only after the First World War were half-hearted attempts made to incorporate unskilled workers. Bastions of white supremacy, unions took little interest in organizing African Americans, and even less effort was put into organizing immigrants of color, including Mexicanos. The only exception of any consequence was the Industrial Workers of the World (IWW), a socialist union formed in 1905, but this short-lived association became a casualty of the postwar Red Scare. In the first decades of the twentieth century, unionized labor was dominated by the American Federation of Labor (AFL). A craft union, the AFL was exclusively concerned with skilled workers. This strategy and the racism that was evident among many of its members precluded any serious interest in mobilizing Mexicanos, the great majority of them unskilled. Mexicano workers had to look, instead, to their own associations; in other words, to the mutualistas. Although these organizations were not primarily intended to fight for economic gains when they emerged in the nineteenth century, mutualistas, in the absence of other alternatives early on, came to play a key role in the struggle to improve working conditions.

Some of the worst abuses were to be found in the mining industry of the Southwest, which by the first decade of the twentieth century centered on the copper fields of Arizona, where Mexicanos, the largest of the immigrant groups in the work force, toiled in mines, mills, and smelters under disgraceful conditions. The Western Federation of Miners (WFM), which would affiliate with the AFL in 1911, was the only viable mining union in the region, but its membership was reticent to include Mexicanos and other immigrants. Dissatisfied with their conditions and unable to break into the WFM, Mexicanos began to organize on their own by 1900, when they initiated a strike in Ray, Arizona, near the important mining center at Globe. Three years later, they joined with Italians to plan, lead, and carry out the great strike at the Clifton, Morenci, and Metcalf mines in eastern Arizona.[26] The WFM stood on the sideline, only one of many reasons the strike failed.

After the 1903 strike, the WFM, divided between those who wanted to recruit immigrants and those who opposed, labeled "inclusionists" and "exclusionists," respectively, by the labor historian Phil Mellinger, reluctantly began to organize foreign and Mexicano miners.[27] For their part, Mexican miners were not eager to enroll in the WFM, looking instead to the Partido Liberal Mexicano. Dissension in the ranks of the labor movement and the panic of 1907 ensured that little would be accomplished in the years before the First World War.

In 1914 and 1915, Mexicanos struck again at Ray. While mutualistas were involved, this work stoppage was led by the Comité por Trabajadores (Committee for Workers), a Mexicano grassroots association, though not a mutualista. The July 1915 strike achieved modest success, in part because Anglo miners were willing to play a supporting role, a harbinger of things to come.

In September 1915, an even bigger strike was initiated at Clifton and Morenci. Once again, Spanish-speaking miners took the initiative, though the leadership was approximately half Anglo and half Mexicano. The agitation lasted four months. In the end, miners won meaningful concessions, but the true significance of these strikes is that Anglos and Mexicanos finally began to work together in the WFM, a milestone in the annals of the working-class movement in the mines of the Southwest.

The victory was short-lived. During and after the war, mining operators went on the offensive, a campaign resulting in the infamous Bisbee Deportations in 1917, when more than one thousand strikers were unceremoniously dumped in the middle of the New Mexican desert by vigilantes after an unsuccessful work stoppage in Arizona, and a series of crushing defeats inflicted on the miners in the aftermath of the Red Scare of 1919. During this "time of troubles," however, Mexicanos preserved their greatest gain—they had joined the mainstream of American organized labor.

Labor organization in the railroad industry was also an exceptionally difficult enterprise for Mexicanos prior to the Depression. But unionization was absolutely essential. The problems Mexicanos encountered in railroad maintenance were similar to those in mining camps. The work was hard, dangerous, and ill paid. Moreover, there was a wage differential that worked to their detriment: most Mexicano rail workers were paid about one dollar for a ten-hour day, while Anglos received seventy-five cents more. Housing was equally dismal; Mexicano families were often forced to live in boxcars.

Organizing was more daunting in railroad work than in mining, mainly because the labor force was constantly on the move. Nonetheless, at the turn of the century, by which time Mexicanos had come to dominate railroad construction and maintenance in the Southwest, they began to organize, again without the help of the struggling American union movement. The first noteworthy agitation occurred in Los Angeles in the spring of 1903, when Mexicano tracklayers launched a strike against Henry Huntington's Pacific Electric Railroad. Mexicanos were making less than eighteen cents an hour. They demanded higher wages. Leadership was provided by the Unión Federal Mexicanos (Mexican Federal Union), "probably the first union of Mexican track workers in the United States."[28] In the end, the strike was a complete disaster because Anglo workers refused to back the Mexicanos and because management was successful in recruiting strikebreakers.

Much more research needs to be done by Chicano scholars on Mexicano attempts to organize track workers. Preliminary studies, however, indicate that workers' efforts to form unions and win concessions were no less active here than in other industries. It is equally clear that victory was elusive, given the many obstacles facing labor organizers, on the one hand, and the strength of the railroad industry, judged to be vital to the national interest by both the government and the public, on the other hand.

In spite of the obstacles described previously, a significant field of labor activity by Mexicanos in the first three decades of the twentieth century was in agriculture, mainly because their numbers were so much greater here than in other areas of employment. Moreover, the perishable nature of many crops provided a lever they could use to their advantage, despite the many obstacles facing unionization in the fields. The most persistent efforts occurred in southern Texas and southern California, the two most advanced areas of agricultural production in the Southwest.

Thanks to Emilio Zamora, Chicano historians have recently become aware of the substantial amount of labor activity, as well as other forms of working-class organization, in southern Texas shortly after the turn of the century.[29] As in other regions, this initial organization owed a great deal to the much-neglected mutualistas. However, as Zamora indicates, the impetus also came from left-wing political organizations on both sides of the border, more specifically, the Texas Socialist Party, established in 1903, during the first decade of the twentieth century, on the American side; and the PLM, during the second decade, on the Mexican side. While these working-class associations did not confine their efforts to agricultural organization, they are noteworthy primarily because they represent the first systematic efforts to unionize Mexicano farmworkers in South and Central Texas.

In the Golden State, efforts to create effective working-class unity, with the aim of improving conditions, have long been the subject of historical study. The initial attempt to chronicle this activity goes back to 1939, when Carey McWilliams published *Factories in the Fields*. The first strike in California agriculture where Mexicanos played a crucial role was in Ventura in 1903, when they joined Japanese workers in a futile effort to gain concessions from beet farmers. Strikes continued sporadically for the next three decades, many of them instigated by the IWW, culminating in the Imperial Valley Cantaloupe Strike of 1928. This confrontation was led by La Unión de Trabajadores del Valle Imperial (the Imperial Valley Workers' Union), formed early in that very year, largely through the efforts of mutualistas, although the Mexican consulate also lent a hand. The strike, which began in May, was prompted not only by a desire for better wages but also by the need to curb the worst abuses of the contratista system. Despite adverse public opinion and the threat of deportation, strikers achieved most of their objectives, the first victory ever recorded in the fields of California, according to Kevin Starr.[30]

Given this legacy of labor militancy, it is not surprising that the 1930s saw a resurgence of labor agitation by Mexicano workers. While strikes occurred throughout the Southwest, they centered on California agriculture. It was here that the American Communist Party focused its efforts, targeting the factory farms that dominated the industry; and it was party members, at least at the outset, who were most active in providing leadership. Agitation lasted throughout the decade, but the most turbulent year was 1933, when there were thirty-seven strikes involving some 47,500 workers from the Sacramento Valley in the north to the Imperial Valley in the south. Two clashes, in particular, are noteworthy: the El Monte Berry Strike and the San Joaquin Valley Cotton Pickers' Strike.

El Monte, a small agricultural community in the San Gabriel Valley, near Los Angeles, was characterized by small farms, many of them leased by Japanese farmers, who grew a variety of berries. The labor force was mixed, but Mexicanos were the largest single ethnic group, and it was they who initiated the strike on 1 June 1933. Some five thousand workers were involved before it was all over. Eventually, on 6 July, the strikers won a minor victory, mainly because the targeted farmers were nonwhite and because the Los Angeles Chamber of Commerce, fearful of losing their business, backed the workers. Unfortunately, the picking season was virtually over by the time of the settlement. Moreover, during the strike, a major schism had developed among the workers, which would have far-reaching consequences. Initiated by a small Mexicano union, the strike had quickly been taken over by the Cannery and Agricultural Workers Industrial Union (CAWIU), a member of the Communist Trade Union Unity League (TUUL). Encouraged by the Mexican consul, Alejandro Martínez, Mexicanos soon affiliated with La Confederación de Uniónes de Campesinos y Obreros Mexicanos (CUCOM, the Confederation of Mexican Farmworkers' and Workers' Unions), an ethnic union recently created by leaders of an older mutualista-inspired association. The split in the ranks of the obreros would provide agribusiness in the next few years with the opportunity to employ the tactics of divide and conquer, which they used with enormous success.

The CAWIU instigated most of the labor agitation in 1933, including the Cotton Pickers' Strike in October, "the longest, largest, and most highly publicized of the many strikes" that year.[31] The work stoppage centered on Corcoran, a small community in the heart of the state's expanding cotton kingdom in the southern San Joaquin Valley, and involved some twelve thousand workers, mostly Mexicano. Strikers were immediately put on the defensive as growers, using red-baiting tactics, convinced the local citizenry that social revolution was imminent. As Kevin Starr points out, however, "If a revolution was occurring in the cotton fields of California, it was a revolution from the right, a *putsch* driven by American Legionnaires and deputized vigilantes, railroading DAs and judges and their shamelessly cooperative juries."[32] Racism played a role, as well. Vigilante violence, which took the lives of three strikers, and the cooperation of local police authorities ensured the complete subjugation of the workers, an omen of things to come in the next few years. Government repression of the CAWIU in the mid-1930s and the subsequent arrival of thousands of Okies, newcomers who harbored pronounced anti-unionist sentiments and strong racial prejudices, meant that serious efforts to organize farmworkers were essentially over.

Mexicano field workers did attempt to resurrect the movement in 1937–1938, when another round of strikes broke out in California. Much of this activity was directed by a new nationwide union, the United Cannery, Agricultural, Packing, and Allied Workers of America (UCAPAWA), formed in Denver in July 1937. Less radical than the Communist CAWIU, the UCAPAWA was nevertheless subject to red-baiting. Moreover, it faced formidable adversaries. By now, agribusiness, fortified by a statewide organization to champion its interests—the Associated Farmers of California (created in 1934)—was clearly in the ascendancy. While growers decried workers' efforts to organize, then and later, they themselves, as Devra Weber expertly depicts in her scholarly investigations, achieved an organization which their counterparts in industry could only envy.[33] The next twenty-five years would be the Golden Age of Agribusiness in California.

The 1930s strikes are notable for a number of reasons. For one, they illustrate the aggressive role played by the Mexican government in protecting the rights of its citizens in the United States. This tradition goes back to the nineteenth century, but the consulates expanded their advocacy activities enormously after the Mexican Revolution, when patriotism surged among expatriate communities. Their numbers also increased; by 1928, there were fifty-eight consulates scattered throughout the country. During the repatriation movement, as Francisco E. Balderrama has argued, consuls served as advocates and benefactors for their compatriots who were harassed by American authorities.[34] Although most Chicano scholars tend to be critical of what they perceive to be modest efforts at best, consuls deserve acknowledgment and credit for alleviating the hardships experienced by the beleaguered community. The aid they lent to the organization of Mexicano workers is one of the least appreciated of their contributions. Especially during the Depression, Mexican consular offices energetically defended the rights of workers, a reflection of the pro-labor sympathies of the Cárdenas administration. Enrique Bravo, the consul at Monterey, for example, was actively involved in the 1933 San Joaquin Valley strike. Joaquín Terrazas, the consul of Calexico, supported Mexicano strikers in the Imperial Valley in 1934. Strikers in the southern California citrus industry in

1935–1936 received valuable assistance from the consul of Los Angeles, Ricardo Hill. Undoubtedly, too, consulate activity in the thirties was prompted by fear that without their intervention, the emerging working-class movement would come under Communist domination.

Conditions became so appalling during the Depression that for the first and only time in American history Communists became meaningful players in efforts to organize labor. Red unions proved to be much more receptive to the idea of recruiting Mexicanos than the traditional unions had ever been. Heirs of the IWW, the CAWIU too chose to recruit from the ranks of the working class, regardless of color. Moreover, Communist unions such as the CAWIU, despite doctrinal precedence given to mobilizing the industrial proletariat, were willing to enter the agricultural fields of California and the Southwest. Generally speaking, Mexicano workers were receptive to CAWIU overtures. Dorothy Ray Healey, who began her long career as a Communist leader by organizing for the CAWIU in the 1930s, later recalled, "Despite charges by the growers that the Communists were conspiring to destroy California's agricultural economy, we were rarely the instigators of these strikes. They usually broke out spontaneously and then the workers would come and find us. Most of the workers we encountered in the early 1930s were Mexican, with some Filipinos, and a scattering of Blacks and Anglos."[35]

Extreme situations call for extreme solutions, and many Mexicanos in desperate straits came to see that there was little to lose in supporting radical unions. Some had recently arrived from Mexico, where the fledgling labor movement had strong left-wing roots, so they were not averse to working with Communist associations. Most Mexicano workers, however, even those in red unions, had little real understanding of Marxist ideology; they needed relief, and they joined Communist unions because mainstream labor unions had failed to cultivate Mexicanos.[36] To many of them, it seemed that only radical organizations were willing to extend a helping hand.

In the end, the strikes of the 1930s failed not because of dissension in the ranks of the strikers, though this was certainly a factor, but because the opposition had preponderant strength. The forces of corporate capitalism, though weakened, turned out to be remarkably resilient. Moreover, the American public, especially the middle class, generally backed management. Big Business was hailed as a bastion against Communism, widely perceived as a threat to the American Way. Class and race considerations also dictated that public opinion would be opposed to the organization of farmworkers, many of them thought to be unassimilable aliens. What little support the workers had garnered was soon undermined by the revival of the economy stimulated by the Second World War.

Beginning with Carey McWilliams, scholars who have studied the history of Mexicanos in the United States have gone to extraordinary lengths to illustrate that their subjects have been assiduous throughout the twentieth century in combating labor exploitation by setting up unions and initiating strikes. Chicano scholars in particular, especially those impacted by Marxist perspectives, have emphasized these struggles.[37] Like McWilliams, they have stressed labor history in an effort to demolish the myth of Mexican docility, a popular stereotype of the Mexicano as a lazy and unprogressive peon. Chicano historians have done well to combat this pernicious view. It seems that in every society there is a need to attribute negative qualities, especially laziness, to some group to promote a more positive self-image among insiders.

The truth of the matter is that Mexicanos have had an unusually strong work ethic. Although Mexico has ostensibly been a welfare state since 1917, when the Constitution instituted a social transformation, in actuality its economy is so fragile that citizens who fail to work risk starvation, hardly a situation calculated to encourage sloth. Anyone who is intimately familiar with Mexican immigrants today recognizes them as people who are willing to do an honest day's job for an honest day's pay—Latino panhandlers are almost as rare as Asian panhandlers—one of the reasons many American employers prefer them over local labor pools. The related, though more generalized, picture of Mexicanos as innately docile hardly needs refutation.

On the other hand, the recitation of a long litany of Mexicano strikes by sympathetic and well-meaning scholars has left a distorted view of Mexicano labor militancy, as Mario T. García has aptly pointed out, especially in agriculture. "Some Mexicans did resort to strikes as an expression of discontent," García observes, "but most Mexicans shied away from such activity and saw no reason for these 'radical' manifestations. Accommodation rather than resistance characterized the Mexican immigrant experience."[38] Historically, and in spite of blatant exploitation, labor agitation among Mexicanos has been the exception, not the rule. "Despite the need for rigorous self-protection," as Mark Reisler has justly observed, "Mexican unions were more ad hoc than permanent."[39] In fact, Mexicanos were used as strikebreakers on many occasions, both in industry and in agriculture.

There are many reasons why the Mexicano masses have failed to live up to the revolutionary expectations of activist university professors, none of them having to do with innate deficiencies of character. In the nineteenth century, there was little possibility of protesting working conditions, quite aside from the absence of an effective labor union movement. There was the class division between old "Spanish" residents and the newer "Mexican" immigrants, the strength of anti-Mexican animosity in the host society, and the relatively modest numbers of Hispanics vis-à-vis Anglos. During the period of the Great Migration, efforts at labor organization were initiated but remained weak. The peasantry is reputed to be the most conservative social class in an agrarian society, certainly the most tradition-bound, and most Mexican immigrants came from these social origins. Furthermore, during the first decades of the twentieth century, while laborers recognized that they were being exploited by mining, railroad, and agribusiness enterprises, they compared their life in the United States with what it had been in Mexico. Even after the Revolution, there was no question that the standard of living was higher in this country than back home. After all, Mexicans came, and they continue to come, to the United States, where many took up residence, of their own volition. Only after they admitted to themselves that they were here to stay, a conclusion that many recent immigrants have still not made, did the immigrants and their children come to appreciate their underprivileged status in American society and the need to change it through their own efforts.

Even with this awareness, it was next to impossible to translate discontent into a viable movement to improve wages and working conditions. The barriers were formidable. This was especially true in the fields, where most of the new-comers eked out a living. To begin with, agricultural work traditionally paid the lowest wages of any job, in part because the work was seasonal and, consequently, migratory. Impoverished workers could not afford to pay union dues. Indeed, they tended to be preoccupied with simply meeting their daily needs. Secondly, the workers lacked education, a luxury they could ill afford given their dismal wages and migratory existence. Many could not speak English. These conditions made it difficult, at best, to develop a cadre of leaders, a prerequisite to any organization. Thirdly, most Mexican immigrants working in the fields had entered the country illegally, which was relatively inconsequential at first, but became a major problem during and after the Depression. Fearing deportation, undocumented workers strove to maintain a low profile. Lastly, and perhaps most crucial in explaining Mexicano failures in the fields, was the enormous power of agribusiness, both before the Second World War and especially afterward. Most of these problems were evident in the industrial sector, though not to the same degree as in agriculture. Given these obstacles, it is surprising that Mexicano workers mobilized at all and, in time, accomplished as much as they did.

MEXICANAS AND THE LABOR MOVEMENT

Though this point has been overstated, the strikes of the 1930s are memorable because they illustrate that Mexicanos were often active agents in determining their fates, not mere pawns in the hands of powerful economic interests. Ultimately, though, the most momentous significance of these activities, as Chicana scholars such as Vicki L. Ruiz have argued, is that they show the dynamic role played by women.[40] Mexicanas, of course, had always been active in contributing to the economic well-being of the family even outside the home. This was particularly the case in lower-class households, where the woman's income was often essential for survival. Financial necessity ultimately overcame the prejudice so pervasive in the culture that a woman's place was in the home. During the Depression, though, a new assertiveness became evident among Mexicanas.

By the thirties, women played a trenchant role in the emerging union movement in the Southwest. This phenomenon was not totally unprecedented. The first in a long line of Mexicana labor leaders was Lucy Gonzales Parsons (1852–1942), a native of Johnson City, Texas, who helped found the IWW shortly after the turn of the century. She has been described as "a figure of great stature," by Martha Cotera, the distinguished chronicler of the history of Mexican women in the United States.[41] Some unions were dominated by Mexicanas, especially in the canning industry where, as the historian Vicki Ruiz and the anthropologist Patricia Zavella have shown, they established a culture of their own.

Mexicanas were often found among the rank and file of the unions, but a measure of the progress they had made within the traditional Mexicano family and Anglo society, both of which often placed barriers to their advancement, was the degree to which they contributed to the leadership of the organizations. Chicano and Chicana historians have only recently brought to light the contributions made by these remarkable women. Since they are not yet household names—only Dolores Huerta seems to have achieved this kind of recognition—something should be said about the most influential of these labor organizers.

Strictly speaking, Luisa Moreno (1906–1992) or Blanca Rosa Rodríguez de León, her real name, was not Mexicana, having been born in Guatemala; however, this Latina worked intimately with Mexicanas during her long career as an organizer and came to be accepted by them as one of their own. Moreno immigrated to the United States in 1928 to pursue an education.[42] After graduating from the College of Holy Names in Oakland, California, she developed a passion for labor reform. She worked as a professional organizer on the East Coast for both the AFL and the Congress of Industrial Organizations (CIO), a more progressive coalition of unions which split from the AFL in 1937. Eventually, she found her way to Texas and California, where she made her mark recruiting Mexican farmworkers and cannery workers for the UCAPAWA, the most progressive agricultural union of the day. Many of the union's leaders were members of the American Communist Party. It is not clear whether Moreno shared that affiliation, but she was certainly sympathetic to the party's humanitarian program. Ultimately, she was elected UCAPAWA vice president, the first woman to achieve this office in any major American labor organization.

Although most of her efforts were focused on labor issues, Luisa Moreno was also active in the fight for civil rights, notably the campaign to end segregation in the Southwest. Perhaps her most meaningful contribution in this regard was the establishment of El Congreso del Pueblo de Habla Española (the Spanish-Speaking

Congress) in 1938, a coalition of middle- and working-class associations in Los Angeles created to protect the civil liberties of the Hispanic population. Retired from public life shortly after World War II, Moreno was forced back into the limelight when she was accused of subversion during the McCarthy witch hunts. She was deported on 30 November 1950. It is only during the past generation that Luisa Moreno, thanks to the efforts of Chicano and Chicana scholars, has received the credit she so richly deserves.

Another early crusader for the rights of Mexicano workers was Emma Tenayuca (1916–1999), who was born in San Antonio, and whose brief career as a union activist was confined to the state of Texas. She initiated her life as a labor organizer in 1934, her senior year in high school. During the next decade, despite her youth, she became the undisputed leader of the labor movement in her native city. She gained national prominence in 1938, when she led a strike of local pecan-shelling workers, most of them Mexicanas. There were occasional victories, but in Texas, as elsewhere, the prosperity brought on by the war undermined the fledgling labor movement. Like Moreno, Tenayuca retired from union activity in the late 1940s, when she left for California. Emma Tenayuca was a pioneer in more ways than one: a reentry student, she eventually graduated magna cum laude from San Francisco State College, one of the first Mexicanas to earn a college degree.

Another Mexicana who made a lasting impact on the labor movement was Josefina Fierro de Bright (1920–1998). Born in Mexico, Josefina was raised in Los Angeles by her mother, a single parent, who introduced her to the anarchist teachings of Ricardo Flores Magón. After working in the fields of the San Joaquin Valley, she enrolled as a student at UCLA but abandoned her studies to marry John Bright, whose left-wing views would reinforce the allure of her mother's progressive views. Entering the workers' movement, the young idealist immediately drew the attention of Luisa Moreno, who encouraged her in her efforts at labor and community organization. Fierro soon became the prime mover behind the Congreso. The organization, which aimed at the betterment of Hispanic peoples, drew enthusiastic support from many sectors of southern California society, including the film industry. Among early backers were Anthony Quinn, Dolores del Río, and John Wayne.[43] Fierro was only one of several women composing the Congreso's leadership. She herself later estimated that about 30 percent of the organization's activists were women.[44] After the war, she helped establish the Independent Progressive Party in California, before voluntarily repatriating to Mexico to escape persecution during the McCarthy era.

The 1930s is generally described in very negative terms by Chicano historians. Clearly, there is good reason to be critical, for on the surface, at least, it was a time of unmitigated disaster for Mexicanos. Economic conditions, as bad as they had been before, now deteriorated in both rural and urban areas. Many members of the ethnic community suffered the humiliation of deportation; others were subjected to intense discrimination. Their efforts to organize into unions and to combat the escalating exploitation collapsed.

By the thirties, though, a ray of hope could be discerned. By now, Mexicanos, many of them born in the United States, were beginning to realize that there would be no returning to the Old Country. This growing awareness was especially evident in the emerging barrios in and out of the Southwest. As Mario T. García demonstrates, the 1930s witnessed the emergence of a meaningful Mexicano middle class, in both numbers and influence, determined to protect the rights of its people as citizens of the United States, perhaps the most portentous accomplishment in an otherwise dismal period in the history of Mexican Americans.

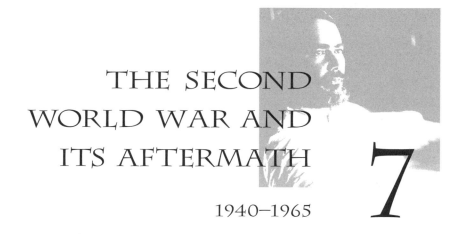

THE SECOND
WORLD WAR AND
ITS AFTERMATH
1940–1965

7

In the annals of American history, the Second World War was probably not as momentous in its consequences for many Americans as had been the Great War a generation before, but such is not the case for Mexicanos in this country. World War II altered life in the Mexicano community profoundly. Its heaviest impact was on the nascent middle class, which grew in both size and influence. In the aftermath of the war, this middle sector, largely composed of children of immigrants rather than immigrants themselves, was eager to win acceptance into American society, but only on its own terms. Much maligned by Chicano historians in the 1960s and 1970s for its lack of concern for the welfare of the ethnic community at large, in recent years this middle class, thanks largely to the efforts of the brothers Mario T. and Richard García, Guadalupe San Miguel Jr., and like-minded historians, has been reevaluated in a much more positive light. Given the intellectual and moral climate engendered by the war, it is clear that options available to this generation were rather limited. Moreover, it is now clear that a substantial number of the middle class *did* attempt to ameliorate working and living conditions for the Mexicano community as a whole, with surprising success.

MEXICANOS IN THE MILITARY

The Japanese attack on Pearl Harbor on 7 December 1941 forced the United States into the war. For Mexicanos, the colossal conflict represented an opportunity to enter the American mainstream. By the 1940s, there were many more of them in the country than there had been during World War I, so their participation was much higher. The military at the time simply counted Latinos as "whites," so accurate numbers are unavailable. According to University of Texas journalism professor Maggie Rivas-Rodríguez, the director of an ambitious Austin-based oral history project to record the experiences of Latinos and Latinas active during the global conflict, estimates of Latinos engaged in active military service vary between 250,000 and 750,000.[1] Estimates for Mexicanos in particular, both immigrants and native-born, run between 250,000 and 500,000, huge numbers considering an overall population of 2.7 million. Most Mexicanos were drafted into the service, like their compatriots—altogether, 10 million men were inducted, twice the number who volunteered. Many Mexicanos, however, were volunteers. Indeed, as is true of other military conflicts in the twentieth century, notably Korea and Vietnam, the Mexicano enlistment rate was probably greater than that of the population at large. There were a number of reasons for this apparent enthusiasm. First of all, the service represented one of the few opportunities for Mexicanos to improve their low socioeconomic status. Often isolated in small communities or trapped in the barrios of larger cities, poorly educated and lacking job skills, they saw the military as the easiest and most immediate way of improving their position. Secondly, while some of them still fostered notions of returning to Mexico, many newcomers, as was typical of immigrant communities, felt a sense of gratitude to their new homeland and joined up out of a sense of sincere patriotism. Finally, the high enlistment rate owed something to the macho ethic permeating Mexicano society; doing military service was a way of proving manhood.

In contrast to World War I, when they were recruited almost exclusively in the Southwest, many Mexicano servicemen now came from other regions. The Midwest was well represented. The Illinois town of Silvis, near Moline, for example, sent 110 Mexicanos off to war, which, according to the U.S. Defense Department, was more than any other comparable town of its size.

As the historian Raúl Morín, a native of Lockhart, Texas, and himself a veteran of the war, has illustrated, Mexicanos were one of the most highly decorated ethnic groups in the U.S. Armed Forces. They served with distinction in both the Pacific and the Atlantic theaters, where they won scores of medals, including the Silver Star, the Bronze Star, the Distinguished Service Cross, the Purple Heart, and the most prestigious military citation of all, the Congressional Medal of Honor. This last decoration, conferred by the U.S. Congress for valor, was first established in 1861. Since that time some thirty-four hundred individuals have been awarded the Medal of Honor, more than three-quarters of them posthumously. Among the recipients have been forty-three Hispanic soldiers, mostly of Mexican descent (see appendix B for a complete list).[2] During World War II, twelve Hispanics, apparently all of them Mexicanos, were bestowed this coveted honor: Luciano Adams, Macario García, Silvestre S. Herrera, José M. López, and Cleto L. Rodríguez from Texas; Harold Gonsalves, David M. Gonzales, and Ysmael R. Villegas from California; José P. Martínez, Alejandro R. Ruiz, and José F. Valdez from New Mexico; and Manuel Pérez Jr., from Oklahoma.

Habitants de Californie, a lithograph by Louis Choris of neophytes in Alta California, which appeared in the artist's *Voyage pittoresque autour du monde* (Paris: Imprimerie de Firmin Dido, 1922). California Historical Society, North Baker Research Library, Templeton Crocker Foundation, FN-30510

Mariano Guadalupe Vallejo and members of his family in
the 1880s. California Historical Society, FN-30504

Carlos Velasco, founder of *La Alianza Hispano-Americana,* and his family about
1880. Courtesy of the Arizona Historical Society/Tucson, AHS#61,860

Juana Elias, member of one of Tucson's ranking families, in 1901.
Courtesy of the Arizona Historical Society/Tucson, AHS#2,138

Mexican miners in Arizona in the early 1900s. Courtesy of
the Arizona Historical Society/Tucson, AHS#64,323

Jovita Idar, Tejana feminist, ca. 1905.
The UT Institute of Texan Cultures at San
Antonio, courtesy of A. Ike Idar, 684-596

Dr. Hector García, founder of the
American G.I. Forum. Dr. Hector P.
García Papers, Special Collections &
Archives, Texas A&M University—Corpus
Christi, Mary & Jeff Bell Library

Campesina in the spinach fields of Robstown, Texas.
Library of Congress, USF34-24829-D

Mexicanas protest during the 1933 cotton strike in California.
Powell Studio Collection, courtesy of the Bancroft Library,
University of California, Berkeley, 1945.007:1-PIC

Santa Fe Railroad track layers, Calwa, California,
1937. Fresno Historical Society Archives

Women railroad workers in Arizona during the Second World War.
Courtesy of the Arizona Historical Society/Tucson, AHS#63,527

Ben Garza, LULAC leader, in 1929.
Benson Latin American Collection,
University of Texas, Austin

M. C. GONZALEZ
Regional Governor of Texas
San Antonio, Texas

M. C. Gonzales, LULAC leader, in
the 1930s. Benson Latin American
Collection, University of Texas, Austin

Mexican funeral, Fresno, California, ca. 1935.
Courtesy of Mrs. Carmen Acuña

Young cotton picker in the San Joaquin Valley in 1936.
Library of Congress, USF34-9950-C, FSA project,
photograph by Dorothea Lange

Poster of Mexican diva Maria Félix in the 1949 film
classic *Doña Diabla.* Courtesy of the Agrasánchez
Film Archive, Harlingen, Texas

Pedro Infante, perhaps the most popular star of Mexico's
Golden Age, in the 1952 film *Dos tipos de cuidado.* Courtesy
of the Agrasánchez Film Archive, Harlingen, Texas

Migrant family passing through San Angelo, Texas, on their way
to the sugar beet fields of Wyoming in 1949. Lee (Russell)
Photograph Collection, Center for American History,
University of Texas, Austin, e_rl_14233_0024

Portrait of tennis great Richard "Pancho" Gonzales in 1950. Herald-Examiner Collection. Los Angeles Public Library

Members of the American G.I. Forum at a soldier's reburial services in Corpus Christi, Texas, in 1949. Lee (Russell) Photograph Collection, Center for American History, University of Texas, Austin, e_rl_13918r2_0021

Given their distinguished but generally unrecognized record, it is easy to understand why the failure of the prolific filmmaker Ken Burns to acknowledge Latinos in his fourteen-hour documentary *The War* elicited such concern, even outrage, in 2007 among many Mexican Americans, particularly veterans and academic organizations. Led by cofounders Dr. Maggie Rivas-Rodríguez and Gus Chávez, and assisted by Armando Rendón, the nationwide protest campaign, dubbed "Defend the Honor," generated immense controversy. In the end, activists gained minimal concessions from Burns and the Public Broadcasting Service, his sponsors; but, more significantly, their actions did bring this valuable Latino contribution to the attention of the general public, at long last. Equally noteworthy, the lengthy and well-publicized campaign also succeeded in mobilizing Spanish-speaking communities across the country.

The largest contingents of Mexicanos who served overseas were probably sent to the Pacific Theater, where they were engaged in battle from the very outset. Hispanos composed a huge proportion of the New Mexico National Guard, which was stationed in the Philippines on the eve of the war, and many of them were among the thirty-six thousand troops forced to surrender to the Japanese. Hundreds of these prisoners died on the infamous Bataan Death March, the murderous eighty-five-mile forced journey through the island jungles in April 1942. Almost three years later, in January 1945, they returned to the Philippines with General Douglas MacArthur and subsequently saw heavy action in the epic island battles, most notably Okinawa, that would finally bring the cataclysmic war against the Japanese to an end.

Undoubtedly the most famous Mexican American soldier to serve in the Pacific was Guy Louis Gabaldón (1926–2006), who made his mark during the Battle of Saipan in 1944. Born in East Los Angeles and raised by a Japanese American family after the age of twelve, young Gabaldón joined the Marine Corps at seventeen. In June and July 1944, he found himself on the island of Saipan, part of the Marianna chain, the site of one of the bloodiest battles of the war. Over three thousand U.S. soldiers and thirty thousand Japanese soldiers died there. Private Gabaldón's acts of bravery during the epic campaign, during which he was twice wounded by machine-gun fire, are the stuff of legends. He killed thirty-three enemy soldiers on the field of battle, for starters. But more incredibly, using his knowledge of the Japanese language, he single-handedly captured more than fifteen hundred enemy combatants and civilians during the two-month period, the most prisoners ever taken by one soldier in the entire history of the U.S. military. After the war, he went into business for many years in Mexico, where he met his Mexican-born Japanese wife. Two of their ten children became Marines. Guy Gabaldón never fully received the recognition that was his due during his lifetime. Outspoken in his views—he was a political reactionary—the aging veteran made many enemies. Recommended for a Medal of Honor for his acts of extraordinary valor by his commanding officer in the aftermath of the battle, he was denied the cherished decoration by the Pentagon, an injustice that Latino civic and veterans' groups have been fighting to rectify ever since.

Mexicanos were also active on the other side of the globe, in North Africa and Europe, where they participated in all major battles. Perhaps their most telling contribution occurred during the Italian campaign, which was initiated on 10 July 1943, with the invasion of Sicily. Company Z of the 141st Regiment of the 36th Division, consisting entirely of Tejanos, most of them from El Paso, was one of the premier American units in Italy. Many members of the company performed heroically, but two individuals in particular stand out: Lieutenant Gabriel Navarette from El Paso and Sergeant Manuel S. Gonzales from Fort Davis, Texas, both of them recipients of Distinguished Service Crosses.

Mexicanos also figured prominently in the assault on "Fortress Europe," which was launched on the beaches of Normandy on D-Day, 6 June 1944. Among the many heroes of the final assault on Germany was Medal of Honor winner Sergeant José M. López (1910–2005), from Brownsville, Texas. A machine gunner with K Company of the 23rd Regiment, 2nd Division, López killed more than one hundred Germans in the Krinkelt Wald, in Belgium, on 17 December 1944. He has the distinction of having killed more enemy soldiers than any other American in World War II. In general, Mexicanos performed valiantly in battle, making sacrifices well beyond what one would expect. It is reported that the heaviest battlefront casualties during the entire war were suffered by the 3rd, 36th, and 45th Infantry Divisions. All contained generous numbers of Mexicanos in their ranks. California congressman Jerry Voorhis observed at the time: "As I read the casualty lists from my state, I find anywhere from one-fourth to one-third of these names are names such as Gonzales or Sanchez, names indicating that the very lifeblood of our citizens of Latin-American descent in the uniform of the armed forces of the United States is being poured out to win victory in the war. We ought not to forget that."[3]

Mexicanos who survived the war gained immeasurably by the experience. Perhaps the most valuable benefit was psychological. Raúl Morín explains:

> These *Chicanos* were different from the Mexican-Americans that we had known before we left the States and went overseas. Although still full of fun and deviltry as ever, they now were well-seasoned and experienced American soldiers. No longer were we chided and shunned by other GI's and Army officers. Where we had been held in contempt by others who disliked us because of our constant Spanish chatter or our lax [sic] in military discipline, we were now admired, respected, and approved by all those around us including most of our commanding officers.[4]

Military service did wonders for self-esteem, but it was meaningful for many young Mexicanos in other ways. Some were forced to deal with Anglos for the first time, and the experience in interethnic relations was generally positive. Cooperating against the common enemy tended to break down mutual prejudices. Some of the friendships forged in battle undoubtedly continued to be cultivated after the war. Although discrimination was not entirely done away with, it was less evident in the service, and Mexicanos and other minorities found career opportunities opening up. Some of them even succeeded in breaking into the officer corps. Manuel Chávez (1910–1996), for example, better known as the poet and historian Fray Angélico Chávez, achieved the rank of major while serving in both Europe and the Pacific in 1943–1946. An even larger number picked up job skills that would be useful in civilian life. Finally, veterans' benefits offered Mexicanos unprecedented opportunities to better their lives by providing education and job training, as well as facilitating the purchase of homes.

The G.I. Bill, in particular, stands out. Signed into law by President Roosevelt on 22 June 1944, this path-breaking act, one of the most powerful legislative forces for social change in U.S. history, paid for the education of 7.8 million soldiers reentering civilian life, many of them Mexicano veterans. Beneficiaries included Américo Paredes (1915–1999), one of the most prolific scholars of the century; Ramón Eduardo Ruiz (1921–), a leading authority on Latin American history; Octavio I. Romano (1923–2005), founder of *El Grito,* the most influential literary magazine of the Chicano movement; Ralph Guzmán (1924–1985), noted educator and civil rights activist; and José Antonio Villarreal (1924–), among the most gifted of contemporary Mexican American writers. Mothers and widows of young soldiers killed in action also received financial aid from the government, a source of family income which often represented the difference between a life of poverty and a relatively comfortable existence.

As neglected as Hispanic men are in conventional histories of the Second World War, the role of Hispanic women has been even more obscure, even among minorities themselves. Indeed, it is not much of an exaggeration to state that mujeres have been totally absent from these accounts, a deficiency that has only recently been addressed by Chicana scholars, among them Christine Marín and Naomi Quiñones. Like their male counterparts, mujeres contributed mightily to the war effort. Some of them, especially Hispanas (Spanish-speaking women from New Mexico and Colorado), served in the military. Their preeminent contribution, though, was on the home front, where they sold war bonds and set up numerous organizations to assist servicemen and servicewomen. The activities of one such organization, Tucson's El Club de Madres y Esposas (the Club of Mothers and Wives), have been thoroughly documented by the historians Christine Marín and Julie A. Campbell.[5] Like other American women, Mexicanas helped to fill the labor vacuum created by servicemen. They continued to toil in the fields, as they had from the very beginning, but now they increasingly discovered opportunities in industry. Some of them even gained employment in defense plants, where jobs were opened up to minorities thanks to Executive Order 8802, which established the Committee for Fair Employment Practices in 1941. Most mujeres in the industrial sector, however, had to settle for less lucrative jobs, such as working in the mushrooming food-processing plants of the Southwest. In general, the war elevated the standard of living for both men and women.[6]

URBANIZATION: TRIALS AND TRIBULATIONS

The best jobs were found in cities. Consequently, during the war years, there was a massive movement of Mexicanos into urban centers. This was true not only along the border but in other parts of the country as well. In the Midwest, the Greater Chicago area saw the Mexicano community surge in numbers, a trend that was evident in Detroit as well. In the Pacific Northwest, the global war witnessed the beginning of Mexicano urbanization as campesinos began to arrive in Portland and Seattle from the Willamette Valley, the Yakima Valley, and other agricultural areas.

As Mexicanos moved into cities in large numbers during the war years, their standard of living began to improve slowly. Some were even able to move beyond the barrio, where, for the first time, they established meaningful contact with Anglos outside a work environment. However, this historic migration was not an unmixed blessing. Discrimination continued to be rampant. Deficient housing, limited economic opportunities, and segregated schools were only the most glaring of the chronic problems plaguing the newcomers. Moreover, in the urban environment, external pressures began to have an adverse impact on the bulwark of Mexicano life, *la familia.*

Chicano nationalists today tend to have a highly idealized picture of the Mexicano family. In fact, this positive assessment is common both within and outside the ethnic community. To a large extent, this perception is a myth. Domestic violence, alcoholism, extramarital affairs, abandonment, and divorce have taken their toll on the modern Mexicano family. These developments are not recent. If one is to believe Ramón Ruiz, social ills were pandemic in Mexico even before the Revolution: "In 1910, more than one out of three births were illegitimate, and the malady, up from 22 percent a decade before, was obviously getting worse."[7] The Revolution was bound to exacerbate the deteriorating situation, given the massive population movements it spawned, as well as the high mortality.

Still, in rural Mexico, as in preindustrial economies in general, the family took on special meaning. "The extended family," the journalist Alan Riding has observed, "is the principal safe haven where emotions can be shown without risk, where unquestioning loyalty is guaranteed, where customs are maintained."[8] Moreover, among the immigrants, most of whom came to toil in the rural areas of the Southwest, the family was revitalized; it was the most immediate source of security in an alien and unfriendly environment, as well as the basic economic unit, a point emphasized by the anthropologist Robert R. Álvarez Jr.[9]

Urban living was bound to weaken traditional family ties. In the countryside, largely isolated from American mainstream culture, the man, as father and husband, could continue to demand that unquestioned obedience—more theoretical than real—he was used to in the Old Country. In the city, though, his wife and children encountered a dominant society which called into question many of their traditional beliefs and relationships. No longer was the ultimate authority of the male unquestioned. Moreover, as economic opportunities opened up to women, a trend accentuated by the war, they naturally demanded more rights, and, as Vicki L. Ruiz has shown, generally received them.[10] Still, changes came amidst staunch resistance, often accompanied by domestic violence. The demand for greater freedom, though inevitable, proved highly disruptive to the family, in part because it occurred so quickly. In his autobiographical novel *Pocho* (1959), José Antonio Villarreal gives a graphic illustration of this corrosive process, which ultimately leads to the complete disintegration of a Mexicano family making a transition from rural to urban life in California's Santa Clara Valley in the thirties and forties.

The advent of *pachuco* gangs in the early 1940s mirrors the breakdown of the traditional family, as well as the discrimination experienced by Mexicano youths in an urban environment. Pachucos, or "zoot-suiters," who apparently first appeared in El Paso on the eve of the war, were youths who represented a unique subculture in the Mexicano community. Much maligned at the time, both in and out of the ethnic community, the pachuco is best known today through Luis Valdez's sympathetic portrayal in his popular and justly acclaimed play, *Zoot Suit* (1978).

Although never very numerous, pachucos made a profound impact on a whole generation of Mexicano youths in the 1940s and 1950s. Children of immigrants, for the most part, pachucos and pachucas felt alienated from their parents, who held on to Old World values, hoping to return to Mexico. Misunderstood by the older generation, the youth also found themselves at odds with the dominant society; Anglos, who denied them jobs and educational opportunities, rejected them as outsiders and criminals. Caught between two worlds, pachucos rebelled by creating their own self-contained society. They wore a distinctive uniform, consisting of a long, loose-fitting coat, high-waisted, baggy pants, and a feathered broad-brimmed hat. Their hair was made up in a ducktail. Dressed in short skirts, pachucas used heavy makeup and wore their hair in a pompadour. Pachuco/a fashions were not unique; these were popular contemporary styles, as any Hollywood movie of the time will attest. What *was* unique was the degree to which the styles were exaggerated, the extremes the youths embraced as a symbol of their defiance. They developed a patois, a strange and fascinating mixture of Spanish, English, and black slang which came to be called *caló*. More extreme was the occasional use of marijuana and a proclivity for tattoos, especially by males. In short, pachucos tried very hard to "shock the bourgeoisie" with their flamboyancy, and did so with a good measure of success.

In his 1961 masterpiece on the Mexican national character, *The Labyrinth of Solitude,* Nobel Prize winner Octavio Paz devoted a controversial chapter, "The *Pachuco* and Other Extremes," to the subject. The Mexican intellectual, who betrayed a not-too-subtle class bias, drew a very unflattering portrait of zoot-suiters. Scorned for his loss of identity, the pachuco, Paz wrote, "is an impassive and sinister clown whose purpose is to cause terror instead of laughter. His sadistic attitude is allied with a desire for self-abasement which in my opinion constitutes the very foundation of his character."[11] Unfortunately, Paz, like many Anglos in the United States, tended to identify pachucos with the entire Mexican American community, which was patently unfair. In fact, zoot-suiters were highly unpopular with many members of their own neighborhoods, if one is to believe Manuel P. Servín, himself a severe critic, who writes: "This writer has yet to find an older, pre–World War II Mexican or Mexican-American defending or offering an apology for the pachucos."[12] However, Paz's view of the pachucos themselves as deeply alienated and insecure is not far off the mark, though he might have been more sensitive to their plight. After all, pachuco youth were more deserving of pity than scorn. While the trend toward victimization was taken too far in later years, pachucos, as educator George I. Sánchez pointed out at the time,[13] *were* victims. Through no fault of their own, they found themselves assailed and rejected on all sides. Left to their own devices, they took refuge in *carnalismo* (brotherhood).

While pachucos and pachucas elicited some sympathy in the barrio, where Mexicanos, as Paz notes, felt an ambivalence toward them, beyond their ethnic community they found only enmity. The war unleashed acute racial tensions in U.S. society, as the internment of the Japanese American population in 1942, a product of intense xenophobia, amply demonstrates. Unfortunately for Mexicanos in general and pachucos more particularly, hostility was soon directed at other ethnic minorities as well. Given the intense racial antipathy of the period, it was predictable that there would be a reemergence of "the Mexican Problem." In fact, a climate of repression soon surfaced, to a marked extent the product of a well-orchestrated media campaign waged by the powerful newspaper publisher William Randolph Hearst. The main targets were pachucos, ideal scapegoats given their distinctive appearance and small numbers.

Two incidents in southern California particularly illustrate the virulence of anti-pachuco sentiment during the war: the Sleepy Lagoon case in 1942 and the so-called Zoot Suit Riots a year later.[14] The Sleepy Lagoon was a small reservoir situated in El Monte, on the eastern outskirts of Los Angeles, where, in early August of 1942, the body of José Díaz was discovered. The young man, a member of a local gang, had apparently been slain the previous evening, possibly by a rival Mexicano gang, the 38th Street Club. Although the evidence was purely circumstantial, authorities were determined to make an example of them, and charges of murder were soon filed against twenty-two members of the 38th Street gang. Except for one youth, all were Mexican Americans.

Spurred on by the local press, which decried a crime wave by "the Mexican element" and advocated a get-tough policy, public opinion was firmly on the side of the prosecution. The trial was conducted under an atmosphere of mass hysteria. Nor did it help that the judge, Charles W. Fricke, had concluded beforehand that the gang was guilty and prejudiced the case in a number of ways throughout the proceedings. For example, he denied the defendants the right to groom themselves properly; they came into the courtroom looking like "criminals." Predictably, no Mexicanos were allowed to sit on the jury. Under these adverse circumstances the verdict was a foregone conclusion. Seventeen youths were found guilty of a variety of crimes. Twelve were charged with first or second degree murder: Jack Meléndez, Victor Thompson, Ángel Padilla, Gus Zamora, John Matuz, Ysmael Parra, Manuel Reyes, Bobby Telles, Manuel Delgado, Chepe Ruiz, Henry Ynostroza, and Henry Leyvas, the leader of the gang.

The Sleepy Lagoon case is very consequential in the annals of Mexican American history for a number of reasons, not the least of which is the fact that it resulted in the first effective mobilization of the Mexicano population in southern California. Mexicanos quickly perceived that it was the entire community, not just pachucos, who were being judged in the case. Racism, it was clear, had a great deal to do with the outcome of the trial.

Perhaps the best indication of racist sentiments during the court proceedings was the testimony presented before the grand jury by Lieutenant Edward Durán Ayres of the Los Angeles Police Department. Ayres felt that Mexicano youth were criminally inclined for genetic reasons. Descended from the bloodthirsty Aztecs, themselves of Mongoloid stock and therefore having "an utter disregard for the value of life," these youths, he argued, had inherited a predisposition toward violence. Ayres explained: "The Caucasian, especially the Anglo-Saxon, when engaged in fighting, particularly among youths, resorts to fisticuffs and may at times kick one another, which is considered unsporting, but this Mexican element considers all that to be a sign of weakness, and all he knows and feels is a desire to use a knife or some lethal weapon. In other words, his desire is to kill, or at least let blood."[15] Convinced that the problem was genetic, Ayres concluded that there was little the authorities could do to combat the malaise—"basically it is biological—one cannot change the spots of a leopard"—save to sentence offenders to lengthy prison terms.

The oft-quoted testimony presented by Ayres—who, ironically, appears to have been Hispanic himself—reflected racial attitudes widely held by the Los Angeles Police Department. In fact, there is some suspicion that Ayres did not author the report at all. However, these biased perceptions were also shared by a large segment of the Anglo American population at the time. And if the root of the problem was indeed biological, it was not only pachucos who stood indicted, but the entire Mexicano community.

The trial was so outrageously unjust, given the dubious procedures that were followed, as well as the racist premises which informed the verdicts, that efforts to overturn the decision were initiated almost immediately. Spearheading the campaign, which focused on the Mexicano barrios of the southland, was a small but determined band of white radicals, notable among them Carey McWilliams and LaRue McCormick, and leaders of the Mexicano community, such as Josefina Fierro. They were assisted by the Spanish-language press, including La Opinión, the city's most respected ethnic newspaper, an organ of the more affluent members of the Mexicano community. Ultimately, the indefatigable efforts of the Sleepy Lagoon Defense Committee paid off: in 1944, the convictions were finally reversed and the defendants released.[16]

In the meantime, Los Angeles was at the center of another series of events that sharply divided the Mexicano and Anglo communities. The Sleepy Lagoon case brought to the surface underlying racial tensions. The string of defeats that the United States encountered in the first months after Pearl Harbor, especially at the hands of the Japanese in the Pacific, undoubtedly exacerbated the situation back home. Indeed, during the war, race riots between blacks and whites broke out in Detroit, New York, and other cities around the country. Violence erupted between Mexicanos and Anglos as well. However, the "Zoot Suit Riots," as these clashes have been labeled, hardly qualify as riots in the usual sense of the word.

There was no love lost between pachucos and U.S. servicemen in southern California, site of a number of military training camps, during the early months of the war. It is hard to imagine two lifestyles so completely at odds. Furthermore, as Mauricio Mazón has argued in his path-breaking psychohistorical study, Zoot-Suit Riots: The Psychology of Symbolic Annihilation (1984), pent-up frustrations and the humiliation experienced in boot camps predisposed the servicemen to acts of violence which would restore their manhood and a sense of community with the civilian population. Given these underlying conditions, confrontation was inevitable. The result was a series of sporadic clashes between the two rival factions. These culminated on 3 June 1943, when, after a relatively minor skirmish, servicemen stationed in San Diego determined to teach the "greasers" a good lesson.

Immediately, a small army of servicemen, mostly sailors and marines on leave, descended on the barrios of Los Angeles. Victims included Mexicano youths, both boys and girls, having little or nothing to do with pachucos but having the misfortune of being in the wrong place at the wrong time. During the next few days, violence escalated, spurred on by the press, which pinned the blame for the so-called riots on the Mexicanos, and tolerated by the police, who simply looked the other way. Local authorities were unable or unwilling to effectively rein in rampaging servicemen. Before too long, similar acts of aggression were launched against Mexicanos in other parts of California and the Southwest, eventually spreading as far as the barrios of the Midwest. The outrages went on for a week, and might have continued longer, except for the intervention of the federal government. The violence stopped only when President Roosevelt had the military revoke passes and order its men back to their bases. But, ultimately, real credit for the termination of this bloody episode belongs to the Mexican government, which lodged a strenuous protest condemning the mistreatment of Mexicanos, some of them Mexican citizens, north of the border. Reluctant to antagonize a valuable ally in the crusade against the Axis Powers—Mexico had declared war on 22 May 1942—FDR was compelled to intervene.

For many Mexicanos living in this country, the Zoot Suit Riots, like the repatriations of the 1930s, left a scar which never completely healed. They wondered how it was possible that they should be subjected to verbal and physical abuse at home at the very time that so many members of their community were fighting overseas to preserve the American Way. The events of the 1930s and 1940s go a long way in explaining the disaffection of the Mexicano population with both the dominant society and the government. For years and years, even those among them who were citizens of the United States would continue to see and identify themselves as "Mexicans," not "Americans."

THE BRACERO PROGRAM

The Bracero Program was another major consequence of World War II. Braceros were Mexican nationals recruited to work in the western United States on a temporary basis as part of a U.S. government–sponsored project during and after the war. The managed migration, an unprecedented and radical solution to America's labor needs, was occasioned by the enormous manpower shortage created by the war. This thorny problem was especially severe in the agricultural fields of the Southwest due to the rapid expansion of the farming industry there and the tendency of farmworkers from the countryside to move to the cities nearby.[17]

The war effectively eliminated Europe as a source of competition on the world market, opening up fabulous opportunities for American farmers. It was the Southwest which benefited most. Growing by leaps and bounds, this region, with its seemingly endless supply of land and its greater propensity to mechanize, forged ahead of the Midwest to become America's breadbasket; by 1945, California had replaced Iowa as the leading agricultural state in the Union. The agricultural boom continued after the war, for the massive destruction wrought by the long conflict left Europe, outside of the Russian sphere of influence, heavily dependent on U.S. imports.

The need for campesinos in the Southwest increased not only because of the growth of the agrarian sector, but also because traditional sources of farm labor were abandoning the countryside for the cities during and after the war. The creation of defense industries served as a catalyst for the transformation of the Southwest into an urban society. Industrial work, more secure and better-paying, was an irresistible magnet for many people living in rural poverty. The expansion of the industrial sector in California, in particular, was so vast that even racial and ethnic minorities were able to take advantage of enhanced employment opportunities, particularly in Los Angeles and the Bay Area.

Already by the time of Pearl Harbor, it had become apparent that a new source of labor was imperative if American agriculture was to meet the emerging challenges successfully. Mexico was the obvious answer. Indeed, it was practically the only solution after Pearl Harbor, when the Pacific was transformed into a Japanese lake, cutting off any possibility of Asian workers. Still, not everyone was enthused about this prospect. Nativists were alarmed over the racial and socioeconomic implications of migration from the south, albeit on a temporary basis. Even the large-scale growers of the Southwest, who were slated to be the chief beneficiaries, had reservations. The last bastion of rugged individualism in America, agribusiness feared the prospects of government regulation that the program entailed. These concerns were most evident in Texas, where farmers were more receptive to the idea of an open border, the absence of any bureaucratic controls at all, for the duration of the war.

So severe was the farm labor shortage, that in the end, and despite the objections of the Texans, an accord was signed on 23 July 1942 by President Roosevelt and Mexico's President Manuel Ávila Camacho and ratified in Mexico City shortly thereafter. The first braceros arrived in California on 29 September. Thanks to this binational agreement, some quarter of a million Mexican nationals, all of them male, were employed as braceros throughout the West before the agreement's expiration in April 1947. During the war itself, some of these men were permitted to work in the railroad industry; however, with this single exception, the agreement specified that workers were restricted to harvesting agricultural products.

Intended as a wartime expedient, the Bracero Program proved to be so efficacious that it was maintained after the defeat of the Axis, albeit in modified forms. Although the original legislation expired, the program itself continued as a series of informal agreements—and was even expanded into Texas, which had refused to participate initially—with slight alterations until the Korean War (1950–1953).

The guest worker program was revitalized in the early fifties, thanks, once again, to a shrinking labor market in the fields. This time, however, Mexican officials were anxious to provide more safeguards for their citizens, especially in the Lone Star State, where abuses were most flagrant. Public Law 78 (PL78), passed by Congress in July 1951, reenacted the program. The new agreement took into account Mexican concerns; though as the years went by, the Mexican government increasingly lost its ability to help shape the pact. Administration continued in the hands of the Department of Labor, where it had been placed three years before, instead of with the Department of Agriculture, notoriously pro-farmer. While agribusiness was not totally satisfied with the revised 1951 legislation, the results were so successful that PL78 was extended every two years, thanks to the efforts of its representatives in Congress. Altogether, the Bracero Program lasted twenty-two years, from July 1942 to December 1964.

Although there were adjustments every time legislation was renewed, the basic outline of the program remained unchanged. Recruitment of workers was the responsibility of the Mexican government. Quotas were set up for the various Mexican states. Because there were so many more volunteers than were needed, a knotty problem that increased over time, the authorities generally resorted to a lottery system. Men fortunate enough to be selected were taken to one of a select number of screening centers in northern Mexico, where criminal records were checked and medical examinations administered. At the height of the program, in the late 1950s, Mexican centers were located in the cities of Hermosillo, Chihuahua, and Monterrey. These hurdles cleared, successful applicants were taken across the border to U.S. recruitment centers located in places like El Centro and El Paso, where, after further medical examinations, employer representatives made the final selection. Typically, workers who failed to secure employment at the end of one week were sent back across the border, to make their way back to native villages at their own expense. Workers who were chosen signed a standard contract and were then transported north to work sites.[18]

The contract spelled out the obligations of the two parties involved, the employer and the employee. The farmer was to provide housing, transportation, and work. The bracero was responsible for health insurance, Mexican social security, and food, all costs that would be deducted from his paycheck. The pact also guaranteed certain conditions of employment, basic living and health needs, and the protection of the worker's civil rights. These stipulations were part of every agreement. Contracts, however, differed in terms of the crop, or crops, to be picked, the county, and the length of tenure (usually three to six months), according to the individual. The U.S. and Mexican governments were responsible for making sure that the contract was honored on both sides.

Official estimates indicate that the Bracero Program employed approximately 4.8 million Mexican nationals during its twenty-two years in existence, but the actual figures were probably closer to 0.5 million individuals, since many men participated year after year.[19] The high-water mark occurred in 1956, when 445,197 contracts were issued to Mexican workers by U.S. authorities. Three-quarters of all braceros found employment in Texas and California, but the program was not limited to the Southwest. Thousands of workers were transported to the Pacific Northwest (before 1947) and the Midwest.

Given the scope of the program and the weakness of government bureaucracy, it was inevitable that abuses would occur. The greatest single complaint by workers was the quality of the food; in an effort to save money, farm owners, generally through their contratistas, provided food and drink that was cheap but often unfamiliar to the Mexican—spaghetti, sandwiches, Kool-Aid, and so forth.[20] Wages were low, housing often inadequate, and race discrimination severe, especially in the states bordering the South. "Although the Bracero agreement contained stipulations with regard to health, housing, food, wages, and working hours," critics charge, "most were disregarded by both the U.S. government and the growers."[21] These chronic abuses have been chronicled in minute detail by Erasmo Gamboa, who has written the most thorough study yet on the workings of the program in a specific geographic area, *Mexican Labor and World War II: Braceros in the Pacific Northwest, 1942–1947* (1990). Interestingly, in the Pacific Northwest, in contrast to other destinations, braceros often went out on strike, which may reflect the difficulty growers experienced in finding alternate sources of farm labor in that particular region.

In spite of the program's shortcomings, it was not difficult to recruit braceros, who clearly derived advantages from the arrangement. The Mexican government, too, found the cooperative venture profitable. Its social security system received a much-needed boost, and, even more propitious, bracero earnings were sent home, where these remittances pumped up local economies. However, the prime beneficiaries, as Ernesto Galarza, one of the most respected Chicano scholars and an early critic of the program, proved in a variety of well-documented studies, were the farmers, particularly the large growers of Texas and California.

Although there was some resistance to the bilateral accord at the outset—and in some quarters there was never complete acceptance—the program was a bonanza for the big farmers, who quickly came to that realization. One of their major concerns historically was the recruitment of labor. How to find workers to harvest crops when needed and to leave the area thereafter, thus avoiding a burden on local schools and public relief funds—this question had never been resolved before. But now that nagging problem was solved at the expense of the government, that is, the taxpayer. Moreover, braceros were ideal laborers when compared to alternative sources of labor: migrant families, undocumented workers, and "winos" (alcoholic derelicts), the last category notoriously unreliable, though the cheapest of all options. Braceros came to the United States for one reason—to make money. Consequently, they were remarkably efficient and unusually reliable. Unlike local laborers, braceros were unlikely to go on strike—the Pacific Northwest was clearly an exception—nor miss work after a weekend of celebration, nor leave the area as the harvest season wound down and became less lucrative. These men, most of them in their twenties and thirties, were selected, usually by a contratista, who found a comfortable niche in the program, solely on the basis of their ability to do the best job possible. The length of the Bracero Program is a testimony to the considerable power wielded by agribusiness in the United States.

On the other hand, the binational program had stalwart opponents, who called for its dismantling by resorting to racist and economic arguments. Nativist organizations were uniformly opposed, of course. Labor unions also found braceros offensive for racist reasons, but economic considerations were predominant. There was persistent concern among union leaders that guest workers remaining in the United States illegally, less than 10 percent of the total, would find their way into the industrial sector, which organized labor saw as its domain, depressing wages and displacing U.S. citizens. Finally, there were small farmers who did not employ braceros but had to compete nationally and internationally against factory farms having the unfair advantage of cheap Mexican labor. Not surprisingly, the campaign to terminate the agreement in Congress was led by George S. McGovern (D-S.Dak.) and Eugene J. McCarthy (D-Minn.), spokesmen for the family farmers of the Midwest. In the end, PL78 was allowed to expire, not only because of pressure exerted by a powerful coalition of opponents but also because of increasing mechanization in the fields. As the labor historian Dennis Nodin Valdés argues: "By the late 1950s, as the effect of mechanization offset the demand for workers in cotton, growers could less easily justify their demand for braceros. Consequently, when the political attack on the bracero program intensified in the late 1950s, traditional bracero users were not as united as before."[22]

The attitude of the Mexicano community in the United States toward the Bracero Program, a managed migration, was as ambivalent as their attitude toward recent Mexican immigration in general. In theory, the agreement had safeguards protecting the rights of native-born farmworkers. For example, the U.S. government was required to certify that there was a genuine labor shortage before local farmers would be eligible to request braceros; and these braceros, once employed, had to be paid "the prevailing wage," that is, the wage that was generally paid for harvesting the particular crop in the particular area—not less than local workers received. In practice, however, given the modest funding and size of the government bureaucracy and the politics of agricultural communities, where large landholders wielded extraordinary power, braceros often displaced native-born workers and tended to depress agricultural wages. This suggests that the attitude toward braceros would likely be more negative among the U.S.-born Mexicano working class, which was adversely affected by the program,[23] and more positive among the ethnic middle class, educated and skilled individuals whose jobs were secure. In general, this may have been the case. However, it should be pointed out that, without exception, Mexican American civil rights organizations, predominantly middle class, took a stand against braceros.

More critical than class considerations was ethnic identification. Those Mexicanos living in the United States, regardless of class, who felt a strong sense of Mexican nationalism were more likely to identify with the braceros and accept them, especially if they themselves were recent immigrants. On the other hand, U.S.-born Mexicanos (Mexican Americans) with weak sentimental ties to the Old Country were likely to reject the guest worker program. In the Mexicano communities of the Southwest, the most consistent and disparaging criticism of the program came from New Mexico's Hispanos, not so much because of competition—agribusiness, concentrated in the Mesilla Valley, was not as powerful here as in other states—but because the Hispanic population, given its long-term residency, was more estranged from its Mexican roots than in other areas. Among southwestern congressmen, Senator Dennis Chávez (D-N.Mex.; 1888–1962) was the most vociferous critic of the Bracero Program.

OPERATION WETBACK

Factory farmers were also willing to dispense with braceros, albeit reluctantly, because by the 1960s they had easy access to other sources of labor that were almost as attractive, notably indocumentados, sometimes referred to as *mojados* (wetbacks) or, less often, *alambristas* (fence-jumpers). Illegal immigration from the south had always been a fact of life along the border, but following the Second World War, it became ubiquitous, reaching flood proportions by the time PL78 was allowed to lapse in the mid-1960s. Some five million illegals were apprehended and returned to Mexico by the U.S. Border Patrol during the twenty-two years of the bracero agreement. In fact, it was the contract-labor program itself, as Manuel García y Griego argues, more than any other single factor, which seems to have stimulated the huge wave of indocumentados.[24]

The increase in illegal entry into the United States, especially in the immediate postwar period, was also a result of the rapid economic development of Mexico. Beginning with the war, a vast economic transformation was initiated. As the economy expanded, Mexicans rushed into the cities to take advantage of new job opportunities. By 1960, the urban population had surpassed the rural population. Unfortunately, while the Mexican bourgeoisie made sizable gains in the 1940s and

1950s, the same could not be said of the lower class. Wages were unable to keep up with inflation. Moreover, a spiraling population ensured that the standard of living would remain low. In 1934, Mexico's population was about 16 million; by 1958, it had skyrocketed to more than 32 million. This phenomenal growth and the problems it fostered were most visible in the cities, where slums proliferated. The historians Michael C. Meyer and William L. Sherman explain: "Drawn by the lure of industry, hundreds of thousands of rural Mexicans flocked to the cities in hope of a better life, but few found it. The industrial revolution required skilled, not unskilled, labor. The need for more jobs, schools, health services, sewage disposal plants, streets, and houses in the cities was now taxing even the extraordinary postwar prosperity."[25] Mexico City, in particular, experienced the many problems associated with urban poverty as the population of the Federal District jumped from 3 million in 1952 to 4.5 million in 1958. The devastating impact of overpopulation and industrialization on the capital's sprawling *vecindades* (slum tenements) during the fifties has been thoroughly analyzed in the classic studies by the American anthropologist Oscar Lewis.

The northern periphery of Mexico became another source of illegal immigration. After the war, this tier of states experienced an unusually rapid economic transformation thanks to irrigation projects initiated during the administration of Miguel Alemán (1946–1952), notably the Morelos Dam on the Colorado River, near Mexicali, and, in the northeast, the Falcón Dam in the Lower Rio Grande Valley. The prospects of employment stimulated a steady northward movement of people from the densely populated central states. The norteño agrarian economy, however, was unable to absorb all the newcomers, resulting in the spectacular growth of border cities. From 1940 to 1967, Ciudad Juárez grew from 55,024 to 501,416; Mexicali from 44,399 to 540,300; and Tijuana from 21,977 to 347,501.

Once on the border, many recent arrivals were unable to resist the temptation to make the crossing to the United States, where jobs were abundant and wages high compared to Mexican standards. Unable to meet the stipulations legal entry required, the overwhelming majority crossed illegally. Since it was virtually impossible to police the international divide, given its length of almost two thousand miles and the modest size of the Border Patrol, deliberately kept understaffed by congressional representatives of southwestern corporate interests, Mexicans found it easy to avoid detection. The volume of traffic increased steadily. In 1950, the number of illegal entrants apprehended and returned to Mexico reached an unprecedented high of 469,000.

In the competition for jobs, undocumented workers held their own against braceros. The sociologist Julián Samora, a specialist on the subject, explains, "Wetback labor is even cheaper [than bracero labor]—no need for contracts, minimum wage, health benefits, housing, transportation, etc. Since the workers are illegal aliens, they have few rights before the law and can be dismissed at a moment's notice."[26]

While corporate farmers may have welcomed the rising tide of undocumented workers, other Americans grew apprehensive. By the early 1950s, anti-immigration fears were exacerbated by the xenophobia accompanying the Cold War. The result was a massive campaign waged by the Immigration and Naturalization Service (INS) to deport undocumented Mexicans. Labeled "Operation Wetback," the program was initiated on 17 June 1954, and lasted for several months.[27] Conducted as a military operation by the Border Patrol, and often employing the intimidation tactics of the thirties, it focused on the Southwest, but eventually it was extended nationally. Over one million people (1,075,168) were apprehended and returned to Mexico in 1954. Operation Wetback was hailed as a huge success, and it is true that in the late 1950s, apprehensions declined noticeably. However, by the early 1960s, illegal entries were on the rise once again. Once the Bracero Program was terminated, this immigration exploded.

With the growth of illegal immigration came the advent of a thriving smuggling operation, a major service industry thereafter from Brownsville to San Diego. At one time, Mexicans could cross the border routinely, no questions asked. As entry became more challenging, as was the case at the time of Operation Wetback, many undocumented immigrants sought help in crossing the border and finding work while escaping detection. Men and women involved in this dangerous and nefarious enterprise came to be known as *coyotes* and *coyotas,* respectively. Some did little more than guide their clients, or *pollos* (chickens), as they came to be called, a few hundred yards under cover of darkness. Others, more fearless, hauled hidden clients across checkpoints in motorized vehicles. For a higher fee—about two hundred dollars in the fifties—they were willing not only to smuggle aliens into the country but to transport them to work sites at a safe distance from the border. On rare occasions it was possible to secure transportation beyond the Southwest, something which became more common after 1965. Often, the client would be provided employment, invariably a low-paying job, since some smugglers either worked for or were themselves contratistas. During this period of illegal immigration, the overwhelming numbers of indocumentados were men, but women occasionally entered the migratory stream, some of them smuggled in to work as *cantineras* (barmaids) and prostitutes. Because the traffic was illicit and because the clients were virtually powerless, the business of smuggling tended to attract an unusually large number of unsavory and unscrupulous individuals. As has been observed on more than one occasion, border populations tend to have more than their share of such predatory types.

THE MEXICAN AMERICAN GENERATION

Until the 1980s, Chicano historians found little to compliment in the emerging middle class in Mexicano communities of the United States, if they bothered to deal with them at all. By and large, the bourgeoisie was written off by some critics as a pack of opportunists motivated exclusively by self-interest, often at the expense of poorer Mexicanos in the barrios. Calling themselves "Latin Americans," "Mexican Americans," or "Spanish Americans," they seemed to be willing to win acceptance into the dominant society at any cost. This exceedingly bleak portrait of the middle class is familiar to anyone who has read the early works of Rodolfo Acuña, the leading exponent of this view. Most Chicano scholars who were products of the 1960s, an age when the downtrodden were glorified and anti-establishment views reigned supreme, shared this perspective, to a greater or lesser extent.

However, this simplistic interpretation eventually came in for increasing criticism by a growing minority of Chicano scholars, led by Mario T. García, one of the most respected historians in the academic community. Calling for a radical reevaluation, García recast the middle class in a positive light. As he pointed out, more affluent members of the Mexicano community were periodically in the forefront of the fight for civil liberties. This was particularly true of the middle class during the years from 1930 to 1960, a cohort that he and other like-minded colleagues refer to as the Mexican American Generation. Consisting primarily of the native-born, the middle class by the thirties began to identify primarily with the United States rather than Mexico; in contrast to the previous generation, which consisted of immigrants whose identity was overwhelmingly conditioned by their love of the Old Country, *México lindo* (beautiful Mexico). Consistent with this new orientation, what the historian Richard García calls the "Mexican-American mind," the second generation, rather than resigning themselves to their degraded condition, as their immigrant parents had been wont to do, began to seek political solutions to the many problems that beset the ethnic community.

Mario García viewed the Great Depression as something of a watershed in this process; however, there was more continuity than he suggests. The League of United Latin-American Citizens (LULAC), for example, which was formed in 1929 and was the most memorable of all the organizations constructed by the Mexican American Generation, was lauded by Professor García as "the oldest Mexican-American civil rights association in the United States." Yet, LULAC itself was an outgrowth of a number of older organizations, including the Orden Hijos de América (Order Sons of America) founded in San Antonio in 1921, which Professor García, in an apparent contradiction, described in this way: "Comprised of mostly lower middle-class professionals, the Sons stressed socializing Mexican Americans to their rights as U.S. citizens and obtaining equal rights for them."[28] LULAC, it could be argued, was the product of developments that could be traced back to World War I, and even further back. The Primer Congreso Mexicanista (First Mexican Congress), which was convened by the highly regarded newspaper editor Clemente N. Idar in Laredo in 1911, was an early champion of the rights of Mexicanos. Indeed, it is clear that even in the nineteenth century, Mexicanos were concerned with protecting their civil liberties and were willing to use political weapons.

Yet it was during the Second World War, as many Chicano scholars conclude, that most Mexicanos in the United States began to see the advantages of remaining in this country rather than returning to Mexico. Moreover, with the war came the rise of a middle class with sufficient interest and ability to provide effective political leadership beyond Texas. It is partly for these reasons that Juan Gómez-Quiñones, in his exhaustive study of contemporary political life, *Chicano Politics: Reality and Promise* (1990), saw the period between 1941 and the 1960s as a distinct stage of cultural development.

In order to appreciate the political advances that were made from the forties to the sixties, however, it is necessary to briefly recap key factors in Mexican American life prior to the Second World War. By the turn of the century, many mutualistas, though primarily immigrant organizations interested in ameliorating the social and economic conditions of their members, were realizing that civil rights could be guaranteed only by entering the political arena. Certainly, this perspective was in evidence, as we saw previously, in the Alianza Hispano-Americana. The First World War spawned a number of mutualistas that resembled the Alianza in their concern for social and political action, notably the Liga Protectora Latina in Phoenix and the Liga Protectora Mexicana in Kansas City. The Alianza, however, remained the most energetic and prestigious mutualista as it expanded its lodges throughout the Southwest, reaching the pinnacle of its popularity in the twenties. During the thirties and forties, under conservative leadership, it shied away from controversy, but it resumed its fight for civil rights after World War II. Kaye Briegel reports that "even as late as 1968 the Alianza remained the best-known Mexican-American organization in Los Angeles."[29] Nevertheless, by this time, it had long since been superseded by more dynamic associations.

The most respected of these other civic organizations was undoubtedly LULAC, which, as mentioned above, grew out of an association that was more obscure but historically meaningful nonetheless, the Orden Hijos de América. The latter was founded in 1921 by prominent leaders of the San Antonio Mexicano community. The association excluded immigrants. "This limitation of membership to American citizens," writes Miguel David Tirado, in a pioneering article, "indicated a growing realization by Mexican-American leaders that political power is essential for the achievement of the minority's aim in this country, and that the political power only arises with the organization of a solid voting bloc of citizens."[30] Although it managed to set up lodges in South Texas, the Orden was soon beset by a multitude of difficulties, not the least of which was ethnic infighting and ultimate schism.

It was some of the more militant members of the Orden who took the initiative in founding LULAC in Corpus Christi on 17 February 1929.[31] Its program was very similar to that of its predecessor. The most charismatic and effective of its early leaders was Alonso S. Perales (1899–1960), who was ably assisted by Manuel C. Gonzales (1900–1986) and Ben Garza (1892–1937).[32] Mirroring the assimilationist attitudes of the time, LULAC too confined its membership to U.S. citizens, and therefore to the middle-class elite. Its stated objective was to inculcate American values among its members. Consistent with this philosophy, it adopted English as its official language. However, it vowed to protect the Mexicano community, not just its own membership, from the discrimination that was rampant at the time. To a surprising extent, it was successful in keeping its promise. Although in public it claimed to be apolitical—its membership included both liberals and conservatives—politics was one avenue it was willing to pursue.

In the past, Chicano historians were hard on LULAC because of its middle-class orientation and assimilationist tendencies. Subsequently, however, while conceding that a strong class bias permeated the organization, Mario García rightly noted that the aim of *Lulacers* was not to deny their Mexican heritage. What they hoped to accomplish, he argued, was "some functional balance between mainstream Anglo-American culture and the culture derived from their Mexican roots."[33]

The success of LULAC was due to its dynamic leadership, its incorporation of youth and women's auxiliaries, and its willingness to change with the times. After the Second World War, LULAC became increasingly active in combating racial prejudice and discrimination in Texas, always its stronghold despite forays into other sections of the country. During the postwar period its effectiveness was aided by its ability to work with a number of powerful Anglo politicians in the state, notably Lyndon B. Johnson.

Perhaps LULAC's most lasting contribution, as Guadalupe San Miguel Jr. has shown in *"Let All of Them Take Heed": Mexican Americans and the Campaign for Educational Equality in Texas* (1987), was in the area of school desegregation, a major problem in Texas and throughout the Southwest. Mexicano children began to be segregated into "Mexican" schools at the turn of the century. The nation's first successful legal challenge to this discriminatory practice occurred in California in 1931, when angry Mexicano parents sued the San Diego County community of Lemon Grove, after their children had been barred from Anglo schools, and won a favorable verdict. Some years later, in 1945, five Mexican American families in Orange County, California, led by Gonzalo and Felícitas Méndez, filed a class action suit against several school districts in an effort to integrate local schools. *Méndez et al. v. Westminster School District of Orange County* (1947), "one of the most significant legal cases in the history of the Southwest," according to Gilbert G. González,[34] effectively ended de jure segregation in California.

Lulacers, while only peripherally involved in the *Méndez* case, were in the forefront of the effort to desegregate Texas schools, which culminated in *Delgado v. Bastrop Independent School District* (1948), which did for the Lone Star State what the former had done for California. While de facto segregation survived until the 1960s in some areas of the Southwest, both of these critical cases served as notable precedents for the landmark *Brown v. Board of Education,* the 1954 Supreme Court decision that mandated school desegregation in the United States and launched the civil rights movements of the sixties.

Finally, the last Mexicano association with a substantial political agenda to emerge before World War II was the Congreso del Pueblo de Habla Española, a federation of Mexicano associations founded, as previously mentioned, in Los Angeles on 4 December 1938. Like all other organizations which aimed at achieving first-class citizenship for Mexicanos, the Congreso mirrored the concerns of the time. Spawned by the Depression, it was a progressive-radical body with a marked Communist influence, as witnessed in the left-wing labor unions active in its creation. Members sought to ensure both economic benefits and civil liberties for Mexicanos.

The Congreso differed from most Mexicano organizations of the interwar period not only because of its radical social program but also because of the degree to which mujeres were involved. Mexicanas have been a significant minority in almost all associations mentioned previously, sometimes segregated into auxiliaries of their own, sometimes integrated into the general membership, as the Chicana historian Cynthia E. Orozco has chronicled so well.[35] Rarely, though, had they played a leading role. The Congreso was an exception. From the very outset, mujeres were among the most active members; the Congreso itself was the brainchild of Luisa Moreno, and its executive secretary for most of its short history was Josefina Fierro de Bright.

The California-based organization had only one national convention, in 1939, before disappearing three years later. The brevity of its existence can be attributed to two main causes: its political radicalism, which though within the reformist tradition, was considered too extreme by most Americans, including many Mexicano obreros themselves; and the onset of the war, which not only required that all citizens work together for the common cause but also generated a multitude of jobs, effectively countering worker dissatisfaction. While the Congreso eschewed electoral politics, it was memorable nonetheless because it provided valuable leadership training for many Mexicano men and women, among them the legendary community organizers Eduardo Quevedo and Bert Corona.

Despite its efforts to expand its membership nationally or at least regionally, the Congreso remained a California organization, with Los Angeles as its power base. Its demise in 1942, on the eve of the Zoot Suit Riots, left a void at precisely the time when a coordinated effort on behalf of civil liberties was most essential. Distressed by the vehemence of anti-Mexican sentiment, Mexicanos in southern California began to set up grassroots organizations for the protection of their communities. Immediately after the war, these efforts led to the formation of Unity Leagues, the first of which arose in the Pomona Valley, east of Los Angeles, in 1946. The effort was guided by a respected champion of the ethnic community, Ignacio ("Nacho") López (1908–1973), editor of a local Spanish-language newspaper, *El Espectador,* in the nearby San Gabriel Valley. Unlike most of the organizations mentioned previously, the Spanish-Speaking Congress being the outstanding exception, the Unity Leagues, which soon proliferated throughout the Los Angeles area, were as interested in mobilizing the working class as they were the middle class. Although their primary mission was to combat discrimination, especially the segregation of schools and other public facilities, Unity League members also sought political office. In 1946, they managed to elect the first Mexicano since the nineteenth century to a California city council, Andrés Morales in the Pomona Valley town of Chino. While encountering only moderate success in achieving their goals, they did lay the foundation for the Community Service Organization (CSO), the most effective Mexican American association to appear in California during the postwar period.

The chief link between the two organizations was Fred W. Ross (1910–1992), a professional organizer and arguably the most important non-Hispanic ever to advance the cause of the Mexicano community. After the war, Ross, a graduate of the University of Southern California, came under the sway of Saul Alinsky (1909–1972). Using Alinsky's techniques of community mobilization and leadership development, Ross exerted an enormous influence on the Mexicano middle class of the City of Angels.

Founded in East Los Angeles in September 1947, CSO grew out of efforts to elect Edward Roybal (1916–2005) to the Los Angeles City Council in that year—1881 was the last time a Mexicano had served on that body. Although he lost the election, Roybal, using Ross's organizational techniques, transformed his small but enthusiastic coterie into an association with more ambitious goals. As its title suggests, the Community Service Organization was intended to meet the many needs of the Mexicano community, but given its genesis as an electoral vehicle, it is not surprising that the nonpartisan group emphasized political action from the very beginning. During its first years, CSO managed to expand throughout the state, successfully running a number of candidates for school and government positions, notably Roybal himself, who was elected to the Los Angeles City Council in 1949. By this time, though, America was in the throes of the Cold War, and CSO leaders, many of them veterans, grew reluctant to advance political candidacies. While continuing to sponsor voter registration drives, CSO focused on educational and police issues during the fifties. Eventually, even these initiatives came to be seen as too controversial, and the organization was virtually transformed into a mutual-aid society by the sixties.

In addition to CSO, the other major community-based organization that developed among Mexicanos in the postwar period, and one that was considerably more effective in achieving its stated goals, was the American G.I. Forum.[36] Founded in Corpus Christi in 1948, the G.I. Forum admitted only veterans, which meant that the membership would be highly patriotic and heavily committed to assimilation. Given its conservative origins and composition, the association's devotion to the American Way was beyond reproach. Consequently, reasonably immune to red-baiting during the McCarthy years, it was less prone to compromise on questions of racial discrimination than its California counterpart. Although its lodges were predominately confined to Texas, the G.I. Forum would be the most celebrated champion of Mexicano civil rights in the country before the advent of the Chicano movement.

Perhaps the key reason for the G.I. Forum's early prominence was the leadership provided by Dr. Héctor Pérez García (1910–1996), one of the most charismatic personalities to emerge from the Mexicano community in the postwar period. According to his biographer, the historian Ignacio M. García, "It would be difficult to identify someone else that most represented his era. If there is a Jeffersonian Age, then there needs to be the acknowledgment of a García Age in Latino history of the United States."[37] Although born in Tamaulipas, Héctor García was raised a Tejano. He received his B.A. from the University of Texas in 1936 and eventually became a physician. He served with distinction in the war, winning a Bronze Star, before returning to South Texas, where he immersed himself in Democratic politics and gained a solid reputation as an indomitable defender of the civil rights of Tejanos. The founder of the Forum, he served as president for many years. He was also active in LULAC and a variety of other ethnic organizations. In 1984, culminating a long and distinguished career of community service, Dr. García was awarded America's highest civilian honor, the Presidential Medal of Freedom.

The most valuable accomplishments of the G.I. Forum came in the area of discrimination, a special concern since there was so much of it in the Lone Star State. Indeed, the organization was founded in the first place as a result of a clamorous example of racial injustice in 1948, when a Mexicano soldier killed in the Philippines, Félix Longoria, was refused burial in the Live Oak County town of

Three Rivers, Texas. After a heated campaign, and with the help of Senator Lyndon Johnson, the beginning of a long and fruitful association, Dr. García and the G.I. Forum were able to secure Longoria a burial at Arlington National Cemetery.

Segregation, the most blatant form of discrimination, was pervasive in Texas during the forties, against not just blacks but also "Meskins," who were generally perceived, as in other parts of the country, as a nonwhite population. During the forties and fifties, the G.I. Forum initiated a series of class-action suits aimed at desegregating schools, recreational facilities, and transportation. It encountered many victories in this area, especially after the 1954 *Brown* decision.

Like the CSO, the G.I. Forum was, and remains, officially nonpartisan, but it always encouraged members to run for elected office and endorsed candidates. Undoubtedly, the legacy of the G.I. Forum goes a long way in explaining why Tejanos have been so much more assertive in politics than have Mexicanos in California and other states during the second half of the twentieth century.

The CSO and the G.I. Forum, though falling short of their lofty goals, were nevertheless able to survive, in contrast to another extraordinary Mexicano civil rights association that was founded in the forties: the Asociación Nacional México-Americana (ANMA, the National Mexican American Association). Founded in Phoenix in February 1949, ANMA functioned only through 1953. Organized by a militant mining union with heavy Mexicano representation, the International Union of Mine, Mill and Smelter Workers (Mine-Mill), ANMA, like the Spanish-Speaking Congress before it, was almost exclusively working class in its membership. Like the old organization, too, its politics were markedly left of center. Dedicated to protecting the rights of Mexicanos, both native- and foreign-born, ANMA was willing to work through alliances with progressive working-class groups, including the American Communist Party, as well as other persecuted ethnic minorities. Another striking similarity with the Congreso was its concern with feminist issues, which was evident in its leadership, where many key positions were held by Mexicanas. Among the members of the first national executive board were Isabel Gonzales, vice president; Xóchitl Ruiz, secretary-general; Virginia Ruiz, executive secretary; and Florencia Luna, secretary-treasurer. Women, too, were conspicuous in leadership roles at the local level.[38]

One of ANMA's most notable campaigns was in support of the famous 1950–1952 miners' strike in Bayard, New Mexico. The fifteen-month work stoppage, immortalized by the film classic *Salt of the Earth* (1954), was initiated by Mine-Mill. The striking miners, most of them Mexicanos, succeeded only when their wives, led by Virginia Chacón, insisted on participating, in spite of their husbands' objections, snatching victory from apparent defeat.

Never very numerous—at its height, membership was a few thousand—ANMA was plagued throughout its brief history by unfounded charges of Communist affiliation, which led to its demise during the McCarthy era. "ANMA eventually declined," recalls Bert Corona, its chief organizer for northern California, "because the FBI intimidated its members and destroyed its organization."[39] The radical tradition of Mexicano political activity, represented by the Congreso and ANMA, would resurface during the Chicano movement in the sixties. Given the temper of the times, however, the only realistic hope for reform during the postwar years rested with more traditional middle-class organizations.

By the late 1950s, winds of change were beginning to sweep through the United States. The Cold War began to thaw, and African Americans, led by Dr. Martin Luther King Jr., initiated a powerful civil rights movement. These momentous changes were reflected in the Mexicano community with the creation of the Mexican American Political Association (MAPA), a middle-class association that unabashedly called for political action by its members. More specifically, this initiative was a direct result of Hispanic dissatisfaction with the Democratic Party. To the extent that they had participated in the electoral process, Mexicanos tended to support the Democrats beginning in the days of FDR—their vote was pretty evenly split between both parties before the Depression. Since Republicans displayed scant interest in courting them, Mexicano votes automatically went to the Democrats, still considered the party of immigrants. Unfortunately, Mexicano support was taken for granted, and patronage for barrio politicos was weak or nonexistent. The final disillusion came with the defeat of Henry ("Hank") López for California secretary of state in 1958, after lukewarm support from the Democratic Party leadership.

Meeting in Fresno, California, disgruntled Mexican leaders organized MAPA on a statewide basis in April 1960. Founders included Roybal, Quevedo, Hermán Gallegos, and Margaret Cruz, who would become the association's first female president in 1973, but the most dedicated and respected single individual was Bert Corona (1918–2001), who came to dominate the short-lived organization. Born in El Paso, Corona was raised in a Methodist household. He attended the University of Southern California briefly, but dropped out during the height of the Depression to work as a labor organizer for CIO. As mentioned previously, he was active in both ANMA and the Congreso, where he had worked with Quevedo. Both men continued their close collaboration in CSO.

Set up as a bipartisan political association, MAPA pledged to support Mexicano candidates to public office, as well as non-Mexicano candidates who promised to work for the Mexicano cause. While *Mapistas* met with moderate success at the polls during the next decade—the election of Roybal to the U.S. House of Representatives in 1962 was especially gratifying—efforts were hampered by internal dissension, a failure to adequately cultivate the working class, and, despite the bipartisan rhetoric, an unwillingness to abandon the Democrats.

The tendency to support the Democratic Party became apparent almost immediately, in the Viva Kennedy movement that helped elect John F. Kennedy to the presidency in 1960. Led by Tejanos Dr. Héctor García, elected national coordinator, and Congressman Henry B. González (1916–2000), this campaign mobilized the Mexicano community solidly behind the youthful Catholic candidate. Mapistas in the Golden State, with few exceptions, were enthusiastic supporters.

The Viva Kennedy clubs were so effective in bringing Mexicanos together that in 1961 it was decided to use the successful campaign as a springboard for the creation of an umbrella organization that would unite the various Mexicano civil rights associations. A precedent had been set ten years before by the American Council of Spanish-Speaking People (ACSSP), but the attempt was abortive, and the organization failed to survive into the sixties. The new initiative was taken by the ubiquitous Dr. Héctor García, who became the founder and first president of the Political Association of Spanish-Speaking Organizations (PASO or PASSO). The organization got off to a promising start in Texas; however, attempts to promote PASSO in the rest of the Southwest stalled, and ultimately the organization petered out. It experienced the obstacles that Mexicano political and cultural associations have always had to overcome at the local level—power struggles, lack of money, class differences, and so on—but apparently the overriding problem was regionalism, the tendency toward parochialism, which translated into an unwillingness of Mexicanos in one section of the country to work with those in another. Although PASSO went through difficult times, it scored occasional victories, among them the stunning election of five Mexicano candidates to the city council of Crystal City, Texas, in 1963.

Latino political advances before the mid-1960s appear rather modest to many critics of the Mexicano middle class. Certainly, it is true that from a purely political perspective little had been gained in terms of representation at any level of government—municipal, county, state, or federal—outside of New Mexico. By 1965, despite a population of between four and five million, Mexicanos had only four representatives in the U.S. Congress: Joseph Montoya (D-N.Mex.) in the Senate and Henry B. González (D-Tex.), Eligio ("Kika") de la Garza (D-Tex.), and Edward R. Roybal (D-Calif.) in the House. It is important, however, to appreciate the monumental obstacles Mexican American leaders faced as they tried to mobilize their ethnic community.

First of all, the immigrant community held a thoroughly negative attitude toward politics. Democracy had never worked well in Mexico. Corruption had been rife, a recurring problem in Mexican political life, as Ramón Eduardo Ruiz's studies show so conclusively. One can hardly blame Mexicans for being cynical, especially peasants, who were traditionally excluded from the political process.

Second, Mexican immigrants came to the United States typically believing that they would return home someday. Third, a large number, possibly the majority, of immigrants entered the country without their papers, which meant they were ineligible for citizenship. Fourth, nationalism came to be so deeply embedded that even immigrants who came in legally and had no intention of returning home were reticent to give up their Mexican citizenship. Fifth, the socioeconomic level of the community made it exceedingly difficult to form political associations. Mexicanos were generally impoverished and often illiterate. Sixth, though there were occasional respites, anti-Mexican feeling was generally pervasive, which meant that the dominant society, consistently maintaining an attitude of ethnic and cultural superiority, discouraged political participation through a variety of tactics, including the poll tax, gerrymandering, and at-large elections.

And yet, from a broader perspective, and in spite of these nagging problems, middle-class leadership could claim some surprising successes by 1965, notably in the field of civil rights. The supreme accomplishment of Mexicano leaders between World War II and the mid-1960s was the effective end of *legal* forms of oppression, a significant victory which paved the way for future gains.[40] Few scholars today would agree with Manuel Servín, who, speaking before the Western History Association in 1965, concluded that "the post–World War II Mexican Americans have been a nonachieving minority."[41]

THE MEXICAN AMERICAN INTELLIGENTSIA

Another positive trend in the period 1940–1965 was the rise of an intelligentsia, a measure of how far the Mexicano middle class in the United States had progressed by the mid-twentieth century. During the nineteenth century, there were individuals who would qualify as intellectuals. Generally, they were clergymen, such as Father Antonio José Martínez, or newspaper editors, such as Francisco P. Ramírez. These were isolated cases, however. After the turn of the century, during the Great Migration, immigrants, especially political refugees, included some well-educated men and women, people of high culture; but many of them were in the country temporarily, and the others mostly had an impact only at the local level.

The Depression brought a fateful departure. Among the most powerful intellects emerging from the barrios was Ernesto Galarza (1905–1984), awarded a Ph.D. at Columbia University, an educator, union organizer, and specialist in labor history.[42] The 1930s, too, witnessed the first successes of the aforementioned Américo Paredes, a folklorist, poet, and novelist who received his doctorate from the University of Texas, where he taught for many years; and a person whose contributions are only now being appreciated, Jovita Mireles Gonzales (1904–1983), a folklorist and historian, the first person of Mexican heritage to be elected president of the Texas Folklore Society.[43]

Three other names, however, deserve special attention because, as Mario García points out, they "helped shape a Mexican-American intellectual culture and scholarship that played a role in the academic world while providing some direction in the realm of ideas to the struggles of the Mexican-American Generation," thus anticipating Chicano scholars who came after: Carlos Castañeda, Arthur Campa, and George Sánchez.[44]

Carlos Eduardo Castañeda (1896–1958) was born in Ciudad Camargo, Chihuahua, but was raised in Brownsville, where his family moved when he was ten. He enrolled at the University of Texas at Austin as an engineering major, but, swayed by the renowned historian Eugene C. Barker, switched to history, earning three degrees in that discipline, including a Ph.D. in 1932. His academic career was spent at his alma mater, where he taught from 1933 to 1958. "No Mexican American historian in the twentieth century," according to his biographer Félix D. Almaráz Jr., "has approximated his solid publishing record of eighteen books and nearly fifty articles."[45] His magnum opus was a massive six-volume study entitled *Our Catholic Heritage in Texas* (1936–1950). The first major historian to write about the history of Mexicanos in the Southwest, Dr. Castañeda is also credited with encouraging U.S. scholars to take an interest in Latin American studies.

Arthur León Campa (1905–1978), too, was an immigrant to Texas. Born in Guaymas, Sonora, to parents who were Methodist missionaries, he grew up near El Paso. Later, his mother moved the family to Albuquerque, where the youth was provided his early schooling. Campa pursued his college education at the University of New Mexico, earning two degrees, before continuing his graduate studies at Columbia University, receiving a doctorate in languages there in 1940. He served in the Second World War, winning a Bronze Star. Subsequently, he turned to an academic career and taught at the University of Denver from 1946 until his retirement in 1972. Although not the first student of Mexicano folklore in the Southwest to achieve fame—the New Mexican Aurelio M. Espinoza Sr., merits that honor—Campa soon acquired a reputation as the outstanding authority in this, his area of expertise. Published posthumously in 1979, *Hispanic Culture in the Southwest* is a summary of Dr. Campa's scholarship during the course of a long and celebrated career.

George I. Sánchez (1906–1972), widely known as "the dean of Mexican-American scholars," was born in Albuquerque. After receiving his B.A. at the University of New Mexico, he attended both the University of Texas and the University of California at Berkeley, where he was awarded his doctorate in educational administration in 1934. A scholar, writer, and educator, Dr. Sánchez first achieved prominence with his impressionistic history of Hispanos, *Forgotten People,* published in 1940, the very year he joined the University of Texas faculty. He is best remembered, though, as a pioneer in the field of bilingual education. An indefatigable worker, Dr. Sánchez also left a mark as a civil rights leader. He was a stalwart member of LULAC, serving as president in 1941. Ten years later, he founded the short-lived American Council of Spanish-Speaking People, an umbrella organization of Mexicano organizations in Texas, mentioned previously.

Probably the outstanding trend in Mexican American history in the period between 1940 and 1965 was the rise of a middle class from virtual anonymity. A generation ago, this assessment would have encountered fierce resistance in emerging Chicana/o studies departments. The pioneering Chicano historians of the 1960s and 1970s generally provided a very unflattering portrait of the fledgling middle sector. Its very weakness, given its low educational level and lack of capital, invited scorn. Moreover, the assimilationist tendency that the middle class displayed historically was completely at odds with the Chicano movement's demand for cultural regeneration at a time when Chicano scholarship was beginning. Not surprisingly, the popular view of the Mexican American middle class as vendidos was mirrored by young scholars of the time.

During the past few years, however, the Chicano perception of these professionals, merchants, and artisans has undergone a dramatic shift, though not one universally endorsed. Now, there is growing appreciation of the fact that during the years between 1940 and 1965, and in spite of the adverse political climate created by two major wars and the fear of Communism, the middle class waged an unremitting struggle to win citizenship rights for all Mexicanos living in the United States. The gains made in the field of civil rights, impressive accomplishments considering the temper of the times, were made primarily because of pressure exerted by middle-class associations, notably LULAC, CSO, and the G.I. Forum. These organizations, even a long-time critic of middle-class elitism like activist-scholar Juan Gómez-Quiñones is forced to admit, had a "creditable record of activity between the forties and the midsixties."[46]

The revisionism apparent today in Chicano historiography reflects a greater maturity on the part of Chicano scholars. Most of these professors are intellectual heirs of the 1960s and 1970s, with Ph.D.s generally earned in the middle of the latter decade, Chicanas somewhat later. Some were militants at the time. Virtually all of them, however, were influenced by Chicanismo, whether they were active participants in the movement or not—which is why they are recognized as Chicano and Chicana scholars—and accepted its natural repugnance of elites. The bias against the bourgeoisie was also reinforced, in many cases, by exposure to Marxist ideas, a tendency more evident at the University of California than elsewhere—and one of the reasons why minority historians trained in California tend to be more militant than their colleagues from Texas. Finally, it should be noted that the overwhelming majority of these scholars have working-class origins.

What accounts for the more sympathetic view of the Mexicano middle class by a growing segment of the scholarly community? The new revisionism mirrors a natural swing of the pendulum; when historians move so far in one direction, there is no place to go but in the other direction. But equally compelling are current demographic and socioeconomic changes in the Mexicano community. The middle class today is expanding. Moreover, Chicano professors in the nation's universities—or even in community colleges, for that matter—are realizing that their students are or will soon become members of that privileged class, albeit with increasing difficulty. Last, and not least, the aging professors themselves have entered into the ranks of the once despised bourgeoisie, which of necessity has softened their attitude toward it.[47]

THE CHICANO
MOVEMENT
1965–1975

8

The decade comprising the midsixties to the midseventies was a period of extraordinary ferment in the Mexicano communities of the United States. Fateful social changes were in the air. Immigration from Mexico, for example, increased markedly, a trend that tended to push many of the older residents of the Southwest into other parts of the country. The most memorable changes, though, were political and psychological.

Following the lead of the African American community, which initiated a far-reaching movement for civil liberties in the fifties, many Mexicanos, now calling themselves Chicanos and Chicanas, embarked on their own campaign to improve socioeconomic conditions and win full recognition of their rights as U.S. citizens.[1] While these concerns had been articulated before, notably by the Mexican American Generation of the post–World War II period, after the midsixties a new aggressiveness developed in the barrios. Socioeconomic gains made in past years seemed woefully inadequate. Many Mexicanos began to demand immediate reform. Some called for revolution. Convinced that changes of whatever kind could be instituted only through the acquisition of power, they emphasized political action as never before. Moreover, in contrast to their postwar predecessors, the leaders of the so-called Chicano Generation stressed pride in their ethnic roots while deemphasizing assimilation into the American mainstream. "A Chicano," Rubén Salazar, a journalist on the periphery of the movement, once said, "is a Mexican-American with a non-Anglo image of himself."[2] Tired of apologizing for their ethnic origins, Chicanos looked to Mexico, especially indigenous Mexico, for inspiration. While there was much disagreement on specific methods—indeed, a substantial minority stood on the sidelines—most of the community was in general agreement with the goals formulated by barrio leaders: cultural regeneration and political power. Since these twin objectives are the crux of the emerging Chicano movement, also called

Chicano Power or Brown Power, the struggle for Mexican American civil rights, it seems reasonable to see this decade in terms of Chicanismo.

THE MEXICANO COMMUNITY IN THE MIDSIXTIES

A portrait of the Mexicano population on the eve of the Chicano movement is helpful in explaining why Chicanismo became so appealing to large segments of the population. The best source of information on Mexicanos in the early sixties, indeed the most comprehensive work on the subject up to this time, was *The Mexican-American People: The Nation's Second Largest Minority* (1970) by Leo Grebler, Joan W. Moore, and Ralph C. Guzmán, a product of research conducted by the Mexican American Study Project at the University of California at Los Angeles in 1964–1968. The UCLA study was based on data taken from the 1960 U.S. census, so the information is very appropriate for our purposes.

The use of government statistics was not without its pitfalls. Since the census had no separate category for Mexicanos but identified them on the basis of "Spanish-surname," a rubric that would include Cubans, Puerto Ricans, and others, it was difficult to interpret the findings. Furthermore, this census, like most government statistical records, was criticized for heavily undercounting Mexicanos, mainly because of the difficulty in keeping track of migrant workers and illegal aliens. Still, the 1960 census and the Grebler study based on it are invaluable demographic sources useful in tracing emerging trends. If allowances are made for the deficiencies alluded to, they present a fairly clear and complete portrait of the community.

The total Mexicano population in 1960, according to Grebler and his colleagues, who interpreted and adjusted the official census figures, was 3,842,000, of which 87 percent (3,344,292) resided in the Southwest and the remaining 13 percent (497,800) in other parts of the country. Texas and California, with about equal numbers, accounted for over 80 percent of the southwestern total. Urbanization was advancing at a brisk pace. By 1960, about two-thirds of the population was urban. Somewhat surprisingly, urbanization was more pronounced in the Southwest, where the proportion approached 80 percent. Roughly one-third of all Mexicanos lived in four cities in this region: Los Angeles, San Antonio, San Francisco, and El Paso. Whether living in cities or the countryside, however, Mexicanos displayed a striking tendency to reside in segregated ethnic communities. Some of these barrios were in the middle of large cities, as was the case in Los Angeles and Albuquerque; some were on the periphery, as in Fresno; some encompassed the entire community, as was true of many agricultural towns of the Lower Rio Grande Valley and, to a lesser extent, the San Joaquin Valley.

During the previous decade, the most trenchant demographic trend was the immigration from throughout the Southwest, especially Texas, to California. There was also heavy immigration into the United States from Mexico. Over 290,000 Mexicans entered the country legally in the fifties. Illegal immigration may have been four times greater. Nevertheless, over 85 percent of the Mexicanos were born in the United States. Indeed, over half of the Spanish-speaking people in the Southwest were native-born of native-born parents; that is, they were at least second-generation U.S. citizens. The fertility rate was very high. Consequently, the population was relatively youthful. The median age was a little over nineteen years, compared to twenty-eight years for the non-Hispanic white population in the Southwest. The high fertility rate and immigration combined to bring about rapid growth: during the fifties, the Mexicano population of the Southwest increased by a remarkable 51 percent. By 1960, Spanish-speakers, almost all of them of Mexican origin, made up 12 percent of the total population in the region.

Impressive social and economic gains had been registered by this time. During the decade of the fifties, the percentage of Latinos in the Southwest classified as laborers declined from 42 to 30 percent. Another positive trend was the entry of Mexican and Mexican American women into the labor force. Their rates of employment outside the home were higher than among Anglos. During the fifties, median income for Mexicano households rose at a substantially higher rate than that of Anglos. Home ownership went up, as well.

Educational levels were improving. During the fifties, the proportions of Spanish-speaking people in the Southwest who completed high school increased almost 75 percent, with California making more progress than other states. The educational gap between Mexicanos and Anglos actually narrowed slightly at this time. Greater numbers of Mexicanos were enrolling in institutions of higher learning. Though brown faces were difficult to find in major universities across the United States, or even in the Southwest, for that matter, the emerging community colleges provided minorities, including Hispanics, a golden opportunity to improve their socioeconomic status. Prominent Mexicanos benefiting from a junior college education, many of them in this period, include scholars Renato I. Rosaldo, Ralph Guzmán, Américo Paredes, Julián Nava, Carlos Muñoz Jr., Armando Navarro, Oscar J. Martínez, and Patricia Zavella; writers Ron Arias, Gary Soto, Denise Chávez, and Floyd Salas; civil rights activists Ignacio López, Dolores Huerta, Cruz Reynoso, José Ángel Gutiérrez, and Edward James Olmos; political leaders Eligio de la Garza, Philip Sánchez, Henry B. González, and Gloria Molina; educators Tomás Rivera and Cecilia Preciado de Burciaga; artists Manuel Neri, José Montoya, and Rupert García; newspaper publisher Mónica Cecilia Lozano; entrepreneur Danny Villanueva; and Tom Flores, the popular athlete and coach.

In general, the decade of the fifties, based on census records, indicated a gradual improvement in the community's socioeconomic condition—this in spite of ongoing immigration from Mexico which skewed the statistics against this positive trend.

Nevertheless, there were many problems. The best indicators of socioeconomic status are education, occupation, and income. According to the Grebler study, Mexicanos ranked close to the bottom in all three categories. In all southwestern states, Mexicanos averaged three to four years less education than Anglos. Roughly 50 percent had less than eight grades of schooling, a lower rate than African Americans. Moreover, the statistics do not indicate the severity of the problem, for they tell us nothing about the quality of instruction. "These years of education," according to the sociologist Joan W. Moore, "probably were obtained disproportionately in rural, small town, and other schools of inferior quality."[3] In institutions of higher learning, the record was dismal. Less than 6 percent of Mexicanos had some college education, half the percentage of the black population and a quarter of the Anglo population. Naturally, the problem was most severe at the university level. In the Golden State, for example, where Mexicanos made up about 10 percent of the population, no branch of the University of California as late as 1967 had as many as one hundred Mexicano students.

In part because of their educational deficiencies, most Mexicanos were employed as unskilled or semiskilled workers in low-wage or marginal jobs, what social scientists call a secondary labor market. Within a particular job category, they tended to be at the bottom, earning the lowest wages. Unemployment rates for Mexicanos were twice as high as for Anglos of comparable ages in 1960. The census of that year indicated that incomes were considerably lower among Spanish-speaking people than other segments of the population. Grebler, Moore, and Guzmán state: "Mexican Americans had only 47 cents for every dollar of Anglo income, and they were worse off than nonwhites."[4] The rural population was significantly more disadvantaged in this respect than the urban population, a disparity that had widened during the previous decade, which helps explain the continuing migration to the cities. According to government criteria, over one-third of the Spanish-speaking population fell under the poverty level—an annual income of three thousand dollars per family. In Texas, over half the Mexicano population was officially poor. Juan Gómez-Quiñones, widely viewed as "the dean of Chicano historians," puts the picture in clear perspective: "Despite the organizational challenge by Mexican Americans to discrimination in the forties, fifties, and sixties and economic gains resulting from postwar economic booms, the unequal position between Mexican Americans and Anglo Americans probably expanded rather than contracted. Mexican advances in education, income, employment, occupational status, and political representation were dwarfed by the much larger gains of Anglo Americans."[5]

The gloomy picture described here had a variety of causes, among them recent immigration, lack of job skills, a scarcity of capital, and language problems. Equally striking, though, was discrimination—based on class, religion, and especially race. Moreover, demographic changes in the Mexicano community worked to increase the climate of intolerance.

ORIGINS OF THE CHICANO MOVEMENT

Still, the socioeconomic condition of the Mexicano community was not notably worse in the early sixties than it had been in the past. Indeed, demographers indicate that steady progress had been made in this regard. Furthermore, despite widespread hostility, *overt* forms of racism were fading. Discrimination was less blatant than before, thanks in part to the efforts of the Mexican American Generation, as well as the waning of the Cold War and the demand for conformity that it fostered. Even Mexicano participation in Vietnam, with its swelling disaffection, is insufficient to explain the rise of Chicanismo; Mexicanos had fought and died in other U.S. wars without turning to militant anti-establishment activity. It was the changing intellectual climate in America, especially the rise of the black civil rights movement, that made the difference.

Brown v. the Board of Education encouraged a new assertiveness by blacks, whose civil rights movement began in 1955, when Rosa Parks, a black woman, refused to give up her bus seat in Montgomery, Alabama. This campaign launched the career of Dr. Martin Luther King Jr. (1929–1968), a young Baptist minister, arguably the most powerful voice for racial justice in the annals of American history. Swayed by Mohandas Gandhi and Henry Thoreau, Dr. King preached the philosophy of militant nonviolence, which had a profound and lasting impact on his contemporaries. Dr. King and the Southern Christian Leadership Conference (SCLC) spearheaded the drive for desegregation and together with the National Association for the Advancement of Colored People (NAACP) dominated the swelling movement during its first years.

By 1966, however, dissatisfied with the seemingly glacial pace of reform, more militant leaders emerged from the African American community, particularly in northern urban ghettos, where Dr. King was less dominant. They included Stokely Carmichael, head of the Student Nonviolent Coordinating Committee (SNCC); Bobby Seale, Huey P. Newton, and Eldridge Cleaver of the Black Panthers; and the most charismatic of the new leaders, Malcolm X (1925–1965), who became the chief spokesman for the Black Muslims. Labeling their movement "Black Power," they called for permanent racial separation and the use of violence.

Both moderate and radical wings of the black civil rights movement, and the riots that broke out in African American ghettos across the country in 1964–1967, had a monumental impact on American society. One of the most immediate responses was the War on Poverty, which was launched by President Lyndon B. Johnson in a quixotic attempt to create the Great Society. A myriad of federally funded programs—Job Corps, Volunteers in Service to America (VISTA), Neighborhood Youth Corps, Head Start, and Upward Bound, among them—were set up to affect the change. While not completely successful, LBJ's domestic programs did ameliorate the plight of many poor people in the country, and they also took the wind out of the sails of black militancy, which had faded by the seventies.

The black civil rights crusade, though, left a powerful legacy. Almost every aspect of American life was impacted, in one way or another. One of the most meaningful consequences of this Second Reconstruction was the stimulus it provided for other people of color to stand up for their rights. These included Mexicanos, who now initiated their own movement of self-awareness.

CHÁVEZ, HUERTA, AND THE UNITED FARM WORKERS

The Chicano movement consisted of hundreds of organizations focusing on a variety of issues. Broadly speaking, these groups were found in barrios, schools, and prisons. In terms of their approaches, they could be divided into those associations that sought to work through the system and those that called for a major restructuring of the system, the moderate and radical wings of the movement, respectively. As the Chicano crusade began, in the midsixties, the moderates predominated. The key organization representing their perspective was undoubtedly the United Farm Workers (UFW).

The history of labor organizing among field workers goes back to the early part of the twentieth century, as we have seen. Both the Industrial Workers of the World, before and during the Great War, and the American Communist Party, in the thirties, made abortive attempts to improve the lives of farmworkers in the agricultural valleys of the West. Before the rise of the UFW, the last serious initiative in the fields was taken by the National Farm Labor Union (NFLU), formed in 1945 and led in California by Ernesto Galarza. In the late forties, the NFLU launched a series of strikes in the Golden State, where it centered its activities. These initiatives failed not only because of the many difficulties inherent in organizing workers in the fields but also because the Bracero Program made it impossible to win concessions from growers, the owners of factory farms. The termination of the bracero agreement in 1964, however, set the stage for the most ambitious unionization attempt to date—the UFW strike that would be launched in California's San Joaquin Valley during the following year. It was led by two extraordinary people: César Chávez and Dolores Huerta.

Despite his rejection of the term *Chicano*, César Chávez (1927–1993) remains the single most important representative of the *movimiento*; indeed, he is the preeminent figure in the history of Mexican Americans.[6] A legend in his own lifetime, it is difficult to separate fact from fiction in relating the outlines of his long and productive career. César Estrada Chávez was born on 31 March 1927, on a small family farm near Yuma, Arizona. During the Depression, his grandfather lost the property, and the Chávez family, forced to move, was reduced to working as migratory farm laborers. For the next few years, they traveled up and down the agricultural valleys of California eking out a living. Education for the Chávez children was sporadic, given their nomadic existence, and young César was forced to abandon his studies altogether after the eighth grade. During World War II, the teenager, short on career options, enlisted in the Navy and served in the Pacific. Upon his release in 1946, armed with greater self-confidence, the young veteran returned to the fields, joining the ill-fated NFLU.

Eventually, Chávez settled down with his wife, Helen, and their growing family in San Jose, California, where he continued to do farm work. It was here in the Bay Area that he met and was influenced by Fred Ross, who recruited him into the Community Service Organization in 1952. Hardworking and dedicated, Chávez made his way up the organizational ladder very swiftly, becoming CSO regional director in 1958. In this capacity, he tried to steer the association toward advocacy of the rights of farmworkers. He met fierce resistance among members who preferred to focus attention on urban and middle-class concerns. Exasperated, Chávez quit the CSO in 1961 and took his family to Delano, his wife's hometown. Using his life savings, he initiated a new union, the Farm Workers Association— known later as the National Farm Workers Association and, later still, the United Farm Workers—which was founded in Fresno on 30 September 1962.

Because the UFW always focused on the family unit, women came to play prominent roles in union activities. Among them, Helen Chávez and Jessie López de la Cruz stand out. From the very outset, though, César Chávez's most trusted lieutenant, often considered cofounder of the union, was Dolores Huerta. Although eclipsed by Chávez throughout most of her life, Huerta remains in many ways, as her biographer Richard A. García has argued, a better symbol of Chicanismo than her friend and mentor.[7]

Dolores Fernández Huerta was born in Dawson, New Mexico, in 1930. Her parents divorced when she was five; and her mother, the seminal force in her life, took the family to the West Coast. Unlike Chávez, Dolores emerged from a middle-class background. Her mother, who started off as a waitress and cannery worker, eventually came to own a hotel in Stockton, California, where Dolores was raised in an integrated neighborhood, received her early education, and met her first husband, an Anglo. After her marriage, she earned a provisional teaching credential by attending community college and taking night classes at College of the Pacific, becoming a grammar school teacher.

In the midfifties, however, she decided to change her life dramatically. Abandoning her middle-class aspirations, she became convinced that personal happiness could be achieved only by helping the underprivileged. Toward that end, she joined the CSO, where she received her initial training as a community organizer under Fred Ross, who taught her the mobilization techniques associated with Saul Alinsky. "The emphasis of Alinsky's message," writes Richard García, "coincided with hers—a pragmatic non-ideological approach to life and change."[8]

It was in the CSO in 1955 that Huerta met Chávez, initiating a lifelong though sometimes turbulent association. A devout Catholic, somewhat puritanical in his value system, Chávez would always have trouble accepting her two divorces and the apparent neglect of her children. These personal difficulties, however, rarely impeded effective collaboration by two individuals equally dedicated to the cause of ameliorating the lives of the downtrodden. When Chávez bolted the CSO in 1961, Dolores Huerta followed. Together, they forged the new union. She was in Delano when the strike began. During the next few years, it would completely consume her life.

THE DELANO STRIKE

The strike against local grape growers in the Kern County city of Delano, just north of Bakersfield, was initiated by the Agricultural Workers Organizing Committee (AWOC), a Filipino union affiliated with the AFL-CIO, on 8 September 1965. Led by Larry Itliong (1913–1977), Filipinos struck to gain higher pay and recognition as a union, a right given to industrial workers by the National Labor Relations Act of 1935 but denied to agricultural laborers. Since most of the field hands in the area were Mexicanos—by the sixties, they constituted at least two-thirds of the agricultural work force in the state—Chávez was asked to join and help conduct the strike. Fearing that his own fledgling union was unprepared, he agreed with some reluctance. However, given his union's superior numbers and his characteristic determination, Chávez soon became the acknowledged leader of the entire operation.

UFW tactics and strategy at Delano mirrored Chávez's personal philosophy. Profoundly impacted by both Gandhi and Dr. King, he had come to embrace the philosophy of militant nonviolence. Like his two renowned mentors, Chávez was against violence on principle; but he also realized, as they did, that violence was self-defeating when directed at a power with a monopoly on armed force. On the other hand, the idea of turning the other cheek, while praiseworthy as a Christian ideal, was calculated to preserve the status quo. It was essential, he felt, that the oppressed unite and assert themselves, using a variety of nonviolent strategies to gain their ends. In the case of farmworkers, those objectives were better working conditions, including higher wages, and recognition of their union. Unlike many other militants of the time, Chávez believed that the American middle class was basically responsive to the needs of poor people and would support them if given the opportunity.

During the long struggle, Chávez recruited help from various disparate sources. These included the trade union movement, especially the AFL-CIO, with which he affiliated in 1966; Christian organizations, both Protestant and Catholic; radical student associations, including the Students for a Democratic Society (SDS); and other civil rights groups. Aside from alliances, he relied, too, on demonstrations, prayer sessions, marches, and fasts. His basic tactic was the strike, the *huelga,* the time-honored weapon of organized labor. Eventually, though, he discovered that a work stoppage had limited potential in small agricultural towns like Delano, where powerful growers could generally count on the support of the local citizenry, including the Mexicano petite bourgeoisie, and even many of the farmworkers themselves. Beginning in 1968, Chávez came to rely on the boycott, a consumer strike, which meant that his success would depend to a large extent on winning support in urban areas throughout the country. His boycott of nonunion grapes in 1968–1975, the first nationwide boycott of any kind, was highly successful. Some 12 percent of the adult American population (17 million people) honored the appeal, effectively wiping out grower profits. Still, the strike was long and hard. It finally ended in 1970, when growers reluctantly agreed to recognize the union and sign contracts with it.

Flushed with victory, the UFW had visions of organizing farmworkers throughout the country. Inspired by Chávez's example, a campesino strike had already occurred in the cantaloupe fields of Starr County in Texas in 1966, the beginning of Chicano militancy in that state. Chávez immediately dispatched Antonio Orendain, an able lieutenant, to mobilize the farmworkers of South Texas. Similar developments would soon take place in Arizona, Colorado, Washington, and other states. Even the Midwest felt repercussions. In 1967, the Toledo-based Farm Labor Organizing Committee (FLOC) was founded by Baldemar Velásquez, a native of Pharr, Texas, to fight for the rights of migrant workers.[9] Concentrating its efforts on Ohio and Michigan, the FLOC achieved its most notable victory in 1986, after an eight-year strike and boycott of the Campbell Soup Company. In neighboring Indiana, the Farm Labor Aid Committee (FLAC) was established by a small coterie of activists, including Gilbert Cárdenas, later an eminent Chicano scholar. Chávez, however, knew that California was the key, and he next tackled the lettuce growers of the Salinas Valley, where labor conditions were as abominable as they had been in the Great Central Valley. Relying on the same tactics as before, the union achieved moderate success.

The UFW was suddenly forced to return to Delano in 1973. Upon the expiration of the old contracts, growers, ignoring Chávez, chose instead to sign new agreements with the Teamsters Union. The International Brotherhood of Teamsters had been expelled by the AFL-CIO in 1957. A maverick union, under the leadership of Jimmy Hoffa, it would be the only major working-class organization to support the Republican Party in the post–World War II period. Moreover, it was the only labor union to embrace the Bracero Program. Efforts to organize field hands were blatantly cynical since the Teamsters had little interest in these workers themselves; their overriding concern was the welfare of the truckers, who would be out of work without fruits and vegetables to transport. The Teamsters were intent on mobilizing campesinos to keep them *from* striking. Since their interests coincided with those of growers, the latter were anxious to end their association with the UFW and sign sweetheart contracts with the Hoffa union.

During the next few years, an acrimonious jurisdictional dispute erupted throughout the agricultural valleys of the West between the two competing unions. It was not resolved until California Governor Jerry Brown, whose sympathies lay with Chávez, entered the fray and forced a compromise: the Teamsters would have jurisdiction over cannery and packing shed workers, the UFW would have free rein over field workers. Surprisingly, the truce held. The 1975 Agricultural Labor Relations Act (ALRA), which Governor Brown guided through the state legislature, helped the UFW initially—it won almost half the 406 elections decided in the first few months—but Republican administrations in California, particularly under Governor Deukmejian, subsequently undermined its effectiveness, causing Chávez to regret his initial support of the legislation.

Unfortunately, successes were few and far between for Chávez during the next few years, as the public mood grew increasingly conservative, boding ill for both trade union and civil rights movements. The upsurge of undocumented workers brought unwelcome competition for agricultural jobs. Internal dissension compounded union problems. When Chávez died in 1993, the union was moribund, having lost 80 percent of its members during the previous decade. The UFW rebounded under his son-in-law, Arturo Rodríguez, but by 1995, when there were an estimated 1.6 million farmworkers in the country, membership was only 26,000, a stark contrast to the 70,000 members during the union's peak years in the mid-1970s. The obstacles to organizing farm labor had proved insurmountable. Moreover, the rapid development of mechanization—machines harvested fewer than 2 percent of California's tomatoes in 1963, but five years later they harvested 95 percent—created another formidable obstacle. An integral part of corporate America, growers were as strong as workers were weak; it truly was a David and Goliath battle.

Still, the failure to unionize farm labor should be seen in a wider perspective. Chávez brought about much-needed reforms in the fields, including medical, pension, and unemployment benefits. The determined UFW leader served as a crucial catalyst in this regard. He was also responsible for focusing national attention on the abuses of agribusiness interests, particularly monopolistic tendencies vis-à-vis land and water.

Moreover, it is a mistake to see and measure Chávez solely in terms of union activity. His movement was much more than an attempt to organize farmworkers;

it was a vital component of the civil rights movement, which partly accounts for the enthusiastic support he found among most churches. Chávez was concerned about the plight of Mexicanos generally, not just those among them who happened to be campesinos. He succeeded in politicizing a large part of the ethnic community, his paramount contribution to the Chicano movement. Indeed, he even found this expanded focus to be too constricting. Like Gandhi and Dr. King, he eventually came to espouse the entire gamut of human rights, irrespective of race, perhaps his most enduring legacy.

In recent years, it has become fashionable to focus on Chávez's shortcomings as both man and leader. Even sympathetic observers have pointed out that he sometimes made poor decisions and fostered authoritarian tendencies within the union. Alienated by these actions, many UFW stalwarts had eventually quit the organization in disgust, including Gilbert Padilla, who had served, together with Dolores Huerta, as its first vice president and had done yeoman duty during its formative years.

Among his own people, Chávez has been criticized from both ends of the political spectrum. Most Mexicanos who have disliked him allege that his movement is un-American. Often products of the Cold War era and middle class in background, these conservative critics are embarrassed by his emphasis on Mexican ethnicity, use of the tactics of confrontation, and alliances with radical groups. Even some farmworkers, usually with economic ties to agribusiness, have withheld their support. Though less evident, there is some criticism of Chávez from the other end of the political spectrum, Chicanos who assail him for his conservatism. These have generally been student radicals, often schooled in Marxist ideas, who felt that his nonviolent approach was misguided, who objected to his emphasis on Catholic symbols, or who were embittered by his rejection of La Raza—"The Race," a self-referent used by Chicano cultural nationalists—that Chávez saw as a new form of racism.[10] Notwithstanding these criticisms from both political extremes, the union leader has been and remains the most respected Mexican American among his own people, three-quarters of whom, at a minimum, see him as a hero. Not surprisingly, at his death, his name was bestowed upon a variety of streets, schools, parks, and community centers, often in the face of outraged Anglo opposition. The most publicized instance occurred in 1993, when Chicano students at UCLA, after a lengthy hunger strike, succeeded in getting university officials to set up a César Chávez Center for Interdisciplinary Study and Chicano and Chicana Studies. Seven years later, California passed legislation making his birthday an official state holiday.

OTHER EARLY CHICANO LEADERS

During the sixties, another extraordinary individual emerged from the ranks of the Mexicano community who received national attention and, for a short while at least, had a profound impact on young Chicano activists, Reies López Tijerina (1926–).[11] Tijerina is assuredly the most fascinating and controversial of movement personalities. Born near Fall City, Texas, the son of migrant farm laborers, he was raised by his father and grandmother after his mother's premature death. At eighteen, he embraced a fundamentalist form of Protestantism and enrolled in the Assembly of God Bible Institute at Isleta (now part of El Paso), where he studied for the ministry. Expelled from the school, he became an itinerant Pentecostal evangelist. His travels took him throughout the country. In 1950, Tijerina and his coreligionists set up a utopian community near Casa Grande, Arizona, but this experiment in communalism did not last long. In 1957, he left Arizona, a fugitive from the law, and headed south, broadening his interests during his brief stay in the country of his forefathers. "Entering Mexico as an itinerant religious leader, he left it deeply motivated by the philosophy of the Mexican revolution."[12] In 1960, Tijerina made his way to New Mexico, where he championed a new cause—the crusade to recover lost Hispano lands. Toward that end, he founded the Alianza Federal de Mercedes (Federal Alliance of Land Grants) in 1963.

This improbable crusade led by an unlikely champion gained surprising support among Hispanos, people notoriously Catholic and conservative. The reasons are largely historical. During World War II, continuing the trend initiated during the Depression, Hispanos were forced to leave their traditional villages in northern New Mexico and southern Colorado in increasing numbers. Many displaced villagers headed to California, but the majority made their way to the cities nearby, notably Albuquerque. This disintegration of village life caused deep alienation. Moreover, poverty continued to be a monumental problem for both rural and urban residents. The war also witnessed the continued immigration of Anglos into the state. Now a minority within the population—by 1960, only 28.3 percent of the state population was Spanish-speaking—Hispanos saw their political clout dissipate rapidly. The rise of Tijerina, an outsider, has to be seen in the context of these desperate and deteriorating conditions.

Disillusionment was most severe in northern New Mexico, where angry villagers blamed their problems on the loss of land. Moreover, it was here that seemingly irresponsible policies established by the National Forest Service threatened the grazing and water rights of the rural Hispano populace. It was in this northern peripheral area, centering on Río Arriba County, where half the residents were on public relief, that Tijerina built a power base. Ultimately, Alianza membership reached twenty thousand.

Tijerina believed that all the problems of "Indo-Hispanos" in the Southwest stemmed from the loss of their patrimony. He charged that this land was taken illegally. The Treaty of Guadalupe Hidalgo, he argued, guaranteed Mexicanos in the United States citizenship rights, including those relating to property. Even land alienated through sale had been taken illegally. Mexicanos, he concluded, needed to organize to win redress through the American court system. The repossession of lost grants was to be a prelude to an even more ambitious and utopian scheme: the creation of a free city-state, the independent Republic of Chama, which would be established in northern New Mexico. Vague and backward looking, the Alianza, as Nancie L. González insightfully notes, represented a "nativistic cult movement."[13]

During the first years, from his headquarters in Albuquerque, Tijerina pursued a moderate path in his efforts to achieve victory. For the most part, he placed his faith on legal avenues; he hoped to regain lost lands through litigation. His research into land grants took him to the archives of Spain and Mexico, where he gathered materials to sustain his claims. He got nowhere; U.S. courts refused to hear the case.

In desperation, Tijerina sought to bring national attention to the plight of Hispanos and to force the government to hear him out through extralegal means. Increasingly, the Alianza resorted to fence-cutting and arson. In 1966, Tijerina occupied Echo Amphitheater, formerly an old land grant, now part of Kit Carson National Forest, arresting forest rangers for trespassing. On 5 June 1967, he and his supporters invaded the courthouse at Tierra Amarilla, county seat of Río Arriba, in an attempt to free jailed Alianza members and make a citizen's arrest of the local district attorney. A shoot-out ensued, with *aliancistas* making a getaway by taking two hostages. The largest manhunt in New Mexico history resulted in the arrest of Tijerina and his closest associates. The chief prosecution witness, a deputy sheriff, was found mysteriously beaten to death in early 1968. Later that year, Tijerina was put on trial for kidnapping and assault during the 1967 shoot-out. While admitting to being present at the courthouse, he denied having anything to do with the violence. A forceful and charismatic speaker, Tijerina handled his own defense and, in a stunning turn of events, succeeded in winning acquittal.

Rey Tigre (King Tiger), as his admirers now called him, was soon in trouble with the law again, and this time his luck ran out. Tried on charges stemming from the Amphitheater episode and for destruction of federal property at a second incident at Kit Carson National Forest, he was found guilty in June 1969 and sentenced to prison. Jailed for two years, he was released on parole from federal prison in Springfield, Missouri, in July 1971, and placed on probation for five years. One of the conditions of his parole was that he sever all ties to the Alianza. He returned to public life, but the old fire was gone. Counseling moderation, he was no longer in the forefront of the Brown Power movement. Soon, even his supporters in New Mexico fell away. Accused of being an Elmer Gantry, a religious charlatan, Tijerina remains an enigmatic figure today. His most meaningful contribution was to dramatize the plight of the impoverished Hispano communities in New Mexico.

Unlike Chávez and Tijerina, Rodolfo ("Corky") Gonzales (1929–2005) realized that the future of the Mexicano community would be in urban areas and that the focus should be on young people.[14] Raised in the barrios of Denver, Gonzales first achieved national prominence as a prize fighter in the early fifties. When he left the ring, he turned to Democratic politics in his hometown. In 1960, he acted as Colorado coordinator of the Viva Kennedy clubs. He then served in a variety of War on Poverty programs. "In no time," according to Stan Steiner, "he was a one-man directory of poverty agencies."[15] Like many other barrio leaders, Gonzales gradually became disillusioned with conventional party politics, and in April 1966, he founded an organization that would permit him to better serve Mexicanos in Denver, La Crusada Para la Justicia (the Crusade for Justice).

An organization to mobilize the ethnic community, the Crusade focused on young people and their problems. It established a whole host of services—school, nursery, gym, art gallery, and community center—as well as its own newspaper, *El Gallo*. During the course of the late sixties, as the political climate became more radical, the Crusade embraced a more militant posture. Gonzales, an ex G.I. Forum member, began to emphasize cultural nationalism. Before too long, he came to espouse a form of separatism. Adopting a widely held view of the time among nationalists, Corky Gonzales became the foremost champion of the idea that Aztlán, the mythical homeland of the México, was to be found in the Southwest, which he and others called "occupied America." The Crusade, going beyond Tijerina, called for the restoration of their ancestral land to Chicanos. In the meantime, Gonzales concentrated on direct action in the schools, launching a series of student walkouts in Denver. The Crusade also participated in Dr. King's 1968 Poor People's March on Washington, D.C., where Gonzales and Tijerina led the Chicano contingent.

By now, the idea had gained currency that militant student groups throughout the country needed a unified organization; and Gonzales, the self-appointed leader of the movement, took the initiative in sponsoring a Chicano Youth Liberation Front, a national convention of barrio youth, in Denver on 27–31 March 1969. The convention attracted more than fifteen hundred Chicanos. It was there that the Spiritual Plan of Aztlán, a call for an autonomous Chicano homeland, was unveiled, and the formation of an independent Chicano party was projected.[16] A second youth conference met in Denver in May of the following year. Gonzales was now firmly committed to the idea of a separatist political party, and immediately after the 1970 conference, he and his allies launched the Colorado Raza Unida Party.

The genesis of the Raza Unida initiative occurred four years earlier. On 28 March 1966, a number of prominent Mexicano delegates walked out of a conference in Albuquerque sponsored by the Equal Employment Opportunity Commission in protest of that agency's failure to address the pressing problems of the barrios. "The walkout in Albuquerque," it has been observed, "marked the first time that the middle-class leadership had engaged in an act of collective protest against the government."[17] President Johnson, looking to placate the dissidents, promised a White House conference of Hispanic leaders to deal with Mexican American issues.

But it soon became obvious that LBJ was having second thoughts about the concession. He had other worries at the time—first and foremost, the conflict in Vietnam. Moreover, he realized that at the proposed meeting, delegates would pressure the administration on a number of potentially embarrassing issues, including the war itself and recognition of the UFW. As the historian Julie Leininger Pycior has ably demonstrated, while he was sympathetic to many Mexicano causes—a compassion stemming from early teaching experience at a "Mexican" school in Cotulla, Texas—LBJ also had to assuage conservative Democrats and political supporters back home who represented agribusiness and ranching interests.[18] Moreover, he realized that many Hispanics, especially outside of Texas, were leaning toward his rivals for the Democratic nomination for the presidency, senators Eugene McCarthy and Robert Kennedy. Mexicano leaders pressed for the conference, but the administration was evasive. Frustration set in. Even his most staunch Mexicano allies in Texas, Dr. Héctor García, Vicente Ximenes, and other G.I. Forum leaders, counseled that he extend some kind of olive branch.

Eventually, the beleaguered Johnson offered a compromise. He would establish an Interagency Committee on Mexican American Affairs, to be chaired by Ximenes. The Committee, in turn, would sponsor a conference in El Paso in late October 1967, when LBJ was scheduled to meet Mexican president Gustavo Díaz Ordaz to sign a treaty returning a small piece of disputed land to Mexico. The compromise package was accepted, and one thousand representatives of Mexicano community organizations throughout the country were invited to El Paso.

These delegates, however, were disappointed that the meeting would not be held at the nation's capital. Moreover, Johnson alienated them by excluding many of their most prominent and radical leaders, including Corky Gonzales and Reies López Tijerina. César Chávez, a zealous Kennedy supporter, was asked to attend, but he turned down the invitation because the El Paso conference refused to deal with farmworker issues.

The meeting was held as scheduled on 27–28 October 1967. Gonzales, Tijerina, and other uninvited radicals, intent on embarrassing the administration, chose to have their own meeting in El Paso, in the Mexicano barrio on the southside. The radicals were joined by a number of representatives who had attended the official meeting but walked out in protest, among them Ernesto Galarza. At the alternate meeting, labeled *La Raza Unida,* the Johnson administration was roundly condemned, and delegates resolved to set up a nationwide organization that would represent Chicano interests in the coming elections. Finally, the delegates endorsed the *Plan de La Raza Unida,* a manifesto affirming Chicano solidarity. A follow-up meeting of La Raza Unida was held in San Antonio in January 1968. It drew twelve hundred delegates representing fifty organizations, both middle-class and student-oriented groups.

The emerging party was mainly the brainchild of José Ángel Gutiérrez (1944–), still another of the key leaders of the Chicano movement. While Chávez and Gonzales might be considered transitional figures from the Mexican American Generation to the Chicano Generation, Gutiérrez, because of his younger age, was firmly rooted in the latter—the idiosyncratic Tijerina belonged in a category all his own.

Gutiérrez was born in the Texas town of Crystal City, in Zavala County, the heart of the Winter Garden area. A dedicated student, he earned his B.A. at Texas A&I University in Kingsville, before moving on to graduate studies at St. Mary's University, a Catholic college in San Antonio. In 1967, while still in graduate school, he became one of the founders of a Chicano student association, the Mexican American Youth Organization (MAYO).[19] Two years later, Gutiérrez and other MAYO leaders, including Mario Campeán and Willie Velásquez, initiated the Winter Garden Project, a Ford Foundation-funded campaign to maximize Tejano political power in a ten-county area along the Rio Grande, centered in Crystal City. Concurrently, Gutiérrez and his MAYO confederates were among the most active promoters and participants at the El Paso and San Antonio La Raza Unida conferences, where they eagerly embraced the concept of a Chicano political party.

In January 1970, translating the popular aspiration into concrete reality, MAYO created El Partido de la Raza Unida, widely known as La Raza Unida Party (LRUP).[20] Established in the Winter Garden area, it was intended to serve as an electoral vehicle in local school board and city council contests. In the spring elections, Gutiérrez and other LRUP leaders ran for office. The party had a spectacularly auspicious beginning: Crystal City Mexicanos won two council seats and three school board seats, one of them belonging to Gutiérrez. These successes were repeated in two other predominantly Mexicano communities nearby, Cotulla and Carrizo Springs. His good fortune prompted the hardworking Gutiérrez to expand his political horizons. He was determined to make LRUP a national association, a third party for Chicanos in competition with the two traditional choices.

In Colorado, meanwhile, Corky Gonzales had similar plans. As we have seen, in the spring of 1970 a Colorado LRUP was established in Denver just a few months after Gutiérrez had initiated his regional organization of the same name in Texas. Beginning in late 1970, prompted by the Tejano, LRUP chapters began appearing in California. It was Gonzales, however, who took the initiative for a nationwide party first. At his urging, three thousand delegates from throughout the Southwest and parts of the Midwest met in El Paso on 1–4 September 1972. The result was the establishment of a national Raza Unida party.

Unfortunately, this first national convention would also be the last. Problems surfaced immediately, as the meeting was marred by massive internal dissension. Two factions emerged, a moderate group looking to Gutiérrez, who saw the party as a vehicle to achieve political power, and a radical contingent headed by Gonzales, who wanted the party to take a more ideological path by dealing with issues of class and gender. Additionally, moderates were willing to consider electoral alliances with the established parties in the coming elections. Radicals were vehemently opposed to this kind of interparty cooperation. Tensions were exacerbated by personal animosity between the two ambitious leaders. The moderates ultimately won out; Gutiérrez was elected chairman of the new party.

Work began immediately on extending LRUP into other parts of the Southwest in preparation for the 1972 primary and general elections. While LRUP was able to gain a small following in New Mexico, Arizona, and California, results at the polls were almost uniformly disappointing. In fact, electoral victories were confined to South Texas.

The party never came close to meeting the lofty expectations of its founders. LRUP declined for the same reasons that the entire Chicano movement, which it claimed to head, fell apart. There were also causes that were particular to its situation. The reticence of Mexicanos, both the leadership and the rank and file, to abandon the Democratic Party was one. Democrats continued to get about three-quarters of the Mexicano vote. Chávez, in particular, was wedded to the Democrats; and in California, his power base, he was constantly at odds with LRUP. Older middle-class organizations, such as the G.I. Forum, LULAC, and even MAPA, kept their allegiance to the Democrats, despite their professed nonpartisan stances. Moreover, using confrontational tactics, LRUP leaders managed to alienate many potential allies. Regionalism also played a role. The Tejanos, who controlled the party, found that other Chicanos in the Southwest were anxious to maintain their freedom of action. Finally, there was the inability of leaders to work together. As would be true in virtually all Chicano and Mexican American organizations, personality clashes were grave impediments to effective teamwork. Increasingly alienated by Gutiérrez, Gonzales left LRUP in 1974, taking his followers with him. Shortly thereafter, the Tejano was challenged for control of the party even in the Winter Garden, his old stronghold. By the mid-1970s, the party was in shambles.

THE CHICANO STUDENT MOVEMENT

To a large extent, the Raza Unida party, notably through the agency of MAYO, mirrored the power of Chicano students. By 1970, the Chicano movement, it appeared, was increasingly dominated by young people, students in high schools and universities concerned especially with the multitude of problems they experienced in these institutions. Among the issues were de facto segregation, racist instructors, the tracking system, and, in institutions of higher learning, inadequate recruitment and funding.

Student activism among Mexicanos was not altogether a recent phenomenon. As with other aspects of the Chicano movement, there were notable historical roots. According to Carlos Muñoz Jr., who has written one of the most insightful studies of the Chicano movement to date, the origins of Mexican student activism "can be traced to 1929 when Ernesto Galarza, then a twenty-four-year-old graduate student in history at Stanford University, spoke out in defense of Mexican immigrant workers."[21] More significantly, in 1942 the Mexican-American Movement, Inc. (MAM), a student association which grew out of YMCA-sponsored Mexican Youth Conferences in Southern California, was formed. Led by Paul Coronel and Félix Gutiérrez, it was dedicated to the promotion of educational opportunities for the Mexicano community. The main precursor of the Chicano student movement was undoubtedly MAM.

By the midsixties, the ferment of the youth movement had impacted Chicanos, who eagerly embraced militant forms of protest. The intellectual sources of student militancy among Chicanos were varied. Almost any form of resistance to oppression was appealing. Students looked to their more militant elders, preeminent among them being Chávez and Tijerina, for inspiration. The Black Power movement was a second major contributor. The Mexican Revolution, personified by Pancho Villa and Emiliano Zapata, was still another source of intellectual inspiration. Many students came under the sway of socialism. They looked to Karl Marx, Mao Zedong, and especially the heroes of the Cuban Revolution, Che Guevara and Fidel Castro.[22] The Vietnam antiwar protest had a weighty impact, as well.

By 1970, after its formative stage, perhaps the cardinal influence on the growing youth movement was that of indigenismo. By now, students were heavily committed to the idea of cultural regeneration, which, as in the case of blacks, meant a glorification of the motherland. It was the Indian legacy, however, that they found attractive, rather than that of the Spanish, who were doubly condemned for being white and imperialist.

The Chicano *student* movement—as contrasted to other aspects of La Causa (the Cause)—began in the midsixties; that is, it emerged simultaneously with the other Chicano efforts previously described. The first of the student organizations espousing some form of Chicanismo was the Student Initiative founded at San Jose State College by Armando Valdez in 1964. Three years later, in 1967, several other militant campus organizations appeared. Texas and California took the lead. In the Lone Star State, besides the aforementioned MAYO in San Antonio, there was the Mexican American Student Organization (MASO) at the University of Texas at Austin. In southern California, the Mexican American Student Association (MASA) appeared at East Los Angeles Community College. It was overshadowed at the outset, however, by the United Mexican American Students (UMAS), which established chapters at the University of California at Los Angeles, the University of

Southern California, Loyola University, and a number of state colleges. In northern California, where the student movement was more radical than in the southland, the dominant organization was the Mexican American Student Confederation (MASC), which grew out of the Student Initiative at San Jose. MASC established chapters at Fresno State, Sacramento State, and Hayward State in 1967, and the University of California at Berkeley the following year.

These student groups all tried to extend their authority beyond their immediate area. The most fortunate in this regard was UMAS, which was able to gain traction beyond California, opening up chapters at the University of Colorado at Boulder in 1968 and penetrating other parts of the Southwest the following year. Soon it also entered the Midwest. Its first chapter there was set up by Gilbert Cárdenas at the University of Notre Dame in South Bend, Indiana.

Beginning at the college level, student militancy quickly spread to younger students. On 3 March 1968, Latino dissatisfaction with the school system became evident at the high school level. On that fateful day, Chicano students in East Los Angeles, in an effort to get school administrations to address their many pressing problems, walked out of several local high schools. They were led by Sal Castro, a Lincoln High School teacher. These "blowouts," as they were called, soon erupted in other schools of what was then the largest school district in the country. Altogether, over fifteen thousand students were involved. Eventually, thirteen strike leaders, including UMAS members Moctezuma Esparza, from UCLA, and Carlos Muñoz Jr., an ex-serviceman, now chapter president at Los Angeles State College, were indicted on conspiracy charges—which were dropped two years later.

The Los Angeles strike received national attention. It also stimulated student activism in other cities. During the next few months, walkouts occurred in high schools throughout the Southwest and beyond. Those in Denver and South Texas were the largest and received the most media attention. Student demands included the hiring of Mexicano instructors, counselors, and administrators; bilingual and bicultural education; and closer cooperation between schools and the barrio.

However, the repercussions of the East Los Angeles blowouts went beyond the high school. A few months later, Mexicano students at San Jose State walked out of their graduation, the first protest activity by Chicanos on a college campus. Other Chicanos participated at the massive strike instigated by the Third World Liberation Front (TWLF) at San Francisco State in November 1968. A TWLF strike ensued at UC Berkeley during the first half of 1969. Chicano students, who had played only a supporting role at San Francisco, were among the most engaged supporters of the Berkeley demonstration. By now, it was clear, the Chicano student movement was rapidly moving to the left and increasingly involved with issues that concerned other radical students.

In early 1969, Chicano students, dispersed in a number of student clubs, sought to achieve a measure of cohesion through the establishment of a nationwide organization. The opportunity arose at a conference held in April at UC Santa Barbara, one of the strongholds of the mushrooming movement. The meeting was called by the Chicano Coordinating Committee on Higher Education (CCHE), formed in 1968 by a group of concerned college students and professors. About one hundred delegates—students, instructors, and administrators—were present. They came from throughout the state of California and other parts of the Southwest. Among the most dynamic participants were Jesús Chavarría, a young professor at UC Santa Barbara and the dominant personality at the meeting; Juan Gómez-Quiñones, who, together with René Núñez, had been one of the prime movers of the meeting; and the ubiquitous Carlos Muñoz Jr., the future chronicler of the Chicano student movement. The three-day Santa Barbara convention had two meaningful results: (1) the drafting of the *Plan de Santa Bárbara,* a program of educational reform calling for the institution of Chicano studies programs, and (2) the establishment of El Movimiento Estudiantil de Aztlán (MECHA or MEChA, the Student Movement of Aztlán), an organization intended to supersede all other student groups by uniting them under the banner of cultural nationalism.[23] The convention, and the organization it spawned, mirrored the increasingly radical notions espoused by Corky Gonzales, whose appeal was at its height at this time. Several weeks before, a number of the delegates at Santa Barbara had attended the Denver Youth Conference, where the Spiritual Plan of Aztlán had been formulated. Gómez-Quiñones had been one of its principal authors.

Naturally, educational issues were of paramount importance to MECHA, as they were to other student associations. Like them, too, it put major emphasis on community involvement, working with a variety of local Chicano community service and political action groups. *Mechistas* were especially active in support of the UFW and LRUP, in spite of the bad blood between the two organizations.

MECHA went into a serious tailspin between 1971 and 1973, from which it never completely recovered. There are many reasons for this diminished status. The enthusiasm that inspired the organization initially could not be sustained after the original leaders left college. Internal divisions took their toll, as well. The dominant nationalist emphasis was challenged in the early seventies by a socialist-inspired wing insisting that class issues receive priority over ethnic considerations. This point of view was ultimately rejected, and distraught socialists abandoned the organization in droves. The same went for frustrated Chicanas who found MECHA reluctant to deal with feminist issues.

Given its numerous problems, it is easy to see why MECHA failed to achieve its ambitious program. It remains today a loose federation of chapters scattered throughout California. The failure of MECHA parallels the ultimate decline of the Chicano student movement in general. Its strengths and weaknesses are best summarized by Juan Gómez-Quiñones, whose participation gives his insights particular cogency: "At its best, the work of student activists has been seminal in its influence on much later activity as well as generously courageous in its militancy; at its worst, it has been anarchic and self-indulgent, given to rhetoric and organizational inconsistency."[24]

THE CHICANO MOVEMENT IN THE COMMUNITY

The Chicano Power movement was not confined to students; Chicanismo was also pervasive in barrios, where it was particularly evident among the working class. The most visible of the militant barrio organizations was the Brown Berets. A paramilitary group, it was founded in East Los Angeles in 1967 by David Sánchez, Carlos Móntez, and Ralph Ramírez, all of them college students at the time. The Brown Berets, however, were relatively unconcerned with the university; their focus was on the barrio, where they targeted police brutality and drug use in the community. They also took a special interest in the youth and played a conspicuous role in the 1968 school walkouts. Sánchez, Móntez, and Ramírez were among the strike leaders put on trial afterward. In 1969, they claimed to have chapters in twenty-seven cities other than Los Angeles, including Denver and San Antonio. By this time, the Vietnam War had become a major priority.

During the previous year, antiwar sentiment in the country had been transformed into a massive movement uniting students and communities throughout the country, and Chicanos were in the forefront of the protest, a fact that has largely escaped mainstream scholarship. As the historian Lorena Oropeza has shown in a path-breaking study, the war forced many Mexican Americans not only to reassess their relationship to other Americans but also to question certain basic values of their own culture, notably machismo.[25] Not all of them opposed the war—the G.I. Forum was an unflagging supporter of U.S. involvement, especially under LBJ— but Chicano students found that their opposition was generally shared by their families in the barrios. This contestation was understandable: the armed conflict had escalated steadily since August 1964, when the infamous Tonkin Resolution gave LBJ carte blanche to stop Communist aggression in Southeast Asia; and, as in World War II and Korea, Mexicanos played a leading role.

Inspired by patriotism, machismo, and the chance to escape dead-end jobs in rural towns and urban barrios—the primary motives cited by the soldiers themselves in Charley Trujillo's absorbing series of interviews, *Soldados: Chicanos in Viet Nam* (1990)[26]—many Mexicano youths volunteered for service. A high percentage entered high-risk branches of the service, such as the U.S. Marine Corps. The majority were drafted. Undereducated, and often ignorant of their rights, Mexicanos were prime targets for draft boards. Hispanos, for example, made up 27 percent of the New Mexican population in 1970, but they supplied 69 percent of all draftees from that state. Even more than most wars, Vietnam was fought by poor people. It is not surprising to find, then, that South Chicago's Mexicano working-class "parish of Our Lady of Guadalupe lost more men in Vietnam than any other parish in the country."[27] Studies conducted by Ralph Guzmán, director of the Mexican American Study Project at UCLA, in 1969 indicated that Mexicanos and other Hispanics were overrepresented in Southeast Asia—on the battlefront and on the casualty lists. Constituting about 11 percent of the population in the Southwest in 1960, Mexicanos apparently represented close to 20 percent of the region's soldiers killed in battle during the following decade.

By the war's end, according to Rubén Treviso, an ex-intelligence case officer in Southeast Asia, "One of every five Hispanics who went to Vietnam was killed in action."[28] This is clearly an exaggeration. However, while it is impossible to determine precisely given the military's policy of not distinguishing them from other "Caucasians" in its official records, impressionistic evidence suggests, as Treviso and minority scholars claim, that Hispanics did indeed make a disproportionate contribution to the war effort. In 2000, two independent researchers, Frederick and Linda Aguirre, went over the 58,202 names inscribed on the Vietnam War Memorial in Washington, D.C., and found that 3,741 of these were Spanish surnames, which would be 6.4 percent of the total.[29] Since, according to the census, Hispanics constituted only about 5 percent of the U.S. population in 1960, they concluded that Latinos were indeed overrepresented in the death rates, albeit slightly.

Many Mexicanos distinguished themselves on the field of battle. Thirteen Hispanics were awarded the Medal of Honor. Among these medal winners was Marine Sergeant Alfredo González from Edinburg, Texas, who died in battle in 1968. Twenty-eight years later, he became the first Mexican American to have a destroyer named after him by the U.S. Navy. Most Mexicanos, however, displayed little enthusiasm for the conflict, and with good reason. In general, the war was fought by minorities and working-class whites. It was not long before the white middle class, who had hailed the war as a moral crusade against Communism at the beginning, came to the conclusion that the escalating conflict was morally indefensible—after most deferments were abolished in early 1970 and the burden of financing the war fell increasingly upon their shoulders. The irony was that those youths being asked to lay down their lives to protect the American Way, the poor of the nation, were largely the very individuals who had gained least from it.

Spearheading Mexicano opposition to the war was the Chicano Moratorium Committee, consisting of both students and members of the community in southern California. The Brown Berets were the most conspicuous of the barrio groups. David Sánchez, Brown Beret prime minister, was cochair of the Chicano Moratorium Committee, together with Rosalío Muñoz, former UCLA student body president and the key figure behind the organization. The Moratorium Committee was responsible for a series of protest marches in East Los Angeles in 1970–1971.[30]

The most memorable demonstration occurred on 29 August 1970, when thirty thousand people gathered at Laguna Park, now named Rubén Salazar Park, to protest U.S. involvement in Vietnam and the disproportionate loss of Latino lives in the conflict. Chicano representatives came from all over the Southwest. Among those in attendance were Corky Gonzales, Bert Corona, and Rudy Acuña. Intended as a peaceful demonstration, the crowd got out of hand when provoked by the police. In the aftermath, three Mexicanos were killed. These included Rubén Salazar, who died under mysterious circumstances.[31] A reporter for the *Los Angeles Times* and news director of KMEX-TV, Salazar was sitting at a bar with some friends when he was struck in the head by a tear-gas projectile fired by a deputy sheriff. Since he was in the process of preparing an exposé on law enforcement in Los Angeles, the circumstances of his death aroused instant suspicion. Even staunch defenders of law and order condemned the injustice: "Whatever the rights and wrongs of what Chicano activists called an Anglo police riot, there was no excuse for what, according to the coroner's inquest, was the unprovoked killing of Salazar."[32] The incident incensed the Latino community in Los Angeles—the officer who shot Salazar was never charged with a crime, though negligence was obvious to many—and angry demonstrations continued for months.

Like the Black Panthers, after whom they patterned themselves, the Brown Berets were subject to intense police repression during this time, and like the black militant group, they gradually changed their emphasis from confrontation to more productive and concrete forms of community service, including educational projects and soup kitchens. Beset by internal dissension, the Brown Berets announced their disbandment in 1972.

Most barrio-based organizations were considerably less conspicuous than the Brown Berets. Yet one of the most effective of these was the Centro de Acción Social Autónoma–Hermandad General de Trabajadores (CASA-HGT, Center of Autonomous Social Action–General Brotherhood of Workers), called by one Chicano scholar, "the most salient progressive organization functioning in the Mexican community" during the seventies.[33] Set up in Los Angeles in 1968 and headed by Soledad ("Chole") Alatorre and Bert Corona, CASA stressed working-class interests. Moreover, it advocated the transnational organization of ethnic Mexican workers without reference to formal citizenship status, a logical orientation given the development of a regional capitalism that seemingly made the Mexican-U.S. border superfluous. However, during the early 1970s, increasingly dominated by "Young Turks" such as Magdalena Mora (1952–1981), CASA moved steadily to the left, becoming a bulwark of Marxism before its demise in 1978. In spite of its brief existence, it had a substantial impact on many other organizations, even after the heyday of the movimiento. According to the historian Rodolfo Acuña, "CASA's legacy is that more than any other organization, it politicized more Chicano and Chicana activists who went on to become labor organizers and politicos in California."[34] Alatorre and Corona, meanwhile, eschewed the more ideological orientation of CASA, choosing instead to focus their efforts on assisting indocumentados in combating deportation and gaining permanent residency through La Hermandad Mexicana Nacional (the Mexican National Brotherhood), an organization established in the early fifties.

Another hotbed of working-class ferment was Chicago, where the Chicano movement was centered on Pilsen, an old Czech neighborhood situated on the southern periphery of the Near West Side that Mexicanos began settling in the late 1950s. Displaced by urban redevelopment, notably the construction of a University of Illinois campus in their midst, and neglected by City Hall, angry barrio dwellers eagerly embraced the movimiento. The Chicano Moratorium Committee established a strong presence in Pilsen, as did CASA, led by the energetic Rudy Lozano. In 1972, the Brown Berets created the Benito Juárez Health Clinic (BJHC) to serve community needs. Shortly afterward, the barrio's educational problems were addressed when residents transformed an old dilapidated school into the new Benito Juárez High School.

Not all community groups were run by working-class residents. Some of the most enduring and consequential were Chicano organizations set up by professionals. Perhaps the two most productive associations of this type were the Mexican American Legal Defense and Education Fund (MALDEF) and the Southwest Council of La Raza (SWCLR). MALDEF was conceived in 1967 by Chicanos in Texas who hoped to provide much-needed legal services to the community.[35] Founders included Peter Tijerina, Gregory Luna, and Mario Obledo. Eventually, MALDEF was able to prosper not only because of its effectiveness in securing funding from private foundations and winning cases but also because of its able leadership, notably executive directors Vilma Martínez, Joaquín Ávila, and Antonia Hernández. Its impact has been profound. "MALDEF," according to the political scientist Maurilio E. Vigil, "has done more to address the problems, needs and concerns of Chicanos than any other contemporary Chicano organization."[36]

The SWCLR was established in 1968 in Phoenix to provide technical assistance and help fund community-based organizations in border states. Four years later, it went national, changing its name to the National Council of La Raza (NCLR) and establishing its headquarters in Washington, D.C. Aided by Hermán Gallegos, Henry Santiestevan, and Maclovio Barraza, Raúl Yzaguirre, from San Juan, Texas, took the initiative in forming the powerful advocacy organization, which he led for almost forty years. Other prominent Chicanos identified with NCLR were Bert Corona and Ernesto Galarza, both of whom seemed to have been involved with virtually every major civil rights initiative during these halcyon years.

From the old SWCLR came the idea, in 1975, for the Southwest Voter Registration Education Project (SWVRP), a Texas-based organization that was extremely effective, under the leadership of ex-LRUP leader Willie Velásquez (1944–1988), in mobilizing Mexicanos to participate in the political process.[37] The SWVRP eventually turned its attention to litigation, working closely with MALDEF.

Educators were some of the most active professionals in the Chicano movement. The oldest of their organizations was the Association of Mexican American Educators (AMAE), established in California in 1965 by teachers and administrators to promote quality education for Mexicano youth. Sal Castro was one of the founders. During its first years, AMAE campaigned vigorously for bilingual and bicultural educational programs.

A more militant educators' organization was the National Association for Chicano Studies (NACS), now called the National Association for Chicana and Chicano Studies (NACCS). The idea of a national Chicano association of activist scholars emerged in 1972–1973. Among the founding fathers were Carlos Muñoz Jr., José Cuéllar, and Jaime Sena-Rivera. A series of informal meetings culminated in the first annual convention in May 1974 at UC Irvine of the National Association of Chicano Social Scientists, the original name. During this formative period, the most dedicated members, in addition to those cited above, included Tomás Almaguer, Lea Ybarra, Adaljiza Sosa Riddell, José Limón, and Mario Barrera, all prominent scholars today. In recent years Julia Curry Rodríguez and Kathryn Blackmer Reyes have steered the organization through trying times.

Although NACS, as NACCS, has survived to the present, it has always experienced internal disputes due to both personality clashes and differences in philosophical approaches. The most recent threats to unity, according to the historian Ignacio M. García, have come from members advocating lesbian-feminism, neo-Marxism, or a militant form of Latinoism.[38] These same difficulties have beset Chicana/o studies programs, which NACCS has unsuccessfully attempted to coordinate into a cohesive network. Since the early 1980s, these programs have suffered a steady decline in enrollment.

THE CHICANA MOVEMENT

After about 1970, a new force began to surface within the movement: feminism. While feminism has a history in the Mexicano community that can be traced at least as far back as the Liga Femenil Mexicanista (Mexican Feminist League), established in 1911 by Jovita Idar (1885–1946) in Laredo, the movimiento at its inception in the sixties displayed little concern for women's liberation, a neglect it shared with other civil rights movements. Although advanced in their political ideas, many Chicanos were very traditional in their views of women and the family.[39] Consequently, in the various Chicano organizations, active participation by Chicanas was discouraged; it seemed that they were inevitably relegated to subordinate positions, such as secretaries, cooks, and janitors. Outright sexual harassment of female members was not uncommon. Many Chicanas gradually came to realize that they were worse off than their *compañeros* (male comrades) since they were subject to triple oppression: exploitation based on race, class, *and* gender.[40] As they sought a greater voice in the movement, they encountered considerable resistance. At the 1969 National Chicano Youth Conference in Denver, delegates, mostly male, resolved that Chicanas were opposed to their own liberation! Middle-class Chicanas also had a difficult time gaining a forum for their views. In 1970, efforts to establish a Chicana caucus at the annual convention of MAPA proved premature.

Some of the feminist criticism came from the ranks of their own sisters. As Anna Nieto-Gómez, herself an early feminist champion, has pointed out, women within the Chicano movement soon came to be divided into two general categories, which she calls the "loyalists" and the "feminists."[41] The first recognized that mujeres were oppressed within their own ethnic communities but felt that ultimately Anglo institutions were to blame. Moreover, they believed that criticism of Hispanic men would serve only to sow the seeds of dissension. Feminists, however, argued that the oppression they experienced within their own communities was as bad as that encountered from the dominant society. They felt that in returning to their cultural roots, many Chicanos had unfortunately come to glorify all aspects of the culture indiscriminately, including the misogynistic elements. Feminists insisted on speaking out against the machismo and sexual abuse rampant in the movement.

This widening schism among women activists came out in the open at the First National Chicana Conference, *Mujeres Por La Raza* (Women for La Raza), in May 1971, when six hundred delegates from the Southwest and Midwest met in Houston. The debates were extraordinarily animated, and the two sides quickly polarized. Eventually, loyalists, almost half the delegates in attendance, including the highly regarded Enriqueta Longeaux y Vásquez, walked out of the meeting in protest, ostensibly because of alleged neglect of mujeres in the barrio.

At first, feminists were put on the defensive by charges of being sell-outs. Labeled traitors, they came to identify with La Malinche, who though much maligned historically for helping Cortés conquer her own people, was now adopted by them as a symbol of womanhood and revered as the mother of the Mexican mestizo. Moreover, their critics also tried to discredit them by identifying emerging feminism with the small lesbian minority within their ranks, thus cashing in on the homophobia that pervades Mexican culture.

Undaunted, Chicana feminists began to form their own caucuses within Chicano conferences. They also initiated their own publications. While not exclusively feminist in its orientation, one of the earliest and most influential was *Regeneración,* which appeared in Los Angeles beginning in 1971. *Encuentro Femenil,* published by Nieto-Gómez and Adelaida del Castillo in 1973–1974, was the first major student publication. Chicana feminists worked with community-based women's service organizations, and before long they created their own associations distinct from those of other members of La Causa. In fact, some of them antedated the Houston Conference. Among these early women's groups were Las Chicanas at San Diego State University and Hijas de Cuauhtémoc at Long Beach State University. The Chicana movement—that is, the movement championing the rights of Mexicanas— was emerging from the shadow of the Chicano movement.

As they encountered increasing hostility by some segments of the Mexicano community, some Chicana groups attempted to make common cause with their counterparts in the white feminist movement, which had resurfaced in the early sixties. In 1973, for example, they formed the Chicana Women's Political Caucus within the National Women's Political Caucus. For the most part, though, these early attempts at cooperation turned out to be disillusioning. Alfredo Mirandé and Evangelina Enríquez explain:

> The Anglo women's movement showed itself to be indifferent to the unique needs of Chicanas, assuming that it could unite all women in the struggle against sexism but minimizing or neglecting the issues of race and poverty.
> . . . What Anglo feminists failed to see was that it was not possible for Chicanas to conceive of a separate women's movement independent of their racial-cultural struggle, just as it had not been possible for them to separate their problems as women from their racial oppression.[42]

Several dynamic leaders emerged from the early Chicana movement. Some of them tended to focus their efforts on the community, others on the schools. Community involvement was particularly stressed by Tejanas like Rosie Castro and Choco Meza, but perhaps the most talented and respected barrio activist of this period was Francisca Flores (1913–1996), from Los Angeles. Together with Ramona Morín, Flores founded the California League of Mexican American Women, a political action association, in the midsixties. Beginning in 1963, she and Delfino Varela published *Carta Editorial* to keep the community informed on issues relating to Mexicanos. When the paper changed its name to *Regeneración* in the seventies, Flores became its chief editor. In October 1970, she was one of the cofounders of the L.A.-based Comisión Femenil Mexicana Nacional (CFMN, National Commission of Mexican Women), the first major national feminista organization, and one which played a leading role in organizing the Houston Conference. A representative of the women's auxiliary of the Pomona G.I. Forum, Flores was among the most outspoken defenders of the feminist perspective at Houston, a defense she continued in the pages of *Regeneración*. Another Flores initiative was the Chicana Service Action Center (CSAC), an employment counseling and manpower training program. For years, she and Alicía Escalante, who founded the East Los Angeles Welfare Rights Organization in 1967, remained the most authoritative voices of Chicana feminism in southern California.

Among the many academicians who were pioneers in the movement, several stand out. Perhaps the most productive and persevering was Martha P. Cotera (1938–). Born in the Mexican state of Chihuahua, Marta Cotera was brought to the United States at the age of eight. After receiving her education at Texas Western University, known today as the University of Texas at El Paso, and Antioch College, she worked as a librarian in Austin until 1968. Two years later, together with her husband, she was one of the founders of Jacinto Treviño College, now defunct, which specialized in preparing teachers for bilingual education programs. By then, Cotera was heavily involved in the Chicano movement and had enough support to run for public office as a member of LRUP, where she joined Rosie Castro and Virginia Músquiz as one of a small group of women in the party leadership. María L. Hernández (1896–1986), a community activist since the twenties, and an LRUP stalwart, served as her mentor. A staunch feminista, Cotera helped found the Texas Women's Political Caucus in 1973, and a year later, she set up a nonprofit Chicana Research and Learning Center in Austin, an umbrella organization which encouraged and helped fund projects aimed at empowering minority women. Her publications on feminism have gained universal acclaim, making Marta Cotera one of the leading educators involved in the Chicana movement.

Chicanas such as Cotera and Elizabeth ("Betita") Martínez were active in championing all the causes Chicanos espoused, but their focus was consistently on women's issues. These included welfare rights, child care, sexual discrimination in employment, abortion, and birth control. Throughout the seventies, they were also adamant in their opposition to involuntary sterilization programs that victimized poor minority women. In colleges, their main contribution was the establishment of Chicana studies classes beginning in 1968 and Chicana studies programs shortly thereafter. These feminist programs were rapidly adopted by institutions of higher learning throughout the Southwest. Their most notable success was in California, the stronghold of Chicana feminism, where Anna Nieto-Gómez, Gracia Molina de Pick, and Corinna Sánchez led the way in their foundation. But in the early seventies, the Chicana movement was only in its infancy. Ultimately, it was to survive the hard years ahead much better than the Chicano movement.

THE DECLINE OF CHICANISMO

The heterogeneous nature of the movement, given the community it represented, was inevitable, but problems were bound to surface. It proved very difficult to get organizations and individuals to lay aside their specific agendas for the common welfare. The growing rift between Chicanos and Chicanas was only the most glaring example. Even *within* organizations, personal squabbles worked against unity. The same factionalism that characterized LRUP was evident in the

Brown Berets and MAPA. The authorities were only too happy to encourage this state of affairs. One well-informed scholar states, "Police provocation to commit not only violent acts but more frequently counterproductive actions was a fact; and of course led to the promotion of dissension within or between groups as well as individuals."[43] Moreover, no one leader emerged from the pack to give direction to the movement—not even Chávez, whose modest education and unbending social conservatism ill suited him for the role that Dr. King played among blacks.

It should also be noted that not all Mexicanos bought into the movement. As might be expected, many older and more affluent Mexican Americans, especially Hispanos in New Mexico and Colorado, had difficulty identifying with the goals of the movement, let alone endorsing the tactics. Called *tapados,* literally "stuffed up people" (i.e., those who refuse to hear the truth) or, worse still, vendidos, by Chicano sympathizers, these conservatives were quickly alienated by what they perceived to be the excesses of the militants. In truth, even elements within the movement—among them, some of the most determined defenders of Mexicano rights, including César Chávez, Bert Corona, and Anthony Quinn—decried extremist tendencies. The point of view of more moderate Chicanos was best expressed by Rodolfo de la Garza, then on the political science faculty of Colorado College, as the movement lost its impetus:

> I am convinced that American society has never dealt justly with Mexican Americans and that Anglo politicians have systematically deprived us of our political rights. Nonetheless, it is also my belief that we must accept some of the responsibility for the situation in which we find ourselves. . . . Too many of us, however, have ignored the example Chávez and the farm workers have given us and instead have resorted to rhetoric and have blamed others for all our problems. We must never allow Anglo society to deny the oppression imposed upon us, but we must also recognize that unless we admit our own weaknesses we can never correct them.[44]

Some working-class people expressed reservations also. Most immigrants, for example, especially recent immigrants, shied away from the movement. To some extent, this reluctance reflects the subtle tension that has always existed between the Mexican immigrant and the native-born Mexican American—as is true historically of almost any immigrant community in U.S. society. Recent immigrants are generally preoccupied with making a living. Moreover, despite their problems, they are grateful for the opportunity to improve their lives.

But ultimately, the failure of the movimiento needs to be seen in a broader context. Despite its deficiencies and weaknesses, the fact of the matter is that all the civil rights movements faded, not just the Brown Power groups. The political and intellectual climate of the country changed drastically with the end of the Vietnam War in 1975. Problems, perceived and real, with the economy altered priorities, as well. As Americans approached the eighties, the concern for human rights was eclipsed by the desire for financial security. Mexicanos were forced to fight hard just to retain their recent gains in a period of conservative ascendancy.

THE CHICANO LEGACY

Writing in the early 1990s about the Chicano movement, one observer tersely commented, "Nothing remains of it now but a handshake practiced by middle-aged men."[45] Granted, outside of the recent immigrant rights marches, there does not appear to be much militancy among Mexicanos since then, either in the barrios or in the schools. Even the term *Chicano* has fallen upon bad times. The meaning of the movimiento, moreover, is much debated these days. While, understandably, participant historians such as Rudy Acuña and Armando Navarro continue to describe Chicanismo and its accomplishments in glowing terms, a point of view best articulated today by the literary scholar/activist George Mariscal, the trend among historians in recent years, especially among younger professors, has been to advance a much more modest assessment.[46] Few of them, however, would go as far as David G. Gutiérrez, who practically reduces the movimiento to a non-happening. After noting that "Chicano activists never came close to exerting the same kind of moral pull on the public's consciousness that their counterparts in the black-liberation and antiwar movements were able to achieve," the highly respected historian, in what appears to be a case of damming with faint praise, concedes that "the movement probably did help to increase general awareness about the 'nation's second largest minority' and to intensify federal, state, and local government efforts on its behalf."[47] A more realistic assessment of the Chicano legacy, however, lies somewhere between the two extremes. On balance, militants had a powerful and positive impact on contemporary society, and their legacy continues to resonate among many Mexicanos today.

Chicano activists were correct when they acted on the premise that American institutions respond to the needs of a minority community only when they are forced to. A good example was the War on Poverty. The programs emanating from that government-sponsored campaign were initially concessions to the black community, thanks in part to the riots of the midsixties, but also to the efforts of the black civil rights movement. It was largely Chicano militancy that forced LBJ to include Mexicanos, who received many benefits from these government-supported programs, not the least of which was the opportunity for leadership training.[48] By the beginning of the twenty-first century, there were literally hundreds of community service organizations serving the Mexicano community that traced their roots to the turbulent decade between 1965 and 1975.

The Brown Power movement brought other gains as well. Reform legislation was one. Bilingual and bicultural education, for example, owed its existence to Chicano pressure. In terms of higher education, the key contribution may well be

Chicana/o studies programs, strongholds of Chicanismo, instituted in more than one hundred universities throughout the nation. A monument to the efforts of student militants, these programs continue to exist—those at UCLA, UC Berkeley, UC Santa Barbara, and CSU Northridge seem to be the most stable—serving the student community and producing innovative scholarly research on a host of topics. Virtually all Latino college professors, in or out of ethnic studies departments, were impacted by the movement. Through them, its values continue to be transmitted to a powerful audience, the future leaders of a multicultural society.

The movement has had a striking impact on artists. Beginning with El Teatro Campesino, established by Luis Valdez as an adjunct to the UFW in the midsixties, Chicanismo became a vital force in the arts. Ultimately, it spurred a cultural renaissance which continues to enrich not only the Mexican-origin community but American society as a whole. Finally, there is the sense of pride that it fostered among Mexicanos, both men and women, especially the youth. Undoubtedly, this is its single most lasting and beneficial contribution.

Themselves products of La Causa, most senior Chicana/o historians who have studied the movimiento tend to see it as the culmination of Mexican American history. In point of fact, as young scholars point out, the militant struggle represents just one episode in that history, albeit a very meaningful one. The movement has come and gone, as the scholars David E. Hayes-Bautista and Gregory Rodríguez candidly observe, but the people are still there.[49]

It is a mistake to identify Chicanismo solely with students. Armando Navarro, who has done the most comprehensive study on MAYO to date, is representative of this view.[50] But this proclivity is most obvious in the work of another political scientist, Carlos Muñoz Jr., himself an ardent activist in his student days.[51] Professor Muñoz makes a very sound point when he insists that students were on the cutting edge of La Causa; however, his propensity to define Brown Power entirely in terms of a youth movement is much too restrictive. He neglects to include the middle-class associations created by the Mexican American Generation, organizations such as LULAC and CSO.

Moreover, the exclusion of other activists of the sixties is unfortunate and highly suspect. For example, in assessing César Chávez, Muñoz avers, "In fact, Chávez has been and remains the leader of a labor movement and later a union struggle that was never an integral part of the Chicano movement."[52] An LRUP member at one point, apparently Muñoz continues to harbor long-standing grievances. To exclude Chávez, Tijerina, and leaders of that ilk is to do grave injustice to them and their contributions.

In sum, the movement was extremely varied. Indeed, it would be more accurate to describe several Chicano movements. Although the students were more vocal and radical, consequently grabbing the headlines, most militant organizations were not student-centered. In fact, as the historian Ignacio García argues, despite appearances, "a closer look at the Movement reveals that it remained dominated not by students or youth but by adults who had experienced Anglo-American prejudice for an extended period."[53] These activists were to be found in a variety of community groups, some operating in urban barrios, others in rural settings. Most served the needs of the working class.

Contrary to Muñoz's interpretation, however, middle-class organizations were also well represented in the movement. In the decade between 1965 and 1975, older middle-class associations such as LULAC, CSO, MAPA, and even the G.I. Forum embraced the concept of La Raza, albeit reluctantly at times. The spectrum within the movement extended from the moderate position endorsed by the G.I. Forum to the radical philosophy of the Brown Berets, with student groups, who were more accommodating than their rhetoric would suggest, somewhere in the middle. What these various organizations had in common was that they all sought, through the tactics of confrontation, to gain political representation in order to protect their civil rights, and they all rejected sacrificing their heritage for break-neck assimilation into the American mainstream, opting instead for some form of cultural pluralism.

GOODBYE TO AZTLÁN

1975–1994

9

The political generation that emerged in barrios after the mid-1970s, labeled by Chicano historians the Post-Chicano Generation—or the Hispanic Generation, given its more conservative nature—lived in a time of rapid and confusing change. Most Chicano scholars, swayed by the high expectations of the preceding decade, have tended to be critical. Political gains from the mid-1970s to the mid-1990s, for the most part a period of Republican ascendancy, appeared to them to be minimal. Socially and economically, too, the vast promise held out by the movimiento remained unfulfilled. And yet, upon closer examination of this disappointing and seemingly unproductive era, it is possible to detect more hopeful signs for the future. This chapter will try to present a balanced portrait of the Mexicano community in the United States during these two decades, a transitional period between Chicanismo and the contemporary age, by focusing on its frustrations and achievements, on its pain and promise.

DEMOGRAPHIC TRENDS

Mexicanos maintained a high profile in American society after the 1970s. There were many reasons for this enhanced visibility. Bilingualism and affirmative action were key factors. But perhaps the most salient was the enormous increase in numbers. Hispanics—a government category used by the U.S. Census Bureau that included Mexicanos, Puerto Ricans, Cubans, and other Latin Americans—increased by 61 percent between 1970 and 1980, and 53 percent between 1980 and 1990. By the latter date, according to census data, these communities numbered 22.4 million, about 9 percent of the total U.S. population (exclusive of indocumentados).[1] About 60 percent of Hispanics, some 13.5 million people, were Mexican in origin.[2] In California alone, according to the census, 109 towns and cities had achieved a Hispanic majority by 1990. This dramatic increase reflected an extraordinarily high birth rate. There were 3.8 persons per family, compared to the 3.2 for a typical American family. A youthful population, Hispanics had a median age of 26.2 years, compared to the 33.0 years for the total population.

By the 1990s, Mexicanos could be found picking citrus fruit in Florida, harvesting tobacco in North Carolina, collecting mushrooms in Pennsylvania, picking orchard crops in Washington, cleaning fish in Alaska, and working in slaughterhouses in Iowa. As the decade opened, some two hundred thousand Mexicanos lived in New York City. Clearly, they had become a national rather than a regional minority. Still, 83 percent of them continued to reside in the Southwest. The greatest number, 6,118,996, lived in California, where the 7.7 million Latinos represented 25.8 percent of the total population, about the same percentage as in Texas (25.5) though lower than New Mexico (38.2). In the Land of Enchantment, interestingly, the trend was different than in other parts of the Southwest. Here the Anglo population was growing at the expense of the Hispano population. For example, in Santa Fe County, the Hispano share of the population fell from 65 percent to 45 percent between 1970 and 1990. Outside the Southwest, the largest number of Mexicanos was found in the Midwest. Over 1.5 million of them resided in Chicago and Detroit and their surrounding areas.

By 1990, 90.5 percent of the Mexicano population in the United States was urban, a higher percentage than the U.S. population at large. The highest concentration of Latinos as of 1992, 4,779,000, was found in the Los Angeles metropolitan area (32.9 percent of the total population), where they constituted the majority of students in the public school system, especially in greater East Los Angeles and the San Fernando Valley. At this time, the Mexicano community of Los Angeles was the fourth largest in the world, after Mexico City, Monterrey, and Guadalajara. In Texas, there were several major cities with heavy Hispanic (overwhelmingly Mexicano) representation, including San Antonio (47.6 percent), Corpus Christi (52 percent), El Paso (69.6 percent), and Laredo (93.9 percent). In Houston, Latino students made up roughly half of the school population. Concurrently, Mexicanos, and other minorities, became part of a major exodus leaving city centers for outlying suburbs, a shift motivated by a multitude of factors, including the desire to escape violence in the barrios.

THE RESURGENCE OF MEXICAN IMMIGRATION

In addition to the high birth rate, the second major cause of the changing demographics, and another obvious reason why Mexicanos were highly visible in the post-Chicano period, was massive immigration from Mexico to the United States. Beginning in the 1960s and accelerating greatly in the 1980s, the movement of people across the border was a source of continual and often acrimonious controversy throughout the nation. This surge, according to Jeffrey Passel, a demographer for the Urban Institute in Washington, D.C., constitutes the greatest historical mass migration to the United States from a single country.[3] While no one can calculate the volume of traffic with any certainty, the number of Mexicans apprehended by the Immigration and Naturalization Service for illegal entry exceeded one million in the sixties and seven million in the seventies. Between 1980 and the early 1990s, when apprehensions of all illegals grew by two-thirds nationwide, according to official records, over one-third of them took place in the San Diego area. By the mid-1990s, the INS estimated that 54 percent of the more than five million illegal immigrants in the country were Mexican nationals. As was true of previous waves of immigration from the south, this recent migration, though generally excluding the absolutely destitute (people with no resources at all), as Jorge Durand of the University of Guadalajara, Laura González of the University of Guanajuato, and other Mexican demographers have shown, was propelled mainly by the inability of Mexico to provide a decent living for many of its citizens.

The outstanding feature of the history of Mexico since World War II was an incredible demographic explosion. By the midnineties, the population exceeded 93 million people, an increase of over 30 million in twenty years. Up until the late 1970s, the Mexican economy had been growing at a steady pace, and the ills associated with a burgeoning population were reasonably contained. But after this time, severe financial and economic problems surfaced, and in 1981–1982, the economy, beset by a fall in oil prices, high inflation, and an unmanageable foreign debt, suddenly plummeted. According to official figures, the number of Mexicans living in poverty mushroomed from 32.1 million to 41.3 million in 1980–1987. The government of President Carlos Salinas de Gotari (1988–1994) responded by instituting severe cost-cutting measures and neo-liberal reforms, the latter facilitating integration of the Mexican economy with that of the United States. Both policies met with vehement opposition, especially from irate nationalists and the beleaguered working classes.

At first, the neo-liberal economic program of Salinas and his successor, Ernesto Zedillo Ponce de León (1994–2000) seemed to be working in spite of massive popular discontent; however, government optimism proved completely unfounded in December 1994, when the peso suddenly crashed. Only U.S. aid in the form of a $13.5 billion rescue package put together by the Clinton administration saved the Mexican economy from total collapse. To pay for the bailout, Mexico was forced to reduce the standard of living for most of its citizens by 20 percent. By 1996, according to a study by the Colegio de México, 80 percent of the Mexican population lived in poverty. Popular dissatisfaction was inevitable, given the country's huge uneven distribution of wealth. The political scientist Howard Handelman notes that by the midnineties, income was more highly concentrated in Mexico than in many considerably poorer countries, such as Pakistan, India, Indonesia, and Peru.[4] The Partido Revolucionario Institucional was further discredited by its failure to carry out democratic political reforms. Government corruption was dramatically exposed during the 1994 presidential elections, when intraparty strife led to widespread violence and the assassination of the party's official candidate, Luis Donaldo Colosio. It was only the safety valve provided by U.S. immigration, many knowledgeable observers have noted, that kept Mexico from plunging into the throes of revolution.

Some newcomers entered the United States through legal channels. The 1965 Immigration Act amended the Immigration and Nationality Act of 1952 by putting a cap, for the first time, of 120,000 a year on immigration from the Western Hemisphere. Eleven years later, immigration from Mexico was restricted to 20,000 a year, a quota which was always filled. In fact, Mexican immigrants generally exceeded this number substantially since the law allowed additional people to enter under a complicated preference system that gave priority to family reunification. Legal immigration from Mexico in the seventies averaged 60,000 persons per year. Moreover, after the demise of the Bracero Program in 1965, pressure by agribusiness and other economic interests in the border states resulted in legislation allowing Mexicans to enter the country as guest workers under a variety of programs. Some, called commuters, entered on a daily basis; others, "green carders" (their permit was originally green), were given permanent residency, allowing them to travel back and forth across the border.

The majority of border crossers, however, were undocumented workers. Motivation was generally the same as before—economic gain. But, beyond the sheer volume, there were striking differences between recent undocumented workers and those of yesteryear. Now immigrants were much more likely than before to come from urban settings; only about a quarter of Mexico's population worked in agriculture by the nineties. "Contrary to the stereotype of Mexican immigrants as overwhelmingly impoverished peasants," researchers Alejandro Portes and Rubén G. Rumbaut have pointed out, "up to 48 percent of the unauthorized have been found to originate in cities of twenty thousand or more, in comparison with 35 percent of all Mexicans."[5] As the postwar economic boom petered out in the seventies and eighties, masses of displaced peasants were forced to abandon overcrowded villages for the cities. Having made a move once, many uprooted newcomers were prepared to relocate again due to failed expectations. Mexico City, possibly the biggest city in the world, was particularly prone to the kinds of pressures that encourage migration, especially after the destructive 1985 earthquake. Many immigrants who left the cities to head north were disillusioned professionals, a class of people largely unrepresented in previous times.

Indigenous people, too, first appeared as a significant component of the immigrant population at this time. California—where today some observers feel the foreign-born outnumber the native-born Mexican population—was a favorite destination. They tended to reside close together, which was only natural since immigration was often the result of kinship networks. Tlacolulenses from Oaxaca, for example, could be found in Santa Monica. A Mixteca colony appeared in the hills near Oceanside. This pattern appeared in cities outside of the Golden State, as well. Houston, for example, developed a substantial Mayan colonia. Since the Indian population was the most traditional in Mexico, their escalating immigrant numbers were a barometer of how desperate the economic plight of the lower classes had become. Anti-Indian sentiment in Mexico was another factor affecting indigenous emigration. As the astute Earl Shorris has aptly noted, "In a nation devoted to celebrating its Indian heritage the terrible irony is that Indians are despised."[6] It was mistreatment of indigenous peoples, who constitute between 10 and 15 percent of the Mexican population, that set the stage for the uprising of the Zapatista National Liberation Army in Chiapas on 1 January 1994. Unrest soon spread to other states with large Native American populations, notably Oaxaca and Guerrero.

Women and entire families were much more evident now than they had been in prior waves of immigration. One survey suggests that mujeres constituted between 60 and 75 percent of those arrested with false documents along the Mexico-U.S. border in 1995. This trend may reflect fundamental changes in family structure in the Old Country, including the decline of extended family networks and compadrazgo, as well as the increasing number of women forced into wage labor in Mexican villages and cities, the latter a factor emphasized by the sociologist Pierrette Hondagneu-Sotelo.[7] Apparently, many people were more determined at this time to maintain permanent residence in the United States—although a 1997 study of illegal immigration to the Golden State from six states in western Mexico, by the San Francisco-based Public Policy Institute of California, concluded that the majority of indocumentados returned home within two years.[8]

Finally, in contrast to earlier times, many of the recién llegados (recent immigrants) from Mexico were not Mexicans at all, but members of other impoverished and persecuted nationalities. Among them were huge numbers of refugees from Central America, where political violence after 1979 uprooted thousands, especially in Nicaragua, El Salvador, and Guatemala.[9] By the midnineties—when the U.S. Census Bureau estimated the Hispanic population was increasing at the rate of nine hundred thousand a year—there were between one-half million and one million Central Americans in Los Angeles, concentrated mainly in the central and south-central parts of the city.

The push-pull paradigm that was so useful in explaining early twentieth-century immigration had less applicability at this time, as both Anglo and Chicano students of immigration have noted.[10] The situation now was more complicated than the old model suggests. For example, in many regions of Mexico, notably the states immediately north and west of the capital, a tradition of immigration had emerged, sometimes from roots in the nineteenth century. For many individuals, the movement north was almost a rite of passage. Moreover, many families were now maintaining dual residence, living in Mexico part of the year and in the United States the rest of the time, often establishing "transnational migrant circuits," as the anthropologist Roger Rouse terms them, a complex immigration pattern inconsistent with the traditional push-pull model.[11]

Many illegal Mexican immigrants, like those from other countries, had entered the country legally—on student, work, or tourist visas—then simply refused to return home. By the 1990s, according to some experts, as much as half of illegal immigration from all countries into the United States—estimated at between three hundred thousand and four hundred thousand individuals annually—may have been initiated in this fashion.

The destination of indocumentados continued to be the Southwest, though California, where the Hispanic population increased dramatically in the 1980s from 4.5 million to 7.6 million, was now a much more attractive magnet than Texas. By 1990, over half of the Hispanics in Los Angeles were immigrants. However, the Borderlands they entered were much different than those encountered by their predecessors in the 1920s, or even the 1950s. No longer were jobs primarily in mining, railroad maintenance, and agriculture. Farm employment, in particular, was difficult to find in the now heavily urbanized Southwest. Moreover, the advent of a so-called postindustrial economy after the sixties meant that available jobs were primarily in the low-wage service sector—typically restaurant, plant nursery, and yard work for men, and child care and paid domestic work for women—rather than in the middle-wage manufacturing area.

In many respects, new immigrants, especially indocumentados, who often worked at two jobs, had it tougher than those in the past. One reason was that although there were more artisans, clerical workers, and even professionals represented than before, immigrants for the most part continued to enter the country as unskilled or semiskilled laborers, while available jobs in the service industry increasingly demanded skills, including the ability to speak English. Opportunities were more limited than they had been fifty years earlier, which may be the reason why a sizable percentage of indocumentados maintained dual residence in Mexico and the United States, coming and going seasonally.

Massive illegal immigration predictably sparked a restrictionist campaign in the United States similar to those of the 1920s and 1950s, with the Mexican immigrant as the focus of attention. Much of the controversy centered on the question, basically economic, of whether immigrants, both legal and illegal, augmented or drained national resources.

Defenders claimed that immigrants performed the work U.S. citizens refused to do. For example, more than 92 percent of California's farm-labor force of nearly one million people in the early nineties was foreign-born. Moreover, although conceding they might put a strain on welfare, health, and educational services, sympathetic observers argued that on balance immigrants made a positive contribution. The Urban Institute, a nonpartisan research organization, agreed, concluding in 1994 that foreigners actually contributed far more tax dollars than they used in services. Mexicans, in particular, it was reported, were unlikely to use welfare services, since they tended to be illegal immigrants. These services disproportionately benefited political refugees, a category that excluded Mexicans. Chicano and other civil rights groups argued that the immigrant, particularly the indocumentado, was being used as a scapegoat for the multitude of problems plaguing the public sector.

On the other hand, critics felt that the labor performed by immigrants did not compensate for the services that they had received. They argued, moreover, that immigrants, many of them illegals, failed to pay a fair share of their taxes. Furthermore, the sheer numbers of immigrants sparked racist sentiments, though these rarely surfaced in the media and other public forums in overt ways. Racial theories, for example, were widely espoused by members of the Federation for American Immigration Reform (FAIR), the leading national advocate of immigration restriction in recent years.

The attitude of the long-standing Mexicano communities in the United States on this heated issue was somewhat surprising. Polls indicated that these communities were even more opposed to illegal immigration than was the American population in general. In 1992, the Latino National Political Survey, headed by respected University of Texas political scientist Rodolfo de la Garza, found that 75 percent of Mexicanos with U.S. citizenship and 84 percent of Mexicanos without U.S. citizenship, compared to 74 percent of non-Hispanic whites, felt that there were too many immigrants in the country. Although anti-Asian sentiment in barrios might partly account for these findings, there was little reason to doubt the survey's basic conclusion, highlighting the fact that the controversy was predominantly economic in nature. Mexicanos residing in the United States legally, whether they had good reason to believe so or not, suspected that their livelihood was being threatened. Tellingly, it was the most recently arrived Mexicans, those who competed for the same kinds of jobs, who were most opposed to a liberal immigration policy. Many Mexican Americans also feared that the backlash against Mexican immigrants would have a detrimental impact on their own communities. For instance, a national identity card, one of the solutions most ballyhooed by restrictionists, would very clearly lead to discrimination against all people of Latino background.

So animated was the popular indignation aroused by both legal and illegal immigration—in some places in California, like Orange County and the San

Fernando Valley, it verged on hysteria—that Congress was forced to act, though not without considerable hesitation, given the complexity of the problem and the powerful lobbies participating in the national debate. Probably the major stumbling block to effective legislation was Republican opposition to imposing sanctions on employers, which many critics felt was the only effective means of curtailing illegal entry. Eventually, a compromise solution was reached. The result was the 1986 Immigration Reform and Control Act (IRCA). Essentially, this legislation was an attempt to deal with all the problems of immigration at once. Under the 1986 law, Mexico continued to supply a large number of legal immigrants (126,561 in 1993). IRCA sought to control *illegal* immigration in two ways: (1) it enacted sanctions against employers of illegal immigrants, and (2) it granted amnesty—and eligibility for citizenship—to undocumented workers who had lived in the United States continuously since 1 January 1982; and, through a Special Agricultural Worker (SAW) program, it legalized indocumentados who had worked a minimum of ninety days in U.S. agriculture between May 1985 and May 1986. Approximately 2.4 million indocumentados applied for and were granted legal status thanks to this legislation.

The 1986 law *did* diminish illegal entry for several years, but by 1990—when another immigration act was passed, increasing immigration levels by 40 percent and doubling the number of visas for skilled workers—the tide had resumed. After that date, the INS apprehended at least 1.5 million people annually. It was estimated that some one hundred thousand to two hundred thousand indocumentados entered the country successfully every year. The total number of Latino illegals in the early nineties was probably around 2 million, though unofficial estimates ranged as high as 12 million—possibly because the first estimate was confined to the settler population while the latter took into account sojourners. A thriving trade in counterfeit documents made it very difficult to enforce the law, but IRCA failed primarily because the U.S. government was unwilling and/or unable to enforce employer sanctions. Employers were rarely caught in violation of the law, hardly surprising since fewer than 350 agents were responsible for supervising 7 million employers. And when offenders *were* caught, penalties were often avoided. Fewer than half of the 12,714 employer cases reported to the INS from 1989 to 1994 resulted in fines.

THE NORTH AMERICAN FREE TRADE ASSOCIATION

The failure of legislation to stymie illegal immigration by 1990 encouraged the supporters of an alternative solution to the problem: those who felt that immigration was inevitable unless the Mexican economy became strong enough to keep Mexicans at home. Efforts in this direction go back to 1965, when American companies, for purely economic motives, began to set up assembly plants, called *maquiladoras,* on the Mexican side of the border to take advantage of cheap labor. Hundreds of thousands of workers were employed assembling parts imported tax-free for appliances, automobiles, and other consumer goods, and sending the finished products north, to be sold in U.S. markets. During the 1980s, maquila-doras became increasingly sophisticated in their operations. Some critics, like the sociologist Devon G. Peña, saw them as high-volume sweatshops exploiting the predominantly female labor force, increasingly married women forced to work by the collapsing Mexican economy.

Eventually, the American government, under both Republican and Demo-cratic administrations, became convinced that the encouragement of U.S. business interests in northern Mexico through the creation of a free-trade zone would yield dual benefits: on the one hand, it would ameliorate the problem of indocumentados by providing Mexicans jobs at home and, on the other hand, it would encourage the economic exploitation of lucrative Mexican markets. By the mid-1980s, the Mexican government, for its part, faced with a glut of unskilled workers and a lack of savings to finance investment, was prepared to wholeheartedly embrace a project which would help modernize the nation's economy, placate its working class, and stabilize political life. Thus, there gradually emerged on both sides of the border the concept of a North American Free Trade Association (Nafta) linking Canada, Mexico, and the United States, the largest trade bloc in the world.

There were many critics. On the Mexican side, nationalists feared the increas-ing penetration of U.S. influence, seen as another form of cultural imperialism. On the American side, resistance to the project was centered in labor unions and con-servationist groups, an alliance led by populist presidential candidate Ross Perot.

Despite formidable opposition, the Nafta agreement was legislated into law in November 1993 and went into effect on 1 January 1994. Among congressional leaders most responsible for its enactment was Representative Bill Richardson, a Mexican-descent Democrat from New Mexico. Then chief deputy majority whip in the House, Richardson would be appointed U.S. ambassador to the United Nations by President Clinton in 1997. The Mexican American communities were divided on Nafta, but Richardson's stance appeared to reflect majority opinion. The growing Latino business community was an avid supporter, and found its leading spokesman in the Santa Barbara-based *Hispanic Business,* edited by ex-militant Jesús Chavarría. Among middle-class organizations, the most enthusiastic endorsement came from the Southwest Voter Registration Education Project, an astute political move, permitting it to gain considerable clout in the Clinton administration.

THE DECADE OF THE HISPANIC: THE UNFULFILLED PROMISE

Looking back, despite misgivings by a minority calling for continuing mili-tancy, there was considerable optimism among Mexicanos throughout the country during the late 1970s. It was apparent that substantial gains had been made in the previous decade, and there was a general expectation that progress would continue on all fronts. The 1980s were heralded as the "Decade of the Hispanic" by Raúl Yzaguirre, director of the National Council of La Raza, and others. This potential, though, was never realized. The Post-Chicano Generation, while compiling a creditable record of achievement, found that it had underestimated the resistance to change in society at large and overestimated its own capacity to resolve long-standing problems.

Disappointment was most obvious in the political arena, where, in spite of alliances with fellow Latinos and other underprivileged segments of society, Mexicanos failed to register anticipated gains. In terms of elective offices, there were a few noteworthy triumphs at the local and state levels, especially in areas with large Mexicano constituencies. Moreover, there was mounting evidence that political clout was expanding beyond the Southwest; already by the mideighties, there were several hundred Hispanic elected and appointed officials in the Midwest. Toney Anaya was elected governor of New Mexico in 1982, continuing a tradition begun in the seventies, when two other Mexicano Democrats had won governorships: Raúl Castro in Arizona and Jerry Apodaca in New Mexico. But electoral victories were few and far between. The Hispanic Caucus in Congress, led by Henry B. González, never fully realized its potential in Washington, despite favorable demographic trends.

One major stumbling block was political apathy in barrios. Yeoman efforts by the National Association of Latino Elected and Appointed Officials (NALEO), MALDEF, and other Chicano civil rights associations notwithstanding, the voter turnout remained embarrassingly low into the nineties. Year in and year out, depending on the election, less than a quarter of Mexicanos eligible to vote actually exercised that privilege.

Internecine squabbles within and between organizations took their toll. Mexicano political organizations were notorious for their inability to work together, an unfortunate characteristic particularly galling to the journalist Rubén Navarrette Jr.: "Ethnic solidarity, a successful economic and political tool for American Jews and other ethnic groups, eludes Latinos. . . . For Latinos, there has been little cooperation or camaraderie. And so little progress. Petty competition, personal intolerance and a refusal to let any of our own progress ahead of us make it unlikely that the children of the sun, however numerous, will ever inherit the earth."[12]

Nor, despite repeated attempts, was there meaningful progress in forming an overall umbrella organization of civil rights associations. Alliances with other ethnic groups, especially African Americans, proved elusive. Although Mexicanos aided Jesse Jackson's Rainbow Coalition, support was lukewarm, hardly surprising given racial and economic tensions between the two minorities. Even pan-Hispanic unity proved elusive. Mexicanos, three-quarters of whom continued to vote Democrat, found little common ground with Cubans, who, though attractive as potential allies given their wealth and political clout, remained solidly united under the GOP banner. The Hispanic Congressional Caucus itself was often divided on whether or not to recognize Cuba. In point of fact, there had always been undisguised admiration for Fidel Castro among most Chicano intellectuals, a sentiment completely at odds with that of the overwhelming majority of Cuban expatriates, who saw the dictator as the Antichrist himself. Generally speaking, as Peruvian American scholar Suzanne Oboler has observed, Spanish-speaking peoples in the United States tended to reject the "Hispanic" label, choosing instead to identify with their particular national group.[13]

The most intractable barrier to Mexicano electoral success in the eighties, however, was the radical change in the climate of opinion, as reflected in Republican ascendancy over political life. This conservatism began to make inroads even into the growing Mexican American middle class. Some of the most damaging criticism of social programs for underprivileged minorities came from within the ranks of the ethnic community, notably from the San Francisco-based journalist Richard Rodríguez (1948–) and the Colorado-born Hispana Linda Chávez (1947–), a staunch and outspoken Republican and a fellow at the Manhattan Institute, a conservative think tank in Washington, D.C.

Educational problems also proved intractable. There was a modicum of progress made in this area, particularly in institutions of higher education, where affirmative action and the Educational Opportunity Program (EOP) helped boost minority enrollment. In the fall semester of 1993, for example, some 14 percent of the 21,593 undergraduates enrolled at UC Berkeley and 17 percent of the 22,892 undergraduates at UCLA were Hispanic, an aggregate category, but overwhelmingly Mexicano. Gains were more impressive at the community college level. By 1996, Hispanics represented 36.3 percent of the 10 million students enrolled in the nation's more than one thousand two-year colleges. These numbers, however, were sadly deficient given the burgeoning, and youthful, communities they represented. Moreover, these small but significant gains in higher education were suddenly threatened in the mid-1990s, when the regents of the University of California, led by Governor Wilson and political ally Ward Connerly voted to terminate admission policies based on affirmative action. This fateful decision was supported by California voters in 1996, when they overwhelmingly endorsed Proposition 209.

The small numbers of Mexicanos in colleges was a consequence of a relatively modest pool of applicants. The high school drop-out rate in the early nineties was over 40 percent—a higher rate than that of African Americans and Puerto Ricans, though slightly better than among Native Americans—not much of an improvement over what it had been before the advent of the Chicano movement. Furthermore, brown students receiving high school degrees were not being prepared to go into higher education: Mexicanos who took the SAT in 1992 averaged 797, while Anglos averaged 933. This distressing record of underachievement was compiled in spite of bilingual and a variety of other academic programs meant to remedy the situation. Conservative critics such as Linda Chávez suggested that these programs themselves were part of the problem.

A product of a 1974 Supreme Court ruling, *Lau v. Nichols,* bilingual education, which mandates that immigrant and other children who speak a language other than English as their primary language be taught in their native tongue as well as English, in particular, was anathema to conservative groups, both in and out of educational circles. Leading the campaign against bilingualism was U.S. English, a California-based organization which promoted the learning of English and attempted to convince Congress to adopt a constitutional amendment to make English the official language of government.[14] Founded in 1983 by John Tanton, a Michigan ophthalmologist who was also instrumental in creating FAIR, the anti-immigration group, and led by ex-senator S. I. Hayakawa, U.S. English grew by leaps and bounds, a reflection of wide-ranging fears of "unassimilable immigrants." One of the national presidents of the organization was Linda Chávez, a champion of the idea that immigrants should assimilate at breakneck speed. Chávez was very vocal in her opposition to all forms of entitlements for minorities because in order to maintain eligibility, she claimed, beneficiaries were encouraged to fail rather than succeed. She and other conservative critics were fond of pointing out the contradiction between segregating students into bilingual programs and the fight for integrated schools that Chicanos and other minorities had persistently waged for most of the twentieth century. The English Only movement, fueled by growing xenophobia and a taxpayers' revolt, flourished in the mideighties. A decade later, twenty-three states, including California, had passed English-only amendments, raising serious questions about the future of bilingual education. Nevertheless, in spite of philosophical, financial, and practical difficulties, bilingualism managed to survive, chiefly because of heavy immigration and aggressive advocacy by ethnic rights groups.

Most Mexicano educators, like the vast majority of the Latino community, supported bilingualism and other progressive measures. In their view, educational reforms after the sixties had been more theoretical than real. Economic problems and reluctant taxpayers meant, unfortunately, that schools were forced to scale down services, and minority-based programs were generally judged to be the most expendable by local school boards. Many Mexicanos suspected that American society at bottom had no real sympathy with these reforms, which were conceded reluctantly in the first place.

There was ample evidence to support this point of view. Certainly, many schools were slow to meet Chicano demands. According to a study by the Tomás Rivera Center, a Hispanic policy research institute in Claremont, California, in 1994, a year after Latinos supposedly reached 10 percent of the total U.S. population, only 3.7 percent of all teachers in American public schools lay claim to that ethnic background. Little wonder, Mexicano parents complained, that many of their children continued to see school as a kind of prison. The failure of American education to meet the needs of the Mexican American community was underlined by an exhaustive interdisciplinary project conducted by Carola and Marcelo Suárez-Orozco of the Harvard Graduate School of Education. They discovered that the attitude toward school was more positive among children of Mexican immigrants than among children of Mexican American parents. The increasing cynicism toward education and poor academic performance of Mexican American adolescents, the researchers concluded, was attributed to a variety of factors, but especially the disparagement and discrimination to which the youths were subjected, both in and out of the classroom.[15]

Still, though governmental and educational policies had much to do with Mexicanos' educational deficiencies, these factors were secondary to impoverished socioeconomic conditions. This depressed status was itself a product of a whole complicated set of circumstances, not the least of which, in recent years, were the public policies of Republican administrations willing to sacrifice the interests of the poor in order to benefit the more affluent segments of American society, thus hastening the trend toward a two-tier society bifurcated largely along ethnic lines. This period, christened "The Rambo Years" by Rodolfo Acuña, is best described by a fellow historian:

> The Reagan era was a period of selfish emphasis, jingoism and chauvinism, and a lack of access. The number of persons in a poverty status increased. The Reagan administration was not only inaccessible; it was generally negative toward the basic social and economic needs of the community, and it undertook specific negative actions concerning immigration and labor. Both antiworker and antiunion policies impacted on the Chicano community.[16]

The reality of poverty was all too apparent. In 1991, according to the U.S. Census Bureau, the median family income for Hispanics was $23,431, as compared to $35,353 for all families in the United States; and the average Latino family income was $29,311, well below the U.S. mean of $42,652. Statistics relating specifically to Mexicanos were daunting. More than a quarter of them (28.1 percent) lived below the poverty line. Their unemployment rate exceeded 10 percent during that year. While 85 percent of the general population had medical insurance, only about 20 percent of the Mexican-origin community could afford health coverage. Moreover, many Mexicanos were immigrants, which meant that they had language difficulties to contend with, on top of financial burdens.

In addition, the record of educational failure can partly be attributed to certain aspects of ethnic culture. Most Chicano historians in the past have tended to dwell on the debilitating impact of outside agencies on the Mexicano community while deemphasizing internal problems—inadvertently and regrettably encouraging the trend among some segments of the community toward victimization that has been so pronounced since the sixties. As the Súarez-Orozcos suggest, this emphasis is understandable since the harm done by schools, police agencies, government organizations, and other Anglo-controlled institutions—as well as the erosive influences that impact all families, Mexicano and non-Mexicano—has been primarily responsible for the majority of ills plaguing the ethnic community. Nevertheless, it is essential to understand that some of these problems are accentuated by cultural factors, which are, of course, products of a historical rather than a genetic inheritance. Among these historical factors, as the anthropologist Oscar Lewis has stressed, is poverty itself.

Perhaps the most serious impediment in Mexicano culture to educational success has been the treatment of children. While exemplary in most respects, child-rearing practices, as in many working-class environments, have often fostered an anti-intellectual streak. The Mexican historian and social critic Carlos Monsiváis makes this very point when he observes: "It is not uncommon in Mexican homes to hear parents scolding their kids for reading when they 'could be doing something useful, like fixing the door.'"[17] Children's questions, especially abstract ones, are all too often discouraged with a "Sólo Dios sabe" (Only God knows), or a "¿Quién sabe?" (Who knows?), leading children to stop asking questions as they grow older, a trait which is hardly conducive to effective scholarship. Mexican parents expect children to be *bien educados,* but, significantly, in Latino culture this phrase means "well-behaved" rather than "well-educated." In spite of prejudice and poverty, other ethnic groups, notably Jews and some Asians, have been much more successful in inculcating their children with a healthy respect for learning.

All of this suggests that another major area of concern, one touched upon previously, was and remains the Mexicano family, a subject of heated debate among sociologists and laypersons alike. Contrary to the popular stereotype of the strong Mexicano family, the first in-depth studies by Anglo social scientists—Ruth Tuck, Pauline R. Kibbe, Celia Heller, and others—portrayed a dysfunctional unit dominated by the macho though distant male who lorded over his submissive wife and children. Since the sixties, Chicano and Chicana scholars have sought to discredit this familial deficiency model, condemning it as a pernicious myth perpetrating negative stereotypes.[18] Quite aside from the obvious criticism that there are all kinds of family units in the heterogeneous Mexicano community, the studies of these ethnic scholars indicate that while patriarchy represents the theory, the reality is quite different. It is the woman, as wife and mother, who is the glue holding the family together, not the authoritarian male. Moreover, decision making is much more egalitarian than previously thought. There are many exceptions, but, in general, Anglo academics see the familia as beset by monumental problems while ethnic studies scholars find it a source of immense security.

Unfortunately, however, some minority champions of the Mexicano family have been overzealous in accentuating the positive, in the process obscuring real problems and creating a mythology of their own. For example, David Hayes-Bautista, director of the Center for the Study of Latino Health at UCLA, concluded in the early nineties that the familia, based on his demographic studies of Los Angeles, was actually quite well-adjusted.[19] In many ways, he argued, it was healthier than Anglo families. Presenting statistical data to back up his contention, he claimed, among other things, that 43 percent of Hispanics maintained traditional households—two parents with children—compared to 16 percent for Anglos. These findings, however, contrasted markedly with data presented by other researchers, as well as impressionistic evidence.

Not all Chicano scholars accepted the rosy picture portrayed by Hayes-Bautista, who apparently set about his work in an effort to prove that Mexicanos were not part of a permanent underclass, an ongoing controversy among urban sociologists. Rodolfo de la Garza, for one, offered a dissenting opinion. "In the modern world," he argued, "the Hispanic family has experienced all the mainstream disruption that America has and perhaps more."[20]

While Hayes-Bautista's findings may have been politically correct, they obscured the reality of the situation. Both statistics and interpretations were highly questionable. His conclusion that more Mexicanos than Anglos in Los Angeles lived in traditional households seemed suspect. Certainly, it was not a typical situation nationally. According to the U.S. Census Bureau, in 1991, 69 percent of the 4.9 million Hispanic families in the country were married couples compared to 78 percent for the entire American population. This disparity casts doubt on the UCLA study.

Also, statistics don't tell the whole story. The rate of abandonment, difficult to extract from the data, has probably been more pronounced in the Mexicano community than among Anglos, because of the high incidence of immigration, if for no other reason. Moreover, there has been a greater aversion to divorce among Mexicanos than in society at large. There are two main reasons for this difference: economic considerations and a Catholic value system which stresses the welfare of children, encourages believers to endure adversity and pay for their mistakes, and generally inculcates the notion that divorced people are "losers." Poverty and the steadfast persistence of these Catholic beliefs in the Spanish-speaking community would suggest that divorce statistics could be a poor indicator of the true condition of the family unit. As Joan W. Moore has suggested, "A cultural image of the 'strong Mexican family' leads to complete disregard for the bleak statistics on desertion and divorce."[21] By the early 1990s, about 20 percent of families of Mexican origin were headed by a female.

To a large extent, the problems of Mexicano families in the United States as the twentieth century drew to a close were those of other American families, and many of the causes were the same as for other groups—urbanization, materialism, drugs, the decline of religion, the impact of television, and so on. But there were other factors as well. One of them was discrimination, although admittedly less severe than in the African American community, where broken homes are endemic and the family is even more fragmented. Discrimination took many forms, from outright police brutality to the destruction of traditional communities through urban renewal or freeway construction.

Poverty, however, was the most salient single problem, one which became increasingly serious among Mexicano workers after the 1960s, when middle-income industrial jobs faded, international immigration increased, and the welfare state contracted, as community-based service organizations were dismantled by the federal government. The rise of homelessness in barrios by the mid-1990s was one of the most visible consequences of these deteriorating conditions. By this time, more than a quarter of the Mexicano community in the United States fell under the official poverty line.

But cultural considerations, once again, should not be neglected in exploring factors impacting family instability. Preeminent was the macho ethic. Often resulting in obviously dysfunctional behavior such as alcoholism, domestic violence, and marital infidelity, machismo has been the cause of a multitude of family problems, some of them less obvious than others. In his fine autobiography, Anthony Quinn shares many valuable examples of the insidious impact of machismo on traditional working-class households, a persistent reality even today.

One episode in particular is poignant. Quinn recalls that when he was about four, he sat at the table with his family eating a steak, a rarity in that impoverished household, that his father, Francisco, had brought home. Before finishing his portion, Anthony, too young to know better, demanded more food. His father pointed out that there was still a large piece of meat on the boy's plate, but the child persisted. Obviously irritated, Francisco proceeded to empty his own plate and that of his surprised wife onto little Anthony's. "All right, you eat it all," he said. Then he watched as the child slowly swallowed the food that he and his wife, both still hungry, had provided. Unable to continue, the brash youngster tried to excuse himself, announcing that he had had enough. But Francisco insisted: "You said you wanted it all and you are going to eat it all." Completely satiated, the contrite child was forced to eat while his father watched impassively. Weeping, Anthony ended up gagging on a piece of meat. The father did not move a muscle to help; he sat sipping his coffee while his son turned blue. His wife Manuela, horrified, was told to leave the child alone. Finally, he got up slowly and disgorged the meat, saving his son's life. Unperturbed, Francisco asked the terrified child if he wanted more to eat! "Don't cry," he admonished his son. "Take your lesson like a man. Be grateful you've learned something." Anthony survived, but his father had made a point—well-behaved children should clean their plates before they ask for second helpings.[22]

This touching anecdote provides a number of illuminating insights on Mexicano working-class culture—Quinn himself used it to illustrate that while a Mexican mother's love is unconditional, the father's love must be earned—but perhaps the most telling has to do with the psychological repercussions of machismo on children. The result of this tyranny was a child's low sense of self-esteem (tellingly, Anthony's family nickname was "the elephant"), as well as a love-hate attitude toward the father—exactly the impact it had on Anthony Quinn.

The psychological damage described here has often been accompanied by physical violence, a major problem that continues to plague Mexicano communities, especially in urban environments. Another reason the UCLA study mentioned above seems unconvincing is that its rosy view of the Chicano family in Los Angeles is inconsistent with the city's reputation as the center of gangs and the violence associated with *cholos* (gang members). By 1989, authorities estimated that there were some 770 gangs in metropolitan Los Angeles, most of them Mexicano. Southern California was not unique. In fact, gangs proliferated in both rural and urban barrios throughout the Southwest and beyond after the 1960s, a phenomenon mirroring the disintegration of the family. As the anthropologist James Diego Vigil has noted, "The gang has become a 'spontaneous' street social unit that fills a void left by families under stress."[23] The majority of cholos, typically second-generation Mexicanos, came from single-parent families, and many were raised by grandparents.

Beyond broken homes and weakened families, the escalation of gang life had other and more profound roots, as the studies of Vigil, Ruth Horowitz, Joan Moore, and Martín Sánchez Jankowski, among others, have shown. These included poverty, discrimination, and alienation, leading young people into difficulties with schools and police. Moreover, during the 1980s, many community-based organizations spawned by the War on Poverty disappeared, destroying a valuable resource that had served to diminish gang activity. Gangs provided much-needed emotional and social support networks left by this void. As membership increased, so did gang-related violence, reflecting racial friction, continuing immigration, the proliferation of firearms, and the popularity of the drug trade. By the 1990s, some barrios had become war zones. This was particularly true in California, where cholo gangs, divided into *sureños* (southerners) and *norteños* (northerners), were engaged in a virtual civil war.

As a result, the Mexicano prison population steadily increased. In 1996, when they represented about 10 percent of the national population, Hispanics constituted 14.3 percent of the prisoners. In California, Hispanics accounted for about 28 percent of the population but about 34 percent of the inmate population. It was clear that Latinos were overrepresented in penal institutions, though admittedly these statistics were somewhat misleading, given legal disadvantages stemming from poverty and inadequate education and a macho proclivity to plead guilty.

Some cholos eventually graduated to one of two major crime syndicates operating in and out of the California state prison system: the Mexican Mafia, or "La Eme" (Spanish for the letter *M*), and Nuestra Familia (Our Family). The former was founded in 1957 at Deuel Vocational Institute in Tracy by Mexicano prisoners from southern California as a mutual protection group. Its numbers expanded to over one thousand members in the seventies, when it came to dominate much of the underworld economy in barrios—drug smuggling, gambling, prostitution, and extortion. Eventually, it was even able to infiltrate federally funded social projects in barrios, notably the Los Angeles-based League of United Citizens to Help Addicts (LUCHA). Nuestra Familia, a rival Mexicano organization, was formed at Soledad Prison in the late 1960s to protect northern California prisoners, mostly of rural background, from La Eme, whose members came mainly from urban southern California. Nuestra Familia, too, had its heyday in the seventies. Both crime syndicates were weakened by intergang warfare and police repression in the eighties, when they lost most of their membership, but both survived into the nineties. Reputedly, La Eme, feeling that its honor had been impugned, put out a contract on Edward James Olmos, the Chicano actor and community activist, who starred in and produced *American Me* in 1992. The film graphically illustrated the ugly side of prison gangs in an effort to discourage Hispanic youth from opting for *la vida loca* (the crazy life).

THE QUEST FOR CRISTO REY

Finally, like the rest of American society, Mexicano communities were beset by a growing spiritual poverty, a void that the Catholic Church was not well equipped to fill. The reasons were partly historical. After their incorporation into the United States in 1848, Mexican Catholics in the Southwest experienced myriad difficulties with the Church. Race was a factor, but equally deleterious, as the church historian Albert López Pulido emphasizes, was the inability of the American clergy to appreciate the folk beliefs and practices, often of Indian and African origin, of their Mexicano flocks.[24] The austere religion of the Irish, who came to dominate the American Church, was far removed from that of the mestizo people they encountered. Hispanic Catholicism was much more concerned with devotions, the festive aspects of religion, and sacramentals like rosaries, scapulars, relics, and candles. The saints tended to command more respect as well, especially the Virgen de Guadalupe, Mexico's patron saint.[25] Also, church attendance was not considered essential by Mexicanos. So vast was the cultural gap that Spanish-speaking parishioners, rather than being treated as practicing Catholics, were often seen by their priests, many of them foreign-born, as pagans requiring missionary activity.

By the first decades of the twentieth century, the unstated policy of the Catholic Church was generally to ignore Spanish-speakers. This was a difficult tendency to combat since, unlike their European counterparts, Mexican immigrants did not bring their own priests with them. Moreover, in the United States, the hierarchy failed to attract Hispanics into the priesthood. Nor, unlike Protestant churches, especially the *evangélicos* (evangelicals), did it prepare Latino laypeople to take leadership roles. The racial segregation of Catholic parishes, to the detriment of Latinos, was still common in the 1950s. Not that barrio needs were totally neglected. Welfare services and catechetical work were usually available. In a few parishes, notably San Antonio, under Archbishop Robert Emmet Lucey, Mexicanos even found sympathetic clergymen who would champion their interests.[26] In general, though, it seemed at this time that the institutional Church, now solidly middle class, had forgotten how to be an immigrant church.

It was not until the 1960s, at about the time of the Second Vatican Council (1962–1965), that the institution, in spite of the intransigence of much of the Irish hierarchy, began to focus on Mexicanos. By now some members of the clergy, especially Hispanics, were calling for greater outreach efforts. Frustrated, many socially conscientious Latina and Latino clerics found that they could best administer to the ethnic community by leaving the Church, a major problem for the institution since its evangelization efforts in colonias were already suffering from its inability to recruit Spanish-speaking clergy.

Margarita Melville (1929–) provides an excellent example. Born in Irapuato, in the Mexican state of Guanajuato, Marjorie (Maggie) Bradford became a Maryknoll nun and was sent to Guatemala as an American missionary in 1954. She was immediately struck by the plight of the local Mayan peasants. Political and economic elites exploited them mercilessly; indigenous people were treated more like animals than humans. All of this was done with the cooperation of the U.S. government after 1954, when President Jacobo Arbenz Guzmán was overthrown by the Central Intelligence Agency. Reaction now reigned supreme in Guatemala. "For the next four decades," Juan González contends, "its people suffered from government terror without equal in the modern history of Latin America."[27] In an effort to combat the genocidal repression, Sister Margarita and her Maryknoll colleagues soon alienated the U.S.-backed dictatorship, which pressured the Church to rein in the increasingly vocal activists. Adamant about continuing her humanitarian efforts to expose the undeclared war that her own country had launched against the Indian masses of Guatemala and other parts of Central America, the frustrated crusader left the order. Returning to the United States, she married Thomas R. Melville, an ex-Maryknoll priest who shared her convictions, took his name, and together with her husband became a zealous critic of the Vietnam War. Part of the "Catonsville Nine," a group of antiwar protesters led by Father Daniel Berrigan who were convicted of burning draft files in Maryland in 1968, the defiant couple served several months in federal prison, before resuming their graduate studies. Eventually, both received doctorates in anthropology. Hired by UC Berkeley's ethnic studies department, Margarita Melville initiated a distinguished academic career as both teacher and administrator. A dedicated scholar-activist, the ex-nun remains a leading advocate of women and minorities, both in the United States and in Central America.[28]

By the sixties, too, Chicano militants were joining with disaffected clergy in demanding that the Church pay more attention to barrio needs. Católicos por la Raza, a student group which came out of Loyola University in Los Angeles, was especially vocal, even confrontational, in its approach. Internal disaffection and militant activity on the part of Chicano laymen, though, were probably less instrumental in swaying Church policies than the specter of Protestant conversions in barrios, an escalating trend by now.

While Protestant efforts to win over Mexicano converts go back to the nineteenth century—by 1900, there were some 150 Spanish-speaking Protestant churches in the Southwest—these had met with scant success; in 1960, less than 3 percent of the ethnic community was Protestant. However, during the decade of the sixties striking inroads into Mexicano communities were made by Protestant denominations, a source of considerable embarrassment and trepidation to the Catholic hierarchy. The more personal approach to religion and the conservative stance on issues such as abortion, crime, homosexuality, and traditional family values within Protestant denominations found a sympathetic audience in barrios. Though the most striking missionary successes were among Puerto Ricans, some experts feel that between 10 and 20 percent of the Mexicano community may have converted to Protestantism, the vast majority of these attracted to evangelical and Pentecostal churches (evangelicals believe in a personal relationship with Jesus Christ, and Pentecostals are evangelicals who stress the role of the Holy Spirit).

Faced with the prospect of losing the allegiance of the barrios, the American Catholic Church successfully responded to the challenge, according to the church historian Anthony M. Stevens-Arroyo.[29] The Church's support of César Chávez and the farmworkers signaled a new orientation. Also, having in 1957 adopted the Cursillo ("little course"), a devotional movement founded on the Spanish island of Mallorca, the Church greatly expanded the innovative program among its Latino parishioners during the 1960s. The Cursillo was a three-day exercise that brought Hispanic laypersons together for Bible study and prayer. The outreach program was extremely successful in increasing church authority in Hispanic barrios. Moreover, it served as a valuable training ground for Catholic lay leadership in these communities. Prominent *cursillistas* included César Chávez himself.

In the 1970s, the Church continued to step up efforts to strengthen its ties with its Spanish-speaking congregations, initiating a series of "Hispanic Pastoral Encounters," or *encuentros,* between Spanish-speaking and Anglo Catholics to bridge the cultural gap in 1972, 1977, and 1985. Also, Latinos were increasingly promoted within the clerical hierarchy. By 1983, there were fifteen Hispanic bishops. The first of them to be appointed archbishop was Roberto Sánchez (1934–), who assumed his office in Santa Fe; but the most effective and popular Hispanic spokesman within the Catholic hierarchy soon became San Antonio Archbishop Patrick Flores (1929–).

A native of Ganado, Texas, Archbishop Flores was convinced at the outset that in order to maintain their hold on the barrios, Catholics needed to deemphasize theology and deal with the practical problems plaguing the community. Accordingly, despite opposition from conservative critics within the institution, he encouraged the Church to set up social action programs throughout Texas. Ultimately, Catholics in the Lone Star State became major supporters of a variety of minority service programs. The most notable was Community Organized for Public Service (COPS), a grassroots organization founded in the early seventies by Ernie Cortés Jr. Aided by the Church, COPS, which employed the mobilization techniques of the late Saul Alinsky, quickly expanded its sway throughout the state. In San Antonio, serving as rector of the city's historic San Fernando Cathedral, Father Virgilio Elizondo, a native son of Mexican immigrants, was allowed to incorporate Mexican religious traditions into the Catholic service, and to develop a mestizo theology that resonated with many of his parishioners. In other parts of the Southwest, however, the Church was more hesitant to respond to Mexicano needs.

In California, reform efforts centered on Padres Asociados para Derechos Religiosos, Educativos y Sociales (PADRES, Priests Organized for Religious, Educational, and Social Rights). Founded in 1970, this Los Angeles-based association of clergymen was dedicated to aiding the Mexicano faithful. This initiative became more effective once Latino leaders within the Church won over powerful Irish prelates to their point of view. In 1975, the United Neighborhood Organization (UNO), the California counterpart of COPS in Texas, was established with Church backing.

Unfortunately, however, during the course of the 1980s, mirroring the conservatism of the Reagan years, the reformist zeal within the Catholic Church slowly faded. By the convocation of the third encuentro, held in Washington, D.C., in

1985, efforts to reach out to Hispanic communities were all but over. By this time, too, a charismatic movement had surpassed the Cursillo in importance among Latino Catholics. Stressing personal salvation, the charismatic movement was less interested in social action than was its predecessor.

Still, by the early 1990s, institutional inertia was momentarily challenged by the enormous resurgence of immigrants, most of them Catholic, from Mexico and the rest of Latin America. Reenergized, some of the clergy focused not only on the spiritual needs of the beleaguered immigrants, especially in the deeply alienated Mexicano communities beyond the Southwest, but also on their material needs. In the rural Midwest, for example, Catholic welfare services were expanded significantly. Equally meaningful, according to researchers, the Church in these communities took on the essential role of intermediary between newly arrived immigrants who were ignorant of their rights and key nonprofit and government welfare agencies.[30] Presumably this expansion of Church social services took place in immigrant communities throughout the country.

The Church also took a firm stand on the controversial immigration question. For example, Cardinal Roger M. Mahony, whose Los Angeles diocese of 5 million was then the largest in the country, became an ardent and consistent supporter of the immigrant rights movement, as were many other members of the hierarchy. Occasionally, priests went as far as establishing sanctuaries in their churches to protect undocumented immigrants from deportation.

These efforts at outreach notwithstanding, by the turn of the century many critics still felt that the Catholic Church was failing to meet changing needs in the Spanish-speaking community. At the parish level, Mexicanos, both native-born and immigrant, continued to abandon their traditional faith in significant numbers; by 2006, according to a 2007 study by the Pew Hispanic Center (PHC), only about 74 percent of them still identified with the Mother Church.[31] Those who left the Church were especially attracted to Protestant denominations that stressed an emotional approach to religion, an alternative that 12 percent of Mexicanos embraced by 2006—the remaining 14 percent joined mainstream Protestant denominations or Jehovah's Witnesses and the Church of Jesus Christ of Latter-day Saints. These thriving evangelical denominations, moreover, were smaller, and their ministers, who tended to speak Spanish, seemed to be better equipped to meet their personal needs.

More recently, some Latinos have begun to look beyond Christianity for spiritual fulfillment. By the turn of the century some twenty-five thousand of them had found Islam to be a viable alternative, particularly in Los Angeles, Chicago, and New York City; but today Muslim groups catering to Hispanics can also be found in small cities like Fresno, California, Plantation, Florida, and Somerville, New Jersey. Buddhism has only recently begun to make modest inroads. However, Latino converts, like the Chicana novelist Sandra Cisneros, are still rare. It is too early to tell whether these more mystical Eastern religions can have the kind of impact on Hispanic colonias that they have had on other minority communities.

Another emerging trend among Mexicanos is their increasing tendency not to affiliate with any church at all, Catholic or non-Catholic. Indeed, the 2007 PHC study found that about 7 percent of Mexicanos identified themselves as atheists— compared to 11 percent of the general U.S. population—and many more admitted to being essentially non-religious even though they continued to identify themselves as Catholics. This trend toward secularization reflects the increasing tendency of Mexicanos to assimilate into mainstream America, which embraces secular human-ism even as it lays claim to religious devotion.

FEMINISTAS: THE SECOND GENERATION

In spite of the disillusionment voiced by many Chicanos about the glacial advances experienced by Hispanic peoples generally and Chicanos in particular, the Mexican-origin community made meaningful gains from the mid-1970s to the mid-1990s. The middle class expanded. Mexicanos became major consumers, together with other Latinos, giving rise to a "Hispanic market," a major target of business corporations. Social advances, however, were probably more fundamental than economic ones. The most momentous social trend in Western civilization during the last few decades has been the progress made by women. Happily, this improvement has been shared by women of color in the United States, including Mexicanas.

During the 1970s, mujeres found that they had more options available to them as traditional attitudes slowly broke down. Urbanization and the mass media were crucial catalysts in effecting this historic change in their status, though per-haps more telling was the increasing entry of women into the work force. While remaining seriously undereducated and underemployed, mujeres nonetheless experienced greater opportunities for personal growth, a positive gain shared by recently arrived immigrant women, as the studies of Pierrette Hondagneu-Sotelo, Julia E. Curry Rodríguez, and others suggest.

By the early nineties, more Latina women than Latino men were going to college and graduating. In 1991, according to the American Council on Education, Latinas earned 20,455 baccalaureates compared to 16,157 for Latinos, the result of long-term trends of which Mexicanas were a part. By the midnineties, there were more Hispanic women in the professions than there were Hispanic men. As educational and career opportunities expanded, some gifted mujeres were able to achieve national prominence in high-profile areas, among them singer Vikki Carr

(1940–) in entertainment, golfer Nancy López (1957–) in sports, and astronaut Ellen Ochoa (1958–) in space exploration.

The progress made by Mexicanas in terms of education and careers was mirrored at the political level. The best example was one of the stellar figures in California politics, Gloria Molina (1948–), *Ms.* magazine's "Woman of the Year" in 1985. A Democrat from East Los Angeles, Molina was the first Chicana elected to the State Assembly (1982) and the Los Angeles City Council (1987). In 1991, she won a seat on the Los Angeles Board of Supervisors, the first woman, of any ethnic background, ever elected to that powerful office.

Other mujeres who enjoyed political success in the post-Chicano era include state senator Polly Baca Barragán (1941–), from Colorado, elected vice-chair of the Democratic National Committee in 1984; Mari-Luci Jaramillo (1928–), an educator from New Mexico, who served as ambassador to Honduras; and Romana Acosta Bañuelos (1925–), Katherine D. Ortega (1934–), and Catalina Vásquez Villalpando (1940–), Republicans who were appointed to the office of treasurer of the United States.

Despite attempts since 1922, when Adelina Otero-Warren unsuccessfully ran for a congressional seat representing New Mexico, no Mexicanas were sent to Congress until 1992, when Edward Roybal's daughter, Lucille Roybal-Allard (1941–), a California Democrat, was elected to the U.S. House of Representatives. An equally striking victory occurred in another House seat election in southern California four years later, when, after a hotly contested race which drew national attention, Loretta Sánchez narrowly defeated nine-term incumbent Bob Dornan, a fiery archconservative, in Orange County, a Republican stronghold. The Democratic newcomer became the 46th Congressional District's first woman and first Hispanic representative.

The steady, though uneven, progress made by mujeres since the seventies was mirrored and to some extent shaped by the Chicana movement, though possibly only a minority of Mexicanas identify with feminism even today. A lingering fear in the community at large of the feminist agenda as destructive of traditional family values and a threat to ethnicity resulted in the early domination of the Chicana movement by women in academia. Since a lesbian component became increasingly evident in university-based feminist circles, the movement grew increasingly distant from the barrio, a trend encouraged by the ascendancy of a conservative political climate in the period under consideration. Chicana lesbians had a difficult time winning acceptance. "Our culture," one of them lamented, "seeks to diminish us by placing us in a context of an Anglo construction, a supposed *vendida* to the race."[32] Anti-lesbian tendencies permeated even Chicana feminist groups, according to the sociologist Irene I. Blea.[33]

In terms of concrete reforms, the most effective women's organizations arose in the barrio, where, in spite of the hostile political climate, they were able to win significant victories. A good example of these kinds of associations, and there were scores of them, was Mothers of East Los Angeles (MELA or MOELA), a lay Catholic group led by Juana Beatriz Gutiérrez.[34] MELA waged a long and ultimately successful campaign in the mideighties to keep the state from building a prison in East Los Angeles, where residents were tired of being exploited by outside political interests. Mujeres also made progress by working in traditional middle-class ethnic organizations. In 1994, for example, LULAC elected its first woman national president, Belén Robles of El Paso, a forceful personality who enjoyed extraordinary power within the U.S. Hispanic community.

On college campuses, strongholds of Chicana feminism, Chicana studies programs steadily proliferated during this period, an indication of the importance accorded women in academic circles. Spearheading this emerging trend was the University of California, especially the Davis campus, where in the early eighties, inspired by Dr. Adaljiza Sosa Riddell, a Chicana/Latina Research Institute was established. Given its university orientation, it is not surprising that the contemporary Chicana feminist movement, as María Linda Apodaca notes, has been a predominantly middle-class phenomenon.[35]

Without a large popular base, Chicana feminists generally had to work through other advocacy groups in order to make a meaningful impact. Some chose to affiliate with white feminist groups such as the National Organization for Women (NOW) or with professional organizations of various kinds, such as the American Psychological Association or the Modern Language Association, forming Chicana caucuses within the general membership. A more popular option was to work within Chicano organizations. Typical was the National Association for Chicano Studies, where Chicanas initiated a campaign in 1982 to make their *compañeros* more responsive to women's issues. A measure of the success of the Chicana caucus, led by the historian Cynthia Orozco, in articulating the feminist agenda was the organization's 1994 name change to the National Association for Chicana and Chicano Studies.

Finally, many Chicana academics felt a need for exclusive associations of their own. These organizations included Mujeres Activas en Letras y Cambio Social (MALCS, Women Active in Letters and Social Change), a national association organized in 1982 by a small group of committed female scholars, foremost among them being Adaljiza Sosa Riddell, who served as president during its first three years, as a support and research network for Chicana professors.

Chicanas also attempted to create national umbrella organizations, but these had little lasting success. The first such initiative on a major scale was the Comisión Femenil Mexicana Nacional, formed in southern California in 1970. The Comisión was instrumental in setting up the Chicana Service Action Center in Los Angeles two years later, with Francisca Flores as founding director. In the mid-1970s, during the presidency of Gloria Molina, the Comisión tried to extend its sway nationally, but it soon clashed with the Mexican American Women's National Association (MANA), apparently in a jurisdictional dispute. Thereafter, despite its best efforts, it remained confined to California.

Like the Comisión, MANA was one of the few nationwide initiatives that arose outside of academia. Founded in Washington, D.C., in October 1974, as a sophisticated advocate for the rights of Hispanic women—not just Mexicanas—it blossomed under the presidency of Elisa Sánchez (1977–1979). By the mid-1980s, according to Sylvia Alicia Gonzales, MANA was "the most prominent Mexican American women's organization nationally."[36] It has become less political in recent years.

By the mideighties, the National Association of Hispanic Women (NAHW), another middle-class women's group with national aspirations, was also at its peak. The brainchild of Sylvia L. Castillo, a clinical social worker, the Los Angeles-based organization was established in order to prepare Latinas for leadership positions in both public and private sectors. Although its membership was modest, about five hundred, the NAHW succeeded in reaching a wider audience through a prestigious journal, *Intercambios Femeniles,* founded in 1980.

THE CHICANO RENAISSANCE

Another positive achievement by the Post-Chicano Generation was a cultural and artistic flowering so vast in scope that the term *Chicano Renaissance* seems entirely appropriate. A growing population, better education, and emergent affluence in many Mexicano communities led, beginning in the 1960s when the movimiento provided the spark, to a veritable explosion of creativity unparalleled in the annals of Mexican American history.

Undoubtedly, the most innovative advances into the early twenty-first century have come in the field of literature, so it is appropriate to begin here before other art forms are surveyed. As in the other arts, recent literary achievements have historical roots antedating the 1960s by many decades. These antecedents in the nineteenth century, especially narratives, have attracted the attention of several distinguished Chicano and Chicana scholars, among them Erlinda Gonzales-Berry, María Herrera Sobek, Rosaura Sánchez, Tey Diana Rebolledo, Genaro Padilla, Ramón Saldívar, José David Saldívar, and Juan Bruce-Novoa.[37] Enormous credit, too, goes to Nicolás Kanellos and the Arte Público Press for launching the Recovering the U.S. Hispanic Literary Heritage project in 1992 in a successful effort to recover and preserve forgotten Latino literary production from the colonial period to 1960.

Imaginative literature, mostly poetry—much of it produced by upper-class political refugees fleeing the Mexican Revolution—generally appeared in the columns of Spanish-language newspapers, which proliferated throughout the Southwest in the second half of the nineteenth century. Among the most popular of these pub-lications were Francisco Ramírez's *El Clamor Público* in Los Angeles (1855–1859); Carlos Velasco's *El Fronterizo* in Tucson (1878–1914); and *La Prensa* in San Antonio (1913–1926) and *La Opinión* in Los Angeles (after 1926), both owned by Ignacio Lozano Sr., a wealthy Mexican immigrant. But researchers have discovered at least one important nineteenth-century novelist, María Amparo Ruiz de Burton (1832–1895), and a host of others in the early twentieth century, including Jovita González, the noted folklorist, and Josefina Niggli (1910–1983), who was born in Monterrey, Mexico. Thanks to the diligent efforts of Chicana/o literary scholars, what Genaro M. Padilla terms "the ethnocentric assumption that Mexican American culture has a meager literary tradition" has largely been exposed as a myth.[38]

The literary production of the Mexican American Generation was rather modest. "When Chicano studies programs and departments were first established in the early seventies," recalls Mary Helen Ponce, "books by Hispanic writers were almost nonexistent."[39] But there was one outstanding exception: *Pocho,* published in 1959 by Doubleday, the first significant novel about the Mexicano experience in the United States written by a Mexican American, José Antonio Villarreal. Largely autobiographical, the work related the difficulties of growing up the son of a Mexican immigrant in California's Santa Clara Valley during the 1920s and 1930s. Although a vast number of themes were introduced, some of them universal in scope, others relating specifically to the immigrant experience, the author was most concerned with the search for identity, one of the dominant motifs in subsequent Chicano literature. Villarreal moved to Mexico in 1973, a surprising turn of events given the assimilationist philosophy that seems to animate the protagonist of his book, and wrote two other novels, *The Fifth Horseman* (1974) and *Clemente Chacón* (1984), neither of which encountered the (belated) success of his initial effort. Given its pioneering features, many literary critics see *Pocho* as the first Chicano novel. Some go so far as to suggest that despite the rapid development of the genre in recent years, it remains the most outstanding novel ever written by a Mexicano author.

The Chicano movement, with its emphasis on cultural regeneration, encour-aged the rise of a vibrant community of authors—novelists, poets, short-story writers, and dramatists—and determined their choice of themes for years to come. Perhaps the most influential literary effort of these turbulent times was the epic poem *I am Joaquín/Yo Soy Joaquín* (1967) by Corky Gonzales. Written in anger, the work denounced racial oppression, hailed the rise of an awakening minority, and called for the restoration of Aztlán, the lost Chicano homeland. Capturing the mood of the times perfectly, the poem was proclaimed almost immediately to be the leading expression of Chicanismo. Other Chicano poets taking their cue from Gonzales included Abelardo Delgado (1931–2004), Raúl Salinas (1934–2008),

Ricardo Sánchez (1941–1995), and Alberto Baltazar Urista Heredia (1947–), who writes under the pseudonym Alurista. "This period," according to Nicolás Kanellos, "was one of euphoria, power, and influence for the Chicano poet, who was sought after almost as a priest, to give his blessings in the form of readings at all cultural and Chicano movement events."[40]

Another powerful force affecting budding Chicano writers was the work of Oscar Zeta Acosta (1936–1974?), a militant Chicano lawyer who wrote two semi-autobiographical novels espousing the philosophy of Chicanismo, *The Autobiography of a Brown Buffalo* (1972) and *The Revolt of the Cockroach People* (1973). The mood of the radical sixties is nowhere better evoked than in this erratic figure, who combined in his personality elements of the *vato loco* (literally, "crazy guy") and the Chicano intellectual. Always living on the edge, addicted to drugs, alcohol, and women, Acosta dropped out of sight in 1974, presumably a drowning victim off the coast of Mazatlán. At the time of his disappearance, Chicano literature was beginning to flower.

The most innovative early Chicano novelists were Tomás Rivera (1935–1984), Rudolfo A. Anaya (1937–), and Rolando Hinojosa (1929–), all of them professors at major southwestern universities. The first of these is generally considered, in spite of his premature death, the preeminent Chicano man of letters. "By any accounts," writes Kanellos, "Tomás Rivera remains the most outstanding and influential figure in the literature of Mexican peoples in the United States, and he deserves a place in the canon of Spanish-language literature in the world."[41] This lofty reputation is largely based on his seminal novel *". . . y no se lo tragó la tierra"* (1971), which deals with Texas migrant workers, a subject the Crystal City native knew intimately. Anaya, a nuevomexicano, wrote copiously—his output includes a number of plays as well as novels—but like his colleague Rivera, his fame rests largely on a single novel, *Bless Me Ultima* (1972), "the best-selling and arguably the most popular Chicano literary work ever."[42] Hinojosa, on the other hand, has produced a vast body of literature, in both English and Spanish, in the form of a cycle of novels (à la Emile Zola)—what he calls the Klail City Death Trip Series—all of it judged to be uniformly outstanding. The setting throughout is a fictional Texas city named Klail, where Hinojosa, himself a native of Mercedes, recreates the life of his people, the Tejanos of the Lower Rio Grande Valley.

By the 1980s, Chicanas were becoming highly visible as professional writers, a barometer of the strides mujeres were beginning to make in education. In their work, feminist themes combined with motifs they shared with their male counterparts: cultural conflict, racial oppression, alienation, and the search for identity. Since the late 1980s, Chicana literary achievements rival those of Chicano authors, especially as regards the novel.[43]

Among the reasons for their popularity was the advent of women's studies programs throughout the country, which, together with the emphasis on multiculturalism in academic institutions at this time, created a heavy demand for their works. Although almost all were committed feminists, the best of them were able to communicate with a variety of audiences. Lucha Corpi (1945–), born in Mexico but eventually based in the Bay Area, evokes the halcyon days of the Chicano movement on college campuses in the 1960s in her novel *Delia's Song* (1989). Among the most prolific Chicana novelists were midwesterners Ana Castillo (1953–) and Sandra Cisneros (1954–), both from Chicago. Castillo began as a poet, but her first novel, *The Mixquiahuala Letters* (1986), an avant-garde epistolary work, firmly established her credentials as a master of that genre among both critics and the public. This reputation was confirmed shortly afterward with the publication of *So Far from God* (1993), winner of a Carl Sandburg Award. Like Ana Castillo, Cisneros succeeded in winning contracts with major American publishing houses, a measure not only of her own considerable skill but also of the increasing respect accorded to Hispanic American literature. Her best efforts included *The House on Mango Street* (1984), a coming-of-age novella; *Woman Hollering Creek, and Other Stories* (1991), a collection of short stories; *My Wicked, Wicked Ways* (1992), a book of poetry; and *Caramelo* (2002), a lengthy semi-autobiographical novel. The San Antonio-based writer was presented the prestigious MacArthur Foundation "genius award" in 1995.[44] Denise Chávez (1948–), a native of Las Cruces, New Mexico, was probably the most versatile Chicana writer. A playwright and poet, she was also proficient as a short-story writer. Her forte, though, seemed to be longer works of fiction, a judgment based on the lavish praise accorded her two novels, *The Last of the Menu Girls* (1986), actually a short-story cycle, and *Face of an Angel* (1993), a work written in a more conventional format. Chávez won a multitude of literary prizes for her vivid portraits of ethnic family life and acquired a solid and well-deserved reputation even beyond Chicano circles.

The short story, "perhaps the strongest genre in Chicano literature today," according to the critic Ray González, is a literary form that has been extremely popular among Mexicano authors in the United States.[45] A master of the art was Estela Portillo Trambley (1927–1998), a Tejana whose short stories—and plays—of the 1970s profoundly impacted feminist writers of the following decade. Though less influential, Helena María Viramontes (1954–), born in East Los Angeles and author of *The Moths and Other Stories* (1985), also left her mark on this burgeoning art form.

Poetry continued to flourish as the Chicano movement faded. The foremost Chicano poet was probably Gary Soto (1952–), whose vision transcended Chicanismo. Soto grew up in the central San Joaquin Valley and attended California State

University at Fresno, where he was affiliated with a school of poets representing different ethnic traditions. There he studied under Phillip Levine, making him the first Mexican American literary figure to be trained by a major American poet. His writing output included short stories, as well as his better-known poetic works. Like Denise Chávez, Soto won many awards and was highly regarded within the literary establishment. Albuquerque-born Jimmy Santiago Baca (1952–), an ex-convict, became one of the Southwest's most respected poets. Pat Mora (1942–), from El Paso, and Lorna Dee Cervantes (1954–), from the Mission District in San Francisco, were also renowned for their poetry, the first for a whole series of published works, including *Communion* (1991), the second for her *Emplumada* (1981), a collection of narrative poems. Gloria Anzaldúa (1942–2004), a native of Hargill, Texas, received acclaim not only because of her verses in *Borderlands/La Frontera: The New Mestiza* (1987) but also because of her work as editor of a splendid anthology, *This Bridge Called My Back: Writings by Radical Women of Color* (1981). One of the most innovative thinkers of her age, Anzaldúa left an intellectual legacy that promises to grow with time. Another prominent poet was the multifaceted Cherríe Moraga (1952–), coeditor of *This Bridge Called My Back*. Like her compañera Anzaldúa, Moraga was a lesbian and strong feminist. Like the Tejana, too, Moraga was best known for her explorations of sexuality—especially in her early essays and poems, published in 1983 under the title *Loving in the War Years*—a topic eliciting increasing interest among university-based Chicano and Chicana intellectuals.

Moraga also made a name for herself in the field of drama, where she continued to explore gender issues. *Giving Up the Ghost* (1984) remains her most celebrated play. Carlos Mortón (1947–), still another Mexicano from Chicago, likewise emphasized sexuality in most of his dramatic works. The foremost playwright, however, remained Luis Valdez (1940–), perhaps the best dramatist, regardless of ethnic background, working in the Southwest at the end of the twentieth century. Born in Delano, Valdez attended San Jose State College and studied drama in San Francisco before returning to his hometown to aid the cause of the farmworkers in the midsixties. A steadfast supporter of Chávez and the UFW, Valdez used the stage as a vehicle to publicize the plight of farmworkers and build working-class unity. El Teatro Campesino, his bilingual theater of farmworkers, was extraordinarily effective in reaching a wide audience because it built on a long tradition of popular theater, both professional and amateur, in Mexico and the Southwest, and because it espoused Indianist elements that appealed to Chicano youth.

Ultimately, El Teatro Campesino spawned over one hundred teatro troupes in barrios and universities throughout the Southwest and beyond, some rural and some urban, but all of them exploring raza themes, thus earning Luis Valdez recognition as the father of Chicano theater. Among the most professional of these theatrical groups were the Teatro Desengaño del Pueblo in Gary, Indiana; the Teatro Urbano in Los Angeles; the Teatro de la Gente in San Jose; and the Teatro de la Esperanza in Santa Barbara, which later relocated to San Francisco's Mission District.

Desiring to expand his artistic horizons, Valdez left Delano in the late sixties and embarked on a series of productions that would win him popular acclaim far and wide. Many of these projects centered around El Teatro Campesino, which in 1971 made its permanent headquarters in San Juan Bautista, on the southern periphery of the Bay Area. Through the years, Valdez gradually moved away from political satire to embrace more mystical and universal themes. His most celebrated theatrical productions were the musical play *Zoot Suit* (1978) and *I Don't Have to Show You No Stinking Badges* (1986), another mainstream work. He was also an accomplished filmmaker and poet. In fact, "Valdez has no peer in the history of Chicano arts," according to the literary critic Ed Morales.[46]

Chicano achievements in film were only slightly less meaningful than those in literature. From the very inception of the industry, movies elicited an enthusiastic response in Mexican-origin communities in the United States. At the outset, the most popular films were those made in Mexico starring Mexican actors. A particularly intimate relationship between audience and actors developed in the Mexican film tradition. It was not unusual, especially in the forties and fifties, to see Mexican matinee idols such as Pedro Infante, Jorge Negrete, Pedro Armendáriz, Tin Tan (Germán Valdez), Cantinflas (Mario Moreno Reyes), Dolores del Río, and María Félix tour the United States, visiting small communities as well as larger cities like San Antonio and Los Angeles.[47]

As Charles Ramírez-Berg, Rogelio Agrasánchez Jr., Rosa Linda Fregoso, George Hadley-García, and other Latino film historians have discovered, Mexicanos have always been represented in Hollywood. Up to the seventies, however, it was almost exclusively as actors and actresses, usually in supporting roles—although there were notable exceptions, from Ramón Novarro (José Ramón Gil Samaniego) to Anthony Quinn. Moreover, they were almost invariably stereotyped into certain "Mexican" roles, mostly negative, as criminal bandits, unfaithful lovers, and immoral mistresses. In the 1970s, however, Mexicanos found enhanced opportunities in the acting profession, often in nontraditional roles, and they began to enter into the production side of the industry.

Boulevard Nights (1979), depicting gang life in the barrios, was a landmark film because it featured an all-Latino cast. Since that time, Mexicano performers have made steady progress. The most accomplished raza actor of the late twentieth century, winner of two supporting actor Oscars, was the ever-popular Anthony Quinn (1915–2001), among the most prolific and celebrated names in international cinema. Together with Ricardo Montalbán (1920–2009), another Mexican immigrant who found fame and fortune in Hollywood, Quinn also worked hard to promote Latinas and Latinos in the mainstream movie industry.

Among the numerous Mexican American actors and actresses who became familiar faces to Hollywood audiences by the end of the twentieth century, Edward James Olmos (1947–) stood out from the rest. His many credits included *Zoot Suit* (1981), based on the Valdez play; *The Ballad of Gregorio Cortez* (1982), a recreation of the popular border corrido; *Stand and Deliver* (1988), where his portrayal of East Los Angeles calculus teacher Jaime Escalante earned him an Academy Award nomination; and *Selena* (1997), a biography of the singing idol.

The most exciting development in the film industry after the movimiento was the sudden appearance of Chicanos behind the camera, as writers, producers, and directors. Most of this work was done outside major studios, as independent productions. The first Chicano film, *I Am Joaquín* (1970), based on Corky Gonzales's poem, was made by Luis Valdez, appropriately enough. Other Chicano filmmakers, many of them products of the UCLA film school in the early 1970s, followed in his footsteps. The vanguard included Moctezuma Esparza, Ricardo Soto, Jesús Salvador Treviñ , Paul Espinosa, and Sylvia Morales. Together these producer-directors and their Chicano colleagues developed an impressive array of documentaries and docudramas. These included *Yo Soy Chicano* (1972) by Treviño, *A La Brava* (1973) by Soto, *Chicana* (1979) by Morales, *The Trail North* (1983) by Espinosa, and *Ballad of an Unsung Hero* (1984) by Espinosa and Isaac Artenstein.[48] Artenstein's *Border Brujo* (1990), featuring Mexican performance artist Guillermo Gómez-Peña, was an innovative merger of cinematography and theater.

Outstanding feature films made by independent Chicano artists included Treviño's *Seguín* (1982); Gregory Nava's *El Norte* (1983); *And the Earth Did Not Part* (1992), an adaptation of Rivera's novel, directed by Severo Pérez and produced by Espinosa; as well as the aforementioned *Ballad of Gregorio Cortez,* directed by Robert Young and produced by Esparza.

Some Chicano directors succeeded in breaking into Hollywood, foremost among them Luis Valdez, who made his play *Zoot Suit* into a feature film in 1981. He followed up this box-office success with a film biography of Ritchie Valens, *La Bamba* (1987), which grossed more than fifty million dollars, sending the signal to the movie industry that Latino movies could be moneymakers. Almost as successful as a commercial and artistic venture was *Born in East L.A.* (1987), a satire by Richard ("Cheech") Marín, who directed and starred in the film. *The Milagro Beanfield War* (1988), coproduced by Esparza; *Stand and Deliver,* directed by Ramón Menéndez; and *My Family* (1995), cowritten and directed by Nava with a strong performance by the Nuyorican, Jimmy Smits, all contributed to the phenomenon known as Hispanic Hollywood.

Another area of creativity where Latinos excelled was in the plastic arts. Here, too, Chicanismo served to stimulate enormous artistic achievement. The basic themes were similar to those pursued by the literary community. Pre-Columbian Indian elements were pronounced, a reflection of the indigenismo resurrected by the movimiento. Spanish themes were decidedly less evident; however, Catholicism, an Iberian legacy, continued to exert a potent impact on artists, as it did on the community at large.[49] The Virgen de Guadalupe was probably the single most appealing motif, a theme best illustrated in the work of the multimedia artist Yolanda López.[50] A concern with Mexican history was evident, too, in the continuing Chicano fascination with the Mexican Revolution, the quintessential symbol of resistance to oppression.

The most popular form of artistic expression was mural painting, which peaked in the seventies, but continues to prosper in Latino communities throughout the country to the present. Undoubtedly, a major influence on barrio artists was that of the three great Mexican muralists produced by the Revolution: José Clemente Orozco, David Alfaro Siqueiros, and Diego Rivera. However, Frida Kahlo (1907–1954), Rivera's wife and a first-rate artist in her own right, had an even more profound impact, especially on Chicana artists.

The Chicano mural movement that surfaced in the late sixties was centered in southern California, with the focal point being Los Angeles, where the leading representative was Judith Baca (1946–). A graduate of California State University at Northridge, Baca studied mural painting techniques in Mexico before initiating her career as one of the most prominent women artists in the United States. In 1976, she was a cofounder of the Social and Public Art Resource Center (SPARC), headquartered in Venice, California. Subsequently, as the organization's artistic director, she sponsored many aspiring minority artists.

Another flourishing southern California art hub was San Diego. Some of the most impressive murals there can be seen in Chicano Park, under the Coronado Bridge, and at the Centro Cultural de la Raza (La Raza Cultural Center), located near the city center in Balboa Park. Many of these San Diego murals were painted by the Congreso de Artistas Chicanos en Aztlán (Congress of Chicano Artists of Aztlán), an art collective previously known as the Toltecas de Aztlán, the brainchild of Salvador Roberto Torres.

The San Francisco Bay Area, a citadel for all the visual arts, also witnessed the proliferation of Chicano murals. Among the most active local groups was Mujeres Muralistas (Women Muralists), founded in 1972 by Texas-born Patricia Rodríguez (1944–), a graduate of the San Francisco Art Institute. Five years later, Susan Cervantes founded the Precita Eyes Mural Arts Center, in the Mission District, the cradle of the mural movement in the city. Stanford University, in nearby Palo

Alto, boasts the impressive series of murals done by the multitalented José Antonio Burciaga (1940–1996) at Casa Zapata.

The Chicano Royal Air Force (CRAF), a Sacramento-based artist cooperative, was founded by Esteban Villa and the late José Montoya. Loyal supporters of Chávez and the farmworkers, these artists combined mural painting with a variety of other art forms, notably posters.

Outside of California the most innovative murals were found in New Mexico and Illinois. In Santa Fe, the Leyba brothers, Samuel, Carlos, and Albert, were instrumental in organizing a group of muralists whose work would win them national recognition. Chicago, with its rich artistic tradition and a relatively prosperous Hispanic population, was soon competing with the barrios of the Southwest as a center of Chicano artistic expression. The chief exponents of the Windy City's muralist movement were two Mexican immigrants, Marcos Raya and José González. The latter can also lay claim to being the founder of the Movimiento Artistico Chicano (MArCh, Chicano Artistic Movement).

Many muralists eventually expanded into easel painting, a form of artistic expression that developed simultaneously with the mural tradition. Thanks to the efforts of Cheech Marín, the leading collector of Chicano art, the work of these painters received wide exposure, and acclaim, in a traveling exhibit, "Chicano Visions: American Painters on the Verge," that toured the United States in 2001–2006. These Chicano painters had worthy predecessors whose work largely antedated the turbulent sixties. Pioneers included Melesio Casas of San Antonio, Eugenio Quesada of Phoenix, and Peter Rodríguez of Stockton. Rodríguez, incidentally, also founded the Mexican Museum in San Francisco in 1972. Under the direction of Marie Acosta-Colón, this institution eventually became the largest and most prestigious Mexican and Chicano art museum in the nation, exerting a major impact on Latino artists everywhere.

Among artists of the sixties who dedicated themselves to both mural and easel painting were the members of the Los Angeles-based Los Four: Frank Romero, Gilbert ("Magú") Luján, Beto de la Rocha, and Carlos Almaráz. Unwavering advocates of Chicanismo, Los Four concentrated on political themes. Almaráz, born in Mexico City in 1941 and raised in East Los Angeles, eventually went on to become one of the most acclaimed Chicano artists in the country before his untimely death in 1989. Also excelling in both major forms of painting was another Angeleño, Glugio Gronk Nicandro, or simply Gronk (1954–). Beginning his career as a member of the collective ASCO ("nausea")—with Patssi Valdez, Willie Herron III, and Harry Gamboa Jr.—his superb talents, according to art expert Max Benavidez, soon elevated Gronk well above his colleagues: "There are certain artists who define a period—Picasso in Paris in the 1920s and 30s, Jackson Pollock and Abstract

Expressionism during the late 1940s and early 50s, Gronk and Almaráz in Los Angeles in the 1980s."[51]

By the beginning of the twenty-first century, Gronk was one of two Mexicano artists who had clearly achieved international renown. The other was Mexican-born Enrique Chagoya (1953–), who mastered a variety of art forms but was perhaps best known for his prints, many of them used as vehicles of political and social satire.

While California was indisputably in the forefront of Chicano artistic developments, Texas was not far behind. For Tejanos, the most promising cultural environment was San Antonio, which produced a number of highly regarded painters, including César Martínez (1944–) from Laredo and Jesse Treviño (1946–), Mexican-born but raised in San Antonio. The Gallería Sin Fronteras (Gallery without Borders), an Austin-based art gallery established by the sociologist Gilbert Cárdenas in 1986, offered local artists an excellent marketplace to display and sell their works, while serving as a valuable source of art education for the Spanish-speaking community.

Printmaking was another medium that attracted Chicanos. The Bay Area continued to be a mecca for graphic artists. Among its principal Latino practitioners were silk-screen artists Malaquías Montoya (1938–) and Rupert García (1941–), both of whom continued to emphasize movimiento themes, true to their Chicano roots. Carmen Lomas Garza (1948–), from south Texas, and Ester Hernández (1944–), from California's Central Valley, the latter an uncompromising feminist, were other celebrated printmakers based in San Francisco.

Chicanos also excelled in sculpture, where there was a rich tradition going back to the New Mexican *santeros* (makers of saints' images) of the eighteenth century. An important bridge linking the traditional santeros with contemporary wood carving was the work of Patrociño Barela (1900–1964), the first Mexican American artist to receive national acclaim, his sculptures having been displayed in New York's Museum of Modern Art in the mid-1930s. Long neglected by art critics and historians, this solitary genius is now gaining appreciation as one of America's most creative artists of his time. Perhaps the most widely recognized sculptor emerging from the Mexicano community since the Second World War was Manuel Neri, born in the San Joaquin Valley town of Sanger in 1930, a professor emeritus at UC Davis. Also significant was the work of two younger sculptors, the Texas-born Luis Jiménez, whose fiberglass creations were thoroughly modern, and installation artist Amalia Mesa-Bains (1943–), an influential teacher whose altars represented a traditional folk art form.

Mexicano achievement in music was less obvious than in other art forms, but even here there was notable progress since the midseventies.[52] As in most artistic fields, a rich musical tradition can be traced back to the nineteenth century, notably in the corridos that first became popular at that time. The early twentieth century saw the rise of two other long-term traditions, both of them Texas-based, as the respected ethnomusicologist Manuel Peña has pointed out: the *conjunto,* catering mainly to the lower classes, and the *orquesta,* middle-class music, considered *jaitón* ("high tone" or snobbish) by the masses.

Polkas, brought into Texas and Mexico from central Europe during the mid-nineteenth century, were the mainstays of conjunto music, the accordion its trademark instrument. The first great conjunto musician was the accordion-ist Narciso Martínez, who immigrated to Texas from Tamaulipas, where he was born in 1911. Exclusively instrumental at the outset, eventually conjunto music added vocals, with one of its most popular interpreters being the legendary Texas songbird, Lydia Mendoza (1916–2007), among the finest singers ever produced by the Borderlands.

While retaining key Mexican elements, orquesta music was markedly im-pacted by American music, specifically by the Big Band sound, the swing music of World War II. Beto Villa, the "father" of Orquesta Tejana, is representative, though his name is not as familiar today as that of Eduardo ("Lalo") Guerrero (1916–2005), another musical legend. Born in Tucson, Guerrero is identified with southern Cali-fornia, where he pursued a long and distinguished career as musician and composer after the late 1930s. Asked to perform at the White House on numerous occasions, he was awarded the National Medal of the Arts in 1996 by President Clinton. Prominent in Guerrero's varied repertoire was *música tropical,* a generic term for a variety of Afro-Latin strains, including boleros, rumbas, cumbias, and cha cha chá, emanating from the Caribbean. This musical genre has been popular among Mexicanos in all regions of the country, especially where they reside in proximity to other Latino communities, as in Chicago and throughout California.

The steady resurgence of Mexican immigration in the late twentieth century meant that musical tastes underwent a slow metamorphosis in the Mexicano com-munities of the United States. The triumph of conjunto over orquesta music was one notable consequence. Concurrently, conjunto began to attract fans outside of its Texas homeland, and eventually the popularity of the Tex-Mex sound extended well beyond the Borderlands. Indeed, some artists, such as Flaco Jiménez, achieved international renown. The rise of *banda* music—a popular musical form related to conjunto, rooted in the brass band tradition, and imported from the northern Mexican states—was another significant tendency, particularly in California, the destination of so many recent norteño emigrants. In general, as the ethnomusi-cologist Steven Loza has illustrated in *Barrio Rhythm* (1993), which focuses on southern California, musical styles were much more eclectic in the Golden State than in Texas.

Still another musical trend was the increased popularity of salsa, the latest manifestation of música tropical. With roots in the Caribbean, where it merged

African and Spanish traditions, it was eventually imported into the United States, where jazz, an African American musical form, altered it in interesting ways. Salsa has always had its most loyal following in this country in the Cuban and Puerto Rican communities of the East. After World War II, however, its infectious rhythm broadened its appeal to other regions. These included the Southwest, where it began to penetrate into Mexicano communities, especially among the nascent middle class, which was gradually abandoning conjunto music. As Mexicanos and their Latino cousins came into closer proximity, a result of Latin American immigration into the Southwest and Mexicano expansion from the Borderlands into other regions, the lure of salsa during its boom years of the 1970s proved irresistible, with the Cuban singer Celia Cruz being a particular favorite. Ultimately, it captivated huge segments of the Mexicano community.

One major exception, though, were recently arrived immigrants who remained faithful to their more traditional musical forms, like the mariachis of El Mariachi Vargas de Tecalitlán, the ballads of Lola ("La Reina") Beltrán, and the *rancheras* of superstar Vicente Fernández. Indeed, given this huge fan base—which included Central American as well as Mexican immigrants—by the early twenty-first century, according to one music critic, "regional Mexican continues to be the strongest genre in Latin music."[53] The most popular interpreter of this music beginning in the 1970s was Los Tigres del Norte, based in San Jose, California, a band virtually unknown in mainstream America.

Some Mexicano artists crossed over into Anglo musical forms, a tendency which will accelerate as acculturation continues. From its very inception in the fifties, rock and roll attracted a number of Mexican American musicians, among them Question Mark and the Mysterians and Sam the Sham (Domingo Samudio) and the Pharaohs. But the most memorable is undoubtedly Ritchie Valens (Ricardo Valenzuela). Born into a migrant farm family in Pacoima, California, the promising pop idol died in an airplane accident in 1959, at the age of seventeen. The crossover tradition was subsequently carried on by Grammy Award winners Tijuana-born Carlos Santana, who combined salsa with rock, and Los Lobos, an East Los Angeles band that experimented with a variety of styles, including norteño music. After the turn of the century, Lila Downs, one of the most innovative singers in contemporary music, achieved international acclaim recording songs not only in Spanish and English, but Mixteca, as well. The crossover tradition was best exemplified, however, by Selena (Quintanilla), the Queen of Tejano, an updated version of Tex-Mex conjunto music. Her rocketing career, then in the process of making a transition to pop, ended tragically in 1995 when the twenty-three-year-old singer was slain by a disgruntled employee. Tejanos even made inroads into country western music. Folk singer Tish Hinojosa, Johnny Rodríguez, and the late Freddie Fender (Andrés Baldemar Huerta) all made valuable contributions to this popular sound, while maintaining a distinctively Latino style.

The enormous fascination with Selena which swept across the country after her untimely death highlights what is perhaps the dominant musical trend since the seventies—the increasing popularity of Latino music in general, undoubtedly a reflection of spiraling demographic patterns. An expanding market has encouraged the rise of small Hispanic record companies and a renewed interest by established labels in recording Latino music, giving rise to unprecedented opportunities for Mexicano and other Latino artists, and incidentally, strengthening this indispensable component of ethnic culture.

By the midnineties, as the second millennium drew to a close, Chicana/o scholars found themselves in an introspective mood. Clearly, an era had ended; it was time to say goodbye to Aztlán. But what had it all meant? And what was in store for the future? Answers were elusive; consensus was impossible. However, the one thing that all ethnic scholars could agree on as they surveyed Mexicano communities across the country was their immense diversity. As to the prospects for these communities in the coming century, most observers were sanguine.

In 1987, the eminent black scholar William Julius Wilson published a controversial study of African American ghettos in Chicago, *The Truly Disadvantaged*, which popularized the notion, current among social scientists for some time, of an urban "underclass."[54] The Harvard sociologist described a lifestyle typically characterized by chronic unemployment, appalling poverty, dysfunctional families, substance abuse, and violence, much of it gang-related. This growing subculture owed its existence to a variety of factors, including deindustrialization and African American middle-class flight to the suburbs. The book initiated a heated controversy in the academic community. One of the numerous questions sparked by the debate was whether the underclass model had validity outside the black community. Before too long, Latino barrios, which shared many of the characteristics of black ghettos—among them, crime, alcohol and drug addiction, and elevated school drop-out rates—came under scrutiny.

In fact, there were segments of Mexicano society, both in and out of the barrios, whose status approached that of an underclass. Scholars Refugio I. Rochín and Mónica D. Castillo, for example, argued that such was the case in the mushrooming Mexicano-dominated towns of California's agricultural valleys.[55] Cholo gangs in the cities were also representative of this unfortunate tendency.

There were grave problems in Mexicano society, especially in impoverished areas. The family, as we have seen, while it continued to be hailed as a pillar of society by some Chicana/o scholars, was beginning to display serious signs of strain. By the midnineties, Mexican Americans had higher out-of-wedlock birthrates than even African Americans. Immigrants were both a blessing and a bane. On the one hand, they replenished the ethnic community with people of unbounded vitality, ensuring the survival of a pluralistic identity; on the other hand, an endless influx of immigrants meant Mexicano communities as a whole would continue to occupy the lower socioeconomic ranks of U.S. society. Moreover, group mobility would be hampered by those anti-progressive aspects of Mexicano culture—continually revitalized by immigration, particularly in transnational communities—that have been previously mentioned. An even greater impediment to socioeconomic progress would be the pervasive racism and discrimination of mainstream society, a point emphasized by UCLA researchers Edward E. Telles and Vilma Ortiz, who argue that in fact educational and economic progress for Mexican Americans wane after the second generation due mainly to these institutional barriers.[56]

Though conceding many of these points, most anthropologists and sociologists rejected the underclass model as applicable to the Mexicano experience. Joel Perlmann, for example, feels that "grim views of eternal poverty seem off the mark."[57] Among the many trenchant differences between black and Mexican urban neighborhoods was that the latter were continually fed by new waves of immigrants eager to make their way in society, an optimism in marked contrast to the frustration and stagnation which seemed to characterize the former. Moreover, while the Mexicano middle class continued to flee to suburbia, ties with the barrios were often maintained through extended families and a variety of other ways. Cholo gangs, as destructive as they might be, by no means dominated barrio life; the anthropologist Carlos G. Vélez-Ibáñez estimated that only between 3 and 10 percent of barrio youths were gang members, even in Los Angeles.[58] An instructive microcosm of the difference was provided by the southern California metropolis, where the despair of Watts, which erupted in the aftermath of the Rodney King decision in 1992, contrasted sharply with the vitality of adjoining Lynwood, a predominantly Mexicano community with even greater poverty. Clearly, and despite important exceptions, Mexicanos had fared better than African Americans. Compared to mainstream America, however, there was little reason for complacency.

By the midnineties, then, Mexicanos were experiencing a transitional period between a Chicano past and a multicultural future, an era marked by both severe obstacles to advancement and great hope for the future, by pain and promise. Geographically, as well, Mexican-origin people in the United States were moving beyond Aztlán as their communities were expanding well outside the confines of their traditional homes in the Greater Southwest, a demographic trend that promised to irrevocably alter the face of contemporary America.

THE HISPANIC CHALLENGE
1994–PRESENT
10

Unlike other social scientists, historians approach the study of contemporary events with some trepidation.[1] While the factual record may be relatively clear, it is difficult to interpret significant trends. Nevertheless, in this chapter an attempt will be made to discover these major currents after 1994 as they relate to Mexicanos in the United States. Since the mid-1990s, a general awareness of Mexican-origin people, who presently represent about 11 percent of the total U.S. population, emerged as a central feature of American life. This recognition reflected an acceleration of two far-reaching demographical tendencies in the United States that were in evidence well before the advent of the North American Free Trade Association: first, the massive immigration of Mexicans, both legal and illegal; and, second, their dispersal to all corners of the Republic. Inevitably, given a whole host of problems that beset U.S. citizens during these turbulent years, not the least of which were the events of 11 September 2001, the appearance of immigrants of color throughout the country, many of them here illegally, fanned those nativist sentiments that were already pronounced before. Beyond xenophobia, Mexicanos, immigrants and residents alike, experienced a multitude of other barriers to advancement. Representing about 65 percent of a Latino population that exceeded 47 million in 2008, Mexicanos, hoping to take advantage of favorable demographic trends, looked to the political arena for relief. While some political gains were registered, however, socioeconomic progress remained uneven. Most Mexicanos, particularly immigrants, continued to live under precarious conditions. On the other hand, the small middle class did expand and continued to make distinguished contributions to American society, especially in the area of popular culture.

MEXICANOS GALORE

It is impossible to know how many immigrants there are in the United States at any given time because the U.S. Census Bureau, while supplying periodic updates, provides comprehensive statistics only every ten years. Moreover, it is widely assumed, by both governmental and non-governmental agencies that have an interest in such matters, that the official census undercounts illegal immigrants by roughly 10 percent. What all these experts can agree upon is that at the turn of the twenty-first century the country was in the midst of a period of massive immigration that rivaled the Great Migration that occurred one hundred years before. It was clear, too, that, unlike the immigrants of the pre–World War I era, the most recent newcomers were primarily non-Europeans, particularly Latin Americans. By all estimates, Mexico accounted for the single greatest stream of immigration, by a sizable margin. In 1990 the decennial census calculated the Mexican immigrant population at 4,198,000. Ten years later, in 2000, it had risen to a whopping 8,088,000. The Census Bureau's March 2007 Current Population Survey (CPS) indicated the presence of 11,671,000 Mexican immigrants in the country, 31.1 percent of a total immigrant population of 37,280,000. There were six times more immigrants from Mexico than the next largest sending country, China.

Beyond its massive numbers, another distinguishing characteristic of Mexican immigration was its large undocumented population. The 2007 CPS placed 11.3 million of the 37,280,000 immigrants in the country in the illegal category. Adjusting for a census undercount, though, demographer Steven A. Camarota of the Center for Immigration Studies (CIS), estimated that the true number could be as much as 12.4 million—perhaps an exaggeration given the center's advocacy of immigrant restriction. About 57 percent of these illegal residents, Camarota concluded, were from Mexico, a figure that would suggest that about 55 percent of all Mexican immigrants in the United States were undocumented.[2]

Mexicans, of course, were part of a broader category of people, Latinos, who were entering the United States at a record-setting pace in the aftermath of the 1986 Immigration Reform and Control Act. To understand the reaction Mexicanos elicited from the mainstream population it is important to know something about this larger group with which they were identified. During the decade of the 1990s, according to the Census Bureau, the Hispanic population increased by well over 50 percent, from 22.4 million to 35.3 million.[3] The rate of growth continued to spiral thereafter. A report issued in December 2007 by the National Hispanic Center, a nonpartisan research institute headquartered in Washington, D.C., indicated that these Latinos, who had now become the nation's largest minority, numbered an incredible 47 million people, about 15.5 percent of the U.S. total.[4] Equally significant, 44 percent of them were non-citizens; and of this number, 55 percent were undocumented immigrants—the other 45 percent were legal aliens. While their fertility rate was high, clearly the burgeoning Latino communities were mainly the product of immigration, a modest movement in the sixties that had become a mammoth human wave by the nineties. Already by 1998, José had become the most popular baby boy's name in both Texas and California. Given their sheer numbers and the large percentage of undocumented among them, it is easy to see why xenophobia ran rampant by the turn of the century. Considering the large percentage of Mexicanos among them—in 2005 their numbers reached 27.5 million—it is clear, too, why national attention was particularly focused on this one ethnic community, to which we now turn in an effort to understand why they had begun to transform large parts of the United States. The answer is to be found in the events of the recent past.

Nineteen ninety-four was a year of momentous political change in both Mexico, where Ernesto Zedillo Ponce de León was elected president, and in the United States, where the mid-term elections saw Republicans, led by Newt Gingrich, regain control of the House of Representatives after forty years of Democratic dominance. The year was also noteworthy in terms of the relationship between the two countries, for beginning on 1 January the free trade provisions of the much-anticipated Nafta agreement went into effect. But if the relationship between the two neighbors was characterized by dramatic changes in 1994, there were equally striking continuities, particularly in regard to immigration, which continued its upward trajectory.

The causes of Mexican immigration after 1994 were largely those that operated before that year. Ultimately, the key factor would be Mexico's failure to provide its citizens a decent living. The rapidly rising level of migration in the midnineties reflected the country's deteriorating social and economic conditions, never very florid, throughout the last decades of the twentieth century. Indeed, Nafta was an attempt, in part, to reverse these trends, but in the short run, at least, the controversial agreement only worsened living conditions for most Mexican citizens. While Canadians and Americans benefited significantly from the free trade provisions of the pact, as did Mexican elites, Mexican workers were not so fortunate; their wages generally declined after Nafta became operational. Moreover, the plethora of jobs anticipated along Mexico's northern border failed to materialize, as many maquiladoras, also known as maquilas, moved to places like China, where they could find even cheaper labor than along the 1,962-mile border.

Economically, farmers in the southern Mexican states, whose tiny plots rarely exceeded twelve acres, were especially vulnerable. Their situation became more and more precarious as protective tariffs on their ancestral crops, beans and corn, were stripped away, finally disappearing altogether on 1 January 2008.[5] During the first decade of the Nafta agreement, U.S. corn exports to Mexico tripled, to the point that they came to provide 20 percent of the corn consumed nationally. Unable to compete against North American producers, who were more efficient and better subsidized, many desperate farmers, perhaps as many as two million, lacking capital and access to credit, were driven off the land. Many of them were forced to become migratory farm laborers—40 percent of this mobile labor force consisting of Indians who spoke Spanish only with difficulty—working for meager wages as they traveled with their families to all corners of the Mexican Republic. The phenomenon was not confined to the South. In the immediate aftermath of Nafta, 20 percent of the quarter million rural families in the central state of Guanajuato packed up and joined the migratory trail. Others, many more of them, found immigration abroad to be their only viable option, especially Indian farmers from the states of Puebla and Oaxaca. These included Zapotecos, Mixtecos, and particularly Mayas. Clearly, Mexico, with a burgeoning population of 106.2 million in 2007, was unable to provide its people a decent living. What happened in that debt-plagued nation, according to Juan González, author of *Harvest of Empire*, is part of a larger pattern of U.S. economic penetration throughout Latin America, where free-trade policies imposed by the United States have impoverished many of the marginal laborers, encouraging and facilitating their immigration to North America.[6]

The dire straits of the southern peasantry were anticipated as soon as the pact was signed, and on 1 January 1994, the very day its provisions went into effect, rebellion broke out in the southern state of Chiapas, whose indigenous population was mainly Mayan. Directed by an enigmatic leader, Subcommander Marcos, the insurgents formed a guerilla organization, the Ejército Zapatista de Liberación Nacional (EZLN), and went on the offensive. Fearing the loss of their traditional lands and way of life, the indigenous population enlisted in large numbers. Bloody skirmishes erupted throughout the South, which soon became a military zone contested by the EZLN on the one hand and right-wing paramilitary groups and federal troops on the other. Prolonged negotiations broke down, leading to a long civil war characterized by massacres of the indigenous populations, a breakdown of law and order reminiscent of Central America in the recent past.

It was not just the South that suffered economically. The entire national economy languished throughout 1994, and just when experts thought the situation could not get worse, it did. Forced to devalue the peso upon his inauguration into office in December, President Zedillo triggered the nation's worst economic crisis in modern history. Almost immediately, the value of its currency dropped by 40 percent, causing widespread discontent. As was mentioned earlier, only an emergency bailout loan by President Clinton and the International Monetary Fund (IMF) in 1995 put a stop to the downward slide, but not until three-quarters of the population had dropped below the poverty level. Economic stagnation remained a fact of life well into the new millennium. Ten years after the bailout, in 2005, government statistics indicated that 47 percent of the country's population lived on less than four dollars a day. Strapped financially, thousands had to flee the country just to survive.

Emigration was encouraged, too, by government instability, a chronic problem in Mexico, but one that was now accentuated by economic collapse. The country seemed to be coming apart at the seams. The defeat of the discredited Partido Revolucionario Institucional (PRI), which had monopolized power continually for seventy-one years, and the triumph of Vicente Fox Quesada, representing the centrist-right Partido de Acción Nacional (PAN), as Mexican president in 2000 failed to restore popular faith in government, as pandemic corruption, scandal, and economic mismanagement continued to plague both local and federal bureaucracies. Felipe Calderón, Fox's handpicked successor as president six years later, was equally ineffective in restoring confidence in democratic institutions.

Next to Chiapas, the breakdown of law and order, a nationwide phenomenon, was most pronounced in the northern border states of Tamaulipas (Nuevo Laredo is the state capital), Chihuahua (Ciudad Juárez), and Baja California Norte (Tijuana), where the traffic in marijuana, cocaine, heroin, and methamphetamines flourished. Columbian in origin, the drugs generally entered Mexico through the southern port of Acapulco. So lucrative was this illicit trade, given the vast U.S. market, that police agencies, offered the choice between "plata o plomo" (silver or lead), were often co-opted by ruthless drug kingpins. Violence all along the border escalated as well-connected drug rings, using high-powered weapons, fought each other to collar the mushrooming trade. In 2006, for example, some 2,000 killings in Mexico were attributed to warring smugglers, a number that jumped to about 2,275 the following year. Most victims were "mules," expendable drug runners paid to make the hazardous crossing. But these mafia-like gangs were not above assassinating police and military authorities, which occurred with troubling frequency along the major drug routes, particularly in border cities such as Agua Prieta, Piedras Negras, and Nuevo Laredo.

In Tijuana, the drug cartel of the Arellano Félix brothers, who routinely tortured and beheaded their rivals, grew so powerful that federal agencies seemed helpless to protect the local citizenry. It was only in 2006, with the intervention of U.S. legal and judicial authorities, that the infamous ring was finally wiped out. Unfortunately, other drug operations immediately rushed in to fill the vacuum, notably the Sinaloa and Gulf cartels. The resulting escalation of the drug war forced President Calderón, encouraged by the Americans, to launch a major offensive against the cartels in 2007, which stemmed the flow of drugs but cost the lives of more than 120 law enforcement officials.

The failure of Mexican law enforcement was dramatically illustrated in another drug-ridden city, Ciudad Juárez, where, beginning in 1993 and continuing through the next decade, more than 350 young women, most of them maquiladora workers, were tortured, raped, and murdered with impunity by unknown assailants.[7] A popular outcry in response to this reign of terror, led by feminist organizations on both sides of the border, with the historian Emma Pérez among the most active coordinators, fell on deaf ears, despite the international attention focused on the city of 1.5 million. Here, too, Mexican authorities seemed unwilling or unable to move effectively to solve seemingly intractable problems, further eroding public confidence in state institutions. A confluence of factors, then, conspired to open up the floodgates.

Finally, one other contributing cause of the mass exodus should be noted, a precondition ever present but little appreciated, according to Sam Quiñones, a U.S. journalist who lived in the southern republic from 1994 to 2004: Mexico continued to be what it had always been—a society of privilege. At the very top sat a small group of businessmen who felt more at home in the United States than in their own homeland. Tellingly, the country's last five presidents—Miguel de la Madrid, Carlos Salinas de Gortari, Ernesto Zedillo, Vicente Fox, and Felipe Calderón—all received graduate degrees from either Harvard or Yale. The rise of the global economy permitted these well-connected businessmen to amass incredible wealth, especially after Nafta, the culmination of neo-liberal economic policies championed by all five Ivy League presidents and the elites they represented. As these privileged few grew more powerful, and more arrogant—"I killed her with one shot. I'm a hero," three-year-old Carlos Salinas declared, according to the Mexico City daily *El Universal,* after he had shot and killed the family's maid with a .22-caliber rifle[8]—their exploitation of the lower classes intensified, fueling smoldering disaffection. The daily humiliations and injustices took their toll. Drug addiction below the border, especially in the northern states, began to proliferate, threatening to become the massive problem that it had long been in the United States. A more popular option was immigration. Uprooted, many immigrants did not look back. Their willingness to put up with conditions in the north that most U.S. citizens would find intolerable can only be understood, Quiñones concludes, in the context of this sad state of affairs back home.

As alarming to most U.S. citizens as the tidal wave of immigration was another major demographic shift pertaining to Mexicanos, one that could well produce more momentous consequences in the long run than a porous southern border—the sudden appearance of Mexican-origin populations in parts of the country where they had never resided in substantial numbers before. This expansion was fed by the record-setting pace of Mexican immigration into the United States. Most arrivals to these new destinations were immigrants, between one-third and one-half of them apparently undocumented; no longer were these border crossers willing to remain exclusively in the traditional gateway states of California, Illinois, and Texas.

Certainly the Greater Southwest continued to attract the majority of Mexican, and Central American, immigrants. Southern Nevada, where construction boomed, witnessed the most dramatic increase in the border region in the nineties, a period during which the state's Latino population tripled.[9] Besides Las Vegas, though, virtually all the major metropolitan areas of the border region, from Houston to the Bay Area, experienced significant Latino growth. At the turn of the century some two-thirds of the Mexican population continued to reside in either Texas or California.

However, given the troubled economy in California, aided by a more stringent U.S. border policy that made it difficult for Mexican immigrants to reach their traditional destinations, by 2000 clearly the escalating trend was migration beyond the southwestern states, the most striking demographic development in Mexican American history during the past generation. Throughout the nineties, and beyond, Nevada notwithstanding, the most rapid proliferation of colonias occurred not in the Greater Southwest, where the percentage of immigrants actually began to drop, but in the rest of the country, including the Midwest, the Mountain West, and the Northeast. Latinos even began to breech the last frontier, Maine, where they found employment on egg farms. Many of these places had virtually no experience with Mexicanos before the nineties. This was true of Iowa, for example, the heart of the Heartland, where Tejanos and other Mexicanos began to appear suddenly in the midnineties. They were drawn to modest rural communities such as Postville, Marshalltown, and Waterloo, where they found ready employment in slaughterhouses. In an effort to avoid paying union wages, the meatpacking industry had recently relocated from large cities like Chicago and Omaha to small towns throughout the Midwest. During the nineties, Iowa's Hispanic population increased a phenomenal 153 percent. Like the Hawkeye State, Wisconsin and Minnesota were other nontraditional settlement areas of the upper Midwest that were beginning to experience the onset of Mexicano migration, and for the same reasons.

While most of these newcomers, regardless of legal status, who ventured beyond the Southwest were attracted to rural settings, many went directly to large metropolitan areas. As is to be expected, Chicago, which is no farther from Mexico City than is Los Angeles, witnessed a major boom in its Hispanic population thanks to immigration from Mexico. Pilsen, the city's main gateway for these newcomers since the sixties, was soon dominated by Mexicanos. Eventually, its Mexican-origin residents grew so numerous that they spilled over into nearby neighborhoods, especially Little Village (la villita) immediately to the west, where the Latino population came to dwarf that of Pilsen itself by the turn of the century. Slowly, southwest Chicago was being transformed into a Little Mexico.

Another metropolitan area that became a major magnate for Mexicanos was New York City. Mexican American journalist María Hinojosa, herself a product of Chicago's South Side, exaggerated only slightly when she recalled that upon her arrival at the Big Apple in 1979, she could not find a single person of her ethnic heritage. Twenty-five years later, the city boasted a Mexicano population of about six hundred thousand, at least 80 percent of them from the state of Puebla.[10] Their reception, according to the geographer Inés M. Miyares, was mixed: "In some neighborhoods, such as Brooklyn's Chinatown in Sunset Park, they are a readily accepted curiosity; in existing Puerto Rican neighborhoods, such as Spanish Harlem ('El Barrio') or Bushwick, they are seen to be taking over the neighborhood."[11]

Undoubtedly, though, the most surprising target of recent Mexicano migration has been the American South, generally perceived as a bastion of nativist sentiment. Of course, Mexicans and Mexican Americans had been entering eastern Texas, the Southern periphery, well before World War I, the ancestors of today's burgeoning colonias in both Dallas and Houston. Since the late 1980s, however, Mexicanos—and to a lesser extent other Latinos—have begun to penetrate the very heart of Dixie. During the 1990s, the Mexicano population in the South tripled. In-migration was focused on Alabama, Arkansas, Tennessee, and particularly the southeastern states of North Carolina, South Carolina, and Georgia. Eventually, the densest ethnic communities in the Southeast would be found in Georgia's Atlanta-Sandy Springs-Marietta metropolitan area, the third largest metropolitan population in the South, and in North Carolina's Charlotte metropolitan area, which witnessed a 49.8 percent increase in its Latino population between 2000 and 2004. North Carolina's Raleigh-Durham area was not far behind.

Why would Mexican-origin job-seekers venture into this unfamiliar terrain, the American South, given not only their distance from their ancestral lands and the absence of pre-existing ethnic communities, but also the region's notorious devotion to white supremacy? During the late twentieth century, the regional economy was undergoing a profound structural transformation. The well-known economic difficulties experienced by the northern rust belt created business opportunities elsewhere, most of all south of the Mason-Dixon Line. Outside investors flocked to the region, lured by cheap labor, weak unions, and incentives offered by local and state governments. The economic boom that ensued attracted skilled workers from across the nation looking for good jobs and houses they could afford. Drawn to metropolitan areas, many wound up in the suburbs of cities such as Atlanta, Charlotte, and Nashville.

The rural economy prospered as well, which gave Mexicanos an opening. The Great Migration of blacks to northern cities during the first half of the twentieth century ensured that the expanding southern economy would create jobs galore in the rural sector. The poultry industry is a case in point.[12] Because of opportunities on chicken farms, the Hispanic population of Siler City, North Carolina, jumped from two hundred in 1990 to over three thousand in 2000. The prospect of decent jobs, then, was the main stimulus for their appearance in the South. Moreover, the region seemed to offer greater security than more traditional areas of settlement, particularly the Southwest, where by the nineties more stringent efforts to enforce

Foreign-Born Mexicans as Percentage of County Population. Migration
Policy Institute, 2004. Courtesy of Migration Policy Institute

immigration laws were centered, with anti-immigrant sentiment most pronounced in California.

It was only in the aftermath of Hurricane Katrina in August 2005, when Latinos poured into New Orleans in search of work in demolition and reconstruction, that most U.S. citizens around the country woke up to the reality of the silent migration that had been transforming the South for more than a decade. By now, too, many of the newcomers themselves were waking up to the reality that they, like previous waves of immigrants, were a source of acute anxiety to the host society. A powerful backlash was emerging throughout the region, with anti-immigrant sentiment emanating from the usual suspects, poor whites; but smoldering resentment was found among all segments of the native population, including blacks, who were beginning to migrate back into the region, reversing a historic trend. Mexicanos were obvious targets of discrimination, given that most of them were foreign-born and many were undocumented. Nevertheless, there is evidence that more and more of them were bringing their families, an indication that they were prepared to make the South their permanent home, despite increasing local opposition.

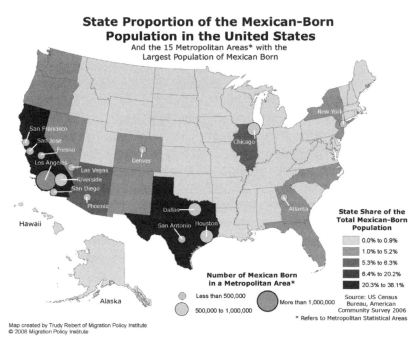

State Proportion of the Mexican-Born Population in the United States
And the 15 Metropolitan Areas* with the Largest Population of Mexican Born

State Share of the Total Mexican-Born Population
- 0.0% to 0.9%
- 1.0% to 5.2%
- 5.3% to 6.3%
- 6.4% to 20.2%
- 20.3% to 38.1%

Source: US Census Bureau, American Community Survey 2006
* Refers to Metropolitan Statistical Areas

Number of Mexican Born in a Metropolitan Area*
- Less than 500,000
- 500,000 to 1,000,000
- More than 1,000,000

Map created by Trudy Rebert of Migration Policy Institute
© 2008 Migration Policy Institute

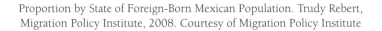

Proportion by State of Foreign-Born Mexican Population. Trudy Rebert, Migration Policy Institute, 2008. Courtesy of Migration Policy Institute

Regardless of where they settled, in or out of the Southwest, Mexican immigrants tended to live among themselves, usually, when possible, within or in proximity to established Mexican American communities. Relations between immigrant and native-born Mexicanos were sometimes strained. As the newcomers settled down and their children began the inevitable process of assimilation, though, there slowly developed a sense of mutual acceptance. And immigrants *were* putting down roots. Given the militarization of the southern border, the tendency among both the documented and the undocumented was to establish permanent residency.

Typically, most immigrants preserved close ties to Mexico, at times maintaining a second residence in their old hometowns. Their remittances, about $23 billion in 2007, continued to flow south, bolstering local economies. After oil exports and tourism, these cash transfers constituted the country's third-largest source of income. By the 1990s, too, many immigrants had established hometown associations to help out not just family and friends, but entire communities. By 2003, there were over 600 Mexican hometown associations registered throughout the United States, 218 in Los Angeles alone.[15] Emigrants were encouraged to maintain these ties by

Mexican officials, who welcomed the vital financial aid received from expatriate communities. In an effort to strengthen transnational bonds, the Mexican government even allowed its nationals abroad the right of dual citizenship after 1998, and Mexican citizens residing in the United States were permitted to vote in the 2006 Mexican presidential elections. This campaign to cultivate nationalist sentiment abroad was promoted not only by Mexican chief executives, particularly Fox and Calderón, but also by state governors, who made regular visits to expatriate communities north of the border. Mexican presidents also did their best to get their U.S. counterparts to extend legal protection to all Mexicanos living in the north, including those who had recently acquired U.S. citizenship. Appeals generally fell on deaf ears, however, as the American government was under increasing pressure from its own citizenry to do something about the southern invasion. We turn now to the U.S. response to "the Hispanic Challenge," beginning with legislative efforts to resolve the border issue.

STEMMING THE TIDE

The ultimate failure of immigration laws like IRCA to stem the southern tide once again resurrected xenophobic sentiments, particularly vis-à-vis Mexicans. The immediate aftermath of IRCA proved to be a major disappointment to nativists. The immense flood of immigration that began in the midsixties showed no sign of receding. On the contrary, both legal and illegal entry seemed to increase as time went by, causing grave concern among many segments of the American population. During the decade following the 1986 IRCA, legal immigration of Mexicans swelled by almost 3 million. By the mid-1990s, many of these legal entrants were beginning to seek naturalization, a prospect that terrified cultural conservatives. Even more menacing was the giant wave of illegal immigration, more than three-quarters of it from Latin America.

The anxiety created around the country by record-setting rates of immigration had a multitude of consequences. The immediate upshot was the escalation of an ongoing national debate on the merits of large-scale immigration, with restrictionists focusing on illegal Mexican immigrants, the so-called Barbarians at the Gate. Clearly, America had lost control of its borders, and a consensus soon developed that drastic measures were in order. More than any other factor, this acrimonious debate fueled the anti-Mexican sentiment which came to typify the 1990s and continued on into the new millennium; FBI reports indicate that between 2004 and 2008, anti-Hispanic hate crimes jumped 25 percent.[14]

Under enormous pressure to act, state and federal authorities responded with a variety of solutions, none of them very effective, as a survey of these legislative responses will illustrate. The fears were most pronounced in California, where denunciations of illegals reached a feverish pitch. The backlash created by border problems was so intense—violence was not uncommon—that a whole series of anti-immigrant initiatives, spearheaded by Republican assemblymen in the southern part of the state, had no trouble gaining popular traction. In 1994, Californians, with a resounding 59 percent of the vote, passed Proposition 187, which denied illegal immigrants and their families health care, welfare, and public education. The bill was endorsed by Republican Governor Pete Wilson, a staunch restrictionist, and heavily subsidized by nativist and racist organizations. Two years later, the confident governor and his conservative backers, capitalizing on escalating anti-immigrant sentiment, decided to dismantle affirmative action. Proposition 209 called for an end to all such programs in the state. Although only indirectly related to the immigrant question, but widely viewed as anti-minority, this ballot measure proved to be even more popular among the non-Hispanic white electorate than Proposition 187, winning by an even wider margin, 63 percent. Finally, in 1998, the voters of the Golden State left no doubt where they stood on the Mexican Question when they overwhelmingly passed Proposition 227, which banished bilingual education from the state. It was not long before other states emulated California by passing anti–bilingual education initiatives. Among them were Arizona in 2000 and Massachusetts two years later. All of these measures effectively polarized the electorate along ethnic lines.

In Texas, authorities were much more cautious in handling the immigrant problem, possibly because the state's economy was relatively healthy in recent years compared to that of California, which had suffered from the drying up of defense industries with the end of the Cold War, as well as from a slump in the real estate business. The Lone Star State also had proportionately fewer illegals—in the late nineties, only 3 percent of its population was illegal, compared with 7 percent in California—and a long-established Mexicano political presence in many border towns.

Meanwhile, as one would anticipate, federal immigration policy also became more stringent. The federal government held out great hopes for Nafta, convinced that once ratified, the pact would in the long run ameliorate or even resolve the immigrant problem. In the short run, however, Washington was under immense pressure to control its borders. The upshot was more legislation. In 1990, Congress increased both the funding for the Border Patrol and penalties for immigration violations. Three years later, the Clinton administration initiated a policy of beefing up border enforcement, Operation Gatekeeper, augmenting the number of Border Patrol agents by about 45 percent. The enactment of another major immigration law in 1996 by the Republican-dominated Congress, the Illegal Immigration and Reform and Immigrant Responsibility Act, upped the ante, again strengthening the Border Patrol, providing more sophisticated surveillance technology, and raising the penalties for both smugglers and illegal migrants. These bold measures also made the status of permanent residents more problematic. Immigrants committing felonies and certain kinds of misdemeanors were now subject to deportation. Moreover, a second piece of federal legislation in 1996, the Welfare Reform Act, excluded permanent residents from the benefits conferred by most social welfare programs.

Still the numbers of immigrants continued to swell, as did opposition to their entry. With vigilante activity on the rise along the southern border, both the Clinton and George W. Bush administrations were forced to escalate the militarization of the border zone, first along the two busiest ports of entry, the sectors around San Diego and El Paso, where seventy-five miles of fences were built. Incredibly, given the tougher enforcement, after a four-year decline—Border Patrol detentions dropped from 1.6 million in 2000 to about 1 million in 2003—illegal immigration resumed tidal proportions by 2004. By the middle of the first decade of the twenty-first century it was estimated that the total number of illegals in the country approached 12 million, with Mexicans perhaps a third of the total. In the post-9/11 world, the threat of illegal immigration was conflated with the threat posed by terrorists and, more realistically, by drug smugglers. Encouraged by the media, nativists grew hysterical. In Congress, they found their champion in Representative Tom Tancredo. Even intellectuals like Harvard political scientist Samuel Huntington joined the anti-immigrant crusade. According to media polls, more than two-thirds of the U.S. population shared their view that the country had lost control of its borders.

In a desperate attempt to placate critics, the federal government increasingly turned to extreme measures. Thanks to the Fence Act signed by President Bush in October 2006, seven hundred more miles of fences began to be constructed along other crucial stretches of the international divide besides San Diego and El Paso. By now the number of Border Patrol agents had grown to about twelve thousand, compared to the thirty-seven hundred agents twenty years before.

The consequences of these stringent policies were dire for Mexicanos, both immigrants and U.S. residents. More and more, the "Tortilla Curtain" forced undocumented workers to enter the country along desolate and often dangerous stretches of desert, lowering their odds of apprehension but dramatically escalating both criminal activity and mortality rates—for example, the number of migrant deaths along the border jumped from 261 in 1998 to 409 in 2003. Moreover, as border expert Douglas S. Massey has shown, many of these undocumented immigrants, unable to return to their Mexican homeland because of the tougher border surveillance, were forced to stay put. "Despite all the rhetoric about floods and invasions," Massey concludes, "the rate of undocumented in-migration from Mexico has not changed in three decades. What has changed is the rate of undocumented outmigration, and that is entirely an artifact of our own policies."[15] In other words, thanks to misguided U.S. strategies after 1986, sojourners increasingly became permanent residents, compounding the problems that nativists feared most.

"BARBARIANS AT THE GATE": THE NEW NATIVISM

The most dramatic response by the American people to immigration was undoubtedly the rise of a widely supported anti-immigrant campaign tinged with elements of racism—European immigrants did not seem to inspire the same nasty reaction as did their Asian and Latino counterparts. As immigration escalated, so too did organized resistance to the newcomers. At the grassroots level this reaction took a variety of forms. Anti-immigration groups sprouted up throughout the country. The movement continued to find its main crusader in the politically powerful Federation for American Immigration Reform (see the previous chapter), the biggest anti-immigration entity within the United States, with some two hundred thousand dues-paying members. A more extreme popular reaction was the advent of vigilante activity, by groups such as the Minutemen, Riders USA, and United for a Sovereign America, which focused primarily on Mexicans. They had been encouraged by the failure of the U.S. Immigration and Customs Enforcement (ICE) to take a firm stand against their unsolicited aid. Some of these extremist groups, according to the Southern Poverty Law Center (SPLC), a nonpartisan organization that monitors hate crimes across the country, were out-and-out hate groups like the Ku Klux Klan. This radical fringe seemed to be most well represented in the West and the South. Even some of the mainstream groups, like FAIR, with its fondness for eugenics, appeared to share many of the racist positions usually associated with those of the radical Right.

FAIR representatives were often invited as guest speakers on talk shows, a disturbing trend which highlights the role of the media in promoting immigrant bashing. Once again, this bigotry was not confined to fringe elements. The mainstream media, taking their cue from CNN's Lou Dobbs, continually demonized immigrants. In 2008, the problem became so egregious that Janet Murguía, president of the National Council of La Raza, was forced to lodge a public protest charging the top three cable news networks—CNN, Fox News, and MSNBC—with complicity in advancing a racist agenda through their endorsement of white supremacist and other bigoted groups.

Most nativists found their home in the Republican Party. This is not surprising; the GOP had a long history of soliciting their electoral and financial support through a consistent policy of immigrant bashing going back to the restrictionist campaigns initiated during the First World War. To understand why it resorted to this tactic, it is necessary to remember that the GOP was then what it is today—the party of

Big Business; that is, its agenda was set by representatives of major corporations and was intended to advance their economic interests. However, in order to win popular elections, the party had to find a way to convince the great middle class to vote against its own best interests, a hard sell. Against great odds, Republicans were able to do just that. They did so by adopting a policy of deception—using bait and switch tactics, demonizing the opposition, starting attention-diverting wars, and the like—essentially resorting to smoke and mirrors. If the GOP operated in strict secrecy from the time of Richard Nixon to that of George W. Bush, it did so for good reason. The strategy was spectacularly successful, resulting in a conservative ascendancy in U.S. political life from the 1960s into the twenty-first century, when it culminated in the two-term presidency of George W. Bush.[16]

Central to party strategy was the use of fear to gain votes, a strategy that began to be employed during the first years of the Cold War, when Senator Joseph McCarthy and his political allies discovered that anti-Communist hysteria paid big dividends at the polls, allowing the party to emerge from the political wilderness. During the civil rights era, the GOP turned to the race card. Its "Southern Strategy," playing on anti-black sentiments by exaggerating the threat to white supremacy posed by the civil rights movement, transformed the South from a Democratic stronghold into the Republican bastion it became by the 1990s, when southern whites regularly voted for GOP candidates by a margin of two to one.

The end of the Cold War did not put an end to the politics of fear. A new scapegoat conveniently appeared—immigrants. Massive immigration in the 1990s, much of it illegal, allowed the party to capitalize on rising nativist sentiments. Using the right-wing media, what critics have labeled "the Republican noise machine," party strategists fanned its fires, often lumping immigrants and terrorists together, and reaped the benefits. Once again the GOP chose to play the race card—white immigrants did not seem to worry people like Tom Tancredo; it was only non-white newcomers who were perceived as a problem—but this racism, whether employed by politicians or right-wing media pundits, was coded rather than overt. Largely neglected before, Latinos, especially Mexicanos, now found themselves demonized, as were terrorists, after the events of 11 September 2001. But not all Republicans were nativists.

In truth, the GOP was deeply divided on immigration, perhaps more so than on any other question. The party base, which included the Christian right, was a stalwart advocate of traditional values and saw immigrants, especially racial minorities, as a threat to the American Dream, as they defined it. Most of the right-wing media shared this perception. Hence, the overwhelming majority of party members, as letters to the editor newspaper sections clearly illustrated, supported policies that would seriously curtail legal immigration and shut off the flow of illegal immigration completely.

Business elites, however, were of another mind. They did not have anything against fear mongering; it had been a tactic that they had endorsed time and again with great success. Immigration was a different matter, though. For most business elites, immigrants represented a cheap source of labor, and in many cases, such as mining, agribusiness, and the lumber industry, an indispensable source of labor. Moreover, a steady flow of immigrants would also depress wages and impede unionization efforts. The last thing the GOP leadership wanted was strict immigration laws, which explains the chronic failure of Republican administrations to enforce tough legislation in the past. Despite the laws, employers were rarely penalized for hiring illegal workers. In 2007, for instance, when ICE officials were forced to ratchet up enforcement efforts by the popular outcry against illegal immigration, there were ninety-two criminal arrests of employers. Now, this sounds like a reasonable number, until one remembers that at this time there were more than six million companies employing more than seven million unauthorized workers. Corporate interests, then, with President George W. Bush as their leading champion, preferred a liberal immigration policy; some employers would even opt for an open border if they had their druthers. Fearing to alienate their base, however, business-oriented members of Congress, which is to say, most legislators, had to be discreet. Ultimately, though, it is important to recognize that throughout the forty-year period of Republican ascendancy, anti-immigrant rhetoric notwithstanding, immigrant policy remained amazingly liberal. GOP administrations continually swung the Golden Door wide open, permitting unprecedented numbers of newcomers to enter, which illustrates better than anything else who really controlled the party agenda.

Any doubts about the party position on immigration were put to rest in 2007, at a time when the immigration debate had reached a feverish pitch, when a much-anticipated and comprehensive compromise immigration bill came before the Senate, a bipartisan effort sponsored by Edward Kennedy (D-Mass.) and John McCain (R-Ariz.). While the party's cultural warriors complained that the proposed legislation provided illegal immigrants with a pathway to citizenship, they were placated by its tough enforcement features, and most of them came around to the idea that its enactment would be a valuable first step toward securing U.S. borders. In the end, however, Republican leaders in the Senate, afraid that the bill would make labor recruitment too difficult, made sure the bipartisan immigration bill went down in flames in a procedural vote on 28 June 2007, bringing about a collapse of federal immigration reform. Despite popular indignation, then, especially among their own rank-and-file, when put to the test, GOP congressional leaders, beholden to their corporate sponsors, demonstrated that they were perfectly willing to settle for the preservation of the status quo—a porous border.

In the meantime, in the absence of federal reform, many cities, counties, and states took matters into their own hands, passing hundreds of anti-immigrant laws.

Much of this legislation was frankly xenophobic, though few initiatives were as mean-spirited as an ordinance passed by the city council of Hazleton, Pennsylvania, which would punish a landlord for *renting* to an undocumented immigrant!

Another momentous reaction to the contemporary reemergence of the Mexican Problem, one more subtle than immigrant bashing, was "white flight," a phenomenon generally associated with black-white confrontations. Actually, what we see by the 1990s was an *acceleration* of white flight, since Mexicanos, like blacks, had first witnessed this reaction to their presence immediately after World War II, an exodus that grew stronger after 1965 in a response to legal restraints imposed by the federal government on racial segregation in schools, on work sites, and later in housing. The sociologist Andrew Barlow correctly argues that these "new suburbs were created by and for whites only, thus enhancing the value of suburbs as sites of racial privileges."[17] From 1950 to 1970, 95 percent of the residents of America's fledgling suburban communities were white. This racial homogeneity began to disappear thereafter, as some minorities too abandoned inner cities for more attractive neighborhoods. The trickle soon became a torrent. By the turn of the century, 32 percent of blacks, 43 percent of Hispanics, and about 50 percent of Asians resided in suburbia.[18]

The classic case in the West was in the great Los Angeles basin, as has been documented by the journalist Mike Davis, the urban affairs expert Joel Kotkin, and a host of other students of urbanization. The white suburban population expanded markedly in the aftermath of the 1965 Watts riots, and then it became a stampede. From 1970 to 2000, the proportion of whites in the city of Los Angeles dropped from 61 percent to 30 percent. Concurrently, however, both blacks and Mexicanos began to find their way into the suburbs. Having expanded the boundaries of East Los Angeles, its burgeoning Spanish-speaking residents, aided by the mushrooming network of freeways, began to migrate in all directions. One major thrust was to the immediate south, into white working-class communities like Huntington Park and South Gate, which in the early 1960s were off-limits to Mexicanos but forty years later had Latino populations in excess of 90 percent.[19] At the same time they migrated to the northeast, to the San Gabriel and Pomona valleys. Still another popular destination was the San Fernando Valley, north of the city center. In the 1960s, the valley was about 90 percent white; by the late 1990s more than 40 percent of the population was Latino.

By the 1980s the transformation of this first ring of white suburbs into Mexicano suburbs, aided now by huge numbers of immigrants coming directly from Mexico, was so far along that critics were already lamenting that Los Angeles in the twenty-first century would be indistinguishable from Tijuana, only much bigger. In fact, already by 2005, Mexicanos constituted about 47 percent of the population of Los Angeles County. By the eighties, too, another key demographic pattern was obvious: as Mexican Americans, and large numbers of blacks, increasingly penetrated older white suburbs, white residents were "forced" to move out to newer suburbs even further from the city center, a pattern that occurred over and over again, until the newest suburbs were way out on the periphery, places like Thousand Oaks, Palmdale, or Dana Point. This recurring process was almost always accompanied by ethnic tensions, sometimes outright violence.

The 1990s witnessed an interesting variation of this pattern. During this decade, the burgeoning Latino population of East Los Angeles, while continuing its inexorable march into white lower- and middle-class communities, also began to move in huge numbers toward the southwest, into South-Central Los Angeles, the heart of the city's black communities, places like Compton and Watts itself. Tensions between the two competing racial minorities would have many consequences, notably in the political arena.

THE AWAKENING GIANT: GRASSROOTS MOBILIZATION

The threat to their civil liberties led Mexican American communities to mobilize politically throughout the country. This grassroots movement was first seen in California. The state's anti-immigration propositions, immediately perceived as an assault on the entire ethnic community, prompted Mexicanos to make their displeasure manifest at the ballot box. According to exit polls taken by the National Association of Latino Elected and Appointed Officials, about 80 percent of Hispanics opposed both Proposition 187, denying illegal immigrants state services, and Proposition 209, outlawing affirmative action, and 65–70 percent opposed Proposition 227, ending bilingual education—all of them passed overwhelmingly despite their opposition.

The controversial legislation also elicited an angry and immediate response in schools and communities by Mexicanos. Street protests began in 1994, when a full-scale mobilization occurred against Proposition 187, culminating in a march in Los Angeles one hundred thousand strong. Two years later the proposition's main stipulations were struck down as unconstitutional by the courts on the grounds that immigration policy was a federal, not a state, prerogative. Other grassroots demonstrations ensued in the aftermath of the passage of Propositions 209 and 227. Latinos viewed the two initiatives as extensions of Proposition 187, and therefore an attack on the entire ethnic community.

The grassroots movement demanding more rights for undocumented workers was a direct response to the increasing militarization of the border, particularly in the aftermath of 9/11. Again, California led the way. Mexicanos took to the streets in 2003, initiating a one-day economic strike on 12 December, the feast of the Virgin of Guadalupe, to protest the repeal of a law allowing undocumented immigrants to apply for driver's licenses. The emerging immigrant-rights movement was gradually gaining momentum beyond the barrios.

It went national in the spring of 2006 as protest marches were organized throughout the country. These massive protests—initiated and coordinated in southern California by UC Riverside professor Armando Navarro and the National Alliance for Human Rights—were a response to proposed legislation sponsored by Representative F. James Sensenbrenner (R-Wis.) which would have made illegal entry a felony and imposed stiff criminal penalties on anyone giving assistance to an illegal immigrant. Thousands of people joined the demonstrations against these draconian measures. The initial protest, in Chicago on 10 March, drew over one hundred thousand participants. On 25 March, in Los Angeles, half a million people took to the streets, and another half million did the same in Houston. Gaining momentum, the agitation culminated with one million protesters staging an economic boycott, accompanied by demonstrations, on 1 May, in what was dubbed "A Day without an Immigrant." The largest of these rallies took place in Chicago and Los Angeles, where estimates of the number of demonstrators ranged once again as high as half a million in each city. A great deal of the credit for the giant turnout in the 2006 spring protests belongs to local community leaders. Spanish-language radio stations played a prominent role as well. Radio disk jockeys were especially instrumental in mobilizing the immigrant community, their main listening audience. Perhaps the most influential of these popular media personalities was Los Angeles–based Renán Almendárez Coello, a native of Honduras, known to an estimated 35 million listeners as "El Cucuy" (the Boogeyman).

Tellingly, Mexicano participation in the emerging immigrant-rights movement was a *nationwide* phenomenon, not one solely confined to the traditional centers of Chicano power. In the Midwest, for example, Voces de la Frontera, an immigrant work center established by Christine Neumann-Ortiz in Milwaukee, was in the vanguard of the pro-immigrant cause, regularly organizing marches, in the face of growing anti-immigrant sentiment among local residents. Though recent arrivals in the South, there too Mexicanos, mostly immigrants, began to mobilize to protect their rights. Protest marches were held throughout the region in March and April 2006. Among the grassroots groups taking the initiative was the Farm Labor Organizing Committee, the Toledo-based union, increasingly active in rural North Carolina.

A year later, on 1 May 2007, sparked by continuing anti-immigration hysteria, another series of nationwide marches, this time more modest in scale, took place in over twenty cities from New York to Los Angeles. The largest rally was in Chicago, "perhaps the epicenter of the immigrant rights movement," according to the historian Juan Mora-Torres.[20]

Some observers saw in these grassroots protests the potential for a populist movement similar to that of Chicanos in the 1960s. These working-class marches were momentous because they marked the first time that illegal immigrants were willing to come in out of the shadows to voice their discontent. "It was the first time," marveled Richard Rodríguez, "I had seen the children of illegality demanding that the United States show respect for their parents. It was the first time I had seen illegal parents, standing fearlessly in public with their children. I tell you it was a momentous time in the history of the Americas."[21] The demonstrations were noteworthy, as well, because they united immigrant and native-born Mexicanos in a common cause. Generally the relations between the two had been marked by distrust and lack of communication. According to pollsters, perhaps a quarter of U.S.-born Latinos were opposed to illegal immigrants. Both groups now came together, united by the recognition that while the proposed legislation was supposedly aimed only at immigrants, it was in fact all Mexicanos who were being targeted.

Playing a key role in protecting the rights of immigrants were the traditional ethnic civil rights organizations. As would be anticipated, MALDEF, the nation's premier legal-advocacy group for the Spanish-speaking, was in the forefront of the campaign. More than any other group, it was MALDEF that was chiefly responsible for the ultimate defeat of California's Proposition 187 in the courts. A variety of other traditional Washington, D.C.–based civil rights groups lent their support, among them the National Council of La Raza, the country's largest advocacy group for Latinos, with over three hundred affiliates. Interestingly, both influential Hispanic organizations elected new leaders in 2004 to succeed renowned predecessors: Ann Marie Tallman, from Wisconsin, was chosen to head MALDEF, succeeding Antonia Hernández; and Janet Murguía, from Kansas, was picked to lead NCLR, succeeding the ailing Raúl Yzaguirre. What was noteworthy here was not that the two new directors were female, for mujeres had held key leadership posts for the past century, but rather their midwestern origins, which reflected a positive trend, a diffusion of Mexican American leadership beyond its traditional bastions in Texas and California.

THE AWAKENING GIANT: ELECTORAL POLITICS

By the early twenty-first century, political mobilization did not just take the form of street protests. At long last, it seemed that the time was ripe for Mexicanos to exert an impact on electoral politics. As we have seen, a start in this direction was initiated in the 1930s, and received a strong impetus as a result of the Second World War. Mexicanos played a leading role, especially in Texas, in the 1960 Kennedy presidential election—the popular Catholic candidate received 85 percent of the Mexicano vote—gaining valuable experience in political organization. The Chicano movement, too, produced a cadre of youthful leaders who increasingly entered the political arena as the movement faded. The extension of the guarantees of the Voting Rights Act of 1965 to Latinos ten years later created new opportunities. Solid gains were made during the last decades of the twentieth century, as both political parties, encouraged by a rapidly escalating number of new Spanish-speaking citizens, began to court Latino voters. Under the Nixon and Reagan administrations, the GOP enjoyed surprising success in weaning Mexicanos, especially the middle class, from their traditional alliance with Democrats. As some GOP strategists pointed out, Latinos tend to be conservative, socially at least. They believe in family, religion, and hard work. So the movement toward Republicans was touted as a natural path.

Most Mexicanos, however, continued to vote for Democrats, an allegiance which was not just a product of inertia. As mentioned before, the GOP has been the party of Big Business, and Mexicanos were, and continue to be, overwhelmingly working class. Moreover, the anti-immigrant sentiments permeating the party, which Latinos took very much to heart, were hard to miss. Throughout the Clinton years, from 1992 to 2000, Mexicanos swung back to the Democrats in large numbers. The Republican-led assault on immigrants, best exemplified by Governor Pete Wilson's support of Proposition 187 in California, was the major cause of this reversal.

During the 1996 presidential campaign, GOP candidate Robert Dole's endorsement of the move to make English the official language of the United States so angered Latinos that Cuban Americans gave President Bill Clinton, running for reelection, almost half of their vote, which speaks volumes, given their right-wing sympathies. Altogether, the incumbent received 72 percent of the Latino vote. In California two years later, Latino voters, venting their frustration with Wilson and his party, were also instrumental in sweeping Democratic candidates into office, among them Cruz Bustamante, elected the state's first Hispanic lieutenant governor.

President Clinton made cultivating Hispanic support a top priority. In his eight years in office, he appointed more Latinos to his cabinet and administration than any other chief executive in history. The most high-profile of these appointments was Bill Richardson, a Mexican American, who served as energy secretary in the second Clinton administration. The impeachment proceedings that marred the last years of his second term failed to diminish Clinton's popularity among Hispanics; all their major advocacy organizations in the nation's capital continued to back the beleaguered president.

By the turn of the century, signs of a massive increase in the size of the Spanish-speaking community were unmistakable, as too were its rising rates of naturalization. According to the Pew Hispanic Center, the number of Mexicans who became naturalized citizens skyrocketed by 144 percent between 1995 and 2005, the most of any national group. Moreover, this population was concentrated in key states, those with huge numbers of electoral votes, such as California, Texas, and Illinois. Republicans were forced to reassess their old strategy, which had generally been either to ignore or to demonize Mexicanos, together with other people of color. Now they, and other Latinos, were to be actively pursued. The architects of this dramatic reversal were George Bush and his chief advisor, Karl Rove.

Living in Texas, with its large Spanish-speaking communities, Bush and Rove had come to appreciate just how conservative many of their neighbors' ethnic values were—among them, the beliefs in the family, religion, and the work ethic, and opposition to abortion—especially as they gained greater affluence. This traditional Mexican value system was reflected in high rates of military service and conversion to Protestantism. Applying a strategy of reaching out to Tejanos, particularly the middle class, paid big dividends in Bush's two successful races for the Texas governorship, the GOP candidate winning almost half the Tejano vote in 1998.

These campaigns led the Bush team to believe that similar results might be achieved at the national level in his 2000 presidential bid. As with LBJ before him, George W. Bush hoped to establish a power base in the barrios. There were many misgivings at the national level among party traditionalists, who feared that a new direction would alienate the party base—white Southerners. The Texas governor was undeterred by the naysayers. His strategy, employing Mexican American operatives such as Raúl Romero and Lionel Sosa, was completely vindicated in the 2000 presidential elections, when, according to the Southwest Voter Registration Education Project, the GOP standard-bearer captured a surprising 37 percent of the overall Latino vote. In 1996, by contrast, Bob Dole, the GOP presidential candidate, had received only 21 percent. In Texas, where the great majority of Latino voters would be of Mexican ancestry, Bush received about 43 percent of the Hispanic vote. Gregory Rodríguez, a senior fellow at the Washington, D.C.–based New America Foundation, a nonpartisan public policy institute, makes an excellent point when he notes that Latinos have been treated so shabbily in the past, either neglected or demonized, that any little gesture, like uttering a couple of Spanish words, eating a tamale, or gaining a Latino celebrity endorsement, is enough to win over many of them. Bush's ability to recognize this fact permitted the GOP to make significant inroads into Mexican American communities.

President Bush promptly repaid the political debt, but it was Cubans who reaped the major benefits. His fourteen-person cabinet included one Hispanic— Cuban American Mel Martínez, who was appointed secretary of housing and urban development. Tejanos were not left completely empty-handed. The president's other top Hispanic appointee was his friend Alberto Gonzales, a Mexican American lawyer from Houston, who was named White House general counsel.

Aided by a coterie of Tejano advisors, including Frank Guerra and Lionel Sosa, President Bush did even better with Hispanic voters in his 2004 reelection, when about 47 percent of those eligible to vote went to the polls, a record 8 million people. His effort to broaden the party base by enticing Mexican Americans, who represent two-thirds of the Latino population, included wooing Mexican president Fox, an ideological soul-mate. Bush's Spanish-language appeals and promises of immigration reform also helped his cause. Ultimately, these strategies netted him between 37 and 44 percent of the Latino vote, depending on which exit polls are consulted. He was particularly successful with Latino Protestants, apparently capturing 56 percent of their vote. The most memorable aspect of the 2004 election for Latinos, however, was the election of the first Hispanic senators in more than a quarter century: Ken Salazar (D-Colo.) and Mel Martínez (R-Fla.).

But the midterm elections of 2006, where Latinos added a third senator, Robert Menéndez (D-N.J.), saw the GOP lose much Hispanic support, despite President Bush's calculated bid during the previous year to win Latinos over with the appointment of Alberto Gonzales as attorney general, the first Hispanic to hold that key post. While the Democrats collected 69 percent of the Latino vote, the GOP settled for just 30 percent. Exit polls by the William C. Velásquez Institute indicated multiple sources of disaffection. Republican policies that benefited the rich at the expense of the poor—deep tax cuts for corporations, deregulation of industries, opposition to minimum-wage hikes—did much to cool enthusiasm for the Bush administration. As with other segments of the population, the continuation of an unnecessary and unpopular war in the Middle East also swayed them. By the previous year, when Latino anti-war activists launched impressive demonstrations in southern California, most Mexicanos had clearly turned against the war in Iraq. But undoubtedly the most telling factor explaining the loss of Mexicano votes in 2006 was the resurgence of the Republican-led anti-immigrant campaign, despite the president's own efforts to distance himself from the party's xenophobic majority. The ethnic backlash at the polls was so pronounced that even the typically pro-Republican Latino Coalition, an influential Hispanic business-advocacy group, endorsed Democrats in several crucial elections. More menacingly, Latino evangelicals, too, began to question their support of the GOP. Captives to the whims of the party base, by now firmly committed to an anti-immigrant agenda, Republican candidates for the 2008 presidential nomination largely abandoned Bush's Hispanic strategy, choosing to dodge virtually all major Hispanic conventions, including those of the NCLR and NALEO, on the eve of the elections. As the only option in a two-party system, Democrats, who did little to merit the gift, were the beneficiaries of the fallout. As Cecilia Muñoz, president of the NCLR, put it: "What this really reflects is a vote away from Republicans, which is not the same thing as a vote affirmatively for Democrats."[22]

In retrospect, perhaps the most meaningful Latino political victory of the decade occurred on 17 May 2005, with the election of Antonio Villaraigosa as mayor of Los Angeles, making him the first Hispanic to occupy that powerful office since 1872. Some political observers viewed this decisive victory—59 percent to 41 percent—by the popular Mexican American Democrat, a onetime UCLA Chicano activist, as a possible turning point for Mexicano political fortunes, the long-awaited awakening of the sleeping giant.[23] After all, by 2005, over six thousand

Hispanics held public office across the country, most of them Mexican Americans. In the future these optimists foresaw a great nationwide Mexicano political upsurge under the aegis of the Democratic Party.

These electoral predictions seem premature, however, on two counts. First, it is not clear that Mexicanos can shake off the political lethargy that characterized their communities throughout the twentieth century. While optimists feel that a change is rapidly coming as they pin their hopes on the new generation, cynics can point to an abundance of statistical evidence to the contrary. For example, in 2003, only 38.5 percent of Hispanic citizens in the country in the 18–24 demographic were registered to vote. In the presidential elections the following year, though both racial minority groups had numerical parity, about 14 percent of the U.S. population, Latinos cast only 6 percent of the vote, compared to 11 percent by blacks. Out of a total population of 40.4 million, only 7.6 million Latinos cast a ballot.

In fairness, it must be admitted that the chronic failure of "the sleeping giant" to wield political clout commensurate with its percentage of the total U.S. population is a product of other factors in addition to political apathy, which, after all, it shares with mainstream society. Many Mexicanos, for example, are illegal immigrants, hence ineligible for citizenship, a prerequisite for voting. Also, their population is extraordinarily young: the median age for Latinos in 2005 was about twenty-seven, compared to about forty for non-Hispanic whites. This means that about a third of them are under eighteen, which makes them ineligible to vote. A final consideration is that oftentimes a prison record will result in disenfranchisement. Many states have passed such laws, and they have had a marked impact on reducing the African American electorate—and, incidentally, the number of Democratic voters—since blacks constitute such a high percentage of the 2.3 million people behind bars and the 5 million who are either on probation or on parole. Altogether, there may be as many as 12 million ex-felons in the country. Less numerous than their black counterparts, Latino *pintos* (convicts and ex-convicts) represent a statistically significant population nonetheless, hence another factor reducing electoral participation.

Second, the rosy prediction above is based on the faulty premise that Mexicano political fortunes are tied to the Democratic Party. However, Mexicano political allegiance cannot be taken for granted by Democrats. There are a number of reasons for this. When in power, Democrats have rarely taken Hispanic concerns very seriously. In fact, in recent years, under the centrist presidency of Bill Clinton, the party seems to have abandoned poor people in general, not too surprising since Democratic lawmakers drink from the same corporate trough as do their Republican rivals. Given this record, is it any wonder that Mexicano support for the Democrats has been lukewarm? Equally important, a deep conservative streak runs through Hispanic culture. Most Latinos continue to espouse traditional values, especially those associated with religion. It is well to remember, then, that by the middle of the first decade of the twenty-first century, roughly 70 percent of Hispanics identified themselves as Catholics and another 15 percent as evangelicals—statistics that clearly suggest a natural affinity with the GOP, a party that emphasizes church-friendly policies. Then, too, many Latinos seem to display a propinquity to cast their vote based on name recognition above all other considerations—GOP incumbent Arnold Schwarzenegger, running in an overwhelmingly Democratic state, took 39 percent of the Latino vote in his 2006 reelection as California governor—which favors the Republicans, who have been very astute in running big name candidates since the time of Ronald Reagan. Finally, the emergence of a more affluent middle class may well lead to more moderate political perspectives in the future, since socioeconomic success generally breeds a desire to maintain the status quo. This trend is well illustrated by the Washington, D.C.–based middle-class organizations advocating for the ethnic community, like MALDEF and NCLR; increasingly dependent on corporate funds, their policies and interests are less community-oriented today than in the past.

Unlike blacks, who overwhelmingly vote Democrat, Latinos have not been consistent supporters of either major party. If the past is any guide, the prospects are that Mexicanos will bounce between red and blue for the foreseeable future. However, in the battle for their votes, Democrats should prevail more often than not. Why is this the case? Tradition is on the side of the Democrats. Excluding Cuban Americans, in Hispanic communities the venerated political figures remain Franklin D. Roosevelt and John F. Kennedy. Even Lyndon B. Johnson has his supporters. In fact, no Republican presidential candidate in recent memory has won the majority of Latino votes. Consider, too, that while some GOP candidates have come close, they have done so by gaining Latino support that is significantly skewed by Cuban Americans, who are ultraconservative. Mexican Americans are another matter. Some Hispanic GOP advisors, like marketing guru Leslie Sánchez, are adamant in arguing that as Mexicanos advance into the middle class there will be a tendency to vote more conservatively, which augurs well for the Republican Party. This contention is undoubtedly true, but only to a certain point. The Mexican American middle class is relatively small, and it will remain that way given the continuing arrival of thousands upon thousands of Mexico's poorer citizens. Most members of the ethnic community will retain working-class ties, and attitudes, for decades to come.[24] The Republicans are hampered, too, by their schizophrenic attitude toward Mexicanos, alternatively cultivating their support and then using them as scapegoats. Perhaps more relevant than Republican disdain, though, are Republican policies. Meant to benefit the haves, the upper half of the population, at the expense of the have-nots, the lower half, the GOP agenda is ultimately inimical to the interests of most Mexicanos.

Whatever their political affiliation, though, it is not unreasonable to believe that Mexicanos will gradually increase their political clout during the course of the twenty-first century, especially if they continue to commit themselves to coalition politics, as Villaraigosa did in Los Angeles. Indeed, the key to advancing Mexicano political power lies in coalition-building. There are a variety of groups that would seem to be natural allies. In the past the most reliable of these have come out of the labor movement, which shows signs of revival recently. This is especially the case in Southern California, where, before his untimely death in 2005, Miguel Contreras rejuvenated the regional trade union movement as head of the Los Angeles County Federation of Labor. His widow, María Elena Durazo, continues to exert a powerful political influence as head of Local 11 of the city's huge hotel and restaurant workers union. Another key labor organization that can be counted on is the AFL-CIO, which in 2000, led by its executive vice president, Linda Chávez-Thompson, embarked on a historic shift when it decided to organize immigrants.

As mentioned previously, since the 1980s there has been a steady push, from both within Hispanic communities and from without, to create a pan-Latino consciousness, in part because of cultural but primarily for political and economic reasons.[25] Despite their modest numbers, Florida's Cuban Americans, given their inordinate economic and political clout, would seem to be desirable allies. Certainly the two Latino communities have much in common, including a strong sense of family values. The stumbling block here, however, has been the Cubans' dyed-in-the wool conservatism, which has precluded interethnic cooperation in the past. Ensconced in the middle class, Cubans are not only socially conservative, they are even more so politically, which is why Cuban American members of Congress have refused to work with the Hispanic Congressional Caucus on a consistent basis. Anti-Castro feeling still borders on the irrational among them, and this sentiment is not just confined to the old émigrés. Apparently the fear of Communism trumps even family values; in 2000, when U.S. courts ruled that six-year-old Elián González—who survived a hazardous sea voyage fleeing Cuba which cost his mother her life—must be returned to his father back home, the Cuban American community in Florida launched massive protests in defiance of the court order. Cubans have always been solidly in the Republican camp. They are the only Latino community in the country that supports the GOP. As we observed previously, since the time of FDR, Mexicanos have always voted Democrat, and many of them, notably the Chicano intelligentsia, see Fidel Castro as a hero. The impending demise of the Cuban dictator will do little to pave the way to improved relations, given class and racial differences.

Relations with the other major Latino community in the United States, Puerto Ricans, are considerably better. Many Mexicanos and Puerto Ricans first came into contact with one another during the Vietnam War, when large contingents from both groups often found themselves in the same fighting units. Given cultural and ethnic affinities, they tended to move in the same circles, and on the battlefield they developed a mutual respect for their fighting prowess. A Chicano soldier from Corcoran, California, later recalled: "The Puerto Ricans were a lot like the *raza,* in action they all did their job. They were pretty good guys. In the rear they would turn into *indios* and throw *chingazos* like the Chicanos. Everyone was a big family. It was togetherness."[26]

On a practical political level, however, issues related to citizenship and race have made cooperation difficult. Such has been the case, for example, in Chicago, the one city where the two groups have a relatively lengthy history of interaction.[27] Nevertheless, common cultural elements such as religion and language and a shared history of mistreatment by mainstream society ultimately paved the way for better relations in the Windy City. Politically, as the historian David A. Badillo has chronicled, interethnic collaboration dates back to the 1970s and 1980s, when Mexicanos and Boricuas came together in the city to challenge the white political machine. As the two groups have increasingly moved on to the other's turf—outside of Chicago, this geographic proximity has been recent—they seem to have inter-mingled reasonably well, even in large metropolitan areas such as New York and Los Angeles. In these Global Cities the two groups occupy the same socioeconomic niche, which creates occasional friction but also encourages mutual sympathy.

In the western states, where the numbers of *Puertorriqueños* and *Cubanos* remain modest, Mexicanos are increasingly coming into contact with recent ar-rivals from Central America, most of them indigenous people, who began to flee their war-torn homelands in the 1970s. Often entering the United States by way of Mexico, many settled down in Florida and Texas, states relatively accessible to their homelands, but most preferred southern California. The majority of Salva-dorian and Guatemalan immigrants to the United States opted for Los Angeles, their communities centering on the city's Pico-Union neighborhood, just east of MacArthur Park. The relationship between Central Americans, themselves a highly diverse group, and Mexicanos has been erratic. Since the 1980s, there has been a history of antipathy between Mexicano prison gangs, on the one hand, and their equally violent Salvadorian counterparts, the 18th Street and Mara Salvatrucha (MS) gangs, on the other. However, Central Americans enthusiastically supported the 2006 marches for immigrant rights, a shared concern that has strengthened ties with their Mexicano neighbors. Continued cooperation between Central Americans and Mexican Americans is likely, given their common culture, as well as their geographical proximity.

The prospects of pan-Latino cooperation, politically or otherwise, are rein-forced, too, by evidence that while Hispanic subgroups continue to prefer terms that emphasize their national roots, more inclusive self-referents—*Latina/o* or

Hispanic—are starting to become more popular among these Spanish-speaking populations. Increasingly, too, despite some misgivings, many Chicana/o studies departments across the nation are changing their names to Latino/a departments, as professors find their student clienteles becoming more diversified.[28] Moreover, as Armando Navarro shows in his impressive survey of Mexicano political organizations, aside from increasing reliance on corporate and foundation funding, the other major trend, in an effort to broaden their base, has been a growing interest in serving all Latino communities.[29]

Together, blacks and Latinos represent more than a quarter of the U.S. population. To some political observers, such as the demographer Jeffrey S. Passel, this suggests that an alliance of Mexicanos, and other Latinos, with blacks might be mutually advantageous. The history of the relationship between the two groups, however, indicates that there are many obstacles to overcome.[30] Mexicanos maintain a highly ambivalent attitude toward their black neighbors. On the positive side, blacks have exerted a profound, though little acknowledged, cultural influence on Latino communities. In the fifties, for example, Elvis Presley, the King of Rock and Roll, was not nearly as popular in Mexicano communities as were Fats Domino, Little Richard, or Chuck Berry. One knowledgeable observer later recalled that during the late 1950s and early 1960s, crowds at "a typical weekend dance" at southern California's El Monte's Legion Stadium, where black music was the rage, "were 90 percent Chicano."[31] More recently, black slang has had a substantial impact on Spanglish, especially in urban settings. Besides popular culture, a common socioeconomic status and ill treatment at the hands of whites have also provided a basis for mutual sympathy.

On the negative side, there is the race issue. Anti-black prejudice has never been as pronounced among Latinos as among whites. Tellingly, there is no Spanish equivalent to the English word *nigger.* None of the Spanish terms of identification used for blacks—*prieto, mayate, tinto, negro*—reflect the same intense level of disdain. The difference is rooted in the past. Ali Mazrui, the eminent African scholar, has pointed out that in East Africa, millions of natives were carried off into slavery after the eighth century by the Arabs, but today blacks are rarely seen in the Middle East. Where are those millions of people, he asks rhetorically. Then he points out that, unlike the United States, blacks were absorbed into the dominant Arab population, reflecting a greater degree of racial tolerance in the Middle East. The same thing could be said of the fate of blacks in Mexico. Many slaves were shipped into New Spain during the colonial period—by 1810, blacks constituted 10 percent of the total population—and yet today there is hardly a trace of blacks as a distinct category.[32] Here, too, in contrast to North America, mestizaje seems to have prevailed, as was the case with indios. Closer to home, in modern-day America, interracial marriages are certainly more common in the brown inner cities than in white suburbia.

Regrettably, however, it must be admitted that race prejudice, albeit more modest in intensity, has been quite common among many, possibly most, segments of the U.S. Hispanic population, including Mexicanos. The African American writer Toni Morrison has famously suggested that the adoption of anti-black attitudes is a "most enduring and efficient rite of passage into American culture" for immigrants attempting to win acceptance in this country.[33] The Chicana historian Vicki L. Ruiz, though, provides a more convincing argument in the case of Latinos: "Color consciousness, with white as the hue of privilege, is not just a twentieth-century by-product of Americanization, but represents historical consciousness rooted in colonial Latin America."[34] This prejudice, then, came with the immigrants, since throughout Latin America, as was true in North America, the exploitation of slaves was justified on racial grounds. Once in the United States, even many of the new-comers who were oblivious to race before naturally adopted this sentiment; the human tendency among downtrodden people, sociologists have found, is to avoid the lowest rung of the socioeconomic ladder. Cultural differences have also served to divide the two; ignorant of the historic plight of blacks in this country, many Latinos like to contrast their relatively stable families with the dysfunction often associated with black ghetto life. Then, too, the ill-will, manifested particularly in big cities such as Chicago, Dallas, and Los Angeles, is augmented by economic competition, since blacks and Latinos are generally vying for the same low-wage jobs.

On their part, blacks, recognizing the racial prejudice, feel that Latinos are unreliable political allies, much more willing to cast their lot with whites. This suspicion was dramatically confirmed in 2008, when Antonio Villaraigosa, who had been aided by black votes in winning his own mayoral election three years before, turned around and endorsed Hillary Rodham Clinton for the Democratic presidential nomination rather than Barack Obama, the overwhelming favorite in the black community, thereby missing a golden opportunity to repair the racial divide in his own backyard.[35] The most crucial factor to consider when explaining anti-Mexican sentiment in black communities, however, is economic.[36] Blacks fear displacement by Spanish-speaking immigrants on the job market, and with good reason. The fact of the matter is that blacks have been hurt badly by cheap im-migrant labor. How many homeowners are going to pay a black laborer sixty-five dollars an hour to build a retaining wall when they can drive down to a day-labor pickup site and find a Mexican *jornalero* (day laborer) willing to do the same job for twenty-five dollars? Blacks, whose ancestors have been in this country for over three hundred years, are often beaten out of jobs by immigrants who arrived just the other day, illegally. Under these circumstances, it would be highly unusual for the black job-seeker to sympathize with the plight of the desperate immigrant, or to make a distinction between immigrant and native-born Mexicans. Many blacks, too, resent that the benefits black leaders fought so hard to achieve in the sixties and seventies have apparently been usurped by outsiders, particularly Latinos.

Conflict is most obvious in urban areas, where traditional black dominance has been challenged by the mushrooming Latino population, as law professor Nicolás C. Vaca documents in his candid study on Latino/black conflict, *The Presumed Alliance: The Unspoken Conflict between Latinos and Blacks and What It Means for America.*[37] East Palo Alto, California, is one such place where these problems have been well-publicized. The best example, though, as the historian Albert M. Camarillo has shown, would be South-Central Los Angeles, where established black communities have been overrun by Mexicanos and forced to play second fiddle or move out entirely.[38] These troubled communities include Camarillo's hometown, Compton. From their 1970 high of 71 percent, that city's black population was reduced to about 40 percent by 2000, with the remaining 60 percent being Latino. Not surprisingly, South-Central has been a virtual battle ground between the two minorities since the nineties, especially in the high schools, where dozens of racial brawls have taken place. Nearby Venice, too, has been wracked by gang violence that reflects brown-black tension. Only the intervention of respected civil rights organizations such as NAACP and MALDEF have prevented an out-and-out race war. In other parts of the country ethnic tensions are more muted than in southern California.

Animosity between the two ethnic minorities is intense, too, in prisons, an environment where natural human feelings most clearly manifest themselves, and where it is difficult for third parties to mediate disputes. Prison clashes between the two minority groups—often encouraged by prison authorities, some cynics have suggested—have been endemic during the past generation. Overcrowded conditions are a factor. So are economic issues, as gangs battle to control money-making enterprises both in prison and out on the streets. But ultimately racial hostilities seem to be at the root of these deadly confrontations. Certainly this appears to be the case in the longstanding war between the Black Guerilla Family and the Mexican Mafia. In prison clashes blacks often find themselves confronted by an alliance of La Eme and the Aryan Brotherhood, a pact that goes back twenty years. Beginning in the midnineties, the lethal violence spilled over onto the streets of Los Angeles, where, according to the Southern Poverty Law Center, the Mexican Mafia launched a ruthless campaign of racial extermination with the intention of driving African Americans out of biracial neighborhoods.

Efforts to build black-brown political alliances have borne some fruit from time to time, in campaigns to combat police brutality or to defend affirmative action programs, for example. Civil rights leaders Tijerina and Chávez, as well as MAPA, all cultivated black support. Interracial cooperation, too, played a major role in the election of Antonio Villaraigosa as Los Angeles mayor. Before that, Angeleños had supported a number of black politicians, including Mayor Tom Bradley and Congresswoman Maxine Waters. Given the rocky relationship described above, however, coalition-building has been disappointing in the past, and all indications suggest that interracial cooperation will continue to be problematic in the foreseeable future, be it in prison, in the community, or in political associations.

SOCIOECONOMIC REALITIES

Since the Reagan era in the 1980s the gap between the haves and the have-nots has widened alarmingly. Impressionistic evidence certainly indicates as much. Gifts in excess of $100 million by well-heeled businessmen to their alma maters became relatively common during the early years of the twenty-first century. At the other end of the social scale, during this same period, the dramatic increase in the number of public school students eligible for subsidized lunches and the rapid growth of cash advance centers located in lower-class neighborhoods both reveal, in stark contrast, the plight of the working poor. On the whole, economic gains eluded U.S. workers in the New Economy. This was certainly true of most Mexicanos, an overwhelmingly working-class population; 66 percent of Hispanics were working class and 33 percent were middle class, according to a 2000 survey conducted by the magazine *Hispanic Business*.[39]

In the period under review, from the mid-1990s to the present, several factors came together to impede social mobility among the masses of Mexican-origin workers. Perhaps the most obvious obstacle, the historian Oscar J. Martínez correctly ascertains, were structural changes in the U.S. economy resulting from globalization. The loss of manufacturing jobs and their replacement by low-wage employment in the service sector made it difficult for workers, especially undereducated Mexicanos, to climb the socioeconomic ladder in the Information Age. Indeed, many immigrants continued to toil in the fields, where it is estimated that 50 to 80 percent of the work force consisted of undocumented laborers.[40]

The consensus of informed opinion was that mass immigration, itself partly an outgrowth of globalization, was another formidable barrier to advancement, a point of view that Martínez shares: "The long-standing influx of large numbers of poor immigrants from Mexico must also be weighed in assessing group disadvantage. The newcomers have skewed the statistical socioeconomic profile of the entire Mexican-origin population in a downward direction. Group progress has been obscured by the constant addition of immigrants with low levels of education, limited job skills, and little or no knowledge of the English language."[41]

Unfortunately, Martínez and most other Chicano scholars neglect a third key factor impeding working-class progress: public policy. Throughout the long period of Republican ascendancy, government policies were geared to disadvantage workers. Every attempt to raise the minimum wage was fought tooth and nail by GOP party leaders. Wages were kept low, too, by liberal immigration policies.

Laws passed to the detriment of workers—as well as consumers—were invariably upheld by a conservative Supreme Court consisting mainly of ex–corporate lawyers. Conversely, particularly since the Reagan years, the one consistent thread running through Republican neo-liberal agendas was the privileging of corporate elites. Deregulation of industries was a case in point. Privatization was another. A third was the war in the Middle East, a bonanza for defense industries and their stockholders. It was a conflict, moreover, that was financed not by taxes, which would necessarily eat into corporate profits, but rather by bonds; which is to say, loans that would have to be paid back by U.S. taxpayers, at high interest, to banks, multinationals, and other bondholders. Clearly, the overwhelming numbers of Mexicanos were on the wrong side of the economic divide, but poverty was just one of their problems.

Earning power reflects educational level, and education among Mexicanos continued to lag far behind almost every other ethnic group in the country, which was unfortunate because to become truly competitive in the Information-Age job market, a good education was crucial. The 2002 No Child Left Behind Act did little or nothing to improve Latino test scores, not only because President Bush underfunded the initiative, but also because its success was hampered by massive immigration. In 2006, the percentage of Hispanics twenty-five and older who had at least a high school education was only 59 percent. Given these early educational failures, and meager financial resources, a college education was an unrealistic option for many members of the working class. My hometown, Huron, California, a small farming town in the western San Joaquin Valley, provides a dramatic example. In this community of more than six thousand residents, 98 percent of them Latino, according to the 2000 federal census, there was not a single person with a college degree. The educational profile was similar in surrounding Westside communities, where the labor force consisted predominantly of immigrants from Mexico and El Salvador. As Armando Navarro points out, unlike the previous two decades, "by the 1990s, Mexicano students entering the universities increasingly came from the ranks of the middle to upper-middle class."[42] To the extent that they advanced beyond high school, Mexicanos and other Hispanics continued to enroll overwhelmingly in two-year colleges. In California, according to the state chancellor's office, Latinos represented 28.9 percent of the state's community college students in 2008.

One of the reasons college degrees were so rare was that even when they were fortunate enough to get into college, Latinos had a hard time staying there. Of all ethnic groups, Latinos were also the most reticent to apply for school loans, according to the National Center for Education Statistics, which undoubtedly contributed to the high college drop-out rate. Undocumented immigrant children, in particular, found it difficult to make ends meet, being ineligible for federal loans.

In some states these students were forced to pay out-of-state tuition even when they were long-term state residents. Fortunately, California was not one of them: Assembly Bill 540, passed in 2001, exempted undocumented students from paying nonresident tuition.

Violence was another severe problem in Latino communities, especially among the youth. Gangs grew more, not less, evident in barrios as time passed. Violence inevitably increased as gangs proliferated. As we have seen, much of this strife was interracial. Though far from typical, many ethnic communities at the turn of the twenty-first century were essentially war zones.

Teen pregnancies, another barometer of dysfunction, appeared to be an intractable problem. Since the midnineties, according to the National Campaign to Prevent Teen and Unplanned Pregnancy, about half of Latinas got pregnant before the age of twenty. Most single mothers faced incredible hardships. Not surprisingly, depression among mujeres was endemic, though the magnitude of the problem was rarely appreciated even by family members.

According to the federal Centers for Disease Control and Prevention, about 37 percent of Mexican Americans were obese in 2007, compared to about 33 percent for the general U.S. population. The main culprits for this growing problem appeared to be lack of exercise and the consumption of fast food. The most alarming consequence was a greater susceptibility to a variety of life-threatening diseases, including diabetes and cancer. Health issues were related, also, to their physical environment. As Devon G. Peña has shown, Mexicanos were more likely to be exposed to pollution and other forms of environmental degradation than other ethnic groups.[43] Diagnosis and treatment continued to be a vexing problem since about one-third of the Mexican-origin population lacked health insurance.

The status of the Mexican American middle class, while by no means florid, was significantly better. While relatively modest in size, they continued to make headway, in terms of both absolute numbers and household wealth. By 2005, the much-sought-after Latino market commanded nearly $600 billion in buying power. The achievement of middle-class status in terms of income was to be expected among second- and third-generation residents. But even some immigrants, overcoming educational deficiencies, were able to make the leap into the highly prized category by working two and sometimes three jobs. As barrio populations soared, many immigrant entrepreneurs who spoke little or no English found unexpected opportunities for social advancement by catering to the needs of the expanding ethnic community. By 2007, the rate of new business growth among Latinos, including Mexicanos, was three times higher than the national average—Chicano scholars, however, have noted a sobering reality in Los Angeles, which is probably generally true: "Despite notable successes, which the media use to illustrate their model-minority narratives, most Latino businesses manage to employ only their entrepreneurs."[44] In Washington, D.C., these owners of small businesses found an increasingly influential advocate in the United States Hispanic Chamber of Commerce (USHCC).

Historically, to a large extent, the most effective leadership in the Mexicano community has come from the ranks of the professions, and happily, beginning in the 1960s, there was a steady increase in the numbers of young Mexican Americans pursuing professional careers. Already by 2000, it was reported that there were about twenty-two thousand members enrolled in the Hispanic National Bar Association and another eight thousand in the Society of Hispanic Professional Engineers. Many of these upwardly mobile individuals were beneficiaries of scholarship aid provided by organizations catering to the financial needs of Latino college students. Most major Hispanic advocacy groups, including LULAC, NCLR, and MALDEF, made scholarships top priorities. Probably the foremost source of financial aid, though, was the San Francisco–based National Hispanic Scholarship Fund (NHSF). Founded in 1975, NHSF greatly expanded its resources under Texas native Sara Martínez-Tucker, who was elected president in 1997.

Those Latinos who finished college soon found themselves in high demand, often in corporate positions. The number of Hispanic households with incomes exceeding one hundred thousand dollars rose 137 percent during the 1990s. Evidence of conspicuous consumption abounded among Mexicanos residing in well-to-do suburbs, and even in more modest neighborhoods. It was not uncommon to find some affluent families spending twenty thousand dollars for *quinceañeras,* elaborate coming-of-age rituals for girls on their fifteenth birthday.

POPULAR CULTURE: MEXICANOS AND THE WIDE WORLD OF SPORTS

Next to the school system, the most common avenue for Americanizing immigrant groups historically has been through sports. Previous chapters have chronicled Mexican American popular culture. However, mirroring scholarly interest in the past, one glaring omission has been athletics, an area that has been a passion in ethnic communities from the very beginning. During the past decade, though, Chicano scholars have begun work in this fascinating field.[45] These pioneering studies make it clear that from the 1920s to the present, Mexicanos have immersed themselves in sports, be it in the semi-professional baseball leagues of the interwar period or today's weekend soccer leagues, not only to win acceptance into American society, but also to bond socially with one another as well as to enhance both individual self-esteem and ethnic pride.

As an oppressed ethnic minority, Mexicanos have desperately sought heroes who could project a positive image in mainstream society. Happily, Latino athletes have been among the most accomplished of sports celebrities, providing key role models to generations of their paisanos, both young and old alike. As was true of many immigrant groups, Mexican-origin athletes made their first impact in the boxing ring. For decades they dominated boxing cards throughout the Greater Southwest, from San Antonio to Stockton. Historically, prize fighting provided the greatest outlet for athletic prowess among the residents of U.S. Spanish-speaking communities. Bert Colima, "el ídolo de Whittier," achieved iconic status in the brown communities of the Southwest before World War II just as Art ("The Golden Boy") Aragón did afterward. Many Mexicanos, both immigrants and natives, excelled in the sport. A surprisingly large number captured coveted professional championships. Among these pugilists reaching the pinnacle of their profession were Manuel Ortiz, Lauro Salas, Vicente Saldívar, Bobby Chacón, Julio César Chávez, Carlos Palomino, Mando Ramos, and Oscar de la Hoya. At the 1984 games in Los Angeles, Paul Gonzales—like de la Hoya, a product of Boyle Heights in East Los Angeles—became the first Mexican American to win an Olympic boxing title. This tradition of success in the ring continues undiminished in Mexicano communities during the first decade of the twenty-first century.

Baseball, the "All-American" sport, has been the other athletic competition where immigrant populations have traditionally performed well. With few exceptions, however, and despite the fact that about a fifth of today's major leaguers come from Latin America, U.S.-born Mexicanos have been underrepresented historically in America's national pastime at the professional level even though since the 1920s they have been skilled and enthusiastic ball players. Arguably the first Mexican American to play in the big leagues was Leo Naja, born Leonardo Alanis, from Mission, Texas, who was drafted by the Chicago White Sox in 1925.[46] However, one exception to their relative anonymity in the sport is particularly noteworthy: Chicano scholars now claim Hall of Famer Ted Williams (1918–2002), perhaps the best hitter of his age, as a member of their ethnic community. Though he rarely mentioned his ethnic roots, the San Diegoan had a Tejana mother, May Venzor. Son of Spanish immigrants, Lefty Gómez, from Rodeo, California, appears to be the only other U.S.-born Latino member of baseball's Hall of Fame.

In 1981, Fernando Valenzuela, the Mexican pitcher, became the first rookie to win the prestigious Cy Young award. Interestingly, in the midst of "Fernandomania," Mexicans on both side of the border came to claim the left-hander as one of their own, bringing together two communities who oftentimes clashed on a variety of issues. It would not be too much of an exaggeration to view the popular athlete as the first true Mexican transnational hero.

The most popular spectator sport for Mexicanos today is professional football. But beyond being avid spectators, they have also performed well on the gridiron. According to San Antonio sports historian Mario Longoria, the first Mexican American to be drafted by a professional team was Joe Aguirre from St. Mary's College in California, who was picked by the Washington club in 1941. In recent years there has been a robust Mexicano presence in the National Football League (NFL). For example, just from the Golden State, Mexican Americans who have excelled as professional football players include quarterbacks Joe Kapp (Salinas), Tom Flores (Sanger), Jim Plunkett (San Jose), and Jeff García (Gilroy); offensive linemen Max Montoya (Montebello) and Anthony Muñoz (Ontario); linebackers Ron Rivera (Fort Ord) and Jack Del Río (Hayward); and defensive lineman Manny Fernández (Oakland). Each of these athletes has either won All League recognition and/or made a vital contribution to a championship team. Additionally, Flores, Rivera, and Del Río have served as NFL coaches. The only Mexicanos in the NFL Hall of Fame are Muñoz and L.A. Rams tight end Tom Fears, a native of Guadalajara, Mexico.

While country-club sports are still largely inaccessible to minorities, this path has been pioneered by a few talented Mexicanos. Already in the 1940s, Pancho Gonzales (1928–1995), born and bred in Los Angeles, had made his mark on the world of tennis. Possibly the only self-taught tennis champion in modern times, the temperamental Gonzales became the sport's dominant American professional player of the 1950s. In the even more exclusive world of professional golf, the quiet Hispana Nancy López and flamboyant Tejano Lee Treviño were considered the best at their sport at some point in their illustrious careers, and eventually both were inducted into golf's Hall of Fame. Synchronized swimmer Tracy Ruiz-Conforto and water polo player Brenda Villa have won Olympic titles, as has speed skater Derek Parra. Rudy Galindo, from San Jose, became the first Mexicano to win a national figure skating championship.

In recent years, much unflattering literature has been written about Latinos in the United States by upper-class, white academics. Generally, these are scholars who have rarely, if ever, wandered into a working-class colonia, much less communicated with its residents. Ignorance breeds contempt. It also makes for misperceptions, sometimes very harmful ones. A good example is Harvard political scientist Samuel P. Huntington (1927–2008), the author of a highly controversial article, "The Hispanic Challenge," published in 2004, on immigration in general but more particularly on Mexican immigration.[47] The work merits some attention here, not only because it reflected popular sentiments on the subject, but also because it has been highly influential, both within the academy and beyond.

Briefly, Huntington argues that immigrants today are changing the face of the United States, which he always refers to as "America," for the worse, and one group in particular is to blame for this deteriorating state of affairs—Mexicans. Legal or illegal, it does not matter, newcomers from Mexico, he argues, are much different than previous immigrants. Among other things, they share a common border with

Americans, which permits easy access; their numbers are unprecedented; and, alone among immigrants, they have a legitimate irredentist claim, land they lost in 1848 as a result of U.S. conquest, the Southwest. Most of all, however, their way of life is completely different from that of U.S. citizens. Products of an Indian and Catholic past, their core values seem to be antithetical to the Anglo-Protestant legacy that Huntington credits for American greatness. This world view, and their racial background, make it almost impossible for Mexicanos, and other Latinos, to assimilate into the mainstream. A nation apart, they threaten the very essence of the American Dream. An unapologetic nativist in the tradition of Madison Grant or John Box, the Ivy League professor in his article warns Americans that they ignore the challenge posed by Latino immigration at their peril.

The Harvard scholar makes some valid points. Mexican immigration *is* unique, and for many of the reasons he suggests. One is that Mexico and the United States do share a common border, possibly the only place on the globe where a modern industrialized state sits right next to a so-called third world nation. The professor is also on the mark when he reminds us that these Spanish-speaking immigrants are predominantly people of color, though there are many exceptions. And, again with significant exceptions, Mexicans do continue to espouse Catholicism, and a Catholic world view.

However, Huntington's analysis is deficient in a number of key areas. For starters, he begins with the assumption that American values and institutions are superior to all others; that is, he completely buys into the myth of American exceptionalism: the idea that Americans are not only different from other people, they are superior. But there is a good reason why historians label this idea a myth. Certainly, Americans do not *look* superior, given their rates of obesity, as any visit to a local shopping mall will illustrate. Nor are they particularly well-educated; in fact, anti-intellectualism is pervasive throughout the society, including among the economic and political elites. Criminality is rampant, if the number of citizens behind bars is any indication. Spiritual poverty is ubiquitous as well. How else to account for the tremendous religious revival we see today in the United States, but not in Europe? And given its constant and unnecessary military aggression throughout the globe, almost exclusively against people of color, it would be a stretch to see the United States as especially virtuous. The idea that Americans are morally and culturally superior, it is important to remember, is held *only* by Americans—not by other people, even Mexicans. Of course, the great Achilles heel of American democracy has always been, at least since 1619, the way the United States has treated—or rather, *mistreated*—blacks, and no amount of rationalization can ever erase the iniquity.

The notion of superior institutions aside, what about the question of assimilation? Differences in culture and race are hardly insurmountable barriers. Their

Catholic background has not precluded the amalgamation of the Irish, Poles, or Italians into the melting pot. Nor has skin color seemed to have kept the Chinese and other Asians from making a successful transition into the American mainstream, something that would leap out at any person scanning the enrollment records of elite universities in this country.

Professor Huntington's main problem, however, is his ignorance of Mexicanos, their past and present. Like other immigrants—more than most, admittedly—Mexicans do retain a sentimental attachment to their homeland, something that was true even of the first white Anglo-Saxon Protestants who came to North America. In time, however, these much-maligned Spanish-speaking immigrants and their children have come to embrace those ideals taught in American schools. In fact, for all the shabby treatment they have received—the theft of their lands, the segregated schools, the repatriation campaigns, and the rest—I am always amazed at how loyal Mexicanos have been, and continue to be, to their new homeland. When this nation has gone to war, as we have seen, Mexicanos have not just wrapped themselves up in a U.S. flag, or put a patriotic sticker on their SUV; they have actually served in the military, and served honorably. Their current representation in the armed forces—an all-volunteer army—speaks volumes about their dedication. While they may be slightly underrepresented in some of the branches of the Armed Forces, research by Professor George (Jorge) Mariscal establishes that "Latinos and Latinas are over-represented in combat positions."[48]

Despite the naysayers, evidence of assimilation is everywhere, if one bothers to look. And the place to look is not among the immigrants themselves—it would be patently unfair to expect a person first setting foot in this country to know and embrace its core values immediately—but among their children and grandchildren. Both of these generations tend to speak English, the third generation almost exclusively. According to Robert Suro, ex-director of the Pew Hispanic Center, Latinos make the transition from Spanish to English in a single generation. Increasingly, too, Mexican Americans live in suburbs, not in ethnic clusters. They have acquired better educations and jobs. By the third generation, exogamy is quite common. The demographer Jeffrey Passel found that about half of marriages in 2000 by third-generation Hispanics were to non-Latino spouses. Huntington himself conceded that more than a quarter of all U.S. marriages involving Latinos had crossed ethnic lines.

The cultural values Mexican immigrants bring from the Old Country are not so different from those Huntington admires. They are basically conservative, and their work ethic rivals that of the seventeenth-century New England Puritans. Even conservative columnist George F. Will is in agreement: "Male Latino work-force participation—80 percent—is the highest of any measured group."[49]

As to irredentist aspirations, the professor's alarming claims border on the ridiculous. The right-wing media has constantly harped on Reconquista—leading fear mongers fixated on this theme include Lou Dobbs and Patrick Buchanan—and Huntington appears to have uncritically accepted these allegations. Yes, during the Chicano movement in the sixties, as we have seen, there was a fringe element that called for the reoccupation of Aztlán, the Chicano homeland they placed in what is now the American Southwest. But outside of the Mechistas, few movimiento militants took these claims seriously. The idea of separatism had little traction in the ethnic community at large then, and has even less today. Not that Mexicanos are completely ignorant of the past. There persists a general awareness, among both immigrants and native-born, that the southwestern part of the United States was once a part of Mexico, but time has dulled the sting. Upward mobility, and increased settlement beyond the Southwest, will further erode the sense of loss.

Huntington and right-wing talk show hosts notwithstanding, Mexicano communities display little rancor toward their Anglo neighbors, certainly much less than these neighbors express toward them. Indeed, the outlook of most Mexicanos, particularly immigrant communities, is quite optimistic. Despite the daily hostility they face, and the all-too-obvious problems that beset their communities as the twenty-first century begins, Mexicanos generally maintain a positive attitude and look hopefully to the future. At the end of 2007, in the midst of one of the most vehement anti-Mexican campaigns in American history, a Pew Hispanic Center study, based on a comprehensive poll taken in October and November of that year, summed up their outlook: "Despite their concerns about the impact of the immigration debate, Hispanics are generally content with their own lives and upbeat about the long-term prospects for Latino children."[50] Rarely does one find in their communities the ennui and cynicism so common among the aging white mainstream population. Against all odds, Mexicanos continue to believe in the American Dream, as their high rates of immigration and fertility attest. And they exude, too, a growing sense of confidence, buoyed by their youth, their increasing numbers, and the small but meaningful gains of the past generation. Warranted or not, Mexicanos feel they are on the eve of a dramatic breakthrough in their quest for political and economic equality, and that is half the battle.

APPENDIX A.

◄O►◄O►◄O►

NATIONAL ASSOCIATION FOR CHICANA AND CHICANO STUDIES SCHOLARS OF THE YEAR

Year	Name	Discipline	Hometown
1981	Américo Paredes	folklore	Brownsville, Texas
	Carey McWilliams	history	Steamboat Springs, Colorado
1982	Julián Samora	sociology	Pegosa Springs, Colorado
1985	Ernesto Galarza	labor organization	Jalcocotán, Nayarit, Mexico
	Tomás Rivera	literature	Crystal City, Texas
1988	Luis Leal	literature	Linares, Nuevo León, Mexico
1989	Rodolfo Acuña	history	Los Angeles, California
	Adaljiza Sosa Riddell	political science	Colton, California
1990	Juan Gómez-Quiñones	history	Parral, Chihuahua, Mexico
1991	Arturo Madrid	literature	Tierra Amarilla, New Mexico
1992	Margarita Melville	anthropology	Irapuato, Guanajuato, Mexico
1996	Yolanda Broyles González	literature	Tucson, Arizona
1997	Jorge Huerta	drama	Los Angeles, California
	Tey Diana Rebolledo	Spanish	Las Vegas, New Mexico
1998	Renato Rosaldo	anthropology	Champaign, Illinois
	Salvador Rodríguez del Pino	literature	Acapulco, Guerrero, Mexico
1999	Mario Barrera	political science	Mission, Texas
	Carlos Muñoz Jr.	political science	El Paso, Texas
2000	Elizabeth "Betita" Martínez	community organization	Washington, D.C.
2001	Cordelia Candelaria	literature	Deming, New Mexico
	Cherríe Moraga	drama	Los Angeles, California
2002	Rodolfo Anaya	literature	Pastura, New Mexico
	Dennis Valdés	history	Detroit, Michigan
2003	Richard Chabrán	library science	El Paso, Texas
	Patricia Zavella	anthropology	Tampa, Florida

Year	Name	Discipline	Hometown
2004	Francisco Lomelí	literature	Sombrerete, Zacatecas, Mexico
2005	Gloria Anzaldúa	literature	Hargill, Texas
2006	Gary Keller-Cárdenas	literature	San Diego, California
2007	Antonia Castañeda	history	Crystal City, Texas
2008	Kevin R. Johnson	legal studies	Culver City, California
	Norma Cantú	literature	Laredo, Texas
2009	Tomás Ybarra-Frausto	cultural studies	New Braunsfels, Texas

APPENDIX B.

⤙◦⤚⤙◦⤚⤙◦⤚

HISPANIC AMERICAN
MEDAL OF HONOR RECIPIENTS

Name	Conflict	Service Branch	Place of Birth or Recruitment
Lucian Adams	World War II	Army	Port Arthur, Texas
John B. Baca	Vietnam	Army	Providence, Rhode Island
David B. Barkley	World War I	Army	Laredo, Texas
Philip Bazaar	Civil War	Navy	Chile
Roy P. Benavidez	Vietnam	Army	Cuero, Texas
Rudolph B. Dávila	World War II	Army	El Paso, Texas
Joseph H. De Castro	Civil War	Army	Boston, Massachusetts
Emilio A. de la Garza Jr.	Vietnam	Marines	East Chicago, Indiana
Ralph E. Dias	Vietnam	Marines	Shelocta, Pennsylvania
Daniel Fernández	Vietnam	Army	Los Lunas, New Mexico
Fernando Luis García	Korea	Marines	Utuado, Puerto Rico
Macario García	World War II	Army	Villa Costaño, Coahuila, Mexico
Edward Gómez	Korea	Marines	Omaha, Nebraska
Harold Gonsalves	World War II	Marines	Alameda, California
David M. Gonzales	World War II	Army	Pacoima, California
Alfredo González	Vietnam	Marines	Edinburg, Texas
Ambrosio Guillén	Korea	Marines	La Junta, Colorado
Rodolfo P. Hernández	Korea	Army	Colton, California
Silvestre S. Herrera	World War II	Army	Camargo, Tamaulipas, Mexico
José Francisco Jiménez	Vietnam	Marines	Mexico City, Mexico
Miguel Keith	Vietnam	Marines	San Antonio, Texas
Baldomero López	Korea	Marines	Tampa, Florida
José M. López	World War II	Army	Mission, Texas
Carlos James Lozada	Vietnam	Army	Caguas, Puerto Rico
Benito Martínez	Korea	Army	Fort Hancock, Texas
Joe P. Martínez	World War II	Army	Taos, New Mexico
Eugene Arnold Obregón	Korea	Marines	Los Angeles, California
John Ortega	Civil War	Navy	Spain
Manuel Pérez Jr.	World War II	Army	Oklahoma City, Oklahoma
Alfred Rascón	Vietnam	Army	Chihuahua, Chihuahua, Mexico
Louis R. Rocco	Vietnam	Army	Albuquerque, New Mexico

APPENDIX B ◄◦►◄◦►◄◦►◄◦►◄◦►◄◦►◄◦►◄◦►◄◦►◄◦►◄◦►◄◦►

308

Name	Conflict	Service Branch	Place of Birth or Recruitment
Cleto L. Rodríguez	World War II	Army	San Marcos, Texas
Joseph C. Rodríguez	World War II	Army	San Bernardino, California
Eurípides Rubio	Vietnam	Army	Ponce, Puerto Rico
Alejandro R. Ruiz	World War II	Army	Loving, New Mexico
Héctor Santiago-Colón	Vietnam	Army	Salinas, Puerto Rico
France Silva	Boxer Rebellion	Marines	Hayward, California
Elmelindo Rodrigues Smith	Vietnam	Army	Honolulu, Hawaii
José F. Valdez	World War II	Army	Governador, New Mexico
Jay R. Vargas Jr.	Vietnam	Marines	Winslow, Arizona
Humbert Roque Versace	Vietnam	Army	Honolulu, Hawaii
Ysmael R. Villegas	World War II	Army	Casa Blanca, California
Máximo Yabes	Vietnam	Army	Lodi, California

APPENDIX C.

─◄○►─◄○►─◄○►─

MEXICAN AMERICAN HISTORICAL NOVELS

Acosta, Oscar Zeta, *Autobiography of a Brown Buffalo,* 1972
————, *The Revolt of the Cockroach People,* 1973
Anaya, Rudolfo, *Alburquerque,* 1995
————, *Bless Me Ultima,* 1972
————, *Heart of Aztlán,* 1976
Arias, Ron, *The Road to Tamazunchale,* 1980
Azuela, Mariano, *The Underdogs,* 1915
Barrio, Raymond, *The Plum Plum Pickers,* 1969
Benítez, Sandra, *Bitter Grounds,* 1997
————, *A Place Where the Sea Remembers,* 1993
————, *The Weight of All Things,* 2000
Brito, Aristeo, *The Devil in Texas,* 1976
Cabeza de Baca Gilbert, Fabiola, *We Fed Them Cactus,* 1954
Candelaria, Nash, *A Daughter's a Daughter,* 2007
————, *Inheritance of Strangers,* 1985
————, *Leanor Park,* 1991
————, *Memories of the Alhambra,* 1977
————, *Not By the Sword,* 1982
Cano, Daniel, *Pepe Ríos,* 1990
————, *Shifting Loyalties,* 1995
Cantú, Norma, *Canícula, Snapshots of a Girlhood en la Frontera,* 1997
Castillo, Ana, *The Guardians,* 2007
————, *The Mixquiahuala Letters,* 1986
————, *Peel My Love Like an Onion,* 1999
————, *Sapogonia,* 1990
————, *So Far From God,* 1994
Chávez, Denise, *Face of an Angel,* 1994
————, *The Last of the Menu Girls,* 1986
————, *Loving Pedro Infante,* 2001
————, *A Taco Testimony,* 2006
Cisneros, Sandra, *Caramelo,* 2003
————, *The House on Mango Street,* 1983
Corpi, Lucha, *Black Widow's Wardrobe,* 1999
————, *Cactus Blood,* 1995
————, *Delia's Song,* 1989
————, *Eulogy for a Brown Angel,* 1992

Cota-Cárdenas, Margarita, *Puppet: A Chicano Novella,* 1985
Cruz, María Colleen, *Border Crossing,* 2003
Del Oro, Donna, *Operation Familia,* 2007
Duarte, Stella Pope, *If I Die in Juárez,* 2008
———, *Let Their Spirits Dance,* 2003
Escandón, María Amparo, *Esperanza's Box of Saints,* 1999
———, *González and Daughter Trucking Co.,* 2005
Espinoza, Alex, *Still Water Saints,* 2007
Esquivel, Laura, *Like Water for Chocolate,* 1992
———, *Malinche: A Novel,* 2006
Estevis, Anne, *Down Garrapata Road,* 2003
Fuentes, Carlos, *The Death of Artemio Cruz,* 1964
García, Guy, *Obsidian Sky,* 1994
García, Lionel, *Hardscrub,* 1989
———, *Leaving Home,* 1985
———, *To a Widow with Children,* 1994
Gaspar de Alba, Alicia, *Desert Blood: The Juárez Murders,* 2007
———, *Sor Juana's Second Dream,* 1999
Gilb, Dagoberto, *The Flowers,* 2008
———, *The Last Known Residence of Mickey Acuña,* 1997
Gonzales, Jovita, *Caballero: A Historical Novel,* 1996
———, *Dew on the Thorn,* 1997
González, Genaro, *The Quixote Cult,* 1998
———, *Rainbow's End,* 1988
González, Rigoberto, *Crossing Vines,* 2003
González Viaña, Eduardo, *Dante's Ballad,* 2007
Grattan-Domínguez, Alejandro, *Breaking Even,* 1997
———, *The Dark Side of the Dream,* 1995
Hinojosa, Rolando, *Dear Rafe,* 1981
———, *Klail City,* 1987
———, *The Valley,* 1983
Islas, Arturo, *La Mollie and the King of Tears,* 1996
———, *Migrant Souls,* 1990
———, *The Rain God,* 1984
Jaramillo, Cleofas, *Romance of a Little Village Girl,* 2000
Juárez, Tina, *Call No Man Master,* 1995
———, *South Wind Come,* 1998
Limón, Graciela, *The Day of the Moon,* 1999
———, *Erased Faces,* 2001
———, *In Search of Bernabé,* 1993
———, *The Memories of Ana Calderón,* 1994
———, *Song of the Hummingbird,* 1996
López, Diana, *Sofia's Saints,* 2002
López-Medina, Sylvia, *Cantora,* 1992
———, *Siguiriya,* 1997
Martínez, Demetria, *Mother Tongue,* 1994
Martínez, Manuel Luis, *Crossing,* 1998
———, *Drift,* 2003
Martínez, Max, *Layover,* 1997
———, *Schoolland,* 1988
———, *White Leg,* 1996

Martínez, Victor, *Parrot in the Oven,* 1998
Masttretta, Ángeles, *Lovesick,* 1996
———, *Tear This Heart Out,* 1985
Mora, Pat, *House of Houses,* 1997
Morales, Alejandro, *The Brick People,* 1988
———, *Death of an Anglo,* 1979
———, *The Rag Doll Plagues,* 1992
———, *Reto en el paraiso,* 1983
Niggli, Josefina, *Mexican Village,* 1945
———, *A Miracle for Mexico,* 1964
———, *Step Down, Elder Brother,* 1947
Paredes, Américo, *George Washington Gómez: A Mexicotexan Novel,* 1990
Pimentel, Ricardo, *House with Two Doors,* 1997
———, *Voices from the River,* 2001
Ponce, Mary Helen, *The Wedding,* 1989
Portillo-Trambley, Estela, *Trini,* 1986
Ramos, Manuel, *The Ballad of Gato Guerrero,* 2004
Rechy, John, *City of Night,* 1976
———, *Miraculous Day of Amalia Gómez,* 2001
Ríos, Isabella, *Victuum,* 1976
Rivera, Rick P., *A Fabricated Mexican,* 1995
———, *Stars Always Shine,* 2001
Rivera, Tomás, *Y no se lo trago la tierra (. . . And the Earth Did Not Part),* 1992
Robinson, Louie García, *The Devil, Delfina Varela and the Used Chevy: A Novel,* 1993
Ruíz, Ronald L., *The Big Bear,* 2003
———, *Giuseppe Rocco,* 1998
———, *Happy Birthday, Jesús,* 2003
Ruíz de Burton, María Amparo, *The Squatter and the Don,* 2nd ed., 1997
———, *Who Would Have Thought It?* 2nd ed., 1995
Rulfo, Juan, *Pedro Páramo,* 1955
Sáenz, Benjamin Alire, *Carry Me Like Water,* 1995
Salas, Floyd, *State of Emergency,* 1996
———, *Tatto the Wicked Cross,* 1967
———, *What Now My Love,* 1994
Soto, Gary, *Nickel and Dime,* 2000
Torrez, Everardo, *Narco,* 2003
Trujillo, Carla, *What Night Brings,* 2003
Trujillo, Charley B., *Dogs from Illusion,* 1994
Urrea, Luis Alberto, *The Hummingbird's Daughter: A Novel,* 2006
———, *In Search of Snow,* 1994
Vásquez, Richard, *Chicano,* 1970
Véa, Alfredo, *La Maravilla,* 1994
———, *The Silver Cloud Café,* 1997
Villanueva, Alma Luz, *Bloodrot,* 1982
———, *Naked Ladies,* 1994
———, *The Ultraviolet Sky,* 1988
Villarreal, José Antonio, *Clemente Chacón,* 1984
———, *The Fifth Horseman,* 1974
———, *Pocho,* 1959
Villarreal, Rosa Martha, *Chronicles of Air and Dreams,* 2000
———, *Doctor Magdalena,* 1995

Villaseñor, Victor, *Macho!* 1973
————, *Rain of Gold,* 1991
————, *Thirteen Senses,* 2001
————, *Wild Steps of Heaven,* 1996
Viramontes, Helena María, *Their Dogs Came with Them,* 2007
————, *Under the Feet of Jesus,* 1996

NOTES

◄○►─◄○►─◄○►

INTRODUCTION

1. When I refer to an academic program or center, rather than the ethnic group, I will employ the adjective *Chicana/o,* which has become standard procedure within the discipline. At present the tendency within the academic discipline, especially among female scholars, is to employ the gender-neutral but grammatically awkward *Chicana/os* (or *Chicano/as*) as a term of reference for the ethnic community generally, both men and women. Writing for a boarder audience than just colleagues in academe, I prefer the older self-referent, *Chicanos.* In my work the term *Chicanos* should be understood to mean *both* men *and* women, unless I indicate otherwise. When I wish to specify males I will use a term like *Chicano men;* to specify females, I will of course use the term *Chicanas.* By their nature, ethnic terms are imprecise. In general, their true meaning can be understood by their context.

2. Deena J. González, *Refusing the Favor: The Spanish-Mexican Women of Santa Fe, 1820–1880* (New York: Oxford University Press, 1999), p. 121.

3. Consult appendix A for a list of annual NACCS Scholar of the Year honorees.

4. Among the most prominent Latino exceptions today are Ralph H. Vigil, Gilbert R. Cruz, and Félix D. Almaráz, the biographer of the pioneer Latino scholar of the Spanish Borderlands , Carlos Eduardo Castañeda. While Latino colonialists remain a small minority, their ranks seem to be growing during the last two decades.

5. In May 2007 there were only 243 faculty members among the 519 dues-paying members of NACCS, according to its newsletter, *Noticias de NACCS* 36 (Summer 2007): 13.

6. See Professor Acuña's revealing interview in José Calderón, "'We Have the Tiger by the Tail': An Interview with Rudy Acuña," *Colorlines* 2 (Summer 1999): 21.

7. For recent examples, see Armando Navarro, *Mexicano Political Experience in Occupied Aztlán: Struggles and Change* (Walnut Creek, Calif.: AltaMira Press, 2005), and George Mariscal, *Brown-Eyed Children of the Sun: A Study of the Chicano Movement* (Albuquerque: University of New Mexico Press, 2005).

8. See Ríos-Bustamante, "General Survey of Chicano/a Historiography," in *Voices of a New Chicana/o History,* ed. Refugio I. Rochín and Dennis N. Valdés (East Lansing: Michigan State University Press, 2000), pp. 245–93, which includes a comprehensive catalogue of virtually all previous historiographic literature on Mexican Americans. For other useful bibliographies on the twentieth century, see *Mexican American Voices,* ed. Steven Mintz (St. James, N.Y.: Brandywine Press, 2000), pp. 227–53, and Manuel Gonzales, "Bibliographic Essay" in *En Aquel Entonces: Readings in Mexican-American History,* ed. Manuel G. Gonzales and Cynthia M. Gonzales (Bloomington: Indiana University Press, 2000), pp. 271–77. For an update of more recent work on Mexican Americans, see the bibliography in the revised edition of Arnoldo De León and Richard Griswold del Castillo, *North to Aztlán: A History of Mexican Americans in the United States* (Wheeling, Ill.: Harlan Davidson, 2006), as well as my own bibliography in this volume.

9. This Marxist orientation informs my recent work, written in collaboration with legal scholar Richard Delgado, *The Politics of Fear: How Republicans Use Money, Race, and the Media*

to Win (Boulder, Colo.: Paradigm Publishers, 2006). For a solid Marxian interpretation of the Mexicano experience in the United States, devoid of ideological baggage, see Yolanda Alaníz and Megan Cornish, *Viva La Raza: A History of Chicano Identity and Resistance* (Seattle, Wash.: Red Letter Press, 2008).

10. Dennis N. Valdés and Refugio I. Rochín, "The Fruitless Search for a Chicana/o Paradigm," in *Voices of a New Chicana/o History,* p. ix.

11. See the lengthy review of *Mexicanos* by Patricia M. Perea and Hector A. Torres, *Aztlán* 28 (Spring 2003): 211–29. For other criticisms of my work by Chicano scholars, see the John Chávez review of *Mexicanos* in *The Journal of American History* 87 (June 2000): 190–91, and Mariscal, *Brown-Eyed Children of the Sun,* p. 286 n52.

12. Rodolfo F. Acuña, "Truth and Objectivity in Chicano History," in *Voices of a New Chicana/o History,* p. 36.

13. Mark McDonald, "Term Limits: Hispanic? Latino? A National Debate Proves No One Name Pleases Everyone," *Dallas Morning News,* 13 Jan. 1993.

1. SPANIARDS AND NATIVE AMERICANS, PREHISTORY–1521

1. Richard Herr, *Spain* (Englewood Cliffs, N.J.: Prentice-Hall, 1971), p. 36.

2. Sachar, *Farewell España: The World of the Sephardim Remembered* (New York: Random House, 1994), p. 5.

3. Eugene K. Keefe et al., *Area Handbook for Spain* (Washington, D.C.: U.S. Government Printing Office, 1976), p. 127.

4. Cooke, *Alistair Cooke's America* (New York: Alfred A. Knopf, 1980), p. 35.

5. The various interpretations of Columbus are surveyed in Alfred W. Crosby, *The Columbian Voyages, the Columbian Exchange, and Their Historians* (Washington, D.C.: American Historical Association, 1987).

6. Timothy Foote, "Where Columbus Was Coming From," *Smithsonian* 22 (Dec. 1991): 29.

7. Wilford, "Columbus and the Labyrinth of History," *Wilson Quarterly* 15 (Autumn 1991): 81.

8. Fernández-Armesto, "Columbus—Hero or Villain?" *History Today* 42 (May 1992): 9.

9. Leobardo Jiménez, quoted by journalist David Kelly, "Indian Enclave at Risk If Duroville Closes," *Los Angeles Times,* 28 Apr. 2008.

10. Washburn, *The Indian in America* (New York: Harper and Row, 1975), p. xvi.

11. Arrell Morgan Gibson, *The American Indian: Prehistory to the Present* (Lexington, Mass.: D.C. Heath, 1980), p. 4.

12. An understanding of Mesoamerican people immediately before and after the Spanish Conquest should begin with Eric R. Wolf's provocative *Sons of the Shaking Earth* (Chicago: University of Chicago Press, 1959).

13. "Although not as large as Teotihuacán, Tula is believed to have been more majestic and extravagant," according to Jaime Suchlicki, *Mexico: From Montezuma to the Fall of the PRI,* 2nd ed. (Washington, D.C.: Brassey's, 2001), p. 20.

14. *The Broken Spears: The Aztec Account of the Conquest of Mexico,* ed. Miguel León-Portilla, trans. Lysander Kemp, rev. ed. (Boston: Beacon Press, 2006), p. xix.

15. Clendinnen, *Aztecs: An Interpretation* (Cambridge: Cambridge University Press, 1991), p. 98.

16. An iconic figure, the "Woman of Many Names" has been subjected to endless controversy. For a brief survey of the voluminous writings on La Malinche, see Emma Pérez, *The Decolonial Imaginary: Writing Chicanas into History* (Bloomington: Indiana University Press, 1999), p. 159 n52. A recent attempt to find the historical figure amidst conflicting

interpretations is made by Camilla Townsend, *Malintzin's Choices: An Indian Woman in the Conquest of Mexico* (Albuquerque: University of New Mexico Press, 2006).

17. Prescott, *History of the Conquest of Mexico* (New York, Bantam Books, 1967).

18. McNeill, *Plagues and Peoples* (Garden City, N.Y.: Anchor Press/Doubleday, 1976), p. 183.

19. See Thomas, *Conquest: Montezuma, Cortés, and the Fall of Old Mexico* (New York: Simon and Schuster, 1994).

20. This "song of sorrow," from the *Cantares mexicanos* collection in the National Library in Mexico City, is quoted in *Broken Spears*, p. 149.

21. Paz, "Reflections (Mexico and the United States)," *New Yorker*, 17 Sept. 1979, p. 140.

22. Forbes, *The Indian in America's Past* (Englewood Cliffs, N.J.: Prentice-Hall, 1964), p. 3.

23. In point of fact, many sixteenth-century Spanish jurists and theologians spoke up in defense of native Americans, leading one Spanish scholar to remark: "Never to this day has a colonial empire been built with such a sense of responsibility and self-criticism." Alfredo Jiménez, "The Spanish Colonial Model," in *Handbook of Hispanic Cultures in the United States: History*, ed. Alfredo Jiménez (Houston, Tex.: Arte Público Press and Instituto de Cooperación Iberoamericana, 1994), p. 77.

24. Fuentes, *The Buried Mirror: Reflections on Spain and the New World* (New York: Houghton Mifflin, 1992), p. 134. It has even been argued by Guillermo Céspedes, *Latin America: The Early Years* (New York: Alfred A. Knopf, 1974), p. 55, that "[c]oming from the racial melting pot of Iberia, Spaniards and Portuguese were not racially ethnocentric," though this seems an exaggeration. The Indian voice on these and other matters, of course, is largely lost, though there are exceptions such as the indigenous chronicles in the León-Portilla anthology cited above. Even today, as in the United States, it is non-Indian scholars who document indigenous societies, past and present. The late great Mexican historian Luis González y González once wryly remarked that the typical Tarascan family in his beloved Michoacán consisted of a father, a mother, their children, and an anthropologist! "El disfrute de la vida en la actualidad," in *Historia General de Michoacán*, ed. Enrique Florescano (Morelia, Mich.: Gobierno del Estado de Michoacán, Instituto Michoacano de Cultura, 1989), 4:294.

25. Neruda, *Memoirs*, trans. Hardie St. Martin (New York: Farrar, Straus and Giroux, 1977), p. 54.

26. Bacalski-Martínez, "Aspects of Mexican American Cultural Heritage," in *The Chicanos: As We See Ourselves*, ed. Arnulfo D. Trejo (Tucson: University of Arizona Press, 1979), p. 19.

27. Richard Rodríguez, *Days of Obligation* (New York: Viking Penguin, 1992), p. 24.

2. THE SPANISH FRONTIER, 1521–1821

1. Turner's essay can be found in *Frederick Jackson Turner: Wisconsin's Historian of the Frontier*, ed. Martin Ridge (Madison: State Historical Society of Wisconsin, 1986), pp. 26–47, and *Where Cultures Meet: Frontiers in Latin American History*, ed. David J. Weber and Jane M. Rausch (Wilmington, Del.: Scholarly Resources, 1994), pp. 1–18.

2. Bannon, *The Spanish Borderlands Frontier, 1513–1821* (New York: Holt, Rinehart and Winston, 1970), p. 3. The starting point for a student of the Spanish frontier is David J. Weber's highly acclaimed *The Spanish Frontier in North America* (New Haven, Conn.: Yale University Press, 1992). During the 1990s, the study of the northern Borderlands experienced a significant revival. See David J. Weber, "The Spanish Borderlands of North America: A Historiography," *Magazine of History* 14 (Summer 2000): 5–11.

3. For an overview of recent scholarly writings in English on New Spain, including the

Far North, see Eric Van Young, "Two Decades of Anglophone Writing on Colonial Mexico: Continuity and Change since 1980," *Mexican Studies/Estudios Mexicanos* 20 (Summer 2004): 275–326. The historical literature on the entire span of Mexican history, in both English and Spanish, is surveyed by Enrique Florescano, *Historia de las historias de la nación mexicana* (México: Taurus, 2002).

4. See Martin A. Favata and José B. Fernández, eds., *The Account: Álvar Núñez Cabeza de Vaca's "Relación"* (Houston, Tex.: Arte Público Press, 1993).

5. Weber, "Reflections on Coronado and the Myth of Quivira," in *Myth and the History of the Hispanic Southwest: Essays by David J. Weber* (Albuquerque: University of New Mexico Press, 1988), p. 4.

6. The Spaniards would continue to explore and settle Florida and other parts of the Southeast during the next few centuries, but this area is not crucial in explaining the roots of the Mexican American people. Consequently, these eastern Borderlands will be dealt with only when they have an impact on the northern frontier of New Spain. Those interested in the Southeast should consult the appropriate sections of Weber's *Spanish Frontier in North America*. Spain also used Mexico as a launching pad into the Pacific. For an overview of Pacific exploration, see Donald D. Brand, "Geographical Exploration by the Spaniards," in *European Entry into the Pacific: Spain and the Acapulco-Manila Galleons*, ed. Dennis O. Flynn, Arturo Giráldez, and James Sobredo (Aldershot, UK: Ashgate/Variorum Press, 2001), pp. 1–54.

7. The standard biography, a minor classic originally published in 1949, remains Herbert E. Bolton, *Coronado: Knight of Pueblos and Plains* (Albuquerque: University of New Mexico Press, 1964).

8. For a fine biography, see Marc Simmons, *The Last Conquistador: Juan de Oñate and the Settling of the Far Southwest* (Norman: University of Oklahoma Press, 1991).

9. For an excellent overview of the indigenous tribes of the Greater Southwest, see *Paths of Life: American Indians of the Southwest and Northern Mexico*, ed. Thomas E. Sheridan and Nancy J. Parezo (Tucson: University of Arizona Press, 1996).

10. The importance of the mission on the Spanish frontier was first established by the great Borderlands historian Herbert Eugene Bolton. See his 1917 essay "The Mission as a Frontier Institution in the Spanish-American Colonies," reprinted in a slightly abridged version in *New Spain's Far Northern Frontier: Essays on Spain in the American West, 1540–1821*, ed. David J. Weber (Albuquerque: University of New Mexico Press, 1979), pp. 51–65.

11. The Franciscans were founded by the Italian San Francesco d'Assisi, in 1209; the Dominicans by the Spaniard Santo Domingo (de Guzmán), in 1217; and the Jesuits by the Spanish Basque Ignacio de Loyola, in 1540.

12. David Weber focuses on the relationship between Spaniards and nomadic tribes in the eighteenth century, throughout the Americas, in *Bárbaros: Spaniards and Their Savages in the Age of Enlightenment* (New Haven, Conn.: Yale University Press, 2005).

13. For a concise description of this revolutionary episode, see Joe S. Sando, "The Pueblo Revolt," in *Handbook of North American Indians*, vol. 9: *Southwest*, ed. Alfonso Ortiz (Washington, D.C.: Smithsonian Institution, 1979), pp. 194–97. See, too, Roberto Mario Salmón, *Indian Revolts in Northern New Spain: A Synthesis of Resistance (1680–1786)* (Lanham, Md.: University Press of America, 1991); Andrew L. Knaut, *The Pueblo Revolt of 1680: Conquest and Resistance in Seventeenth-Century New Mexico* (Norman: University of Oklahoma Press, 1995).

14. De la Teja, "Forgotten Founders: The Military Settlers of Eighteenth-Century San Antonio de Béxar," in *Tejano Origins in Eighteenth-Century San Antonio*, ed. Gerald E. Poyo and Gilberto M. Hinojosa (Austin: University of Texas Press, 1991), p. 37.

15. *Handbook of Texas Online*, s.v. "Spanish Texas," http://www.tshaonline.org/handbook/online/articles/SS/nps1.html.

16. Robert C. West, *Sonora: Its Geographical Personality* (Austin: University of Texas Press, 1993), p. 43.

17. Jesuit efforts on the peninsula are traced in minute detail by Harry W. Crosby, *Antigua California: Mission and Colony on the Peninsular Frontier, 1697–1768* (Albuquerque: University of New Mexico Press, 1994).

18. Simmons, "Settlement Patterns and Village Plans in Colonial New Mexico," *Journal of the West* 8 (Jan. 1969): 19.

19. Hall, *Social Change in the Southwest, 1350–1880* (Lawrence: University Press of Kansas, 1989), p. 147.

20. Jackson and Castillo, *Indians, Franciscans, and Spanish Colonization: The Impact of the Mission System on California Indians* (Albuquerque: University of New Mexico Press, 1995), p. 44.

21. For a recent life of the famous explorer, see Donald T. Garate, *Juan Bautista de Anza: Basque Explorer in the New World* (Reno: University of Nevada Press, 2003).

22. Tjarks, "Comparative Demographic Analysis of Texas, 1777–1793," *Southwestern Historical Quarterly* 77 (Jan. 1974): 301.

23. Hurtado, *Indian Survival on the California Frontier* (New Haven, Conn.: Yale University Press, 1988), p. 22.

24. Bustamante, "'The Matter Was Never Resolved': The *Casta* System in Colonial New Mexico, 1693–1823," *New Mexico Historical Review* 66 (Apr. 1991): 145.

25. See, for example, Ramón A. Gutiérrez, *When Jesus Came, the Corn Mothers Went Away: Marriage, Sexuality, and Power in New Mexico, 1500–1846* (Stanford, Calif.: Stanford University Press, 1991).

26. Ríos-Bustamante, "New Mexico in the Eighteenth Century: Life, Labor and Trade in la Villa de San Felipe de Albuquerque, 1706–1790," *Aztlán* 7 (Fall 1976): 372–73.

27. Nostrand, "Hispano Cultural Distinctiveness: A Reply," *Annals of the Association of American Geographers* 74 (1984): 168 n3. For a relatively comprehensive list of Spanish families entering New Mexico during the colonial period, and their known origins, see José Antonio Esquibel, "The People of the Camino Real: A Genealogical Appendix," in the beautifully illustrated *The Royal Road: El Camino Real from Mexico City to Santa Fe* (Albuquerque: University of New Mexico Press, 1998), pp. 145–76.

28. Marc Simmons, "History of Pueblo-Spanish Relations to 1821," in *Handbook of North American Indians,* 9:192.

29. Swadesh, *Los Primeros Pobladores: Hispanic Americans on the Ute Frontier* (Notre Dame, Ind.: University of Notre Dame Press, 1974), p. 40.

30. Based on the 1790 census, and taking into account that many people of mixed blood were designated *españoles,* Antonio Ríos-Bustamante estimates that "anywhere from 70 to 80 percent of the population of Albuquerque were mestizo in fact, if not in convention by 1790." "New Mexico in the Eighteenth Century," p. 380.

31. Tijerina, *Tejanos and Texas under the Mexican Flag, 1821–1836* (College Station: Texas A&M University Press, 1994), pp. 7–8.

32. Pfefferkorn, *Sonora: A Description of the Province,* trans. Theodore E. Treutlein (Tucson: University of Arizona Press, 1989), p. 284.

33. Servín, "California's Spanish Heritage: A View into the Spanish Myth," *Journal of San Diego History* 19 (1973): 3.

34. Jack D. Forbes, "Hispano-Mexican Pioneers of the San Francisco Bay Region: An Analysis of Racial Origins," *Aztlán* 14 (Spring 1983): 178, and Antonio Ríos-Bustamante and Pedro Castillo, *An Illustrated History of Mexican Los Angeles, 1781–1985* (Los Angeles: Chicano Studies Research Center Publications, University of California, 1986), p. 33.

35. Castañeda, "Sexual Violence in the Politics and Policies of Conquest: Amerindian Women and the Spanish Conquest of Alta California," in *Building with Our Hands: New Di-*

rections in Chicana Studies, ed. Adela de la Torre and Beatríz M. Pesquera (Berkeley and Los Angeles: University of California Press, 1993), pp. 23, 29.

36. Hernández, "The Secret Jews of the Southwest," *Outlook* 63 (Fall 1992): 12. Mainstream Jewish scholars, defining Jewish identity much more strictly, generally scoff at these claims.

37. David J. Weber, *The Mexican Frontier, 1821–1846: The American Southwest under Mexico* (Albuquerque: University of New Mexico Press, 1982), pp. 278–79. See, too, Oakah L. Jones Jr., *Los Paisanos: Spanish Settlers on the Northern Frontier* (Norman: University of Oklahoma Press, 1979), p. 253.

3. THE MEXICAN FAR NORTH, 1821–1848

1. The best overview of this period remains David J. Weber, *The Mexican Frontier, 1821–1846: The American Southwest under Mexico* (Albuquerque: University of New Mexico Press, 1982), which contains the most comprehensive bibliography on the subject up to its publication.

2. See Palmer, *The Age of the Democratic Revolution: A Political History of Europe and America, 1760–1800,* 2 vols. (Princeton, N.J.: Princeton University Press, 1964).

3. David J. Weber, "American Westward Expansion and the Breakdown of Relations between *Pobladores* and '*Indios Bárbaros*' on Mexico's Far Northern Frontier, 1821–1846," in *Myth and the History of the Hispanic Southwest: Essays by David J. Weber* (Albuquerque: University of New Mexico Press, 1988), p. 121.

4. Anti-clericalism was especially pronounced among Mexican Liberals, according to the celebrated Latin Americanist Charles A. Hale, *Mexican Liberalism in the Age of Mora, 1821–1853* (New Haven, Conn.: Yale University Press, 1968).

5. Almaguer, "Interpreting Chicano History: The World-System Approach to Nineteenth-Century California," *Review* 4 (Winter 1981): 482.

6. For example, Bernardo Yorba, whose family owned the Rancho Santiago de Santa Ana, had twenty-two children, according to Lisabeth Haas, *Conquests and Historical Identities in California, 1769–1936* (Berkeley and Los Angeles: University of California Press, 1995), p. 49. The historian Douglas Monroy disagrees on the size of frontier families. He feels that fathers usually had three or four children, but immediately thereafter quotes Angustias de la Guerra Ord, who had a dozen siblings (and gave birth to another dozen). *Thrown among Strangers: The Making of Mexican Culture in Frontier California* (Berkeley and Los Angeles: University of California Press, 1990), p. 141.

7. "Women, like men, had the right to acquire property not only through grants but also through endowments, purchases, gifts, and inheritance." Chávez-García, *Negotiating Conquest: Gender and Power in California, 1770s to 1880s* (Tucson: University of Arizona Press, 2004), p. 54. While this privilege also extended to Indian women, in practice they "acquired little or no" property (ibid., p. 75). Cf. Michael J. González, who claims that the legal rights extended to women were more apparent than real. *This Small City Will Be a Mexican Paradise: Exploring the Origins of Mexican Culture in Los Angeles, 1821–1846* (Albuquerque: University of New Mexico Press, 2005), p. 169.

8. A generation ago David Weber noted the dearth of biographies of important Hispanic figures living in 1821–1848. Happily, this deficiency is beginning to be addressed. Two of the best full-scale biographies are devoted to members of the Hispanic elite: Alan Rosenus, *General M. G. Vallejo and the Advent of the Americans* (Albuquerque: University of New Mexico Press, 1995), and Robert Ryal Miller, *Juan Alvarado: Governor of California, 1836–1842* (Norman: University of Oklahoma Press, 1998).

9. Sherburne Cook, one of the leading authorities on early-nineteenth-century native Americans in California, disagrees. He feels that life improved for Indians after secularization because they gained greater freedom, an argument he develops in his 1943 essay "The

Indian versus the Spanish Mission," in Sherburne F. Cook, *The Conflict between the California Indian and Western Civilization* (Berkeley and Los Angeles: University of California Press, 1976), pp. 1–194.

10. For the treatment of native Americans by Hispano-Mexican and Anglo masters in the nineteenth century, see Monroy, *Thrown among Strangers,* and Albert L. Hurtado, *Indian Survival on the California Frontier* (New Haven, Conn.: Yale University Press, 1988). The diverse perceptions of the indigenous people by their Hispanic and Anglo conquerors at this time are the subject of James J. Rawls, *Indians of California: The Changing Image* (Norman: University of Oklahoma Press, 1984).

11. Weber, *Mexican Frontier,* p. 105.

12. Sandoval, "Montezuma's Merchants: Mexican Traders on the Santa Fe Trail," in *Adventure on the Santa Fe Trail,* ed. Leo E. Oliva (Topeka: Kansas State Historical Society, 1988), p. 43. Cf. Susan Calafate Boyle, *Los Capitalistas: Hispano Merchants on the Santa Fe Trail* (Albuquerque: University of New Mexico Press, 1997), who feels that "it is not possible to establish positively which ethnic group controlled the trade" (p. xiii).

13. See Daniel Tyler, "Gringo Views of Governor Manuel Armijo," *New Mexico Historical Review* 45 (Jan. 1970): 23–36.

14. Lecompte, "Manuel Armijo and the Americans," *Journal of the West* 19 (July 1980): 51–63.

15. In fact, according to some scholars, the status of New Mexican women was even more exalted than that of their counterparts in California. See Janet Lecompte, "The Independent Women of Hispanic New Mexico, 1821–1846," *Western Historical Quarterly* 12 (Jan. 1981): 17–35. For Anglo views of Hispanas during this period, see Deena J. González, "La Tules of Image and Reality: Euro-American Attitudes and Legend Formation on the Spanish-Mexican Frontier," in *Building with Our Hands: New Directions in Chicana Studies,* ed. Adela de la Torre and Beatríz M. Pesquera (Berkeley and Los Angeles: University of California Press, 1993), pp. 75–90. Regrettably, and despite its subtitle, there is virtually nothing on New Mexican society during this period in Ramón A. Gutiérrez, *When Jesus Came, the Corn Mothers Went Away: Marriage, Sexuality, and Power in New Mexico, 1500–1846* (Stanford, Calif.: Stanford University Press, 1991).

16. See González, *Refusing the Favor: The Spanish-Mexican Women of Santa Fe, 1820–1880* (New York: Oxford University Press, 1999). Relying heavily on archival records, both Miroslava Chávez-García and Deena González agree on the legal protections accorded Mexicanas in California and New Mexico, respectively. Both agree, too, that these protections eroded under U.S. rule. However, Chávez-García feels that women gained some new freedoms in compensation, while González sees the period of American hegemony as one of unmitigated disaster for Hispanas.

17. See James E. Officer and Henry F. Dobyns, "Teodoro Ramírez: Early Citizen of Tucson," *Journal of Arizona History* 25 (Autumn 1984): 221–44.

18. Tijerina, *Tejanos and Texas under the Mexican Flag, 1821–1836* (College Station: Texas A&M University Press, 1994), chap. 1.

19. Limerick, *The Legacy of Conquest: The Unbroken Past of the American West* (New York: W. W. Norton, 1988), p. 229.

20. De León, *They Called Them Greasers: Anglo Attitudes toward Mexicans in Texas, 1821–1900* (Austin: University of Texas Press, 1983), pp. 1–13. Raymund A. Paredes, on the other hand, feels that anti-Mexican sentiment among Texans before the War of Independence was largely based on Hispanophobia and anti-Catholicism. "The Origins of Anti-Mexican Sentiment in the United States," *New Scholar* 6 (1977): 158.

21. Juan Gómez-Quiñones, *Roots of Chicano Politics, 1600–1940* (Albuquerque: University of New Mexico Press, 1994), p. 134.

22. Craver, *The Impact of Intimacy: Mexican-Anglo Intermarriage in New Mexico, 1821–1846* (El Paso: Texas Western Press, 1982), p. 75.

23. For a good survey of foreign migration into California during the Mexican period,

see Doyce B. Nunis Jr., "Alta California's Trojan Horse: Foreign Immigration," *California History* 76 (Summer and Fall 1997): 299–330.

24. Fontana, *Entrada: The Legacy of Spain and Mexico in the United States* (Tucson: Southwest Parks and Monuments Association and the University of New Mexico Press, 1994), p. 217.

25. Hurtado, *John Sutter: A Life on the North American Frontier* (Norman: University of Oklahoma Press, 2006).

26. For Smith's two forays into California, see David J. Weber, *The Californios versus Jedediah Smith, 1826–1827: A New Cache of Documents* (Spokane, Wash.: Arthur H. Clark, 1990).

27. Trujillo, *Tejanos and Texas*, p. 133.

28. For a concise review of the pietistic interpretations of the Alamo U.S. historians have generally embraced, see David J. Weber, "Refighting the Alamo: Mythmaking and the Texas Revolution," in *Myth and the History of the Hispanic Southwest*, pp. 133–51. The ambivalent role played by Tejanos in the war, a subject usually neglected in mainstream histories, is the subject of Arnoldo De León, "Tejanos and the Texas War for Independence: Historiography's Judgment," *New Mexico Historical Review* 61 (Apr. 1986): 137–46.

29. Navarro and Seguín are two of the six individuals highlighted in my short monograph, *The Hispanic Elite of the Southwest* (El Paso: Texas Western Press, 1989).

30. See David Montejano, "Old Roads, New Horizons: Texas History and the New World Order," in *Mexican Americans in Texas History*, ed. Emilio Zamora, Cynthia Orozco, and Rodolfo Rocha (Austin: Texas State Historical Association, 2000), p. 25. The twenty-one biographies in Sammye Munson's *Our Tejano Heroes: Outstanding Mexican-Americans in Texas* (Austin: Panda Books, 1989) include that of Gregorio Esparza, who died defending the Alamo, as well as those of Juan Seguín and José Antonio Navarro.

31. The Treaty of Velasco is reproduced in *Between the Conquests: Readings in the Early Chicano Historical Experience*, ed. Michael R. Ornelas, 3rd ed. (Dubuque, Ia.: Kendall/Hunt, 2000), pp. 195–97.

32. Dennis N. Valdés, "The Spanish-Mexican Borderlands and Chicano History," *Latin American Research Review* 35, no. 1 (2000): 258.

33. Ibid., p. 257.

34. This view is shared by most Chicano historians. See, for example, Carlos E. Cortés, "Mexicans," in *Harvard Encyclopedia of American Ethnic Groups*, ed. Stephen Thernstrom (Cambridge, Mass.: Harvard University Press, 1980), p. 701.

35. Meyer and Sherman, *The Course of Mexican History* (New York: Oxford University Press, 1979), p. 345.

36. The war is the subject of the Emmy Award-winning PBS documentary, *The U.S. Mexican War (1846–1848)*. The four-hour series, a product of collaborative efforts by U.S. and Mexican historians, was produced by Paul Espinosa and directed by Ginny Martin (Dallas/Fort Worth: North Texas Public Broadcasting, 1998).

37. This is a major theme running through his highly speculative study, *This Small City*. Michael J. González, who teaches at the University of San Diego, should not be confused with Michael J. Gonzales, also a historian, who teaches at Northern Illinois University.

38. For a copy of the treaty, see *Major Problems in Mexican American History*, ed. Zaragosa Vargas (New York: Houghton Mifflin, 1999), pp. 136–40.

39. Gómez-Quiñones, *Roots of Chicano Politics*, p. 188.

40. Meyer and Sherman, *Course of Mexican History*, p. 334.

41. Happily, this historical judgment has been reversed by recent scholarship; at the end of the twentieth century even high school textbooks "recognize American responsibility for the war." Richard Griswold del Castillo, *The Treaty of Guadalupe Hidalgo: A Legacy of Conflict* (Norman: University of Oklahoma Press, 1990), p. 113.

42. Smith, *War with Mexico*, vol. 2 (Gloucester, Mass.: Peter Smith, 1919), p. 311.

43. Reséndez, *Changing National Identities at the Frontier: Texas and New Mexico, 1800–1850* (New York: Cambridge University Press, 2004), p. 5.

44. Whitman, *Brooklyn Daily Eagle*, 7 July, 1846, quoted in Reginald Horsman, *Race and Manifest Destiny: The Origins of American Racial Anglo-Saxonism* (Cambridge, Mass.: Harvard University Press, 1981), p. 235.

4. THE AMERICAN SOUTHWEST, 1848–1900

1. Judith Sweeney, "Chicana History: A Review of the Literature," in *Essays on La Mujer*, ed. Rosaura Sánchez and Rosa Martínez Cruz (Los Angeles: Chicano Studies Center Publications, University of California, Los Angeles, 1977), p. 103.

2. Campa, *Hispanic Culture in the Southwest* (Norman: University of Oklahoma Press, 1979), p. 184.

3. Almaguer, "Ideological Distortions in Recent Chicano Historiography: The Internal Model and Chicano Historical Interpretation," *Aztlán* 18 (Spring 1987): 15.

4. Gonzales-Day, *Lynching in the West, 1850–1935* (Durham, N.C.: Duke University Press, 2006).

5. See Arnoldo De León, "Texas Mexicans: Twentieth-Century Interpretations," in *Texas through Time: Evolving Interpretations*, ed. Walter L. Buenger and Robert A. Calvert (College Station: Texas A&M University Press, 1991), pp. 48–49.

6. Ríos-Bustamante, "The Barrioization of Nineteenth-Century Mexican Californians: From Landowners to Laborers," *Masterkey* 60 (Summer/Fall 1986): 32.

7. Camarillo, *Chicanos in a Changing Society: From Mexican Pueblos to American Barrios in Santa Barbara and Southern California, 1848–1930*, rev. ed. (Dallas: Southern Methodist University Press, 2005).

8. Rojas, *Joaquín Murrieta: "El Patrio"* (Mexicali, B.C.: Estado de Baja California, 1986).

9. The complex motives leading to accommodation among the elite are examined in Manuel G. Gonzales, *The Hispanic Elite of the Southwest* (El Paso: Texas Western Press, 1989).

10. Shinn, "Pioneer Spanish Families in California," *Century Magazine* 41 (Jan. 1891): 385.

11. Acuña, "The Making of *Occupied America*," in *Occupied America: A Chicano History Symposium*, ed. Tatcho Mindiola Jr. (Houston, Tex.: Mexican American Studies Program, University of Houston, 1982), p. 23.

12. Barrera, *Beyond Aztlan: Ethnic Autonomy in Comparative Perspective* (Notre Dame, Ind.: University of Notre Dame Press, 1988), p. 13.

13. Emilio Zamora, *The World of the Mexican Worker in Texas* (College Station: Texas A&M University Press, 1993), p. 93.

14. González, *The Spanish-Americans of New Mexico: A Heritage of Pride* (Albuquerque: University of New Mexico Press, 1967), p. 76.

15. Ibid., p. 28.

16. Guillermo Lux and Maurilio E. Vigil, "Return to Aztlán: The Chicano Rediscovers His Indian Past," in *The Chicanos: As We See Ourselves*, ed. Arnulfo D. Trejo (Tucson: University of Arizona Press, 1979), p. 3.

17. Swadesh, *Los Primeros Pobladores: Hispanic Americans of the Ute Frontier* (Notre Dame, Ind.: University of Notre Dame Press, 1974), p. 133.

18. Marc Simmons, *The Little Lion of the Southwest: A Life of Manuel Antonio Chaves* (Chicago: Swallow Press, 1973), p. 23.

19. Robert A. Roessel Jr., "Navajo History," in *Handbook of North American Indians*, vol. 10: *Southwest*, ed. Alfonso Ortiz (Washington, D.C.: Smithsonian Institution, 1983), p. 506.

20. Miller, "Cross-Cultural Marriages in the Southwest: The New Mexican Experience, 1846–1900," in *New Mexico Women: Intercultural Perspectives*, ed. Joan M. Jensen and Darlis A. Miller (Albuquerque: University of New Mexico Press, 1986), p. 100.

21. For a sympathetic biography, see Deena J. González, "La Tules of Image and Reality: Euro-American Attitudes and Legend Formation on a Spanish-Mexican Frontier," in *Building with Our Hands: New Directions in Chicana Studies*, ed. Adela de la Torre and Beatríz M. Pesquera (Berkeley and Los Angeles: University of California Press, 1993), pp. 75–90.

22. For biographical information, see Sandra L. Stephens, "The Women of the Amador Family, 1860–1940," in *New Mexico Women*, p. 258.

23. See Simmons, *Little Lion of the Southwest*.

24. See Nostrand, "The Hispano Homeland in 1900," *Annals of the Association of American Geographers* 70 (Sept. 1980): 382–96.

25. David J. Weber, *Foreigners in Their Native Land: Historical Roots of the Mexican Americans* (Albuquerque: University of New Mexico Press, 1973), p. 157.

26. The legal battles waged over the most famous of the two hundred New Mexican land grants, the 1.7-million-acre tract awarded to Lucien Maxwell in the 1840s, have been traced in minute detail by the historian María E. Montoya, *Translating Property: The Maxwell Land Grant and the Conflict over Land in the American West, 1840–1900*, rev. ed. (Lawrence: University Press of Kansas, 2005).

27. For an engaging study on the brotherhood, see Marta Weigle, *Brothers of Light, Brothers of Blood: The Penitentes of the Southwest* (Albuquerque: University of New Mexico Press, 1976).

28. Chávez, "The Penitentes of New Mexico," *New Mexico Historical Review* 29 (Apr. 1954): 94–123.

29. Simmons, *New Mexico: An Interpretive History* (Albuquerque: University of New Mexico Press, 1988), p. 164.

30. See, for example, De León, *Mexican Americans in Texas: A Brief History* (Arlington Heights, Ill.: Harlan Davidson, 1993).

31. David Montejano, *Anglos and Mexicans in the Making of Texas, 1836–1986* (Austin: University of Texas Press, 1987).

32. Gómez-Quiñones, *Roots of Chicano Politics, 1600–1940* (Albuquerque: University of New Mexico Press, 1994), p. 270.

33. For a Chicano perspective on this episode, see Mary Romero, "El Paso Salt War: Mob Action or Political Struggle?" *Aztlán* 16 (1985): 119–44.

34. Carlos Larralde and José Rodolfo Jacobo, *Juan N. Cortina and the Struggle for Justice in Texas* (Dubuque, Iowa: Kendall/Hunt Publishing, 2000), is a useful biography of the famous rebel, but a more complete portrait emerges in Jerry Thompson, *Cortina: Defending the Mexican Name in Texas* (College Station: Texas A&M University Press, 2007).

35. See Américo Paredes, *With His Pistol in His Hand* (Austin: University of Texas Press, 1958).

36. For a recent study, see Elliott Young, *Catarino Garza's Revolution on the Texas-Mexico Border* (Durham, N.C.: Duke University Press, 2004).

37. Mills, *Forty Years at El Paso, 1858–1898*, ed. Rex Strickland (El Paso, Tex.: Carl Hertzog, 1962), pp. 22–23.

38. McWilliams, *North from Mexico: The Spanish-Speaking People of the United States* (New York: Greenwood Press, 1968), chap. 2.

5. THE GREAT MIGRATION, 1900–1930

1. The best work on the Great Migration is Mark Reisler's deeply researched and comprehensive *By the Sweat of Their Brow: Mexican Immigrant Labor in the United States, 1900–1940* (Westport, Conn.: Greenwood Press, 1976).

2. Marilyn P. Davis, *Mexican Voices/Mexican Dreams: An Oral History of Mexican Immigration to the United States* (New York: Henry Holt, 1990), p. 4.

3. The difficulties in establishing an accurate demographic record of Mexicans in the United States are examined in Reisler, *Sweat of Their Brow,* pp. 265–73.

4. McWilliams, *The Mexicans in America* (New York: Teachers College Press, 1968), pp. 8–15.

5. See Sánchez, *Becoming Mexican American: Ethnicity, Culture, and Identity in Chicano Los Angeles, 1900–1945* (New York: Oxford University Press, 1993), chap. 1.

6. Gonzales, *The Mexican Revolution, 1910–1940* (Albuquerque: University of New Mexico Press, 2002), p. 2.

7. For a copy of *El Plan de San Diego,* see *Testimonio: A Documentary History of the Mexican American Struggle for Civil Rights,* ed. F. Arturo Rosales (Houston, Tex.: Arte Público Press, 2000), pp. 63–65.

8. See James A. Sandos, *Rebellion in the Borderlands: Anarchism and the Plan of San Diego, 1904–1923* (Norman: University of Oklahoma Press, 1992).

9. Ruiz, *Triumphs and Tragedy: A History of the Mexican People* (New York: W. W. Norton, 1992), p. 311.

10. A modest estimate, according to Michael C. Meyer and William L. Sherman, *The Course of Mexican History* (New York: Oxford University Press, 1979), p. 552.

11. For life in a typical peasant community, see the classic study of a village in Michoacán by one of Mexico's greatest historians, Luis González, *San José de Gracia: Mexican Village in Transition,* trans. John Upton (Austin: University of Texas Press, 1974).

12. Richard Griswold del Castillo and Arnoldo De León, *North to Aztlán: A History of Mexican Americans in the United States* (New York: Twayne Publishers, 1996), p. 23, see a significant rise of Mexican immigration after 1880; consequently, they believe there is a good deal of continuity in Mexican American history between the nineteenth and the twentieth centuries. This point of view is challenged by scholars who believe that an entirely new phase of that history is initiated at about 1900 with the beginning of mass immigration. See Gilbert G. González and Raúl Fernández, "Chicano History: Transcending Cultural Models," *Pacific Historical Review* 63 (Nov. 1994): 488–89.

13. Cardoso, *Mexican Emigration to the United States, 1897–1931* (Tucson: University of Arizona Press, 1980), p. 34.

14. De León, *Mexican Americans in Texas: A Brief History* (Arlington Heights, Ill.: Harlan Davidson, 1993), p. 71.

15. Chávez, *The Lost Land: The Chicano Image of the Southwest* (Albuquerque: University of New Mexico Press, 1984), p. 1.

16. See, for example, Roberto R. Álvarez Jr., *Familia: Migration and Adaptation in Baja and Alta California, 1800–1975* (Berkeley and Los Angeles: University of California Press, 1987).

17. Gordon, *The Great Arizona Orphan Abduction* (Cambridge, Mass.: Harvard University Press, 1999), p. 51.

18. McWilliams, *North from Mexico: The Spanish-Speaking People of the United States* (New York: Greenwood Press, 1968), p. 186. For the life of Mexicanos living in southwestern mining communities during this period, see Gordon, *Great Arizona Orphan Abduction,* which focuses on Clifton and Morenci—both predominantly Mexican towns—shortly after the

turn of the century, and Christine Marín, "Always a Struggle: Mexican Americans in Miami, Arizona, 1909–1951" (Ph.D. diss., Arizona State University, 2005).

19. For the significance of this landmark legislation, see Marc Reisner, *Cadillac Desert: The American West and Its Disappearing Water,* rev. ed. (New York: Penguin Books, 1993), p. 111.

20. See Neil F. Foley, "Chicanos and the Culture of Cotton in Central Texas, 1880–1900: Reshaping Class Relations in the South," in *Community Empowerment and Chicano Scholarship,* ed. Mary Romero and Cordelia Candelaria (Los Angeles: National Association for Chicano Studies, 1992), p. 112.

21. In constructing this composite biography, I have relied heavily on oral interviews found in *The Life Story of the Mexican Immigrant: Autobiographic Documents Collected by Manuel Gamio,* comp. Manuel Gamio (1931; reprint, New York: Dover Publications, 1971).

22. Manuel Gamio attempted to ascertain the home state of Mexican immigrants in the United States in the summer of 1926 by tabulating the destination of their money orders. The top three states, in rank order, were Michoacán (20 percent), Guanajuato (19.6 percent), and Jalisco (14.7 percent). "Sources of Mexican Immigrants and the Distribution of Immigrants in the United States," in *Mexican Immigration to the United States* (Chicago: University of Chicago Press, 1930), p. 13.

23. For this unique society, see Chad Richardson, *Batos, Bolillos, and Pelados: Class and Culture on the South Texas Border* (Austin: University of Texas Press, 1999), and Daniel D. Arreola, *Tejano South Texas: A Mexican American Cultural Province* (Austin: University of Texas Press, 2002), works which supersede the much older, though still useful, William Madsen, *Mexican-Americans of South Texas* (New York: Holt, Rinehart and Winston, 1964).

24. Colonel J. G. Boswell and his nephew, J. G. Boswell II, are the focus of an excellent family biography by Mark Arax and Rick Wartzman, *The King of California: J. G. Boswell and the Making of a Secret American Empire* (New York: Public Affairs, 2003).

25. Representative works include Frances Esquibel Tywoniak and Mario T. García, *Migrant Daughter: Coming of Age as a Mexican American Woman* (Berkeley and Los Angeles: University of California Press, 2000), and Rose Castillo Guilbault, *Farmworker's Daughter: Growing Up Mexican in America* (Berkeley: Heyday Books, 2005). A series of intimate interviews of campesinos and their families is the basis for an informative study by Ann Aurelia López, *The Farmworkers' Journey* (Berkeley and Los Angeles: University of California Press, 2007).

26. For the role of Mexicanas in the Revolution—and other wars in Mexican history—see Elizabeth Salas, *Soldaderas in the Mexican Military: Myth and History* (Austin: University of Texas Press, 1990).

27. Anthony Quinn, *The Original Sin: A Self-Portrait* (Boston: Little, Brown, 1972), p. 55.

28. See, for example, Sánchez, *Becoming Mexican American,* and F. Arturo Rosales, "Mexican Immigrant Nationalism as an Origin of Identity for Mexican Americans: Exploring the Sources," in *Mexican American Identity,* ed. Marta E. Bernal and Phylis C. Martinelli (Encino, Calif.: Floricanto Press, 1993), pp. 43–45.

29. González, "Labor and Community: The Camps of Mexican Citrus Pickers in Southern California," *Western Historical Quarterly* 22 (Aug. 1991): 298. Professor González explores this topic more systematically in *Labor and Community: Mexican Citrus Worker Villages in a Southern California County, 1900–1950* (Urbana: University of Illinois Press, 1994).

30. Weber, *Dark Sweat, White Gold: California Farm Workers, Cotton, and the New Deal* (Berkeley and Los Angeles: University of California Press, 1994), pp. 9, 53.

31. Leonard, *Making Ethnic Choices: California's Punjabi Mexican Americans* (Philadelphia: Temple University Press, 1992), p. 71.

32. The Colorado sugar beet industry, and the hand-to-mouth existence it generated among Mexicano families, with a focus on women, is described by Mary Romero and Eric Margolis, "Tending the Beets: Campesinas and the Great Western Sugar Company," *Revista*

Mujeres 2 (June 1985): 17–27. See, too, José Aguayo, "Los Betabeleros (The Beetworkers)," in *La Gente: Hispano History and Life in Colorado,* ed. Vincent C. De Baca (Denver: Colorado Historical Society, 1998), pp. 105–19.

33. The best two studies on the Mexicano presence in the Midwest are Juan R. García, *Mexicans in the Midwest, 1900–1932* (Tucson: University of Arizona Press, 1996), and Dionicio Nodín Valdés, *Barrios Norteños: St. Paul and Midwestern Mexican Communities in the Twentieth Century* (Austin: University of Texas Press, 2000).

34. Vargas, *Proletarians of the North: A History of Mexican Industrial Workers in Detroit and the Midwest, 1917–1933* (Berkeley and Los Angeles: University of California Press, 1993), pp. 23–24.

35. García, *Mexicans in the Midwest,* p. 89.

36. See Bodnar, *The Transplanted: A History of Immigrants in Urban America* (Bloomington: Indiana University Press, 1985).

37. Nugent, *Crossings: The Great Transatlantic Migrations, 1870–1914* (Bloomington: Indiana University Press, 1992), p. 35.

38. Zamora, *The World of the Mexican Worker in Texas* (College Station: Texas A&M University Press, 1993), pp. 15–17.

39. Apparently, a low degree of social mobility was characteristic of urbanized Mexicans, as well. "Among first-, second-, and third-generation semiskilled and unskilled male Mexican laborers in Los Angeles, not a single individual moved upward to a white-collar position during the ten years between 1918 and 1928," according to Ricardo Romo, *East Los Angeles: History of a Barrio* (Austin: University of Texas Press, 1983), p. 122.

40. Galarza, "Mexicans in the Southwest: A Culture in Process," in *Plural Society in the Southwest,* ed. Edward H. Spicer and Raymond H. Thompson (New York: Weatherhead Foundation, 1972), p. 283.

41. As Peter Skerry has observed in *Mexican Americans: The Ambivalent Minority* (New York: Free Press, 1993), Mexicanos in the United States seem unsure about their racial identity. However, this confusion is more apparent than real; though they recognize and for the most part take pride in their Indian heritage, Mexicanos at times identify themselves as white in an attempt to avoid discrimination. This trend was most evident among middle-class Hispanos and Tejanos between the 1920s and the 1950s. And, of course, there is a small minority within the Spanish-speaking community who *are* white.

42. Michael Omi and Howard Winant, *Racial Formation in the United States: From the 1960s to the 1980s* (New York: Routledge and Kegan Paul, 1986), p. 57.

43. See, for example, Juan Gómez-Quiñones, *Mexican American Labor, 1790–1990* (Albuquerque: University of New Mexico Press, 1994), p. 334.

44. This negative assessment is shared by the respected political scientist Jorge G. Castañeda in "Mexico and California: The Paradox of Tolerance and Dedemocratization," in *The California-Mexico Connection,* ed. Abraham F. Lowenthal and Katrina Burgess (Stanford, Calif.: Stanford University Press, 1993), p. 42. See, too, Alejandro Portes, "The Longest Migration," *New Republic,* 26 Apr. 1993, p. 40, who recognizes "the significant progress made by many U.S.-born Mexican-Americans" in the recent past but concludes with this sobering thought: "Their collective achievements get buried in figures skewed by the continuously arriving mass of poor immigrants."

45. Portes and Rumbaut, *Immigrant America: A Portrait* (Berkeley and Los Angeles: University of California Press, 1990), p. 238.

6. THE DEPRESSION, 1930–1940

1. Deutsch, *No Separate Refuge: Culture, Class, and Gender on an Anglo-Hispanic Frontier in the American Southwest, 1880–1940* (New York: Oxford University Press, 1987), chap. 7.

2. Monroy, *Rebirth: Mexican Los Angeles from the Great Migration to the Great Depression* (Berkeley and Los Angeles: University of California Press, 1999), pp. 117–18.

3. Starr, *The Dream Endures: California Enters the 1940s* (New York: Oxford University Press, 1997), pp. 172–73.

4. See Rosales, *¡Pobre Raza! Violence, Justice, and Mobilization among México Lindo Immigrants, 1900–1936* (Austin: University of Texas Press, 1999).

5. See, for example, Patricia Preciado Martin, *Songs My Mother Sang to Me: An Oral History of Mexican American Women* (Tucson: University of Arizona Press, 1992).

6. Focusing on the Orange County community of Santa Ana, Lisbeth Haas has a fascinating chapter on the role of theater and cinema in Mexicano working-class culture in southern California during the interwar period. See *Conquests and Historical Identities in California, 1769–1936* (Berkeley and Los Angeles: University of California Press, 1995), chap. 4.

7. Romo, *East Los Angeles: History of a Barrio* (Austin: University of Texas Press, 1983), p. 10. "The barrio is not a ghetto," concurs the historian Julián Nava. "It is a haven." Quoted in "Chicanos on the Move," *Newsweek,* 1 Jan. 1979, p. 24.

8. The Midwest, like all geographic regions in the United States, is difficult to define precisely, but for our purposes the area shall consist of the following states: the Dakotas, Illinois, Indiana, Iowa, Kansas, Michigan, Minnesota, Missouri, Nebraska, Ohio, and Wisconsin.

9. According to James A. Garza, Hispanos began to establish small settlements on the Canadian River during this period. "The Long History of Mexican Immigration to the Rural Midwest," *Journal of the West* 45 (Fall 2006): 57. But not everyone would agree that the lower Plains are part of the Midwest. And besides, these small settlements were quickly abandoned, as the author admits.

10. For a concise historiography of Mexicanos in the Midwest, see Dennis N. Valdés, "Region, Nation, and World System: Perspectives on Midwestern Chicana/o History," in *Voices of a New Chicana/o History,* ed. Refugio I. Rochín and Dennis N. Valdés (East Lansing: Michigan State University Press, 2000), pp. 115–40.

11. David A. Badillo, focusing on Detroit, is representative of this view: "Intermarriage with Anglo-Americans . . . blurred the formation of the kind of fixed caste lines that characterized discrimination against Mexicans in Texas. Discrimination undeniably occurred at various points, but the immigrant context of the Midwestern mosaic more readily muffled ethnic conflicts." *Latinos in Michigan* (East Lansing: Michigan State University Press, 2003), p. 14.

12. Valdés, "The New Northern Borderlands: An Overview of Midwestern Chicano History," in *Perspectives in Mexican American Studies,* vol. 2: *Mexicans in the Midwest,* ed. Juan R. García (Tucson, Ariz.: Mexican American Studies and Research Center, 1989), p. 2. In a more recent study, however, the author tends to stress the parallel experiences of Mexicanos in both regions. See Dionicio Nodín Valdés, *Barrios Norteños: St. Paul and Midwestern Mexican Communities in the Twentieth Century* (Austin: University of Texas Press, 2000).

13. Cohen, *Making a New Deal: Industrial Workers in Chicago, 1919–1939* (New York: Cambridge University Press, 1990), pp. 165–66.

14. Arredondo, *Mexican Chicago: Race, Identity, and Nation, 1916–39* (Urbana: University of Illinois Press, 2008).

15. Focusing on southern California, these dynamics are graphically described by William Deverell, *Whitewashed Adobe: The Rise of Los Angeles and the Remaking of Its Mexican Past* (Berkeley and Los Angeles: University of California Press, 2004). See, too, Nathan Daniel Gonzales, "'Visit Yesterday, Today': Ethno-Tourism and Southern California, 1884–1955" (Ph.D. diss., University of California, Riverside, 2006).

16. See, for example, Charles Ramírez-Berg, "Colonialism and Movies in Southern California, 1910–1934," *Aztlán* 28 (Spring 2003): 75–96. For an excellent overview of Latino stereotypes in the film industry, see the documentary *The Bronze Screen: 100 Years of*

the Latino Image in Hollywood, DVD, directed by Nancy De Los Santos (Chicago: Questar, 2002).

17. Quoted in Rodolfo Acuña, *Occupied America: The Chicano's Struggle for Liberation* (San Francisco: Canfield Press, 1972), p. 140.

18. Cardoso, *Mexican Emigration to the United States, 1897–1931* (Tucson: University of Arizona Press, 1980), p. 144.

19. Hoffman, *Unwanted Mexican-Americans in the Great Depression: Repatriation Pressures, 1929–1939* (Tucson: University of Arizona Press, 1974), pp. 174–75. Some Chicano historians have argued that as many as one million Mexicanos were repatriated during the 1930s. A recent study by a Mexican scholar using Mexican records, however, arrives at a more modest figure of about 425,500. Fernando Saúl Alanís Enciso, "¿Cuántos fueron? La repatriación de mexicanos en los Estados Unidos durante la Gran Depresión: Una interpretación," *Aztlán* 32 (Fall 2007): 86.

20. For the impact of repatriation on deported Mexicans, see Camille Guerin-Gonzales, *Mexican Workers and American Dreams: Immigration, Repatriation, and California Farm Labor, 1900–1939* (New Brunswick, N.J.: Rutgers University Press, 1994), and Francisco E. Balderrama and Raymond Rodríguez, *Decade of Betrayal: Mexican Repatriation in the 1930s,* rev. ed. (Albuquerque: University of New Mexico Press, 2006).

21. Neil Betten and Raymond A. Mohl, "From Discrimination to Repatriation: Mexican Life in Gary, Indiana, during the Great Depression," *Pacific Historical Review* 42 (Aug. 1973): 379.

22. Gregory, *American Exodus: The Dust Bowl Migration and Okie Culture in California* (New York: Oxford University Press, 1989), p. 17.

23. Haslem, *The Other California: The Great Central Valley in Life and Letters* (Reno: University of Nevada Press, 1994), p. 113.

24. Robert Kelley, *The Shaping of the American Past,* 4th ed. (Englewood Cliffs, N.J.: Prentice-Hall, 1986), p. 608.

25. For the history of labor activism by the Mexican-origin population in the United States, consult Juan Gómez-Quiñones, *Mexican American Labor, 1790–1990* (Albuquerque: University of New Mexico Press, 1994), and Rodolfo Acuña, *Corridors of Migration: The Odyssey of Mexican Laborers, 1600–1933* (Tucson: University of Arizona Press, 2007).

26. For labor agitation by Arizona's copper miners, see Andrea Yvette Huginnie, "'Strikitos': Race, Class, and Work in the Arizona Copper Industry, 1870–1920" (Ph.D. diss., Yale University, 1991). The story of Mexican copper miners in Arizona from 1903 to 1947, with a focus on Clifton-Morenci, is told in dramatic fashion—Luis Valdez does the narration—in the fine documentary *Los Mineros,* DVD, directed by Hector Galán (Scottsdale, Ariz.: Espinosa Productions, 1991).

27. Mellinger, "'The Men Have Become Organizers': Labor Conflict and Unionization in the Mexican Mining Communities of Arizona, 1900–1915," *Western Historical Quarterly* 23 (Aug. 1992): 323–47.

28. Charles Wollenberg, "Working on El Traque: The Pacific Electric Strike of 1903," *Pacific Historical Review* 42 (Aug. 1973): 361.

29. See Zamora, *The World of the Mexican Worker in Texas* (College Station: Texas A&M University Press, 1993).

30. Starr, *Endangered Dreams: The Great Depression in California* (New York: Oxford University Press, 1996), p. 66.

31. Ronald W. López, "The El Monte Berry Strike of 1933," *Aztlán* 1 (Spring 1970): 101–102.

32. Starr, *Endangered Dreams,* p. 80.

33. Weber, *Dark Sweat, White Gold: California Farm Workers, Cotton, and the New Deal* (Berkeley and Los Angeles: University of California Press, 1994), pp. 118–21.

34. See Balderrama, *In Defense of La Raza: The Los Angeles Mexican Consulate and the Mexican Community, 1929–1936* (Tucson: University of Arizona Press, 1982).

35. Dorothy Ray Healey and Maurice Isserman, *California Red: A Life in the American Communist Party* (Urbana: University of Illinois Press, 1993), p. 44.

36. Juan Gómez-Quiñones, *Roots of Chicano Politics, 1600–1940* (Albuquerque: University of New Mexico Press, 1994), p. 394, estimates that Communist Party membership "may have numbered approximately five hundred Mexicans."

37. See, for example, Yolanda Alaníz and Megan Cornish, *Viva la Raza: A History of Chicano Identity and Resistance* (Seattle, Wash.: Red Letter Press, 2008), a Marxist study of Mexican American working-class agitation.

38. García, *Desert Immigrants: The Mexicans of El Paso, 1880–1920* (New Haven, Conn.: Yale University Press, 1981), p. 235.

39. Reisler, *By the Sweat of Their Brow: Mexican Immigrant Labor in the United States, 1900–1940* (Westport, Conn.: Greenwood Press, 1976), p. 249.

40. See Vicki L. Ruiz, *From Out of the Shadows: Mexican Women in Twentieth-Century America* (New York: Oxford University Press, 1998), chap. 4. The book title is misleading since this sketchy study falls short of a comprehensive examination of Mexicanas, nor even of their activism, during the entire span of the twentieth century.

41. Martha Cotera, *Profile on the Mexican American Woman* (Austin: National Educational Laboratory Publishers, 1976), pp. 62–63.

42. Moreno's early career as a labor organizer is treated extensively in Carlos C. Larralde and Richard Griswold del Castillo, "Luisa Moreno: A Hispanic Civil Rights Leader in San Diego," *Journal of San Diego History* 41 (Fall 1995): 284–311.

43. Apparently John Wayne was not yet the vehement anti-Communist conservative he would later become. Interestingly, all three wives of the Hollywood icon were Latinas: Josephine Sáenz, a Panamanian; Esperanza ("Chata") Bauer-Díaz, a Mexicana; and Pilar Palette, a Peruvian.

44. García, *Mexican Americans: Leadership, Ideology, and Identity, 1930–1960* (New Haven, Conn.: Yale University Press, 1989), p. 165.

7. THE SECOND WORLD WAR AND ITS AFTERMATH, 1940–1965

1. The goal of the U.S. Latino and Latina World War II Oral History Project is to create an archive of primary source materials documenting Mexicano participation in the war. The project's website is www.lib.utexas.edu/ww2latinos.

2. The number of Hispanic Medal of Honor winners is much disputed. For example, only thirty-eight Hispanic Medal of Honor recipients are listed in "On the Front Lines," *Hispanic Magazine,* Aug. 1993, p. 39. Twenty-nine of these heroes were Mexicanos, according to José "Pepe" Villarino, "Mexican American Military War Heroes, Congressional Medal of Honor Winners," in *Aztlán: Chicano Culture and Folklore,* ed. José "Pepe" Villarino and Arturo Ramírez (New York: McGraw-Hill, 1998), pp. 71–77.

3. Quoted in Ronald Takaki, *A Different Mirror: A History of Multicultural America* (New York: Little, Brown, 1993), p. 393.

4. Morín, *Among the Valiant: Mexican-Americans in WWII and Korea* (Alhambra, Calif.: Borden Publishing, 1966), p. 256.

5. Marín, "La Asociación Hispano-Americana de Madres y Esposas: Tucson's Mexican American Women in World War II," *Renato Rosaldo Lecture Series Monograph* 1 (Summer 1985): 5–18, and Campbell, "Madres y Esposas: Tucson's Spanish-American Mothers and Wives Association," *Journal of Arizona History* 31 (Summer 1990): 161–82.

6. Not all scholars share this rosy assessment. The historian Dennis Valdés, for example, finds that most Mexicanos in the Midwest came out of the war with "limited occupational advancement and ongoing segregation," a thesis he advances in "The Mexican American

Dream and World War II: A View from the Midwest," in *Mexican Americans and World War II*, ed. Maggie Rivas-Rodríguez (Austin: University of Texas Press, 2005), p. 137.

7. Ruiz, *Triumphs and Tragedy: A History of the Mexican People* (New York: W. W. Norton, 1992), p. 285. The debilitation of the Mexican family at midcentury is well chronicled by the anthropologist Oscar Lewis in his classic study *Five Families* (New York: Basic Books, 1959).

8. Riding, *Distant Neighbors: A Portrait of the Mexicans* (New York: Vintage Books, 1989), pp. 7–8.

9. Álvarez, *Familia: Migration and Adaptation in Baja and Alta California, 1800–1975* (Berkeley and Los Angeles: University of California Press, 1987).

10. Ruiz, "'Star Struck': Acculturation, Adolescence, and the Mexican American Woman, 1920–1950," in *Building with Our Hands: New Directions in Chicana Studies,* ed. Adela de la Torre and Beatríz M. Pesquera (Berkeley and Los Angeles: University of California Press, 1993), p. 122.

11. Paz, *The Labyrinth of Solitude* (New York: Grove Press, 1961), p. 16. Cf. David Alfonso José Rojas, "The Making of Zoot Suiters in Early 1940s Los Angeles" (Ph.D. diss., University of California, Berkeley, 2001).

12. Servín, "The Post–World War II Mexican-Americans, 1925–65: A Nonachieving Minority," in *An Awakened Minority: The Mexican-Americans,* ed. Manuel P. Servín, 2nd ed. (Beverly Hills, Calif.: Glencoe Press, 1974), p. 173.

13. Sánchez, "Pachucos in the Making," in *Readings on La Raza: The Twentieth Century,* ed. Matt S. Meier and Feliciano Rivera (New York: Hill and Wang, 1974), pp. 122–26.

14. For an interesting study on these unsavory episodes, see Eduardo Obregón Pagán, *Murder at the Sleepy Lagoon: Zoot Suits, Race, and Riot in Wartime L.A.* (Chapel Hill: University of North Carolina Press, 2003).

15. Quoted in "Edward Durán Ayres Report," in *Readings on La Raza,* p. 131.

16. For this successful effort, see Frank P. Barajas, "The Defense Committees of Sleepy Lagoon: A Convergent Struggle against Fascism, 1942–1944," *Aztlán* 31 (Spring 2006): 33–62.

17. Braceros were also recruited to work on U.S. railroads during the war, a little known program that worked better than its agricultural counterpart, according to Barbara A. Driscoll's fine study, *The Tracks North: The Railroad Bracero Program of World War II* (Austin: Center for Mexican American Studies, University of Texas at Austin, 1999).

18. For a firsthand account of bracero life in the late fifties, see the testimony of Manuel Sánchez in Oscar Lewis, *The Children of Sánchez: Autobiography of a Mexican Family* (New York: Vintage Books, 1961), pp. 323–70. For the Bracero Program, see Ernesto Galarza, *Merchants of Labor: The Mexican Bracero Story* (Charlotte, N.C.: McNally and Loftin, 1964); Richard Craig, *The Bracero Program: Interest Groups and Foreign Policy* (Austin: University of Texas Press, 1971); and Kitty Calavita, *Inside the State: The Bracero Program, Illegal Immigrants and the INS* (London: Routledge, 1992). The Bracero Program also receives extensive coverage in Gilbert G. González, *Guest Workers or Colonized Labor? Mexican Labor Migration to the United States* (Boulder, Colo.: Paradigm Publishers, 2006).

19. González, *Guest Workers,* p. 2.

20. A U.S. citizen, I was employed in the Bracero Program in the early sixties; my main charge was to deliver these much-maligned sack lunches to the field hands. I was a farmworker, on and off, from the age of five to the age of twenty-six, when, as a newlywed, I was employed as a tractor driver hauling newly picked tomatoes out of the fields. My wife, the only white woman on an otherwise all-Mexicana crew, worked sorting the tomatoes, making for a memorable honeymoon.

21. Julián Samora and Patricia Vandel Simon, *A History of the Mexican-American People,* rev. ed. (Notre Dame, Ind.: University of Notre Dame Press, 1993), p. 140.

22. Valdés, "Machine Politics in California Agriculture, 1945–1990s," *Pacific Historical Review* 63 (May 1994): 223.

23. A point emphasized by Matt García, *A World of Its Own: Race, Labor, and Citrus in the Making of Greater Los Angeles, 1900–1970* (Chapel Hill: University of North Carolina Press, 2001), p. 13.

24. García y Griego, "The Importation of Mexican Contract Laborers to the United States, 1942–1964," in *Between Two Worlds: Mexican Immigrants in the United States,* ed. David G. Gutiérrez (Wilmington, Del.: Scholarly Resources, 1996), p. 71.

25. Meyer and Sherman, *The Course of Mexican History* (New York: Oxford University Press, 1979), p. 647.

26. Samora, *Los Mojados: The Wetback Story* (Notre Dame, Ind.: University of Notre Dame Press, 1971), p. 9.

27. For the most comprehensive study, see Juan Ramón García, *Operation Wetback: The Mass Deportation of Mexican Undocumented Workers in 1954* (Westport, Conn.: Greenwood Press, 1980).

28. García, *Mexican Americans: Leadership, Ideology, and Identity, 1930–1960* (New Haven, Conn.: Yale University Press, 1989), p. 43.

29. Briegel, "Alianza Hispano-Americana and Some Mexican-American Civil Rights Cases in the 1950s," in *An Awakened Minority,* p. 178.

30. Tirado, "Mexican American Community Political Organization, 'The Key to Chicano Political Power,'" *Aztlán* 1 (Spring 1970): 56.

31. García, *Mexican Americans,* pp. 25, 29.

32. A major shortcoming of Chicano scholarship is in the area of biography. Although Cynthia E. Orozco provides mini-biographies of all three in *The Handbook of Texas,* none of these important leaders has been treated in a comprehensive study. Interestingly, it is a much less influential member of LULAC, a Tejano who led the national association in the late1950s, who has been the subject of a major biography: Thomas H. Kreneck, *Mexican American Odyssey: Felix Tijerina, Entrepreneur and Civic Leader, 1905–1965* (College Station: Texas A&M University Press, 2001).

33. For a scholarly study of the association, see Benjamin Márquez, *LULAC: The Evolution of a Mexican American Political Organization* (Austin: University of Texas Press, 1993).

34. González, *Chicano Education in the Era of Segregation* (Philadelphia: Balch Institute Press, 1990), p. 149.

35. For the active role played by mujeres in Mexican American associations, see Cynthia E. Orozco, "Beyond Machismo, La Familia, and Ladies Auxiliaries: A Historiography of Mexican-Origin Women's Participation in Voluntary Associations and Politics in the United States, 1870–1990," in *Perspectives in Mexican American Studies,* vol. 5: *Mexican American Women: Changing Images,* ed. Juan R. García (Tucson, Ariz.: Mexican American Studies and Research Center, 1995), pp. 1–34.

36. For a well-researched study, see Carl Allsup, *The American GI Forum: Origins and Evolution* (Austin: Center for Mexican American Studies, University of Texas, 1982).

37. García, *Hector P. García: In Relentless Pursuit of Justice* (Houston, Tex.: Arte Público Press, 2002), p. xvii.

38. See Liliana Urrutia, "An Offspring of Discontent: The Asociación Nacional México-Americana, 1949–1954," *Aztlán* 15 (Spring 1984): 177–84.

39. Corona, *Memories of Chicano History: The Life and Narrative of Bert Corona,* ed. Mario T. García (Berkeley and Los Angeles: University of California Press, 1994), p. 189.

40. Juan Gómez-Quiñones, *Chicano Politics: Reality and Promise, 1940–1990* (Albuquerque: University of New Mexico Press, 1990), p. 88.

41. Servín, "The Post–World War II Mexican-Americans," p. 168.

42. Galarza has been called "the foremost Chicano activist scholar" by a person who is often described in this fashion himself: Rodolfo Acuña, *Occupied America: A History of*

Chicanos, 5th ed. (New York: Pearson/Longman, 2004), p. 473 n117. Galarza has left an important autobiography, *Barrio Boy* (Notre Dame, Ind.: University of Notre Dame Press, 1971).

43. Jovita González is now a subject of considerable interest. A good analysis of one aspect of her legacy is found in Leticia M. Garza-Falcón, *Gente Decente: A Borderlands Response to the Rhetoric of Dominance* (Austin: University of Texas Press, 1998), chap. 3: "The Historical Fiction of Jovita González: Complex and Competing Class Identities," pp. 74–132. See, too, "Appendix B: Biographical Outline of Jovita González's Life," ibid., pp. 258–61.

44. García, *Mexican Americans,* p. 232.

45. Almaráz, *Knight without Armor: Carlos Eduardo Castañeda, 1896–1958* (College Station: Texas A&M University Press, 1999), p. xiii.

46. Gómez-Quiñones, *Chicano Politics,* p. 85.

47. The growing conservatism of aging Chicana/o studies faculty is described by Ignacio M. García, who tends to be critical, in "Juncture in the Road: Chicano Studies Since 'El Plan de Santa Bárbara,'" in *Chicanas/Chicanos at the Crossroads,* ed. David R. Maciel and Isidro D. Ortiz (Tucson: University of Arizona Press, 1996), pp. 181–203.

8. THE CHICANO MOVEMENT, 1965–1975

1. For the etymology of the term *Chicano,* see Edward Simmen, "Chicano: Origin and Meaning," in *Pain and Promise: The Chicano Today,* ed. Edward Simmen (New York: Mentor, 1972), pp. 53–56.

2. Salazar, *Los Angeles Times,* 6 Feb. 1970.

3. Moore, *Mexican Americans* (Englewood Cliffs, N.J.: Prentice-Hall, 1970), p. 67.

4. Leo Grebler, Joan W. Moore, and Ralph C. Guzmán, *The Mexican-American People* (New York: Free Press, 1970), p. 19.

5. Gómez-Quiñones, *Chicano Politics: Reality and Promise, 1940–1990* (Albuquerque: University of New Mexico Press, 1990), p. 99.

6. "The importance of César Chávez in creating the faction that became known as the Chicano Movement cannot be overestimated," according to Rodolfo Acuña, *Occupied America: A History of Chicanos,* 5th ed. (New York: Pearson/Longman, 2004), p. 312. There are a score of Chávez biographies, virtually all of them sympathetic. Though dated in many respects, the most objective biography remains John Gregory Dunne, *Delano,* rev. ed. (New York: Farrar, Straus and Giroux, 1971); the most widely used in Chicana/o studies, Richard Griswold del Castillo and Richard A. García, *César Chávez: A Triumph of Spirit* (Norman: University of Oklahoma Press, 1995).

7. García, "Dolores Huerta: Woman, Organizer, and Symbol," *California History* 72 (Spring 1993): 70.

8. Ibid., p. 65.

9. For a solid study of FLOC, see W. K. Barger and Ernesto M. Reza, *The Farm Labor Movement in the Midwest: Social Change and Adaptation among Migrant Farmworkers* (Austin: University of Texas Press, 1994).

10. For the left-wing criticism of Chávez, from a socialist perspective, see Yolanda Alaníz and Megan Cornish, *Viva la Raza: A History of Chicano Identity and Resistance* (Seattle, Wash.: Red Letter Press, 2008), pp. 157–80.

11. "Most researchers credit the birth of the Chicano Movement to the activities of Reies López Tijerina," according to Lisa Magaña, *Mexican Americans and the Politics of Diversity: ¡Querer es poder!* (Tucson: University of Arizona Press, 2005), p. 24. For Tijerina, see his autobiography, *They Called Me "King Tiger": My Struggle for the Land and Our Rights,* trans. José Angel Gutiérrez (Houston, Tex.: Arte Público Press, 2000). See, too, Rudy V. Busto, *King Tiger: The Religious Vision of Reies López Tijerina* (Albuquerque: University of New Mexico

Press, 2006). For a recent re-examination of the fiery crusader, see Lorena Oropeza, "The Heart of Chicano History: Reies López Tijerina as a Memory Entrepreneur," *The Sixties: A Journal of History, Politics and Culture* 1 (June 2008): 49–67.

12. Clark S. Knowlton, "Tijerina, Hero of the Militants," in *An Awakened Minority: The Mexican-Americans,* ed. Manuel P. Servín, 2nd ed. (Beverly Hills, Calif.: Glencoe Press, 1974), p. 198.

13. González, "Alianza Federal de Mercedes," in *The Mexican-Americans: An Awakening Minority,* ed. Manuel P. Servín (Beverly Hills, Calif.: Glencoe Press, 1970), p. 202.

14. For an older but still useful biography, see Christine Marín, "Rodolfo 'Corky' Gonzales: The Mexican-American Movement Spokesman, 1962–1972," *Journal of the West* 14 (Oct. 1975): 107–20.

15. Steiner, *La Raza: The Mexican Americans* (New York: Harper and Row, 1969), p. 382.

16. See the *Plan Espiritual* in *Aztlán: Essays on the Chicano Homeland,* ed. Rudolfo A. Anaya and Francisco Lomelí (Albuquerque: University of New Mexico Press, 1989), pp. 1–5.

17. Carlos Muñoz Jr., *Youth, Identity, Power: The Chicano Movement* (London: Verso, 1989), p. 56.

18. Pycior, "From Hope to Frustration: Mexican Americans and Lyndon Johnson in 1967," *Western Historical Quarterly* 24 (Nov. 1993): 468–94.

19. For this key association, see Armando Navarro, *Mexican American Youth Organization: Avant-Garde of the Chicano Movement in Texas* (Austin: University of Texas Press, 1995).

20. For a participant-history of LRUP, see Ignacio M. García, *United We Win: The Rise and Fall of the Raza Unida Party* (Tucson: Mexican American Studies and Resource Center, University of Arizona, 1989).

21. Muñoz, *Youth, Identity, Power,* p. 21.

22. George Mariscal correctly sees the Cuban Revolution as a seminal influence on Chicanos. See *Brown-Eyed Children of the Sun: Lessons from the Chicano Movement* (Albuquerque: University of New Mexico Press, 2005), chap. 3. Curiously, however, while pages and pages are devoted to Che Guevara, Mariscal barely mentions Fidel, who was, after all, *the* dominant figure of the revolution—and one of the greatest leaders of the twentieth century.

23. For the *Plan de Santa Bárbara,* see *Introduction to Chicano Studies,* ed. Livie Isauro Durán and H. Russell Bernard (New York: Macmillan, 1973), pp. 535–45.

24. Gómez-Quiñones, *Chicano Politics,* pp. 119–20.

25. Oropeza, *¡Raza Sí ¡Guerra No! Chicano Protest and Patriotism during the Viet Nam War Era* (Berkeley and Los Angeles: University of California Press, 2005).

26. Charley Trujillo, ed., *Soldados: Chicanos in Viet Nam* (San Jose, Calif.: Chusma House Publications, 1990). See, too, the moving documentary of the same name, VHS, directed by Charley Trujillo and Sonya Rhee (San Jose, Calif.: Chusma House Documentary, 2003). Lea Ybarra has compiled a more recent, and comprehensive, set of war narratives, *Vietnam Veteranos: Chicanos Recall the War* (Austin: University of Texas Press, 2004). See, too, George Mariscal's fascinating anthology of Chicano writings on the war, including veterans' narratives, *Aztlán and Viet Nam: Chicano and Chicana Experiences of the War* (Berkeley and Los Angeles: University of California Press, 1999).

27. Edward James Olmos, Lea Ybarra, and Manuel Monterrey, *Americanos: Latino Life in the United States/La Vida Latina en los Estados Unidos* (Boston: Little, Brown, 1999), p. 79.

28. Treviso, "Hispanics and the Vietnam War," in *Vietnam Reconsidered: Lessons from a War,* ed. Harrison E. Salisbury (New York: Harper and Row, 1984), p. 184.

29. Aguirre and Aguirre, "Fact Sheet: Latinos and the Vietnam War," 7 Nov. 2000, http://www.latinoadvocates.org/filteredwebapge.htm. There are many problems with this approach. The most obvious is that many Latinos do not have Spanish surnames. The sociologist Lea Ybarra, who had eighteen cousins, as well as her only brother, serving in Vietnam, claims

that more than ten thousand Hispanics died in the war. *Fresno Bee,* 24 Dec. 1989. For a complete list of the names inscribed on the wall, see *Vietnam Veterans Memorial: Directory of Names* (Washington, D.C.: Vietnam Veterans Memorial Fund, 1994).

30. The Moratorium Committee and these marches, set in the context of a broad cultural and national perspective, are the subjects of Lorena Oropeza's thoroughly researched study, *¡Raza Sí! ¡Guerra No!*

31. For Salazar's life and work, see *Border Correspondent: Selected Writings, 1955–1970,* ed. Mario T. García (Berkeley and Los Angeles: University of California Press, 1996).

32. L. H. Gann and Peter J. Duignan, *The Hispanics in the United States: A History* (Boulder, Colo.: Westview Press, 1986), p. 301. Both authors were fellows at the Hoover Institution, the ultraconservative think tank at Stanford University.

33. Gómez-Quiñones, *Chicano Politics,* p. 150.

34. Acuña, *Occupied America,* 5th ed., p. 353.

35. For its origins, see Pete Tijerina, "The Birth of MALDEF," *La Prensa* (San Antonio), 29 Nov. 1998.

36. Vigil, "MALDEF: Chicano Advocate for Educational, Economic and Political Reform," in *Community Empowerment and Chicano Scholarship,* ed. Mary Romero and Cordelia Candelaria (Los Angeles: National Association for Chicano Studies, 1992), p. 231.

37. For a sympathetic biography by a protégé, see Juan A. Sepúlveda Jr., *The Life and Times of Willie Velásquez: Su Voto es Su Voz* (Houston, Tex.: Arte Público Press, 2003).

38. García, "Chicano Studies Since 'El Plan de Santa Bárbara,'" in *Chicanas/Chicanos at the Crossroads,* ed. David R. Maciel and Isidro D. Ortiz (Tucson: University of Arizona Press, 1996), p. 189.

39. "Mexican society," observes Carlos Fuentes, "is founded on very chauvinistic principles inherited from the Aztecs, the Spaniards, and the Arabs. We have a triple misogynistic inheritance that is very hard to overcome." Quoted by Anne-Marie O'Connor, "The Sum of Unequal Parts," *Los Angeles Times,* 24 Oct. 1997.

40. Given the homophobia typical of Mexican American culture, it was not long before a small number of Chicanos and Chicanas began to focus on the issue of sexual orientation, as well. For the lesbian-gay contribution to the movimiento, a subject almost completely neglected before, see the pioneering work of Alaníz and Cornish, *Viva la Raza,* pp. 272–79.

41. Nieto-Gómez, "La Femenista," *Encuentro Femenil* 1 (1974): 34–47. For Nieto-Gómez and the first Chicana feminists, see Naomi Helena Quiñones, "Hijas de la Malinche (Malinche's Daughters): The Development of Social Agency among Mexican American Women and the Emergence of First Wave Chicana Cultural Production" (Ph.D. diss., Claremont Graduate School, 1997).

42. Mirandé and Enríquez, *La Chicana: The Mexican-American Woman* (Chicago: University of Chicago Press, 1979), p. 239. For feminist difficulties in forging interethnic alliances, see Benita Roth, "On Their Own and For Their Own: African-American, Chicana, and White Feminist Movements in the 1960s and 1970s" (Ph.D. diss., University of California, Los Angeles, 1998).

43. Gómez-Quiñones, *Chicano Politics,* p. 140.

44. Rudolph O. de la Garza, "The Politics of Mexican Americans," in *The Chicanos: As We See Ourselves,* ed. Arnulfo D. Trejo (Tucson: University of Arizona Press, 1979), p. 119.

45. Earl Shorris, *Latinos: A Biography of the People* (New York: W. W. Norton, 1992), p. 100.

46. See, for example, Ernesto Chávez, *"¡Mi Raza Primero!" (My People First!): Nationalism, Identity, and Insurgency in the Chicano Movement in Los Angeles, 1966–1978* (Berkeley and Los Angeles: University of California Press, 2002), and Stephen J. Pitti, *The Devil in Silicon Valley: Northern California, Race, and Mexican Americans* (Princeton, N.J.: Princeton University Press, 2003). Even Lorena Oropeza, who is generally supportive, refuses to turn a blind eye to the movement's failures: "At its worst, Chicano cultural nationalism harbored racist and

destructive tendencies," she cautions, ¡Raza Sí! ¡Guerra No!, p. 191. Sexual exploitation, she adds, was one of these destructive tendencies.

47. Gutiérrez then drives the nail in the coffin by concluding: "even at its peak, the rhetoric of militant Chicanismo, and even self-identification as 'Chicano,' appealed only to a fraction of the ethnic Mexican population." "Globalization, Labor Migration, and the Demographic Revolution: Ethnic Mexicans in the Late Twentieth Century," in The Columbia History of Latinos in the United States Since 1960, ed. David G. Gutiérrez (New York: Columbia University Press, 2004), p. 59.

48. The political impact of Chicanismo is explored in John A. García, "The Chicano Movement: Its Legacy for Politics and Policy," in Chicanas/Chicanos at the Crossroads, pp. 83–107.

49. Hayes-Bautista and Rodríguez, "The Chicano Movement: More Nostalgia than Reality," Los Angeles Times, 17 Sept. 1995.

50. See Navarro, Mexican American Youth Organization.

51. See Muñoz, Youth, Identity, Power.

52. Ibid., p. 7.

53. García, Chicanismo: The Forging of a Militant Ethos among Mexican Americans (Tucson: University of Arizona Press, 1997), p. 134. See, too, Marguerite V. Marín, Social Protest in an Urban Barrio: A Study of the Chicano Movement, 1966–1974 (Lanham, Md.: University Press of America, 1991), and Guadalupe San Miguel Jr., "Actors Not Victims: Chicanas/os and the Struggle for Educational Equality," in Chicanas/Chicanos at the Crossroads, p. 159. San Miguel again stresses the leadership role of non-student adults in the movement in Brown, Not White: School Integration and the Chicano Movement in Houston (College Station: Texas A&M University Press, 2001), as do Jorge Iber, Hispanics in the Mormon Zion, 1912–1999 (College Station: Texas A&M University Press, 2000), p. 104, and Lydia R. Otero, "La Placita Committee: Claiming Place and History," in Memories and Migrations: Mapping Boricua and Chicana Histories, ed. Vicki L. Ruiz and John R. Chávez (Urbana: University of Illinois Press, 2008), p. 61.

9. GOODBYE TO AZTLÁN, 1975–1994

1. The figures relating to the 1990 census in this chapter are taken from Statistical Record of Hispanic Americans, ed. Marlita A. Reddy (Detroit: Gale Research Inc., 1993).

2. Most Spanish-speakers prefer Latinos to Hispanics, although both terms are equally imprecise, according to Mexican-born writer Ilan Stavans, The Hispanic Condition: Reflections on Culture and Identity in America (New York: Harper Perennial, 1996), p. 26.

3. Quoted by Patrick J. McDonnell, "Immigrants Not Lured by Aid, Study Says," Los Angeles Times, 29 Jan. 1997.

4. Handelman, Mexican Politics: The Dynamics of Change (New York: St. Martin's Press, 1997), p. 176.

5. Portes and Rumbaut, Immigrant America: A Portrait (Berkeley and Los Angeles: University of California Press, 1990), p. 11.

6. Shorris, Latinos: A Biography of the People (New York: W. W. Norton, 1992), p. 164.

7. Hondagneu-Sotelo, Gendered Transitions: Mexican Experiences of Immigration (Berkeley and Los Angeles: University of California Press, 1994), pp. 31, 187.

8. Wall Street Journal, 29 Apr. 1997.

9. The life of Yamileth López, a Nicaraguan woman, illustrates the troubles and tribulations experienced by undocumented workers from Central America in crossing Mexico and escaping detection in the United States. See Undocumented in L.A.: An Immigrant's Story, ed. Dianne Walta Hart (Wilmington, Del.: SR Books, 1997).

10. See, for example, Portes and Rumbaut, Immigrant America, p. 231.

11. See Rouse, "Mexican Migration and the Social Space of Postmodernism," *Diaspora* 1 (Spring 1991): 8–23.

12. Navarrette, "Ethnic Envidia: When Achievement Means Selling Out," *Los Angeles Times*, 30 Aug. 1992. Navarrette returns to this theme in his autobiography *A Darker Shade of Crimson: Odyssey of a Harvard Chicano* (New York: Bantam Books, 1993), p. 224.

13. See Suzanne Oboler, *Ethnic Labels, Ethnic Lives: Identity and the Politics of (Re)Presentation in the United States* (Minneapolis: University of Minnesota Press, 1995), chap. 6.

14. For U.S. English and its relation to the English Only movement, see Luis A. Torres, "The National English Only Movement, Past and Future," in *Community Empowerment and Chicano Scholarship,* ed. Mary Romero and Cordelia Candelaria (Los Angeles: National Association for Chicano Studies, 1992), pp. 217–30.

15. Suárez-Orozco and Suárez-Orozco, *Transformations: Migration, Family Life, and Achievement Motivation among Latino Adolescents* (Stanford, Calif.: Stanford University Press, 1995), p. 188.

16. Juan Gómez-Quiñones, *Chicano Politics: Reality and Promise, 1940–1990* (Albuquerque: University of New Mexico Press, 1990), p. 185.

17. Monsiváis, "The Immigrants' View of Education," *Los Angeles Times,* 25 Aug. 1996.

18. See, for example, Alfredo Mirandé and Evangelina Enríquez, *La Chicana: The Mexican American Woman* (Chicago: University of Chicago Press, 1979), p. 116, who insist that the familial deficiency model is a myth, arguing instead that "[t]he Chicano family has proved remarkably resilient and impervious to external forces."

19. See Michael Meyer, "Los Angeles 2010: A Latino Subcontinent," *Newsweek,* 9 Nov. 1992, pp. 32–33.

20. Quoted in Adam R. Jacobson, "Changing with the Times," *Hispanic Magazine,* Mar. 1994, p. 20. For a bleak portrait of the Hispanic family—one that seems excessively pessimistic, in my view—see Stavans, *Hispanic Condition,* p. 112.

21. Moore, *Mexican Americans* (Englewood Cliffs, N.J.: Prentice-Hall, 1970), p. 9.

22. Anthony Quinn, *The Original Sin: A Self-Portrait* (Boston: Little, Brown, 1972), pp. 45–46. For an insightful analysis of this book, see Marcos Portales, *Crowding Out Latinos: Mexican Americans in the Public Consciousness* (Philadelphia: Temple University Press, 2000), chap. 8. Described as "one of the most engaging autobiographies yet published by a Mexican American who has achieved success in the America," *The Original Sin,* Portales feels, "ought to occupy an increasingly significant position in the history of Mexican American thought and American culture" (p. 100). For additional biographical information, see Tino Villanueva, "Autobiographical Disclosures: Tino Villanueva Interviews Anthony Quinn," *Americas Review* 16 (Fall/Winter 1988): 110–43.

23. Vigil, *Barrio Gangs: Street Life and Identity in Southern California* (Austin: University of Texas Press, 1988), p. 90.

24. See Pulido, "Mexican American Catholicism in the Southwest: The Transformation of a Popular Religion," *Perspectives in Mexican American Studies,* vol. 4: *Emerging Themes in Mexican American Research,* ed. Juan R. García (Tucson, Ariz.: Mexican American Studies and Research Center, 1993), pp. 93–108.

25. According to tradition, the Virgin Mary appeared before a converted Indian, Juan Diego, on the outskirts of Mexico City in 1531. The apparition occurred on the hill of Tepeyac, where the Aztecs had worshipped Tonantzin, mother of gods. Taking on the characteristics of Tonantzin, the brown-skinned virgin is known as Our Lady of Guadalupe. Her day is celebrated on 12 December. Given the conflation of indigenous goddesses with the Virgin Mary throughout the Catholic third world, the Marist cult remains as strong there today as it was in Europe during the Middle Ages. For the veneration of Guadalupe in the United States, see Jeanette Rodríguez, *Our Lady of Guadalupe: Faith and Empowerment among Mexican American Women* (Austin: University of Texas Press, 1994), and Jacqueline Orsini Dunnington, *Guadalupe: Our Lady of New Mexico* (Santa Fe: Museum of New Mexico Press, 1999).

26. Some nuns, too, played a supportive role, notably in east Texas, where they sought to protect Mexicanos from white racism. "By the mid-twentieth century," Roberto R. Treviño notes, "Catholic Sisters labored among those helping to usher in the Civil Rights Era of the post-World War II years." "Facing Jim Crow: Catholic Sisters and the 'Mexican Problem' in Texas," *Western Historical Quarterly* 34 (Summer 2003): 142.

27. González, *Harvest of Empire: A History of Latinos in the United States* (New York: Viking Press, 2000), p. 137.

28. *Notable Hispanic American Women,* ed. Diane Telgen and Jim Kamp (Detroit: Gale Research, 1993), s.v. "Margarita Melville." Another Latina ex-nun whose career followed a similar trajectory was social activist Lupe Anguiano. Ibid., s.v. "Lupe Anguiano."

29. See Stevens-Arroyo, "From Barrios to Barricades: Religion and Religiosity in Latino Life," in *The Columbia History of Latinos in the United States,* ed. David G. Gutiérrez (New York: Columbia University Press, 2004), pp. 303–54.

30. Ken R. Crane and Ann V. Millard, "'To Be with My People': Latino Churches in the Rural Midwest," in *Apple Pie and Enchiladas: Latino Newcomers in the Rural Midwest,* ed. Ann V. Millard and Jorge Chapa (Austin: University of Texas Press, 2004), p. 190.

31. *Changing Faiths: Latinos and the Transformation of American Religion* (Washington, D.C.: Pew Hispanic Center, 2007), p. 13, http://pewhispanic.org/files/reports/75.pdf. Most religious scholars agree that roughly two-thirds of the Hispanic community have maintained their allegiance to Catholicism at this time, but estimates vary widely. For example, according to a poll of Latinos over the age of forty by the American Association of Retired People (AARP) released in early 2008, only 41 percent of them identified themselves as practicing Catholics, while 29 percent espoused Protestant denominations. For complete poll results, see http://assets.aarp.org/rgcenter/general/hispanic_spirituality.pdf.

32. Carla Trujillo, ed., *Chicana Lesbians: The Girls Our Mothers Warned Us About* (Berkeley: Third Woman Press, 1991), p. ix.

33. Blea, *La Chicana and the Intersection of Race, Class, and Gender* (New York: Praeger, 1992), p. 134.

34. For an in-depth study of MELA, see Mary Pardo, *Mexican American Women Activists: Identity and Resistance in Two Los Angeles Communities* (Philadelphia: Temple University Press, 1998).

35. Apodaca, "A Double Edge Sword: Hispanas and Liberal Feminism," *Crítica* 1 (Fall 1986): 96–114.

36. Gonzales, *Hispanic American Voluntary Organizations* (Westport, Conn.: Greenwood Press, 1985), p. 62.

37. For Chicano efforts to find a literary past, see *Recovering the U.S. Hispanic Literary Heritage,* ed. Ramón Gutiérrez and Genaro Padilla (Houston, Tex.: Arte Público Press, 1993), and *Reconstructing a Chicano/a Literary Heritage: Hispanic Colonial Literature of the Southwest,* ed. María Herrera-Sobek (Tucson: University of Arizona Press, 1993).

38. Padilla, *My History, Not Yours: The Formation of Mexican American Autobiography* (Madison: University of Wisconsin Press, 1993), p. 5.

39. Ponce, "Hispanic Writers Contribute to the U.S. Literary Landscape," *Hispanic Magazine,* May 1999, p. 33.

40. Kanellos, "Literature," in *The Hispanic Almanac: From Columbus to Corporate America,* ed. Nicolás Kanellos (Detroit: Visible Ink Press, 1994), p. 390.

41. Ibid., p. 392.

42. Frank N. Magill, ed., *Masterpieces of Latino Literature* (New York: Harper Collins, 1994), p. 41.

43. See Teresa McKenna, *Migrant Song: Politics and Process in Contemporary Chicano Literature* (Austin: University of Texas Press, 1997), p. 21.

44. According to *Hispanic Magazine,* Nov. 1997, p. 12, sixteen Hispanics had won this coveted award since its inception in 1981. Mexican-origin winners include former MALDEF president Joaquín Avila, COPS founder Ernie Cortés Jr., performance artist Guillermo

Gómez-Peña, historian Ramón Gutiérrez, artist Amalia Mesa-Bains, and FLOC director Baldemar Velásquez.

45. González, *Mirrors beneath the Earth: Short Fiction by Chicano Writers,* ed. Ray González (Willimantic, Conn.: Curbstone Press, 1992), p. 1.

46. Morales, "Shadowing Valdez," *American Theatre* 9 (Nov. 1992): 14.

47. For the impact of touring Mexican superstars such as Pedro Infante and María Félix on audiences in small Mexican American communities, see Manuel G. Gonzales, "Arturo Tirado and the Teatro Azteca: Mexican Popular Culture in the Central San Joaquin Valley," *California History* 83 (Summer 2006): 46–63. For an appreciation of the bigger picture, see Rogelio Agrasánchez Jr., *Mexican Movies in the United States: A History of the Films, Theaters and Audiences, 1920–1960* (Jefferson, N.C.: McFarland, 2006).

48. A relatively complete list of these films to about 1990 is found in Gary D. Keller, "Film," in *Hispanic Almanac,* pp. 497–559.

49. Geoffrey Fox, *Hispanic Nation: Culture, Politics, and the Construction of Identity* (Tucson: University of Arizona, 1996), p. 213.

50. López is described as "one of the most important, powerful, and challenging voices in women's art." Rita Sánchez, "Chicanas in the Arts, 1970–1995: With Personal Reflections," in *Chicano San Diego: Cultural Space and the Struggle for Justice,* ed. Richard Griswold del Castillo (Tucson: University of Arizona Press, 2007), pp. 177–78.

51. Benavidez, "Chicano Art: Culture, Myth, and Sensibility," in Cheech Marín, *Chicano Visions: American Painters on the Verge* (Boston: Little, Brown, 2002), p. 19.

52. For a concise survey of the historical evolution of Mexicano music in the United States, see Glenn Appell and David Hemphill, *American Popular Music: A Multicultural History* (Belmont, Calif.: Thomson Schirmer, 2006), chap. 9. For a comprehensive treatment of U.S. Latino music, see Ed Morales, *The Latin Beat: The Rhythms and Roots of Latin Music from Bossa Nova to Salsa and Beyond* (Cambridge, Mass.: Da Capo Press, 2003). The acclaimed documentary, *Songs of the Homeland,* VHS, directed by Hector Galán (Austin: Galán Productions, 1996), is a riveting introduction to Tejano music.

53. Ernesto Lechner, "The Other Latin Music," *Hispanic Business,* July/Aug. 2001, p. 88.

54. For the underclass controversy, see *In the Barrios: Latinos and the Underclass Debate,* ed. Joan Moore and Raquel Pinderhughes (New York: Russell Sage Foundation, 1993).

55. Rochín and Castillo, *Immigration and Colonia Formation in Rural California,* CLPP Working Paper, vol. 2 (Berkeley: Institute for the Study of Social Change, University of California, Berkeley, 1995), p. 14.

56. Telles and Ortiz, *Generations of Exclusion: Mexican Americans, Assimilation, and Race* (New York: Russell Sage Foundation, 2008).

57. Perlmann, *Italians Then, Mexicans Now: Immigrant Origins and Second-Generation Progress, 1890 to 2000* (New York: Russell Sage Foundation, 2005), p. 117. Perlmann believes that Mexican Americans today are on the same path of assimilation as Italian Americans were one hundred years ago, but it will take Mexicanos longer to advance into the middle class, given racial discrimination and rising wage inequality.

58. Vélez-Ibáñez, *Border Visions: Mexican Cultures of the Southwest United States* (Tucson: University of Arizona Press, 1996), pp. 189–90.

10. THE HISPANIC CHALLENGE, 1994–PRESENT

1. My chapter title is taken from Samuel P. Huntington, "The Hispanic Challenge," *Foreign Policy* (Mar.–Apr. 2004): 30–45.

2. Center for Immigration Studies, "Immigrants in the United States, 2007: A Profile of America's Foreign-Born Population," Nov. 2007, http://www.cis.org/articles/2007/back1007.html.

3. The tendency in official government statistics, and increasingly in non-governmental sources, is to look at the Latino category without breaking it down into national subgroups. This is unfortunate for scholars interested in a specific ethnic group—Mexicanos, in our case. Of necessity, then, some of the statistics used in this chapter pertain to the general Latino population, and therefore they give only an approximate idea of the Mexicano condition. When interpreting these statistics, students should keep in mind that Cuban Americans generally skew the numbers for Latinos significantly, in one way or another (usually in a more positive direction). However, when extrapolating, keep in mind that in 2006, the 1,517,028 Cuban Americans represented less than 4 percent of the Latino total.

4. Pew Hispanic Center, "2007 National Survey of Latinos: As Illegal Immigration Issue Heats Up, Hispanics Feel a Chill," 19 Dec. 2007, http://pewhispanic.org/reports/report.php?ReportID=84.

5. For the plight of Mexican farmers, see Víctor Quintana, "The Mexican Rural Sector Can't Take It Anymore," in *Labor versus Empire: Race, Gender and Migration,* ed. Gilbert G. González et al. (New York: Routledge, 2004).

6. Alluding to the massive immigration from Latin America, Juan González observes: "Whether we regard this human stream as curse or fortune does not matter, for it is the harvest of empire and it will not be stopped until the empire's expansion is redirected and its prosperity shared more equitably." *Harvest of Empire: A History of Latinos in America* (New York: Viking, 2000), p. 205. See, too, Gilbert G. González and Raúl Fernández, *A Century of Chicano History: Empire, Nations and Migration* (New York: Routledge, 2004).

7. Some scholars feel that the Juárez murders are an exaggerated manifestation of the kind of violence that women have traditionally experienced in Mexican society. See, for example, Kathleen Staudt, *Violence and Activism at the Border: Gender, Fear, and Everyday Life in Ciudad Juárez* (Austin: University of Texas Press, 2008).

8. Quoted by Andrés Oppenheimer, *Bordering on Chaos: Guerrillas, Stockbrokers, Politicians, and Mexico's Road to Prosperity* (New York: Little, Brown, 1996), p. 201.

9. For an insightful look at the lives of Mexicans in the Las Vegas construction industry during this period, see chap. 7, "Aztlán in Neon: Latinos in the New City," in Hal Rothman, *Neon Metropolis: How Las Vegas Started the Twenty-First Century* (New York: Routledge, 2002).

10. An excellent essay on the Mexicano community in the Big Apple is Robert Courtney Smith, "Racialization and Mexicans in New York City," in *New Destinations: Mexican Immigration in the United States,* ed. Víctor Zúñiga and Rubén Hernández-León (New York: Russell Sage Foundation, 2006), pp. 220–43.

11. Miyares, "Changing Latinization of New York City," in *Hispanic Spaces, Latino Places: Community and Cultural Diversity in Contemporary America,* ed. Daniel D. Arreola (Austin: University of Texas Press, 2004), p. 153.

12. The role Latinos, especially Mexicanos, have played in the restructuring of this key industry in the nine southeastern states is explored by William Kandel and Emilio A. Parrado, "Hispanics in the American South and the Transformation of the Poultry Industry," in *Hispanic Spaces, Latino Places,* pp. 255–76.

13. Xóchitl Bada, "Mexican Hometown Associations," 31 Aug. 2004, http://www.pbs.org/pov/pov2003/thesixthsection/special_mexican.html.

14. Jessica Ramírez, "When Hate Becomes Hurt," *Newsweek,* 10 Mar. 2008, p. 14.

15. Massey, "Understanding America's Immigration 'Crisis,'" *Proceedings of the American Philosophical Society* 151 (Sept. 2007): 310.

16. Focusing on the role of fear mongering, this ascendancy is traced in Manuel G. Gonzales and Richard Delgado, *The Politics of Fear: How Republicans Use Money, Race, and the Media to Win* (Boulder, Colo.: Paradigm Publishers, 2006).

17. Barlow, *Between Fear and Hope: Globalization and Race in the United States* (Lanham, Md.: Rowman and Littlefield, 2003), p. 17.

18. Joel Kotkin, "Business: Grass-Roots Business; A Revival of Older Suburbs as Ethnic Businesses Take Hold," *New York Times,* 27 Feb. 2000. For the Mexicano migration to the suburbs, see David R. Ruiz, "Barrio Urbanism and the Cities of the Southwest," *Journal of the West* 45 (Fall 2006): 12–20.

19. This transformation is documented by James R. Curtis, "Barrio Space and Place in Southeast Los Angeles, California," in *Hispanic Spaces, Latinos Places,* pp. 125–41.

20. Mora-Torres, "La Primavera del Inmigrante: Media and Voice in the Making of Chicago's Immigrant Rights Movement, 2005–2007," 20 Mar. 2008 oral presentation, 35th annual convention of the National Association for Chicana and Chicano Studies, Austin, Texas.

21. Rodríguez, "Mexicans in America," *Cato Unbound,* 8 Sept. 2006, http:www.cato-unbound.org/contributors/richard-rodriguez/.

22. Quoted in Arian Campo-Flores, "A Latino 'Spanking,'" *Newsweek,* 4 Dec. 2006, p. 40.

23. "Villaraigosa's meteoric political rise was a metaphor for the maturation of Mexican American politics," according to Gregory Rodríguez, *Mongrels, Bastards, Orphans, and Vagabonds: Mexican Immigration and the Future of Race in America* (New York: Pantheon Books, 2007), p. 253. As the title of his book indicates, what distinguishes Rodríguez's work from the growing number of histories of Mexican Americans is its emphasis on racial factors.

24. Many Republicans concede this point. "Above all, insofar as there is a modest drift rightwards among Hispanics as they rise economically, that is more than canceled out by the fact that continuing immigration channels new, poor Hispanic voters into the Democratic ranks." John O'Sullivan, "Hasta la Vista, Baby: Bush's Hispanic Strategy Comes Unraveled," *National Review,* 8 Apr. 2002, http://www.nationalreview.com/8apr02/jos04802.shtml.

25. A precursor in calling for the creation of a Latino identity in order to foster political and economic power was Ignacio L. López, editor of *El Espectador.* Joseph A. Rodríguez, "Becoming Latinos: Mexican Americans, Chicanos, and the Spanish Myth in the Urban Southwest," *Western Historical Quarterly* 29 (Summer 1998): 173.

26. Miguel Lemus, quoted in *Soldados: Chicanos in Viet Nam,* ed. Charley Trujillo (San Jose, Calif.: Chusma House Publications, 1990), pp. 34–35. Some 47,000 Puerto Ricans served in the Vietnam War.

27. Nicholas De Genova and Ana Y. Ramos-Zayas, *Latino Crossings: Mexicans, Puerto Ricans, and the Politics of Race and Citizenship* (New York: Routledge, 2003), p. 30.

28. Some Chicano scholars fear that the broader orientation "will dilute and weaken Chicana/o History," José Cuéllo, "Introduction: Chicana/o History as a Social Movement," in *Voices of a New Chicana/o History,* ed. Refugio I. Rochín and Dennis N. Valdés (East Lansing: Michigan State University Press, 2000), p. 4.

29. Navarro, *Mexicano Political Experience in Occupied Aztlán: Struggles and Change* (Walnut Creek, Calif.: AltaMira Press, 2005).

30. These obstacles are well documented by Roberto Suro, *Strangers among Us: Latino Lives in a Changing America* (New York: Vintage Books, 1999), chap. 15. The author is pessimistic on the prospects for better relations; instead, he foresees continuing Latino-black tension "in a battle to avoid being left in sole possession of last place in American society. It is a battle at the bottom that is certain to be bloody even though neither contestant can hope for more than a Pyrrhic victory" (p. 244). Also pessimistic on interracial cooperation is law professor Steven W. Bender, who bases his assessment on mutual perceptions: "African Americans and Latinas/os tend to hold negative stereotypical views of each other." *Greasers and Gringos: Latinos, Law, and the American Imagination* (New York: New York University Press, 2003), p. 164.

31. Rubén Guevara, quoted in Steven Loza, *Barrio Rhythm: Mexican American Music in Los Angeles* (Urbana: University of Illinois Press, 1993), p. 82.

32. "By the time New Spain became independent Mexico in 1821, blacks had almost

disappeared into a mixed race society," notes Rodríguez, *Mongrels, Bastards, Orphans, and Vagabonds*, p. 80.

33. Morrison, "On the Backs of Blacks," *Time*, 2 Dec. 1993, p. 57.

34. Ruiz, "Morena/o, blanca/o y café con leche: Racial Constructions in Chicana/o Historiography," *Mexican Studies/Estudios Mexicanos* 20 (Summer 2004): 348. This point is made too by Rutgers University law professor Tanya K. Hernández, "Roots of Latino/black Anger," *Los Angeles Times*, 7 Jan. 2007.

35. Once Barack Obama won his party's presidential nomination, however, Villaraigosa enthusiastically backed his fellow Democrat against Republican Senator John McCain. In fact, Obama, the nation's first black president, captured 67 percent of the Latino vote in this historic 2008 election. The president-elect promptly rewarded Hispanic supporters by appointing two Mexican-origin Democrats to his cabinet: Colorado Senator Ken Salazar, secretary of the interior; and Hilda Solis, a four-term member of the U.S. House of Representatives from southern California, secretary of labor. In an unprecedented move, a third Latino, Bill Richardson, former energy secretary and U.N. ambassador under President Bill Clinton, was also named to the cabinet, as secretary of commerce; but the New Mexican governor was forced to withdraw from consideration due to an ongoing federal investigation into possible financial improprieties while serving in state office.

36. Black respondents indicated as much to Tomás Rivera Policy Institute researchers in a study on interracial tensions in South Los Angeles. See the TRPI Policy Brief, prepared by David Fabienke, *Beyond the Racial Divide: Perceptions of Minority Residents on Coalition Building in South Los Angeles* (Los Angeles: Tomás Rivera Policy Institute, June 2007), p. 2.

37. Vaca, *The Presumed Alliance: The Unspoken Conflict between Latinos and Blacks and What It Means for America* (New York: HarperCollins, 2004).

38. Camarillo, "Cities of Color: The New Racial Frontier in California's Minority-Majority Cities," *Pacific Historical Review* 76 (Feb. 2007): 18–19.

39. Middle-class households were defined in the study as those earning between $40,000 and $140,000 annually. Robert R. Brischetto, "The Hispanic Middle Class Comes of Age," *Hispanic Business*, Dec. 2001, pp. 21–32.

40. An appreciation of the plight of these workers can be gained by consulting the portrait of strawberry workers along the California coast, many of them Mixtecos, in Eric Schlosser, *Reefer Madness: Sex, Drugs, and Cheap Labor in the American Black Market* (Boston: Houghton Mifflin, 2003), pp. 75–108.

41. Martínez, *Mexican-Origin People in the United States: A Topical History* (Tucson: University of Arizona Press, 2001).

42. Navarro, *Mexicano Political Experience*, p. 498.

43. Peña, *Mexican Americans and the Environment: Tierra y Vida* (Tucson: University of Arizona Press, 2005), p. xxxiii.

44. Victor M. Valle and Rodolfo D. Torres, *Latino Metropolis* (Minneapolis: University of Minnesota Press, 2000), p. 179.

45. See, for example, the essays in Jorge Iber and Samuel O. Regalado, eds., *Mexican Americans and Sports: A Reader on Athletics and Barrio Life* (College Station: Texas A&M University Press, 2007). Other path-breaking studies include José M. Alamillo, "Peloteros in Paradise: Mexican American Baseball and Oppositional Politics in Southern California, 1930–1950," *Western Historical Quarterly* 34 (Summer 2003): 191–211, and Juan Javier Pescador, "¡Vamos Taximaroa! Mexican/Chicano Soccer Associations and Transnational/Translocal Communities, 1967–2002," *Latino Studies* 2 (Dec. 2004): 352–76.

46. The title of the biography by Noe Torres, *Baseball's First Mexican-American Star: The Amazing Story of Leo Naja* (Tamarac, Fla.: Llumina Press, 2006), is misleading: Naja achieved his stardom in the minor leagues, both in Mexico and the United States.

47. The contents of this article would later appear in Huntington's book, *Who Are We? Challenges to American National Identity* (New York: Simon and Schuster, 2004).

48. Mariscal, "Latinos on the Frontlines: Again," *Latino Studies* 1 (July 2003): 348.

49. Will, "'We Have Been Here Before': Similarities between Irish, Italians and Jews Then, and Blacks, Latinos and Asians Now," *Newsweek,* 11 June 2001, p. 64.

50. "2007 National Survey of Latinos: As Illegal Immigration Issue Heats Up, Hispanics Feel a Chill," Pew Hispanic Center Report, 9 Dec. 2007, http://pewhispanic.org/reports/report.php?ReportID=84.

SELECT BIBLIOGRAPHY
OF WORKS SINCE 1985

◄○►◄○►◄○►

Practical considerations preclude a complete bibliography here. For the most important scholarly work in Chicana/o studies before 1985, the foundational literature of the first generation, see the "Select Bibliography of Works after 1965" in the first edition of *Mexicanos*.

BOOKS

Acosta, Teresa Palomo, and Ruthe Winegarten. *Las Tejanas: 300 Years of History.* Austin: University of Texas Press, 2003.

Acosta-Belén, Edna, and Barbara R. Sjostrom, eds. *The Hispanic Experience in the United States: Contemporary Issues and Perspectives.* New York: Praeger, 1988.

Acuña, Rodolfo. *Anything but Mexican: Chicanos in Contemporary Los Angeles.* New York: Verso, 1996.

———. *Corridors of Migration: The Odyssey of Mexican Laborers, 1600–1933.* Tucson: University of Arizona Press, 2007.

———. *Occupied America: A History of Chicanos.* 6th ed. New York: Pearson Longman, 2007.

———. *U.S. Latino Issues: Contemporary American Ethnic Issues.* Westport, Conn.: Greenwood Press, 2003.

Agrasánchez, Rogelio, Jr. *Mexican Movies in the United States: A History of the Films, Theaters and Audiences, 1920–1960.* Jefferson, N.C.: McFarland, 2006.

Águilar Camín, Héctor, and Lorenzo Meyer. *In the Shadow of the Mexican Revolution.* Trans. Luis Alberto Fierro. Austin: University of Texas Press, 1993.

Alamillo, José M. *Making Lemonade Out of Lemons: Mexican American Labor and Leisure in a California Town, 1880–1960.* Urbana: University of Illinois Press, 2006.

Alaníz, Yolanda, and Megan Cornish. *Viva la Raza: A History of Chicano Identity and Resistance.* Seattle, Wash.: Red Letter Press, 2008.

Alarcón, Norma, Ana Castillo, and Cherríe Moraga, eds. *Third Woman: The Sexuality of Latinas.* Berkeley, Calif.: Third Woman Press, 1989.

Alba, Richard, and Victor Nee. *Remaking the American Mainstream: Assimilation and Contemporary Immigration.* Cambridge, Mass.: Harvard University Press, 2003.

Aldama, Frederick Luis. *Brown on Brown: Chicano/a Representations on Gender, Sexuality, and Ethnicity.* Austin: University of Texas Press, 2006.

Almaguer, Tomás. *Racial Fault Lines: The Historical Origins of White Supremacy in California.* Berkeley and Los Angeles: University of California Press, 1994.

Almaráz, Félix D., Jr. *Knight without Armor: Carlos Eduardo Castañeda, 1896–1958.* College Station: Texas A&M University Press, 1999.

Alonzo, Armando. *Tejano Legacy: Rancheros and Settlers in South Texas, 1734–1900.* Albuquerque: University of New Mexico Press, 1998.

Alvarado, Victoria. *Mujeres de Conciencia/Women of Conscience.* Encino, Calif.: Floricanto Press, 2008.

Álvarez, Luis. *The Power of the Zoot: Youth Culture and Resistance during World War II.* Berkeley and Los Angeles: University of California Press, 2008.

Álvarez, Robert R., Jr. *Familia: Migration and Adaptation in Baja and Alta California, 1800–1975.* Berkeley and Los Angeles: University of California Press, 1987.

Anderson, Gary Clayton. *The Conquest of Texas: Ethnic Cleansing in the Promised Land, 1820–1875.* Norman: University of Oklahoma Press, 2005.

Anzaldúa, Gloria. *Borderlands/La Frontera: The New Mestiza.* San Francisco: Spinsters/Aunt Lute Book Co., 1987.

Arredondo, Gabriela F. *Mexican Chicago: Race, Identity, and Nation, 1916–39.* Urbana: University of Illinois Press, 2008.

Arreola, Daniel D., ed. *Hispanic Spaces, Latino Places: Community and Cultural Diversity in Contemporary America.* Austin: University of Texas Press, 2004.

———. *Tejano South Texas: A Mexican American Cultural Province.* Austin: University of Texas Press, 2002.

Artico, Ceres I. *Latino Families Broken by Immigration: The Adolescents' Perceptions.* New York: LFB Scholarly Publishing, 2003.

Ávila, Eric. *Popular Culture in the Age of White Flight: Fear and Fantasy in Suburban Los Angeles.* Berkeley and Los Angeles: University of California Press, 2004.

Badillo, David A. *Latinos in Michigan.* East Lansing: Michigan State University Press, 2003.

Balderrama, Francisco E., and Raymond Rodríguez. *Decade of Betrayal: Mexican Repatriation in the 1930s.* Rev. ed. Albuquerque: University of New Mexico Press, 2006.

Barger, W. K., and Ernesto M. Reza. *The Farm Labor Movement in the Midwest: Social Change and Adaptation among Migrant Farmworkers.* Austin: University of Texas Press, 1994.

Barkan, Elliott Robert. *From All Points: America's Immigrant West, 1870s–1952.* Bloomington: Indiana University Press, 2007.

Barrera, Mario. *Beyond Aztlán: Ethnic Autonomy in Comparative Perspective.* Notre Dame, Ind.: University of Notre Dame Press, 1988.

Barton, Paul. *Hispanic Methodists, Presbyterians, and Baptists in Texas.* Austin: University of Texas Press, 2006.

Bean, Frank, and Marta Tienda. *The Hispanic Population of the United States.* New York: Russell Sage Foundation, 1987.

Bejarano, Cynthia L. *¿Qué Onda? Urban Youth Culture and Border Identity.* Tucson: University of Arizona Press, 2005.

Bixler-Márquez, Dennis J., et al., eds. *Chicano Studies: Survey and Analysis.* Rev. ed. Dubuque, Ia.: Kendall/Hunt, 1997.

Blanton, Carlos Kevin. *The Strange Career of Bilingual Education in Texas, 1836–1981.* College Station: Texas A&M University Press, 2004.

Bonilla, Frank, et al., eds. *Borderless Borders: U.S. Latinos, Latin Americans, and the Paradox of Independence.* Philadelphia: Temple University Press, 1998.

Boyle, Susan Calafate. *Los Capitalistas: Hispano Merchants on the Santa Fe Trail.* Albuquerque: University of New Mexico Press, 1997.

Broyles-González, Yolanda. *Lydia Mendoza's Life in Music: La Historia de Lydia Mendoza (Norteño Tejano Legacies).* New York: Oxford University Press, 2001.

Burgos, Adrian. *Playing America's Game: Baseball, Latinos and the Color Line.* Berkeley and Los Angeles: University of California Press, 2007.

Burke, John Francis. *Mestizo Democracy: The Politics of Crossing Borders.* College Station: Texas A&M University Press, 2002.

Burt, Kenneth C. *The Search for a Civic Voice: California Latino Politics.* Claremont, Calif.: Regina Books, 2007.

Busto, Rudy V. *King Tiger: The Religious Vision of Reis López Tijerina.* Albuquerque: University of New Mexico Press, 2005.

Camarillo, Albert. *Chicanos in a Changing Society: From Mexican Pueblos to American Barrios in*

Santa Barbara and Southern California, 1848–1930. Rev. ed. Dallas: Southern Methodist University Press, 2005.

Cárdenas, Gilberto, ed. *La Causa: Civil Rights, Social Justice and the Struggle for Equality in the Midwest.* Houston, Tex.: Arte Público Press, 2004.

Carlson, Alvar W. *The Spanish-American Homeland: Four Centuries in New Mexico's Río Arriba.* Baltimore: Johns Hopkins University Press, 1990.

Carrasco, Davíd, et al., eds. *Mesoamerica's Classic Heritage: From Teotihuacan to the Aztecs.* Boulder: University Press of Colorado, 2000.

Carroll, Michael P. *The Penitente Brotherhood: Patriarchy and Hispano-Catholicism in New Mexico.* Baltimore: Johns Hopkins University Press, 2002.

Carroll, Patrick J. *Felix Longoria's Wake: Bereavement, Racism, and the Rise of Mexican American Activism.* Austin: University of Texas Press, 2003.

Casas, María Raquél. *Married to a Daughter of the Land: Spanish-Mexican Women and Interethnic Marriage in California, 1820–1880.* Reno: University of Nevada Press, 2007.

Castañeda, Alejandra. *The Politics of Citizenship of Mexican Migrants.* New York: LFB Scholarly Publishing, 2006.

Castillo-Speed, Lillian, ed. *Women's Voices from the Borderlands.* New York: Simon and Schuster, 1995.

Castro, Rafaela G. *Chicano Folklore: A Guide to the Folktales, Traditions, Rituals, and Religious Practices of Mexican Americans.* New York: Oxford University Press, 2001.

Chacón, Justin Akers, and Mike Davis. *No One Is Illegal: Fighting Violence and State Repression on the U.S.-Mexico Border.* Chicago: Haymarket Books, 2006.

Chance, Joseph E. *José María de Jesús Carvajal: The Life and Times of a Mexican Revolutionary.* San Antonio, Tex.: Trinity University Press, 2006.

Chávez, Ernesto. *"¡Mi Raza Primero!" (My People First): Nationalism, Identity, and Insurgency in the Chicano Movement in Los Angeles, 1966–1978.* Berkeley and Los Angeles: University of California Press, 2002.

Chávez, Fray Angelico, and Thomas E. Chávez. *Wake for a Fat Vicar: Father Juan Felipe Ortiz, Archbishop Lamy, and the New Mexican Catholic Church in the Middle of the Nineteenth Century.* Albuquerque: LPD Press, 2004.

Chávez, John R. *Eastside Landmark: A History of the East Los Angeles Community Union, 1969–1993.* Stanford, Calif.: Stanford University Press, 1998.

Chávez, Leo. *Shadowed Lives: Undocumented Immigrants in American Society.* Fort Worth, Tex.: Harcourt Brace Jovanovich, 1992.

Chávez, Linda. *Out of the Barrio: Toward a New Politics of Hispanic Assimilation.* New York: BasicBooks, 1991.

Chávez, Lydia. *The Color Bind: The Battle to End Affirmative Action.* Berkeley and Los Angeles: University of California Press, 1998.

Chávez, Thomas E. *Manuel Alvarez, 1794–1856: A Southwestern Biography.* Niwot: University Press of Colorado, 1990.

———. *New Mexico: Past and Future.* Albuquerque: University of New Mexico Press, 2006.

Chávez-García, Miroslava. *Negotiating Conquest: Gender and Power in California, 1770s to 1870s.* Tucson: University of Arizona Press, 2004.

Cockcroft, James D. *Outlaws in the Promised Land: Mexican Immigrant Workers and America's Future.* New York: Grove Press, 1986.

Cole, Stephanie, and Alison M. Parker, eds. *Beyond Black and White: Race, Ethnicity, and Gender in the U.S. South and Southwest.* College Station: Texas A&M University Press, 2004.

Connor, Walker, ed. *Mexican-Americans in Comparative Perspective.* Washington, D.C.: Urban Institute Press, 1985.

Contréras, Sheila Marie. *Blood Lines: Myth, Indigenism, and Chicana/o Literature.* Austin: University of Texas Press, 2008.

Crane, Ken. *Latino Churches: Faith, Family, and Ethnicity in the Second Generation.* New York: LFB Scholarly Publishing, 2003.

Cruz, Gilbert R. *Let There Be Towns: Spanish Municipal Origins in the American Southwest, 1610–1810.* College Station: Texas A&M University Press, 1988.

Cuéllar, Carlos E. *Stories from the Barrio: A History of Mexican Fort Worth.* Fort Worth: Texas Christian University Press, 2003.

Cutter, Charles R. *The Legal Culture of Northern New Spain, 1700–1810.* Albuquerque: University of New Mexico Press, 1995.

Dávila, Arlene. *Latinos, Inc.: The Marketing and Making of a People.* Berkeley and Los Angeles: University of California Press, 2001.

Davis, Marilyn, ed. *Mexican Voices, Mexican Dreams: An Oral History of Mexican Immigration to the United States.* New York: Henry Holt, 1990.

Davis, Mike. *Magical Urbanism: Latinos Reinvent the US City.* London: Verso, 2000.

De Anda, Roberto M. *Chicanas and Chicanos in Contemporary Society.* Boston: Allyn and Bacon, 1996.

De Genova, Nicholas. *Working in Boundaries: Race, Space, and "Illegality" in Mexican Chicago.* Durham, N.C.: Duke University Press, 2005.

De Genova, Nicholas, and Ana Y. Ramos-Zayas. *Latino Crossings: Mexicans, Puerto Ricans, and the Politics of Race and Citizenship.* New York: Routledge, 2003.

de la Garza, Beatriz. *A Law for the Lion: A Tale of Crime and Injustice in the Borderlands.* Austin: University of Texas Press, 2002.

de la Garza, Rodolfo, and Harley L. Browning. *Mexican Immigrants and Mexican Americans: An Evolving Relation.* Austin: Center for Mexican American Studies, University of Texas, 1986.

de la Teja, Jesús F., and Ross Frank, eds. *Choice, Persuasion, and Coercion: Social Control on Spain's North American Frontiers.* Albuquerque: University of New Mexico Press, 2005.

de la Torre, Adela. *Moving from the Margins: A Chicana Voice on Public Policy.* Tucson: University of Arizona Press, 2002.

de la Torre, Adela, and Antonio Estrada. *Mexican Americans and Health: ¡Sana! ¡Sana!* Tucson: University of Arizona Press, 2001.

de la Torre, Adela, and Beatríz M. Pesquera, eds. *Building with Our Hands: New Directions in Chicana Studies.* Berkeley and Los Angeles: University of California Press, 1993.

De León, Arnoldo. *Ethnicity in the Sunbelt: A History of Mexican-Americans in Houston.* Houston, Tex.: Mexican American Studies Program, University of Houston, 1989.

———. *Mexican-Americans in Texas: A Brief History.* 2nd ed. Arlington Heights, Ill.: Harlan Davidson, 1999.

———. *Racial Frontiers: Africans, Chinese, and Mexicans in Western America, 1848–1890.* Albuquerque: University of New Mexico Press, 2002.

———, ed. *Tejano Epic: Essays in Honor of Félix D. Almáraz, Jr.* Austin: Texas State Historical Association, 2005.

De León, Arnoldo, and Richard Griswold del Castillo. *North to Aztlán: A History of Mexican Americans in the United States.* 2nd ed. Wheeling, Ill.: Harlan Davidson, 2006.

de Varona, Frank, ed. *Hispanic Presence in the United States: Historical Beginnings.* Washington, D.C.: National Hispanic Quincentennial Commission, 1993.

Del Castillo, Adelaida R., ed. *Between Borders: Essays on Mexican/Chicana History.* Encino, Calif.: Floricanto Press, 1990.

Delgado, Héctor L. *New Immigrants, Old Unions: Organizing Undocumented Workers in Los Angeles.* Philadelphia: Temple University Press, 1993.

Delgado, Richard, and Jean Stefancic, eds. *The Latino/a Condition: A Critical Reader.* New York: New York University Press, 1998.

Denner, Jill, and Bianca L. Guzmán, eds. *Latina Girls: Voices of Adolescent Strength in the United States.* New York: New York University Press, 2006.

Deutsch, Sarah. *No Separate Refuge: Culture, Class, and Gender on an Anglo-Hispanic Frontier in the American Southwest, 1880–1940.* New York: Oxford University Press, 1987.

Deverell, William. *Whitewashed Adobe: The Rise of Los Angeles and the Remaking of Its Mexican Past.* Berkeley and Los Angeles: University of California Press, 2004.

Dimas, Pete. *Progress and a Mexican American Community's Struggle for Existence: Phoenix's Golden Gate Barrio.* New York: Pete Lang, 1999.

Dolan, Jay, and Allan Figueroa Deck, eds. *Hispanic Catholic Culture in the U.S.: Issues and Concerns.* Notre Dame, Ind.: University of Notre Dame Press, 1994.

Dolan, Jay, and Gilberto M. Hinojosa, eds. *Mexican Americans and the Catholic Church, 1900–1965.* Notre Dame, Ind.: University of Notre Dame Press, 1994.

Driscoll, Barbara A. *The Tracks North: The Railroad Bracero Program of World War II.* Austin: Center for Mexican American Studies, University of Texas at Austin, 1999.

Espinosa, Gastón, and Mario T. García, eds. *Mexican American Religions: Spirituality, Activism, and Culture.* Durham, N.C.: Duke University Press, 2008.

Espinosa, Gastón, Virgilio Elizondo, and Jesse Miranda, eds. *Latino Religions and Civic Activism in the United States.* New York: Oxford University Press, 2005.

Estrada, William David. *The Los Angeles Plaza: Sacred and Contested Space.* Austin: University of Texas Press, 2008.

Fernández, José E. *The Biography of Casimiro Barela.* Albuquerque: University of New Mexico Press, 2003.

Flores, William V., and Rina Benmayor, eds. *Latino Cultural Citizenship: Claiming Identity, Space, and Rights.* Boston: Beacon Press, 1997.

Foley, Douglas E., et al. *From Peones to Politicos: Ethnic Relations in a South Texas Town, 1900–1977.* Austin: Center for Mexican American Studies, University of Texas, 1988.

Foley, Neil. *The White Scourge: Mexicans, Blacks, and Poor Whites in Texas Cotton Culture.* Berkeley and Los Angeles: University of California Press, 1997.

Fontana, Bernard. *Entrada: The Legacy of Spain and Mexico in the United States.* Tucson: Southwest Parks and Monuments Association and the University of New Mexico Press, 1994.

Forrest, Suzanne. *The Preservation of the Village: New Mexico's Hispanics and the New Deal.* Albuquerque: University of New Mexico Press, 1989.

Fox, Geoffrey. *Hispanic Nation: Culture, Politics, and the Constructing of Identity.* Tucson: University of Arizona Press, 1996.

Frank, Ross. *From Settler to Citizen: New Mexican Economic Development and the Creation of Vecino Society, 1759–1820.* Berkeley and Los Angeles: University of California Press, 2000.

Fregoso, Rosa Linda. *The Bronze Screen: Chicana and Chicano Film Culture.* Minneapolis: University of Minnesota Press, 1993.

———. *Mexican Encounters: The Making of Social Identities on the Borderlands.* Berkeley and Los Angeles: University of California Press, 2003.

Galindo, D. Letticia, and María Dolores Gonzales, eds. *Speaking Chicana: Voice, Power, and Identity.* Tucson: University of Arizona Press, 1999.

Gallegos, Bernardo P. *Literacy, Education, and Society in New Mexico, 1693–1821.* Albuquerque: University of New Mexico Press, 1992.

Gamboa, Erasmo. *Mexican Labor and World War II: Braceros in the Pacific Northwest, 1942–1947.* Austin: University of Texas Press, 1990.

Gann, L. H., and Peter J. Duignan. *The Hispanics in the United States: A History.* Boulder, Colo.: Westview Press, 1986.

Ganster, Paul, and David E. Lorey. *The U.S.-Mexican Border into the Twenty-First Century.* 2nd ed. Lanham, Md.: Rowman and Littlefield, 2007.

García, Alma M., ed. *Chicana Feminist Thought: The Basic Historical Writings.* New York: Routledge, 1997.

———. *Narratives of Mexican American Women: Emergent Identities of the Second Generation.* Walnut Creek, Calif.: AltaMira Press, 2004.

García, Eugene E. *Hispanic Education in the United States: Raíces y Alas.* Lanham, Md.: Rowman and Littlefield, 2001.

García, Ignacio M. *Chicanismo: The Forging of a Militant Ethos among Mexican Americans.* Tucson: University of Arizona Press, 1997.

———. *Hector P. García: In Relentless Pursuit of Justice.* Houston, Tex.: Arte Público Press, 2002.

———. *United We Win: The Rise and Fall of the Raza Unida Party.* Tucson: Mexican American Studies and Resource Center, University of Arizona, 1989.

———. *Viva Kennedy: Mexican Americans in Search of Camelot.* College Station: Texas A&M University Press, 2000.

———. *White But Not Equal: Mexican Americans, Jury Discrimination, and the Supreme Court.* Tucson: University of Arizona Press, 2008.

García, Jaime, ed. *Beginning a New Millennium of Chicana and Chicano Scholarship: Selected Proceedings of the 2001 NACCS Conference.* Berkeley: National Association for Chicana and Chicano Studies, 2006.

García, Jorge J. E. *Hispanic/Latino Identity: A Philosophical Perspective.* Malden, Mass.: Blackwell, 2000.

García, Juan R. *Mexicans in the Midwest, 1900–1932.* Tucson: University of Arizona Press, 1996.

García, Juan R., Julia Curry Rodríguez, and Clara Lomas, eds. *In Times of Challenge: Chicanos and Chicanas in American Society.* Houston, Tex.: Mexican American Studies Program, University of Houston, 1988.

García, Mario T. *Católicos: Resistance and Affirmation in Chicano Catholic History.* Austin: University of Texas Press, 2008.

———. *Mexican Americans: Leadership, Ideology, and Identity, 1930–1960.* New Haven, Conn.: Yale University Press, 1989.

———, ed. *Memories of Chicano History: The Life and Narrative of Bert Corona.* Berkeley and Los Angeles: University of California Press, 1994.

García, Matt. *A World of Its Own: Race, Labor, and Citrus in the Making of Greater Los Angeles, 1900–1970.* Chapel Hill: University of North Carolina Press, 2001.

García, Nasario, and Demetria Martínez, eds. *Comadres: Hispanic Women of the Río Puerco Valley.* Santa Fe: Western Edge Press, 2002.

García, Richard A. *Rise of the Mexican American Middle Class: San Antonio, 1929–1941.* College Station: Texas A&M University Press, 1991.

Garrison, Philip. *Because I Don't Have Wings: Stories of Mexican Immigrant Life.* Tucson: University of Arizona Press, 2006.

Garza, Humberto. *The Mexican-American War of 1846-1848: A Deceitful Smoke Screen.* San Jose, Calif.: Sun House Publishing, 2006.

Garza-Falcón, Leticia M. *Gente Decente: A Borderlands Response to the Rhetoric of Dominance.* Austin: University of Texas Press, 1998.

Getz, Lynne Marie. *Schools of Their Own: The Education of Hispanos in New Mexico, 1850–1940.* Albuquerque: University of New Mexico Press, 1997.

Gómez, Laura E. *Manifest Destinies: The Making of the Mexican American Race.* New York: New York University Press, 2007.

Gómez-Quiñones, Juan. *Chicano Politics: Reality and Promise, 1940–1990.* Albuquerque: University of New Mexico Press, 1990.

———. *Mexican American Labor, 1790–1990.* Albuquerque: University of New Mexico Press, 1994.

————. *Roots of Chicano Politics, 1600–1940*. Albuquerque: University of New Mexico Press, 1994.

Gonzales, Manuel G. *The Hispanic Elite of the Southwest*. El Paso: Texas Western Press, 1989.

Gonzales, Manuel G., and Richard Delgado. *The Politics of Fear: How Republicans Use Money, Race, and the Media to Win*. Boulder, Colo.: Paradigm Publishers, 2006.

Gonzales, Manuel G., and Cynthia M. Gonzales, eds. *En Aquel Entonces: Readings in Mexican-American History*. Bloomington: Indiana University Press, 2000.

Gonzales, Phillip B., ed. *Expressing New Mexico: Nuevomexicano Creativity, Ritual, and Memory*. Tucson: University of Arizona Press, 2007.

Gonzales, Sylvia Alicia. *Hispanic American Voluntary Organizations*. Westport, Conn.: Greenwood Press, 1985.

Gonzales-Berry, Erlinda, and David R. Maciel, eds. *The Contested Homeland: A Chicano History of New Mexico*. Albuquerque: University of New Mexico Press, 2000.

Gonzales-Day, Ken. *Lynching in the West, 1850–1935*. Durham, N.C.: Duke University Press, 2006.

González, Arturo. *Mexican Americans and the U.S. Economy: Quest for Buenos Días*. Tucson: University of Arizona Press, 2002.

González, Deena J. *Refusing the Favor: The Spanish-Mexican Women of Santa Fe, 1820–1880*. New York: Oxford University Press, 1999.

González, Gilbert G. *Chicano Education in the Era of Segregation*. Philadelphia: Balch Institute Press, 1990.

————. *Culture of Empire: American Writers, Mexico, and Mexican Immigrants, 1880–1930*. Austin: University of Texas Press, 2004.

————. *Guest Workers or Colonized Labor? Mexican Labor Migration to the United States*. Boulder, Colo.: Paradigm Publishers, 2006.

————. *Labor and Community: Mexican Citrus Worker Villages in a Southern California County, 1890–1950*. Urbana: University of Illinois Press, 1994.

González, Gilbert G., and Raúl A. Fernández. *A Century of Chicano History: Empire, Nations and Migration*. New York: Routledge, 2004.

González, Juan. *Harvest of Empire: A History of Latinos in the United States*. New York: Viking Press, 2000.

González, Michael J. *This Small City Will Be a Mexican Paradise: Exploring the Origin of Mexican Culture in Los Angeles, 1821–1846*. Albuquerque: University of New Mexico Press, 2005.

Griswold del Castillo, Richard, ed. *Chicano San Diego: Cultural Space and the Struggle for Justice*. Tucson: University of Arizona Press, 2007.

————. *The Treaty of Guadalupe Hidalgo: A Legacy of Conflict*. Norman: University of Oklahoma Press, 1990.

————, ed. *World War II and Mexican American Civil Rights*. Austin: University of Texas Press, 2008.

Griswold del Castillo, Richard, and Richard A. García. *César Chávez: A Triumph of Spirit*. Norman: University of Oklahoma Press, 1995.

Griswold del Castillo, Richard, and Manuel Hidalgo, eds. *Chicano Social and Political History in the XIX Century*. Encino, Calif.: Floricanto Press, 1992.

Guerin-Gonzales, Camille. *Mexican Workers and American Dreams: Immigration, Repatriation, and California Farm Labor, 1900–1939*. New Brunswick, N.J.: Rutgers University Press, 1994.

Guerrero, Vladimir. *The Anza Trail and the Settling of California*. Santa Clara, Calif.: Heyday Books, 2006.

Guilbault, Rose Castillo. *Farmworker's Daughter: Growing Up Mexican in America*. Berkeley: Heyday Books, 2005.

Gutiérrez, David G., ed. *Between Two Worlds: Mexican Immigrants in the United States*. Wilmington, Del.: Scholarly Resources, 1996.

———, ed. *The Columbia History of Latinos in the United States since 1960*. New York: Columbia University Press, 2004.

———. *Walls and Mirrors: Mexican Americans, Mexican Immigrants, and the Politics of Ethnicity*. Berkeley and Los Angeles: University of California Press, 1995.

Gutiérrez, José Ángel. *Making of a Chicano Militant: Lessons from Cristal*. Madison: University of Wisconsin Press, 1998.

Gutiérrez, Ramón A. *When Jesus Came, the Corn Mothers Went Away: Marriage, Sexuality, and Power in New Mexico, 1500–1846*. Stanford, Calif.: Stanford University Press, 1991.

Gutiérrez-Jones, Carl. *Rethinking the Borderlands: Between Chicano Culture and Legal Discourse*. Berkeley and Los Angeles: University of California Press, 1994.

Haas, Lisabeth. *Conquests and Historical Identities in California, 1769–1936*. Berkeley and Los Angeles: University of California Press, 1995.

Habell-Pallán, Michelle, and Mary Romero, eds. *Latina/o Popular Culture*. New York: New York University Press, 2002.

Hadley-García, George. *Hispanic Hollywood: The Latins in Motion Pictures*. New York: Carol Publishing, 1990.

Hall, Thomas D. *Social Change in the Southwest, 1350–1880*. Lawrence: University Press of Kansas, 1989.

Haney López, Ian F. *Racism on Trial: The Chicano Fight for Justice*. Cambridge, Mass.: Harvard University Press, 2003.

Hayes-Bautista, David E. *La Nueva California: Latinos in the Golden State*. Berkeley and Los Angeles: University of California Press, 2004.

Hellman, Judith Adler. *The World of Mexican Migrants: The Rock and the Hard Place*. New York: New Press, 2008.

Herrera-Sobek, María. *The Mexican Corrido: A Feminist Analysis*. Bloomington: Indiana University Press, 1990.

———. *Northward Bound: The Mexican Immigrant Experience in Ballad and Song*. Bloomington: Indiana University Press, 1993.

———, ed. *Reconstructing a Chicano/a Literary Heritage: Hispanic Colonial Literature of the Southwest*. Tucson: University of Arizona Press, 1998.

Heyck, Denis Lynn Daly, ed. *Barrios and Borderlands: Cultures of Latinos and Latinas in the United States*. London: Routledge, 1994.

Hondagneu-Sotelo, Pierrette. *Doméstica: Immigrant Workers Cleaning and Caring in the Shadows of Affluence*. Berkeley and Los Angeles: University of California Press, 2001.

———. *Gendered Transitions: Mexican Experiences of Immigration*. Berkeley and Los Angeles: University of California Press, 1994.

Hordes, Stanley M. *To the End of the Earth: A History of the Crypto-Jews of New Mexico*. New York: Columbia University Press, 2005.

Huntington, Samuel. *Who Are We? The Challenges to America's National Identity*. New York: Simon and Schuster, 2004.

Hurtado, Aída, and Patricia Gurin. *Chicana/o Identity in a Changing U.S. Society: ¿Quién Soy? ¿Quiénes Somos?* Tucson: University of Arizona Press, 2004.

Hurtado, Albert L. *Indian Survival on the California Frontier*. New Haven, Conn.: Yale University Press, 1988.

———. *Intimate Frontiers: Sex, Gender, and Culture in Old California*. Albuquerque: University of New Mexico Press, 1999.

———. *John Sutter: A Life on the North American Frontier*. Norman: University of Oklahoma Press, 2006.

Hutchinson, Sydney. *From Quebradita to Duranguense: Dance in Mexican American Youth Culture*. Tucson: University of Arizona Press, 2007.

Iber, Jorge. *Hispanics in the Mormon Zion, 1912–1999.* College Station: Texas A&M University Press, 2000.

Iber, Jorge, and Arnoldo De León. *Hispanics in the American West.* Santa Barbara, Calif.: ABC–CLIO, 2005.

Iber, Jorge, and Samuel O. Regalado, eds. *Mexican Americans and Sports: A Reader on Athletics and Barrio Life.* College Station: Texas A&M University Press, 2007.

Jackson, Robert H. *From Savages to Subjects: Missions in the History of the American Southwest.* Armonk, N.Y.: M.E. Sharpe, 2000.

————. *Missions and Frontiers of Spanish America.* Scottsdale, Ariz.: Pentacle Press, 2005.

Jankowski, Martin Sánchez. *City Bound: Urban Life and Political Attitudes among Chicano Youth.* Albuquerque: University of New Mexico Press, 1986.

Jiménez, Alfredo, ed. *Handbook of Hispanic Cultures in the United States.* Houston, Tex.: Arte Público Press and Instituto de Cooperación Iberoamericana, 1994.

Jiménez, Carlos M. *The Mexican American Heritage.* Berkeley: TQS Publications, 1993.

Jiménez, Francisco, Alma M. García, and Richard A. García. *Ethnic Community Builders: Mexican-Americans in Search of Justice and Power; The Struggle for Citizenship Rights in San José, California.* Walnut Creek, Calif.: AltaMira Press, 2007.

Jirasek, Rita Arias, and Carlos Tortolero. *Mexican Chicago.* Charleston, S.C.: Arcadia Publishing, 2001.

Johnson, Benjamin Heber. *Revolution in Texas: How a Forgotten Rebellion and Its Bloody Suppression Turned Mexicans into Americans.* New Haven, Conn.: Yale University Press, 2003.

Johnson, Benjamin Heber, and Jeffrey Gusky. *Bordertown: The Odyssey of an American Place.* New Haven, Conn.: Yale University Press, 2008.

Johnson, Kevin R. *How Did You Get to Be Mexican? A White/Brown Man's Search for Identity.* Philadelphia: Temple University Press, 1999.

Johnson-Webb, Karen D. *Recruiting Latino Labor: Immigrants in Non-Traditional Areas.* New York: LFB Scholarly Publishing, 2003.

Jones, Richard C. *Ambivalent Journey: U.S. Migration and Economic Mobility in North-Central Mexico.* Tucson: University of Arizona Press, 1995.

Kanellos, Nicolás, ed. *The Hispanic-American Almanac: A Reference Work on Hispanics in the United States.* Detroit: Gale Research, 1993.

————. *A History of Hispanic Theatre in the United States: Origins to 1940.* Austin: University of Texas Press, 1990.

Kalpowitz, Craig A. *LULAC: Mexican Americans and National Policy.* College Station: Texas A&M University Press, 2005.

Kearney, Milo, and Manuel Medrano. *Medieval Culture and the Mexican American Borderlands.* College Station: Texas A&M University Press, 2001.

Keefe, Susan E., and Amado M. Padilla. *Chicano Ethnicity.* Albuquerque: University of New Mexico Press, 1987.

Kells, Michelle Hall. *Héctor P. García: Everyday Rhetoric and Mexican American Civil Rights.* Carbondale: Southern Illinois University Press, 2006.

Kessell, John L. *Pueblos, Spaniards, and the Kingdom of New Mexico.* Norman: University of Oklahoma Press, 2008.

————. *Spain in the Southwest: A Narrative History of Colonial New Mexico, Arizona, Texas, and California.* Norman: University of Oklahoma Press, 2002.

Krauze, Enrique. *Mexico: Biography of Power: A History of Modern Mexico, 1810–1996.* New York: Harper Collins, 1997.

Kreneck, Thomas H. *Mexican American Odyssey: Felix Tijerina, Entrepreneur and Civic Leader, 1905–1965.* College Station: Texas A&M University Press, 2001.

Langley, Lester D. *MexAmerica.* New York: Crown, 1988.

Laó-Montes, Agustín, and Arlene Dávila, eds. *Mambo Montage: The Latinization of New York City.* New York: Columbia University Press, 2001.

Larralde, Carlos, and José Rodolfo Jacobo. *Juan N. Cortina and the Struggle for Justice in Texas.* Dubuque, Ia.: Kendall/Hunt, 2000.

Leclerc, Gustavo, Raúl Vila, and Michael J. Dear, eds. *Urban Latino Cultures: La Vida Latina en Los Angeles.* Thousand Oaks, Calif.: SAGE Publishers, 1999.

Leonard, Karen Isaksen. *Making Ethnic Choices: California's Punjabi Mexican Americans.* Philadelphia: Temple University Press, 1992.

Limón, José. *Mexican Ballads, Chicano Poems: History and Influence in Mexican-American Social Poetry.* Berkeley and Los Angeles: University of California Press, 1992.

Longoria, Mario. *Athletes Remembered: Mexicano/Latino Professional Football Players, 1929–1970.* Tempe, Ariz.: Bilingual Press, 1997.

López, Ann Aurelia. *The Farmworkers' Journey.* Berkeley and Los Angeles: University of California Press, 2007.

Loza, Steven. *Barrio Rhythm: Mexican American Music in Los Angeles.* Urbana: University of Illinois Press, 1993.

Lugo, Alejandro. *Fragmented Lives, Assembled Parts: Culture, Capitalism, and Conquest at the U.S.-Mexico Border.* Austin: University of Texas Press, 2008.

Machado, Daisy L. *Of Borders and Margins: Hispanic Disciples in Texas, 1888–1945.* New York: Oxford University Press, 2002.

Macías, Thomas. *Mestizo in America: Generations of Mexican Ethnicity in the Suburban Southwest.* Tucson: University of Arizona Press, 2006.

Maciel, David R., and María Herrera-Sobek, eds. *Culture across Borders: Mexican Immigration and Popular Culture.* Tucson: University of Arizona Press, 1998.

Maciel, David R., and Isidro D. Ortiz, eds. *Chicanas/Chicanos at the Crossroads: Social, Economic, and Political Change.* Tucson: University of Arizona Press, 1996.

Magaña, Lisa. *Mexican Americans and the Politics of Diversity: ¡Querer es poder!* Tucson: University of Arizona Press, 2005.

Marín, Marguerite V. *Social Protest in an Urban Barrio: A Study of the Chicano Movement, 1966–1974.* Lanham, Md.: University Press of America, 1991.

Mariscal, George, ed. *Aztlán and Viet Nam: Chicano and Chicana Experiences of the War.* Berkeley and Los Angeles: University of California Press, 1999.

———. *Brown-Eyed Children of the Sun: Lessons from the Chicano Movement.* Albuquerque: University of New Mexico Press, 2005.

Márquez, Benjamin. *Constructing Identities in Mexican-American Political Organizations: Choosing Issues, Taking Sides.* Austin: University of Texas Press, 2003.

———. *LULAC: The Evolution of a Mexican American Political Organization.* Austin: University of Texas Press, 1993.

———. *Power and Politics in a Chicano Barrio: A Study of Mobilization Efforts and Community Power in El Paso.* Lanham, Md.: University Press of America, 1985.

Martin, Patricia Preciado. *Songs My Mother Sang to Me: An Oral History of Mexican American Women.* Tucson: University of Arizona Press, 1992.

Martinez, Elizabeth "Betita," ed. *500 Years of Chicana Women's History.* Piscataway, N.J.: Rutgers University Press, 2007.

Martínez, Elizabeth Coonrod. *Josefina Niggli, Mexican American Writer: A Critical Biography.* Albuquerque: University of New Mexico Press, 2007.

Martínez, Juan Francisco. *Sea la Luz: The Making of Mexican Protestantism in the American Southwest, 1829–1900.* Denton: University of North Texas, 2007.

Martínez, Oscar J. *Mexican-Origin People in the United States: A Topical History.* Tucson: University of Arizona Press, 2001.

———. *Troublesome Border.* Tucson: University of Arizona Press, 1988.

Martínez, Richard Edward. *PADRES: The National Chicano Priest Movement.* Austin: University of Texas Press, 2005.

Martínez, Rubén. *Crossing Over: A Mexican Family on the Migrant Trail.* New York: Metropolitan Books, 2001.

————. *The Other Side: Notes from the New L.A., Mexico City, and Beyond*. New York: Vintage Books, 1993.

Massey, Douglas S., ed. *New Faces in New Places: The Changing Geography of American Immigration*. New York: Russell Sage Foundation, 2008.

Massey, Douglas S., Jorge Durand, and Nolan J. Malone. *Beyond Smoke and Mirrors: Mexican Immigration in an Era of Economic Integration*. New York: Russell Sage Foundation, 2002.

Massey, Douglas, et al. *Return to Aztlán: The Social Process of International Migration from Western Mexico*. Berkeley and Los Angeles: University of California Press, 1987.

Matovina, Timothy. *Guadalupe and Her Faithful: Latino Catholics in San Antonio, from Colonial Origins to the Present*. Baltimore: Johns Hopkins University Press, 2005.

————. *Tejano Religion and Ethnicity: San Antonio, 1821–1860*. Austin: University of Texas Press, 1995.

McDonnell, Jeanne Farr. *Juana Briones of Nineteenth-Century California*. Tucson: University of Arizona Press, 2008.

McFarland, Pancho. *Chicano Rap: Gender and Violence in the Postindustrial Barrio*. Austin: University of Texas Press, 2008.

McKenna, Teresa, and Flora Ida Ortiz, eds. *The Broken Web: The Educational Experience of Hispanic American Women*. Claremont and Berkeley: Tomás Rivera Center and Floricanto Press, 1988.

McKenzie, Phyllis. *The Mexican Texans*. College Station: Texas A&M University Press, 2004.

McWilliams, Carey. *North from Mexico: The Spanish-Speaking People of the United States*. Rev. ed. Westport, Conn: Greenwood Press/Praeger, 1990.

Meier, Matt S. *Mexican American Biographies: A Historical Dictionary, 1836–1987*. Westport, Conn.: Greenwood Press, 1988.

Meier, Matt S., and Feliciano Rivera. *Mexican Americans/American Mexicans: From Conquistadors to Chicanos*. Rev. ed. New York: Hill and Wang, 1993.

Meier, Matt S., and Margo Gutiérrez, eds. *Encyclopedia of the Mexican American Civil Rights Movement*. Westport, Conn.: Greenwood Press, 2000.

Melville, Margarita B., ed. *Mexicanas at Work in the United States*. Houston, Tex.: Mexican American Studies Program, University of Houston, 1988.

Menchaca, Martha. *Mexican Outsiders: A Community History of Marginalization and Discrimination in California*. Austin: University of Texas Press, 1995.

Millard, Ann V., and Jorge Chapa, eds. *Apple Pie and Enchiladas: Latino Newcomers in the Rural Midwest*. Austin: University of Texas Press, 2004.

Miller, Robert Ryal. *Juan Alvarado: Governor of California, 1836–1842*. Norman: University of Oklahoma Press, 1998.

Mindiola, Tatcho, Jr., and Emilio Zamora, eds. *Chicano Discourse: Selected Conference Proceedings of the National Association for Chicano Studies*. Houston, Tex.: Mexican American Studies Program, University of Houston, 1992.

Mintz, Steven, ed. *Mexican-American Voices*. New York: Brandywine Press, 2000.

Minutaglio, Bill. *The President's Counselor: The Rise to Power of Alberto Gonzales*. New York: HarperCollins, 2006.

Miranda, M. L. *A History of Hispanics in Southern Nevada*. Reno: University of Nevada Press, 1997.

Mirandé, Alfredo. *The Chicano Experience: An Alternative Perspective*. Notre Dame, Ind.: University of Notre Dame Press, 1985.

————. *Hombres y Machos: Masculinity and Latino Culture*. Boulder, Colo.: Westview Press, 1997.

Monday, Jane Clements, and Frances Brannen Vick. *Petra's Legacy: The South Texas Ranching Empire of Petra Vela and Mifflin Kenedy*. College Station: Texas A&M University Press, 2007.

Molina, Natalia. *Fit to Be Citizens? Public Health and Race in Los Angeles, 1879–1939*. Berkeley and Los Angeles: University of California Press, 2006.

Monroy, Douglas. *The Borders Within: Encounters between Mexico and the U.S.* Tucson: University of Arizona Press, 2008.

———. *Thrown among Strangers: The Making of Mexican Culture in Frontier California*. Berkeley and Los Angeles: University of California Press, 1990.

Monsiváis, George I. *Hispanic Immigrant Identity: Political Allegiance vs. Cultural Preference*. New York: LFB Scholarly Publishing, 2004.

Montejano, David. *Anglos and Mexicans in the Making of Texas, 1836–1986*. Austin: University of Texas Press, 1987.

———, ed. *Chicano Politics and Society in the Late Twentieth Century*. Austin: University of Texas Press, 1999.

Montgomery, Charles. *The Spanish Redemption: Heritage, Power, and Loss on New Mexico's Upper Rio Grande*. Berkeley and Los Angeles: University of California Press, 2002.

Montoya, María E. *Translating Property: The Maxwell Land Grant and the Conflict over Land in the American West, 1840–1900*. Rev. ed. Lawrence: University Press of Kansas, 2005.

Moore, Joan W., and Raquel Pinderhughes, eds. *In the Barrios: Latinos and the Underclass Debate*. New York: Russell Sage Foundation, 1993.

Mora-Ninci, Carlos. *Latinos in the West: The Student Movement and Academic Labor in Los Angeles*. Lanham, Md.: Rowman and Littlefield, 2007.

Mora-Torres, Juan. *The Making of the Mexican Border: The State, Capitalism, and Society in Nuevo León, 1848–1910*. Austin: University of Texas Press, 2001.

Morales, Ed. *The Latin Beat: The Rhythms and Roots of Latin Music from Bossa Nova to Salsa and Beyond*. Cambridge, Mass.: Da Capo Press, 2003.

Muñoz, Carlos, Jr. *Youth, Identity, Power: The Chicano Movement*. New York: Verso, 1989.

Murcia, Rebecca Thatcher. *Américo Paredes*. Bear, Del.: Mitchell Lane Publishers, 2004.

Murguía, Alejandro. *The Medicine of Memory: A Mechica Clan in California*. Austin: University of Texas Press, 2002.

Murphy, Arthur D., Colleen Blanchard, and Jennifer A. Hill, eds. *Latino Workers in the Contemporary South*. Athens: University of Georgia Press, 2001.

Navarrete, Rubén, Jr. *A Darker Shade of Crimson: Odyssey of a Harvard Chicano*. New York: Bantam Books, 1993.

Navarro, Armando. *The Cristal Experiment: A Chicano Struggle for Community Control*. Madison: University of Wisconsin Press, 1998.

———. *La Raza Unida Party: A Chicano Challenge to the U.S. Two-Party Dictatorship*. Philadelphia: Temple University Press, 2000.

———. *Mexican American Youth Organization: Avant-Garde of the Chicano Movement in Texas*. Austin: University of Texas Press, 1995.

———. *Mexicano Political Experience in Occupied Aztlán: Struggles and Change*. Walnut Creek, Calif.: AltaMira Press, 2005.

Nieto-Phillips, John M. *The Language of Blood: The Making of Spanish-American Identity in New Mexico, 1880s–1930s*. Albuquerque: University of New Mexico Press, 2004.

Noriega, Chon, ed. *Chicanos and Film: Representation and Resistance*. Minneapolis: University of Minnesota Press, 1992.

Nostrand, Richard L. *El Cerrito, New Mexico: Eight Generations in a Spanish Village*. Norman: University of Oklahoma Press, 2003.

———. *The Hispano Homeland*. Norman: University of Oklahoma Press, 1992.

Ochoa, Enrique C., and Gilda L. Ochoa, eds. *Latino Los Angeles: Transformations, Communities, and Activism*. Tucson: University of Arizona Press, 2005.

Ochoa, Gilda L. *Becoming Neighbors in a Mexican American Community: Power, Conflict, and Solidarity*. Austin: University of Texas Press, 2004.

Officer, James E. *Hispanic Arizona, 1536–1856*. Tucson: University of Arizona Press, 1987.

Olivas, Louis, ed. *Arizona Hispanics: The Evolution of Influence.* Tempe: Arizona State University, 2002.

Ornelas, Michael R., ed. *Beyond 1848: Interpretations of the Modern Chicano Experience.* Dubuque, Ia.: Kendall/Hunt, 1999.

Oropeza, Lorena. *¡Raza Si! ¡Guerra No! Chicano Protest and Patriotism during the Viet Nam Era.* Berkeley and Los Angeles: University of California Press, 2005.

Orozco, E. C. *Republican Protestantism in Aztlán: The Encounter between Mexicanism and Anglo-Saxon Secular Humanism in the United States Southwest.* 2nd ed. Glendale, Calif.: Petereins Press, 1991.

Padilla, Félix M. *Latino Ethnic Consciousness: The Case of Mexican Americans and Puerto Ricans in Chicago.* Notre Dame, Ind.: University of Notre Dame Press, 1985.

Pagán, Eduardo Obregón. *Murder at the Sleepy Lagoon: Zoot Suits, Race, and Riot in Wartime L.A.* Chapel Hill: University of North Carolina Press, 2003.

Pardo, Mary S. *Mexican American Women Activists: Identity and Resistance in Two Los Angeles Communities.* Philadelphia: Temple University Press, 1998.

Paredes, Américo. *Folklore and Culture on the Texas-Mexican Border.* Ed. by Richard Bauman. Austin: Center for Mexican American Studies, University of Texas, 1993.

Pastor, Robert A., and Jorge G. Castañeda. *Limits to Friendship: The United States and Mexico.* New York: Vintage, 1993.

Peña, Devon G. *Mexican Americans and the Environment: Tierra y Vida.* Tucson: University of Arizona Press, 2005.

———. *The Terror of the Machine: Technology, Work, Gender, and Ecology on the U.S.-Mexico Border.* Austin: Center for Mexican American Studies, University of Texas, 1997.

Peña, Manuel. *Música Tejana.* College Station: Texas A&M University Press, 1999.

———. *The Texas-Mexican Conjunto: History of a Working-Class Music.* Austin: University of Texas Press, 1985.

Perea, Juan F., ed. *Immigrants Out! The New Nativism and the Anti-Immigrant Impulse in the United States.* New York: New York University Press, 1997.

Pérez, Emma. *The Decolonial Imaginary: Writing Chicanas into History.* Bloomington: Indiana University Press, 1999.

Pérez-Torres, Rafael. *Mestizaje: Critical Uses of Race in Chicano Culture.* Minneapolis: University of Minnesota Press, 2006.

Perlmann, Joel. *Italians Then, Mexicans Now: Immigrant Origins and Second-Generation Progress, 1890 to 2000.* New York: Russell Sage Foundation, 2005.

Perrigo, Lynn I. *Hispanos: Historic Leaders in New Mexico.* Santa Fe: Sunstone Press, 1985.

Phillips, Michael. *White Metropolis: Race, Ethnicity, and Religion in Dallas, 1841–2001.* Austin: University of Texas Press, 2006.

Pitt, Leonard. *The Decline of the Californios: A Social History of the Spanish-Speaking Californians, 1846–1900.* Rev. ed. Berkeley and Los Angeles: University of California Press, 1999.

Pitti, Stephen J. *The Devil in Silicon Valley: Northern California, Race, and Mexican Americans.* Princeton, N.J.: Princeton University Press, 2003.

Portales, Marco. *Crowding Out Latinos: Mexican Americans in the Public Consciousness.* Philadelphia: Temple University Press, 2000.

Portes, Alejandro, and Robert L. Bach. *Latin Journey: Cuban and Mexican Immigrants in the United States.* Berkeley and Los Angeles: University of California Press, 1985.

Portes, Alejandro, and Rubén G. Rumbaut. *Immigrant America: A Portrait.* Berkeley and Los Angeles: University of California Press, 1990.

———, eds. *Legacies: The Story of the Immigrant Second Generation.* Berkeley and Los Angeles: University of California Press, 2001.

Poyo, Gerald E., and Gilberto M. Hinojosa, eds. *Tejano Origins in Eighteenth-Century San Antonio.* Austin: University of Texas Press, 1991.

Privett, Stephen A., S.J. *The U.S. Catholic Church and Its Hispanic Members: The Pastoral Vision of Archbishop Robert E. Lucey.* San Antonio, Tex.: Trinity University Press, 1988.

Prouty, Marco G. *César Chávez, the Catholic Bishops, and the Farmworkers' Struggle for Social Justice.* Tucson: University of Arizona Press, 2006.

Pulido, Laura. *Black, Brown, Yellow, and Left: Radical Activism in Los Angeles.* Berkeley and Los Angeles: University of California Press, 2006.

Quezada, J. Gilberto. *Border Boss: Manuel B. Bravo and Zapata County.* College Station: Texas A&M University Press, 1999.

Quinn, Anthony. *One Man Tango.* New York: HarperCollins, 1995.

Quiñones, Sam. *Antonio's Gun and Delfino's Dream: True Tales of Mexican Migration.* Albuquerque: University of New Mexico Press, 2007.

Quiroz, Anthony. *Claiming Citizenship: Mexican Americans in Victoria, Texas.* College Station: Texas A&M University Press, 2005.

Radding, Cynthia. *Wandering Peoples: Colonialism, Ethnic Spaces, and Ecological Frontiers in Northwestern Mexico, 1700–1850.* Durham, N.C.: Duke University Press, 1997.

Ramírez, Elizabeth C. *Chicanas/Latinas in American Theatre: A History of Performance.* Bloomington: Indiana University Press, 2000.

Ramírez, Ricardo. *Faith Expressions of Hispanics in the Southwest.* San Antonio, Tex.: Mexican American Cultural Center, 1990.

Ramírez Berg, Charles. *Poster Art from the Golden Age of Mexican Cinema.* Austin: University of Texas Press, 1997.

Ramos, Henry A. J. *The American G.I. Forum: In Pursuit of the Dream, 1948–1983.* Houston, Tex.: Arte Público Press, 1998.

Ramos, Raúl A. *Beyond the Alamo: Forging Mexican Ethnicity in San Antonio, 1821–1861.* Chapel Hill: University of North Carolina Press, 2008.

Rebolledo, Tey Diana, ed. *Nuestras Mujeres: Hispanas of New Mexico, Their Images and Their Lives, 1582–1992.* Albuquerque, N.M.: El Norte Publications/Academia, 1992.

Reichman, Jill S. *Immigration, Acculturation, and Health: The Mexican Diaspora.* New York: LFB Scholarly Publishing, 2006.

Regalado, Samuel O. *Viva Baseball! Latin Major Leaguers and Their Special Hunger.* 3rd ed. Urbana: University of Illinois Press, 2008.

Reséndez, Andrés. *Changing National Identities at the Frontier: Texas and New Mexico, 1800–1850.* New York: Cambridge University Press, 2005.

———. *A Texas Patriot on Trial in Mexico: José Antonio Navarro and the Texan Santa Fe Expedition.* Dallas, Tex.: DeGolyer Library and William P. Clements Center for Southwest Studies, 2005.

Reyes, David, and Tom Waldman. *Land of a Thousand Dances: Chicano Rock 'n' Roll from Southern California.* Albuquerque: University of New Mexico Press, 1998.

Richardson, Chad. *Batos, Bolillos, and Pelados: Class and Culture on the South Texas Border.* Austin: University of Texas Press, 1999.

Ríos-Bustamante, Antonio. *Mexican Los Angeles: A Narrative and Pictorial History.* Encino, Calif.: Floricanto Press, 1992.

———. *Regions of La Raza: Changing Interpretations of Mexican American Regional History and Culture.* Encino, Calif.: Floricanto Press, 1992.

Ríos-Bustamante, Antonio, and Pedro Castillo. *An Illustrated History of Mexican Los Angeles, 1781–1985.* Los Angeles: Chicano Studies Research Center, University of California, 1986.

Rivas-Rodríguez, Maggie, ed. *Mexican Americans and World War II.* Austin: University of Texas Press, 2005.

Rivas-Rodríguez, Maggie, et al. *A Legacy Greater Than Words: Stories of U.S. Latinos and Latinas of the WWII Generation.* Austin: U.S. Latino & Latina WWII Oral History Project, University of Texas Press, 2006.

Rocard, Marcienne. *The Children of the Sun: Mexican-Americans in the Literature of the United States*. Trans. by Edward G. Brown Jr. Tucson: University of Arizona Press, 1989.

Rochín, Refugio I. *Economic Perspectives of the Hispanic Community*. San Antonio, Tex.: Tomás Rivera Center, 1988.

Rochín, Refugio I., and Dennis N. Valdés, eds. *Voices of a New Chicana/o History*. East Lansing: Michigan State University Press, 2000.

Rodríguez, Gregory. *Mongrels, Bastards, Orphans, and Vagabonds: Mexican Immigration and the Future of Race in America*. New York: Pantheon Books, 2007.

Rodríguez, Jeanette. *Our Lady of Guadalupe: Faith and Empowerment among Mexican American Women*. Austin: University of Texas Press, 1994.

Rodríguez, Luis J. *Always Running, La Vida Loca: Gang Days in L.A.* Willimantic, Conn.: Curbstone Press, 1993.

Rodríguez, Marc S., ed. *Repositioning North American Migration History: New Directions in Modern Continental Migration, Citizenship and Community*. Rochester, N.Y.: University of Rochester, 2004.

Romero, Mary. *Maid in the USA*. New York: Routledge, 1992.

Romero, Mary, and Cordelia Candelaria, eds. *Community Empowerment and Chicano Scholarship*. Los Angeles: National Association for Chicano Studies, 1992.

Rosales, F. Arturo. *Chicano! History of the Mexican American Civil Rights Movement*. Houston, Tex.: Arte Público Press, 1997.

———. *¡Pobre raza! Violence, Justice, and Mobilization among México Lindo Immigrants, 1900–1936*. Austin: University of Texas Press, 1999.

———, ed. *Testimonio: A Documentary History of the Mexican American Struggle for Civil Rights*. Houston, Tex.: Arte Público Press, 2000.

Rosales, Rodolfo. *The Illusion of Inclusion: The Untold Political Story of San Antonio*. Austin: University of Texas Press, 2002.

Rosenus, Alan. *General M. G. Vallejo and the Advent of the Americans*. Albuquerque: University of New Mexico Press, 1995.

Ruiz, Vicki L. *Cannery Women/Cannery Lives: Mexican Women, Unionization, and the California Food Processing Industry, 1930–1950*. Albuquerque: University of New Mexico Press, 1987.

———. *From Out of the Shadows: Mexican Women in Twentieth-Century America*. New York: Oxford University Press, 1998.

Ruiz, Vicki L., and John R. Chávez, eds. *Memories and Migrations: Mapping Boricua and Chicana Histories*. Urbana: University of Illinois Press, 2008.

Ruiz, Vicki L., and Virginia Sánchez, eds. *Latina Legacies: Identity, Biography, and Community*. New York: Oxford University Press, 2005.

Ruiz, Vicki L., and Susan Tiano, eds. *Women on the U.S./Mexican Border: Responses to Change*. London: Allen and Unwin, 1987.

Salas, Elizabeth. *Soldaderas in the Mexican Military: Myth and History*. Austin: University of Texas Press, 1990.

Saldívar, José David. *Border Matters: Remapping American Cultural Studies*. Berkeley and Los Angeles: University of California Press, 1997.

Saldívar, Ramón. *Chicano Narrative: The Dialectics of Difference*. Madison: University of Wisconsin Press, 1990.

Salmerón, Roberto M. *Indian Revolts in Northern New Spain: A Synthesis of Resistance, 1680–1786*. Lanham, Md.: University Press of America, 1991.

Samora, Julián, and Patricia Vandel Simon. *A History of the Mexican-American People*. 2nd ed. Notre Dame, Ind.: University of Notre Dame Press, 1993.

Sánchez, George J. *Becoming Mexican American: Ethnicity, Culture and Identity in Chicano Los Angeles, 1900–1945*. New York: Oxford University Press, 1993.

Sánchez, Leslie. *Los Republicanos: Why Hispanics and Republicans Need Each Other.* New York: Palgrave Macmillan, 2007.

Sánchez, Marta. *"Shakin' Up" Race and Gender: Intercultural Connections in Puerto Rican, African American, and Chicano Narratives and Culture (1965–1995).* Austin: University of Texas Press, 2006.

Sánchez, Rosaura. *Telling Identities: The Californio Testimonios.* Minneapolis: University of Minnesota Press, 1995.

Sandos, James A. *Converting California: Indians and Franciscans in the Missions.* New Haven, Conn.: Yale University Press, 2004.

Santa Ana, Otto. *Brown Tide Rising: Metaphors of Latinos in Contemporary American Public Discourse.* Austin: University of Texas Press, 2002.

Santiago, Myrna I. *The Ecology of Oil: Environment, Labor, and the Mexican Revolution, 1900–1938.* New York: Cambridge University Press, 2006.

San Miguel, Guadalupe, Jr. *"Let All of Them Take Heed": Mexican Americans and the Campaign for Educational Equality in Texas, 1910–1981.* Austin: University of Texas Press, 1987.

———. *Tejano Proud: Tex-Mex Music in the Twentieth Century.* College Station: Texas A&M University Press, 2002.

Schultze, George E. *Strangers in a Foreign Land: The Organizing of Catholic Latinos in the United States.* New York: Rowman and Littlefield, 2007.

Sepúlveda, Juan A., Jr. *The Life and Times of Willie Velásquez: Su Voto es Su Voz.* Houston, Tex.: Arte Público Press, 2003.

Shaw, Randy. *Beyond the Fields: Cesar Chavez, the UFW, and the Struggle for Justice in the 21st Century.* Berkeley and Los Angeles: University of California Press, 2008.

Sheridan, Thomas E. *Los Tucsonenses: The Mexican Community in Tucson, 1854–1941.* Tucson: University of Arizona Press, 1986.

Shorris, Earl. *Latinos: A Biography of the People.* New York: W. W. Norton, 1992.

———. *The Life and Times of Mexico.* New York: W. W. Norton, 2004.

Skerry, Peter. *Mexican Americans: The Ambivalent Minority.* New York: Free Press, 1993.

Soltero, Carlos R. *Latinos and American Law: Landmark Supreme Court Cases.* Austin: University of Texas Press, 2006.

Staudt, Kathleen. *Violence and Activism at the Border: Gender, Fear, and Everyday Life in Ciudad Juárez.* Austin: University of Texas Press, 2008.

Stavans, Ilan. *The Hispanic Condition: Reflections on Culture and Identity in America.* New York: HarperCollins, 1995.

Strachuitz, Chris, with James Nicolopulos, comp. *Lydia Mendoza: A Family Autobiography.* Houston, Tex.: Arte Público Press, 1993.

Street, Richard Steven. *Beasts of the Field: A Narrative History of California Farmworkers, 1769–1913.* Stanford, Calif.: Stanford University Press, 2004.

Suárez-Orozco, Carola, and Marcelo Suárez-Orozco. *Transformations: Migration, Family Life, and Achievement Motivation among Latino Adolescents.* Stanford, Calif.: Stanford University Press, 1995.

Súarez-Orozco, Marcelo M., ed. *Crossings: Mexican Immigration in Interdisciplinary Perspectives.* Cambridge, Mass.: Harvard University Press, 2002.

Súarez-Orozco, Marcelo M., and Mariela M. Páez, eds. *Latinos: Remaking America.* Berkeley and Los Angeles: University of California Press, 2002.

Tatum, Charles M. *Chicano Popular Culture: Que Hable el Pueblo.* Tucson: University of Arizona Press, 2001.

Telles, Edward E., and Vilma Ortiz. *Generations of Exclusion: Mexican Americans, Assimilation, and Race.* New York: Russell Sage Foundation, 2008.

Thompson, Jerry. *Cortina: Defending the Mexican Name in Texas.* College Station: Texas A&M University Press, 2007.

Tijerina, Andrés. *Tejanos and Texas under the Mexican Flag, 1821–1836.* College Station: Texas A&M University Press, 1994.

Tijerina, Reies López. *They Called Me "King Tiger": My Struggle for the Land and Our Rights.* Trans. José Angel Gutiérrez. Houston, Tex.: Arte Pùblico Press, 2000.

Torres, Noe. *Baseball's First Mexican-American Star: The Amazing Story of Leo Naja.* Tamarac, Fla.: Llumina Press, 2006.

Treviño, Roberto R. *The Church in the Barrio: Mexican American Ethno-Catholicism in Houston.* Chapel Hill: University of North Carolina Press, 2006.

Treviño, Roberto R., and Richard V. Francaviglia, eds. *Catholicism in the American West: A Rosary of Hidden Voices.* College Station: Texas A&M University Press, 2007.

Truett, Samuel, and Elliott Young, eds. *Continental Crossroad: Remapping U.S.-Mexican Borderlands History.* Durham, N.C.: Duke University Press, 2004.

Trujillo, Charley, ed. *Soldados: Chicanos in Viet Nam.* San Jose, Calif.: Chusma House Publications, 1990.

Tywoniak, Frances Esquibel, and Mario T. García. *Migrant Daughter: Coming of Age as a Mexican American Woman.* Berkeley and Los Angeles: University of California Press, 1999.

Vaca, Nicolás C. *The Presumed Alliance: The Unspoken Conflict between Latinos and Blacks and What It Means for America.* New York: Harper Collins, 2004.

Valdés, Dennis Nodín. *Al Norte: Agricultural Workers in the Great Lakes Region, 1917–1970.* Austin: University of Texas Press, 1991.

Valdés, Dionicio. *Mexicans in Minnesota.* St. Paul: Minnesota Historical Society Press, 2005.

Valdés, Guadalupe. *Con Respeto: Bridging the Distances between Culturally Diverse Families and Schools--An Ethnographic Portrait.* Williston, Vt.: Teachers College Press, 1996.

Valencia, Reynaldo Anaya, et al. *Mexican Americans and the Law: ¡El pueblo unido jamás será vencido!* Tucson: University of Arizona Press, 2004.

Valle, Victor M., and Rodolfo D. Torres. *Latino Metropolis.* Minneapolis: University of Minnesota Press, 2000.

Vargas, Zaragoza. *Labor Rights Are Civil Rights: Mexican American Workers in Twentieth-Century America.* Princeton, N.J.: Princeton University Press, 2005.

———. *Proletarians of the North: A History of Mexican Industrial Workers in Detroit and the Midwest, 1917–1933.* Berkeley and Los Angeles: University of California Press, 1993.

Vásquez, Francisco H., and Rodolfo D. Torres, eds. *Latino/a Thought: Culture, Politics, and Society.* Lanham, Md.: Rowman and Littlefield, 2003.

Velasco Ortiz, Laura. *Mixtec Transnational Identity.* Tucson: University of Arizona Press, 2005.

Vélez-Ibáñez, Carlos G. *Border Visions: Mexican Cultures of the Southwest United States.* Tucson: University of Arizona Press, 1996.

Vento, Arnoldo Carlos. *Mestizo: The History, Culture and Politics of the Mexican and the Chicano.* Lanham, Md.: University Press of America, 1998.

Vigil, Ernesto B. *The Crusade for Justice: Chicano Militancy and the Government's War on Dissent.* Madison: University of Wisconsin Press, 1999.

Vigil, James Diego. *Barrio Gangs: Street Life and Identity in Southern California.* Austin: University of Texas Press, 1988.

———. *The Projects: Gang and Non-Gang Families in East Los Angeles.* Austin: University of Texas Press, 2007.

Vigil, Maurilio E. *Hispanics in American Politics: The Search for Political Power.* Lanham, Md.: University Press of America, 1987.

———. *The Hispanics of New Mexico: Essays on History and Culture.* Bristol, Ind.: Wyndham Hall Press, 1985.

Vigil, Ralph H., Frances W. Kaye, and John R. Wunder, eds. *Spain and the Plains: Myths and Realities of Spanish Exploration and Settlement on the Great Plains.* Niwot: University Press of Colorado, 1994.

Villarino, José (Pepe), and Arturo Ramírez, eds. *Aztlán: Chicano Culture and Folklore, An Anthology.* New York: McGraw-Hill, 1998.

Villarreal, Roberto E., and Norma G. Hernández, eds. *Latinos and Political Coalitions: Political Empowerment for the 1990s.* Westport, Conn.: Greenwood Press, 1991.

Walsh, Casey. *Building the Borderlands: A Transnational History of Irrigated Cotton along the Mexico-Texas Border.* College Station: Texas A&M University Press, 2008.

Weber, David J. *Bárbaros: Spaniards and Their Savages in the Age of Enlightenment.* New Haven, Conn.: Yale University Press, 2005.

———, ed. *Myth and the History of the Hispanic Southwest: Essays by David J. Weber.* Albuquerque: University of New Mexico Press, 1988.

———. *The Spanish Frontier in North America.* New Haven, Conn.: Yale University Press, 1992.

Weber, Devra. *Dark Sweat, White Gold: California Farm Workers, Cotton, and the New Deal.* Berkeley and Los Angeles: University of California Press, 1994.

Wells, Mariam J. *Strawberry Fields: Politics, Class and Work in California Agriculture.* Ithaca, N.Y.: Cornell University Press, 1996.

Weyr, Thomas. *Hispanic U.S.A.: Breaking the Melting Pot.* New York: Harper and Row, 1988.

Whaley, Charlotte. *Nina Otero-Warren of Santa Fe.* Albuquerque: University of New Mexico Press, 1994.

Williams, Norma. *The Mexican American Family: Tradition and Change.* Dix Hills, N.Y.: General Hall, 1990.

Young, Elliott. *Catarino Garza's Revolution on the Texas-Mexico Border.* Durham, N.C.: Duke University Press, 2004.

Zamora, Emilio. *The World of the Mexican Worker in Texas.* College Station: Texas A&M University Press, 1993.

Zavella, Patricia. *Women's Work and Chicano Families: Cannery Workers of the Santa Clara Valley.* Ithaca, N.Y.: Cornell University Press, 1987.

Zlolniski, Christian. *Janitors, Street Vendors, and Activists: The Lives of Mexican Immigrants in Silicon Valley.* Berkeley and Los Angeles: University of California Press, 2006.

Zolov, Eric. *Refried Elvis: The Rise of the Mexican Counterculture.* Berkeley and Los Angeles: University of California Press, 1999.

Zúñiga, Víctor, and Rubén Hernández-León, eds. *New Destinations: Mexican Immigration in the United States.* New York: Russell Sage Foundation, 2006.

ARTICLES

Alamillo, José M. "More Than a Fiesta: Ethnic Identity, Cultural Politics, and Cinco de Mayo Festivals in Corona, California, 1930–1950." *Aztlán* 28 (Fall 2003): 57–85.

———. "Peloteros in Paradise: Mexican American Baseball and Oppositional Politics in Southern California, 1930–1950." *Western Historical Quarterly* 34 (Summer 2003): 191–211.

Alemán, Jesse. "Assimilation and the Decapitated Body Politic in *The Life and Adventures of Joaquín Murieta.*" *Arizona Quarterly* 60 (Spring 2004): 71–98.

Alfaro, Juan. "The Spirit of the First Franciscan Missionaries in Texas." *U.S. Catholic Historian* 9 (Spring 1990): 49–66.

Almaráz, Felix D., Jr. "Franciscan Evangelization in Spanish Frontier Texas: Apex of Social Contact, Conflict, and Confluence, 1751–1761." *Colonial Latin American Historical Review* 2 (Summer 1993): 253–87.

———. "Harmony, Discord, and Compromise in Spanish Colonial Texas: The Río San Antonio Experience, 1691–1741." *New Mexico Historical Review* 67 (Oct. 1992): 329–56.

———. "An Uninviting Wilderness: The Plains of West Texas, 1534–1821." *Great Plains Quarterly* 12 (Summer 1992): 169–80.

Alonzo, Armando C. "Hispanic Farmers and Ranchers in the Soil and Water Conservation Movement in South Texas, 1940s to Present." *Agricultural History* 78 (Spring 2004): 201–21.

Álvarez, Robert. "*Los Re-mexicanizados: Mexicanidad,* Changing Identity and Long-term Affiliation on the U.S.-Mexico Border." *Journal of the West* 40 (Spring 2001): 15–23.

Arbeláez, María Soledad. "The Sonoran Missions and Indian Raids of the Eighteenth Century." *Journal of the Southwest* 33 (Autumn 1991): 366–86.

Arredondo, Gabriela F. "Navigating Ethno-Racial Currents: Mexicans in Chicago, 1919–1939." *Journal of Urban History* 30 (Mar. 2004): 399–427.

Ávila, Eric. "Popular Culture in the Age of White Flight: Film Noir, Disneyland, and the Cold War (Sub) Urban Imaginary." *Journal of Urban History* 31 (Nov. 2004): 3–22.

Badillo, David A. "Between Alienation and Ethnicity: The Evolution of Mexican-American Catholicism in San Antonio, 1910–1940." *Journal of American Ethnic History* 16 (Summer 1997): 62–83.

Barajas, Frank P. "The Defense Committees of Sleepy Lagoon: A Convergent Struggle against Fascism, 1942–1944." *Aztlán* 31 (Spring 2006): 33–62.

———. "Resistance, Radicalism, and Repression on the Oxnard Plain: The Social Context of the Betabelero Strike of 1933." *Western Historical Quarterly* 35 (Spring 2004): 29–51.

Bauman, Robert. "The Black Power and Chicano Movements in the Poverty Wars in Los Angeles." *Journal of Urban History* 33 (Jan. 2007): 277–95.

Bebout, Lee. "Hero Making in El Movimiento: Reies López Tijerina and the Chicano Nationalist Imaginary." *Aztlán* 32 (Fall 2007): 93–121.

Beltrán, Mary. "Dolores Del Río, the First 'Latin Invasion,' and Hollywood's Transition to Sound." *Aztlán* 30 (Spring 2005): 55–85.

Benavides, José Luis. "'Californios! Whom Do You Support?' *El Clamor Público's* Contradictory Role in the Racial Formation Process in Early California." *California History* 84 (Winter 2006–2007): 54–66.

Benton-Cohen, Katherine. "Common Purposes, Worlds Apart: Mexican-American, Mormon, and Midwestern Women Homesteaders in Cochise County, Arizona." *Western Historical Quarterly* 36 (Winter 2005): 429–52.

Burt, Kenneth C. "Tony Rios and Bloody Christmas: A Turning Point between the Los Angeles Police Department and the Latino Community." *Western Legal History* 14 (Summer/Fall 2001): 159–92.

Bustamante, Adrian. "'The Matter Was Never Resolved': The Casta System in Colonial New Mexico, 1693–1823." *New Mexico Historical Review* 66 (Apr. 1991): 143–64.

Camarillo, Albert. "Cities of Color: The New Racial Frontier in California's Minority-Majority Cities." *Pacific Historical Review* 76 (Feb. 2007): 1–28.

———. "Perspectives on Mexican-American Urban Life and Culture." *Journal of American Ethnic History* 5 (Spring 1986): 72–79.

Campa, Arthur. "Immigrant Latinos and Resident Mexican Americans in Garden City, Kansas: Ethnicity and Ethnic Relations." *Urban Anthropology* 19 (Winter 1990): 345–60.

Carrigan, William D., and Clive Webb. "The Lynching of Persons of Mexican Origin or Descent in the United States, 1848 to 1928." *Journal of Social History* 37 (Winter 2003): 411–38.

Castañeda, Antonia I. "Engendering the History of Alta California, 1769–1848: Gender, Sexuality, and the Family." *California History* 76 (Summer and Fall 1997): 230–59.

———. "Gender, Race, and Culture: Spanish-Mexican Women in the Historiography of Frontier California." *Frontiers* 11, no. 1 (1990): 8–30.

Chávez, Ernesto. "Imagining the Mexican Immigrant Worker: (Inter)Nationalism, Identity, and Insurgency in the Chicano Movement in Los Angeles." *Aztlán* 25 (Fall 2000): 109–35.

Chávez, Leo R. "Settlers and Sojourners: The Case of Mexicans in the United States." *Human Organization* 47 (Summer 1988): 95–108.

Chávez, Sergio. "Community, Ethnicity, and Class in a Changing Rural California Town." *Rural Sociology* 70 (Sept. 2005): 314–35.

Chávez-García, Miroslava. "Intelligence Testing at Whittier School, 1890–1920." *Pacific Historical Review* 76 (May 2007): 193–228.

―――. "Youth, Evidence, and Agency: Mexican and Mexican American Youth at the Whittier State School, 1890–1920." *Aztlán* 31 (Fall 2006): 55–83.

Christian, Carole E. "Joining the American Mainstream: Texas's Mexican Americans during World War I." *Southwestern Historical Quarterly* 92 (Apr. 1989): 559–95.

Cohen, Deborah. "Caught in the Middle: The Mexican State's Relationship with the United States and Its Own Citizen Workers, 1942–1954." *Journal of American Ethnic History* 20 (Spring 2001): 110–32.

Conde, Carlos D. "Huntington and the Mexican Peril." *Hispanic Outlook in Higher Education* 14 (23 Aug. 2004): 8.

Coronado, Raúl, Jr. "Selena's Good Buy: Texas Mexicans, History, and Selena Meet Transnational Capitalism." *Aztlán* 26 (Spring 2001): 59–100.

Cortés, Carlos E. "Mexican Americans in Twentieth-Century California." *Masterkey* 60 (Summer/Fall 1986): 36–48.

Cortés, Enrique. "Mexican Colonies during the Porfiriato." *Aztlán* 10 (Summer–Fall 1979): 1–14.

Cuéllo, José. "The Persistence of Indian Slavery and Encomienda in the Northeast of Colonial Mexico, 1577–1723." *Journal of Social History* 21 (Summer 1988): 683–700.

Dash, Robert C., and Robert E. Hawkinson. "Mexicans and 'Business as Usual': Small Town Politics in Oregon." *Aztlán* 26 (Fall 2001): 87–123.

de la Garza, Rodolfo O., and Muserref Yetim. "The Impact of Ethnicity and Socialization on Definitions of Democracy: The Case of Mexican Americans and Mexicans." *Mexican Studies/Estudios Mexicanos* 19 (Winter 2003): 81–104.

de la Teja, Jesús Francisco. "Indians, Soldiers, and Canary Islanders: The Making of a Texas Frontier Community." *Locus* 3 (Fall 1990): 81–96.

De León, Arnoldo. "Tejanos and the Texas War for Independence: Historiography's Judgment." *New Mexico Historical Review* 61 (Apr. 1986): 137–46.

De León, Arnoldo, and Kenneth L. Stewart. "A Tale of Three Cities: A Comparative Analysis of the Socio-Economic Condition of Mexican-Americans in Los Angeles, Tucson, and San Antonio, 1850–1900." *Journal of the West* 24 (Apr. 1985): 664–74.

Delgado, Edmundo. "A Spanish Ranker in New Mexico: Captain Manuel Delgado of Santa Fe, 1738–1815." *New Mexico Historical Review* 66 (Jan. 1991): 1–13.

Durand, Jorge, Douglas S. Massey, and Emilio A. Parrado. "The New Era of Mexican Migration to the United States." *Journal of American History* 86 (Sept. 1999): 518–36.

Engstrand, Iris H. W. "Perception and Perfection: Picturing the Spanish and Mexican Coastal West." *Western Historical Quarterly* 36 (Spring 2005): 4–21.

Escobar, Corinne. "Here to Stay: The Mexican Identity of Moapa Valley, Nevada." *Nevada Historical Society Quarterly* 36 (Summer 1993): 71–89.

Escobar, Edward J. "The Dialectics of Repression: The Los Angeles Police Department and the Chicano Movement, 1968–1971." *Journal of American History* 79 (Mar. 1993): 1483–1514.

―――. "The Forging of a Community: The Latino Experience in Northwest Indiana." *Latino Studies Journal* 2 (Jan. 1991): 38–57.

Escobedo, Elizabeth R. "The Pachuca Panic: Sexual and Cultural Battlegrounds in World War II Los Angeles." *Western Historical Quarterly* 38 (Summer 2007): 133–56.

Espinosa, J. Manuel, and W. Charles Bennett Jr. "Don Diego de Vargas: Portrait of a Seventeenth-Century Conquistador." *New Mexico Historical Review* 64 (July 1989): 305–17.

Espinoza, Dionne. "'Revolutionary Sisters': Women's Solidarity and Collective Identification among Chicana Brown Berets in East Los Angeles, 1967–1970." *Aztlán* 26 (Spring 2001): 15–58.

Estrada, Daniél, and Richard Santillán. "Chicanos in the Northwest and the Midwest United States: A History of Cultural and Political Commonality." *Perspectives in Mexican American Studies* 6 (1997): 195–228.

Ettinger, Patrick. "'We Sometimes Wonder What They Will Spring on Us Next': Immigrants and Border Enforcement in the American West, 1882–1930." *Western Historical Quarterly* 37 (Summer 2006): 159–83.

Foley, Douglas E. "The Legacy of the *Partido Raza Unida* in South Texas: A Class Analysis." *Ethnic Affairs* 2 (Spring 1988): 47–73.

Foote, Cheryl. "Spanish-Indian Trade along New Mexico's Frontier in the Eighteenth Century." *Journal of the West* 24 (Apr. 1985): 25–30.

Gamboa, Erasmo. "Braceros in the Pacific Northwest: Laborers in the Domestic Front, 1942–1947." *Pacific Historical Review* 61 (Aug. 1987): 378–98.

García, Alma M. "The Development of Chicana Feminist Discourse, 1970–1980." *Gender and Society* 3 (June 1989): 217–38.

García, Gilberto. "Beyond the Adelita Image: Women Scholars in the National Association for Chicano Studies, 1972–1992." *Perspectives in Mexican American Studies* 5 (1995): 35–61.

García, Ignacio M. "Constructing the Chicano Movement: Synthesis of a Militant Ethos." *Perspectives in Mexican American Studies* 6 (1997): 1–19.

García, Richard A. "César Chávez: A Personal and Historical Testimony." *Pacific Historical Review* 63 (May 1994): 225–33.

———. "Dolores Huerta: Woman, Organizer, Symbol." *California History* 72 (Spring 1993): 56–71.

García-Acevedo, María Rosa. "Politics across Borders: Mexico's Policies toward Mexicans in the United States." *Journal of the Southwest* 45 (Winter 2003): 533–55.

Garcilazo, Jeffrey M. "McCarthyism, Mexican Americans, and the Los Angeles Committee for Protection of the Foreign-Born, 1950–1954." *Western Historical Quarterly* 32 (Autumn 2001): 273–95.

Garza, James A. "The Long History of Mexican Immigration to the Rural Midwest." *Journal of the West* 45 (Fall 2006): 57–64.

Gómez, Arthur. "Royalist in Transition: Facundo Melgares, the Last Spanish Governor of New Mexico, 1818–1822." *New Mexico Historical Review* 68 (Oct. 1993): 371–87.

Gonzales, Manuel G. "Arturo Tirado and the Teatro Azteca: Mexican Popular Culture in the Central San Joaquin Valley." *California History* 83 (Summer 2006): 46–63.

———. "Dr. Mariano Samaniego, Citizen of the El Paso Valley." *Password* 35 (Winter 1990): 159–70.

———. "Mariano G. Samaniego." *Journal of Arizona History* 31 (Summer 1990): 141–60.

Gonzales, Phillip B. "El Jefe: Bronson Cutting and the Politics of Hispano Interests in New Mexico, 1920–1935." *Aztlán* 25 (Fall 2000): 67–108.

———. "The Hispano Homeland Debate: New Lessons." *Perspectives in Mexican American Studies* 6 (1997): 123–41.

———. "Struggle for Survival: The Hispanic Land Grants of New Mexico, 1848–2001." *Agricultural History* 77 (Spring 2003): 293–324.

Gonzales, Phillip B., and Ann Massmann. "Loyalty Questioned: Nuevomexicanos in the Great War." *Pacific Historical Review* 75 (Nov. 2006): 629–66.

González, Gilbert G. "Labor and Community: The Camps of Mexican Citrus Pickers in Southern California." *Western Historical Quarterly* 22 (Aug. 1991): 289–312.

———. "The Mexican Citrus Picker Union, the Mexican Consulate, and the Orange County Strike of 1936." *Labor History* 35 (Winter 1994): 48–65.

————. "The 'Mexican Problem': Empire, Public Policy, and the Education of Mexican Immigrants, 1880–1930." *Aztlán* 26 (Fall 2001): 199–207.

————. "Segregation of Mexican Children in a Southern California City: The Legacy of Expansionism and the American Southwest." *Western Historical Quarterly* 16 (Jan. 1985): 55–76.

————. "Women, Work, and Community in the Mexican *Colonias* of the Southern California Citrus Belt." *California History* 74 (Spring 1995): 58–67.

González, Gilbert G., and Raúl Fernández. "Empire and the Origins of Twentieth-Century Migration from Mexico to the United States." *Pacific Historical Review* 71 (Feb. 2002): 19–58.

González, Michael J. "'The Child of the Wilderness Weeps for the Father of Our Country': The Indian and the Politics of Church and State in Provincial California." *California History* 76 (Summer and Fall 1997): 147–72.

Gray, Paul Bryan. "Francisco P. Ramírez: A Short Biography." *California History* 84 (Winter 2006–2007): 20–38.

Greenleaf, Richard E. "The Inquisition in Eighteenth-Century New Mexico." *New Mexico Historical Review* 60 (Jan. 1985): 29–60.

Griswold del Castillo, Richard. "Mexican Intellectuals' Perceptions of Mexican Americans and Chicanos, 1920–Present." *Aztlán* 27 (Fall 2002): 33–74.

Guest, Francis F. "An Inquiry into the Role of Discipline in California Mission Life." *Southern California Quarterly* 71 (Spring 1989): 1–68.

Gutiérrez, David G. "*Sin Fronteras?:* Chicanos, Mexican Americans, and the Emergence of the Contemporary Mexican Immigration Debate, 1968–1978." *Journal of American Ethnic History* 10 (Summer 1991): 5–37.

Gutiérrez, Ramón A. "Honor Ideology, Marriage Negotiation, and Class-Gender Domination in New Mexico, 1690–1848." *Latin American Perspectives* 12 (Winter 1985): 81–104.

Hall, G. Emlen. "San Miguel del Bado and the Loss of the Common Lands of New Mexico Community Land Grants." *New Mexico Historical Review* 66 (Oct. 1991): 413–32.

Heidenreich, Linda. "The Colonial North: Histories of Women and Violence from Before the U.S. Invasion." *Aztlán* 30 (Spring 2005): 23–54.

Hernández, Frances. "The Secret Jews of the Southwest." *Outlook* 63 (Fall 1992): 12–13, 30.

————. "The Secret Legacy of Christopher Columbus in the Southwest." *Password* 35 (Summer 1990): 55–70.

Hernández, Kelly Lytle. "The Crimes and Consequences of Illegal Immigration: A Cross-Border Examination of Operation Wetback, 1943 to 1954." *Western Historical Quarterly* 37 (Winter 2006): 421–44.

Hernández, Salomé. "No Settlement without Women: Three Spanish California Settlement Schemes, 1790–1800." *Southern California Quarterly* 72 (Fall 1990): 203–34.

Hinojosa, Gilberto Miguel. "Friars and Indians: Towards a Perspective of Cultural Interaction in the San Antonio Mission." *U.S. Catholic Historian* 9 (Spring 1990): 7–25.

Hurtado, Albert L. "Sexuality in California's Franciscan Missions: Cultural Perceptions and Sad Realities." *California History* 71 (Fall 1992): 370–85.

Iber, Jorge. "Hispanics and Community in the American West." *Journal of the West* 45 (Fall 2006): 7–11.

————. "Mexican Americans of South Texas Football: The Athletic and Coaching Careers of E.C. Lerma and Bobby Cavazos, 1932–1965." *Southwestern Historical Quarterly* 105 (Apr. 2002): 617–33.

————. "Mexican Workers in Utah: Life and Labor in Two Tourist Towns," *Journal of the West* 40 (Spring 2001): 60–66.

John, Elizabeth A. H. "Bernardo de Gálvez on the Apache Frontier: A Cautionary Note for Gringo Historians." *Journal of Arizona History* 29 (Winter 1988): 427–30.

————. "Crusading in the Hispanic Borderlands: An Essay Review." *Journal of the Southwest* 30 (Summer 1988): 190–99.

Kanellos, Nicolás. "*El Clamor Público:* Resisting the American Empire." *California History* 84 (Winter 2006–2007): 10–18.

Katz, Michael B., Mark J. Stern, and Jamie J. Fader. "The Mexican Immigration Debate: The View from History." *Social Science History* 31 (Summer 2007): 157–89.

Kearney, Michael. "From the Invisible Hand to Visible Feet: Anthropological Studies of Migration and Development." *Annual Review of Anthropology* 15 (1986): 331–61.

Kelsey, Harry. "European Impact on the California Indian." *Americas* 41 (Apr. 1985): 494–511.

————. "Finding the Way Home: Spanish Exploration of the Round-Trip Route across the Pacific Ocean." *Western Historical Quarterly* 17 (Apr. 1986): 145–64.

Kessell, John L. "Juan Bautista de Anza, Father and Son: Pillars of New Spain's Far North." *New Mexico Historical Review* 79 (Spring 2004): 159–87.

Larralde, Carlos. "J. T. Canales and the Texas Rangers." *Journal of South Texas* 10 (1997): 38–68.

————. "Juan Cortina's Spy: Elena Villarreal de Ferrer." *Journal of South Texas* 11 (1998): 104–24.

Larralde, Carlos M., and Richard Griswold del Castillo. "Luisa Moreno and the Beginnings of the Mexican American Civil Rights Movement in San Diego." *Journal of San Diego History* 43 (Summer 1997): 159–75.

————. "North from Mexico: Carey McWilliams' Tragedy." *Southern California Quarterly* 80 (Summer 1998): 231–45.

————. "San Diego's Ku Klux Klan, 1920–1980." *Journal of San Diego History* 46 (Spring/ Summer 2000): 68–89.

Leal, Luis. "Américo Paredes and Modern Mexican American Scholarship." *Ethnic Affairs* 1 (Fall 1987): 1–11.

Lecompte, Janet. "Coronado and the Conquest." *New Mexico Historical Review* 64 (July 1989): 279–304.

Ledesma, Irene. "Texas Newspapers and Chicana Workers' Activism, 1919–1974." *Western Historical Quarterly* 26 (Autumn 1995): 309–31.

Lewthwaite, Stephanie. "Race, Paternalism, and 'California Pastoral': Rural Rehabilitation and Mexican Labor in Greater Los Angeles." *Agricultural History* 81 (Winter 2007): 1–35.

López, Felipe H., and Pamela Munro. "Zapotec Immigration: The San Lucas Quiaviní Experience." *Aztlán* 24 (Spring 1999), 129–49.

Lowe, John. "Joaquín Murieta, Mexican History, and Popular Myth of Freedom." *Journal of Popular Culture* 35 (Fall 2001): 25–40.

Machado, Manuel A., Jr. "Mexican Labor in the United States: The View from Mexican Cantinas." *Journal of the West* 25 (Apr. 1986): 59–64.

Macías, Anthony. "Latin Holidays: Mexican Americans, Latin Music, and Cultural Identity in Postwar Los Angeles." *Aztlán* 30 (Fall 2005): 65–86.

Magnaghi, Russell M. "Plains Indians in New Mexico: The Genízaro Experience." *Great Plains Quarterly* 10 (Spring 1990): 86–95.

Marcelli, Enrico. "The Changing Profile of Mexican Migrants to the United States: New Evidence from California and Mexico." *Latin America Research Review* 36, no. 3 (2001): 105–32.

Marez, Curtis. "Signifying Spain, Becoming Comanche, Making Mexicans: Indian Captivity and the History of Chicana/o Popular Performance." *American Quarterly* 53 (June 2001): 267–307.

Marín, Christine. "Mexican Americans on the Home Front: Community Organizations in Arizona during World War II." *Perspectives in Mexican American Studies* 4 (1993): 75–92.

Mariscal, Jorge. "Negotiating César: César Chávez in the Chicano Movement." *Aztlán* 29 (Spring 2004): 21–56.

Márquez, Benjamín. "The Politics of Race and Assimilation: The League of United Latin American Citizens, 1929–40." *Western Political Quarterly* 42 (June 1989): 355–75.

———. "The Politics of Race and Class: The League of United Latin American Citizens in the Post–World War II Period." *Social Science Quarterly* 68 (Mar. 1987): 85–101.

Martínez, Ana Luisa. "Pablo Cruz and *El Regidor*: The Emergence of a Bicultural Identity in San Antonio, 1888–1910." *Journal of the West* 45 (Fall 2006): 21–28.

Martínez, Arthur D. "Los de Dodge City, Kansas: A Mexican-American Community in the Heartland of the United States." *Journal of the West* 24 (Apr. 1985): 88–95.

Martínez, María Elena. "The Black Blood of New Spain: Limpieza de Sangre, Racial Violence, and Gendered Power in Early Colonial New Mexico." *William and Mary Quarterly* 61 (July 2004): 479–520.

Meier, Matt S. "Esteban Ochoa, Enterpriser." *Journal of the West* 25 (Jan. 1986): 15–21.

———. "'King Tiger': Reies López Tijerina." *Journal of the West* 27 (Apr. 1988): 60–68.

Meighan, Clement W. "Indians and California Missions." *Southern California Quarterly* 69 (Fall 1987): 187–201.

Mellinger, Phil. "'The Men Have Become Organizers': Labor Conflict and Unionization in the Mexican Mining Communities of Arizona, 1900–1915." *Western Historical Quarterly* 23 (Aug. 1992): 323–47.

Michelson, Melissa R., and Amalia Pállares. "The Politicization of Chicago Mexican Americans: Nationalization, the Vote, and Perceptions of Discrimination." *Aztlán* 26 (Fall 2001): 63–85.

Miranda, Gloria E. "Racial and Cultural Dimensions in Gente de Razon Status in Spanish and Mexican California." *Southern California Quarterly* 70 (Fall 1988): 265–78.

Mitchell, Pablo. "You Just Don't Know Mrs. Baca: Intermarriage, Mixed Heritage, and Identity in New Mexico." *New Mexico Historical Review* 79 (Fall 2004): 437–58.

Mize, Ronald L., Jr. "Mexican Contract Workers and the U.S. Capitalist Agricultural Labor Process: The Formative Era, 1942–1964." *Rural Sociology* 71 (Mar. 2006): 85–108.

Monroy, Douglas. "The Creation and Re-creation of Californio Society." *California History* 76 (Summer and Fall 1997): 173–95.

Montgomery, Charles. "'Becoming Spanish-American': Race and Rhetoric in New Mexico Politics, 1880–1928." *Journal of American Ethnic History* 20 (Summer 2001): 59–84.

Montoya, Fawn-Amber. "From Mexicans to Citizens: Colorado Fuel and Iron's Representation of Nuevo Mexicans, 1901–1919." *Journal of the West* 45 (Fall 2006): 29–35.

Montoya, María E. "The Roots of Economic and Ethnic Divisions in Northern New Mexico: The Case of the Civilian Conservation Corps." *Western Historical Quarterly* 26 (Spring 1995): 15–34.

Mora, Anthony. "Resistance and Accommodation in a Border Parish." *Western Historical Quarterly* 36 (Autumn 2005): 301–26.

Mora-Torres, Juan. "Pilsen: A Mexican Global City in the Midwest." *Diálogo* (DePaul University), no. 9 (Fall 2005): 3–7.

Moreno, Deborah. "'Here the Society Is United': 'Respectable' Anglos and Intercultural Marriage in Pre-Gold Rush California." *California History* 80 (Spring 2001): 2–17.

Moreno, E. Mark. "Mexican American Street Gangs, Migration, and Violence in the Yakima Valley." *Pacific Northwest Quarterly* 97 (Summer 2006): 131–38.

Navarro, Armando. "The Post Mortem Politics of the Chicano Movement: 1975–1996." *Perspectives in Mexican American Studies* 6 (1997): 52–79.

Nixon-Méndez, Nina L. "Los Fundadores Urbanos (Urban Pioneers): The Hispanics of Dallas, 1850–1940." *Journal of the West* 32 (Oct. 1993): 76–82.

———. "Mexican-American Voluntary Associations in Omaha, Nebraska." *Journal of the West* 28 (July 1989): 73–85.

Nostrand, Richard L. "The Century of Hispano Expansion." *New Mexico Historical Review* 62 (Oct. 1987): 361–86.

Nuñez-Janes, Mariela. "Bilingual Education and Identity Debates in New Mexico: Constructing and Contesting Nationalism and Ethnicity." *Journal of the Southwest* 44 (Spring 2002): 61–78.

Nusz, Nancy, and Gabriella Ricciardi. "Our Ways: History and Culture of Mexicans in Oregon." *Oregon Historical Quarterly* 104 (Spring 2003): 110–23.

Ochoa, Enrique C. "Constructing Fronteras: Teaching the History of the U.S.-Mexico Borderlands in the Age of Proposition 187 and Free Trade." *Radical History Review* 70 (Winter 1998): 119–30.

Oppenheimer, Robert. "Acculturation or Assimilation: Mexican Immigrants in Kansas, 1900 to World War II." *Western Historical Quarterly* 16 (Oct. 1985): 429–48.

Orenstein, Dara. "Void of Vagueness: Mexicans and the Collapse of Miscegenation Law in California." *Pacific Historical Review* 74 (Aug. 2005): 367–407.

Oropeza, Lorena. "The Heart of Chicano History: Reies López Tijerina as a Memory Entrepreneur." *The Sixties: A Journal of History, Politics and Culture* 1 (June 2008): 49–67.

Pardo, Mary. "Mexican American Women Grassroots Community Activists: 'Mothers of East Los Angeles.'" *Frontiers* 11, no. 1 (1990): 1–7.

Peña, Manuel. "From Ranchero to Jaitón: Ethnicity and Class in Texas-Mexican Music (Two Styles in the Form of a Pair)." *Ethnomusicology* 29 (Winter 1985): 29–55.

Perales, Mónica. "Fighting to Stay in Smeltertown: Lead Contamination and Environmental Justice in a Mexican American Community." *Western Historical Quarterly* 39 (Spring 2008): 41–63.

Pescador, Juan Javier. "¡Vamos Taximaroa! Mexican/Chicano Soccer Associations and Transnational/Translocal Communities, 1967–2002." *Latino Studies* 2 (Dec. 2004): 352–76.

Pichardo, Nelson A. "The Establishment and Development of Chicano Voluntary Associations in California, 1910–1930." *Aztlán* 19 (Fall 1988–1990): 93–155.

Pinheiro, John C. "'Religion without Restriction': Anti-Catholicism, All Mexico, and the Treaty of Guadalupe Hidalgo." *Journal of the Early Republic* 23 (Spring 2003): 69–96.

Poyo, Gerald E., and Gilberto M. Hinojosa. "Spanish Texas and Borderlands Historiography in Transition: Implications for United States History." *Journal of American History* 75 (Sept. 1988): 393–416.

Preece, Harold. "Jacob de Cordova: A Jew Deep in the Heart of Texas." *Western States Jewish History* 29 (Jan. 1997): 166–90.

Pulido, Alberto L. "Are You an Emissary of Jesus Christ? Justice, the Catholic Church, and the Chicano Movement." *Explorations in Ethnic Studies* 14 (Jan. 1991): 17–34.

———. "Mexican American Catholicism in the Southwest: The Transformation of a Popular Religion." *Perspectives in Mexican American Studies* 4 (1993): 93–108.

Quintana, Frances León. "Land, Water, and Pueblo-Hispanic Relations in Northern New Mexico." *Journal of the Southwest* 32 (Autumn 1990): 288–99.

Quiroz, Anthony. "Class and Consensus: Twentieth-Century Mexican American Ideology in Victoria, Texas." *Southwestern Historical Quarterly* 106 (Jan. 2002): 31–54.

Ramírez-Berg, Charles. "Colonialism and Movies in Southern California, 1910–1934." *Aztlán* 28 (Spring 2003): 75–96.

Reséndez, Andrés. "Getting Cured and Getting Drunk: State versus Market in Texas and New Mexico, 1800–1850." *Journal of the Early Republic* 22 (Spring 2002): 77–103.

Richards, Susan V. "From Traders to Traitors? The Armijo Brothers through the Nineteenth Century." *New Mexico Historical Review* 69 (July 1994): 215–28.

Richmond, Douglas W. "The Climax of Conflicts with Native Americans in New Mexico: Spanish and Mexican Antecedents to U.S. Treaty Making during the U.S.-Mexico War, 1846–1848." *New Mexico Historical Review* 80 (Winter 2005): 55–86.

Ríos-Bustamante, Antonio. "The Barrioization of Nineteenth-Century Mexican Californians: From Landowners to Laborers." *Masterkey* 60 (Summer/Fall 1986): 26–35.

Robinson, Robin. "Accommodation to Domination: Demise of the Tejano Elite in the Lower Rio Grande." *Journal of South Texas* 10 (1997): 69–87.

Rodríguez, Alicia E. "Disfranchisement in Dallas: The Democratic Party and the Suppression of Independent Political Challenges in Dallas, Texas, 1891–1894." *Southwestern Historical Quarterly* 108 (July 2004): 42–64.

Rodríguez, Marc Simon. "A Movement Made of 'Young Mexican Americans Seeking Change': Critical Citizenship, Migration, and the Chicano Movement in Texas and Wisconsin, 1960–1975." *Western Historical Quarterly* 34 (Autumn 2003): 275–300.

Rodríguez Domíguez, Víctor M. "The Racialization of Mexican Americans and Puerto Ricans: 1890s–1930s." *CENTRO Journal* 17 (Spring 2005): 71–105.

Rojas, Maythee. "Re-membering Josefa: Reading the Mexican Female Body in California Gold Rush Chronicles." *Women's Studies Quarterly* 35 (Spring 2007): 126–49.

Romero, Mary, and Eric Margolis. "Tending the Beets: Campesinas and the Great Western Sugar Company." *Revista Mujeres* 2 (June 1985): 17–27.

Romero, Roberto Chao. "'El destierro de los Chinos': Popular Perspectives on Chinese-Mexican Intermarriage in the Early Twentieth Century." *Aztlán* 32 (Spring 2007): 113–44.

Romero, Tom I., II. "Wearing the Red, White, and Blue Trunks of Aztlán: Rodolfo 'Corky' Gonzales and the Convergence of American and Chicano Nationalism." *Aztlán* 29 (Spring 2004): 83–117.

Rosales, Francisco A. "Mexicans, Interethnic Violence, and Crime in the Chicago Area during the 1920s and 1930s: The Struggle to Achieve Ethnic Consciousness." *Perspectives in Mexican American Studies* 2 (1989): 59–97.

Rosario Rodríguez Díaz, María del. "Mexico's Vision of Manifest Destiny during the 1847 War." *Journal of Popular Culture* 35 (Fall 2001): 41–50.

Rose, Margaret. "Traditional and Nontraditional Patterns of Female Activism in the United Farm Workers of America, 1962–1980." *Frontiers* 11, no. 1 (1990): 26–32.

Rose, Susan, and Sarah Hiller. "From Migrant Work to Community Transformation: Families Forming Transnational Communities in Peribán and Pennsylvania." *Oral History Review* 34 (Winter/Spring 2007): 95–142.

Rouse, Roger. "Mexican Migration and the Social Space of Postmodernism." *Diaspora* 1 (Spring 1991): 8–23.

Ruiz, David R. "Barrio Urbanism and the Cities of the Southwest." *Journal of the West* 45 (Fall 2006): 12–20.

Ruiz, Vicki L. "California's Early Pioneers: Spanish/Mexican Women." *Social Science Review* 29 (Fall 1989): 24–30.

———. "Morena/o, blanca/o y café con leche: Racial Constructions in Chicana/o Historiography." *Mexican Studies/Estudios Mexicanos* 20 (Summer 2004): 343–59.

———. "Nuestra América: Latino History as United States History." *Journal of American History* 93 (Dec. 2006): 655–72.

———. "A Promise Fulfilled: Mexican Cannery Workers in Southern California." *Pacific Historian* 30 (Summer 1986): 50–61.

———. "Una Mujer sin Fronteras: Luisa Moreno and Latina Labor Activism." *Pacific Historical Review* 73 (Feb. 2004): 1–20.

Sánchez, Federico A. "Rancho Life in Alta California." *Masterkey* 60 (Summer/Fall 1986): 15–25.

Sandos, James A. "Junípero Serra's Canonization and the Historical Record." *American Historical Review* 93 (Dec. 1988): 1253–69.

Sandoval, David A. "The American Invasion of New Mexico and New Mexican Merchants." *Journal of Popular Culture* 35 (Fall 2001): 61–72.

———. "Gnats, Goods, and Greasers: Mexican Merchants on the Santa Fe Trail." *Journal of the West* 28 (Apr. 1989): 22–31.

San Miguel, Guadalupe, Jr. "Culture and Education in the American Southwest: Towards an Explanation of Chicano School Attendance, 1850–1940." *Journal of American Ethnic History* 7 (Spring 1988): 5–21.

———. "The Rise of Recorded Tejano Music in the Post-World War II Years, 1946–1964." *Journal of American Ethnic History* 19 (Fall 1999): 26–49.

Santiago, Mark. "Virtue, Character, and Service: The Spanish Officer Corps in Sonora, 1779." *Journal of Arizona History* 44 (Spring 2003): 45–72.

Saragoza, Alex M. "The Significance of Recent Chicano-Related Historical Writings: An Appraisal." *Ethnic Affairs* 1 (Fall 1987): 24–62.

Schilz, Thomas Frank, and Donald E. Worcester. "Spread of Firearms among the Indian Tribes on the Northern Frontier of New Spain." *American Indian Quarterly* 11 (Winter 1987): 1–10.

Segura, Denise A., and Beatríz M. Pesquera. "Beyond Indifference and Antipathy: The Chicana Movement and Chicana Feminist Discourse." *Aztlán* 19 (Fall 1988–1990): 69–92.

Sheridan, Clare. "Contested Citizenship: National Identity and Mexican Immigration Debates of the 1920s." *Journal of American Ethnic History* 21 (Spring 2002): 3–35.

Smith, Michael M. "Mexicans in Kansas City: The First Generation, 1900–1920." *Perspectives in Mexican American Studies* 2 (1989): 29–57.

Solórzano, Armando. "The Making of Latino Families in Utah." *Beehive History* 25 (1999): 18–21.

South, Scott J., Kyle Crowder, and Erick Chávez. "Migration and Spatial Assimilation among U.S. Latinos: Classical versus Segmented Trajectories." *Demography* 42 (Aug. 2005): 497–522.

Szasz, Ferenc Morton. "A New Mexican 'Davy Crockett': Walt Disney's Version of the Life and Legend of Elfego Baca." *Journal of the Southwest* 48 (Autumn 2006): 261–74.

Telles, Edward. "Mexican Americans and the American Nation: A Response to Professor Huntington." *Aztlán* 31 (Fall 2006): 7–23.

Treviño, Roberto R. "Facing Jim Crow: Catholic Sisters and the 'Mexican Problem' in Texas," *Western Historical Quarterly* 34 (Summer 2003): 139–64.

———. "*Prensa y patria:* The Spanish-Language Press and the Biculturation of the Tejano Middle Class, 1920–1940." *Western Historical Quarterly* 22 (Nov. 1991): 451–72.

Valdés, Dennis Nodín. "Betabeleros: The Formation of an Agricultural Proletariat in the Midwest, 1877–1930." *Labor History* 30 (Fall 1989): 536–62.

———. "Machine Politics in California Agriculture, 1945–1990s." *Pacific Historical Review* 63 (May 1994): 203–24.

———. "Settlers, Sojourners, and Proletarians: Social Formation in the Great Plains Sugar Beet Industry, 1890–1940." *Great Plains Quarterly* 10 (Spring 1990): 110–23.

Valerio-Jiménez, Omar S. "Neglected Citizens and Willing Traders: The Villas del Norte (Tamaulipas) in Mexico's Northern Borderlands, 1749–1846." *Mexican Studies/Estudios Mexicanos* 18 (Summer 2002): 251–96.

Vargas, Zaragoza. "In the Years of Darkness and Torment: The Early Mexican American Struggle for Civil Rights, 1945–1963." *New Mexico Historical Review* 76 (Oct. 2001): 383–414.

———. "Life and Community in the 'Wonderful City of the Magic Motor': Mexican Immigrants in 1920s Detroit." *Michigan Historical Review* 15 (Spring 1989): 47–68.

———. "Tejana Radical: Emma Tenayuca and the San Antonio Labor Movement during the Great Depression." *Pacific Historical Review* 66 (Nov. 1997): 553–80.

Vigil, Maurilio. "The Ethnic Organization as an Instrument of Political and Social Change: MALDEF, A Case Study." *Journal of Ethnic Studies* 18 (Spring 1990): 15–31.

Vigil, Ralph H. "John Francis Bannon and the Historiography of the Spanish Borderlands: Retrospect and Prospect." *Journal of the Southwest* 29 (Winter 1987): 331–63.

———. "Spanish Exploration and the Great Plains in the Age of Discovery: Myth and Reality." *Great Plains Quarterly* 10 (Winter 1990): 3–17.

Weber, David J. "The Spanish Legacy in North America and the Historical Imagination." *Western Historical Quarterly* 23 (Feb. 1992): 5–24.

———. "Turner, the Boltonians, and the Borderlands." *American Historical Review* 91 (Feb. 1986): 66–81.

Wells, Miriam J. "Power Brokers and Ethnicity: The Rise of a Chicano Movement." *Aztlán* 17 (Spring 1986): 47–77.

Zamora, Emilio. "The Failed Promise of Wartime Opportunity for Mexicans in the Texas Oil Industry." *Southwestern Historical Quarterly* 95 (Jan. 1992): 323–50.

Zavella, Patricia. "'Abnormal Intimacy': The Varying Work Networks of Chicana Cannery Workers." *Feminist Studies* 11 (Fall 1985): 541–57.

DOCTORAL DISSERTATIONS

Alamillo, José Manuel. "Bittersweet Communities: Mexican Workers, Citrus Growers on the California Landscape, 1880–1941." University of California, Irvine, 2000.

Aldama, Arturo James. "Disrupting Savagism in the Borderlands of Identity: Violence, Resistance, and Chicana/o, Native American, Mexican Immigrant Struggles for Representation." University of California, Berkeley, 1996.

Alonzo, Armando C. "*Tejano* Rancheros and Changes in Land Tenure, Hidalgo County, Texas, 1848–1900." Indiana University, 1991.

Alvarado, Rudolph Valier. "A History of Teatro in Lubbock, Texas." Texas Tech University, 1995.

Álvarez, Luis Alberto. "The Power of the Zoot: Race, Community, and Resistance in American Youth Culture, 1940–1945." University of Texas, Austin, 2001.

Andrade, Juan, Jr. "A Historical Survey of Mexican Immigration to the United States and an Oral History of the Mexican Settlement in Chicago, 1920–1990." Northern Illinois University, 1998.

Apodaca, María Linda. "They Kept the Home Fires Burning: Mexican-American Women and Social Change." University of California, Irvine, 1994.

Armbruster, Ralph Joseph. "Globalization and Cross-Border Labor Organizing in the Garment and Automobile Industries." University of California, Riverside, 1998.

Arredondo, Gabriela F. "'What! The Mexican Americans?': Race and Ethnicity, Mexicans in Chicago, 1916–1939." University of Chicago, 1999.

Badillo, David A. "From South of the Border: Latino Experiences in Urban America." City University of New York, 1988.

Baker, Anthony. "The Social Production of Space of Two Chicago Neighborhoods: Pilsen and Lincoln Park." University of Illinois, Chicago Circle, 1995.

Baker, Susan González. "Many Rivers to Cross: Mexican Immigrants, Women Workers, and the Structure of Labor Markets in the Urban Southwest." University of Texas, Austin, 1989.

Bakewell, Elizabeth Avery. "Picturing the Self: Mexican Identity and Artistic Representation, Post-1968." Brown University, 1991.

Baraza, Eva. "Central American Immigrants and the Democratization of Los Angeles: 'La cadena de oppressión y la resistencia.'" Northern Arizona University, 2005.

Barker, E. Shannon. "Los Tejanos de San Antonio: Mexican Immigrant Family Acculturation, 1880–1929." George Washington University, 1996.

Barrera, Baldemar James. "'We Want Better Education': The Chicano Student Movement for Educational Reform in South Texas, 1968–1970." University of New Mexico, 2007.

Barton-Cayton, Amy Elizabeth. "A Woman's Resistance Is Never Done: The Case of Women Farm Workers in California." University of California, Santa Cruz, 1988.

Bernal, Dolores Delgado. "Chicana School Resistance and Grassroots Leadership: Providing an Alternative Framework for the 1968 East Los Angeles Blowouts." University of California, Los Angeles, 1997.

Bouvier, Virginia Mayo. "Women, Conquest, and the Production of History: Hispanic California, 1542–1840." University of California, Berkeley, 1995.

Brune, Betty Jean. "Mexican-American and Anglo-American Attitudes toward Women: An Investigation of Traditionalism, Biculturalism, and Ethnicity." University of Texas, Austin, 1989.

Buelna, Enrique Meza. "Resistance from the Margins: Mexican American Radical Activism in Los Angeles, 1930–1970." University of California, Irvine, 2007.

Busto, Rudy V. "Like a Mighty Rushing Wind: The Religious Impulse in the Life and Writing of Reies López Tijerina." University of California, Berkeley, 1991.

Cabrera-Mereb, Claudine. "The Biocultural Profile of a Population at Risk in the U.S.-Mexican Border." University of Arizona, 1992.

Cadena, Gilbert Ramón. "Chicanos and the Catholic Church: Liberation Theology as a Form of Empowerment." University of California, Riverside, 1987.

Calderón, José Zapata. "Mexican American Politics in a Multi-Ethnic Community: The Case of Monterey Park, 1985–1990." University of California, Los Angeles, 1991.

Calderón, Roberto Ramón. "Mexican Politics in the American Era, 1846–1900: Laredo, Texas." University of California, Los Angeles, 1993.

Canelo, María José. "Carey McWilliams and the Question of Cultural Citizenship in the 1940s." New York University, 2003.

Carrasco, Nicolás. "The Relationship between Parental Support and Control and Adolescent Self-Esteem in Mexican, Mexican American, and Anglo American Families." University of Texas, Austin, 1990.

Castañeda, Antonia I. "*Presidarias y Pobladoras:* The Journey North and Life in Frontier California, 1770–1821." Stanford University, 1990.

Castañeda Gómez del Campo, Alejandra. "Politics of Citizenship: Mexican Migrants in the United States." University of California, Santa Cruz, 2003.

Chapa, Jorge. "The Increasing Significance of Class: Class, Culture and Chicano Assimilation." University of California, Berkeley, 1988.

Chaves, María Judith Feliciano. "Mudejarismo in Its Colonial Context: Iberian Cultural Display, Viceregal Luxury Consumption, and the Negotiation of Identities in Sixteenth-Century New Spain." University of Pennsylvania, 2004.

Chávez, Anthony Joseph. "The Religious Call in Early Adult Development: Seven Life Studies of Mexican-American Sisters." Wright Institute, Berkeley, 1986.

Chávez, Ernesto. "Creating Aztlán: The Chicano Movement in Los Angeles, 1966–1978." University of California, Los Angeles, 1994.

Chávez, Marisela Rodríguez, "Despieren Hermanas y Hermanos! (Awaken Sisters and Brothers): Women, the Chicano Movement, and Chicana Feminisms in California, 1966–1981." Stanford University, 2005.

Chávez, Miroslava. "Mexican Women and the American Conquest in Los Angeles: From the Mexican Era to American Ascendancy." University of California, Los Angeles, 1998.

Chavira, Alicia. "Women, Migration, and Health: Conditions and Strategies of a Mexican Migrant Population in the Midwest." University of California, Los Angeles, 1987.

Churchill, Charles Bradford. "Adventurers and Prophets: American Autobiographies in Mexican California, 1828–1847." University of California, Santa Barbara, 1989.

Contréras, Raoul. "The Ideology of the Political Movement for Chicano Studies." University of California, Los Angeles, 1993.

Crimm, Ana Caroline Castillo. "Success in Adversity: The Mexican Americans of Victoria County, Texas, 1800–1880." University of Texas, Austin, 1994.

Cruz, Wilfredo. "The Nature of Alinsky-Style Community Organizing in the Mexican-American Community of Chicago." University of Chicago, 1987.

Cuádraz, Gloria Holguin. "Meritocracy (Un)Challenged: The Making of a Chicano and Chicana Professoriate and Professional Class." University of California, Berkeley, 1993.

Cuéllar, Carlos Eliseo. "Stories from the Barrios: A History of Mexican Fort Worth." Texas Christian University, 1998.

Dávalos, Karen May. "Ethnic Identity among Mexican and Mexican-American Women in Chicago, 1920–1991." Yale University, 1993.

De Borhegyi-Forrest, Suzanne Sims. "The Preservation of the Village: The Origins and Implementation of New Mexico's Hispanic New Deal." University of Wyoming, 1986.

De Genova, Nicholas. "Working the Boundaries, Making the Difference: Race and Space in Mexican Chicago." University of Chicago, 1999.

de la Teja, Jesús Francisco. "Land and Society in 18th Century San Antonio de Béxar: A Community on New Spain's Northern Frontier." University of Texas, Austin, 1988.

Deutsch, Sarah Jane. "Culture, Class, and Gender: Chicanas and Chicanos in Colorado and New Mexico, 1900–1940." Yale University, 1985.

Díaz, Rosemary T. "El Senador, Dennis Chavez: New Mexico Native Son, American Senior Statesman, 1888–1962." Arizona State University, 2006.

Dietrich, Lisa Christine. "Coming of Age in the Barrio: Girls, Gangs, and Growing-Up." University of California, San Diego, 1996.

Dimas, Pete Rey. "Progress and a Mexican-American Community's Struggle for Existence: Phoenix's Golden Gate Barrio." Arizona State University, 1991.

Donato, Rubén. "In Struggle: Mexican-Americans in the Pajaro Valley Schools, 1900–1979." Stanford University, 1987.

Dunn, Timothy J. "Immigration Enforcement in the U.S.-Mexico Border Region, the El Paso Case: Bureaucratic Power, Human Rights, and Civic Activism." University of Texas, Austin, 1999.

Durán, Tobías. "We Come as Friends: Violent Social Conflicts in New Mexico." University of New Mexico, 1985.

Echeverria, Darius V. "Aztlán Arizona: Abuses, Awareness, Animosity, and Activism amid Mexican-Americans, 1968–1978." Temple University, 2006.

Escobedo, Elizabeth Rachel. "Mexican American Home Front: The Politics of Gender, Culture, and Community in World War II Los Angeles." University of Washington, 2004.

Espinosa, Kristin Elizabeth. "Helping Hands: Social Capital and the Undocumented Migration of Mexican Men to the United States." University of Chicago, 1997.

Espinoza, Dionne Elaine. "Pedogogies of Nationalism and Gender: Cultural Resistance in Selected Representational Practices of Chicana/o Movement Activists, 1967–1972." Cornell University, 1996.

Fish, Luise Ann. "All Rise: Reynaldo G. Garza, the First Mexican American Federal Judge." Texas A&M University, 1996.

Flores, Lisa Angela. "Shifting Visions: Intersections of Rhetorical and Chicana Feminist Theory in the Analysis of Mass Media." University of Georgia, 1994.

Foley, Neil Francis. "The New South in the Southwest: Anglos, Blacks, and Mexicans in Central Texas, 1880–1930." University of Michigan, 1990.

Frank, Ross Harold, "From Settler to Citizen: Economic Development and Cultural Change in Late Colonial New Mexico, 1750–1820." University of California, Berkeley, 1992.

Galán, Francis X. "Last Soldiers, First Pioneers: The Los Adaes Border Community on the Louisiana-Texas Frontier, 1721–1779." Southern Methodist University, 2006.

Gallegos, Bernardo P. "Literacy, Schooling, and Society in Colonial New Mexico: 1692–1821." University of New Mexico, 1988.

García, Ignacio M. "The Politics of Aztlán: The Forging of a Militant Ethos among Mexican Americans." University of Arizona, 1995.

García, Jorge. "*Forjando Ciudad:* The Development of a Chicano Political Community in East Los Angeles." University of California, Riverside, 1986.

García Bedolla, Lisa. "Fluid Borders: Latino Identity, Community and Politics in Los Angeles." Yale University, 1999.

García y Griego, Larry Manuel. "The Bracero Policy Experiment: U.S.-Mexican Responses to Mexican Labor Migration, 1942–1955." University of California, Los Angeles, 1988.

Garcilazo, Jeffrey Marcos. "'Traqueros': Mexican Railroad Workers in the United States, 1870 to 1930." University of California, Santa Barbara, 1995.

Garza, Lisa. "Crossing the Educational Border: Mexican-American Women in Higher Education." Texas Women's University, 1995.

Gerardo, Galadriel Mehera. "Misunderstood Masculinities: Competing Expressions of Manhood, the Zoot Suit Riots, and Young Mexican American Masculine Identity in World War II Los Angeles." University of California, Los Angeles, 2007.

Getz, Lynne Marie. "Progressive Ideas for New Mexico: Educating the Spanish-Speaking Child in the 1920's and 30's." University of Washington, 1989.

Gonzales, Gabriela. "Two Flags Entwined: Transborder Activists and the Politics of Race, Ethnicity, Class, and Gender in South Texas, 1900–1950." Stanford University, 2005.

Gonzales, Gilbert Ramírez. "Strategy and Stopes: Mines, Management, and Community in Superior and Jerome, Arizona, 1900–1955." Arizona State University, 2004.

Gonzales, Nathan Daniel. "'Visit Yesterday, Today': Ethno-Tourism and Southern California, 1884–1955." University of California, Riverside, 2006.

Gonzales, Nicki Margaret. "'Yo Soy Loco Por Esa Sierra': The History of Land Rights Activism in San Luis, Colorado, 1863–2002." University of Colorado, 2007.

Gonzales, Phillip B. "A Perfect Furor of Indignation: The Racial Attitude Controversy of 1933." University of California, Berkeley, 1985.

González, Deena J. "The Spanish-American Women of Santa Fe: Patterns of Their Resistance and Accommodation, 1820–1880." University of California, Berkeley, 1986.

González, Michael J. "Searching for the Feathered Serpent: Exploring the Origins of Mexican Culture in Los Angeles, 1830–1850." University of California, Berkeley, 1993.

González, Suronda. "Immigrants in Our Midst: Grace Abbot, the Immigrants' Protective League of Chicago, and the New American Citizenship, 1908–1924." State University of New York, Binghamton, 2005.

Gordillo, Luz María. "Engendering Transnational Ties: Mexicans and Other Sides of Immigration, 1942–2000." Michigan State University, 2005.

Green, Susan Marie. "Zoot Suiters: Past and Present." University of Minnesota, 1997.

Guerin-Gonzales, Camille. "Cycles of Immigration and Repatriation: Mexican Farm Workers in California Industrial Agriculture, 1900–1940." University of California, Riverside, 1985.

Guerra, Fernando Javier. "Ethnic Politics in Los Angeles: The Emergence of Black, Jewish, Latino, and Asian Officeholders, 1960–1989." University of Michigan, 1990.

Guevarra, Rudy P. "Mexipino: A History of Multiethnic Identity and the Formation of the Mexican and Filipino Communities of San Diego, 1900–1965." University of California, Santa Barbara, 2007.

Guidotti-Hernández, Nicole. "Made by Violence: Chicana Narrative and the Remaking of the World, 1851–1996." Cornell University, 2004.

Gutiérrez, David G. "Ethnicity, Ideology, and Political Development: Mexican Immigration as a Political Issue in the Chicano Community, 1910–1977." Stanford University, 1988.

Gutiérrez, Gabriel. "Bell Towers, Crucifixes, and Cañones Violentes: State and Identity Formation in Pre-Industrial Alta California." University of California, Santa Barbara, 1997.

Gutiérrez, Henry Joseph. "The Chicano Education Rights Movement and School Segregation, Los Angeles, 1862–1970." University of California, Irvine, 1990.

Gutiérrez, Ramón A. "Marriage, Sex, and the Family: Social Change in Colonial New Mexico, 1660–1846." University of Wisconsin, Madison, 1980.

Haas, Mary Lisbeth. "The Barrios of Santa Ana: Community, Class, and Organization." University of California, Irvine, 1985.

Habell-Pallán, Michelle. "'Cutting the Label Out': Performing Identity, Cultural Politics, and Transnational Subjects in Chicana/o and Latina/o Cultural Production." University of California, Santa Cruz, 1997.

Hackel, Steven W. "Indian-Spanish Relations in Colonial California: Mission San Carlos Borromeo, 1770–1834." Cornell University, 1994.

Hansberger, Bernd. "Mining and Colonisation on the Northwest Frontier of New Spain: Aspects of the Economical and Social History of Sonora, 1640–1767." University of Vienna, 1990.

Haverluk, Terence William. "Mex-America: The Maintenance and Expansion of an American Cultural Region." University of Minnesota, 1993.

Hayes-Bautista, David E. "Latino Health Indicators and the Underclass Model: From Paradox to New Policy Models." University of California, Los Angeles, 1990.

Hernández-Fujigaki, Jorge. "Mexican Steelworkers and the United Steelworkers of America in the Midwest: The Inland Steel Experience (1836–1976)." University of Chicago, 1991.

Herrera, Carlos R. "The King's Governor: Juan Bautista de Anza and Bourbon New Mexico in the Era of Imperial Reform, 1778–1788." University of New Mexico, 2000.

Heyman, Josiah. "The Working People of the United States–Mexico Border in the Region of Northeastern Sonora, 1886–1936." City University of New York, 1988.

Hidalgo de la Riva, Teresa (Osa). "Mujerista Moviemaking: Chicana Filmmakers Sylvia Morales and Lourdes Portillo." University of Southern California, 2004.

Hondagneu, Pierrette María. "Gender and Politics of Mexican Undocumented Migrant Settlement." University of California, Berkeley, 1991.

Huaco-Nuzum, Carmen Juana. "Mestiza Subjectivity: Representation and Spectatorship in Mexican and Hollywood Films." University of California, Santa Cruz, 1993.

Huginnie, Andrea Yvette. "'Strikitos': Race, Class, and Work in the Arizona Copper Industry, 1870–1920." Yale University, 1991.

Iber, Jorge. "Ethnicity in Zion: A History of Hispanics in Northern Utah, 1912–1997." University of Utah, 1997.

Inda, Xavier. "Matter Out of Place: Mexican Immigrants, National Terrains." University of California, Berkeley, 1997.

Innis-Jiménez, Michael D. "Persisting in the Shadow of Steel: Community Formation and Survival in Mexican South Chicago, 1919–1939." University of Iowa, 2006.

Jarvinen, Lisa. "The American Film Industry and the Spanish-Speaking Market during the Transition to Sound, 1929–39." Syracuse University, 2007.

Jungmeyer, Robert L. "The Bracero Program, 1942–1951: Mexican Contract Labor in the United States." University of Missouri, Columbia, 1988.

Latorre, Guisela María. "Chicana/o Murals of California: Indigenist Aesthetics and the Politics of Space, 1970–2000." University of Illinois, Urbana-Champaign, 2003.

Ledesma, Irene. "Unlikely Strikers: Mexican-American Women in Strike Activity in Texas, 1919–1974." Ohio State University, 1992.

León, Luis Daniel. "Religious Movement in the United States-Mexico Borderlands: Toward a Theory of Chicana/o Religious Poetics." University of California, Santa Barbara, 1997.

Levario, Miguel Antonio. "Cuando Vino la Mexicanada: Authority, Race, and Conflict in West Texas, 1895–1924." University of Texas, Austin, 2007.

Levinson, Irving Walter. "Wars within War: Mexican Guerillas, Domestic Elites and the Americans, 1846–1848." University of Houston, 2003.

Lopes, Shirley. "Remembering the Brave Women: Chicana Literature on the Texas-Mexico Border, 1900–1950." University of Iowa, 2004.

López, César. "El Descanso: A Comparative History of the Los Angeles Plaza Area and the Shared Racialized Space in the Mexican and Chinese Communities, 1853–1933." University of California, Berkeley, 2003.

Loza, Stephen Joseph. "The Musical Life of the Mexican/Chicano People in Los Angeles, 1945–1985: A Study in Maintenance, Change, and Adaptation." University of California, Los Angeles, 1985.

Lugo, Alejandro. "Fragmented Lives, Assembled Goods: A Study in Maquilas, Culture, and History at the Mexican Borderlands." Stanford University, 1995.

Luján, Joe Roy. "Dennis Chavez and the Roosevelt Era, 1933–1945." University of New Mexico, 1987.

Machado, Daisy Lucrecia. "Of Borders and Margins: Hispanic Disciples in Texas, 1888–1945." University of Chicago, 1996.

Macías, Anthony Foster. "From Pachuco Boogie to Latin Jazz: Mexican Americans, Popular Music, and Urban Culture in Los Angeles, 1940–1965." University of Michigan, 2001.

Maldonado, Carlos Saldívar. "'The Longest Running Death in History': A History of Colegio Cesar Chavez, 1973–1983." University of Oregon, 1986.

Mantovina, Timothy Matthew. "San Antonio Tejanos, 1821–1860: A Study of Religion and Ethnicity." Catholic University of America, 1993.

Marchevsky, Alejandra E. "Flexible Labor, Inflexible Citizenship: Latina Immigrants and the Politics of Welfare Reform." University of Michigan, 2004.

Marín, Christine. "Always a Struggle: Mexican Americans in Miami, Arizona, 1909–1951." Arizona State University, 2005.

Mariscal, Jorge O. "The Economics of International Migration: Mexican Undocumented Migrants in the U.S." New York University, 1986.

Martínez, Ana Luisa. "The Voice of the People: Pablo Cruz, El Regidor, and Mexican American Identity in San Antonio, Texas, 1888–1910." Texas Tech University, 2003.

Martínez, Anne M. "Bordering on the Sacred: Religion, Nation, and U.S.-Mexican Relations, 1910–1929." University of Minnesota, 2003.

Martínez, Camilo Amado, Jr. "The Mexican and Mexican-American Laborers in the Lower Rio Grande Valley of Texas, 1870–1930." Texas A&M University, 1987.

Martínez, Fredda Gregg. "Familism in Acculturated Mexican Americans: Patterns, Changes, and Perceived Impact on Adjustment to U.S. Society." Northern Arizona University, 1992.

Martínez, Juan Francisco. "Origins and Development of Protestantism among Latinos in the Southwestern United States, 1836–1900." Fuller Theological Seminary, 1996.

Martínez Saldaña, Jesús. "At the Periphery of Democracy: The Binational Politics of Mexican Immigrants in Silicon Valley." University of California, Berkeley, 1993.

Mata, Jennifer Rebecca. "Creating a Critical Chicana Narrative: Writing the Chicanas at Farah into Labor History." Washington State University, 2004.

Mattingly, Doreen Jeanette. "Domestic Service, Migration, and Local Labor Markets on the United States-Mexico Border." Clark University, 1996.

Maturo, Carol L. "Malinche and Cortés, 1519–1521: An Iconographic Study." University of Connecticut, 1994.

McCarthy, Malachy Richard. "Which Christ Came to Chicago: Catholic and Protestant Programs to Evangelize, Socialize, and Americanize the Mexican Immigrant, 1900–1940." Loyola University, Chicago, 2002.

McCoyer, Michael. "Darkness of a Different Color: Mexicans and Racial Formation in Greater Chicago, 1916–1960." Northwestern University, 2007.

Menchaca, Martha. "Chicano-Mexican Conflict and Cohesion in San Pablo, California." Stanford University, 1987.

Mendoza, Valerie Marie. "The Creation of a Mexican Immigrant Community in Kansas City, 1890–1930." University of California, Berkeley, 1997.

Mireles, Gilbert Felipe. "Picking a Living: Farm Workers and Organized Labor in California's Strawberry Industry." Yale University, 2005.

Montes de Oca Ricks, María. "Mediating the Past: Continuity and Diversity in the Chicano Literary Tradition." University of South Carolina, 1991.

Montgomery, Charles H. "History as Culture: The Making of Spanish Heritage in New Mexico, 1883–1940." Cornell University, 1995.

Montoya, Fawn-Amber. "Mines, Massacres, and Memories: Colorado Fuel and Iron's Creation of a Community in Southern Colorado, 1880–1919." University of Arizona, 2007.

Montoya, Lisa JoAnn. "Latino and African-American Legislative Activism in the U.S. House of Representatives, 1989–1992." Washington University, 1995.

Montoya, María Elaine. "Dispossessed People: Settler Resistance on the Maxwell Land Grant, 1860–1901." Yale University, 1993.

Mora, Joshua Al. "Man's Inhumanity to Man: Justice and Injustice in Three Mexican-American Playwrights." Texas Tech University, 1994.

Muñoz, Laura K. "Desert Dreams: Mexican American Education in Arizona, 1870–1930." Arizona State University, 2006.

Navarro, Julian A. "Our Southern Brethren: National Identity and Pan-Americanism in Early United States-Mexico Relations, 1810–1830." University of Michigan, 2005.

Noreiga, Chon A. "Road to Aztlán: Chicanos and Narrative Cinema." Stanford University, 1991.

O'Brien, William Patrick. "Independence, Missouri's Trade with Mexico, 1827–1860: A Study in International Consensus and Cooperation." University of Colorado, 1994.

Ochoa, Gilda Laura. "Animosity and Unity: Mexican American and Mexican Immigrant Relations in La Puente, California." University of California, Los Angeles, 1997.

Ochoa, Ricardo. "Biographical Factors and Their Use as Predictors of Tenure and Absenteeism in a Tijuana Maquiladora." United States International University, 1990.

Ochoa-Serrano, Alvaro. "Michoacanos in Los Angeles: United States-Mexican Transitional Culture, 1920–1970." University of California, Los Angeles, 1998.

Okoh, Gaye T. M. "A Sifting of Centuries: Political and Musical Crossroads of African-Americans and Chicanos in Los Angeles." University of Minnesota, 2004.

Oropeza, Lorena. "¡La Batalla Esta Aqui! Chicanos Oppose the War in Vietnam." Cornell University, 1996.

Orozco, Cynthia E. "The Origins of the League of United Latin American Citizens (LULAC) and the Mexican American Civil Rights Movement in Texas with an Analysis of Women's Political Participation in a Gendered Context, 1910–1929." University of California, Los Angeles, 1992.

Orozco, José. "Esos altos de Jalisco!: Emigration and the Idea of Alteño Exceptionalism, 1926–1952." Harvard University, 1998.

Otero, Lydia R. "Conflicting Visions: Urban Renewal, Historical Preservation and the Politics of Saving a Mexican Past." University of Arizona, 2003.

Pagán, Eduardo Obregón. "Sleepy Lagoon: The Politics of Youth and Race in Wartime Los Angeles, 1940–1945." Princeton University, 1996.

Palmer, Susan L. "Building Ethnic Communities in a Small City: Roumanians and Mexicans in Aurora, Illinois, 1900–1940." Northern Illinois University, 1986.

Pardo, Mary Santoli. "Identity and Resistance: Mexican American Women and Grassroots Activism in Two Los Angeles Communities." University of California, Los Angeles, 1990.

Parker, Heather Rose. "The Elusive Coalition: African American and Chicano Political Organization and Interaction in Los Angeles, 1960–1973." University of California, Los Angeles, 1996.

Pastrano, José Guillermo. "Industrial Agriculture in the Peripheral South: State, Race, and the Politics of Migrant Labor in Texas, 1890–1930." University of California, Santa Barbara, 2006.

Peña, Manuel Heriberto. "The Emergence of Texas-Mexican Conjunto Music, 1935–1960: An Interpretive History." University of Texas, Austin, 1987.

Peñaloza, Lisa N. "Atravesando Fronteras/Border Crossings: An Ethnographic Exploration of the Consumer Acculturation of Mexican Immigrants." University of California, Irvine, 1990.

Pérez, Robert Cristian. "Indian Rebellions in Northwestern New Spain: A Comparative Analysis, 1695–1750's." University of California, Riverside, 2003.

Pesquera, Beatríz Margarita. "Work and Family: A Comparative Analysis of Professional, Clerical and Blue-Collar Chicana Workers." University of California, Berkeley, 1985.

Pichardo, Nelson Alexander. "The Role of Community in Social Protest: Chicano Working Class Protest, 1848–1933." University of Michigan, 1990.

Pitti, Gina Marie. "To 'Hear about God in Spanish': Ethnicity, Church, and Community Activism in the San Francisco Archdiocese's Mexican American Colonias, 1942–1965." Stanford University, 2003.

Pitti, Stephen Joseph. "Quicksilver Community: Mexican Migrations and Politics in the Santa Clara Valley, 1800–1960." Stanford University, 1998.

Prichard, Nancy Lee. "Paradise Found? Opportunities for Mexican, Irish, Italian and Chinese Born Individuals in the Jerome Copper Mining District, 1890–1910." University of Colorado, 1992.

Privett, Stephan A. "Robert E. Lucey: Evangelization and Cathesis among Hispanic Catholics." Catholic University of America, 1985.

Pubols, Helen Louise. "The Casa De La Guerra: Family and Community in Nineteenth Century Santa Barbara." University of California, Santa Barbara, 1991.

Pulido, Alberto López. "Race Relations within the American Catholic Church: An Historical and Sociological Analysis of Mexican-American Catholics." University of Notre Dame, 1989.

Quiñones, Naomi Helena. "Hijas de la Malinche (Malinche's Daughters): The Development of Social Agency among Mexican American Women and the Emergence of First Wave Chicana Cultural Production." Claremont Graduate School, 1996.

Radding, Cynthia. "Ethnicity and the Emerging Peasant Class of Northwestern New Spain, 1760–1840." University of California, San Diego, 1990.

Ramírez, José A. "'To the Line of Fire, Mexican-Texans': The Tejano Community and World War I." Southern Methodist University, 2007.

Rentería, Tamis Hoover. "The Culture of Mexican-American Professionals Today: Legacy of the Chicano Movement." Stanford University, 1992.

Reséndez, Andrés. "Caught between Profits and Rituals: National Contestation in Texas and New Mexico, 1821–1848." University of Chicago, 1997.

Reyes, Bárbara O. "Nineteenth-century California as Engendered Space: The Public/Private Lives of Women of the Californias." University of California, San Diego, 2000.

Reyes, José Roberto. "Machismo, Marianismo and Marital Adjustment among Mexican Immigrants and Mexican American Couples." Fuller Theological Seminary, 1995.

Ríos-Bustamante, Antonio José. "Los Angeles, Pueblo and Region, 1781–1850: Continuity and Adaptation on the North Mexican Periphery." University of California, Los Angeles, 1985.

Rodríguez, Julia Curry. "Reconceptualizing Undocumented Labor Immigration: The Causes, Impact and Consequences in Mexican Women's Lives." University of Texas, Austin, 1988.

Rodríguez, Marc S. "Obreros Unidos: Migration, Migrant Farm Workers' Activism, and the Chicano Movement in Wisconsin and Texas, 1950–1980." Northwestern University, 2000.

Rodríguez, María Elena. "Mary Dilley, Curandera: A Modern South Texas Folk Healer." Texas A&M University, 1993.

Rodríguez, Ralph Edward. "Chicana and Chicano Fiction into the Nineties: Genre and Contestation." University of Texas, Austin, 1997.

Rojas, David Alfonso José. "The Making of Zoot Suiters in Early 1940s Los Angeles." University of California, Berkeley, 2001.

Romero, Tom I., Jr. "Of Race and Rights: Legal Culture, Social Change, and the Making of a Multiracial Metropolis, Denver, 1940–1975 (Colorado)." University of Michigan, 2004.

Romero, Yolanda García. "The Mexican American Frontier Experience in Twentieth Century Northwest Texas." Texas Tech University, 1993.

Rosales, Rodolfo. "The Rise of Chicano Middle Class Politics in San Antonio, 1951–1985." University of Michigan, 1991.

Rosales, Steven. "Soldados Razos: Chicano Politics, Identity, and Masculinity in the U.S. Military, 1940–75." University of California, Irvine, 2007.

Rose, Margaret. "Women in the United Farm Workers: A Case Study of Chicana and Mexicana Participation in a Labor Union." University of California, Los Angeles, 1988.

Roth, Benita. "On Their Own and For Their Own: African-American, Chicana, and White Feminist Movements in the 1960s and 1970s." University of California, Los Angeles, 1998.

Rouse, Roger. "Mexican Migration to the United States: Family Relations in the Development of a Transnational Migrant Circuit." Stanford University, 1989.

Salas, Elizabeth. "*Soldaderas* in the Mexican Military: Myth and History." University of California, Los Angeles, 1987.

Salinas, Susan Mary. "The Effect of Domestic Values on Marriage between Anglos and Hispanics." University of Texas, Arlington, 1986.

Sánchez, George J. "Becoming Mexican American: Ethnicity and Acculturation in Chicano Los Angeles, 1900–1943." Stanford University, 1989.

Sandoval, Denise Michelle. "Bajito y Suavecito/Low and Slow: Cruising through Lowrider Culture." Claremont Graduate School, 2003.

Sego, Eugene B. "Six Tlaxcalan Colonies on New Spain's Northern Frontier: A Comparison of Success and Failure." Indiana University, 1990.

Segura, Denise Anne. "Chicanas and Mexican Immigrant Women in the Labor Market: A Study of Occupational Mobility and Stratification." University of California, Berkeley, 1986.

Soldatenko, María Angelina. "The Everyday Lives of Latina Garment Workers in Los Angeles: The Convergence of Gender, Race, Class, and Immigration." University of California, Los Angeles, 1992.

Sommers, L. K. "Alegría in the Streets: Latino Cultural Performance in San Francisco." University of Michigan, 1986.

St. John, Rachel C. "Line in the Sand: The Desert Border between the United States and Mexico, 1848–1934." Stanford University, 2005.

Street, Richard Steven. "'We Are Not Slaves': A History of California Farmworkers, 1769–1869--The Formative Years." University of Wisconsin, Madison, 1995.

Tirres, Allison. "American Law Comes to the Border: Law and Colonization on the U.S./Mexico Divide, 1848–90." Harvard University, 2008.

Treviño, Roberto R. "*La fe:* Catholicism and Mexican Americans in Houston, 1911–1972." Stanford University, 1993.

Trujillo, Armando J. "Community Empowerment and Bilingual/Bicultural Education: A Study of the *Movimiento* in a South Texas Community." University of Texas, Austin, 1993.

Tsu, Cecilia. "Grown in the 'Garden of the World': Race, Gender, and Agriculture in California's Santa Clara Valley, 1880–1940." Stanford University, 2006.

Turpen, Twila Faye. "Cohesion, Inequality, and Interethnic Conflict in Territorial New Mexico." University of New Mexico, 1987.

Valerio-Jiménez, Omar S. "*Indios Bárbaros,* Divorcées, and Flocks of Vampires: Identity and Nation on the Rio Grande, 1749–1892." University of California, Los Angeles, 2001.

Valle, María Eva. "MEChA and the Transformation of Chicano Student Activism: Generational Change, Conflict, and Continuity." University of California, San Diego, 1996.

Van Handel, Robert Michael. "The Jesuit and Franciscan Missions in Baja California." University of California, Santa Barbara, 1991.

Vaquera-Vásquez, Santiago R. "Wandering Stories: Place, Itinerancy, and Cultural Liminality in the Borderlands." University of California, Santa Barbara, 1997.

Vargas, George. "Contemporary Latino Art in Michigan, the Midwest, and the Southwest." University of Michigan, 1988.

Verduzco Chávez, Basilio. "Transnational Activism and Environmental Conflicts in the United States-Mexico Border Region." Rutgers University, 1997.

Vila, Pablo Sergio. "Everyday Life, Culture and Identity on the Mexican-American Border: The Ciudad Juárez-El Paso Case." University of Texas, Austin, 1994.

Villar, María de Lourdes. "From Sojourners to Settlers: The Experience of Mexican Undocumented Migrants in Chicago." Indiana University, 1989.

Villarreal, Mary Ann. "*Cantantes y Cantineras:* Mexican American Communities and the Mapping of Public Space." Arizona State University, 2003.

Young, Elliott Gordon. "Twilight on the Texas-Mexico Border: Catarino Garza and Identity at the Cross-Roads, 1880–1915." University of Texas, Austin, 1997.

Walsh, Jane MacLaren. "Myth and Imagination in the American Story: The Coronado Expedition, 1540–1542." Catholic University of America, 1993.

Weber, Devra Anne. "The Struggle for Stability and Control in the Cotton Fields of California: Class Relations in Agriculture, 1919–1942." University of California, Los Angeles, 1986.

Wilson, Tamar Diana. "Vamos Para Buscar La Vida: A Comparison of Patterns of Outmigration from a Rancho in Jalisco and Immigration to a Mexicali Squatter Settlement." University of California, Los Angeles, 1992.

Yáñez-Cávez, Aníbal. "Development and Crisis: Geographical Industrialization in Coahuila and Mexico-U.S. Economic Integration." University of California, Berkeley, 1994.

INDEX

◄◊►◄◊►◄◊►

Italicized page numbers indicate illustrations.

INDEX ►─◄◦►─◄◦►─◄◦►─◄◦►─◄◦►─◄◦►─◄◦►─◄◦►─◄◦►─◄◦►─◄◦►─◄◦►─

MANUEL G. GONZALES is Professor of History at Diablo Valley College. A specialist in both modern Europe and the American Southwest, he has been a visiting professor of Chicano history in the ethnic studies department at the University of California, Berkeley. His publications include *Andrea Costa and the Rise of Socialism in the Romagna* and *The Hispanic Elite of the Southwest.* He is editor (with Cynthia Gonzales) of *En Aquel Entonces* (Indiana University Press, 2000).